NAPOLEON AT LEIPZIG

NAPOLEON AT LEIPZIG

Battle of the Nations 1813

George Nafziger

Helion & Company

Helion & Company Limited
Unit 8 Amherst Business Centre
Budbrooke Road
Warwick
CV34 5WE
England
Tel. 01926 499 619
Fax 0121 711 4075
Email: info@helion.co.uk
Website: www.helion.co.uk
Twitter: @helionbooks
Visit our blog http://blog.helion.co.uk/

Originally published by The Emperor's Press 1996
This new edition published by Helion & Company 2018
Designed and typeset by Mach 3 Solutions Ltd (www.mach3solutions.co.uk)
Cover designed by Paul Hewitt, Battlefield Design (www.battlefield-design.co.uk)
Printed by Gutenberg Press Limited, Tarxien, Malta

Text © George Nafziger 1996
Images open source
Maps drawn by George Anderson © Helion & Company Limited 2018
Front cover: The Grenadiers à Cheval of the Imperial Guard at Hanau, by Richard Knötel.

ISBN 978-1-912390-11-3

British Library Cataloguing-in-Publication Data.
A catalogue record for this book is available from the British Library.

For details of other military history titles published by Helion & Company Limited contact
the above address, or visit our website: http://www.helion.co.uk.

We always welcome receiving book proposals from prospective authors.

Contents

List of Illustrations

List of Maps

Sketch Maps

Color Maps

* Map has key. Map keys can be found at the end of the color section.

Acknowledgements

I would like to acknowledge the assistance of a number of people, without whom this work could not have been what it is. I would like to again acknowledge the kindness and support of Mr. Peter Harrington, curator of the Anne S. K. Brown Military Collection, Brown University. He graciously and repeatedly opened this famous collection and gave me access to anything that could assist my researches.

Similarly, Mr. J. J. Slonaker of the US Army Military History Institute opened the doors of the Army's historical library to me, allowing me to have copies made of numerous rare and obscure works that contributed significantly to this work.

It is with special pleasure that I acknowledge the assistance of several personal friends. First is Mr. Peter Hofschröer, who selflessly opened up his library, and provided copies of the artwork, editorial comments, and other assistance for which I am much in his debt.

Significant assistance was provided by Mr. Gustav Bergman, who most kindly ran down to the Stockholm archives and dug up a number of tidbits on the Swedish participation in this campaign. Without his selfless assistance, the actions of the Swedes would most certainly not have been as well covered.

Mr. Soren Anderson, of Aalborg, Denmark, provided significant assistance and details on the Danish portion of the campaign, which would certainly have been unobtainable without his kind assistance.

I also owe a debt to Major Hartmut Nagel and Dr. Thomas Scheben of the Cairo Egypt Office of the Konrad-Adenauer-Foundation, both of whom took the time to read the manuscript and provide their insight. An insight, I might add, which sprang from and led to a number of interesting exchanges on the fluidity of the spelling of German town names and the proper use of German words in the English grammar environment.

I also need to acknowledge the assistance of CDR Chris Janiec, USN, who, from the middle of the Pacific Ocean and between catapult shots, took the time to read and provide editorial comments and a fresh perspective.

Finally, a special acknowledgement and most humble thanks again goes to Mr. Warren Worley, who continues to act as a technical editor, helping to flesh out the text with technical details, catching discrepancies in the source documents that slipped past me, as well as providing an extra comma here and there.

Notes on Translation

In order to add to the flavor of this work, as many German (and French) terms as possible have been used. It is recognized that German grammar requires a variety of changes to its vocabulary, depending on usage. However, as this would be confusing to non-German speakers, for whom this book is written, the nominative declension has always been used and plurals are formed using the English method. To those who are concerned about this, I apologize for this corruption of the German language.

The term used for an infantry captain in German has changed over the years and varies from source to source. All of the following terms are common forms of the German for "captain": Hauptman, Kapitain, Kapitän, and Capitain. As no documents were found indicating that the Saxons used one form, or that the Prussians, Württembergers, etc., used specific other forms, the form encountered in the original source is used throughout the text.

Both the Russians and Germans used the word *Jäger* to describe light troops. However, since there is no *umlaut* in the Russian Cyrillic alphabet, and to facilitate the identification of the nationality of these often somewhat vaguely identified light troops, every time a Russian *Jager* unit is referenced, it will be in the Anglicized form—*Jager*. The German units will always be referred to as *Jäger*.

Abbreviations and Terminology

For simplicity's sake some abbreviations are used for many officer's ranks. In some instances, the full title is used where it is not particularly long. The ranks and their equivalents in current ranks are:

French

Maréchal	Field Marshal
Général de division	Major General (GD)
Général de brigade	Brigadier General (BG)
Colonel	Colonel
Major	Lt. Colonel
Chef d'escadron	Major (cavalry and horse artillery)
Chef de bataillon	Major (infantry and foot artillery)
Capitaine	Captain
Lieutenant	1st Lieutenant
Sous-lieutenant	2nd Lieutenant

Prussian, Russian, and most German states

Feldmarschall	Field Marshal (FM)
General der Kavallerie	Lieutenant General (GdK)
General der Infanterie	Lieutenant General (GdI)
Generallieutenant	Major General (GL)
Generalmajor	Brigadier General (GM)
Oberst	Colonel
Oberstleutnant	Lt. Colonel
Major	Major
Rittmeister	Captain (cavalry)
Hauptman, Kapitän	Captain (infantry)
Leutnant	1st Lieutenant
Unterleutnant	2nd Lieutenant

Austrian

Feldmarschall	Field Marshal (FM)
General der Kavallerie	General "of Cavalry" (GdK)
General der Infanterie	General "of Infantry" (GdI)
Feldzeugmeister	Lieutenant General (FZM)
Feldmarschal-lieutenant	Major General (FML)
Generalmajor	Brigadier General (GM)
Oberst	Colonel
Oberstleutnant	Lt. Colonel
Rittmeister	Captain (cavalry)
Hauptman, Kapitän	Captain (infantry)
Leutnant	1st Lieutenant
Unterleutnant	2nd Lieutenant

Introduction

August had been a disappointing month for Napoleon. Though he had personally defeated the Army of Bohemia at Dresden, his armies had lost the battles of Gross-Beeren, Katzbach, Löwenberg, Kulm, and Hagelberg. His losses in troops and equipment had been substantial, with the I Corps destroyed at Kulm and the 17th Division destroyed at Löwenberg. If the results were totaled, they were definitely tilted against Napoleon.

It was a most disappointing continuation of what had been a most promising and successful spring campaign that had been crowned with little other than victory. Obviously, the summer armistice had been a mistake, a tragic and substantial one for Napoleon. Despite his efforts to continue the rapid rebuilding of his armies, the allies had made better use of the armistice than he had. They were reinforced by the armies of a new belligerent, Austria. Burning with a desire for revenge, Austria's white coated legions marched from their mountainous domain down onto the Saxon plains and pointed their bayonets at their old nemesis. They had enjoyed seven full months to rebuild and recover their strength from the Russian campaign, and four years to recover from their disastrous 1809 campaign. If they had not entered the fray it is probable that Napoleon's luck from the spring would have continued. The great Corsican eagle was wounded, however, and the Austrians saw an opportunity to strike.

The worst result of August was probably that the allies had escaped every blow Napoleon threw at them, save the one at Dresden. The allies had developed a terrible new tactic—they ran away—and it worked! Blow after blow fell into thin air as the usually aggressive, but plodding allied armies suddenly danced and jabbed. Each powerful blow struck nothing, while each wasted effort drained both the physical and morale strength from the French army.

September had started with the another major calamity when Ney was pummeled at Dennewitz. With the collapse of Napoleon's second thrust at Berlin, both sides settled down into what would be two months of relative calm. Much like the calm in the eye of a hurricane, after Dennewitz, September was a month of maneuvers, but little combat. Soon, however, the second round of the great, climactic struggle would be joined and the final resolution both armies sought would be found in the fury and terror of a shrieking tempest of shot and shell.

Both sides strove to catch their wind so they could renew the fight; both sides filled in their depleted ranks and reorganized their armies. Napoleon disbanded whole corps and combined their shattered remains to form usable and viable formations. The allies rebuilt their units and filled depleted ranks. Each side with an eye on the other, striving to be the first to be ready to resume the fight, the two tired adversaries rose to their feet again and staggered towards each other. Their jaws set, their fists clenched, tired to the bone and wishing they could build their strength longer, but knowing that the first to strike a major blow would probably win the war.

1

The Eye of the Hurricane
September 1813

Napoleon, in his operational plans of 30 August, had resolved to move to Hoyerswerda with Marmont's VI Corps, the Imperial Guard, and Latour-Maubourg's I Cavalry Corps. Once established there with two infantry corps and three cavalry divisions, Napoleon was centrally located where he could support Ney in his march on Berlin, act against the Armies of Bohemia or Silesia, keep Blücher separated from Schwarzenberg, and cover Dresden from a renewed attack.[1]

Napoleon had left St-Cyr's XIV Corps in Pirna and Victor's II Corps in Freiberg to contain the Army of Bohemia. Their task was to contain Schwarzenberg, if he acted, until Napoleon could arrive with his central reserve.

The I Corps had been reconstituted under the GD Mouton with the 15,000 men who escaped from the disaster at Kulm and 18,000 men in various *bataillons de marche* that arrived from Mainz. GD Teste's 23rd Division was ordered to rejoin this force in Dresden.[2] The corps, with three divisions, was established in Dresden so it might complete its reorganization and to act as a last reserve. The 42nd Division was rebuilt, and the XIV Corps again had four divisions, and Reuss' former brigade was rebuilt and reassigned to the II Corps.

The VIII Corps (Poniatowski) was posted in Zittau and Macdonald commanded the III, V, and XI Corps, which were posted around Görlitz.

On 2 and 3 September, the Young and Old Guard, I Cavalry Corps, the French bridging train, and the Imperial Headquarters started moving towards Königsbrück and Hoyerswerda. The VI Corps moved out of Dippoldiswalda and marched towards Königsbrück and Hoyerswerda as well.

On the central front alarming news stirred the army. A convoy of material destined for Macdonald was taken by allied partisans a few miles from Dresden.

Napoleon decided that he was no longer able to gather his *masse de manoeuvre* in Hoyerswerda, and decided that he would have to move to Macdonald's assistance. He directed, as a result, that those units already heading for Königsbrück were to move to Bautzen via Camentz. Two divisions of Young Guard, which were under Curial and still stood in Pirna, were to move to Bautzen by 5 September or earlier.

Poniatowski was ordered to hold the VIII Corps ready to move out of Zittau and turn Blücher's left flank when so ordered. Latour-Maubourg's I Cavalry Corps was also directed to Bautzen.[3]

With these dispositions complete, Napoleon wrote to Ney that he intended to attack the allies on 4 September, and would press on towards Berlin in "great haste" after that. He also sent instructions to St-Cyr, in Dresden, and directed him to reinforce the city's defenses.[4]

At 4:00 p.m., on 3 September, Napoleon departed for Hartha. During the morning of 4 September, he was on the road to Bautzen, driving his forces on. His gendarmes and staff officers hustled up and down the columns, pushing stragglers back into their units.

Once in Bautzen, Napoleon encountered Macdonald's forces and immediately redirected his dispositions to allow a resumption of the offensive. Murat was given command of the III Corps (Souham) and I Cavalry Corps (Latour-Maubourg) and told to follow the road to Görlitz through

Wurschen. Macdonald was to advance with the V Corps, XI Corps, and the II Cavalry Corps on the southern route, attacking on the right of Murat. At the same time the VIII Corps (Poniatowski) was to move to Löbau.

At the same time Napoleon made these dispositions, Blücher was advancing in pursuit of Macdonald with his army, led by a strong advanced guard of 10,000 men under the command of GL Vassil'shikov. This advanced guard was vigorously attacked by the French II Cavalry Corps, followed by Macdonald, as they recrossed the Löbauer-Wasser. At the same time, Murat threw Nansouty's Guard Cavalry Corps forward into Reichenbach and forced back the Prussians in that city.

The vigor of the French attacks told Blücher that Napoleon was once again present, and he immediately began withdrawing his forces during the night of 4/5 September. The reports from Nansouty and Latour-Maubourg on the morning of 5 September, announced the withdrawal of the allied forces. Napoleon personally rode forward with d'Ornano's 1st Guard Cavalry Division and watched it throw back a force of allied cavalry in Reichenbach.

The allied positions on 5 September were as follows: GL Vassil'shikov stood with his cavalry on the right bank of the Löbauer-Wasser.[5] He moved the infantry of the advanced guard and some artillery into Reichenbach. In case of attack, Vassil'shikov had orders to withdraw back to Lanskoi's cavalry.

At 6:45 a.m., Katzeler sent a report from Glossen, stating that the French camps on the opposite bank were quiet. Two reconnaissance forces were sent to Löbau, one consisting of 10 mounted men, the other was formed with 30 mounted men under an officer. They were charged to verify if the French were preparing to move on Zittau. A Russian colonel soon appeared from that direction, reporting that there were no French in that village.

However, at 9:00 a.m., it was learned that large masses of French infantry were forming near Glossen. In response Katzeler sent six battalions and three cavalry regiments towards Glossen, and a second column down the main road to the same point. A third column was dispatched towards Löbau.[6]

Vassil'shikov estimated the French force at 30,000 men. A prisoner had informed him that this force included the 2nd Division, 2nd Cavalry Corps. Vassil'shikov withdrew his cavalry rearguard slowly before this mass, and by 11:00 a.m., it still stood to the west of Reichenbach. Somewhat later it was reported that the bulk of the French forces had marched on Görlitz.

These movements convinced Blücher of Napoleon's arrival with large reinforcements, and confirmed his decision that he should maneuver to avoid the decisive battle that Napoleon was seeking. He prepared to withdraw into Bohemia via Zittau and Annaberg, and moved his forces to a position to the east of the village on the Topfenberg.

A French force of four light cavalry regiments and two cuirassier regiments moved to cut off the allied withdrawal. The Prussian cavalry closed on the French and received a volley of musketry,[7] which broke the lead regiment—the East Prussian Dragoon Regiment. They fled backwards, disorganizing a hussar regiment which was following them and was preparing to charge. At the same instant, the hussars received several discharges of canister; they too collapsed. The 1st and 2nd Squadrons and the jägers were thrown back, and would have found themselves in a bad situation, if the 3rd and 4th Squadrons (Major Knobloch) had not struck back at the moment when the French cavalry prepared to envelop the two wings of the Prussian cavalry. The French cavalry was not driven back, but the shock of the attack sufficed to prevent them from successfully destroying the Prussian cavalry.[8]

The intention of GL Vassil'shikov had been to retake Reichenbach and to defend himself there to the last. However, he gave up this project when he saw the overwhelming French forces before him. Katzeler was charged with covering his retreat. About 2:00 p.m., the Russian infantry stood in a position behind Markersdorf. The French do not appear to have pursued him.

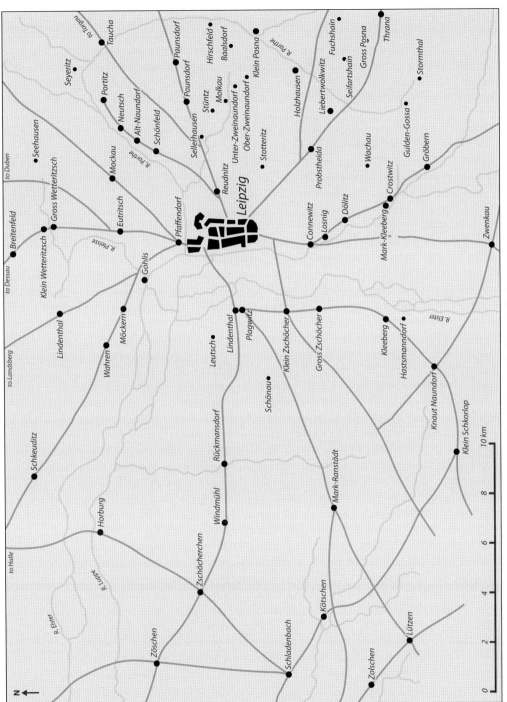

Sketch Map 1 The Leipzig Region.

The French columns did, however, continue to advance. Oberst Hiller withdrew with his rearguard by "echelon" as far as Landskrone, suffering at the hands of French artillery during his withdrawal.

Murat arrived in Markersdorf and changed the direction of the French to the right, not wishing to follow the allies into the narrow defiles before them. On Murat's left, Delmas' 9th Division moved down the main road. On his right advanced the V Corps, supported by Charpentier's 36th Division.[9]

On the same day, Blücher recrossed the Neisse to the south of Görlitz, closely followed by Macdonald. The Prussian 1st and 2nd Brigades crossed over a pontoon bridge below Görlitz. Langeron's Corps and the 7th and 8th Prussian Brigades crossed on another pontoon bridge upstream from the city. The 6th and 7th Russian Corps covered the crossing.

The 6th and 7th Russian Corps, menaced on their left by Murat's turning maneuver, withdrew under the cover of Vassil'shikov's cavalry towards Görlitz. Part of the rearguard, two battalions and two squadrons of the 1st Brandenburg Uhlan Regiment, stopped just to the west of the village. The first pontoon bridge, brought under French cannon fire, was set afire and became unusable. The infantry moved to the second pontoon bridge upstream and the cavalry crossed at the ford. The rest of the rearguard withdrew into the suburb to watch the bridge in Görlitz, waiting for the last of the infantry to cross before they destroyed the bridge.

Blücher was worried because of his proximity to the mountains to the south. He knew that he stood the chance of being trapped by Napoleon against those mountains and suffering a fate similar to Vandamme's I Corps at Kulm. He was also afraid of being cut off from the Army of Bohemia.

Macdonald occupied Görlitz on 5 September, as the allies abandoned it, but he did not judge it appropriate to force passage over the river. He sent part of his infantry into the villages between Reichenbach for the night and crossed the Neisse in the morning.[10]

Napoleon stopped the pursuit once the French had Görlitz. He did not wish to advance too far from Dresden, nor did he wish to get too far from Ney or the forces around Dresden should they require support. Though no engagement of note occurred, the resumption of the offensive did improve the sagging morale of Macdonald's forces.

Later on the 5th, Napoleon returned to Bautzen, arriving at 2:00 a.m., on 6 September. There he found word that Schwarzenberg had resumed the offensive, and appeared to be crossing over the mountains once again. Napoleon did not take this news seriously and responded by sending Latour-Maubourg's I Cavalry Corps and Marmont's VI Corps to Hoyerswerda. A separate brigade (Nordmann) was sent to Luckau.

These forces had been moving as order or only two hours when the I Cavalry Corps received orders to move in has Dresden. This resulted from a letter from St-Cyr announcing that the Army of Bohemia was in three lines, preparing to advance against Dresden once again, between Töplitz and the frontier. St-Cyr anticipated a serious engagement at any time.

Napoleon responded to St-Cyr on 7 September that he perceived this as only a diversion to distract him from his designs on Berlin and to cause him to disengage from his actions against Blücher.

The Allied Movements

Schwarzenberg learned of Napoleon's departure for Bautzen and made his dispositions to move on Dresden again. His goal was to distract Napoleon from Blücher and allow Blücher to once again assume the offensive. He hoped to fatigue the French army and break its morale by forcing it to engage in continuous countermarches to face each new threat.

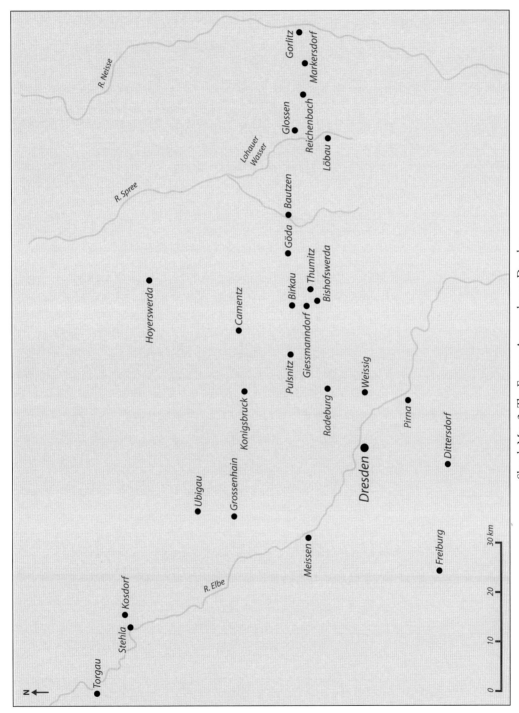

Sketch Map 2   The Eastern Approaches to Dresden.

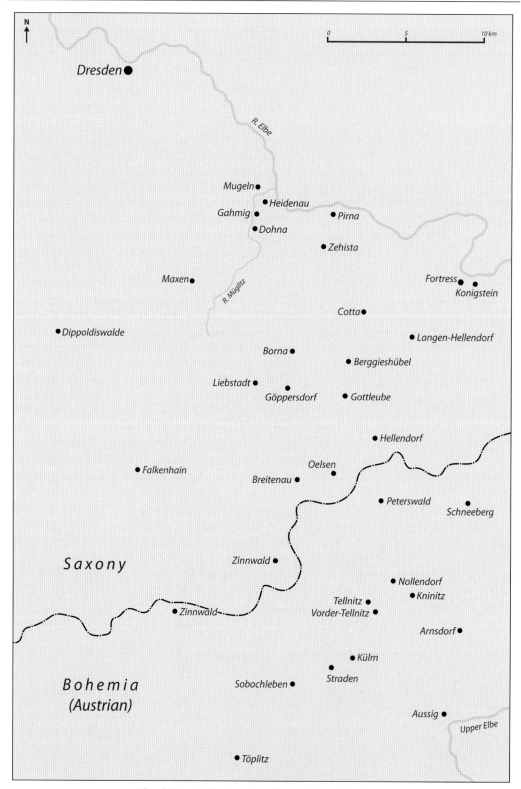

Sketch Map 3 The Southern Approaches to Dresden.

Napoleon's ability to react to this type of strategy was limited. He could not afford to ignore any threat. His recent experiences with the morale of Macdonald's troops showed that he had to keep them advancing towards the enemy. His problem was finding some method of motivating his generals and marshals to the same level of activity, plus ensuring that they would not find themselves outgeneraled by the allies, as had been happening with alarming regularity since 15 August.

The Army of Bohemia

St-Cyr had his XIV Corps spread around Dresden. The 42nd Division (Mouton-Duvernet) was in Pirna, with a few battalions in Königstein. The 45th Division was in Bornstein. Pajol's 10th Light Cavalry Division stood near Dittersdorf and the 43rd and 44th Divisions were around Berggieshübel.

On 4 September, the Prussians and Russians of the Army of Bohemia crossed over the mountains. The Austrians remained behind. Wittgenstein moved into Peterswald, Kleist moved to Hellendorf, Gortschakov moved towards Königstein, and Pahlen and Württemberg moved to Neumannsdorf, on the road from Tellnitz to Fürstenwalde.[11]

During the night of 4/5 September it was supposed, in St-Cyr's headquarters in Pirna, that the allies had augmented their forces on the right and, in an effort to separate St-Cyr from Victor, Wittgenstein had pushed a corps into the gap between them. In fact, Wittgenstein's orders to his troops were:

1. Ziethen's advanced guard shall advance down the main road to Hellendorf, being supported by the Russian 1st Corps (Gortschakov).
2. The 2nd Russian Corps (Württemberg) shall move through Oelsen and Gottleube on the same point in a manner so as turn the ravine which runs there.
3. Pahlen shall march from Falkenhain towards Liebstadt after having been relieved by Moritz Liechtenstein's Division.
4. Kaisarov shall move on Dohna via Liebstadt,[12] and Prince Württemberg, after taking Hellendorf, shall move on Göppersdorf and join Pahlen there.

However, despite the issuance of those orders for 5 September, they remained largely unexecuted. The Austrian division did not arrive, Pahlen and Kaisarov remained immobile, the former in Falkenhain and the latter in Borchen.[13]

Württemberg, however, did move into Oelsen, where he encountered a French detachment that required some persuading before it departed. Württemberg states that he arrived in the evening of 5 September.[14] However, Plotho[15] states that he arrived during the following morning.[16] Regardless, it appears that there were two or three French battalions camped behind Hellendorf. The village itself was occupied only by skirmishers, two companies forming a skirmish line across the front of the village and a battalion covering the right of the village. Württemberg sent Ziethen, leading four squadrons of cavalry, to turn Hellendorf and moved to send the bulk of his forces in a frontal attack against the French. His assault overran the French position. The French forces, part of the 43rd Division, pulled back to the edge of the nearby woods and maintained themselves there until 10:30 p.m., when the battle ended.[17]

St-Cyr, after confirming the allied movements, moved Mouton-Duvernet's 42nd Division to Königstein and drew the three others to Dohna (45th) and Zehista (43rd and 44th). Through this maneuver, St-Cyr established a line formed by these two villages, facing the allies. Gortschakov stood facing Mouton-Duvernet before Königstein. Kleist and Wittgenstein faced the rest of the line.

On 6 September, Wittgenstein and Kleist moved to Gieshabel and Cotta, respectively, while the other columns remained stationary. It was the movement of these two corps that had so alarmed St-Cyr. Napoleon's assessment of the situation was correct.

On the same day, the French Imperial Guard arrived in Dresden as did Latour-Maubourg's I Cavalry Corps and Marmont's VI Corps. Napoleon began making plans to act against the Army of Bohemia immediately after his arrival.

During the night of 7/8 September, Napoleon started receiving confused reports of Ney's action at Dennewitz. This disaster obliged Napoleon to rethink his actions once again and move to support Ney, once he was sure that the Army of Bohemia was not a serious threat around Freiberg, Chemnitz and Dippoldiswalda. He directed Victor to move from Freiberg to Dresden, Latour-Maubourg to move to Pirna, and the Guard to Dohna.

On the morning of 8 September, the three divisions of the XIV Corps attacked Wittgenstein and Kleist. Dohna was overrun by the Imperial Guard. The two allied generals either deduced Napoleon's presence from the arrival of the Imperial Guard or recognized his touch in these attacks. As a result they broke off from the engagement quickly and withdrew to the Zehista heights. The Austrians, who had remained in Bohemia, withdrew to Tetschen and Leitmeritz.

On the French side, the XIV Corps established itself south of Dohna, the I Corps moved to Zehista, three divisions of Young Guard under Mortier and the Guard Cavalry moved to Mugeln, and Latour-Maubourg's I Cavalry Corps moved into Müglitz.

The remainder of the Young Guard, the Old Guard, and Marmont's VI Corps were in Dresden. Victor's II Corps was moving on Dohna, leaving one division to watch the road to Freiberg.[18]

In the morning of 8 September, the advanced posts of St-Cyr's Corps were attacked behind Zehista and Zuschendorf. The 43rd Division, which formed this advanced guard with Pajol's 10th Light Cavalry Division, was attacked frontally by Pahlen's troops supported by a division from Württemberg's 2nd Corps. Prince Gortschakov marched to the right in a feint simulating the allied move against Dresden in August.

Gortschakov was to encounter only the forces of Ziethen's Brigade, part of Kleist's Corps. The Austrian corps had supported the movement of the Russo-Prussian army in the move to the left. Prince Liechtenstein had moved to Freiberg, Klenau moved to Chemnitz. Kaisarov was in Maxen covering lines of communication. He was also charged with turning the French left and moving against the rear of the XIV Corps. Constantine's reserves lay behind Gieshübel. Schwarzenberg, with 50,000 to 60,000 men of the Austrian army, was moving on the right bank of the Elbe with the assistance of bridges established by Aussig and Leitmeritz.[19]

During the evening of 9 September Napoleon learned the full extent of Ney's defeat at Dennewitz. Napoleon ordered Ney to withdraw his forces to Torgau. Napoleon realized, as he mulled over the actions of the last two weeks, what the allies were attempting to do to him. No doubt he realized that they were deliberately avoiding combat with him, choosing instead to engage only his lieutenants. He also realized that he had before him the opportunity of inflicting a substantial check to the allies if he took it. To effect this, all he had to do was to move Mortier's Young Guard to a position behind Pirna and Latour-Maubourg to the Müglitz.

On 9 September Napoleon resumed the march. He did not know the location of the Austrians, so he feared they might be in a position to move against Fürstenwalde and Dresden, while he was moving on Peterswald. To prevent this he ordered Victor to take the first of these roads and sent the Comte de Lobau and St-Cyr along the second. Mortier was to follow their movement with the Young Guard while the 42nd Division moved through Königstein and on to Hellendorf. Lefèbvre-Desnoëttes, and his cavalry were to move down the road from Dippoldiswalda to Altenburg.

Dumonceau's 2nd Division, which formed the head of the I Corps, attacked Wittgenstein, who had assumed a defensive position between Cotta and Zehista. Shortly later Mortier, who had not waited for orders, arrived in Gieshübel via Kriswitz, supported Dumonceau, and together they passed the allied right flank. At the same time, Lobau's I Corps turned the Russian's left flank. Wittgenstein was an impossible position, realized it, and quickly withdrew on Nollendorf.[20]

The morning of 9 September, found St-Cyr's front lines being struck again by Pahlen's cavalry, supported by Vlasov's Division and part of the Russian 2nd Corps. GD Bonet held them at bay with considerable effort.

Ziethen began to turn St-Cyr's left. St-Cyr was marching down the main road from Pirna to Dresden. Bonet formed his 45th Division in echelons and prepared to evacuate his position in Gross-Seydlitz. He withdrew in good order through the Müglitz valley, and took up a position on the left bank of this stream. The 43rd Division stood on the Gahmig heights and the 44th Division stood closer to Müglen. The XIV Corps, now concentrated, awaited Napoleon's orders.[21]

The allies, wishing to take the French position before them, moved against the left bank of the Müglitz. However, the French were able to hold the position and resist the allied attacks. The French sought to hold their line with its left on the village of Heidenau and its right on the village of Dohna. The allies, seeing the importance of these two positions, repeatedly struck at them. Ziethen moved against Heidenau and Pahlen attacked Dohna. Three battalions of the 42nd Division, holding Heidenau and supported by the 44th Division, threw Ziethen back.

Napoleon, after reviewing the situation, turned to and began questioning a number of captured Russian officers. He then began to ask St-Cyr where he could move his troops, once they had arrived before the allied position. St-Cyr showed him Dohna and Heidenau, which he had been holding all day. The one stood as master of the main road to Pirna. The other stood to the right of the road to Töplitz.[22]

Here Napoleon could form his columns under the protection of the other French units there and pass them across the Müglitz fords. However, it would be two more hours before the rest of the French forces arrived, and Napoleon lapsed into a period of inactivity. After some discussion it was decided that the XIV Corps should prepare for the assault. The 1st Brigade, 45th Division moved through Dohna and the 2nd Brigade, 45th Division, moved to the left of the village, with Pajol's 10th Light Cavalry Division accompanying it. The brigades of the 43rd and 44th Divisions formed to the left of the 45th Division. The 44th Division was to follow the 43rd Division across the Müglitz, once the 43rd and 45th Divisions had cleared enough terrain to allow it sufficient room to deploy. As the XIV Corps moved across the Müglitz and over the crest of the ridge before it, they found the allies organized in echelons and beginning to withdraw.[23]

Despite the allied withdrawal, the French attack continued. Pajol, despite the weakness of his forces, executed several successful attacks and took many prisoners.

A squadron of the 14th Hussars arrived. On 22 August it had been cut off by Klenau's Corps and was unable to return to French lines until that moment. It was immediately assigned duties with the advancing XIV Corps. It was soon engaged by the Grodno Hussars and destroyed, with only an officer and two non-commissioned officers surviving.

As the allies withdrew, the II Corps arrived in Maxen, the I Corps, XIV Corps, and Young Guard found themselves on the old road to Bohemia, and St-Cyr occupied Fürstenwalde. Dumonceau's 2nd Division remained in contact with Wittgenstein's withdrawing forces, and pursued them from Peterswald. Dumonceau attacked both Kleist and Wittgenstein again and again in an effort to delay their withdrawal and allow the flanking French corps time to get into position, so a decisive battle could occur.

During the evening of 9 September, the Comte de Lobau and St-Cyr bivouacked in Fürstenwalde. Mortier and the Young Guard continued to follow Dumonceau.

During the 10th Napoleon sent the I and XIV Corps through the passes at Geyersberg and directed them on to Ebersdorf. The passes were difficult and once there, the roads were worse.

Napoleon moved with the armies and took up a position where he found he could overlook the battlefield of Kulm. There he saw the Austrians, who had moved towards Tetschen and made a turn to Aussig in order to withdraw. They had left a rearguard under Raevsky to cover the Geyersberg passes. Bonet's force, XIV Corps, attacked vigorously, but because his artillery had not been able to move through the Geyersberg passes, the results were not substantial and did not open the pass.[24]

Efforts were made to mount some guns on the crags by Geyersberg, but they were unsuccessful, losing more precious time and letting Wittgenstein and Kleist open the gap even more.

Napoleon thought of withdrawing back the way he'd come, and then moving through Nollendorf, but the roads there were even worse. On the other hand, he feared that the Austrians might maneuver behind him, by passing through Zinwald, so he abandoned any idea of changing his line of march.

Finally, during the evening, Bonet's force occupied Kraupen and the pass out of the mountains. Dumonceau's 2nd Division arrived at Peterswald, followed by the Young Guard about the same time. The terrain had conspired to prevent Napoleon's maneuver from succeeding, and during the 10th, when he learned that he no longer had the opportunity of striking the allied flanks, he abandoned his maneuver.

On 11 September, Napoleon stood on the heights above Nollendorf, overlooking the fateful field at Kulm, where he saw the allied armies arrayed before him. Rather than expose his columns to being attacked one at a time by an overwhelming force as they cleared the mountain passes., he renounced any further effort against the Army of Bohemia and withdrew to Pirna. Once there Napoleon directed St-Cyr to take command of the I and XIV Corps. The I Corps was to withdraw by Breitenau towards Hellendorf. Dumonceau's 2nd Division, which occupied a position around Nollendorf, was to remain there. The two other divisions which occupied Peterswald, Hellendorf, and Gieshübel were to support him. The 42nd Division was to withdraw to Königstein. The XIV Corps was to watch the passes at Geyersberg and Borna. Victor's II Corps was to watch the passes at Dippoldiswalda and Freiberg.

Macdonald's Army

By 6 September, Blücher had withdrawn behind the Queiss River, and Macdonald had occupied Görlitz with his advanced guard and established the remainder of his army between Bautzen and Wurschen. Their right was covered by Poniatowski's VIII Corps in Löbau. The III, V, and XI Corps, with Sébastiani's II Cavalry Corps, totaled about 65,000 men. They were facing the 85,000 men of the Army of Silesia.

Prior to his departure, Napoleon had ordered Macdonald to hold firm in his positions and to not pass over the Spree if he was forced to withdraw. Macdonald's troops, however, were very fatigued from their travails and their morale left much to desired. Macdonald's army assumed a passive posture, and except for a skirmish between Decouz's 3rd Young Guard Division and the allies by Reichenbach, took no aggressive action.

On 8 September, Souham's attached cavalry, the 23rd Light Cavalry Brigade, three guns, and the 4/10th Légère Regiment were sent forward as a flying corps, to observe the movements of the allies around Rothenburg.

The V Corps, which had suffered tremendous casualties during the last few weeks, stood by Löwenberg. It was reinforced by the 10th Division, which was detached from the III Corps. The III Corps also had the 39th Division permanently detached to the XI Corps. Though shorn of two divisions and a brigade of light cavalry, the III Corps still had three infantry divisions and all of its artillery.[25]

During the day of 8 September, the VIII Corps and IV Cavalry Corps found themselves subject to a strong allied reconnaissance. GB Uminski (27th Light Cavalry Brigade), who occupied a post before the main camp, decided on 9 September to drive the allied cavalry away. He was ordered to penetrate the allied cavalry screen as far as possible, supporting his movement with an infantry battalion. The Advanced Guard Regiment[26] charged the Cossacks, while the Polish 14th Cuirassiers maneuvered against the dragoons. The Cossacks were thrown back and lost a standard. The Russian dragoons also fell back, losing about 80 killed and wounded and a large number of prisoners. Uminski's forces pursued them about a league, when they saw before them a large number of allied columns moving down the roads to Herrhuth and Ostritz.

An hour and a half later, the allies appeared before Poniatowski's position with a force of light cavalry that was charged by the 27th Light Cavalry Brigade and driven back. The Russians sent forward a force of skirmishers, who were countered by Polish skirmishers. This inconclusive skirmish yielded prisoners, who informed Poniatowski that this was Langeron's Corps and that he was advancing against the Poles.

The Russians began to feed more men into the battle and reinforced their infantry with a 12-pdr battery. By about 4:00 p.m., the Russians had 6,000 men deployed before the VIII Corps and began to turn Poniatowski's flank. Being unable to hold Löbau, he withdrew to Neustadt.[27]

Blücher, finding he was no longer being pursued, realized that Napoleon was no longer present, and resolved to resume the offensive. On 9 September, he set his forces forward again. St.-Priest's Division, followed by the rest of Langeron's Corps, passed over the Neisse at Ostritz. Yorck's Corps crossed between Ostritz and Görlitz. The goal of the maneuver was to cut off Macdonald's advanced guard, which occupied these two cities, but the movement was detected by the French in Görlitz, who withdrew to Reichenbach and later to Hochkirch.[28]

On the same day, Macdonald withdrew to Bautzen. On 11 September, he was in Godau, leaving only a small advanced guard across the Spree. On 12 September he resumed his withdrawal and moved to Bischofswerda, because he believed his left was threatened. His retrograde movements continued, and on 15 September, his forces were positioned as follows: Poniatowski (VIII Corps) in Stolpen, Lauriston (V Corps) in Dröbnitz, Gérard (XI Corps) in Schmiedefeld, and Souham (III Corps) in Radeberg. Macdonald's retreat was effected without firing a shot or with any serious pursuit or pressure. It cannot be explained by other than the morale of the troops and their commanders.

Napoleon in Dresden

Napoleon returned to Dresden on 12 September. Ney's defeat at Dennewitz had driven him back on Torgau, and Macdonald had surrendered the eastern frontier. Napoleon had begun to realize that Dresden would be the site of yet another major battle and resolved to prepare for it. He could not abandon the line of the Elbe. The geography of Germany and the significance of the Elbe and its cities forced Napoleon to continue holding it.[29] Davout was to continue holding Hamburg, Ney was between Torgau and Wittenberg, Girard was in Magdeburg, and Napoleon would remain in Saxony with the remainder of the army facing the main allied armies.

To prepare, Napoleon directed that Macdonald's forces (III, V, VIII, and XI Corps) should establish themselves between Radeberg and Stolpen. Maréchal St-Cyr was to establish a series of fortifications on the Saxon side of the Bohemian mountains. These works were to be on the plateaus of Pirna and Berggieshübel and across the road from Liebstadt to Töplitz.[30]

St-Cyr's forces were distributed with the 42nd Division on the Pirna plateau, holding Libenstein and Königstein. The three divisions (1st, 2nd, and 23rd) of the I Corps, now commanded by GD Mouton, Comte de Lobau, were positioned by Berggieshübel, the remaining three divisions of the XIV Corps (the 42nd Division being assigned to I Corps) were on the road from Liebstadt to Töplitz. Two divisions of Young Guard were posted behind Pirna, where they were to act as a reserve for St-Cyr. The Old Guard and the remainder of the Young Guard were in Dresden as a general reserve. Victor's II Corps was in Freiberg, to watch the routes from Bohemia to Leipzig, and the VI Corps (Marmont) and the I Cavalry Corps (Latour-Maubourg) were in Grossenhain, to maintain contact with Ney in Torgau.

In an effort to stop the partisan actions in his rear, Napoleon detached Lefèbvre-Desnoëttes with his Guard cavalry and the corps cavalry of II Corps.[31]

After the defeat of Ney's army at Dennewitz a reorganization was necessary. The XII Corps was dissolved and its forces distributed between the IV and VII Corps.

A pontoon bridge was erected at Pirna which, with those in Lilienstein and Königstein, assured communications between Macdonald's forces east of the Elbe with those of St-Cyr on the left bank.

However, before adopting this project, Napoleon had formed another. He had resolved to move his center to Torgau, because Dresden was too close to the Bohemian mountains, which limited his maneuvering room. This allowed the Army of Bohemia to always be within two days march of his main army, and limited his ability to respond by reducing his reaction time. Between the allied cavalry superiority and the impenetrable nature of the mountains, he would always find himself liable to an immediate demand for his attention on that quarter. He was unable to execute the move because of Ney's retreat on Torgau and that of Macdonald on Radeberg.

In addition, Napoleon also felt that Dresden was too far from Berlin. His one major opportunity to force the allies to negotiate would be if he could knock out the Prussians and force them to sue for peace. The Russians and Austrians were not vulnerable to any such geopolitical defeat, and as the allies were refusing battle with him, the opportunity for a decisive battlefield victory was slim. That left only the hope that a quick rush and seizure of Berlin could yield the decisive results he wanted.

There were disadvantages to this concept, because it uncovered Saxony, and the capture of Dresden and Leipzig would have a serious impact on the fragile loyalty of the Confederation of the Rhine.

On 12 September Napoleon had issued instructions for the preparation of Torgau for such an operation, but events intervened. The result was that Napoleon was forced to execute the campaign with two major forces, one in Hamburg and the other at Dresden, plus a liaison corps between Torgau and Wittenberg.

The Army of Bohemia Advances Again

The Austrians under Schwarzenberg, who were, at the moment, separated from the Prussians and Russians of the Army of Silesia, realized the futility of actions by Kleist and Wittgenstein alone against Dresden. On 12 September they withdrew back to Töplitz.

In Töplitz a council of war was held. Here it was decided to chase all the French troops from their positions on the heights before them, and as soon as that was complete, to move the bulk of the army to the left, via Marienberg towards Saxony, in the direction of Leipzig and Chemnitz.

A letter arrived from Blücher and a new conference was assembled. Though the details of the conference are lost, it is known that the Austrians were opposed to a general reunion of all the allied forces. GM Radetzky stated, in essence, that Napoleon had repeatedly proven to the allies that he could maneuver his forces and bring them to battle by gathering superior forces against them. His personality was inspiring his generals, who were otherwise fatigued with war, while without him his soldiers had to be driven at the allies. He advocated that Napoleon's "manner of conducting war should not be [theirs]. [Napoleon] should seek battles and they [the allies] should evade them."[32] This attitude appears to have been accepted by the allies, with the understanding that nothing was more disadvantageous than the reunion of large forces at a single point. The union of the Army of Bohemia with either that of Bernadotte or Blücher, would be a colossal error that only God could command, personalities being what they were. This would permit Napoleon to concentrate his forces and fall on part of the allied army in a decisive manner.

Knesebeck was sent to Blücher to advise him of the perceived advantages and disadvantages of a union of the allied armies. These advantages were enumerated as follows:

Advantages
1. The combined army could begin a march in this direction (Töplitz) without awaiting the arrival of GdK Bennigsen, and during those days that the Army of the Reserve would be marching from Guntzlau to Görlitz, the Army of Silesia could move on the road to Bautzen.
2. The Army of Silesia would remain near its resources.
3. Blücher would continue to remain in contact with the Army of the North.

Disadvantages
1. A reinforcement of allied forces on the middle Elbe or in the vicinity of Torgau would shorten French supply lines and give them time to move reinforcements to the threatened area.

It was felt that if Blücher did not move his army into Bohemia to support the Army of Bohemia, the Army of Bohemia alone was not sufficiently strong to risk moving towards Chemnitz. It would have to detach 40,000 men before the Erzgebirge to cover that point. Napoleon, by virtue of his central position, would be able to move in three marches from Dresden to Töplitz and in a further three marches to Sebastianberg, concentrating his forces as necessary to protect or attack those points. The Army of Silesia was, therefore, unable to move against the French lines of communication. However, if the Army of Silesia remained on the Elbe, then the Army of Bohemia could move with assurance into Saxony.

If the Army of Silesia found difficulties in crossing the Elbe in the vicinity of Torgau, or if it and the Army of the North could not cross elsewhere, the entire French army could move against the Army of Bohemia.

If, however, the Army of Silesia succeeded in passing the Elbe, it could well be forced into a battle with the river at its back and would be unable to withdraw. A battle before the union with the Army of the North would be too risky.

The Army of Silesia, once unified with the Army of the North, would lose its independence, which would bring into play all the disadvantages of combining the smaller armies into a larger, less maneuverable one.

There was also the problem of politics. Bernadotte's two victories, Gross-Beeren and Dennewitz, had somewhat embarrassed the Russians and Austrians and there was talk of placing the combined Armies of Silesia and the North under the command of Bernadotte. The Prussians, not wishing to lose their one command, sought to retain their freedom of action and command.

Wittgenstein, on learning that Napoleon had returned to Dresden, assumed the offensive again on 13 September. Kleist and Colloredo quickly joined him. Schwarzenberg decided to send forward a strong reconnaissance to cross the Erzgebirge to examine the French positions.[33]

Wittgenstein moved to the right, via Hellendorf, against the Comte de Lobau's force. Colloredo and Prinz August von Preussen's 12th Brigade of Kleist's Corps moved through Breitenau against the XIV Corps.

The fortifications that Napoleon had ordered raised by Gieshübel and on the road to Liebstadt had not yet been erected. GD Dumonceau's 2nd Division, I Corps, which was the most advanced

French force, was attacked in Nollendorf by the allies and obliged to withdraw on Peterswald. This movement uncovered the XIV Corps, which also withdrew.

Napoleon attempted to seize the opportunity, as he had a week earlier. On 15 September he moved to Berggieshübel with the Guard, and ordered I Corps and the 42nd Division to arrange themselves in echelons on the right of Wittgenstein's Corps. He ordered St-Cyr to march by Fürstenwalde to the Geyersberg Heights. Wittgenstein, seeing he was being flanked, quickly withdrew.

Between 2:00 and 3:00 p.m., Napoleon began to attack the allied positions. Kaisarov was obliged to evacuate Markersbach and the French movement began to turn the Russian right, forcing the Russian 3rd Division to withdraw to the heights to the north of Hellendorf. At the same time, the Russian 5th Division occupied the village of Hellendorf and Kaisarov moved there as well. The Russian 3rd and 14th Divisions continued their retreat to the middle of the village of Peterswald. On learning of Kaisarov's retreat, Prinz August von Preussen detached two battalions under Oberstleutnant Blücher into the forest to the east of the Hellendorf-Raitza road to cover the right, and on the left, he positioned another battalion and two Russian cannon.

At 5:30 p.m., Napoleon stood before Pirna. Two divisions of the Imperial Guard stood at Langen Hennersdorf, and two more stood at Gieshübel. When he learned that the allies were withdrawing, he ordered GD Mouton-Duvernet to push his 42nd Division forward to the Peterswald Heights. When that movement was complete, the advanced guard of the 42nd Division stood on the heights and the main body occupied Gieshübel, where it began constructing redoubts. The 43rd Division continued to guard the road to Königstein.[34]

On 16 September Napoleon continued to advance. Wittgenstein withdrew to Kulm, Colloredo to the heights of Striegwitz, and Kleist to Serberchen. The French troops pursued the allies without rest, and despite an intense rain all day, occupied the Nollendorf heights and the Geyersberg pass by evening.

Combat by Peterswald

Until 11:00 a.m., on 17 September, everything remained quiet between the two armies. At that time, however, French columns surged forward preceded by about 25 cavalry squadrons. Pahlen was under orders not to engage in any serious combat and withdrew his forces towards Nollendorf. Pahlen's troops were disposed as follows. The Russian cavalry, having the 1st Prussian Hussar Regiment on their right, stood to the north of Peterswald. The Russian 5th Division stood to the south of Peterswald and the Prussian 12th Brigade (Prince August von Preussen) stood to the west of the village. Pahlen stood near the 5th Division on the edge of the Jungferndorf Woods, where he observed the retreat of the 12th Brigade.[35]

Kleist, by Wittgenstein's orders, was advancing on their position with the Prussian 2nd Corps. He had departed his camp in Soborten with the Prussian 10th and 11th Brigades. The Prussian 9th Brigade remained to guard the passages at Graupen and Geiersberg. The Prussian 12th Brigade was to march towards Eulau and occupy the mountain passages around Schneeberg. The 11th Brigade was assigned the mission of occupying the advanced posts between Peterswald and Hellendorf, while the 10th Brigade stood as a reserve by Nollendorf.

The Russian and Prussian artillery, with the exception of one battery, withdrew towards Nollendorf at the approach of the French cavalry. The French cavalry moved to the east of Peterswald, and threw back the 1st Silesian Hussar Regiment, which sought to cover the retreat of the allied artillery. The Russian 5th Division occupied a position on the edge of the woods by Jungferndorf while the 12th Brigade and the cavalry found themselves taking heavy casualties from the French attacks. The single Russian battery remaining in support barely escaped.

In this action, the 1st Silesian Hussars, on the right of the Russian artillery, found itself against the 9th Chevaulégers-lanciers Regiment. Knowing that Russian Uhlan regiments were operating in the area, the commander of the 9th Chevaulégers-lanciers advanced waving a handkerchief and calling out to the Prussians to not charge, that they were Russian cavalry. Puzzled by the ploy, Oberstleutnant von Blücher's cavalry did not charge, allowing the 2/, 3/9th Chevaulégers-lanciers to pass through a hole between the 2/, 3/1st Silesian Hussars. They reunited with the first squadron and struck the flank of the 4/1st Silesian Hussars, driving them back.

The question of friend or foe now being answered, the 1/, 2/Silesian Hussars swung around and struck the flank of the 9th Chevaulégers-lanciers and drove them back in turn behind the supporting Anhalt Chasseur Regiment. The 9th Chevauléger-lanciers' colonel appears to have lost his life as a result of his perfidious attack.[36]

Ziethen chose not to stand on the Peterswald Heights and receive the French attack, so he withdrew. At 12:30 p.m., the 11th Brigade assumed a position to the north of Nollendorf to cover Pahlen's retreat. However, during the poorly organized withdrawal, Wittgenstein's Corps mixed with Pirch's Brigade and the artillery and train clogged the defile. The situation seemed grave, but the crisis passed before the French appeared.

At 1:30 p.m., Kleist's advanced guard found a position on the Nollendorf heights, and at the same time Pahlen was moving through the Tellnitz defile, with the French close behind him. Kleist ordered Ziethen to occupy a position on the heights. Pirch placed two battalions to the right of the chapel and a battalion in Streckenwald to cover the road to Tellnitz, while the rest of his brigade and the reserve cavalry moved towards Kulm.[37]

After a heavy artillery preparation, a division of I Corps attacked through a storm of sleet and snow and struck Ziethen's Brigade, which had been left as a rearguard between Tellnitz and Kunitz. At 3:00 p.m., Ziethen was pushed back and the French division marched on Kulm, where it did not hesitate to engage Wittgenstein's Corps.

The night of 16/17 September passed with the allies slowly withdrawing towards Kulm. At 11:00 p.m., Schwarzenberg ordered the dispositions for the next day for the allied army. They were as follows:The 2nd Armeeabteilung (Merveldt): Longueville's Brigade in Aussig, where it was to watch the road to Tetschen. Giffing's Brigade was to be in Klein Kaudern. It was to hold the Arnsdorf and Niesenbahm passes. The Kienmayer Regiment covered the front and right by München and Spansdorf. The Gradiscaner Grenz Battalion was to stand on the wooded heights by Saara. The Johann Dragoon Regiment was to stay in reserve. Kloppstein's Brigade was to stand on the heights by Postitz and Gartitz. Merczery's Brigade was to stand in the valley behind them as a reserve.1st Armeeabteilung (Colloredo): the advanced guard was to occupy the villages of Jonsdorf, Tillisch, Auschine, and Tannischberg. Torry's Brigade was to occupy Strisowitzerberg, Schöbritz, and the sheep fold. The Hessen-Homburg Hussars and Reisch Dragoons were to form the liaison between the advanced guard in the sheep pens and Deutsch-Neudörf. Their positions were to be occupied before daybreak. Czervinka's Brigade was to be in the tile works. Greth's Division was to stand in reserve to the left of Ziegelhütte.A Russian corps of 10,000 to 12,000 men was to occupy Kulm with advanced posts in Nieder- and Ober-Arbesau and Schande. The army reserve was to stand before Dux, by Döplitz on Wiklitz and to establish itself on the Bihane by 9:00 a.m.

The 3rd Armeeabteilung (Gyulai) was to stand in reserve by Brix. The Russian army was to move to Sobochleben and cover the left of the army by occupying Ebersdorf, Geiersberg, and Mückenthurmel.

Kleist ordered Ziethen's Brigade, reinforced by two battalions from the 12th Brigade and the 4th Russian Jager Regiment, deployed between Kulm and Vorder Tellnitz. The 10th and 11th Brigades, and the artillery reserve stood to the south of Kulm. The 9th Brigade stood towards Sobochleben, by the mountains.

The Russian 2nd Corps established itself with Mamonov's Brigade on the left of Kulm, the 34th Jagers in Kulm, and the 20th and 21st Jagers in the small woods to its east. The Russian 3rd Division and the Tobolsk and Minsk Regiments stood in reserve behind Kulm with three supporting batteries. The Russian 1st Corps was to the east of Sobochleben, having its right wing covered by Pahlen's cavalry. General Barclay de Tolly issued the order for the Russo-Prussian Reserve to take positions by Sobochleben and to defend his left wing with a detachment by Ebersdorf and by occupying the mountain passes through Graupen and Geiersberg.[38]

Ziethen was ordered, in case he was obliged to withdraw, to move down the main road and take up a position by Kulm, leaving the 4th Jagers in the woods with orders to withdraw to the west of the large heights. Württemberg, concerned for his left, requested that Wittgenstein send a corps in that direction. Wittgenstein advised him that Gortschakov was marching on Sobochleben and that he would support Württemberg.[39]

In Battle at Kulm Again

During the morning a thick fog covered the Kulm valley and slowed movements, until about noon when the sky began to clear. Before him, Napoleon saw 40,000 to 50,000 allied infantry standing ready. The French troops moved down the Nollendorf Road and attacked Vorder Tellnitz. Ziethen left two Prussian battalions behind an abatis and sent the Russian 4th Jager Regiment to the west. The rest of his brigade stood behind Kulm. He retained his position for two hours, despite the French attacks. However, around 2:00 p.m., he was forced to withdraw once the French columns turned his left. A battery positioned on the heights to the north of Kulm protected his retreat.[40]

Ziethen's infantry and artillery fell back to the edge of the mountain and linked up with Württemberg's forces by Schande. His cavalry moved to a new position between Kulm and Deutsch-Neudörfel. Around 2:30 p.m., Württemberg established Ziethen's Brigade to the east of Kulm and placed four battalions and two guns on Ziethen's left. The Russian 4th Jager Regiment was to later join this force. The rest of the Russian 3rd and 4th Divisions (11 battalions) stood to the south of Kulm.

The French attack at 3:00 p.m. was supported by ten guns. Count Lobau's I Corps prepared itself quickly for the assault, while Mouton-Duvernet's 42nd Division occupied the villages of Ober-Arbesau, Nieder-Arbesau, and Tillisch. At the same time, a French force pushed down the main road towards Kulm and Schande. A French battery of 10 guns, soon reinforced by more guns, occupied a ridge northeast of Schande and opened fire on the Prussian battery on the Horka, driving it off. A column marched against the Russian 20th Jager Regiment and another, larger column moved against Kulm. The allied artillery redoubled its fire and silenced the French battery supporting the attack. However, the French brought forward more guns and renewed the fight. The French infantry moved into the woods to the west of Kulm.

Other French infantry columns marched quickly through Arbesau, Tillisch, Johnsdorf, and Auschine to turn the allied flank. Colloredo decided to repeat the allied maneuver of 30 August and wrote to Merveldt, "The enemy are advancing against Kulm and are beginning to press me. I am going to attack in concert with Wittgenstein, if the 2nd Corps comes in time to attack the French left flank."

The Austrian offensive began at 3:30 p.m. Colloredo left Striegwitz, and with his 1st Armeeabteilung, moved to the heights to the south of the village. He posted two batteries to the left of Auschine that fired principally on the French battery by Schande. He stopped there an hour and a half to allow the Russian 2nd Corps time to intervene.

The Russian 2nd Corps moved into a position between Zuckmantel and Bohna. Lederer's Division moved from Saara to Zuckmantel, where his advanced guard took the village after the third attempt. Liechtenstein's Division marched from Gartitz and Postitz via Trosching towards Bohna, and threw the French from Vorder Tellnitz towards Kninitz. It was around 4:30 p.m., as Merveldt organized his corps in Bohna. Liechtenstein's Division stood in the first line and Lederer's Division stood in the second line. Merveldt ordered Liechtenstein to move his first brigade towards Kninitz and to move his second against Vorder Tellnitz.

As Merveldt's 2nd Armeeabteilung moved on Kunitz and Nollendorf, Colloredo's 1st Armeeabteilung was forming in echelon to its left and moving on Gartitz and Arbesau. At 5:00 p.m., Lederer's Division quickly pushed the French out of Tillisch.

In response, Ornano's 1st Guard Cavalry Division dispatched two squadrons of the Berg Lancers, under Colbert, which made a stunning attack against the Austrians and overran both Austrian batteries by Schande. The guns were retaken in an Austrian counterattack by a squadron of the Hessen-Homburg Hussars, supported by a number of Prussian squadrons[41] and a battalion of the de Ligne Infantry Regiment.

The brigade of Young Guard, which occupied Arbesau, was heavily attacked. Despite its efforts, it suffered the loss of a battalion and three cannon and was forced to withdraw. It was also in this engagement that the 21st and 33rd Line Regiments lost their eagles.[42] On the left the battle deteriorated into a skirmish duel where the French superiority told and the allies were forced to withdraw.

The allies began a general advance. The Prussians and Russians between Schande and the mountains attacked the French with their bayonets and drove them towards Tellnitz. At the same time Wittgenstein's troops moved from Kulm and Schande towards Tellnitz. The fire of the French battery by Schande fell silent and Colloredo's Austrian batteries played upon the lines of French infantry.

The Austrian 1st Corps moved from Arbesau and Auschine against Tellnitz, Tannischberg, and Tillisch. General Merveldt advanced with the Austrian 2nd Armeeabteilung against Deutsch Neudörfel and Schöbritz and reached the region of Zuckmantel and Kninitz.

GM Ziethen, convinced of the importance of maintaining his position, counterattacked with four battalions, and captured BG Creutzer before being forced to stop before Vorder Tellnitz.

As Napoleon received word of the Austrian move against Kninitz, he directed an infantry division forward to counter the Austrian move. The French moved into the woods by Vorder Tellnitz. Around evening a two-hour rain began to fall, accompanied by a heavy fog, making further combat impossible. That evening the Russian Jagers reoccupied Tellnitz. Napoleon rode back to Peterswald where he spent the night.

Though not militarily defeated, the French were obliged to withdraw. Rather than face another Kulm, they fell back to Berggieshübel and the allies reoccupied Peterswald.

This operation, like those that had preceded it, produced no results other than to fatigue the soldiers of the I and XIV Corps without inflicting compensating damage on the allies. The French losses are reported by Austrian sources at about 2,000 dead and wounded and another 2,000 prisoners, including General Creutzer. In addition, they lost two eagles, a flag, and seven cannon. The allies reputedly lost 1,000 men.[43]

The action over, Napoleon left the I and XIV Corps on the heights of Gieshübel and on the road to Liebstadt. The II Corps moved to maintain contact with Macdonald, whose forces held positions in Radeberg and Stolpen. Marmont (VI Corps) and Latour-Maubourg (I Cavalry Corps) were in Grossenhain. The Guard now moved to Pirna where it became a general reserve ready to act on either bank of the Elbe by virtue of the bridge there.

His dispositions made, Napoleon again sat back to await events. He had under his immediate control the forces of Macdonald and St-Cyr, that is to say eight army corps and the Imperial Guard.

One weak point in this arrangement was Napoleon's contact with Ney. After his defeat at Dennewitz, Ney had withdrawn to Torgau and Bernadotte had taken advantage to move up to the Elbe and throw bridges across it between Roslau and Acken. He then sent Czernichev across the Elbe at Acken to harass the French rear areas with his Cossacks. Bülow was sent towards Wittenberg and Tauentzien marched on Mühlberg and Liebenwerda in an effort to link with Blücher.

Combat by Cosdorf

The northern front facing Blücher was not quiet either. On 14 September Tauentzien moved Wobeser forward against Torgau. Blücher left Ubigau at 1:30 p.m., and soon heard that a large corps under Murat stood in Grossenhain. He responded by reinforcing his post in Cosdorf, formed by two squadrons of cavalry, with two companies of infantry under the orders of Major Kospboth.

On arriving in Cosdorf, the French observed a number of barges near Stehla, which seemed to be loaded with food. Kospboth had deployed part of his infantry as skirmishers in an advanced guard, while he held the bulk of his forces 1,000 paces to the rear to guard the convoy. His cavalry stood in Cosdorf. His situation was superior to the French position, as the terrain offered him some cover, but the convoy could not move because of the weak wind. Kospboth soon learned that a large force of French cavalry was closing on his position after chasing his cavalry from Cosdorf. He quickly formed his tiny force of infantry into square and prepared for the assault. The French cavalry struck and succeeded in cutting off a few Prussians attempting to defend the convoy. The convoy was then captured.

At noon, Tauentzien learned of the French crossing to the right bank. The French assembly point at Grossenhain was risky, with Tauentzien on their left flank and the Army of Silesia on their right. Tauentzien perceived that Napoleon intended to push this force towards the Elbe and ordered Wobeser to move back to Ubigau. This order was received by Wobeser at 5:00 p.m., as he reached Zschakau. He immediately moved back up the road and learned of the fall of Cosdorf to Chastel's cavalry, as well as the occupation of Elsterwerda, Liebenwerda, and Mühlberg by the French cavalry. At 10:00 p.m., he arrived in Ubigau. His advanced guard moved to Lönnewitz and established cavalry posts in Falkenberg, Schmerkendorf, and Beiersdorf. This action obliged Tauentzien to stop his move on Torgau and establish his force at Herzberg.[44]

On 17 September Murat, who commanded the VI Corps (Marmont) and the I Cavalry Corps (Latour-Maubourg), moved against Tauentzien and pushed him back from Mühlberg and Liebenwerda, but on the 18th, the Prussians counterattacked and recaptured Mühlberg. Tauentzien then moved back up the Schwarz-Elster River and occupied Elsterwerda, obliging Murat to push his advanced posts to Grossenhain.

Allied Plans

The movement of Tauentzien towards the Army of Silesia was not unsupported. Macdonald perceived that the Army of Silesia was, itself, moving towards Zittau to link up with the Army of Bohemia. Concern began to arise in the French general staff that the three allied armies were seeking to link up and act in unison against them.

The allies, themselves, were beginning to speak of "the decisive battle." The three sovereigns, who were with the Army of Bohemia, once again began to speak of crossing through the mountains to strike the French. However, this time, in lieu of striking at Dresden, the target was Leipzig, with the allies moving through Chemnitz and Commotau. The numerous partisans of Thielmann and Platov, spread between the Saale and the Elster, were to prepare the path for the Army of Bohemia.

The plan was a solid plan, but in order for it to work the allies had to join two of their armies, those of Bohemia and Silesia, so as to have sufficient strength to deal with Napoleon. This was demonstrated by the results of the battles at Katzbach and Dresden earlier in the year.

If it was not possible for Blücher to effect a junction with the Army of Bohemia, the plan would have to wait until the allied Army of the Reserve,[45] under Bennigsen, could arrive.

In addition, if these armies were to make their junction in the field, by marching through the relatively open terrain around Dresden, they would offer Napoleon the opportunity to block the passage of one of the two armies while concentrating his strength against the second and destroying it.

In view of the many difficulties involved with Blücher attempting to join the Army of Bohemia, it was decided that Bennigsen would move through Breslau and into Bohemia, so as to join Schwarzenberg's proposed movement against Leipzig. The movement of Bennigsen through Breslau, Zittau, and Töplitz would, in its turn, be covered by Blücher's Army of Silesia. Once that movement was complete, the Army of Silesia would make a thrust towards Dresden, so as to draw the French attention away from the mountain passes, and Schwarzenberg would begin his movement on Leipzig. At the same time, the Army of the North would cross the Elbe at Wittenberg and move up the Mulde.[46]

The first action, as a result of this agreement, was that Bennigsen was ordered to take his 50,000 men and move through Zittau and Tetschen towards Töplitz. Once there he would join the Army of Bohemia. He would then cover the Peterswald defiles, move into Saxony through Commotau, and advance on Chemnitz.

Blücher would advance, make his demonstrations against Dresden, and then move to his right and cross the Elbe at Roslau, so as to link up with the Army of the North. Once joined together, Blücher's and Bernadotte's two armies would march on Leipzig from the north.

Bennigsen reached the gorges of Zittau on 17 September, and arrived in Töplitz on 22/23 September. Schwarzenberg's combined forces now totaled about 200,000 men. While this juncture was being effected, Tauentzien and Bülow demonstrated before Torgau and Blücher acted before Dresden.

The new allied plan was superior to that of Trauchenberg. Now, instead of three independent forces, none of which were sufficiently large to survive a major engagement with the French, they would now have only two forces, of 200,000 and 120,000 men respectively.

Napoleon Reacts

On 21 September, like the predator waiting in its lair for its prey to appear, Napoleon moved out of Dresden, and on 22 September he was in Hartha where he joined Macdonald's headquarters. Instead of the usual small reconnaissance that Macdonald had been sending out to watch Blücher, Napoleon directed the III, V, and VIII Corps to advance towards Bischofswerda, which was occupied by an advanced guard under Rudsevich. Napoleon and the Imperial Guard followed the operation. Rudsevich found himself confronted with a massively superior force, and quickly retired into the forests around Bischofswerda and on Godau.

On 23 September, Macdonald's army continued its march towards Bautzen, but it was stopped by the presence of a large allied force. The French were led by Exelman's 4th Light Cavalry Division of Sébastiani's II Cavalry Corps. The III Corps established itself east of Bischofswerda and Geissmannsdorf, covered on its left by Beurman's 23rd Light Cavalry Brigade. Delmas' 9th

Division stood in Pulsnitz. The V Corps formed in echelon by division in Drebnitz, Putzkau, and Tröbigau, with parties of cavalry pushed forward to Gaussig to cover their front.

At 5:00 a.m., on 24 September, Katzeler reported to Blücher that the French had remained motionless since the last report of their positions, with the exception of the French advanced posts. Shortly after his report was delivered, Souham's III Corps began to march forward in three columns. The right column, composed of cavalry and artillery, moved through Bischofswerda. The center column consisted solely of infantry and crossed open fields as it marched on Geissmannsdorf. The left column consisted of all arms.[47]

Major Klüx was under orders not to engage in a serious battle and withdrew to Göda covered by his skirmishers. As soon as the heads of the French columns appeared before his new position, he once again withdrew, covered by his skirmishers and three platoons of infantry which formed his rearguard. The French pursued them until they moved into a forest. Then the formed French ceased the pursuit and only French skirmishers moved into the woods in pursuit.

The French left column continued its quick marching pace. Oberst Katzeler faced this column with three battalions and some light infantry, under Major Klüx, with orders to cover his right flank.

Unfortunately for Katzeler, the terrain prevented him from observing the size of the French forces opposing, so he resolved to make a stand and to test the French strength. Wedel's battalion (4/15th Silesian Landwehr Regiment) evacuated the forest to the west of Welcke and took a new position on the side of the road behind a swamp. As the French arrived, his battalion fired on them with "battalion fire," but was obliged to withdrew as the French skirmishers swept towards the flanks. Katzeler resumed his retreat with orders to move to Klein Praga where he joined Rudsevich's advanced guard.

During the pursuit of Katzeler, the bulk of the XI Corps remained behind on the edge of the forest between Thumitz and Wölkau, as if to reform before resuming its advance. Large numbers of its skirmishers continued moving forward to Rothnauslitz. Katzeler took advantage of the village and the separation of the skirmishers from the main body of the French XI Corps to charge them with 11 squadrons[48] supported by the skirmishers and Jägers of his advanced guard, plus some formed Russian infantry. His cavalry advanced in columns by platoon through the defile between Rothnauslitz and Potschapplitz at the gallop, with the East Prussian National Cavalry Regiment in the lead. The first regiment moved towards Potschapplitz and the two others moved on Rothkretscham. Part of the allied cavalry dismounted and fought on foot in the village streets with the French skirmishers, while the remainder found themselves facing three regiments of French cavalry which appeared in the direction of Thumitz, formed in columns and facing the allied infantry.

Two squadrons of the Brandenburg Hussar Regiment moved through the village and struck at the leading French regiment, which, believing itself secure in the narrow road, accepted their charge without countercharging. The Prussians were thrown back. After rallying, they were joined by two squadrons of the Brandenburg Uhlan Regiment. These four squadrons then threw themselves against the French a second and third time. Both times their attacks were supported by a fifth squadron coming from Potschapplitz. After the melee they fell back and deployed across the French front as the Prussian skirmishers pushed into Rothnauslitz. The 2/Brandenburg Hussars and 3/Brandenburg Uhlans then advanced against the skirmishers to their right and left. The 3/Brandenburg Uhlans, after pushing through Rothnauslitz, captured 320 fusiliers of the Westphalian Guard who had little taste for the battle. By this time the French had brought their artillery into action, and as the Prussian cavalry withdrew, it was hastened on its way by more than a little cannon fire. The Prussian skirmishers covered the withdrawal of their cavalry.[49]

The energetic Prussian attack deceived Macdonald into believing that he faced 12,000 to 15,000 allies with 30 cannon. As a result, when he resumed his movement forward his advanced guard was supported by a strong battery of artillery. The French soon moved over the Praga and Göda heights with little opposition. At 5:00 p.m., Macdonald wrote to Napoleon stating that he had cleared the woods and that the allies appeared to have fallen back to Birkau. As night was beginning to fall, Macdonald ordered the XI Corps to echelon its three divisions between Thumitz and Birkau with its head covered by the ravine of the latter city. He returned to Goldbach around 6:00 p.m., after establishing his advanced guard in its positions. Maison's Division remained in Stolpen to cover his right while the divisions of Albert and Rochambeau moved towards Rückersdorf and Drebnitz. After some quick engagements Lauriston believed that the allies had a camp between Neustadt and Neukirch. This news caused Macdonald to believe his position was overextended and in great jeopardy. Believing serious threat existed to its right flank, Macdonald ordered his forces to fall back.

The battle renewed at 6:30 p.m., after Macdonald departed. Night was beginning to fall as the French advanced guard arrived before Göda, which Major Klüx defended with the 2/East Prussian Infantry Regiment. Two companies occupied the village bridge and its adjacent houses. One company each was on the right and the left of the bridge. Two Jäger companies stood on the south of the bridge and another stood in reserve to the right behind the village. The 1/Brandenburg Regiment supported them to the east. The rest of the troops were in position on a hill a quarter of a league to the rear.

The French artillery showered a hail of shells on Göda in support of the French attack. The frontal attack was a demonstration, as the main assault was against the Prussian company established on the left of the bridge. The Prussians were driven back and took up a new position in a nearby cemetery. Katzeler acted quickly to keep Klüx from being cut off. He sent the 1/Brandenburg Infantry Regiment forward to strike the French columns.[50] The French had just gained possession of the village as the 1/Brandenburg Regiment sent forward a platoon on each side of the village. The rest of the battalion then moved forward at the *geschwindschritt*[51] in a column of platoons down the main street of the village. They quickly overran the cemetery, but the darkness and the fatigue of his troops obliged Katzeler to withdraw. His two battalions withdrew to rejoin the main body of the advanced guard and only the Prussian pickets remained facing Göda. Macdonald remained convinced that he faced 15,000 allies.

During the evening Lauriston position the XI Corps in echelon by division between Birkau to Thumitz. On its left he positioned a heavy cavalry division in Geissmannsdorf and Pickau. The Light cavalry was in Thumitz, Damitz, Wölkau, and Rothnauslitz. Marchand's 39th Division (Hessians and Badeners) stood before and behind Bischofswerda. It had detached a battalion to support the heavy cavalry and another to Goldbach to serve the headquarters. The III Corps had two divisions in Harthau and Frankenthal. The third division was in Radeberg. Macdonald intended to march on Bautzen with the XI Corps, supported by two divisions of the III Corps the following morning.[52]

French prisoners interrogated by the Prussians inclined Blücher to believe that Napoleon had departed the army and caused him to decide it was time to turn on the French. He moved Sacken from Marienstern to Göda and ordered a night attack on Macdonald's left. The advanced guards of Langeron's and Yorck's Corps were warned to prepare for the attack. Unfortunately for the Prussians, Blücher made up his mind to attack too late for it to be executed, and Sacken's Corps stopped in Pietzschwitz.

The left of the Army of Silesia, St.-Priest, withdrew towards Wilthen. His move uncovered Bubna's left flank, causing him to move his advanced guard to Lobendau and his main body to Hainspach. When the French V Corps appeared on the Lauterbach and Langen-Wolmsdorf Heights, Bubna estimated he faced 16,000 French troops. Albert's 10th Division, 4,000 men, deployed and overran Rückersdorf. General Neipperg counterattacked with part of the Austrian Jager Battalion #5, two squadrons of the Blankenstein Hussars, and the Russian 29th and 45th

Jager Regiments, pushing the French back to their artillery. The allied advanced posts resumed their old positions.

Lauriston's subsequent reports to Napoleon were vague. He reported that before him stood two battalions of Austrian Jägers, three squadrons of the Blankenstein Hussars, and six Russian infantry battalions. He reported that only a few allied bivouac fires illuminated the hillsides, not enough to indicate a major force. Interrogations of the local inhabitants revealed that there were forces of Austrian cavalry and Cossacks in Neustadt, but their numbers had steadily declined over the last several days. He did learn that there were significant Russian cavalry forces in Lauterbach, but that they too had been withdrawing since noon.[53]

In view of the fatigue of the army and the tactical situation, Napoleon ordered the French to withdraw and on 24 September, the three corps were massed in Weissig, about four miles from Dresden.

Napoleon concentrated his forces and prepared his position in and around Dresden, but he could not forget Ney. As a result, he organized a force in Meissen. Macdonald was discharged as overall commander of the III, V, and VIII Corps and resumed command of the XI Corps, but also retained command of the II Cavalry Corps.[54] The army was then redistributed as follows:

- The XI Corps (Macdonald) was to remain in Weissig.
- The V Corps (Lauriston) occupied Dresden.
- The III (Souham) and VI (Marmont) and the I Cavalry Corps (Latour-Maubourg) moved to Meissen.
- The VIII Corps (Poniatowski) was posted on the road between Waldheim and Leipzig to assist Lefèbvre-Desnoëttes in his action against the allied partisan forces.
- St-Cyr's army was deployed with I Corps (Lobau) in Berggieshübel, XIV Corps in Pinta and Borna, and the II Corps (Victor) in Freiberg.[55]

Facing them, the Army of Silesia had an advanced post in Schandau and its main body between Bautzen and Kamentz. The Army of Bohemia was in Töplitz.

Seeing the forces arrayed before him, and knowing of the arrival of 60,000 more men under Bennigsen, Napoleon had begun to think of withdrawing his forces and facing the allies on the Rhine. He had already written Clarke to prepare for his arrival and to prepare the border fortresses for operations.

In order to effect such a movement, it would be necessary for Napoleon to have secure lines of communications, and to this end, he ordered Augereau (IX Corps) to cover those lines as well as to send forward a division destined to join the I Corps. The remainder of the IX Corps was to move to Jena, where it could assure the loyalty of the Bavarians. If the Bavarians were to defect while the IX Corps was still in Würzburg, it would be too isolated and would collapse. Its security was greater if it stood closer to the Grande Armée, and in Jena it could cover the passes through the Thüringian Forest.

The Allied Partisan Forces

GL Thielmann had organized 2,000 Austrian and Prussian cavalry and two guns for operations behind the French lines. He arrived in Töplitz on 2 September, and was ordered to move up the Eger River to Carlsbad. From there he was to move through the mountains to Annaberg and on to Zwickau, where he could operate against the French communications between Mainz and Leipzig. In general, he was to operate on the left bank of the Mulde and the right bank of the Mensdorf.

Thielmann arrived in Altenburg on 7 September, about 60 miles into Saxony, and dispatched a squadron to Walsenburg on the Mulde. This detachment was detected and word reached Napoleon of Thielmann's presence on 12 September. In response, Napoleon dispatched Lefèbvre-Desnoëttes to chase him down. Lefèbvre-Desnoëttes left Altenburg and moved on Waldheim. Margaron, who commanded in Leipzig, was at the same time advised to increase his vigilance.[56]

However, by 12 September, Thielmann's forces had put many miles between themselves and their last known location. They struck at Weissenfels, dispersing the French they found there. From there they moved against Naumburg, where the French garrison surrendered.

At the same time as Lefèbvre-Desnoëttes began to move, Ney was ordered to send Piré's 1st Light Cavalry Brigade to Leisnig and have them scout the area towards Altenburg.

Victor, who was in Freiberg, was to hold a column of 1,200 cavalry and eight companies of voltigeurs ready to move if Thielmann came near him. Nansouty was ordered to send Ornano's 1st Guard Cavalry Division to Nossen, where it would form a reserve for Lefèbvre-Desnoëttes.

Augereau's IX Corps, which was en route to Jena, promised to close the back door on Thielmann's little force and possibly also that of Mensdorf. Margaron, the commandant of the Leipzig garrison, dispatched 1,000 infantry and 500 cavalry on a raid to recapture Weissenfels, which they had done during the night of 14/15 September. Unfortunately, Thielmann had already departed and was en route to Merseburg. The force he left in Weissenfels escaped and moved to Zeitz as ordered. They led Margaron's forces after them, straight into the trap that Thielmann had planned for them.

In Merseburg, Thielmann destroyed the war materials he found and broke the bridge over the Saale. He then divided his forces into two columns in an effort to confuse the pursuing French columns, and ordered them to rendezvous at Naumburg.

As Thielmann arrived in Merseburg, Lefèbvre-Desnoëttes began his move on Weissenfels and Naumburg. Thielmann, learning of the presence of Girardin's Brigade near Apolda, suspected an enveloping movement, abandoned his goal of Naumburg, and moved towards Freiburg, where he rallied on 19 September.[57]

As the first allied troops arrived in Freiburg they found themselves faced by one of the forces that Lefèbvre-Desnoëttes had organized from the French depots in Saxony. Minutes later, when Thielmann arrived with his second column, he found himself separated from the first column. After some quick maneuvering, he skirted past the French flank and led his column to Zeitz, where he arrived on 21 September and met Mensdorf's forces.

Lefèbvre-Desnoëttes, who was moving to Weissenfels and Pegau, redirected his movement to Altenburg, covering the roads to Chemnitz and Zwickau. Mensdorf found himself faced by Piré at Leisnig and withdrew towards Grimma. Lefèbvre-Desnoëttes threw himself after Mensdorf, but Mensdorf had already decamped and fled towards Rötha. Prior to reaching Rötha, Mensdorf turned aside and moved to Zeitz, where he rejoined Thielmann and both moved to Zwickau to await Platov and his forces.

Czernichev's Partisans

To the north, Bernadotte had detached Czernichev with 3,000 cavalry and directed him to move on Kassel in the Kingdom of Westphalia. Kassel was garrisoned by 4,000 men under GD Allix.

Czernichev crossed the Elbe at Acken on 22 September.[58] His forces moved quickly into Westphalia. In a quick engagement near Halchter and in Brunswick his Cossacks captured one colonel, 25 officers and 350 men. Many of the young Westphalian soldiers, expressing their nationalism, joined Czernichev and were used to form *a freiwillige Jäger* squadron for the 3rd Kurmark Landwehr Cavalry Regiment.[59]

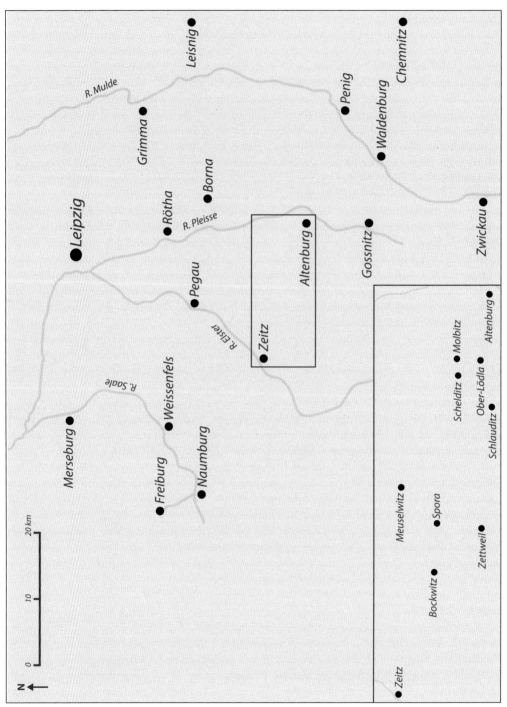

Sketch Map 4   The Partisan Front.

On 28 September he arrived before the gates of Kassel, and attacked the city.[60] Jérôme fled to Benkendorf, escorted by two Guard battalions, eight squadrons, and a number of guns. Jérôme left GD Allix in command of the city and the remaining troops.

Czernichev divided his forces into three columns. The first contained about 1,000 Cossacks under Benkendorf. It swam the Fulda and moved against the Frankfurt road. The second column contained the Isoum Hussars and two Cossack regiments under Colonel Bedraga. It moved against Bettenhausen, which was defended by the Jägergarde Battalion, the depots of the light infantry battalions, and a two-gun battery.[61] The third column, under General Bastineller, contained the remainder of the forces and moved against Kassel.[62]

At Bettenhausen Major Bödicker deployed his troops. The 6th Company, Jägergarde, was deployed in a skirmish line with a support in front of the main position. The 2nd Company remained formed behind them while the remaining four companies of the Jägergarde, the depots of the light infantry, and the two guns stood behind the bridge, on the Wahlebach stream.[63]

About 200 Cossacks approached down the road and encountered the Westphalian Guard skirmish line. They executed a swarm attack, rushing forward in a wild and savage attack. The Westphalian skirmishers pulled back on their support and were slowly forced back to their main position on the bridge.

Colonel Bedraga led the first major attack against the bridge. He rode at the head of the Isoum Hussars and was shot dead by three musket balls. Enraged, the Isoum Hussars drove against the Westphalians, capturing their guns and capturing one of the two battalions. The second battalion fled, crossing over the Fulda and occupying a number of houses, from which it set up a crossfire using the cannons defending the gate. Stabscapitain Lischin advanced with cannon and quickly dismounted one of the Westphalian guns. That done, the Isoum Hussars charged the position and carried it.

At the same time Benkendorf's forces swam the Fulda and pursued Jérôme as he fled. They had a quick skirmish with his advanced guard and purportedly captured 250 men and some of Jérôme's baggage. They then continued their pursuit of Jérôme all the way to Marburg.

General Bastineller's forces advanced against Kassel and set up two howitzers to fire on the city. When Bastineller arrived in Rothenburg, 200 of his Cossacks caught a small Westphalian detachment and captured them. This force consisted of about 100 infantry, the two companies of the 2nd Cuirassier Regiment under Oberstleutnant von Mentzhausen, and perhaps two guns.[64] So many of the Westphalians captured during the assault on Kassel later volunteered to serve with Czernichev that an infantry battalion was organized and placed under Major Dörnberg.[65]

The city of Kassel did not defend itself and after a couple of cannon shots,[66] on 29 September, GD Allix surrendered the city.[67] Once in possession of the city, Czernichev reported to Winzingerode that he had captured a considerable quantity of munitions and arms of all sorts, the sum of 79,000 thalers, 1,000 sick and wounded French, and 22 cannon which were sent to Berlin. Of the funds, 15,000 thalers were distributed to the partisan force, 4,000 thalers were given to Major Dörnberg to outfit the newly formed battalion of Westphalian deserters, and 60,000 thalers were sent to Winzingerode.[68]

The relief column, under the Westphalian General Sandt, stopped upon learning of Jérôme's flight and the fall of the city. Czernichev did not attempt to hold the city, but contented himself with destroying the French war material he found there and then moved back across the Elbe.

The Affair at Altenburg

GD Lefèbvre-Desnoëttes had been pursuing the partisans for over two weeks when he occupied Altenburg. However, the allied force that he faced on the morning of 28 September was far stronger than he had anticipated.

That morning another streifkorps under Hetman Platov arrived before Altenburg. His forces were deployed in three columns. The right, under the command of Colonel Illesky, contained 600 infantry, two guns, and three squadrons of the Austrian Hessen-Homburg Hussars. Illesky led his column down the road to Penig. The center column was under Prince Kudaschov and consisted of 1,500 to 1,800 cavalry moving down the road to Waldenburg. The streifkorps of Mensdorf and Thielmann, about 2,000 men total, moved down the road to Zwickau. All three columns, consisting of 3,000 Austrian infantry, 20 Cossack regiments, a brigade of Austrian hussars, and a few Austrian and Russian guns, arrived at a point two and a half miles (four kilometers) from Altenburg at 10:00 a.m.[69]

French at Altenburg
2nd Guard Division
  4/, 5/, 6/, 7/1st Guard Lancer Regiment
  7/, 8/, 9/, 10/Guard Chasseurs à Cheval Regiment
  5/, 6/Guard Grenadiers à Cheval
Brigade: Piré
  1/, 2/6th Hussar Regiment
  1/, 2/, 3/7th Hussar Regiment
  1/, 2/, 3/8th Hussar Regiment
Brigade: Valle
  1/, 2/8th Chasseurs à Cheval Regiment
  1/, 2/9th Chasseurs à Cheval Regiment
  1/, 2/25th Chasseurs à Cheval Regiment
5th Light Cavalry Division: Général de division Lorge
  12th Light Cavalry Brigade: Général de brigade Jacquinot
    3/, 4/, 5/5th Chasseurs à Cheval Regiment
    3/, 4/10th Chasseurs à Cheval Regiment
    5/, 6/13th Chasseurs à Cheval Regiment
  13th Light Cavalry Brigade: Général de brigade Merlin
    4/ & 1 Co 5/15th Chasseurs à Cheval Regiment
    3/, 4/21st Chasseurs à Cheval Regiment
    3/, 4/22nd Chasseurs à Cheval Regiment
Baden Brigade: Generalleutnant Hochberg
  1/, 2/2nd Baden Regiment
  Lingg Jäger Battalion
Division: Margaron
  French Brigade:
    4/35th Légère Regiment
    1/36th Légère Regiment
    2/96th Line Regiment
    2/103rd Line Regiment
    1/132nd Line Regiment
    1st Provisional Cavalry Regiment
    2nd Provisional Cavalry Regiment
    3rd Provisional Cavalry Regiment
    4th Provisional Cavalry Regiment

The attack against Lefèbvre-Desnoëttes began from the right, to allow Colonel Illesky to turn Altenburg and to cut the French line of retreat to Borna. According to Thielmann, Platov's goal was to turn the French left and strike the battalion and three guns believed to be holding the road to Borna. The signal to attack was given by the firing of a cannon from the left wing.

Mensdorf's journal states that Platov assumed that a column of about 5,000 men had entered Mittweida and decided to attack Altenburg prior to Thielmann's arrival.

The French soon caught wind of the planned attack. Lefèbvre-Desnoëttes reported intercepting a letter from GM Paumgarten to an Austrian colonel which advised him of the pending attack by "4,400 cavalry, 600 infantry and six guns." Lefèbvre-Desnoëttes quickly evacuated Altenburg and moved to a position on Ober Lödla, facing Altenburg. His artillery and cavalry stood in the center, while his infantry covered his wings, reaching to positions on the edge of the Moblitz Forest on the left and the Schlauditz defile on the right.

Lefèbvre-Desnoëttes then dispatched Chef d'escadron Dulimbert to GD Lorge with a request that he bring his cavalry forward to a position by the Zeitz defiles, placing his infantry and artillery on the heights before that village to cover Lefèbvre-Desnoëttes' retreat. The bridges on the Elster between Pegau and below Zeitz were destroyed.

A second officer, sent to the Duke of Padua, GD Arrighi, announced that if infantry was not sent to support Lefèbvre-Desnoëttes, his division would be obliged to withdraw that night to Weissenfels.[70]

The French were struck frontally by GM Kudaschov, from Platov's Corps. They held off the Russians until a Cossack Pulk succeeded in finding its way around the French northern flank. Then the French were forced to withdraw.

At the defile at Scheldditz, formed by the Gerstenbach, Lefèbvre-Desnoëttes stopped his withdrawal and moved four companies of the 2nd Baden Infantry Regiment across the stream. A company of Baden infantry (Moller) was detached to hold the bridge. The French cavalry then executed two strong attacks, supported by the French artillery to the west of the village.

After the charges, the French cavalry withdrew across the bridge. Once across, the Baden infantry placed itself astride of the bridge and was charged three times by two squadrons of Austrian Chevaulégers and some Cossacks in dense mass. The Baden infantry repelled these attacks by firing by sections.

Mensdorf, who formed the advanced guard, and Thielmann began their movement at 6:00 a.m. As they reached Gössnitz, the sound of Platov's cannon reached them. Their streifkorps advanced at the trot "to the sound of the cannon," moving a distance of seven and a half miles (12 kilometers) and reached Lefèbvre-Desnoëttes' right flank, by Zettwitz, at 7:30 a.m.

Once in position, the advanced guard, 1/, 2/2nd Silesian Hussars, moved to Sposa. They arrived at 9:00 a.m., encountering several French squadrons, which covered Lefèbvre-Desnoëttes' flank. The French withdrew down the road to Zeitz.

The 2nd Silesian Hussars, and Puchner's squadron, threw themselves against what they estimated to be two squadrons of cuirassiers.[71] The cuirassiers were thrown back into a forest, with part being killed and the rest eventually taken prisoner.[72]

The French, seeing this situation, sent forward a squadron of Young Guard Grenadiers à Cheval to rescue their comrades. They were met by the Prussian hussars in *ordre serré*.[73] The French were thrown back and they fell in behind three Baden infantry companies. The Baden infantry had time to fire only a single ragged volley before it was surrounded and obliged to surrender.

As the Prussians gathered up their prisoners, they were struck by some squadrons of the Young Guard Lancers and Chasseurs. A call for help went to Thielmann, who then attacked the Young Guard Lancers and Chasseurs in the right flank. The Prussian cavalry reformed and moved against the French, supported by a squadron of the Austrian Chevaulégers. The French were being forced back, but pursuit became impossible with the arrival of a large, fresh force of French cavalry.[74]

A battery of French artillery inflicted many casualties on the squadron of the Austrian Hessen-Homburg Hussars and the Silesian National Cavalry Regiment until GM Kudaschov came up with the Don horse battery and took the French artillery in the flank, forcing it to withdraw. The French then withdrew towards Rockwitz. There were five further charges by the French.

The French guard cavalry withdrew and the forces of Platov, Thielmann, and Mensdorf united before Menschwitz and renewed their attack. Lefèbvre-Desnoëttes pushed his forces through Zeitz, taking an hour and a half to do so, despite constant harassment by the Cossacks.

At this time Lefèbvre-Desnoëttes' rearguard was formed by two squadrons of Grenadiers à Cheval, three guns, and the French 4/35th Légère.[75] As they withdrew through Zeitz, they were charged by the allies. The Grenadiers à Cheval countercharged and threw the Austrian infantry back in disorder. A countercharge by the Austrian Chevaulégers, however, pushed back the Grenadiers à Cheval and burst into the village.

The French gunners panicked and cut the traces of their guns, abandoning all three to the allies. The French cavalry was badly handled and also fled from the village. What infantry remained, about 200 men, threw themselves into the bridgehead works, but were soon obliged to surrender when the allied cavalry dismounted and moved against them.[76]

The French them withdrew towards Naundorf, pursued only by Puchner's squadron. Lefèbvre-Desnoëttes sent word to the Duke of Padua and Napoleon of his setback and reorganized his force. Platov reunited with Thielmann and also reorganized his forces, forswearing any serious effort to finish off the badly bruised French force.

The massive superiority of numbers on the allied side told and the tiny French force was badly handled. The allies reported capturing 55 officers, 1,380 men, three cannon, a howitzer, and three guard standards.[77] The actual French casualties reported came to 144 wounded and 1,277 killed or taken prisoner. Among the many wounded was GB Castex.[78]

French Casualties at Altenburg

	Sqns	Strength	Killed		Wounded or Prisoner	
			Off	Troop	Off	Troop
Provisional Cavalry Regiment	4		3	40	7	153
9th Chasseurs à Cheval	2	18/271				
25th Chasseurs à Cheval	2	19/375				
Piré's Brigade			–	–	12	144
6th Hussar Regiment	2	21/377				
7th Hussar Regiment	3	29/447				
8th Hussar Regiment	3	28/525				
1st Guard Lancer Regiment	4	47/724	–	38	2	50
Guard Chasseurs à Cheval	4	41/1,602	4	32	–	49
Guard Grenadiers à Cheval	2	22/402	3	12	2	38
2nd Baden Infantry Regiment			–	–	9	408
4/35th Légère Infantry Regiment			1	11	9	394

That evening Platov returned to Altenburg; Thielmann did not return until 29 September. Platov then moved to Chemnitz during the nights of 29 and 30 September. Thielmann and Mensdorf moved part of their forces, during the night of 30 September, to Zwickau. The rest were caught by the advanced guard of Poniatowski's VIII Corps and driven back or sabered. Poniatowski sent strong forces to both sides to rid the countryside of remaining partisans, while the bulk of his forces moved towards Chemnitz and Zwickau to pursue the fleeing allied partisans.[79]

2

Operations on the Lower Elbe August–September 1813: The Battle of the Göhrde

When hostilities were resumed the allies detached a 30,000 man corps of Russians, Prussians, Swedes, Hanoverians, and Mecklenburgers, under the command of the Russian general Graf Wallmoden, into Schwerin to operate against Hamburg. Wallmoden's army corps consisted of 29 battalions, 40 squadrons, 60 guns, half an English rocket battery, and four Cossack regiments.[1]

Facing Wallmoden, Maréchal Davout commanded the XIII Corps in Hamburg. Davout's force consisted of three divisions of infantry, a light cavalry brigade, the Hamburg garrison, and a corps of 15,000 Danes.

On 8 August, Napoleon wrote Davout, describing to him his plans for the upcoming campaign. He described his intentions for Oudinot to move against Berlin and the "active role" he expected Davout to play in that operation. Napoleon directed Davout to leave Hamburg, as soon as he knew that the armistice was broken, and act with alacrity against the allies.

The XIII Corps and the Danes were to move on Berlin as Oudinot and Girard did. Girard's Division, from Magdeburg, was to be the link between the two marshals.

On 12 August, Napoleon informed Davout that he should be ready to move out on 18 August, attack the allies if possible, and place himself between Stettin and Berlin, cutting Berlin from the sea and British aid.[2]

On the allied side, Wallmoden had moved a light force of two battalions up to the Elbe by Lauenburg, under the command of Major von Lützow. Though the bulk of his forces remained in Schwerin, Wallmoden pushed his right forward to Lübeck and his left as far as Grabow.

In accordance with his orders, Davout marched his corps out of Hamburg on 18 August, and began moving through Lauenburg and Boitzenburg en route to Berlin. As he arrived in Boitzenburg, however, he turned towards Wittenburg and Schwerin to cut Wallmoden off from the sea.[3]

Wallmoden ordered his forces to concentrate. The cavalry concentrated behind the Boize stream, Arentschildt's Division stood in bivouac behind Wittenburg and Lyon's Division was in Hagenow.[4]

During the evening of the 18th, the advanced guard of the XIII Corps attacked Lauenburg, which was organized for defence. Though the attack was inconclusive, von Lützow abandoned his positions during the following morning, and with Tettenborn's Cossacks, withdrew to Vellahn, pursued by a small force of French.

On 20 August, von Lützow and Tettenborn were attacked again and withdrew on Zarrenthin, where they found the Swedish General Vegesack.

On the same day, Davout seized the bridge at Zahrensdorf and moved towards Wittenburg, covering his left by the detachment which he had sent after allied Cossacks.[5]

The Skirmish at Camin

Early, about 6:00 a.m., on 21 August, Dörnberg, Arentschildt, and Tettenborn drew their forces together. Tettenborn's advanced guard stood on the left wing by Vellahn. Right from there, behind the woods by Kloddram, were five battalions of Arentschildt's Division. The 4th Russo-German Legion (RGL)[6] Battalion was detached to Camin to form the right wing. Behind the same place, stood General von Dörnberg with the Hanoverians, the 3rd KGL[7] Hussar Regiment and half of the 1st RGL Horse Battery von Scheele. The 1st RGL Hussar Regiment watched the open area between Camin, the Schaalsee, and Zarrenthin. The 2nd RGL Hussar Regiment stood in the middle of the corps' position, with the half-Horse Battery von Görtzen to bind the two flanks and to hold the road to Goldenbow.[8] Lyon's Division remained in Hagenow. Wallmoden's forces waited in these positions for the first attack of Davout's advancing forces. Around 4:00 p.m., the heads of two French columns appeared. One came from the direction of Damin and the other passed through Marsow and was advancing on Goldenbow.

Before the village of Camin, which stood in the Schildebach stream valley, Major von Horn placed his 4th RGL Battalion in a dry ditch. He placed his skirmishers in a small woods on a hill by the ditch. Here they waited.

About 5:00 p.m., General Lallemand's 30th Light Cavalry Brigade, three battalions of the Danish Auxiliary Division, and 10 guns, approached Wallmoden's positions. The cavalry swung to the right and moved towards Goldenbow. The Danish light forces pushed into the woods concealing the skirmishers of the 4th RGL Battalion under Lieutenants Ehrhardt and Dollman. A skirmish broke out and the Danish Colonel Waldeck sent forward three companies of the Holstein Sharpshooters and French voltigeurs to sweep the legionaires out of the woods. The fight lasted about 45 minutes, and the legion skirmishers fell back on their battalion. The Danes then brought forward a battery of six guns which began pounding the battalion, driving it behind the crest of the hill.

The Danes remained stationary when the 4th RGL Battalion withdrew. Major von Horn pulled his battalion into Camin and set a watch until 9:00 p.m., when he was ordered to withdraw his battalion to Hagenow. He had lost a total of three dead and 26 wounded.[9]

The Skirmish by Marsow

The 2nd RGL Hussar Regiment had been accompanied, during the withdrawal through Goldenbow, by a half-battery. As it fell back, it encountered a column of infantry and artillery from Loison's 3rd Division passing through Marsow. The French artillery immediately deployed and began to bombard the hussars, supported by skirmishers which passed through the two small woods and over the old wall around Marsow. The hussars found themselves trapped between a ditch, the old city wall, and a marsh which made a counterattack or withdrawal impossible. The hussars were obliged to stand and suffer the French fire. The hussars sent out flankers to try to hold the French at a distance, but their casualties began to mount.[10]

The hussars were saved from a terrible end by the timely arrival of Wallmoden's KGL and Hanoverian cavalry plus a division of artillery[11] coming from Camin. The artillery quickly unlimbered and drove back the French skirmishers. It then turned its attention to the French artillery. The skirmishers of the 1st RGL Battalion under Premier-Leutnants von Danowsky and von Lösen arrived shortly after and engaged the French skirmishers on the village walls, driving them back. The skirmish soon ended, but the situation remained dangerous for Wallmoden.[12] The 2nd RGL Hussars lost 11 men dead, 49 wounded, and 14 missing. They also lost 75 horses. The KGL cavalry lost a few men and horses from the French fire and the allied battery lost two men.

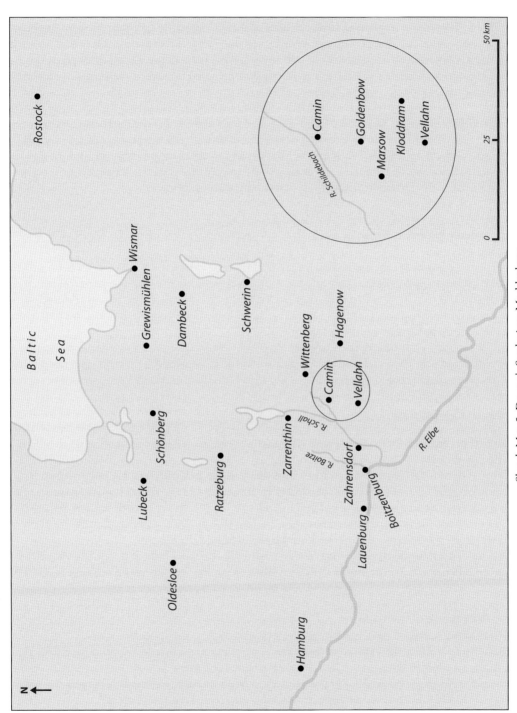

Sketch Map 5   Davout's Stroke into Mecklenburg.

The Skirmish by Kloddram

A part of the French forces that had moved through Marsow passed on towards the woods by Kloddram. They were accompanied by artillery and approached the position held by Leutnant von Görtzen, near the woods. Görtzen's four guns answered the French artillery and the 5th RGL Battalion withdrew back into the woods to escape the French fire. The skirmishers of the 1st RGL Brigade advanced to the edge of the woods and prepared to engage the French, when they advanced.

However, the situation with the 2nd RGL Hussars up by Marsow had become critical and the skirmishers of the 1st RGL Battalion were withdrawn and sent to their assistance. After they departed, the French sent forward their skirmishers to engage the skirmishers of the 2nd RGL Battalion. General Tettenborn sent forward his Cossacks to chase the French back and the legionnaires in the woods made as much noise as they could to convince the French that a large force was hiding there. As the French fell back night fell, ending the engagement.[13]

Wallmoden's Retreat Continues

Faced by the advance of superior French forces, Wallmoden withdrew his forces to Grewismühlen, between Wismar and Lübeck. The Swedes under Vegesack then withdrew their center from Wittenburg and the troops under Schwerin moved to the right, by Grabow. The allied forces were then divided into two groups, opening Schwerin up to Davout's advance and one of his objectives was surrendered to Davout without a fight.

On 23 August, Davout and the Danes entered Wittenburg and on 24 August, they occupied Schwerin. Vegesack, then at Dambeck, began to fear that he would be cut off and rapidly fell back to Wismar, and then on to Rostock. Loison (3rd Division) pursued Vegesack and occupied Wismar without a fight.

The XIII Corps stopped its advance, because it had received no news of Oudinot's advance. This was fortunate, for Oudinot lost the battle of Gross-Beeren on 23 August, and if Davout had continued his advance, Bernadotte could have easily overwhelmed him. Davout chose to hold his position in Wismar and Schwerin.[14]

When Davout did learn the news of Gross-Beeren, on 2 September, he ordered Loison to abandon Wismar. Davout withdrew the forces in Schwerin and pulled back on Schönberg. The XIII Corps regrouped itself with the Danes in Oldesloe, on the Trave. Lübeck was garrisoned and Loison occupied the fortifications on the right bank of the Stegnitz, towards Ratzeburg. Davout then withdrew the bulk of his corps back to the right bank of the Elbe.

Wallmoden, taking advantage of Davout's withdrawal, occupied Schwerin, but left Vegesack in Grewismühlen. The two antagonists had, basically, reoccupied their armistice positions.

Prelude to the Battle of Göhrde

Wallmoden faced Davout with an inferior force and his actions would continue to reflect that reality. In an effort to compensate for the reinforcements he knew he could not expect from the Army of the North, he raised 20,000 landsturm[15] in Mecklenburg and Swedish Pomerania. It was a force of these landsturm, acting as guerrillas, who intercepted a dispatch from Davout directing General Pécheux to move to Magdeburg with a force of six battalions and a battery. Once there, he was to clear the left bank of the Elbe of the various guerrilla formations that were operating there.

Pécheux was ordered to follow the road from Harburg, to Pattensen, Lüneburg, Danneburg, and to Seehausen.

Having Pécheux's itinerary, Wallmoden saw an opportunity to destroy a sizable force without much danger to himself. Orders were prepared. Vegesack and his Swedes were left to garrison Schwerin and Grewismühlen. Wallmoden advanced with 16,000 men towards Dömitz, where a bridge had been constructed. On 16 September Wallmoden's advanced guard, under Tettenborn, moved to Dannenberg and found Pécheux's advanced guard.[16]

About 9:00 a.m. 100 of Tettenborn's Cossacks began skirmishing with Pécheux's advanced posts. Tettenborn withdrew, drawing Pécheux's column after him, causing Pécheux to expose his flank to Wallmoden's main body, which had crossed the Elbe near Dömitz.

Pécheux did not take the bait, realizing that he was facing a superior force. He had good reason not to be too aggressive. Over half of his force was formed of fresh conscripts, trained in haste, very inexperienced, and for the most part, too young. In addition, they were already greatly fatigued by their long march.[17] He stopped and took up a position near Göhrde, with his forces in two columns. Wallmoden, forming his forces into three columns, advanced in echelon and moved to envelop Pécheux's tiny force.

Arentschildt's column moved to the left of the main road over the Riebrau and into the woods. His column encountered no enemy posts. He drew his column back, moved past the Röthen forest house, and to the right, where he encountered a few scattered French pickets. The French fell back towards Dalenburg. Arentschildt's column then rejoined the main force under Graf Wallmoden, and their advanced guard moved down the Dannenberg-Lüneburg road to strike Pécheux.

The Cossacks swept to the right of the woods, supported by the infantry of the advanced guard. Behind them came the 3rd Division, under General Lyon. Dörnberg then led his cavalry division against the French left.[18]

Major von Lützow's forces drove down the road to Lüneburg. Its skirmishers were sent into the woods to the left and right of the road, supported by the Jäger detachment of Lützow's 1st Battalion.[19]

About 3:00 p.m., Wallmoden's forces pushed into the woods where Pécheux had positioned a battalion of the 3rd Line Regiment. Lützow's Battalion and Reiche's Battalion, part of Tettenborn's advanced guard, engaged the battalion and drove it back. As the French battalion came out of the far side of the woods, it was beset by Tettenborn's Cossacks. It then pulled back into the woods and took up a position on the edge of the woods, in a ditch. From there it engaged in a half-hour fire fight. It was able to escape because of the supporting fire of Pécheux's battery, and the arrival of a squadron of the 28th Chasseurs à Cheval Regiment that came up and chased off the remaining Cossacks. Tettenborn then led Spoormann's Hanseatic battery into the woods, under the cover of the 4/Lützow Freikorps Hussars, where it began firing on the French guns on the left wing of their line.[20]

Pécheux's Positions

Pécheux had taken up a position on the Steinker Hill, which ran parallel to the Göhrde woods. Behind the hill stretched a plateau that extended to Oldendorf and Röthen. The Lübben Stream ran between the Steinker Hill and the woods and was crossed by the post road. It was passable by horses.

Pécheux had arranged his forces with four battalions in the first line, supported by two guns on the right and five guns on his left wing.[21] His artillery stood on a slight knoll which was higher than the rest of the ridge. On the right, on a small knoll, he had posted his squadron of Chasseurs with a skirmisher screen to cover the exit from the woods, should Tettenborn's Cossacks attempt

Sketch Map 6 Pécheux's Route to Göhrde.

to push forward. Two grenadier companies stood in Oldendorf to cover the escape route, should that become necessary. The remaining battalions were on the Mur Hill, by Breese as a reserve and to protect against a possibility of Arentschildt's Division striking at Pécheux's right flank.

As the allies fought their way through the woods to close on Pécheux's position, Lützow's Battalion had deployed entirely as skirmishers. Reiche's Battalion, which remained formed to support von Lützow's skirmishers,[22] advanced into the dry ditch behind the French, encouraging the French departure with their bayonets. It was about 4:30 p.m.[23] To the right of Reiche's Battalion came the Kielmansegge Jägers. To the left were the four squadrons of the Lützow Hussars which covered the flank of the woods. As Major von Lützow's infantry came out of the woods, they found themselves faced by French skirmishers backed by a Chasseur squadron of 80 men. In addition, as he attempted to lead his men forward, he was greeted by a volley of fire from the French battalion and artillery on the hill.[24]

The three squadrons of Lützow's Hussars, supporting the skirmishers, charged the French Chasseurs. The outnumbered French wisely refused to stand and withdrew behind the French infantry, which had formed square. Lützow's Hussars charged the square, but musketry and supporting canister broke the Prussian charge.[25] The Reiche and von Lützow infantry then attacked the French, but they too were driven back with heavy losses. The French battalion had fought off both attacks, but was forced to withdraw because of the other developments on the battlefield. Major von Lützow was seriously wounded during this exchange, but his skirmish line drove forward, capturing a howitzer drawn by farm horses.[26] The 4/von Lützow's Hussar Regiment stood protecting Spoormann's Hanseatic Foot Battery and had not taken part in the attack.[27]

As this skirmish battle progressed, the heads of the three columns, forming Wallmoden's main body, advanced out of the woods. First came General von Arentschildt's column, then von Dörnberg's, and finally that of General Lyon. The heads of all three columns arrived on the battlefield between 4:00 p.m. and 5:15 p.m.

When the first artillery fire began, von Arentschildt was in the middle of the forest. On hearing the artillery fire, he sent his artillery and hussars forward at a trot. A half-hour later his column broke out of the woods, about 2,000 paces from the French position. Once there he was joined by General Wallmoden, who had been waiting for his arrival.

The battle began with a violent artillery duel as Arentschildt's artillery, the 1st RGL Battery, deployed its six guns and opened fire. The initial placement of his battery was wrong and its fire did not reach the French position. Then, the allies observed two of the French battalions withdrawing to form a reserve on the Mur Hill by Breese. Two squadrons of allied cavalry sprang forward in an effort to strike these two battalions, but the French cannon fire was too accurate, inflicting many casualties on them.

The second squadron moved to the left against Eichdorf, where it encountered the French Chasseurs and two French cannon. The allied cavalry sought a flank to turn, but did not succeed.

Fifteen minutes later, Arentschildt's infantry broke through the leading edge of the woods. The 1st RGL Brigade swung to the right to link up with General Lyon's column. The small remaining breach was filled by the skirmishers from the 6th RGL Battalion, under Captain von Brun. The 1st RGL Battalion swung into line, and advanced against the French without waiting for the 2nd RGL Battalion. The 2nd RGL Battalion remained in column and moved against the French right wing, too far from the 1st RGL Battalion for mutual support. The two battalions were taken under artillery fire and musketry separately, the 2nd RGL Battalion suffering numerous casualties. The 5th RGL Battalion, initially remained in the woods as a reserve, but now it advanced out to form a second line.[28]

The 2nd RGL Brigade marched forward and assumed a position to the left of the 1st RGL Brigade, placing itself on the road from Röthen to Oldendorf.

Lyon's Division Arrives

As the advanced guard's skirmish battle began, Lyon and von Dörnberg's columns stood 1,500 paces from the Göhrde hunting lodge. When they heard the cannon fire, they quickened their march. At the head of the column stood the Bremen-Verden Battalion, of Martin's Brigade. It was ordered to move through the woods at a run and in 15 minutes cleared them. At the same time von Dörnberg ordered forward Kuhlmann's 2nd KGL Horse Battery, covered by two squadrons of the 3rd KGL Hussar Regiment. They moved forward at a gallop and cleared the woods at the same time as the Bremen-Verden Battalion. Once clear Kuhlmann's 2nd KGL Horse Battery moved to the right of the Hanoverian troops and opened fire against the French.[29] Wiering's Battery also moved forward, but to the left. It took up a position near the 5th RGL Battalion.[30]

Martin's Brigade moved to the left in the woods, in an effort to link up with Arentschildt's Brigade. Lyon's Division marched by battalion in columns of companies. Halkett's Brigade, moving to the right, cleared the woods with the Lauenburg Battalion in the lead. As it broke the cover of the woods, it was immediately engaged by the French artillery. This was more than the Hanoverians could handle and the battalion fell backwards into the woods.

The Langrehr and Bennigsen Battalions then deployed and formed the first line between Martin's Brigade and the post road. As the Lauenburg Battalion pulled itself back together, it joined the British 73rd Regiment of Foot forming the second line.[31] At the same time, the allied artillery obliged Pécheux to withdraw behind the crest of the hill, to shelter his troops from their fire.

Von Dörnberg Arrives

As von Dörnberg's column emerged from the woods, it moved to the right of the post road. He moved his Division between Dübbekold and Lübben. The 3rd KGL Hussar Regiment led the way with Sympher's 1st KGL Battery and Strangeway's Rocket Battery following. They deployed to take the French position in the left flank.[32] At least one rocket was observed to strike the French battalion on heights.

The Attack of the 3rd KGL Hussars

The 3rd KGL Hussar Regiment moved to the right. The 4th Squadron remained by Kuhlmann's Battery to cover them. The 1st Squadron, under Rittmeister von Beila moved forward at the trot. The 2nd and 3rd Squadrons moved forward as well, but without orders. As the 1st Squadron arrived within 15 paces of the French infantry, it received a devastating volley that killed Rittmeister von Beila and emptied many saddles. Pécheux had held his infantry in a dense column formation, so that they could defend themselves against cavalry attack, without having to form square.[33]

The other two squadrons passed the French, who had formed square, taking fire from it as they passed, and moved into the middle of the French position. Here, aside from being pounded by artillery fire and skirmish fire, they encountered the second French square. At 50 paces from that square, they received a volley that shook their ranks, but they still closed and slashed at the French with their sabers. Their commander, Rittmeister von Hugo, was killed with a bayonet thrust.[34] During this attack, the skirmishers from the 1st RGL Battalion advanced and fired on the French squares.

Artillery Duel

As the hussars engaged the French infantry the 2nd RGL Horse Battery (von Tiedemann), which had been with the Hanoverian hussars in the tail of Dörnberg's Division as it came through the woods, joined Sympher's 1st KGL Horse Battery and Strangeway's Rocket Battery. They held their fire as the hussars withdrew from their attack. When they resumed firing, the effect was limited by a haze thick enough to seldom provide a clear view of the French artillery and the battalion next to it.

General Lyon held back his attack until the artillery had time to soften up the French before his assault. Natzmer's Brigade of the Russo-German Legion was tied down in a skirmish battle with the French battalion on the right wing. This skirmish fight was beginning to take on a very bloody nature.

The French stood in closed columns or square because of the threat of the allied cavalry. The French battalion on the left flank had, after the attack of the 3rd KGL Hussars, withdrawn in good order behind the foot of the heights to the plateau. Here it was also sheltered from the fire of the three allied batteries. Only Sympher's 1st KGL Horse Battery was able to inflict any casualties on it. The battalion now stood 60 to 80 paces behind the edge of the plateau.

The Skirmish Fight

The skirmishers of the 1st RGL Battalion, under Premier-Leutnant von Danowsky, and those of the 2nd RGL Battalion, under Captain von Bronsart, moved against the French again. The heads of the two French columns defended themselves with a heavy skirmish fire. This fire was very effective and the French skirmishers inflicted heavy casualties on the Russo-German Legion. The RGL lost three officers and several of its skirmishers to this fire.[35]

Despite the casualties the allied skirmishers pressed forward until they were 100 paces from the French, and they too inflicted heavy casualties on the French columns. But the French did not surrender a foot of ground to the allies. This skirmish battle lasted about an hour.

The French Right is Crushed

About 6:00 p.m., Arentschildt's Division was ordered forward. The six battalions of the first line moved forward. The Schapler (1st) and Fircks (2nd) RGL Battalions moved forward in a bayonet attack in columns formed on the middle.[36] The French artillery fired on them, inflicting casualties and wounding Major Fircks.

The French waited, firmly planted in their position, for the advancing Russo-German Legion. When the RGL was 80-100 paces from the French, a Congreve rocket, which had been fired at a range of 2,000 paces, struck the ground between the French and allied battalions. The Russo-Germans fell back and then pushed forward again to 150 paces, when they began a heavy skirmish fire with the French. The French musketry was murderous and the 2nd RGL Battalion lost six officers and 55 men killed or wounded. The losses in the 1st RGL Battalion were slightly lower.[37]

The French fell back pursued by the allied skirmishers. The 1st and 2nd RGL Battalions caught their breath and began the advance again. Scheele's 1st RGL Horse Battery moved against Eichdorf in an effort to slow the French withdrawal. At the same time, the skirmishers from the 4th RGL Battalion moved up and struck the French column from behind.

The 1st RGL Hussars had been moving forward during the entire battle. The 1st Squadron stood facing forward, while the 3rd and 4th Squadrons, under Oberstleutnant von der Goltz, moved

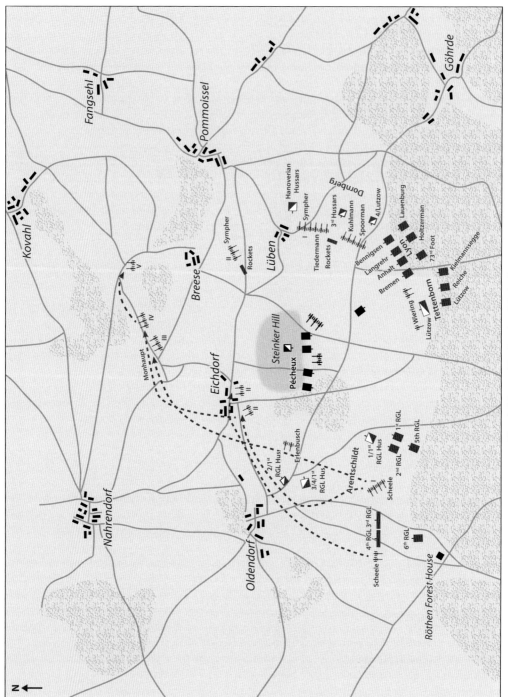

Sketch Map 7 The Battle of Göhrde.

The Battle of Göhrde, by Röchling.

to the left in an open column of squadrons, against the right flank of the French infantry. They advanced towards Oldendorf. Only the 2nd Squadron moved to the left and Eichdorf.

The 3rd and 4th Squadrons, under Rittmeister von der Horst, were sent forward to attack a withdrawing column of French infantry. The French stopped and formed themselves to receive the attack. The hussars struck the middle and left of the column, despite the heavy rolling fire. The attack was successful, breaking in the French left flank, and part of the battalion was crushed. Many of the French fled into the near by houses, while the remainder threw themselves to the ground.[38]

Though most of the battalion of the 105th Line Regiment was crushed, its right wing remained intact and was able to continue its withdrawal. The hussars, in their excitement did not succeed in completely destroying the battalion, and many of those who threw themselves to the ground were able to scamper over to those who remained formed. The remainder fled and were either run down or taken prisoner by the Cossacks, who now began swarm over the field.

The Attack on the French Left

Lyon's Division was charged with the assault on the French left. Martin's Brigade moved against the second French battalion on the left wing. However, due to an error by the Brigade-Adjutant, the Bremen-Verden Battalion became confused whether it was advancing against the French or allied infantry. As the battalion reached foot of the Steinker Hill it stopped, and the battalion commander went forward to see where his battalion was to go. A few quick words brought the battalion forward and as it broke the crest of the plateau, it found itself 60-80 paces from a waiting French battalion.

The stunned Hanoverians found their surprise punctuated by the roar of the French muskets. The French stood with their battalion in column of companies and brought about 66 muskets to bear on the advancing Hanoverians. The battalion commander, a major, two other officers and 25 men fell dead and wounded. The lead company collapsed backwards, while the rear companies continued forward, pushing through them. A tangled, milling mass of confused soldiers took yet another volley from the French and fell back, retreating towards their starting positions.[39]

To the right, the Anhalt-Dessau Battalion attempted to deploy, but the collapse of the Bremen-Verden Battalion and the fire it took itself caused its morale to collapse and the battalion withdrew. At this critical moment, Lieutenant d'Hüvelé brought forward the Hanoverian foot battery. He placed his battery on the left of the French battalion and began to take it under canister fire. At the same time the 3rd KGL Hussars went forward, and when the artillery paused, it advanced against the French column. The von Lützow cavalry also came up.

As the attack of Martin's Brigade was floundering, Halkett brought his brigade forward against the French left flank. His attack was led by a screen of skirmishers. As the brigade reached the foot of the hill, it began to receive French volley fire. The Bennigsen Battalion continued to advance, while the Langrehr Battalion stopped to return fire. The French allowed the Bennigsen Battalion to advance to within 10 paces before they fired. It would appear, however, that many of the front rank of the French lost their nerve, threw down their guns, and pushed back through their line. The French collapsed and turned to the rear, withdrawing. They were then struck in one flank by the 3rd KGL Hussars and in the other by Cossacks.

The area between Eichdorf and Breese was now filled with fugitives from the earlier fight. They fled into the various houses seeking cover from the hussars and Cossacks. The rockets and Sympher's 1st KGL Horse Battery moved forward through Lübben towards Breese, where they deployed and took the withdrawing French under fire once again.[40]

Wardenburg's Brigade

As Wardenburg's Brigade passed through the woods, the 3rd and 4th RGL Battalions moved to take the French in the rear. The 6th RGL Battalion remained in reserve and covered Scheele's 1st RGL Battery, while its schützen were detached to join Arentschildt's and Lyon's skirmishers. The 3rd and 4th RGL Battalions advanced against Oldendorf, taking fire in their flank and rear as they marched. The brigade soon stopped, and the remaining skirmishers deployed under the command of Capitain von Funcke and Premier-Leutnant von Gilsa. The skirmishers advanced to clear the village. The attack was under the direction of Leutnant von Staff, from the division staff, and he had a Zug (platoon) of hussars at his disposal, to support this attack.

Captain von Funcke sent his forces in the eastern entrance of the village, while Leutnant von Gilsa advanced into the western end. Here they encountered the two grenadier companies that Pécheux had sent to garrison the village, and a skirmish battle began. They fought at a range of about 120 paces, until the French decided to take the mass of their forces and cut their way out. At this time, the hussar platoon drove forward and the French resistance collapsed. The allies captured three officers and 113 men.[41]

The Fall of Eichdorf

As the French right wing fell back after Natzmer's attack, Oberstleutnant Monhaupt moved forward against Eichdorf with a force of cavalry and a small battery of two licornes[42] and two cannon. Two guns moved to the edge of the gardens and the remaining four guns, under Premier-Leutnant von Scheele, remained on the hill by Oldendorf. At the same time, the 6th RGL Battalion advanced against Eichdorf. The combination of the artillery support and the infantry caused Eichdorf to fall with little resistance. One officer and 36 French were taken prisoner.

Monhaupt left four guns with the 6th RGL Battalion and took the last two guns, escorted by 100 Cossacks, to pursue the retiring French. He deployed his guns and bombarded the French as they withdrew, inflicting casualties on them with little risk of being attacked himself, even though the French still had some artillery with them. One such retiring column had 800-1,000 men and a number of refugees withdrawing after it. They had organized themselves in a small village with two guns and four caissons. This force was attacked by the 4/3rd KGL Hussars who successfully drove them out. It was 7:30 p.m. and night was beginning to fall.

Pécheux formed what remained of his six battalions in squares and began to withdraw down the road in good order. Eventually, he fought his way out of Wallmoden's trap and began to move towards Harburg, pursued by Tettenborn's Cossacks. Pécheux lost between 500 and 1,200 men and his six guns. Wallmoden appears to have lost 566 men in the battle.[43]

This battle is interesting for many reasons. It was, by no means, a fair fight. Wallmoden's force numbered about 14,000 men and Pécheux had only around 4,000. Pécheux was outnumbered in every category, infantry, cavalry, and artillery. That he was not simply surrounded, overwhelmed, and crushed is a testimony to his generalship and to the leadership of his officers. It might also be considered a testimony to the courage engendered in any soldier when he is faced by hopeless odds and the recognition that his only hope of survival is to fight *à l'outrance,* to the death.

Wallmoden did maneuver to envelop Pécheux's tiny force in a manner that should have resulted in a clean and crushing victory, but those efforts failed to bring about that victory. The problem was not so much of Wallmoden's plan, but of the ability of any army in this period to coordinate such enveloping maneuvers. It would appear that Göhrde was not as big a victory as it might have been because of a number of factors, 1) the frontal attack by Wallmoden's infantry occurred before the envelopment was completed, 2) the infantry and cavalry attacks did not wait until the superior allied artillery had time to break up the French infantry, though careful use of the terrain by Pécheux may well have contributed to the inability of the allied artillery to do this, and 3) the allied infantry appears to have been very fragile. This latter point is exemplified collapse and withdrawal of the Bremen-Verden and Anhalt-Dessau Battalions from the battle after suffering very low numbers of casualties in a single volley, 30 and 20 dead and wounded respectively. This "fragility" could extended to all of the infantry Wallmoden commanded, except the 73rd Highland and the KGL infantry. The RGL, the single largest block of infantry, had been formed by German nationals captured during the 1812 campaign. Their enthusiasm is questionable, as they had chosen to join the Russian army rather than face a prisoner of war camp in Russia. Having escaped one horror by returning to the battlefield, would it be reasonable to think that they would eagerly throw themselves at the French bayonets?

It would appear, therefore, that even though Wallmoden had an overwhelming number of troops, their caliber was far below that necessary to overwhelm one-third of their numbers in desperate French conscripts.

On 18 September, Wallmoden withdrew back across the Elbe and returned to Schwerin. At the end of September, Davout moved his forces slightly. Loison was moved to Ratzeburg and the Danes occupied Oldesloe. The allied positions remained unchanged.[44]

3

The Allies Execute Their Plan to the North 1–15 October 1813: The Battle of Wartenburg

North of Dresden, Blücher began his march. He masked his march to the west with Vassil'shikov's cavalry and his advanced guard was commanded by Sacken. Vassil'shikov's cavalry quickly encountered Latour-Maubourg's I Cavalry Corps in Grossenhain. Murat's reaction was to order Latour-Maubourg to fall back on Meissen, but Vassil'shikov followed him and cannonaded the bridge over the Elbe.

Bülow's 3rd Corps, part of the Army of the North, marched to Wartenburg and Tauentzien's 4th Corps marched on Jessen. The other corps of the Army of the North moved to Rosslau and Barby. Bülow threw a bridge over the Elbe at Wartenburg and made preparations to allow passage over the Elbe at two other points.[1]

On 25 September the first move was made. A broken bridge stood over the Elbe River by Elster and the allies needed to secure it. The attack was placed under the command of Oberst Lieutenant von Schön, commander of the 1st Pomeranian Infantry Regiment. His assault detachment consisted of the 2/2nd Kurmark Landwehr Regiment, a company of the East Prussian Jäger Battalion, a squadron of the West Prussian Uhlan Regiment, and half of 6-pdr Foot Battery #19.[2]

On 29 September the assault force was reinforced by the assignment of the Pomeranian Grenadier Battalion, the 1/1st and 2 companies of 2/1st Pomeranian Infantry Regiment, and 12-pdr Foot Battery #4, but still the attack was not sent forward.

Maréchal Ney, fearing to be cut off from Dresden, ordered the IV Corps to move to Wartenburg the night of 1/2 October.

Blücher arrived in Jessen on 30 September and Sacken rejoined him there. Blücher had left only the Russian 6th Corps under GM Scherbatov and Bubna's 2nd (Austrian) Light Division facing Dresden. Blücher then moved into Wartenburg and Jessen, relieving the corps of Bülow and Tauentzien, who returned to the Army of the North. These two corps moved two marches from Wittenberg and prepared to cross the Elbe there.

On 1 October Blücher began organizing boats on the Elster and on 2 October a pontoon bridge was erected at Wartenburg to replace the one that Bülow had taken with him, when he moved north.

The Battle of Wartenburg

On 1 October Yorck's 1st Prussian Corps of the Army of Silesia arrived at the Elster bridge and established itself on the east bank of the Elbe. Near the village of Elster, the Elbe formed an ox bow bend that enveloped on the left bank a large parcel of marshy terrain, in which the Wartenburg castle stood. The castle stood on the extreme north of a dike, that cut across the loop of the bend

The French division of Morand at Wartenburg, 3 October, by Philippoteaux.

in the river. At the other extremity of the dike stood the village of Bleddin. The road by which the Prussians intended to pass, cut through the middle of the dike. The dike itself stood 10-12 feet high and was a perfect breast work behind which to deploy infantry. Before it, extended a marshy pasture that was absolutely flat and almost devoid of any cover behind which troops might seek shelter. Being pasture, the cattle that grazed on these fields kept all brush mown flush with the ground. It was an ideal killing ground.

Bertrand's IV Corps had not yet been joined by Guilleminot's 12th Division, which was assigned to the corps after the dissolution of the XII Corps. However Beaumont's cavalry was present, providing seven squadrons of Westphalian and Hessian cavalry for the corps.

The three original divisions of the IV Corps were deployed with Morand's 12th Division in and around the castle, extending to the road crossing the dike. Fontanelli's 15th (Italian) Division was deployed between Globig and Wartenburg, in reserve. A six-gun battery was positioned on the northern part of the Sandberg, and on its left wing stood an eight-gun battery. Slightly further to the south stood a six-gun battery. Two guns were posted north of Rödkolks, in the sheep pens, and two further guns stood on the southern end of the village of Wartenburg. One more stood behind the dike, on the road between Wartenburg and the sheep pens, another one stood slightly further north, and one stood in the Kossä Schumann garden.[3]

On the extreme southern end of the dike, in the village of Bleddin, was Franquemont's 38th (Württemberg) Division. The 38th Division was in terrible condition after the battle of Dennewitz. The 9th and 10th Infantry Regiments were merged into a Combined Light Infantry Battalion. The 1st, 4th, and 6th Regiments were formed into the 1st, 2nd, and 3rd Combined Infantry Battalions. The 2nd and 7th Regiments were broken up and their forces distributed between the first three regiments. The division had, as a result, a strength of four battalions and six guns. The 1st and 3rd Württemberg Cavalry Regiments were reduced to a single squadron, each with three Züge (platoons).[4]

The Württembergers were deployed with Döring's Brigade, two battalions, in Schuberg, about 1,000 paces from Bleddin, with its front facing the bridgehead. The 2nd Combined Battalion stood to the left and the 3rd Combined Battalion stood to the right, behind the Elbe dike. Their reserve stood in the old dike watch house. Four guns stood before them.

Stockmayer's Brigade (Combined Light Infantry and 1st Combined Battalion) stood before Bleddin in reserve and to cover the right flank. The Württemberg cavalry, about 100 horse, stood behind Bleddin as well so they could watch the Elbe bank and cover the 38th Division's rear.[5]

Beaumont's cavalry stood between the divisions of Morand and Franquemont to provide a liaison and to act as a reserve for either force, should they need it.

During the day of 2 October, Yorck's Corps erected a pontoon bridge over the Elbe river. During the evening Oberstleutnant von Siöholm brought forward the 1/, 2/2nd East Prussian Infantry and Fischer's Landwehr Battalion (1/6th Silesian), supported by 6-pdr Foot Battery #1 (Huet) to defend the bridgehead.

The actual assault over the river began during the evening of 2 October, when 100 Pomeranian Grenadiers were sent over the bridge covered by skirmishers. They were supported by 1/2 6-pdr Foot Battery #19, and 1/2 12-pdr Foot Battery #4 below Elster, and 1/2 12-pdr Foot Battery #4 above Elster. The erection of a pontoon bridge was begun, once the far bank was securely in the Prussian hands. The attack began at 9:00 p.m., and the bridge was in place by dark. The bridge was erected by the Russian pioneer companies of Ivanov and Schiskin and a Prussian Pioneer Company.[6]

During 3 October, 6-pdr Horse Battery #6 (von Steinwehr) and its cavalry escort arrived from the Reserve Cavalry of Bülow's 3rd Corps and joined the Prussian forces at the river.

On the same day, at 5:00 a.m., Yorck's 1st Corps stood in two columns. The first column was formed by the 1st and 2nd Brigades, plus the Reserve cavalry. It moved by Hemsendorf and over the Elster. The second column, consisting of the 7th and 8th Brigades and the reserve artillery, had earlier crossed the Elster by Jessen.

Prinz Carl von Mecklenburg led the first column, and was ordered to take Wartenburg with Oberstleutnant Siöholm's detachment. As soon as Wartenburg was in Mecklenburg's hands, the rest of the column was to cross over.[7]

The pontoon bridge was made ready and at 6:30 a.m., Siöholm's detachment moved across the bridge.[8] His column moved towards Wartenburg in a fog, but at about 100 paces from the French advanced posts, he was seen and began to receive fire. However, the terrain was so cut by ditches and so marshy, that Mecklenburg was obliged to stop the advance of his three battalions.[9]

About 7:00 a.m., Yorck sent across the 1st East Prussian Grenadiers, the Silesian Grenadiers, and the Seydlitz Landwehr Battalion (3/5th Silesian). In order to support the three battalions already across the river and to secure the right flank, the 1st East Prussian Grenadiers were ordered to the right, where they took up a position by the Elbe. Their skirmishers were detached and sent forward with the forces in the first line. Mecklenburg's forces pushed back the French skirmish lines, through the sodden and marshy terrain, capturing 40 prisoners.

Blücher's forces were unable to maneuver in the marsh and were obliged to move down the single road to the dike. Bertrand lay in wait, but his attention was not on his flanks, because he presumed they were safe. He was to pay for that error.

In order to protect his position, Siöholm's detachment, three battalions, plus the East Prussian Grenadiers, were deployed along the river's edge. The 1st East Prussian Grenadiers were moved to the right and stood on the bank of the Elbe. The Seydlitz Landwehr Battalion (3/5th Silesian), the 1/2nd East Prussian Regiment and the Fischer Landwehr Battalion (1/6th Silesian) were posted on the road between Elster and Wartenburg.[10]

The Silesian Grenadiers, Fus/1st East Prussian and 2/2nd East Prussian Infantry plus Kossecky's Landwehr Battalion (4/5th Silesian), supported by half of 6-pdr Foot Battery #1, crossed. As they moved to the left the entire 1st Brigade, under Oberst von Steinmetz and half of 6-pdr Foot Battery #2, crossed the pontoon bridge. He took command of what units stood on the west bank of the bridgehead, bring his force to a strength of eight battalions: 1st East Prussian Grenadiers, 1/2nd East Prussian Regiment and the Landwehr Battalions of Seydlitz (3/5th Silesian), Mumm (1/5th Silesian), Walter von Krosigk (1/13th Silesian), Larisch (2/13th Silesian), and Marwitz (4/13th Silesian).[11] The four cannon that they had tried to take with through the marsh were sent back because of the problems attempting to move them.[12]

The landwehr battalions of Walter von Krosigk (1/13th Silesian) and Mumm (1/5th Silesian) were placed in the second line, while the Landwehr Battalions Larisch (2/13th Silesian) and Marwitz (4/13th Silesian) were pulled back as a reserve.

In the meantime, Siöholm personally led his skirmishers forward towards Wartenburg. As he closed on the dead arm of the Elbe and the earthen dike, he was received by the French with a murderous volley of canister and musketry. Morand and Fontanelli had allowed the Prussians to advance, and once they were within range, opened fire with their massed musketry and artillery, including the guns in the Wartenburg Castle.

Steinmetz reacted by pulling his forces behind the woods that separated him from the French positions. The landwehr battalions of Larisch (2/13th Silesian) and Marwitz (4/ 13th Silesian) were sent forward to the edge of those woods, while Steinmetz sent forward more skirmishers to support Siöholm.

The half of 6-pdr Foot Battery #2 (Lang) which stood with the 1st Brigade, attempted to maneuver to a position where it could fire on the French battery on the left. Lieutenant Lang had great difficulty in attempting to find a position from which he could fire. He was only able to initially bring a single howitzer to bear on the French. He was eventually reinforced by the half of 6-pdr Foot Battery #1 that Mecklenburg sent back and the half-battery on the far bank of the Elbe, by Elster. These nine guns began to fire on the French line, supporting their infantry.[13]

The surprise caused by the French return fire had been nearly total and the destruction incredible. Yorck's 1st Corps collapsed and the remains of the Prussian attack fell back to the bridge in confusion. Blücher, however, remained undaunted, rallied Yorck's stunned troops and sent them forward again, in an effort to hold his bridgehead, and to give the rest of his force sufficient room to deploy.

To cover this attack, Blücher ordered Prinz Carl von Mecklenburg to pass upstream of Bleddin, and to strike the 38th Division, as Yorck moved against the French center. Prinz Carl von Mecklenburg led his four battalions forward towards the dike. At 9:00 a.m., his lead elements moved towards Bleddin, skirting behind the woods.

The Prinz left the 2/2nd East Prussian Regiment, whose skirmishers were with Siöholm, before the earthen dike. At the same time, the Kossecky Landwehr Battalion (4/5th Silesian) arrived slightly to the right, while the Fus/1st East Prussian and the Silesian Grenadiers moved to take Wartenburg in the flank. To do this, they moved to pass through Bleddin, in order to get into the open fields, and have a clear line of advance against Wartenburg.[14]

Prinz Carl von Mecklenburg led the two battalions personally. He soon advanced to the point where the four Württemberg guns took him under fire, and he stopped.

Franquemont had been advised by Bertrand, once Siöholm's skirmishers were engaged, that the Prussians had crossed the Elbe in strength. He was also told that he was to hold Bleddin at all costs.

Yorck had stopped the advance of Steinmetz's forces. He rode forward to the skirmish line, near Wartenburg, to study the situation. His entourage was showered with canister, some of which struck Kapitain Delius in the mouth and wounded Oberstleutnant von Schmidt's horse. While there Yorck watched his skirmishers falling back and assuming a defensive position.[15] He then ordered 12-pdr Battery #2, on the far bank of the Elbe, to take the French artillery north of Wartenburg under fire.

The Prussian 7th Brigade's assault on Wartenburg, 3 October, by Becker.

Yorck's 12-pdr Foot Battery #2 stood on the far bank of the Elbe, south of Elster. Four cannon and two howitzers of Battery #1 stood on the southern edge of the Elster. On the north side of Elster stood 12-pdr Foot Battery #4 (Bülow's Corps) to cover the bridge. Oberstleutnant von Schmidt ordered 6-pdr Foot Battery #1 (Witte), to find a location where he could take the French artillery under fire. Witte moved to the left bank of the Elbe, to find a position.

At 11:00 a.m., the Prussian situation stood as follows. The 1st Brigade stood facing the French on the left flank. The 7th Brigade remained between the 1st Brigade and the bridgehead. On the left flank, Prinz Carl von Mecklenburg was moving against Bleddin, in an effort to turn the French right flank, swing north, and take Wartenburg in the rear. The 8th Brigade remained as a reserve by the pontoon bridge.

The plan was that once the 2nd Brigade took Bleddin and began to move north the 1st Brigade, supported by the 7th Brigade, would strike the French line frontally.[16] To support this plan, Prinz Carl von Mecklenburg was reinforced by the two battalions of the 1st East Prussian Regiment, the Mecklenburg Hussar Regiment (four squadrons) and the 2nd Leib Hussar Regiment (three squadrons). General von Horn supported Mecklenburg with five guns of 6-pdr Foot Battery #3 (Ziegler) and 6-pdr Foot Battery #1 (Stern), which was on the far bank of the Elbe.[17]

As a support force for Mecklenburg's advance, General von Horn stood with the eight battalions of the 7th Brigade. This force consisted of 1/, 2/, Fus/Leib Infantry Regiment, the Thuringian Battalion, and the Landwehr Battalions of Sommerfeld (1/15th Silesian), Pettingkoser (2/15th Silesian), Reichenbach (3/4th Silesian), Knorr (4/4th Silesian), and Kottulinsky (2/4th Silesian).[18] This force was supported by three guns from 6-pdr Foot Battery #3.

The 8th Brigade (Hünerbein) remained south of the road from Elster to Wartenburg, about 2,000 paces from the pontoon bridge. It consisted of the 2/, Fus/Brandenburg Regiment and the 1/, Fus/12th Reserve Regiment and the Brixen Landwehr Battalion (4/14th Silesian). The Fus/Brandenburg Regiment and two guns of 6-pdr Foot Battery #15 stood about 2,000 paces further down the road from the rest of the 8th Brigade. The other six guns of 6-pdr Foot Battery #15 stood behind the brigade in reserve.[19]

As Mecklenburg began his advance, the 2/2nd East Prussian Regiment stood on the Elbe dike, and the Silesian Grenadier Battalion stood in the Eich Woods, north of the Schützberg, with its skirmishers and *freiwillige Jägers* engaging in a lively skirmish with the Württembergers. Mecklenburg's forces advanced, supported by the fire of 6-pdr Foot Battery #2 and a 12-pdr battery on the far bank of the Elbe.

The 38th Division had a strength of about 1,500 men at this time. Döring's Brigade stood 1,000 paces from Bleddin by the bridgehead. The Kronprinz Regiment (1st Combined Battalion) stood on the right wing by the Elbe dike, the 4th Regiment (2nd Combined Battalion) stood on the left. Four guns were distributed along the brigade's front.[20]

About 600 paces of the terrain was clear from the river bank back to a woods. About 400 paces to the north stood the 6th Regiment (3rd Combined Battalion) in a strong defensive position.

Stockmayer's Brigade stood as a reserve before Bleddin, covering the right flank and the park, which stood behind the village. The cavalry stood behind the village where it could watch the Elbe as far as Pretsch. The village itself was little more than two rows of houses on either side of the road that paralleled the dike. The houses were typical of the area, "*fachwerk*" or timbered framework construction with the gaps in the walls between the timber skeleton filled in with a lattice of slats or small limbs. This lattice was then plastered with clay to fill in the gaps. Some brick work was evident, but scarce and the only truly substantial building was the small church, which was built of stone.

When the Prussians under Mecklenburg pushed forward, the 1/, 2/1st East Prussian Regiment struck the Württemberg Kronprinz Regiment. They were followed by the Mecklenburg Hussars and the 2nd Leib Hussars, supported by the fire of 6-pdr Foot Battery #1 and five guns from 6-pdr Battery #3, and followed by the entire 7th Brigade.[21]

Mecklenburg formed his Prussians into three echelons, each with two battalions. He placed his cavalry behind the right wing and advanced. On the left wing stood the 1/, 2/1st East Prussian Regiment, the 2/2nd East Prussians, Kossecky's Landwehr Battalion (4/5th Silesian), and finally the Silesian Grenadiers and the Fus/1st East Prussian Regiment.

Franquemont reinforced the Kronprinz Regiment (1st Combined Battalion), which stood behind the dike watch house, with the combined light battalion. Their combined fire drove back the Prussian skirmishers and *freiwillige Jägers*, so the Prussian line was reinforced by the two Züge of the 2/2nd East Prussian Infantry, that had been detached earlier.[22] Shortly later half of the 1st Regiment was sent forward to try to hold the line. Seeing that the Württembergers had no further reserves, Oberstleutnant Lobenthal sent a half-battalion forward. The Württemberg artillery fired on them, but did not stop their advance.

The combined effects of the Prussian infantry and cavalry was more than the tiny force of Württembergers could handle. Franquemont sent a message to Bertrand asking for reinforcements. At 2:00 p.m., the Württembergers were obliged to withdraw from Bleddin. The 4th Württemberg Regiment (2nd Combined Battalion) was the rearguard as the division withdrew.[23] As they withdrew, they were pursued by the Leib Hussars, who captured five cannon and six caissons.[24]

At 2:00 p.m., the Fus/1st East Prussian Regiment moved into the woods to the right of Bleddin, and joined with the 7th Brigade. The 2/1st East Prussian Regiment passed over the Elbe and the two other battalions of the first echelon moved down the road to Wartenburg, in order to capture what prisoners they could. The Prussian skirmishers followed the Württembergers closely.[25]

The Württembergers moved south, and 800 paces from Bleddin, they sought to establish a new defensive position. They placed their six guns on their left flank.

As the skirmishers of the Prussian second line moved across the dike running from Bleddin to Wartenburg, they observed Beaumont's two cavalry brigades. Word was passed back to the

Prussian cavalry which came forward. The Mecklenburg Hussars had one squadron detached to support the infantry, so the Prussians advanced with six squadrons, supported by half of 6-pdr Foot Battery #1.[26] The 3/Mecklenburg Hussars stood on the right flank. To their left stood the 2/,1/Mecklenburg and the 2/, 3/2nd Leib Hussars. The 4/2nd Leib Hussars formed the rear rank, behind the left flank, serving as a reserve. Beaumont's cavalry[27] stood near Globig. It swung by platoons to the left and advanced at a trot. Beaumont's cavalry did not stand the charge, broke 10 paces in front of the Prussians, and were driven from the field. The Westphalian and Hessian cavalry were nearly obliterated in this defeat.[28] The 4/2nd Leib Hussars pursued Beaumont's shattered regiments a few hundred paces and rallied to their formation.[29]

Around the swamp, the Württemberg infantry attempted another stand. The combined light infantry, and the 1st, 4th, and 6th Regiments[30] took up positions to the left of the swamp.

Oberst von Weltzien led his Prussians forward. Horn sent the 2/Leib Regiment to the left and held the 2/, 3/, 4/4th Silesian Landwehr Regiment behind them as support. The Prussians advanced in a bayonet attack.[31] The Württemberg defensive effort was valiant, but unsuccessful. For its efforts the enfeebled 38th Division lost another 500 men killed, wounded, and missing.[32]

A Württemberg battalion with the division staff passed over the Leine passage. It was attacked by a squadron of the Prussian cavalry and formed square. The Prussian cavalry surrounded it and tried to break it. The VVürttembergers, however, pushed through, retreating off the field. An extemporaneous squadron of mounted officers formed itself and attacked in an effort to liberate a number of captured guns, but failed and was also driven off.

In Bleddin

A squadron of the Mecklenburg Hussars, three Prussian battalions, and half of 6-pdr Battery #1 remained by Bleddin, to control that flank, should a French force appear from Torgau. The Silesian Grenadiers and Kossecky's Landwehr Battalion (4/5th Silesian), supported by nine guns, swung to the right to move against Wartenburg. At the same time St.-Priest held the 8th Corps near Bleddin, and General Kapzevich crossed the bridge with the 10th Corps.[33]

During the attack on Bleddin, in the center, the East Prussian Grenadier Battalion moved to the right, Walter von Krosigk's Landwehr Battalion (1/13th Silesian), 1/2nd East Prussian, and Fischer's Landwehr Battalion (2/6th Silesian) stood in the first line with the Landwehr Battalions of Mumm (1/5th Silesian), Seydlitz (3/5th Silesian), Marwitz (4/13th Silesian), and Larisch (2/13th Silesian) remaining in reserve. As the Prussians advanced, a skirmish battle erupted between the two lines.[34]

Hulot's Brigade, 12th Division, counterattacked Yorck's advancing columns and destroyed two battalions.

When Bleddin fell, General von Horn threw forward the Fus/Leib Regiment and the Thuringian Battalion. The Prussians began to roll up the French flank. The French skirmishers proved such a problem that both the Fus/Leib and the Thuringian Battalion were totally deployed as skirmishers. The Fus/ Brandenburg was sent over to support Horn's attack, because his formed units consisted only of the 2/Leib Regiment.

The French counterattacked with little success. The Fus/Leib deployed into skirmish formation, supported by Walter von Krosigk's Landwehr Battalion (1/13th Silesian), 8th Brigade.

With its flank turned, the IV Corps had no alternative, but to withdraw. The dike and all the entrenchments were now enfiladed, Russians were now beginning to pass over the Elbe, and having no reserve force with which to engage the Duke of Mecklenburg, Bertrand withdrew after four hours of battle to Kemberg. From there he withdrew to Dilben on the Mulde, where he reestablished contact with the VII Corps (Reynier), which stood between Düben and Dessau.

The Results of the Battle

The losses of the IV Corps were 500 killed and wounded and 150 prisoners. The Prussians admit losing 67 officers, 17 non-commissioned officers, 18 musicians, and 1,824 soldiers, or a total of from 1,926 to 2,099 men, depending on the source consulted. However, they claim to have captured 11 cannon, 70 caissons, and 1,000 prisoners from the IV Corps, and having inflicted 500 casualties, and captured five guns and four caissons from the 38th Division.[35] They also lost General Horn to one of the last canister discharges of the French artillery, as it withdrew.

On 4 October Blücher passed the remainder of his forces across the Elbe, with the exception of Thümen's Brigade, which remained before Wittenberg, besieging it. In addition, Wobeser's Brigade remained before Torgau, to keep it under observation.

As the Army of Silesia crossed the Elbe at Wartenburg, the Army of the North crossed the Elbe at Rosslau and at Barby. From there it moved up the Mulde. Ney found himself with Bernadotte moving across his northern flank and Blücher moving across his southern flank. He had little choice but to retire.[36]

It is true that Ney had at his disposition the bridges of Düben, Bitterfeld, and Dessau over the Mulde, and one might think that positioned as he was, between two enemy forces that were separated one from the other by two days march, that he could have operated on the concept of interior lines of communication, attacked one belligerent and resolved that battle, before he had to face the combined forces of both. However, Ney had only about 40,000 men, while Blücher had 60,000 and Bernadotte had more than 70,000. This eliminated any chance of action by Ney and he retired on Delitzsch.

Yorck salutes the Leib Regiment after the Battle of Wartenburg, 3 October, by Knötel.

Operations on the Düben

On 2 October, Napoleon ordered Murat to move that night to Freiberg, and to take command of the V Cavalry Corps (L'Héritier), II Corps (Victor), V Corps (Lauriston), and the VIII Corps (Poniatowski).

At that time the Army of Bohemia was once again crossing through the mountains, but not towards Dresden as they had before, but towards Leipzig. On 2 October 70,000 men of this army stood at the passes through the mountains, on the line from Eibenstock, Annaberg, and Marienberg. The remainder of the Army of Bohemia, 80,000 men, stood to the south of the mountains, on a line running from Komotou to Karlsbad. Finally, Bennigsen, with his 50,000 men, stood in Töplitz and Aussig.

On the same day, 3 October, the Army of Silesia, with 64,000 men, was on the left bank of the Elbe and engaged in the battle of Wartenburg. After detaching Thümen (4,000 men) and Wobeser (4,000 men), Blücher still retained 56,000 men. Bernadotte's Army of the North, which included Tauentzien's Corps, contained 70,000 men and commanded the passages over the Elbe at Rosslau, Acken, and Barby.

On 4 October, Klenau's advanced guard, of the Army of Bohemia, entered Chemnitz. Lauriston, whose V Corps occupied the area around the city, attacked Klenau with part of his corps, dislodging them. However, Platov, with his corps of Cossacks, was in the vicinity of Zwickau and moved against the right flank of the V Corps, driving it back on Mittweida. The following day Schwarzenberg established his headquarters in Marienberg.

Napoleon did not learn of Blücher's passage over the Elbe until 5 October, but he knew of its march. He was not troubled by the double offensive of the allies and announced that he was seeking the general battle that would come of this offensive.

To face the allies Napoleon had organized his army into three masses. The southern one, under Murat, was to operate against the Army of Bohemia. The northern one, under Ney, was to operate against the northern allied offensive and Napoleon, himself, was to remain in command of the central reserve.[37]

To effect this plan, Napoleon ordered Murat on 5 October, to take a strong position between Chemnitz and Penig. Napoleon sent Marmont (VI Corps) and Souham (III Corps) to join Ney, who already commanded the IV and VII Corps, and the III Cavalry Corps.

Napoleon's central reserve consisted of the XI Corps under Macdonald and the Imperial Guard. This force was then moved towards Meissen. Macdonald's forces marched along both banks of the Elbe. Seven battalions and a few squadrons were sent along the right bank, through Fischbach towards Stolpen. En route they encountered Bubna's 2nd Light Division, which Blücher had left before Dresden, but the engagement was of little significance. They rejoined the XI Corps without much difficulty.

The IX Corps of Augereau was moving from Jena towards Leipzig, to form the garrison of that city, with the 6,000 men already in garrison under the command of Arrighi.

With his orders issued, Napoleon waited for news of the allied maneuvers. On 6 October, not knowing how or if Blücher or Bernadotte were marching on Leipzig, he wrote to Marmont, stating that he intended to be in Meissen that evening with 80,000 men. His advanced guard was to be on the road between Leipzig and Torgau. Napoleon was considering the option of moving on Torgau, along the right bank of the Elbe, in order to cut off the allies from their bridges, and forcing them into a battle, to defend or regain their passage to the east. As an alternative, he was considering marching up the left bank of the Elbe, which had the benefit of marching through Wittenberg, but could allow the allies to recross the Elbe.[38]

Napoleon awaited news that would tell him which alternative was preferable. He stood with his *masse de manoeuvre* poised on the intersection of the main roads from Meissen to Torgau, and to

Leipzig. He was able to move against the Army of the North and of Silesia, be it on the Düben, or Leipzig, or Mittweida. He was able to join either Murat or Ney, which ever was to find himself faced with a general battle.

In view of the prospect for a general battle, he concentrated the bulk of his forces near Würzen and left St-Cyr's Corps to garrison Dresden. This concentration at Würzen was ordered on 7 October.

In a note dated 7 October, Napoleon made the following dispositions. He and his headquarters, with Sébastiani's II Cavalry Corps, the Guard and Oudinot's I Young Guard Corps were to position themselves four leagues from Würzen, so that they could be in Leipzig on 8 October.

The III Corps (Souham) was to be in Würzen, while the VI Corps (Marmont) was to move towards the Mulde. The V Corps (Lauriston) was to take a position in Rochlitz, the II Corps (Victor) was to move to Mittweida and maintain contact with the VIII Corps (Poniatowski) in Frohburg. The following day the II Corps was to move into Frohburg.

St-Cyr was to deploy the I and XIV Corps around Dresden, move to Meissen on 8 October, evacuating Dresden and moving on Würzen. On 8 October Napoleon wanted his army in Würzen and on 10 October St-Cyr was also to be in Würzen. Napoleon was concentrating his forces between the two advancing allied wings, so that he could deal with either allied force separately, or, if necessary, withdraw over the Saale.

While this concentration was executed, Murat stood before the Army of Bohemia with the II, V, and VIII Corps, and the IV and V Cavalry Corps. His function was to keep the Army of Bohemia at a distance so Napoleon could strike at the Armies of Silesia and of the North. Once they were beaten, Napoleon would return to his earlier plans of moving against Berlin.

Once having beaten those two armies, the reasons for the detachments and garrisons in Dresden, Lilienstein, Königstein, and Pirna would vanish, and the evacuation of those formations he had ordered would be irrelevant.

Napoleon left Dresden on 7 October, convinced that he would engage Blücher and Bernadotte before they effected their junction with Schwarzenberg. To ensure this, Napoleon's plan depended on Murat. Napoleon stated in a letter to Berthier, that Murat's principal goal was to be to slow the march of the Army of Bohemia on Leipzig, and to never allow him to cross the Mulde. Napoleon did not want all of the various armies to approach Leipzig at the same time, where Napoleon anticipated his general battle.[39]

Despite the plans laid out in the letter of 7 October, the I and XIV Corps remained in Dresden after the proposed departure dates. Napoleon, however, arrived in Würzen on 8 October where he found the Guard, the III, and XI Corps.

On 7 October the allies stood with 30,000 men of the Army of the North in Dessau and 40,000 on the line from Zörbig to Jesnitz, between the Saale and Mulde. The Army of Silesia occupied the bridges at Mühlbeck, Düben, and Eilenburg. Blücher had only the Corps of Yorck and Langeron with him in Düben, while Sacken's Corps was in Mockrehna, on the road from Eilenburg to Torgau.

The Overall French Situation Falters

The Army of Bohemia was slowly proceeding out of Bohemia. Its lead corps stood on the line from Chemnitz to Altenberg. The right was formed by Bennigsen's army, which continued to march on Dresden, and whose advanced guard had reached the line running from Liebstadt to Altenberg.

Things were already going afoul for the French. Ney and Marmont were squabbling. Feeling his position compromised, Ney withdrew after the battle of Wartenburg and he called Marmont to his aid. Marmont advanced to Eilenburg, but at exactly that moment, Ney abandoned his position and crossed behind the VI Corps, to close with the Elbe in the direction of Torgau. This left Marmont extremely exposed and opened up to the allies a path to Leipzig. Ney, not having communicated the reasons for his maneuver, forced Marmont to retire on Taucha. In fact, Ney's objective was to gather Souham's III Corps in to his army as soon as possible, because he did not have much faith in those of Bertrand (IV) and Reynier (VII), after their failures at Gross-Beeren and Dennewitz. Nonetheless, this thoughtlessness engendered a considerable amount of ill will towards Ney from Marmont.

On 8 October Ney's forces stood strung along the line from Taucha, Eilenburg, and Schildau. Arrighi guarded Leipzig with 6,000 men, and Augereau's IX Corps was moving into Naumburg with 12,000 men.

Murat occupied the line from Frohburg and Mittweida. Napoleon stood in Würzen and Dahlen with 140,000 men facing Blücher's 60,000 men. Napoleon and Blücher were so close that their light forces were in contact. Bernadotte's army stood one days march north of Blücher.

Napoleon believed that the Army of Silesia stood in Düben, and during the night of 8/9 October, ordered all of his forces to move against that point. He hoped to lift the siege of Wittenberg, move down the right bank of the Elbe, destroy the allies' bridges, and engage Blücher in a decisive battle.

Blücher and Bernadotte were not unaware of Napoleon's activities. Bernadotte wrote to Blücher on 8 October, about the reported movements of Napoleon to Meissen and his apparent project to strike Blücher's left flank. Bernadotte advised him to accept that prospect, with the goal of paralyzing Napoleon's forces, and keeping them away from the Army of Bohemia, as it struck towards Leipzig and moved against his flanks and rear.

Bernadotte further advised that if Blücher advanced too far, he would allow Napoleon to interpose himself between him and his bridges. He also stated that he believed that Napoleon intended to strike at the head and flank of the Army of Silesia, in which instance they could withdraw back to the right bank of the Elbe, or cross over to the left bank of the Saale.

In the latter case, Bernadotte stated he felt that Blücher would have to cross over the Wartenburg bridge and move rapidly towards the bridge that Bernadotte would raise at Ferchland. Bernadotte stated in this last case, that he too would withdraw and burn the bridge at Rosslau, leaving only six battalions in Acken, to hold the bridgehead, while the two combined armies disputed Napoleon's passage over the Saale, or passed back over the Elbe as circumstances permitted.

In either circumstance, the goal was to delay and distract Napoleon, and both situations would accomplish the goal. Bernadotte stated very specifically, that wasting Napoleon's time and effort was necessary to "prepare for the success of the Army of Bohemia."[40] He also stated that if Napoleon was to turn and pursue Blücher with serious intent, Blücher was not to waste a second withdrawing to the safety of the right bank of the Elbe or the Saale.

Napoleon's Thrust on the Düben

On 9 October Napoleon began his march up the two banks of the Mulde towards Düben. Sébastiani's II Cavalry Corps led the march up the right bank, followed by Dombrowski's 27th (Polish) Division and Souham's III Corps. On the left bank of the Mulde stood Reynier's WI Corps. About halfway between the Mulde and the Elbe stood Bertrand's IV Corps. These three corps moved on the same front, forming a first line.

In what amounted to second line, Napoleon placed the I Cavalry Corps, followed by the Imperial Guard. Marmont's VI Corps marched behind Reynier and Macdonald's XI Corps marched behind Bertrand.

Ney, with his advanced guard, stood between Wurzen and Eilenburg. He began his movement at 6:00 a.m., and during the days march, encountered a few small enemy detachments, which were thrown back. At 3:00 p.m., Ney's forces arrived before Düben. Sébastiani encountered the first of Sacken's forces by Probsthain and dispersed them. This cavalry and Bertrand's IV Corps followed Sacken towards Kemberg and Mockrehna, which the allies abandoned.

Blücher learned of the French advance quite late and immediately began to withdraw his army up the Mulde. He crossed the Mulde at Mühlbeck and Jesnitz, moving to the west and seeking an opening on the left bank. Langeron's Corps abandoned Düben in such haste, that they left behind a just completed bridge. The Prussian general staff fled with the French cavalry barking at their heels. Sacken retired by forced marches on Raguhn, where he crossed the Mulde. The bridges were destroyed in order to stop the French pursuit.

A large quantity of baggage, a Russian convoy, and many prisoners were captured by the French in their rapid advance, but the allies escaped. Ney's advanced guard passed Düben and the VII Corps occupied the city. The III Corps occupied Haussig. Dombrowski stopped in Pristäblich, and Napoleon established his headquarters in Eilenburg, where the Imperial Guard also stopped.[41]

Blücher rejoined Bernadotte on 10 October, in the area of Zörbig and Radegart, about eight leagues from Düben.

If Napoleon had succeeded in catching Blücher, there is no question that the 120,000 Frenchmen at his disposal would have overwhelmed the 60,000 Prussians and Russians under Blücher.

On 10 October the French army once again began to move up the Mulde. However, in order to permit Napoleon to move on Wittenberg and relieve it, Ney was left to watch the territory between the road from Bitterfeld to Wittenberg and that from Düben to Pretsch.

Napoleon wrote to Ney advising that it appeared that, before the French advance, Sacken had been ordered to occupy the Eilenburg bridge, while Langeron was to occupy the Düben bridge and Yorck was to occupy the Bitterfeld bridge. This would allow the Army of Silesia to advance rapidly on Leipzig, when it chose to do so. A Swedish advanced guard of 3,000 men was reported in Delitzsch on 9 October. After relating the directions of withdrawal of the various allied generals and their corps, Napoleon stated that he had ordered Macdonald to move to Mockrehna and on to Weidenhain, following Sacken. If Sacken retired to Dommitzsch or Kemberg, Macdonald was to follow him. Sébastiani and Bertrand were ordered to Pressel and Ney was to order the III Corps and the I Cavalry Corps to take up a position before Düben.

Reynier (VII Corps) was to support Poniatowski (VIII Corps) in Kemberg and Fournier (6th Light Cavalry Division) was to recross the bridge at Düben and join Marmont, who was in Hohenleina, moving on Düben.

Marmont (VI Corps) was ordered to watch the movements of the allies around Bitterfeld, Delitzsch, and Leipzig. If the northern armies moved against Leipzig, Marmont was to occupy a position parallel to their advance, with Düben on his lines of operation, and covering the bridge at Eilenburg. Lefèbvre-Desnoëttes was to scout the territory between Düben and Leipzig, watching for the movements of the allied advanced guards towards Leipzig.

On 10 October Napoleon established his headquarters in Düben. Around noon, he received word from Murat that he had occupied Frohburg, Gerthain, Rochlitz, and Borna. Napoleon also learned that the Army of Bohemia had moved through Penig, and that Wittgenstein was advancing through Altenberg and Leitz. He realized that it was probable that Murat would be obliged to withdraw towards Leipzig, but hoped that Murat would delay them long enough to allow him sufficient time to finish dealing with Blücher.

That afternoon, at 3:00 p.m., Napoleon learned that Sacken had left Leipnitz at 6:00 a.m., that morning for Raguhn. This news raised in Napoleon the suspicion, that the Army of Bohemia was acting in concert with the northern armies, to draw him away from Leipzig. Though Napoleon did not renounce his plans to relieve Wittenberg, he ordered a redeployment, which would allow him to fall back, in case of an attack on Leipzig. That morning he renewed his order to occupy Wittenberg that evening, with the V, VII, and XI Corps and Sébastiani's II Cavalry Corps. They were to cross the Elbe the following day, 11 October. Ney was sent with III Corps to Gräfenhainichen, with the order to scout towards Dessau, Jesnitz, and Bitterfeld. The same order was given the Guard cavalry. The I and II Young Guard Corps (Oudinot and Mortier) were sent to a position before Düben and the Old Guard was in Düben. In addition, all of the convoys in Leipzig were rerouted to Eilenburg.

Then, at 5:30 a.m., Napoleon wrote to Murat.[42] In that letter he stated that during the next day, 11 October, he would have either swept up the enemy, or he would have destroyed his bridges and thrown him back across the Elbe. After running the Army of Silesia back across the Elbe, he planned to turn south and be in Leipzig on 13 October.

He calculated Murat's forces, at that time, would be:

II Corps	Victor	16,000 infantry	1,200 cavalry
V Corps	Lauriston	12,000 infantry	800 cavalry
VIII Corps	Poniatowski	5,000 infantry	3,000 cavalry
IX Corps	Augereau	8,000 infantry	3,000 cavalry
Leipzig Garrison	Arrighi	8,000 infantry	3,000 cavalry
V (bis) Cavalry Corps Milhaud		2,000 cavalry	
Total			62,000 men

Napoleon felt that he could, during the 12th, send Murat 20,000 men, which would raise Murat's strength to 80,000 men. Napoleon speculated that Murat had between 50,000 and 80,000 men facing him, and that there was little about which to be concerned.

Indeed, he appears to have been relishing the developing situation and the impending battle.

That evening Napoleon wrote to Arrighi, advising him that Murat and Augereau would soon be joining him in Leipzig. He stated that it was his intention to retreat across the Mulde by the bridges at Eilenburg and Düben, and, if it became necessary, on the Elbe by Wittenberg and Torgau. His objective was to disconcert the allies, if he did not have the opportunity to strike the northern allied armies, before the Army of Bohemia arrived before Leipzig.

Having reaffirmed to Murat his mission, Napoleon then crossed to the right bank of the Elbe, to cut the communications of Bernadotte and Blücher. Napoleon realized that he was allowing these two generals to come between his army and France, but was unconcerned. He felt that the allies would be more concerned for their communications, than he was for his own. Their actions in that past, most particularly the Prussian sensibilities about any threat to their capital, supported Napoleon's position.

Napoleon perceived the northern armies had three choices. In the first, Blücher would await his arrival and offer battle. Napoleon was assured of success in this case. In the second, Blücher would fall back and join Bernadotte, in which case Napoleon would cross the Elbe, and assume a new line of strategic operations. In the third case both the Armies of Silesia and of the North would cross back behind the Elbe, allowing Napoleon to force a battle before Berlin.

If the latter happened, it is true that Napoleon would be facing 200,000 allied troops, but Murat was in a position to rapidly dispatch three corps from the Freiberg area, and leave the Army of Bohemia hung up in the mountain passes, unable to shift its direction of march, so as to aid in the pending battle. After Napoleon crushed Bernadotte and Blücher, what matter the territories that the Army of Bohemia had occupied? It would be quickly obliged to withdraw once again into its mountain fastness, as the victorious Napoleon swept back down upon them.

The plan was brilliant, but it was irreparably damaged by the defection of Bavaria from the Confederation of the Rhine on 8 October, which cost Napoleon a division, threatened his communications with France, and shook the political foundations of his German empire. It also suffered as a result of Augereau's failure to proceed quickly enough to participate in the offensive.

The day of 11 October saw little change and few results. Ney stood in Gräfenhainichen. Reynier was before Wittenberg, Macdonald was in Rackith, and Bertrand was busy destroying the bridge-head at Wartenburg. The news received by the French provided little of use, and did not allow them to identify where the allied armies were located.

III Corps Moves on Dessau

During the day of 11 October, the III Corps occupied Gräfenhainichen. The 8th Division stood before the village, straddling the road. The corps park and artillery stood behind the infantry. The 9th Division and the 23rd Light Cavalry Brigade moved to Judenberg that day, and took up a position. The 8th Division also detached a battalion to Radis, under the orders of General Fournier.[43]

During the night, General Delmas (9th Division) was ordered to attack Dessau. In order to execute his orders, he was given command of the light cavalry. On 12 October the 9th Division began its march forward at 7:00 a.m. The light cavalry formed the advanced guard with the 3/2nd Légère Regiment. About a mile from Judenberg, this advanced guard encountered allied pickets in the edge of the forest by Pölnitz. About 1,000 Cossacks moved to stop the French advance, while two Prussian battalions and 300-400 Prussian cavalry withdrew down the road to Oranienbaum. General Beurman charged them, without giving them time to examine the terrain, sabered them, and took the bridge to Pölnitz.

The 10th Hussars then found themselves facing a substantial force of Prussian infantry in the village of Jonitz, where they covered the retreat of their fellows. General Estève, with three battalions of his brigade and the rest in reserve, marched forward with lowered bayonets and cleared the village of the Prussians. The pursuit was so aggressive, that the Prussians were unable to destroy the bridge over the first arm of the Mulde. Indeed, the pursuit was such that the Prussians fell back pell-mell into Dessau, where the main bridge and its guard were captured intact.

As the infantry charged forward so successfully, the 10th Hussars, with three squadrons, turned the village of Jonitz by the right, and chased the Cossacks towards Rosslau, along the right bank of the Mulde, capturing 150 men and 200 horses. A total of about 1,200 allies were captured during the action around Dessau.[44]

Napoleon had received word from Murat of an engagement between the French and the Army of Bohemia at Borna. Wittgenstein, he was told, had been beaten and was withdrawing on Frohburg. Based on that he ordered Reynier and Dombrowski to push on Rosslau. Macdonald was to move to Wittenberg, and if the allies resisted the move into Rosslau, he was to move to support Reynier. If not, he was to remain there.

Napoleon ordered Ney to move with the III Corps (Souham) and the cavalry at his disposal to occupy Dessau and the bridgehead there. When Reynier was master of Rosslau, Ney was to destroy the bridgehead and erect two pontoon bridges. Napoleon felt that Ney's cavalry could do considerable damage to the allies, if it were to advance onto the Dessau plain. Ney was also authorized to take command of the IV Corps, when it finished its operations in Wartenburg. Oudinot's I Young Guard Corps was ordered to remain in Gräfenhainichen and watch Raguhn.

Marmont was ordered to move to Delitzsch in order to watch Halle and Leipzig. Mortier (II Young Guard Corps) and the Guard stood near Kremberg and were to remain there. However, they were to hold themselves ready to march with Marmont if necessary. Sébastiani was to move across the Elbe at Wittenberg and strike at the allies on the right bank. Latour-Maubourg was to remain in Kemberg, until sufficient information was received to judge how he was to be used.

Napoleon's instructions to Marmont were that he was to find a position where he could cover Düben, Jesnitz, and Leipzig. Lefèbvre-Desnoëttes was to scout on Marmont's left, and small forces of infantry, cavalry, and artillery were to be posted on the roads to Halle, Köthen, and Leipzig.

During the night of 10/11 October, Blücher and Bernadotte withdrew their armies to the Saale. The former moved to Rothenburg and the latter to Halle. Tauentzien remained in contact with Dessau to cover the bridges and protect Berlin, while Thümen continued the siege of Wittenberg.

During the day of 11 October, Reynier moved on Wittenberg and on the 12th, he passed through the village on the right bank. He drove Thümen's Corps back beyond Coswig, but then stopped. If he had continued his advance, he would have arrived in Rosslau in time to come on Tauentzien's rear, as Ney struck his front. This was an opportunity missed. Instead, Tauentzien recrossed the Elbe and destroyed the bridge at Rosslau. He joined Thümen and they retired towards Potsdam and Berlin, passing through Zerbst.[45]

On the same day the French cavalry passed over the Elbe. Sébastiani (II Cavalry Corps) moved against Acken, Roussel's 2nd Light Cavalry Division moved to Zerbst, Exelmans' 4th Light Cavalry Division moved on Belzig, Treuenbrietzen, and Zahna. In the last two Exelmans encountered the columns of Thümen and Tauentzien, who were retiring in disorder on Berlin.

Sébastiani sought to capture the pontoon bridge at Acken. When he arrived, he found 4,000 men under the command of Hirschfeld, positioned in a fortified village defending the bridgehead. The French cavalry overran a few works and engaged in a lively cannonade of the position, but was unable to take the position, and withdrew back to the right bank of the Elbe. On 12 October Augereau and the IX Corps arrived in Leipzig.

On his side, Ney sent his cavalry columns towards Köthen and Acken. He also sent part of Souham's Corps towards Acken as well, but was obliged to withdraw them. The bridge there was destroyed by a few shots of the artillery assigned to Brayer's 8th Division.

Napoleon had quite suddenly decided to stop the advances of Ney and Reynier, calling them back, and ordering them to move to Leipzig for the hoped for general battle. Ney was to move through Düben, and arrive in Taucha on 14 October. Macdonald was also ordered to be in Düben, no later than the 14th. Reynier and Dombrowski were ordered to move through Düben on the 13th, and be in Taucha on the 14th. Bertrand, Sébastiani, and Latour-Maubourg were also to move to Düben, as quickly as possible.

The reasons for this abrupt change in plans is not clear, but it is highly likely that it was the defection of Bavaria, and Napoleon himself later stated that was the reason. It is possible that Murat's situation contributed to this decision, but it certainly was not the principal driving factor.

Murat's Actions Around Penig

On 8 October, Murat had arrived in Mittweida, with orders to move to Penig, and to chase the Austrians out of that position. On the 9th, Klenau recaptured Penig, and one of his divisions occupied Luntzenau, on the right of the VIII Corps. In order not to be flanked, Poniatowski withdrew to Rochlitz, where he joined Murat.

On 10 October, the IV Cavalry Corps engaged Pahlen's cavalry outside Frohburg. Pahlen was defeated, but Murat learned that Wittgenstein was moving on Borna, and decided to withdraw to Eila. On 11 October Murat assumed a position with the II, V, and VIII Corps and his cavalry between Wachau and Liebertwolkwitz, practically in the suburbs of Leipzig. His advanced posts were in Thrana, Gross-Pössna, and Naunhof. Murat's announcement that he had assumed this disposition, arrived at the same time as the news of Bavaria. No doubt Napoleon felt it was time to act.

It is also possible that the capture of papers from the Austrian Counselor Kraff, being sent from Schwarzenberg to Bernadotte, influenced this decision. Those papers clearly defined the allied plans and objectives in a very precise manner, particularly with relation to Bernadotte's operations at Bernburg on the Saale.[46]

On 11 October Schwarzenberg's headquarters were in Altenberg. Wittgenstein, Kleist, and Klenau were concentrated around Borna. Bennigsen and Colloredo, who had been left by Schwarzenberg to cover Prague, had advanced towards Leipzig as well.

The Skirmish at Dohna

On 8 October Colloredo's lead elements were in Zehista, and Bubna attacked the bridgehead at Pima. During the morning of 9 October, GM Paskievich, while at his advanced posts, learned that the French of Lobau's I Corps were withdrawing. He ordered his forces to advance and not lose contact with the French.

At the same time, Count Hardegg's cavalry column had moved out of Breitenau. By Geppersdorf, on a ridge, stood the French infantry. An Austrian hussar regiment charged them, broke them, and obliged them to withdraw. The French infantry attempted another stand by Neumannsdorf, but they were once again pushed back.[47]

In the meantime the Allied Polish Reserve Army moved westwards to take its place with the converging allied armies marching on Leipzig. General Markov had moved forward from Zehista, and stood before the French by Gross-Seydlitz. He struck them and drove them back, through the Burhardswalde Forest to Dohna.

The French were estimated to be about 20,000 strong in their Dohna position. Their right wing stood on the small city of Dohna, and their left wing stood on Klein-Seydlitz and the Elbe, through which the main road to Dresden ran.

General Bennigsen assumed personnel command of the battle, with General Bulatov (16th Division) commanding the right wing and Paskievich (26th Division) commanding the left wing.[48] General Hardegg brought his division forward, through Borna to turn the French right flank.

Bulatov's column stormed the village of Klein-Seydlitz, while Bennigsen personally led the cavalry attack against the French artillery. After the storming of Klein-Seydlitz, the French brought forward a howitzer, and began to bombard the village with shells. The village was set afire and the Russians were obliged to abandon it. However, Bulatov reorganized his forces and drove forward, supported by Bubna's artillery firing from the far bank of the Elbe, and drove the French from their second position by Heidenau.[49]

Paskievich's column, on the left, struck Dohna proper and penetrated into the village. The French reserves, which had stood by the village of Gahmig, behind Dohna, sent in their skirmishers to reinforce Dohna, and the French artillery pounded his forces. Paskievich sent forward his skirmishers and renewed the attack. During the attack, he succeeded in striking two French battalions in the flank.

After a hard fought battle, Paskievich's forces finally forced the village. The French responded by sending forward two columns from their reserves by Gahmig. Bennigsen personally directed two battalions to counter the French attack. At the same time, General Hardegg passed through Sirsen and was marching against the French right flank. When the French observed this, they withdrew, leaving Heidenau in flames. Darkness fell, and under the protective fire of their artillery, the French withdrew to the heights behind Gahmig, Meuscha, and Heidenau. The French reportedly lost 1,500 men dead and wounded, plus 300 prisoners. The Russians lost 800 men from Paskievich's Division and Bulatov's losses were no less serious.[50]

On 10 October Bennigsen pushed a reconnaissance force to the outskirts of Dresden, leaving Count Ostermann-Tolstoy, who commanded the left wing of the Reserve Army, facing the city with 20,000 men, and moved towards Leipzig, with the remainder of his force. Only Chasteler remained in Töplitz with 10,000 men, to cover Bohemia.[51]

Napoleon retained St-Cyr in Dresden, in case Schwarzenberg should decide to withdraw once again into the Austrian mountains. By holding Dresden, Napoleon was in a position to either close the gate, or to pursue the Army of Bohemia and push it far back into those mountains.

Bernadotte and Blücher

The commanders of the two northern armies learned of Napoleon's thrusts against their rears, that Thümen and Tauentzien were withdrawing, and that the French had passed four corps across the Elbe. They also decided that they would continue their advance to the west. The French actions in their rear were not going to distract them from their goals.

As Bertrand began to withdraw from Wittenberg, Bernadotte's advanced guard arrived in Acken, but as the bridge had been destroyed, the Army of the North was obliged to remain on the left bank of the Elbe.

The situation, as it stood on 14 October, had the major portions of the allied and French forces concentrating in the Leipzig area. However, Napoleon's dispositions had caused him to detach the III, VII, and XI Corps at some distance. The allies had inferior forces, with the 3rd and 4th Corps of Bülow and Tauentzien positioned too far away to be deployed quickly, in the pending battle.

The French Move on Leipzig

On 14 October, an apprehensive Napoleon made the trip from Düben to Leipzig watching to the west and northwest for the anticipated attack of Blücher's army. At the moment, only Marmont's VI Corps was available to face such an attack. Individual cannon shots could be heard in that direction, and this increased his unrest. As a result Général de division Latour-Maubourg was ordered to send a reconnaissance force from the I Cavalry Corps from Göbschelwitz towards Radefeld. Napoleon also heard more cannon fire to the south, which gave the situation a very threatening aspect.

Napoleon did not go to Leipzig, but set up his headquarters in Reudnitz at the fork in the Wurtzen-Eilenburg road. His anxieties, which were driven by the prospect of an allied attack on his scattered forces, were so great, that he ordered Bertrand to make arrangements for a possible withdrawal over the Mulde by Düben. A force of 2,000 men, 200 cavalry, and six guns from the IV Corps was dispatched and occupied the passage. Napoleon learned of the occupation of the passage, while on the Halle-Zörbig road and was reassured.[52]

Ordnance officer Captain Caraman[53] was sent by Maréchal Marmont to Napoleon, and reported that the marshal had occupied a favorable position on the Breitenfeld-Lindenthal-Stahmeln line. Though the allies were near, they had only sent forward a little cavalry and some artillery. An attack was anticipated here on 15 October. The only concern remaining that afternoon was Murat's battles to the south. As a result, Napoleon did not dispatch the Young Guard to support Marmont, but drew them towards Reudnitz, where they joined Friant's 1st Old Guard Division and the 1st and 3rd Guard Cavalry Divisions under Ornano and Walther, forming a general reserve.

Curial's Guard column, moving from Eilenburg towards Taucha, consisted of the 2nd Old Guard Division and the 2nd Guard Cavalry Division of Léfèbvre-Desnoëttes. It was ordered to Holzhausen, evidently in order to counter an anticipated allied effort to turn Murat's left flank.

Latour-Maubourg (I Cavalry Corps), who had encountered and overcome numerous allied light troops occupying the village of Radefeld, now received the order, to move down the road to Grimma, and at the same time, support Murat.

When this order was sent, Murat sent word that the allies had been thrown back, and that he had succeeded in holding his position between Liebertwolkwitz and the White Elster. Calmed with the knowledge that the allies were moving against the western and not the eastern wing, Napoleon's anxieties declined. There also came word that Macdonald had, at 2:00 a.m., crossed the bridge by Düben. Napoleon knew now that on 15 October, he would have a considerable force at his disposal, to face the anticipated allied attack. The showdown battle was coming and Napoleon wanted as much of his army present as possible.[54]

Bertrand was sent orders that the IV Corps was to move to the fork in the road that led to Eutritzsch. He was to cover the right wing of Mockau, leaning on the Parthe, with his left behind Marmont's right, standing in echelon. This would permit him to serve the VI Corps as a reserve, while also observing the bridges over the Partha by Plösen, Schönefeld, and Pfaffendorf. Should the allies make a major attack in this area, the Guard could be sent forward quickly. Orders were sent to Macdonald to hasten his march, and he same order was sent to Ney and Reynier. Marmont was ordered to fortify his position.

As a precaution, the small headquarters north of the Partha in Mockau, as well as the ambulances were ordered to move to Reudnitz. Latour-Maubourg sought passage aver the Parthe and found a bad ford by Mockau. Though his cavalry could cross, his artillery was unable to follow and remained on the north bank. Latour-Maubourg drew the rest of the I Cavalry Corps together by Schönefeld. That his force was unable to move quickly was welcomed, as his horses had no forage since 13 October, and had been saddled the entire day of 14 October. That night he rode to Stötteritz, where he arrived at 8:30 p.m. Once there he gave orders to stop for the day.[55] Napoleon had reason to be glad that no major battle had occurred on 15 October.

The advance of the main column from Düben was delayed for many reasons. A quick allied strike against the scattered forces could have had disastrous results. Around 7:00 p.m., Bertrand had reached Hohenossig. He hoped that the advanced division would arrive in Eutritzsch at midnight. The artillery however, advanced slowly over a poor road, and it was doubtful that it would reach Hohenossig that evening. The number of the stragglers was uncommonly great.

Macdonald moved the XI Corps to Lindenhain, where he came under the protection of Defrance's 4th Heavy Cavalry Division, placed by Ney near Reibitz. Sébastiani's II Cavalry Corps was unable to pass through Düben. Ney had set out from Pölnitz in the early morning. His column hurried forward and when he arrived in Düben around noon, he found the bridge and the village so filled with train units, that he advised Reynier, whose VII Corps and Dombrowski's Division stood by Kemberg, to march towards Eilenburg instead.

Ney also ordered the III Corps to move towards Leipzig via this detour at the same time. Dombrowski was, however, sent towards Döbeln. Ney hoped that the III Corps, under Souham, would cross the Mulde that evening, and shortly later, around 2:00 a.m., join Macdonald, who was emerging from Lindenhain. In fact, Brayer's 8th and Richard's 11th Divisions of the III Corps, and Fournier's 6th Light Cavalry Division, arrived that night on the heights east of the Mulde. Delmas' 9th Division and the corps cavalry served as the corps advanced guard and moved only as far as Schköna.[56]

Napoleon received news from Marmont during the night of 15 October that the VI Corps had, during the day, encountered only a strong force of allied cavalry and some artillery, but no infantry. Part of this cavalry had moved down the road from Halle, and part had moved down the road from Zörbig. Marmont sent a strong advanced guard forward and secured the village of Radefeld. He evidently was under the impression, that he would soon face an overwhelming attack, as he had learned from prisoners, of the march of Army of the North towards Halle. Marmont felt his position was so good that even a strong allied force could not attack him frontally, so he feared a flanking movement around his left wing, down the road to Halle. The cavalry on the Halle road fueled these fears.

Napoleon presumed that Bernadotte would march towards Halle, where Blücher would soon arrive. The only risk would be if Marmont was threatened with an attack. This junction of the two armies on the road, predicted a massing for an attack. Napoleon knew that when Blücher had sufficient forces gathered, he would pass over to the offensive and attack. It was also logical that the Army of the North would pass through Zörbig and Landsberg, to join in the undertaking. The appearance of large cavalry forces before Marmont indicated this condition, and predicted an attack.

In the early morning, Murat reported that the allies facing him had been advancing since 4:00 p.m. During the night very few camp fires were visible, and in the early morning, reconnaissance parties were sent forward to investigate the allied position.[57]

Napoleon had based his forces on the western bank of the Elbe and concentrated his forces to defend Leipzig. Obviously he hoped, by pushing the war as far to the east as possible, to hold as much of Germany as possible, as well as to keep the war on German soil as long as possible. However, the allied movements had passed him to the west, and were seriously threatening to cut him off from his lines of communications with France. Napoleon's actions *vis-à-vis* the allied movements, indicate imperial contempt of an universally recognized principle in the art of war that a general must protect his lines of communication. Napoleon was violating this with perfect impertinence.

Instead, Napoleon looked on the maneuvers as the gathering for the decisive battle for which he had so longed. This desire for a decisive battle had caused him to accept an inferior position and would have long-range ramifications in the event that he lost. But he was confident of the superiority of his leadership, and the influence of his presence on friend and enemy. He was mesmerized by the impending chance to strike his enemies.[58]

4

The Army of Bohemia in the South 1–15 October 1813: the Battle of Liebertwolkwitz

Skirmish by Penig and Zehma

Murat had, as a result of the arrival of Napoleon's orders, resolved on 5 October to order an attack for early on 6 October. The goal of this attack was to secure Chemnitz, but Murat believed that the expulsion of the allied forces by Schellenberg had to occur first. Therefore, he decided to send all of Victor's II Corps and the V Cavalry Corps against the allied position.

Lauriston ordered a reconnaissance in force by V Corps in the morning. Two divisions by Liechtenau and the third by Ottendorf were directed to move against Chemnitz. When Murat had taken Schellenberg, the II and V Corps were ordered to attack Chemnitz. In preparation, Poniatowski was directed to send a strong reconnaissance detachment from Penig against Chemnitz, as well as to send another from Altenburg towards Zwickau. A further force was sent towards Gera and Zeitz, to reconnoiter, and perhaps to join Augereau's IX Corps, which by 5 October had already reached Jena. The VIII Corps no longer found itself in the peaceful backwater of the campaign.

During the afternoon of 5 October, as word came from Leipzig of the allied crossing of the Elbe by Wittenberg, which was to greatly influence Napoleon's next decisions, Murat held Victor's troops in readiness for the attack and kept himself ready for Napoleon's order to advance.[1]

When Poniatowski learned that the movement of Sokolnicki's 7th Light Cavalry Division towards Penig was canceled, he decided upon the occupation of this village. He felt this was necessary to strengthen his position and lessen the strain on his corps. The battle strength of his corps had been greatly reduced, as a result of the levy sent to Dombrowski's Division and the assignment of the 20th Light Cavalry Brigade to the I Corps during the campaign. However, the Polish contingent had been heavily reinforced with artillery in an effort to make up for this.

With a need to reconnoiter towards the Saale, on 6 October Poniatowski sent a strong reconnaissance detachment towards Zwickau and Werdau, to confirm or deny the ever present threat of a general allied advance. Also GD Sokolnicki dispatched a small cavalry force towards Chemnitz, as ordered by Murat. This movement was, however, stopped as a result of an early morning attack by the Austrian Oberst Desfours.

At 1:00 a.m., on 6 October, Oberst Desfours had advanced from his lines by Röhrsdorf with 1/Koburg Infantry Regiment, two squadrons of the O'Reilly Chevaulégers, two squadrons of the Hohenzollern Chevaulégers, and two horse guns. His force advanced through Hartmannsdorf, against Penig. In order to not draw the attention of the Polish advanced posts by the noise of the guns on the paved streets, the guns were left by Hartmannsdorf, and a company was detached to Mühlau, to serve as a reserve.

At 5:00 a.m., the 1/Koburg Infantry Regiment moved down both sides of the road to a hill, about one mile (1.6 kilometers) northwest of Mühlau. The cavalry advanced down the road in column.

The leading squadron of the O'Reilly Chevaulégers encountered and drove back a small Polish cavalry advanced post, and quickly moved to the Galgenberg Heights, about 1 mile (1.6 km) southeast of Penig, in order to strike the infantry positioned there. The Polish infantry was supported by two guns. The first attack of the Austrian cavalry failed, as did the attack of the main cavalry body, when it arrived.[2]

At the direction of Hauptmann Heim, the general staff officer of the detachment, the entire third rank of infantry was immediately detached and deployed as skirmishers. The skirmishers moved through the cavalry and advanced against the Poles on the heights. At the same time, Heim brought forward the two guns from Hartmannsdorf, and the infantry reserve left by Mühlau.

The Austrian artillery quickly dismounted one of the two Polish guns, and as it was supported by the strength of the Austrian skirmish line, the Poles soon found they were unable to hold their position. The attempts of the Polish cavalry to strike the flank of the attacking Austrian battalion, were stopped by the rallied chevaulégers. The Poles withdrew from their position on the Galgenberg Heights, leaving behind them the dismounted gun, 50 dead and wounded, as well as 10 captured Polish Uhlans. The Poles fell back through Penig.

The Austrian skirmishers started to move forward, but Oberst Desfours called them back. He had no order to occupy Penig. In addition, in order to hold Penig, the Austrians would have had to expel the Poles from the nearby heights, without which the village would be untenable. Furthermore it was learned that the Poles could quickly be reinforced to 3,500 men. It is understandable that the Austrians did not undertake a second attack and around 8:00 a.m., they began to withdraw.

Sokolnicki held Penig strongly and threw his advanced posts forward, as soon as the Galgenberg was abandoned by the Austrians. From a reconnaissance towards Chemnitz, he learned of the presence of a battalion of the Erzherzog Karl Infantry Regiment and a half-battery by Hartmannsdorf, which FML Mohr had sent forward during the engagement before Penig. Sokolnicki reported to his corps commander, that he had repulsed the attack of 3,000 men and several guns.[3]

The Polish reconnaissance detachment sent towards Zwickau, encountered the advanced guard of Pahlen's cavalry corps, south of Gössnitz, which was moving towards Altenburg. This Russian division appeared before Zehma with 1,000 Cossacks, three regiments of hussars, an Uhlan regiment, and some horse artillery. The Poles were driven back, losing about 60 prisoners. The collision with the Poles caused Pahlen to detach three hussar regiments by Gössnitz. He then dispatched only GM Illowaiski XII's Cossacks, to reconnoiter the Polish lines.

Wittgenstein had, in the meantime, advised Schwarzenberg that he had complied with his orders, and that the main body of the Russians had at 2:00 p.m., marched into Götzenthal by way of Meerane. Kleist, had advanced with his corps from Schneeberg. By 7:00 a.m., two brigades and the reserve cavalry were in the village and the other two brigades stood by Zwickau. As a reserve, the 1st Light Division, stood on the Saale. In addition, Thielmann's Streifkorps was with them. Thielmann's advanced guard consisted of GM Kaisarov with the Olviopol Hussars, a Jager battalion, and two guns, which moved to attack Gera.

With the movement orders issued, it was hoped that Pahlen could, by 6 October, seize the city of Altenburg, and the Russian 14th Division (Helfreich) supporting the reconnaissance force, would be south of Gössnitz. Pahlen set his cavalry in motion, and advanced towards Zehma, where he struck the Polish advanced guard and drove it back. The Poles pulled their infantry and cavalry back to a position by Möckern.[4] Pahlen, with his cavalry, had not initially considered renewing the attack against the Poles. However, the Polish cavalry took matters into its own hands.[5]

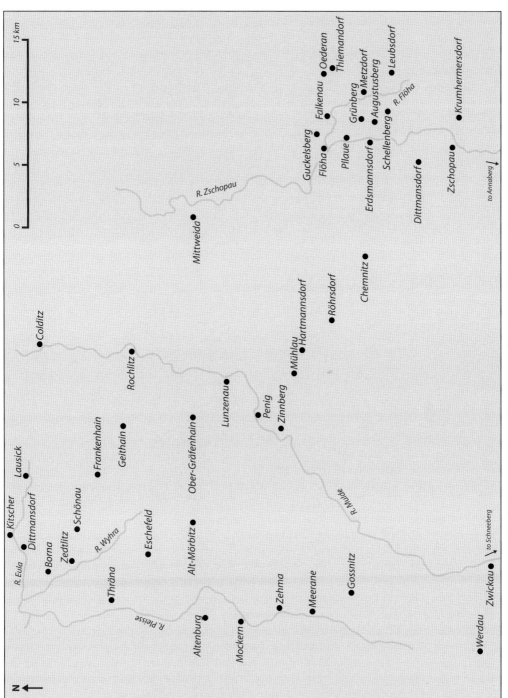

Sketch Map 8 The Area of Operations of the Army of Bohemia 1-15 October.

The Poles attacked and drove the Russians back to Pahlen's reserve, capturing one officer and 29 men. The Poles then pulled back to the Pleisse. As they withdrew, the Cossacks and Lubno Hussars counterattacked, and took two officers and 20 men prisoner. The Polish advanced posts were once again pushed back to Möckern.

Another Polish reconnaissance towards Werdau learned from prisoners that it faced M. Liechtenstein's 1st Light Division near Gera. The Polish efforts confirmed that Wittgenstein was marching on Altenburg.[6]

The skirmishes on 6 October had cost the Poles more than 100 men. Poniatowski bought with his efforts important and indisputable information. He now knew of the march of the 1st Light Division and Thielmann's Streifkorps through Gera against Jena, as well as the advance of Wittgenstein's Corps. Poniatowski had instructions to hold Penig, but in consequence of the many detachments, only 3,000 men remained in his reserve by Frohburg. As a result, he resolved, on early on 7 October, to abandon Altenburg and move his main body to Rochlitz, to join Sokolnicki. He believed that the road to Leipzig could be safely uncovered. He knew that Arrighi had ordered the 2nd Guard Cavalry Division of GD Lefèbvre-Desnoëttes, to move to Leipzig, in order to cover the movement of the transport of sick and wounded. In addition, Merlin's 13th Light Cavalry Brigade stood in Weissenfels, in the region between Lützen and Mark-Ranstädt.[7]

Skirmish by Schellenberg

During the morning of 6 October, FML Murray's forces stood as follows. On the heights southeast of Plaue stood Oberstleutnant Graf Stürgkh with the 2/Erzherzog Ludwig, two squadrons of the Klenau Chevauléger Regiment, and two guns. The line of security posts consisted of a half-company strung between the bridge over the Zschopau by Erdmannsdorf, along the Zschopau and Flöha to Gückelsberg. There the pickets touched the second advanced post group, the 2/Würzburg Infantry Regiment, which stood on the heights north of Grünberg. Both were covered by two guns stationed southwest of Grünberg, and the 1/Erzherzog Ludwig Regiment, which served as a reserve. The 1/Würzburg Regiment stood by Hohenfichte, with a squadron of the Klenau Chevauléger Regiment and two more guns. This battalion had detached a half-company to the Metzdorf bridge, and the other half-company and a cavalry platoon to the heights by Thiemendorf. A company was sent to the hill top by Leubsdorf.

As a further reserve, Murray held back four companies of the 3/Erzherzog Ludwig Regiment and two guns. From this, a half-company served to assure liaison with the left wing's and Crenneville's advanced posts, near Leubsdorf.

The movements of the French in the morning, and the disappearance of the camp on the heights by Oederan, with an advance of the Poles towards Chemnitz, to reinforce the skirmish line by Penig, distracted the Austrians. As a result, the Austrians paid little attention to the movement, about 8:00 a.m., of about 600 cavalry and two battalions from Oederan, towards that side of Metzdorf. Murray believed that it was only a reconnaissance or other inconsequential movement, and therefore failed to notify Gyulai of its movement.

The advance of this advanced guard was the prelude to a battle that Murat had ordered for 8:00 a.m., in response to newly received orders from Napoleon. Dufour's 5th Division and the French V Cavalry Corps were pushed forward from Flöha and Gückelsberg, to the area between the Zschopau and Flöha streams. Vial's 6th Division and that part of Berkheim's 1st Light Cavalry Division's advanced posts, which had been present, stood by Gross-Waltersdorf. The remainder of Berkheim's 1st Light Cavalry Division stood in a strong position by Schellenberg, facing Metzdorf. Dubreton's 4th Division stood to the south, on the flank of these forces, to defend against any flank attack.[8]

The advanced guard of Vial's 6th Division struck around 9:00 a.m., hitting the half-company of the Würzburg Infantry Regiment standing northeast of Metzdorf. While the cavalry moved around its right flank, Vial's infantry engaged the Austrian infantry frontally in a skirmish. The French cavalry vainly sought a chance to break the infantry, but failed. The Austrian infantry, supported by a platoon of the Klenau Chevauléger Regiment, which kept the French cavalry and skirmishers at a respectful distance, withdrew across the bridge.

In the meantime, about 9:30 a.m., GD Dufour had begun his flank attack. The V Cavalry Corps moved from the woods north of Gückelsberg, where it had concealed itself as it organized for the attack, and quickly moved towards Flöha, ignoring the fire from the weak pickets of the Erzherzog Ludwig Infantry Regiment in the forest south of Falkenau. The cavalry attacked in a deep column with "unbelievable quickness" through the gap between the two posts occupying the heights. The two Austrian battalions were unable to detain them.

The 1/Erzherzog Ludwig Regiment, supported by two guns, formed square in its position west of Grünberg. Both guns were on the corners of the square, as they awaited the attack. A few good cannon shots inflicted a number of casualties on the leading cavalry detachment. That cavalry then moved through the interval and into the Schellenberg Woods, in order to hit the battalion in the flank and rear, while the following French detachments marched up. The battalion drew itself to the rear, before the French cavalry could prepare a coordinated attack. It occupied the village of Grünberg, and joined with the half-company of the 2/Würzburg Regiment that stood there. Combined they fought the advanced guard of Vial's 6th Division.[9] The battle became serious and Murray was obliged to send forward his reserve. The French were to prevail, and as the last Austrians withdrew across the bridge, they set it afire.

Dufour's 5th Division stood by Schellenberg, while Pajol's V Cavalry Corps stood in two groups moving from Flöha and Falkenau, against the heights by Plaue and Grünberg. These maneuvers quickly made Murray's position untenable. Oberstleutnant Stürgkh, seeing the threatening moves, took advantage of a gap between the cavalry and the main French body, to withdraw to Erdmannsdorf. He crossed over the Zschopau and positioned a battalion, covered by a half-company of infantry and a cavalry platoon, in Paumgarten, to cover his withdrawal to the heights on the western bank. When the French detachments came over the river, he resumed his withdrawal towards Dittmansdorf.

The situation was worse for Major Stiller and the 2/ Würzburg Regiment. The advance of the right wing of Vial's 6th Division cut him off. He dispersed his entire battalion into skirmishers, and deployed them to defend Flöha. As the left group of Dufour's 5th Division passed quickly through a woods, Stiller found his position threatened, and his battalion hurriedly drew back to the heights in the rear. His battalion moved towards the safety of a small woods.

However, part of Pajol's V Cavalry Corps noticed the withdrawal of the battalion, and advanced against them. Stiller formed his forces into "*divisionsmasse*"[10] and drove off two attacks. But, more squadrons of Berkheim's 1st Light Cavalry Division had crossed over the Flöha, and a third attack came at Stiller's Battalion from all sides. The French attack crushed part of the battalion, taking the battalion's flag and many prisoners.[11]

Murray learned the bad news of Stiller's fate, and soon saw French infantry on the heights north of Grünberg, moving against his left flank. The bulk of Pajol's V Cavalry Corps had been standing by Schellenberg, but now set itself in motion in order to cut off the Austrian escape route.

Despite the infantry and canister fire, the French pushed after the Austrians. Murray reached the heights south of the village of Schellenberg, where two of his battalions put up a long and stubborn resistance, as the remainder of his forces moved to a new position south of the forest church.

The French did not strike again as the Austrians withdrew, and the Austrians succeeded in pulling out of the battle about 3:00 p.m.[12]

Murat was moving as quickly as possible towards the Augustusburg Palace, in order to reach the region beyond the Zschopau. Once there he saw troop masses by Chemnitz, Zschopau, and Marienberg. The presence of these allied forces was further confirmed by prisoners and local peasants. Murat was uncertain whether or not he should push towards Chemnitz, or pursue Murray's beaten forces. This was because he had learned that the two allied Emperors were in Marienberg, and that the Russian and Prussian forces, under Wittgenstein, were moving from Annaberg to Zwickau. He realized that he was facing the entire Army of Bohemia. After the first flush and shock of that revelation passed, he decided to strike the heights before him and then fall behind the Flöha. He quickly dispatched news to Napoleon of his discovery, stating "I think that Your Majesty has not an instant to lose, in making a decision of what to do."[13]

Murat recovered his composure when no general allied attack occurred. No attack came mostly because the roads between the allied positions and his were very poor. Earlier, at 10:30 a.m., Murray had sent a message to Gyulai requesting reinforcements, stating that he must withdraw if not soon supported. Yet Gyulai made no move to send assistance. Gyulai had orders not to become entangled in a major battle. He contented himself with calling the main body to arms, while sending two squadrons to support Murray at the forest church, and Csollich's Brigade moved towards Krumhermersdorf.

Feldmarschal Schwarzenberg, who rode forward to join Klenau in a personal reconnaissance of Chemnitz, likewise sent no assistance to Murray, because he did not know of the French attack. Klenau had been busy with the movement of the 4th Armeeabteilung in the morning, along the road to Zwickau, and likewise knew nothing. When word of the battle finally arrived in Chemnitz, the fight was long since over.

Murat decided that the allies would remain inactive. His cavalry stood with four battalions of Vial's 6th Division by Metzdorf, where a bridge been erected. The 27th Chasseurs à Cheval Regiment stood on the heights to the left of Augustusburg. Dufour's 5th Division went with the remaining light cavalry of the V Cavalry Corps, to a position behind the Flöha. The main body of Vial's 6th Division moved near Oederan, where the dragoons of the 5th (l'Héritier) and 6th (Milhaud) Heavy Cavalry Divisions, V Cavalry Corps, also took up positions. The other half of Dubreton's 4th Division and Berkheim's 1st Light Cavalry Division were likewise withdrawn in the direction of Oederan.

Murat ordered GB Valory's 1st Brigade, 6th Division, to withdraw back behind the Flöha, and permitted the allies to reoccupy the heights. Murat consolidated his forces in case Napoleon should send orders to march on Chemnitz. As it was, Napoleon had marched through Nossen. Murat nevertheless made preparations, should the Emperor come. The bridge over the Flöha was ready. Lauriston's V Corps stood by Mittweida and Poniatowski's VIII Corps stood by Penig, ready to act.[14] However, the action against the Army of Bohemia was not to occur.

Skirmish by Penig and Eschefeld on 9 October

GdK Klenau had learned, during the night of 9 October, that the French were advancing down the main road from Waldheim and Mittweida, towards Rochlitz. In order to check this French flank march, Wittgenstein was ordered by Schwarzenberg to occupy the Mulde crossings by Penig. Klenau, who had reconnoitered the far bank of the Mulde by Penig, had also come to the conclusion, prior to learning from Wittgenstein, that Poniatowski's VIII Corps was advancing from Frohburg towards Rochlitz, in an effort to turn and strike their left wing. The French were to be occupied by FML Mohr, whose orders were to contain any flanking movement.[15]

GM Schäffer dispatched the Zach Infantry Regiment, two squadrons of the O'Reilly Chevaulégers, and a half-brigade battery, to seek a passage over the Mulde by Lunzenau, and from there move against the French left flank. In order to divert Poniatowski's attention, Klenau ordered GM Baumgarten to demonstrate against Rochlitz. In addition, a small force under Major Piret, consisting of a battalion of the Lindenau Infantry Regiment and a half-squadron of the Hohenzollern Chevaulégers, were ordered to pass over the Mulde by Zinnberg. A request was also sent to Pahlen to send troops towards Frohburg. Mohr received the order to wait for the results of Schäffer's flanking movement before moving, so the main body of the army group remained behind Mühlau in its bivouac and prepared its meal.

Mohr, who commanded the 1st Division, 3rd Armeeabteilung, contented himself with limited actions. Between 7:00 and 8:00 a.m., his six guns began to fire on the six Polish guns facing him. Armeeabteilung Artillery Director Oberst von Stein supervised this exchange, which proved effective and forced the Polish artillerists to draw back.. In the meantime, the skirmishers of a battalion of the Wallachian-Illyrian Grenz Regiment, engaged Sokolnicki's Polish skirmishers occupying the village. Though the Polish general's forces stood in strength behind Mühlau, Sokolnicki, commander of the 7th Light Cavalry Division, was aware of his danger, and sent repeated requests for assistance. Despite these requests, Murat had contented himself with ordering Kellerman (IV Cavalry Corps) to stop the passage by Penig, without strengthening Sokolnicki's position.

As the cannonade began, Sokolnicki once again sent a request for support to Kellerman. Kellerman responded at 8:00 a.m., by sending him a battalion of 600 men and the bulk of Sulkowski's 700 man, 8th Light Cavalry Division. Murat faced a decision. No word of the Austrian flank move had been received, and there was no attack by Penig, but Poniatowski had sent word of a strong allied corps by Altenburg. Murat decided, at 9:00 a.m., to order the II Corps to march to Frohburg.[16]

Sokolnicki soon learned that an Austrian column was advancing against Lunzenau. He immediately sent a column of infantry, supported by a small force of cavalry and two horse guns, to support the forces about to be struck by this column. However, these reinforcements were to arrive too late. About 8:30 a.m., Schäffer had begun bombarding the Polish position in Lunzenau with his two cannon. He sent forward two companies of the Zach Infantry Regiment, supported by some chevaulégers, to find a passage over the Mulde. They found it, crossed the Mulde, and drove off the Polish observation posts after a short skirmish. The remaining Austrian companies crossed and advanced against the Polish infantry positioned on the left bank. The limited Polish cavalry did not counterattack. After a long skirmish, the Austrians resumed their advance towards Ober-Gräfenhain.

Upon learning of the passage of the Austrian detachment by Lünzenau, Kellerman abandoned thoughts of a passive, defensive stand by Penig. The Polish garrison of the village was given the order to advance.

The Austrian attack continued. The right wing of the Wallachian-Illyrian Grenz Regiment, formed by two companies, was strengthened by a division[17] of the 2/ Erzherzog Karl Infantry Regiment. This division moved into the Mulde River valley by Lünzenau, and attacked the Poles, initially with success. The attacking companies of the Erzherzog Karl Regiment struck the Polish right flank and forced them into a walled garden in front of the village. The Austrian battle group, now reinforced by yet another company of the same regiment, stormed the garden at 9:00 a.m. The last division of the 2nd Battalion, joined the rest of the battalion and moved forward in an attack against Penig. At Penig the Austrians found the Chemnitz Gate was barred, and diverted their march, advancing towards the Mulde bridge. This bridge had been stripped of its planking, and only the girders stood in place." Rushing across the girders, the sudden rush of the Grenzers did not permit the Poles on the far bank much chance to resist their attack.

Hauptmann Horn, after the capture of the gardens, also led his division of the 2/Erzherzog Karl Regiment to the banks of the Mulde. He crossed the river, expelled the skirmishers on the far side, and quickly struck against the heights, where a Polish battery stood. Despite suffering two guns dismounted, this Polish battery fought bravely as long as they could, only withdrawing its guns and munition wagons as the Austrians arrived.

At the same time as Lünzenau fell, a reconnaissance detachment of the Neumärk Dragoons was moving towards Alt-Mörbitz on the Frohburg Road. This force was moving only just ahead of a detachment of Sulkowski's Polish cavalry. The loss of Penig had forced Sulkowski to move with the rest of his brigade towards Ober-Gräfenhain. In addition, Kellerman moved his entire IV Cavalry Corps towards Geithain, to join Maison's 16th Division.

It was about 10:00 a.m., as Mohr reached the heights by the Mulde. Klenau soon learned from Wittgenstein that Frohburg had been occupied by the French. Not contenting himself with his present position, Mohr moved to a position on the far side of Penig and then moved against Rochlitz. Baumgarten was ordered to advance his infantry brigade towards Wiederau, and the main body of Mohr's Division was to be left between Penig and the Mühlau bivouac, where it would serve as a reserve. Schäffer stopped and remained in Lunzenau to unite with the two parts of the advanced guard. His reluctance to advance was easily explained, because the French were rapidly advancing, in force, towards Leipzig, in order to engage in a major battle between that city and Eilenburg. Any isolated Austrian detachments encountered by the French would be in a dire situation, and such a situation was to be avoided.[19]

Around 1:00 p.m., Murat approached Frohburg with the II Corps. He still assumed that Kellerman had delayed the Austrian passage over the Mulde. He stated that if the allies came over the Mulde with a strong force, which he did not feel was likely, he would send the entire army against them, and drive them back across the river.

Poniatowski had delayed his advance until the II Corps arrived. About 2:00 p.m., the head of Vial's 6th Division appeared northeast of Frohburg. GD Berkheim sent Murat two cavalry regiments to secure the south, as far as Gnaudstein.

Poniatowski drove away a Cossack Pulk from behind the Eschefeld swamp with little effort. The Poles drove forward, but they soon encountered Russian infantry. After a long struggle, the Russians were forced back towards Windischleuba. The allied resistance to the Polish advance quickly grew, and from prisoners it was learned that Wittgenstein's entire corps stood before them. Murat ordered the Poles to advance against Eschefeld, where he swung to the right, in order to strike the Russians.

While executing this maneuver, the King of Naples learned of the fall of Penig. Murat realized that from that position Wittgenstein could seriously threaten his flank. In addition, Wittgenstein could move through Gera and Altenburg towards Leipzig, threatening that city. Action was necessary on Murat's part.[20]

When Victor learned of the Poles' situation north of Frohburg and by Roda, about 9:00 p.m., he immediately sent two battalions, a light cavalry regiment and two horse guns to Borna. This detachment took up positions there, in order to cover the lines of communication with Leipzig. Lauriston had, during the night, moved Maison's 16th Division near Roda, and moved the 17th (Albert) and 19th (Rochambeau) Divisions from Rochlitz and Colditz, towards Geithain and Frankenhain. The Mulde bridge by Rochlitz was destroyed, and a garrison placed in Colditz. Kellerman's mostly Polish IV Cavalry Corps,[21] was ordered to join Poniatowski's Polish VIII Corps. All trains were ordered on the road to Lausick.

Skirmish by Borna 10 October

During the morning of 10 October, Wittgenstein was, based on his earlier decision, marching towards Frohburg. He feared that Murat's entire army would attack, and therefore, wanted first to defeat the force that stood before him. As a result he planned an attack during the afternoon, but he was having second thoughts and considered waiting until 11 October, when Klenau's forces would join him. Only Kleist's 2nd Prussian Corps by Altenburg was readily at hand, so this hesitation was understandable.

At dawn, Ziethen sent three battalions and four squadrons to Eschefeld, where they quickly found themselves in a serious skirmish with Poniatowski's advanced posts. His exaggerated announcements that the Poles had significantly more infantry than on the previous day, troubled Wittgenstein, and caused him to further delay his attack. As he pondered what action to take, word came of the skirmish by Borna, and he found the decision was made for him. He sent Ziethen and his Prussian 11th Brigade, as reinforcements to attack Frohburg, and he rejoined his Russians by Borna, where the ever stronger sound of cannon fire indicated an earnest battle.

At daybreak, Gorchakov was relieved by Württemberg near Thräna, northwest of Frohburg. As he moved with his advanced guard into Zedtlitz and closed on the Wyhra, he saw large masses of French troops moving towards Borna, on the far side of the river. In addition, Pajol's attack had alerted Pahlen, who hurriedly prepared himself to receive the next French attack. The only infantry available to him were Jager Regiments #24 and #26 from Helfreich's 14th Division, which were on the eastern bank of the Wyhra by Borna.

Soon Murat's Polish advanced guard encountered Pahlen's forward posts, pushing them back into the old part of Borna, along the Frohburg road. Poniatowski's VIII Corps was followed at a large distance by Victor's II Corps and Pajol's V Cavalry Corps. On the far side of the Wyhra, Murat saw an allied column approaching, and began to deploy his forces on the left bank of the Wyhra. Gorchakov's artillery opened fire from the heights by Zedtlitz. The King of Naples issued orders for the French main body to move from the road into the woods between Borna and Schönau. The advanced guard was reinforced by the addition of the French 3rd Hussar Regiment. The advanced guard then moved against the old city of Borna, attacking the flanks and front of the Russian Jager regiments that Gorchakov had sent over the river. Gorchakov's main body remained by Zedtlitz. In the meantime, Helfreich sent infantry reinforcements into the old city. The Russians went over to the attack, and except for the intervention and successful attack of the Krakus and the 3rd Hussar Regiment, would have defeated the Polish advanced guard, before Poniatowski arrived with the main body of the VIII Corps east of Borna.[22]

The ensuing attack of the Polish advanced guard forced Pahlen and Gorchakov to send their cavalry, which stood by Zedtlitz, across the river and against Victor's columns advancing through the woods. Pajol threw himself with the V Cavalry Corps against the Russians, forcing a heated cavalry fight. Unsuccessful, the allies were pushed back.

Soon the II Corps stood behind the VIII Corps. Murat then ordered Victor to relieve Poniatowski's VIII Corps with Dubreton's 4th Division. Victor was then to march with his two other divisions to a position behind the Eula stream. Pajol went ahead, in order to strike the Russian troops crossing the river by Gestewitz and Kitzscher. At the same time, Lauriston ordered the V Corps forward and drew the army trains from Lausick behind the Eula. The trains moved to a new position by the Thierbach, to the left of the II Corps.

With the arrival of Dubreton's 4th Division, Poniatowski led the VIII Corps to the heights to the north of Borna. In order to occupy the allies, the Poles struck the old city from the north. The Poles twice succeeded in forcing their way into the town.

It was 11:00 a.m., as Murat dispatched GD Arrighi's corps towards Leipzig with orders that those forces stay between the allies and Leipzig. Murat was convinced the best position Arrighi could find for his forces was behind the Eula stream. His instructions were to maintain the security of Leipzig. Arrighi received his orders that evening and ordered Lefol's Independent Division,[23] which stood by Connewitz, forward.[24]

About 11:00 a.m., Wittgenstein was also moving towards Borna, and had ordered Gorchakov to advance through Zedtlitz towards Schönau. Murat feared that the allies were about to attack, while Victor moved the 4th Division to a new position with Poniatowski. Murat feared this attack would permit Wittgenstein, covered by a few battalions, to move a large force of cavalry and several guns along the Wyhra to Rötha.

The Poles had moved to the right flank of the II Corps, and during the night the IV Cavalry corps had joined them. They arrived by Lausick that afternoon. From there the VIII Corps moved once again to Otterwisch. The Polish advanced guard was followed by Wittgenstein's forces, without being molested as it placed itself in a strong position, south of the Eula crossings. Murat began to realize that the possibility of attack by Wittgenstein was minimal. His move had been successful. He had lost none of his baggage and only a few hundred prisoners were taken by the allies. He was greatly satisfied and looked with great confidence to the future. He believed he had won a position, that must cause the failure of the allied plans. Murat wrote Napoleon saying, "Wittgenstein is not strong enough to be able to undertake something against me, and it is less probable that Schwarzenberg will support him. One such plan would expose him to the danger of being cut off from Bohemia and it would, therefore, be preferable to strike at Dresden."[25]

Wittgenstein believed that Gorchakov's advance would permit him to intercept the Poles. He also believed that Ziethen had engaged in battle, which would permit him to again march against Priessnitz. However, Gorchakov's movement was too slow, and he arrived too late to intercept the Poles, as they withdrew. Gorchakov only reached the region around Flössberg, where he encamped for the night. He limited his aggressive moves against the Poles, to having them pursued by the 2nd Silesian Hussars, the Silesian Uhlans, and an artillery battery. This force was drawn into a small cavalry battle. The Prussian cavalry followed as far as the crossing over the Eula stream by Kitzscher, where they were stopped. Pahlen had, in the meantime, pushed his advanced guard up to the Eula stream, where it became involved in a battle over the occupation of Dittmansdorf. The French, nevertheless, maintained their possession of the village.

Württemberg was by Borna, Ziethen with the 10th and 11th Brigades stood by Frohburg, and Kleist, with the rest of the Prussian forces, stood stationary by Altenburg. At noon the advanced guard of FML Mohr, of Klenau's 4th Armeeabteilung, arrived in Frohburg. The main body of Klenau's forces, at Wittgenstein's request, moved up the Altenburg-Frohburg road from Penig to support him. Schäffer reached Geithain, Baumgarten moved over the Mulde and took a position in Rochlitz.

Wittgenstein was of the opinion, that Murat would abandon his position behind the Eula, as soon as all his troops had united. He was convinced that Gorchakov's march would encourage Murat to withdraw. He decided to expedite the advance and ordered Pahlen's advance to Rötha. But Wittgenstein soon recognized that Murat intended a long stay behind the Eula. It was on 11 October that Wittgenstein decided to bring Kleist's 2nd Corps forward to the position behind the Eula, in case the French were not inclined to withdraw.

The order was first issued to Kleist. In response, on 11 October, Ziethen immediately marched his group from Altenburg towards Borna. Furthermore, Schwarzenberg's order directed that a detachment be sent to Zeitz. The order then arrived to break out from Altenburg due west.[26]

Schwarzenberg learned from Klenau, in the course of the afternoon, of the capture of Frohburg. He then learned from reading captured letters, that Napoleon had moved to Wurzen, during the night of 8-9 October. At the same time, he finally received news from the Army of the North. Bernadotte had sent an officer named Oberskov to the Czar. This officer had passed through Pegau, where he met Platov. He brought information that Bernadotte's headquarters were in Radegast on 8 October, and those of Blücher were in Düben. The Russian officer reported that on 7 October, the two army commanders had a meeting, and were beginning their march against Leipzig.

Blücher and Bernadotte were convinced that Napoleon would gather his forces by Leipzig. It was still felt that Murat was faced with the need to evacuate Rochlitz and Geithain, so Schwarzenberg had no reason to vary from his previous intentions. On 11 October, Wittgenstein and Kleist took up positions by Borna. Their advanced guards stood by Rötha on one wing, and on the other wing reached through Lausick towards Grimma. Klenau's forces occupied Frohburg, Geithain, and Röchlitz. The Austrian Reserve, 2nd, and 3rd Armeeabteilungs were in Altenburg, the Russian Grenadiers and the 3rd Cuirassier Division were in Langeleuba, while the Russo-Prussian Guard and the artillery reserve were in Penig.[27]

On the morning of 11 October, news arrived from Bubna that he had, on 8 October, stormed the bridgehead at Pirna, and had raised a small pontoon bridge. He also sent word that there were no more French outside Dresden. GM Knorring had struck a post in Nossen and urged an advance into Dresden. Platov's Streifkorps, moving towards Lützen, sent word that the union with the Army of the North would be made.

The one major concern for the allies was Augereau's IX Corps, which formed Napoleon's main reserve, and had stood by Jena, looking over the Saale, for sometime. Its movements and actions could unhinge the allied plans.

Skirmish by Wethau and Stössen on 10 October

On 8 October FML Moritz Liechtenstein and GL Thielmann advanced towards Eisenberg, after learning that Augereau had abandoned the bridges by Dornburg and Camburg. The two generals advanced over the Saale, but avoided risking an encounter with Augereau's forces in their strong position by Jena. Instead, they chose to send out a cavalry detachment, under Rittmeister Freiherr von Wüsthof, towards Weimar.[28] Liechtenstein hoped, through this to so alarm the French, that Augereau would be induced to move to defend Weimar.

However, during the night of 8 October, Augereau received Napoleon's order to march on Leipzig. At the same time Arrighi ordered GD Lefol to move his division from Naumburg, to serve as the first line of Augereau's forces and also ordered Lefèbvre-Desnoëttes' cavalry to join him. The movement of these detachments offered Augereau the opportunity to strike a heavy blow against the allies, with this excellent cavalry from the V (bis) Cavalry Corps. They were veteran solders from Spain, and he plotted to bring the allies within his grasp. Despite his written orders, on the morning of 8 October, he moved down the road to Weimar. He hoped to lure Liechtenstein, by this maneuver, over the Saale, and by sudden move from Weimar towards Apolda, force the allies into a battle.

The planned blow failed, because Augereau's march from Jena was observed. Oberst Mensdorf, on whom the attack was intended, was to have marched to Klosterlausnitz. However he had not advanced, when he did not meet Liechtenstein's 1st Light Division as planned. His decision not to advance was reinforced, when he received word from Rittmeister Wüsthof, in Apolda, that he had seen a column from 10,000 to 12,000 men on to the road from Weimar to Naumburg. Statements from the civilians related that few French troops were standing by Jena. Liechtenstein quickly decided to join both streifkorps to his forces, and be ready to act if Jena was truly evacuated or only weakly occupied. Mensdorf was to advance through Jena towards Eckhartsberga and to attach himself to the French. Liechtenstein and Thielmann intended to move between Kösen and Naumburg, where the French column must cross over the Saale, in order to either stop Augereau or crush his advanced guard.[29]

During the morning of 9 October, as Mensdorf's detachment, stood ready to send patrols towards Jena, Mensdorf received, via GM Kaisarov, Wittgenstein's order to march on Lützen. He was to observe the French activities there. FML M. Liechtenstein relieved Oberst Mensdorf by ordering GM Prinz von Hessen-Homburg to march to Jena. Wittgenstein's note arrived later, authorizing the use of Mensdorf's forces to secure the left flank. Liechtenstein considered the possibly of sending Mensdorf to Teuchern, in order the observe the Naumburg-Weissenfels road. During the night Mensdorf took by surprise the French posts at Teuchern.

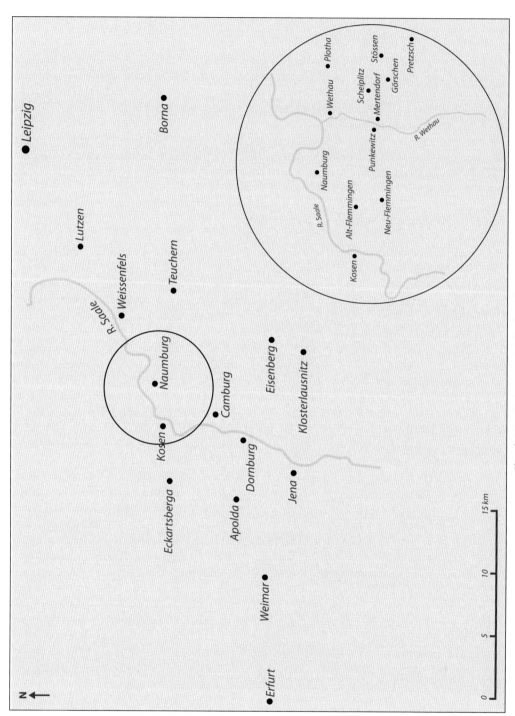

Sketch Map 9 Augereau's March on Leipzig.

Augereau had hoped, by 9 October, to have reached Weissenfels, however the march had by 8 October already gone awry. His forces moved down bad roads that wore hard on his young infantrymen, and on 9 October, Rittmeister Wüsthof raided his train. Augereau was obliged to turn back a large portion of his column to rescue his train, further slowing his advance.[30]

Augereau felt himself obliged to move his forces to Naumburg, and allowed Thielmann to pass unhindered over the Saale by Kösen. He sent GB Subervie's 9th (bis) Light Cavalry Division with some voltigeur companies towards Wethau, where there was a ford over the Wethau stream. The 1/19th and 1/, 2/22nd Dragoon Regiments (three squadrons) joined the rest of Queunot's 5th (bis) Heavy Cavalry Division in Neuflemmingen. The main body of the corps remained in Naumburg.

Thielmann's Streifkorps moved to the south, driving the French Dragoons from Neuflemmingen, taking a number of prisoners and bombarded Naumburg. Colonel Mermet, commanding Montéléger's 1st Brigade, drew together his brigade and advanced from Alt-Flemmingen against Thielmann's Streifkorps. He brought Thielmann to battle and drove him through Mertendorf towards Scheiplitz-Görschen.

Liechtenstein had not received the report of the evacuation of Jena until the afternoon. Once he did, he moved through Roda towards Stössen. He sent forward a force of Grenz and Jäger Companies, plus a few squadrons of the Vincent Chevauléger Regiment, on a reconnaissance patrol. They reported back that the French were already at Wethau and that any effort to capture the Wethau Bridge would result in large losses. Liechtenstein decided, therefore, to strike before daybreak. During the night he sent forward numerous small detachments to harass the French garrison of Wethau, to keep them agitated and under constant alarm throughout the night. The goal was to bring the French security forces to the point, where they took little or no notice of the allied troops, so that when the actual assault came, it would not be recognized as a major attack until too late.

Liechtenstein hoped, that by capturing the bridge, he could cost Augereau at least a day's march, if not totally block his march on Leipzig. Mensdorf was invited to cooperate by moving to Plotha, so as to block the road to Weissenfels.[31]

The plans drawn up at midnight, set the attack on the bridge to occur at 6:00 a.m. Mensdorf was to operate on Liechtenstein's right flank, while Thielmann cooperated on the left. However, a later report from his scouts about the visibly alarmed nature and attentiveness of the French posts, induced Liechtenstein to revise the time of his planned assault to 4:00 a.m.

Oberst Freiherr Veyder von Malberg led his 7th Austrian Jäger Battalion in the assault, and the attack succeeded completely. It was supported by the 2nd Jäger Battalion as it advanced.[32] The French detachment in Wethau was overthrown, GB Subervie escaped being taken prisoner dressed "only in his shirt". Liechtenstein believed that, with the occupation of the bridge, the game had been won. However, Augereau saw the weak position held by the allies, and resolved to attack them and clear the road. As GB Aymard, with the battalions of the 3/10th and 2/21st Légère Regiments and four guns moved directly against the bridge, GB Lagarde, with four battalions, moved the upstream to the ford by Punkewitz-Mertendorf, and crossed to the far bank. This combined attack struck the defenders of the bridge, which consisted only of the 7th Jäger Battalion and a company of the Broder Grenz Regiment. The allied bridge garrison was driven back to GM Scheither, who commanded the 2nd Jäger Battalion, a squadron of the Vincent Chevaulégers, and the entire artillery of the 1st Light Division (18 guns).[33]

Behind them stood Thielmann's cavalry, four Austrian and four Prussian squadrons,[34] and two Don Cossack Regiments. FML Liechtenstein had the bulk of his division, consisting of two battalions,[35] 11 squadrons,[36] and his general reserve standing by Stössen. When he learned of the French capture of the bridge, he ordered a general advance towards Stössen. He occupied Stössen with five companies of the 1st Jäger Battalion. The sixth company was placed in Görschen, to cover the left flank. His cavalry moved into the plain behind Stössen, to allow a junction with Thielmann's forces when they might arrive.[37]

The advance of the 7th Jäger Battalion proved very difficult. The French light infantry struck with great vigor, so that the Jägers repeatedly counterattacked, supported by Rittmeister Devaux's squadron of the Vincent Chevaulégers, in order to win some breathing room. Soon the French cavalry column moved over the bridge, with Subervie's 9th (bis) Light Cavalry Division in the lead. Devaux broke the attack of the first squadron against the Jägers with an attack by his chevaulégers in their flank.[38] This gave the Jägers time to form "*klumpen*"[39] and defend themselves against the following attacks. At the same time, the French infantry attacked. The French drove the Austrian infantry back and nearly caught the Austrian artillery, as it struggled to escape. The timely arrival and attack of Thielmann's rearguard, especially the squadron of the Klenau Chevaulégers under Rittmeister Franz Graf Kesselstadt, allowed them to escape. The Jägers of the 7th Jäger Battalion deployed in skirmish formation and covered the withdrawal of the defeated Austrians.[40]

Holding the bridge, Maréchal Augereau immediately resumed his march towards Leipzig. Because of the constant threat of the allied cavalry and forces that he had just driven away, he gave GD Milhaud, V (bis) Cavalry Corps, the order, to follow the allies with his cavalry and to attack them, if possible.

Followed by the fire of Subervie's horse batteries, the allied artillery and Thielmann's cavalry withdrew behind Stössen. Stössen was occupied by the 1st Jäger Battalion, which soon found itself in a fierce fight as the French advanced. The French artillery fire inflicted many losses on the allies. Liechtenstein was not willing to allow himself to be drawn into another battle and his position was not favorable, so he ordered a withdrawal to Pretzsch. His infantry and artillery quickly moved through the cavalry line. At the same time, he prepared a withdrawal by echelons, when the left flank of Subervie's light cavalry appeared and began their attack.

Thielmann did not waste a second and placed himself at the head of four Prussian squadrons, leading them forward. On the left flank he was accompanied by his Cossacks, while the Levenehr Dragoons followed as a reserve. All the other allied cavalry detachments, however, were withdrawing at this time.

Subervie's leading squadrons showered their attackers with carbine fire, but the allies broke through their line. Despite their success, the Prussians were themselves driven back by the remaining squadrons of the French light brigade. The Levenehr Dragoons were obliged to come to their assistance.

In the meantime, Milhaud had moved his dragoons forward in column. Montéléger's 6th (bis) Heavy Cavalry Division and Colonel Mermet's Brigade of the 5th (bis) Heavy Cavalry Brigade (Queunot) moved down the road with one squadron behind the other. According to French sources, they threw the leading squadron of the 6th Dragoon Regiment against the Vincent and Kaiser Chevaulégers before they could interfere in the light cavalry battle. As GB Queunot led the remaining squadrons of his division into the battle, Milhaud marked the Hohenzollern Dragoon and the Prussian 2nd Silesian Hussars as his target. The two allied cavalry regiments were struck in the flank by the 2nd Dragoon Regiment and disordered. All did not go well for Queunot's 5th (bis) Heavy Cavalry Division and a squadron of the 13th Dragoon Regiment was surrounded by the allied cavalry. It balled itself into a clump, in order to face the attacks from every direction. During this time Mermet deployed his brigade, and the attack of the 18th and 19th Dragoon Regiments, freed Subervie's surrounded 9th (bis) Light Cavalry Division. At the same time the entire mass of Montéléger's 6th (bis) Heavy Division came to their assistance and the cavalry battle turned to the French favor.

The attack of Thielmann's cavalry and the Levenehr Dragoons was unsuccessful. Oberst Franz von Gallois stood before his two and a half squadrons of the Vincent Chevauléger Regiment, with orders not to allow himself to be drawn into the battle. However, seeing the battle turning against his fellows, he placed himself in the front of his chevaulégers and led them against the French flank. The attack of the old Walloon Regiment, broke the French attack and they gave way, allowing the allied squadrons to reunite and reorganize for the withdrawal. Oberst von Gallois was awarded the Theresa Cross for his failure to follow orders.[41]

The battle was fought with great bitterness on both sides. The French had defeated the allied cavalry, and this was a shock to the allies, who had heretofore enjoyed uncontested cavalry superiority. They had encountered veteran French cavalry drawn from Spain, when they were used to meeting only poorly trained recruits in the French cavalry.

The allied cavalry once again turned back towards Pretzsch. The threatening posture of two squadrons of the Kaiser Chevaulégers held back as a reserve, slowed the advancing French. Once the French encountered the allied infantry and artillery by Pretzsch, they were too fatigued to engage in another fight. In addition, the appearance of Mensdorf's cavalry to the north and Thielmann's Cossacks to the south, encouraged Milhaud to leave the allied cavalry by Pretzsch undisturbed, as it reorganized itself. He did not resume his pursuit, until the allied cavalry resumed their withdrawal. The pursuit was not very aggressive as Liechtenstein had left behind a rearguard.

Liechtenstein's forces had suffered nearly 1,000 casualties in this battle. He had been visibly hurt by this undertaking. Not willing to resume the fight, he broke off actual contact, but he did not permit Augereau out of his sight.[42]

He clearly felt that his orders had authorized this action, but having been bested while acting outside the letter of his orders, he began writing his justifications. His reports to Schwarzenberg and Wittgenstein contained lengthy explanations, validating his actions, and stated that Thielmann had also felt the necessity to block Augereau's march to the Leipzig. Indeed, the actual delay he inflicted on Augereau's advance may well have had a significant effect on the outcome of the battle of Leipzig. Had Augereau arrived on the Leipzig battlefield during the first day his corps may well have been the decisive forces that Napoleon needed to defeat the Army of Bohemia.[43]

Undisturbed, on 11 October, Augereau pushed his corps to Weissenfels. On 12 October he received troubling word of numerous allied light troops in region to the west of Leipzig, through which he must pass, before he could support Murat in a serious battle.

The same news of these allied light cavalry patrols caused orders to be sent to Poniatowski, to send a strong reconnaissance detachment to the bridge by Crostewitz. He was also to send patrols towards Zwenkau, in order to capture a few Cossacks, and to gather information from the population of the surrounding villages.

The French strategic situation was difficult, yet filled with opportunities. The French stood on interior lines of communication between two detached allied armies. Concentrating his forces against either one, should have given Napoleon the chance for the decisive victory he sought. Yet, it was necessary to unite the army on 15 October, and to determine the intent of the allies that stood around Halle.

Napoleon was inclined to strike against the allied main army, but wanted a favorable opportunity to settle accounts with Blücher. Admittedly to concentrate his forces would require time, time Napoleon did not have. Operating on the internal lines of communication would require him to either detach a large rearguard to hold one of the two allied pincers at bay, or to march against an allied force, with enough distance to protect him from a blow to his rear. Unfortunately, his first effort at this, his push to the north after Blücher and Bernadotte, had failed. A second effort would probably have resulted in the same situation, but with the main allied army in his rear capturing Leipzig. Obviously the geo-political considerations heavily influenced Napoleon's plans for the following days more than the military.

The strategic situation of early October, changed into a grand tactical situation. As the allies converged on Leipzig, he was obliged to detach a large force to serve as a rearguard, north of the Parthe.

Napoleon in camp near Leipzig, 14 October.

With this in mind, Napoleon sent Macdonald the order to march to Taucha, northeast of Leipzig, but not to cross the Parthe. While he passed through Naunhof, he could also strike Klenau's right flank, should the opportunity arise. Ney was again sent the order to march down the main road, while Reynier was to move to the left bank of the Mulde by Düben.[44]

Marmont once again reported that he required reinforcements, especially cavalry, in order to be able to effectively block the Halle-Leipzig road. Napoleon did not accept this suggestion, sending his Généraladjudant GB Flahaut to the Maréchal, telling him to maintain a constant reconnaissance towards Halle and Landsberg, penetrating as far as the Herz.

As this order was dispatched, Napoleon mounted his horse and rode with Murat towards Liebertwolkwitz. From there they moved to the west of the Galgenberg Heights. The I Cavalry Corps of Latour-Maubourg followed the main staff, in order to be able to renew the battle the following day, as well as to support Pajol's 10th Light Cavalry Division.

The area around Leipzig remained peacefully quiet. The allies were not, however, marching off as Murat had reported that morning. The allied advanced posts still stood opposite the French, but at a slightly greater distance.

Schwarzenberg was still pressed by his worries that Murat would follow the main body of the allied army, and that Napoleon might have joined Murat. Towards 3:00 p.m., a French parliamentarian arrived at the allied advanced posts, with a note, requesting if Schwarzenberg was to be found in the vicinity, and stating that Berthier wished to communicate with him. The response was that Schwarzenberg had no time to confer.

At this time Napoleon rode to Poniatowski's VIII Corps, which was crossing the Pleisse and taking up a position on this wing. On the left flank, the positions were handed over to three of Poniatowski's Regiments with the customary ceremony. The presence of the opposing allied forces gave the act a special meaning.

Napoleon swept back through Zweinaundorf in the darkness, as he rode to his headquarters in Reudnitz. Murat's troops by Zweinaundorf fell back to their bivouac, with the I Cavalry Corps in support.[45]

Austrian Maneuvers

During the night of 13/14 October, Prince Schwarzenberg advised FZM Gyulai that the anticipated attack by GL Kleist against Leipzig, would occur during the morning of 14 October, preceded by a reconnaissance by GdK Wittgenstein, and that on his side, FZM Gyulai should push down the road from Pegau as far as Lützen.[46]

As directed by this order, the Light Division of Crenneville moved towards Lützen, from where Gyulai personally led a reconnaissance in force towards Leipzig, as far as Schönau. The French avoided a serious conflict, and withdrew after light resistance to their position by Lindenau.

As a result of this the Austrian 3rd Abteilung marched to Muschwitz, leaving the Würzburg Regiment, a battalion of the Erzherzog Louis Regiment, and a half-battery under the orders of FML Murray in Weissenfels. Two other battalions, a squadron of the Rosenberg Chevauléger Regiment and two cannon under GM Salins were posted in Naumburg, in order to cover the passages over the Saale for later operations. In addition, another squadron was detached for ordinance (orderly) service. The 3rd Abteilung was, as a result, diminished by five battalions and two squadrons, leaving only 15 battalions and 11 squadrons for the attack on Leipzig.[47]

During this reconnaissance, all the troops moved to the indicated points. Hessen-Homburg's Division moved into Muschwitz and Czollich's Brigade moved near Röcken, on the road to Lützen. Mensdorf's Streifkorps took up a position in Döhlen, between Lützen and Mark-Ranstädt.

On 15 October, the 3rd Abteilung was ordered to first move to Lützen, then to push its advanced guard to Mark-Ranstädt, leaving two battalions and a battery to occupy the château and the bridge at Weissenfels. Two other battalions were to be sent to the Kösen bridge. The Austrian 1st Light Division (Prince M. von Liechtenstein) and Thielmann's Streifkorps were put under the orders of FZM Gyulai. The former became the advanced guard for the Austrian 3rd Abteilung. The 1st Light Division then moved from Muschwitz, via Starsiedel, towards Lützen, where it was rejoined by Czollich's Brigade, and the main force of the corps. They then bivouacked around the village. Crenneville's Austrian Light Division stood by Mark-Ranstädt, where it was joined by M. von Liechtenstein's 1st Light Division. Liechtenstein's Division had 2,657 men and 1,857 horses.

Liechtenstein had left a detachment in Zschocher and another in Pristablich. Oberst Mensdorf moved his troops to Schönau, so that his Cossacks and partisans could communicate on the left with GL St.-Priest. The communications to the right were opened with the advanced guard of the 2nd Abteilung, which occupied Zwenkau and had a post in Nauendorf.[48]

The French had considerably reinforced their advanced post around Lindenau. Towards the evening, orders were received by the allies to execute an attack, on 16 October, against Leipzig.

The Cavalry Battle at Liebertwolkwitz

Being intent on a major battle in the vicinity of Leipzig, the allies resolved, on 13 October, to send forward a offensive grand reconnaissance. Toll sent a note to Wittgenstein, at 3:15 p.m., that day, to inform him that the advance would begin the next day. Murat, however, fearing he would be overrun by the large force of the allies, proposed to Napoleon, that he be allowed to withdraw to the far side of the Partha. Napoleon sent Gourgaud to advise Murat that he was arriving in Leipzig on the 14th. Murat, reassured by this promise, decided to accept battle.

Unfortunately, Murat chose to abandon his position by Cröbern and Gülden-Gossa, and withdraw towards Leipzig during the night of 13/14 October. During the morning of the 14th, his forces were deployed as follows: Poniatowski (VIII Corps) was between Connewitz and Mark-Kleeberg. Poniatowski commanded 12 battalions, six squadrons and six and a half batteries, about 5,400 infantry, 600 cavalry, and 30 guns. Victor (II Corps) was on the heights of Mark-Kleeberg and extended to Wachau. Victor commanded 32 battalions and eight batteries, about 15,000 men and 58 guns. Lauriston (V Corps) was on the heights between Wachau and Liebertwolkwitz. He commanded 35 battalions, seven squadrons and eight batteries, about 12,000 infantry, 700 cavalry, and 53 guns. The village of Liebertwolkwitz was prepared for defense and occupied by Maison's 16th Division. Augereau's IX Corps or Corps de Réserve stood to the rear, towards Leipzig. It contained 9,500 infantry and 14 guns. The combined forces of the IV and V Cavalry Corps, about 1,800 and 4,000 men respectively, stood in Liebertwolkwitz, behind the left wing of the French line. The command of these two corps was confided in GD Kellerman. A division of Young Guard stood as a reserve by Holzhausen.[49]

Wittgenstein had, on his side, organized his troops in two columns. The left column had Pahlen's troops in the lead, and moved on Magdeborn with the Soum, Grodno, and Loubny Hussar Regiments, three Cossack regiments under Illowaiski XII, and Horse Battery #7. Pahlen's forces totaled about 1,800 cavalry. Ten Prussian squadrons from the Neumärk Dragoons, the East Prussian Cuirassiers, and the Silesian Uhlan Regiment,[50] supported by Horse Battery #10, came next. Behind them was the Reserve Cavalry Brigade of GM Röder consisting of the Silesian and Brandenburg Cuirassiers, the 2nd Silesian Hussars, the 7th and 8th Silesian Landwehr Cavalry, and Horse Batteries #7 and #8.[51]

GL Pahlen occupied the bank of the Goselbach with GM Helfreich's 14th Division and bivouacked the cavalry in groups on the southern bank of the stream. Pahlen got Wittgenstein's order to advance against Störmthal at 5:00 a.m. Similar orders were sent to Klenau, but they there not received until around 9:30 a.m. These orders required the pushing forward of the Russian advanced guard posts, to ascertain the presence or departure of the French from their positions. The certainty that the French still occupied their last known positions was not in question as the advanced troops had remained unchanged and the watch fires still burned. Furthermore, in the morning hours thick fog covered the ground. It was not until about 8:00 a.m., as the French advanced troops drew back, that it was ascertained with certainty that the French had vacated their positions by Störmthal, Gülden-Gossa, and Cröbern.[52]

Wittgenstein ordered a pursuit of the French. However, the pursuers were to do so "without getting entangled in an a unequal battle." Pahlen, with the reinforced advanced guard, moved towards Störmthal, where on 13 October the French main body was presumed to be. He did so by moving "in front" of the French through Magdeborn (Tanzberg)-Gülden-Gossa. Helfreich's

14th Division, with the Radjanov #2, Jaroslav, and Illowaiski #12 Cossack Regiments screening its advance, moved through Cröbern.

Behind the mass of cavalry came Helfreich's 14th Infantry Division, which marched on Cröbern; the 4th Infantry Division (Pischnitzky), which moved on Gülden-Gossa; the 5th Infantry Division (Mezentzov), which moved against Störmthal; and finally Kleist's 2nd Prussian Corps.[53]

As a reserve, Gorchakov held back the 3rd Division from Württemberg's 2nd Russian Corps and the Prussian 9th and 12th Brigades under Kleist's personal command. They passed through Gülden-Gossa, followed by GM Ziethen with the Prussian 10th and 11th Brigades. The Prussian light cavalry moved through Störmthal.

GdK Klenau sent a short order: "The French retire, they must therefore be struck on all sides." Later GL Pahlen, supported by the Prussian reserve cavalry and the Russian 3rd Cuirassier Division, followed Helfreich's 14th Division to Cröbern. The two Prussian battalions standing by Raffia also moved to Cröbern.[54] The right hand column, formed by Klenau's Corps, moved out of the University Forest to seize Liebertwolkwitz.

Pahlen advanced. The Russian Grodno, Loubny, and Soum Hussar Regiments, plus the Russian Horse Battery #7, departed their bivouacs in Göselbach at 8:30 a.m., and began moving through Gülden-Gossa. The attached Prussian cavalry, with their horse battery, received orders to follow them and began movement in the same direction at 9:00 a.m. Pahlen had, at this time, arrived on the heights south of Gülden-Gossa. The Illowaiski #12 Cossacks encountered, and signaled to him, the presence of a large French force supported by 30 guns near Mark-Kleeberg. Pahlen stopped his movement and detached GM Rudinger with the Grodno Hussars to support the Illowaiski #12 Cossacks.

Pahlen then sent the Grodno Hussars towards Mark-Kleeberg, and the Loubny Hussars towards Liebertwolkwitz, to reconnoiter, while he rode with the Soum Hussars and the horse battery, towards the heights north of Gülden-Gossa. Once there he awaited the arrival of the Prussian cavalry. The Loubny Hussars soon reported a large French force stood there as well, convincing Pahlen of the numerical superiority of the French standing before him. He decided it would be prudent to wait for the arrival of the Prussian cavalry, before resuming his advance. He was joined by Diebitsch,[55] who wanted him to fall immediately on the French. However, Pahlen refused to move before the arrival of the Prussian Cavalry Reserve and Duka's 3rd Russian Cuirassier Division. When they did arrive, he sent forward the Soum Hussars, Horse Battery #7, and the Neumärk Dragoon Regiment.'[56] As Pahlen maneuvered his cavalry, Württemberg brought his 2nd Corps to a position north of Gülden-Gossa.

Württemberg was, at this time, marching his corps through Magdeborn towards Gülden-Gossa under the cover of a hussar squadron posted on the heights north of Gülden-Gossa. The hussars were to warn him of any threatening French movements. Shortly later he was taken under fire by a group of French cavalry. Behind the French hussars, a French general and his retinue galloped from the north, to the heights overlooking Württemberg's advance. Württemberg then moved to the south of Gülden-Gossa, to join Pahlen and GM Diebitsch. He informed them he had found strong French forces on the Wachau-Liebertwolkwitz line, and that his corps would not be able to advance through Gülden-Gossa without becoming embroiled in an unequal battle. Diebitsch did not believe the French would resist such a move seriously. As he rode through Magdeborn, Prussian GM von Hake had told him, "The enemy will withdraw, as soon as we fire a few cannon shots," so he obviously doubted any serious French resistance.[57]

Württemberg and Diebitsch joined with Pahlen's advanced guard, as Diebitsch observed the French cavalry marching from the heights north of Gülden-Gossa. Now even Diebitsch realized that a major battle was about to occur.

About the same time, shortly before 9:00 a.m., Gorchakov's advanced guard reached Störmthal. His column contained the Grekov VIII Cossack Regiment, and the Tchougouiev Uhlan Regiment.

It was later was joined by six Prussian squadrons.[58] They advanced through Störmthal, and charged repeatedly into the whirling cavalry battle.

Helfreich's 14th Division and the two Prussian battalions under Oberstleutnant Löbel had reached Cröbern. GM Rüdiger advised Pahlen that the French were reinforcing their forces between Mark-Kleeberg and Wachau. Pahlen sent him nine squadrons of landwehr cavalry, which took position near Auenhain without being observed by the French. His Cossacks and landwehr cavalry, later supported by the Grodno Hussar Regiment, skirmished east of Crostewitz, with the Polish cavalry standing between Mark-Kleeberg and Wachau. They held the ground until the arrival of the 3rd Cuirassier Division.

Pahlen moved the Soum Hussar Regiment to the plateau north of Gülden-Gossa. The Prussian cavalry was in the order in which it had departed its bivouacs that morning. First came the Neumärk Dragoon Regiment, the 1/, 4/Silesian Uhlan Regiment, the East Prussian Cuirassier Regiment, and Horse Battery #9 "Tuchsen." East of Wachau and by Liebertwolkwitz, there were posted a number of French batteries, which flanked and began firing on the Russian hussars, marching between the villages on the height.[59]

Russian Horse Battery #10 moved forward to a position on the northern rim of the plateau by Gülden-Gossa and began to fire on the French cavalry. It was supported by the Soum Hussars. Its target was formed in a deep column. The French regiments were formed in columns of divisions along the eastern side of the Erlen Woods. The battery began to put howitzer shells into the thick mass of French cavalry.[60]

Murat, who had held his cavalry on the heights behind Wachau, noted that the Russian horse battery was very exposed, and sent forward some of Pajol's Regiments to stop this battery from tormenting them. The battery was very exposed and only supported by the Soum Hussars, who were thrown back. The battery itself quickly withdrew to a position by the Prussian artillery. The French cavalry was then taken in the flank by the Neumärk Dragoon Regiment. Their attack was followed by an attack by the East Prussian Cuirassiers, in a platoon column, and the Silesian Hussars. At the same time, the two squadrons of Silesian Uhlans swung to the left, and struck the rear echelons of the French. The attack was too much for the French cavalry, who withdrew rapidly.[61]

GM von Röder, with his reserve cavalry, and the landwehr cavalry, under the command of Oberst von Mutius, passed through Cröbern, and as they passed through the defile, they found the Cossacks and hussars locked in battle with overwhelming forces. They deployed as they advanced out of the village. The Brandenburg Cuirassier Regiment and Prussian Horse Battery #2 moved to the north of Cröbern.[62]

The Grekov #8 Cossacks and the Tchougouiev Uhlan Regiment arrived on the battlefield at that time. The Silesian and Brandenburg Cuirassiers took up positions to the left of the East Prussian Cuirassiers, while the Neumärk Dragoons and Soum Hussars rallied and formed the second line.

Röder sent the landwehr cavalry, under von Mutius, to support the Cossacks north of Cröbern, and placed himself with the Silesian Cuirassier Regiment and Horse Battery #2. He ordered them to advance at a trot, and ordered the Brandenburg Cuirassiers to follow behind quickly. As he reached the Leipzig Road, he saw on the plateau a mass of French cavalry to the north. The Silesian Cuirassier Regiment were ordered forward to attack them.

The Brandenburg and Silesian Cuirassiers deployed to the left in platoon column and trotted forward on Pahlen's left. The Silesian Cuirassiers deployed to the left and the Brandenburg Cuirassiers deployed to the right, both in echelons. They advanced forward on either side of the East Prussian Cuirassier Regiment. The three regiments drove forward and struck the head of Milhaud's column of dragoons, the 22nd and 25th Dragoons, who had formed in line. Behind the 22nd and 25th Dragoons came a column formed of the 20th, 19th and 18th Dragoon Regiments.[63]

The death of Lieutenant von Lippe as he attempts to capture Murat, by Knötel.

The battle continued, in an uninterrupted series of charges and countercharges. Murat ignored his position as commander by once again reducing himself to the position of brigade or regimental commander and leading one charge after another. He lost overall control of the battle.

Towards noon, the exhaustion of both sides was so great, that, for a short while, the two belligerent forces on the plateau by Gülden-Gossa stood 300 to 400 paces from one another, resting their panting horses and recovering their wounded. The further course of the battle consisted solely of the constant and uncoordinated pushes of small groups of cavalry without a plan.

In one instance, Murat had personally led forward a regiment. It broke in the attack and was falling back, when Lieutenant Guido von der Lippe, of the Neumärk Dragoon Regiment, spotted Murat alone and undefended. He promptly led forward a small force of men, in an effort to seize Murat, but was shot dead by the single trooper standing by Murat.[64]

Pahlen, seeing the turn taken by the battle, resolved to hold his position, until the arrival of Klenau's column. He refused his left wing and supported it with two Prussian batteries. He pushed forward his right wing. The French, on their side, reinforced their right and established, between Wachau and Liebertwolkwitz, a number of strong batteries, whose fire took the allied left in enfilade.

Murat, believing the moment had come to finish the allied force, formed a single large column, with the cavalry of the V Cavalry Corps, and threw them against the allied batteries. The allied artillery responded with canister, that inflicted many casualties on the head of the French column. The Russian Hussars, the Prussian Uhlans and the Brandenburg Cuirassiers took advantage of this, to throw themselves on the French. It was now 2:00 p.m., and the battle had begun at 9:00 a.m.

Klenau's Corps

The 4th Armeeabteilung was, during the night of 13/14 October, so exhausted from its strenuous march of the previous day, that it collapsed near Threna, without establishing itself on the important terrain features of the battlefield. The advanced guard had stood idly by and allowed the French to occupy the point of the University Forest and the village of Gross-Pösna.

At 6:00 a.m., Klenau answered Wittgenstein's note of 13 October. This note requested that he and his Armeeabteilung attack the French as soon as the cannon fire from the left wing was heard. Klenau sent Wittgenstein word that he wished to be excluded from the beginning of the attack because of the condition of his forces. GL Pahlen, however, had been assured that he would cooperate with the attack. At the same time, Schwarzenberg sent out a corrected note acknowledging Klenau's situation. The proposed attack would be difficult, because of the isolated location of the his forces, the bad communications and the limited support he could expect. In addition, he noted there was a small chance of an attack, by the French forces gathered by Leipzig.

According to Klenau's statements, around 7:00 a.m., two notes arrived. The first was an order from the allied headquarters. It arrived directing the 4th Armeeabteilung to move to Borna around 4:00 a.m. The second message was from Wittgenstein with typical supporting orders for the first.[65]

Yet Klenau did not move. It cannot be assumed that Klenau totally ignored these orders, and on the other side, there is not the least indication to be found in any documents, that he made any preparation for the departure to Borna. It is certain that Klenau's behavior on 14th October, was influenced by other factors. There are circumstantial indications that Baron Toll intervened. For Klenau to ignore written orders without a reprimand, indicates some verbal communication occurred. It is, therefore, very probable that in the morning Toll either personally carried word to Klenau, or that he sent a general staff officer ordering the 4th Armeeabteilung to attack Liebertwolkwitz. Only in this situation, can Klenau's holding back be understood. Otherwise the order to march on towards Borna would certainly have been carried out.

Wittgenstein's short order "The enemy retires…" was received by Klenau around 9:00 a.m. Opposite the 4th Armeeabteilung the French stood quietly, making no effort to advance. Liebertwolkwitz was entrenched and strongly held by the French. On the heights to the south of Liebertwolkwitz, by the windmill, stood about 100 cavalry. To the west was a force of 10,000 to 12,000 French deployed in battle order. Twenty guns stood on the Galgenberg Heights. The slope south of Liebertwolkwitz was covered with swarms of French skirmishers. It is understandable why Klenau showed so little inclination to attack the exceedingly strong position by Liebertwolkwitz, especially when the allied column advancing through Störmthal was still not present. Also the report from GL Pahlen arrived, stating that he not yet begun acting in accordance with Wittgenstein's order to advance towards Störmthal.[66]

The cannon fire from Wittgenstein grew louder and Klenau did not appear Toll sent a direct order from Schwarzenberg to Klenau, directing he attack Liebertwolkwitz and the heights lying behind it. This finally motivated Klenau, who, around 10:00 a.m., ordered preparations made for the attack. He then issued orders for only part of his corps to undertake the attack; only his cavalry and the advanced guard under Mohr were ordered forward. Splenyi's Brigade was to follow behind as a reserve. The other troops remained in their positions.

Klenau understood Liebertwolkwitz was occupied by 3,000 men and supported by 24 guns on a nearby hill. He knew that Lauriston's V Corps stood nearby, supporting the village's defenders. He ordered GM Baumgarten to attack the village from the direction of Holzhausen, and take on the French left flank. He sent 10 to 15 guns to occupy a small knoll between Liebertwolkwitz and Holzhausen, to support the attack, and established a strong skirmish line in front of his troops.[67]

On the north edge of the University Forest stood the Wallachian-Illyrian Grenz Battalion, which in conjunction with the Hohenzollern Chevaulégers and the Erzherzog Ferdinand Hussars, drove back the French skirmishers on the southern slope of Liebertwolkwitz. At the same time, the Erzherzog Karl Infantry Regiment and the 3/Lindenau Infantry Regiment sent detachments into the Niederholz, in order to hold themselves ready to attack towards Liebertwolkwitz. An Austrian horse battery positioned itself under the protection of the grenz and hussars west of Gross-Pösna. Here it opened fire, and cleared the slope south of Liebertwolkwitz of the French.[68]

The Erzherzog Karl Infantry formed itself in two lines, the 2nd Battalion in the first line and the 1st Battalion in the second line. The regiment then began advancing towards Liebertwolkwitz. The 3/Lindenau remained as a reserve behind the left flank. Klenau then sent Splenyi's Brigade and 10 squadrons of Desfours' Cavalry Brigade towards Gross-Pösna and moved Schäffer's Brigade's battery forward.

Klenau then formed two batteries, one by Gross-Pösna and one on the Kolmberg hill. From these positions he could fire on the east exit from Liebertwolkwitz. The two 12-pdr batteries of the corps reserve were sent forward somewhat later to Gross-Pösna.

At 11:30 a.m., the 2/Erzherzog Karl advanced at the *doublierschritt*, without stopping to fire, to a position 100 paces from the village of Liebertwolkwitz, and then broke into a dead run. They quickly pushed into the village. The gardens, lanes, and houses of Liebertwolkwitz were heavily defended, and the French fought furiously to hold the village. The 1st Battalion was soon forced to join the battle, supporting the 2nd Battalion, as they pushed through the entire village. Only the western portion and the church court remained in the possession of the French. The situation was stabilized about 2:15 p.m.[69]

Three times the French tried to retake the village, but the two Austrian battalions held on, eventually firing off all of their ammunition. Now the Lindenau Regiment advanced into the village. Its 3rd Battalion relieved the Austrians fighting in the eastern part of Liebertwolkwitz. The battalion commander, Hauptmann Petsch, was shot in the head during the battalion's advance, yet despite his wound he remained in command, leading his battalion to its place, and setting up its defense. Finally, however, he was obliged to leave the battle line. The 2/Lindenau, under Major Freiherr von Harnach, along with part of the 3rd Battalion, occupied the middle of the village. The 1/Lindenau began a new effort to drive the French out of the western portion of the village. However, the French force in this part of the village was especially strong, and they were supported by heavy artillery fire from the Galgenberg Heights. The battalion, despite its tremendous effort, failed and was pushed back to the Windmill Heights south of the village. The Erzherzog Karl Regiment reorganized itself shortly later to the east of the village, where the Württemberg Infantry Regiment had also taken up positions.

Klenau's light cavalry of the advanced guard formed behind the Wallachian-Illyrian Grenz Battalion, in echelons to the left. Behind them was Desfours' Cavalry Brigade. It was formed with the O'Reilly Chevauléger Regiment in the first line, and Kaiser Cuirassier Regiment in the second line. Despite the heavy French fire artillery fire, Oberst Rothkirch, upon seeing the situation of the Lindenau Regiment in Liebertwolkwitz, sent a number of Austrian batteries to the Windmill Heights to support the infantry.

Murat Renews the Assault

At this time, about 2:00 p.m., Murat chose to send his cavalry forward once again in a massive column. Milhaud's 6th Heavy Cavalry Division led the attack, followed by l'Hériter's 5th Heavy Cavalry Division forming the first line, Subervie's 9th Light Cavalry Division, and Berkheim's 1st Light Cavalry Division forming behind L'Héritier. On the Galgenberg plateau, between the two artillery lines, Murat formed his cavalry mass. Once formed, Murat sent his forces towards Gülden-Gossa, with Pahlen's cavalry as its target.

Klenau observed the French from his vantage point, and sent Oberstleutnant Kothmayer, with the six platoons of the Hohenzollern Chevaulégers assigned to defend his headquarters, to attack the French dragoons in the flank. Rittmeister Czen of the Erzherzog Ferdinand Hussars stood with his squadron to the west of the Windmill Heights, guarding the Austrian artillery stationed there. He saw the critical nature of the French attack, and without awaiting orders, he led his squadron forward into the French flank as the French moved past his position on the heights. Desfours' Brigade, consisting of the Kaiser Cuirassier Regiment and the O'Reilly Chevauléger Regiment, also received an order from Klenau to follow the Ferdinand Hussars, and strike the left flank of Murat's cavalry.

Klenau's horse artillery, supported by a squadron of the Erzherzog Ferdinand Hussars and the Hohenzollern Chevauléger Regiment, took up a position and established a crossfire with the Prussian and Russian batteries already on the field.

The fire of the main allied battery, slightly to the right of the advancing French column was devastating. This battery consisted of the 36 guns of the Prussian Horse Batteries #7, #8, and #10, and Russian Horse Battery #7. As the French assault slowed, the Olviopol and Soum Hussars and the Brandenburg Cuirassiers struck to the right of the head of Milhaud's column. They were supported by the Silesian Cuirassier Regiment. The Silesian Uhlans struck the left of the French column, supported by the Loubny Hussars and the Tchougouiev Uhlans. Behind them advanced the East Prussian Cuirassier Regiment and the Neumärk Dragoon Regiment. The Grekov #8 Cossacks stood behind the Tchougouiev Uhlans.

The squadrons of the Ferdinand Hussars and Hohenzollern Chevaulégers supporting the Austrian horse artillery also joined in the attack, once the artillery was no longer able to fire without hitting its own cavalry.

The assault on the head and flank of the French column was more than the French cavalry could take, and they quit the battlefield. As they withdrew, the French artillery redoubled its fire, inflicting considerable losses on the allied cavalry.[70]

On Pahlen's left flank, the Grodno Hussars, the Silesian Landwehr Cavalry, and the Illowaiski #12 Cossacks held off the Polish cavalry, until the arrival of the Russian 3rd Cuirassier Division.

The shattered French cavalry moved to Probstheida and through the infantry standing there. The allied pursuit moved against that infantry, as the last phase of their pursuit. During this attack, part of the French artillery positioned on the Galgenberg Heights, found its position compromised when the Lindenau Regiment had driven the French infantry completely out of Liebertwolkwitz. The French infantry was driven back to the heights between Liebertwolkwitz and Probstheida. French artillery moved up and soon showered the Austrians with shot and shell.[71] Klenau moved to the Windmill Heights, in order to join with Oberst Stein and direct the fire of the Austrian artillery. Oberst Rothkirch, at Klenau's side, was killed by a cannonball.

Despite the success of his infantry, Wittgenstein stopped the advance. At this time the English military attaché, Major General Wilson, and somewhat later Oberst Latour from Schwarzenberg's headquarters, bought orders to avoid a decisive battle. Perhaps Klenau had also received an earlier verbal order. He transferred the direction of the battle to FML Hohenlohe, and moved towards Pomssen.

Around 5:30 p.m., Maison's 16th Division, V Corps, began a new attack towards Liebertwolkwitz. Hohenlohe left the defense to the Württemberg and Erzherzog Karl Infantry Regiments. The attack was so powerful, and perhaps so surprising, that the Austrians were thrown back, abandoning Liebertwolkwitz. They fell back to Gross-Pösna. The Austrian artillery on the Windmill Heights was suddenly in danger of being taken by the French. Kapitänleutnant Smikal, with the 5th Company, Württemberg Infantry Regiment,[72] held back the French attacks against the artillery. The French did not push beyond Liebertwolkwitz. FML Mohr held the University

Forest-Niederholz line with his advanced posts. The remainder of his troops were withdrawn from the battle, and pulled back to their bivouacs for the night.

The line of Wittgenstein's advanced posts ran from the University Forest through the plateau north of Gülden-Gossa, to the sheep pens by Auenhain and on to Crostewitz. The Russian light cavalry moved to a position, to the right of Gülden-Gossa. Gorchakov, with his corps, the Prussian reserve cavalry brigade under Röder, the Neumärk Dragoon Regiment, and their horse artillery, stood northwest of Störmthal. The Prussian landwehr cavalry took up a position before Cröbern. Württemberg's corps bivouacked, with the 9th Prussian Brigade, southwest of Gülden-Gossa. Klenau, who had been pushed out of Liebertwolkwitz, assumed a position by Pombsen. Helfreich's 14th Division, the 10th, 11th, and 12th Prussian Brigades, and the 3rd Russian Cuirassier Division were by Cröbern, and Raevsky's supporting Grenadier Corps stood north of Espenhain. Kleist's headquarters were in Dechwitz and those of Wittgenstein was in Mölbis.

There is very little information on the activity of Baumgarten's detachment during 14 October. It appears that the GM Baumgarten and his weak forces advanced through Seifertshain, towards Holzhausen. However, he encountered a force of French infantry and about 10 guns, which hindered his march. As a result, he was unable to join the battle by Liebertwolkwitz. Instead, he was in the first line, securing the northern flank, and the line of retreat. He passed the day directing the fruitless skirmishing of the 2/Kerpen Regiment. As evening fell, Baumgarten was by Naunhof, while Oberst O'Brien and his detachment moved up from Rochlitz and occupied Grimma.

The losses of the Austrians in the battle of Liebertwolkwitz were very heavy, especially the heavy losses of the Lindenau Regiment and artillery. In fact, of the 12 Austrian guns lost in the battle five were dismounted.[73] Klenau appears to have lost about 1,000 men *hors de combat*, while the Silesian Cuirassiers alone lost 13 officers and 96 men *hors de combat*. The losses of the other regiments varied considerably.

The battle of Liebertwolkwitz had cost the French 500 to 600 casualties, including GD Pajol and GB Montmarie, who were wounded, and about 1,000 men, who were lost as prisoners to the allies.[74]

Liebertwolkwitz was not a conclusive fight in any sense. It showed the superiority of allied cavalry over that of the French, which is not a surprise. However, neither side gained and held significant terrain, neither side inflicted significant casualties on the other, and it does not appear to have had any effect on the battle that was developing around Leipzig. One could argue that it was simply the skirmish of the advanced guards before the actual battle began.

5

The Battle to the South
16 October 1813

The battle at Leipzig was to be the largest battle in history to that date. The combined might of the allied and French armies were about to meet and decide the fate of Europe for the next 150 years.

The allied forces initially on the battlefield consisted of the Army of Bohemia, to the south, and the Army of Silesia, to the north. They were to be joined later by the Army of Poland and the Army of the North. At this time, the strength of the allied armies were:

Army of Bohemia—FM Fürst Schwarzenberg	Men	Guns
4 Austrian Corps, the Austrian Reserve, and the 1st Light Division	110,451	242
Prussian 2nd Corps—Kleist	29,000	112
Russian Corps—Wittgenstein	10,900	274
Guard Cavalry—Galitzin	6,800	0
Corps Cavalry—Pahlen	2,600	0
Cossacks—Platov	3,364	0
Russian Reserve—Constantine	7,170	0
Total Army of Bohemia	*170,285*	*628*
Army of Silesia—GdK Blücher		
Prussian 1st Corps—Yorck	21,475	104
Russian Corps—Langeron	30,341	146
Russian Corps—Sacken	3,579	60
Total Army of Silesia	*55,395*	*310*
Army of the North—Crown Prince Bernadotte		
Swedish Army—Stedingk	18,485	62
Russian Corps—Winzingerode	23,091	86
Prussian 3rd Corps—Bülow	16,281	94
Total Army of the North	*57,857*	*242*
Army of Poland—GdK Bennigsen		
Advanced Guard—Stroganov	8,258	
Infantry—Docturov	27,842	
Cavalry—Tschaplitz	4,641	
Austrian 2nd Light Division—Bubna	7,262	
Total Army of Poland	*48,003*	*134*
Total Allied Armies Present	**351,540**	**1,314**

The French had been fighting on internal lines of communications against the circling allied armies and Napoleon had concentrated most of his army at Leipzig for the final showdown. The only major formations of the French army not at Leipzig were the I and XIV Corps in Dresden under St-Cyr, the X Corps under Rapp besieged in Danzig, and the XIII Corps under Davout in Hamburg. There were no other major portions of the French army that were not already at Leipzig on the first day of the battle. Napoleon was to receive no reinforcements. His army consisted of:

Imperial Guard—Mortier and Oudinot	Men	Guns
Old Guard	10,919	
Young Guard	21,776	
Guard Artillery	3,911	
Guard Cavalry	6,318	
Guard Total	*42,924*	*202*
II Corps—Victor	15,304	55
III Corps—Souham	17,168	61
IV Corps—Bertrand	8,953	6
V Corps—Lauriston	13,072	51
VI Corps—Marmont	18,830	82
VII Corps—Reynier	12,637	48
VIII Corps—Poniatowski	5,000	44
IX Corps—Augereau	8,647	12
XI Corps—Macdonald	15,862	68
Independent Divisions	8,899	34
I Cavalry Corps—Latour-Maubourg	6,480	27
II Cavalry Corps—Sébastiani	5,679	12
III Cavalry Corps—Arrighi	4,000	9
IV Cavalry Corps —Kellerman	3,000	18
V Cavalry Corps—Pajol	5,000	3
Total	191,455	732

The battle of Leipzig would see 542,995 men locked in combat for four days. It would be the climax of the 1813 fall campaign and the battle that finally broke the power of Napoleon's empire.

The Battlefield

Leipzig lies in the northwestern corner of the Kingdom of Saxony. It lies on the eastern bank of a bend in the Elster and Pleisse Rivers. They merge just north of the city and run parallel past the city from the Erzgeberg Mountains. The two rivers meander and are linked in several places by canals and various natural branches that produce a series of heavily wooded and marshy islands between the two main channels. Both rivers are deep and generally unfordable. The Pleisse could be forded in a few places, but the Elster was not fordable and both proved to be serious military obstacles.

To the north of Leipzig runs the Parthe River which runs from Taucha southwest into the Elster. It is crossed by several bridges and fords. As it flows south it breaks into a number of branches and its right bank is covered with forests.

Wachau.

Leipzig is the hub of 10 major roads. Seven of those roads enter the city from the eastern side of the twin rivers, crossing the open plains of northwestern Saxony. Three of the roads approach the city from the west and merge into a single road at Lindenau that then passes across the Elster and Pleisse on a series of bridges and causeways, forming a natural choke point.

The principal road to the west is the road to Lützen. It passes through a mile-and-a-half-long defile from its first bridge over the Pleisse River and reaches Leipzig by the Luppe Bridge. It crosses five principal bridges and six minor bridges before it traverses the entire Elster valley. In the middle of the Elster valley it passes through the Raths brickworks.

The plains to the east and west of the city were generally unobstructed by large tracts of woods, though there were a few small forests that were to play significant roles in the upcoming battle. The rolling nature of the plain was marked with many ridges providing the tactically important high ground and would be the object of many of the battles to come. However, the only major hills were on the western bank of the Elster between Lindenau and Mark-Ranstädt.

The city itself was surrounded by walls, but they were remnants of older wars and not designed to withstand the rigors of a modern siege. They were pierced by numerous gates and the suburbs of the city came right up to them. There had not been time to clear the suburbs away from the walls, nor to put the walls into a condition to withstand a siege, nor had there been time to provision the city for a siege. The French had time however to prepare a number of earthworks and entrenchments from which they planned to defend the city.

The Battle of Wachau: The Allied Plan of Attack

At midnight, Wittgenstein established his forces in their positions. Between 3:00 and 4:00 a.m., he issued his orders. He arrayed his attack in four columns.

The first column, under GdK Klenau, consisted of the Austrian 4th Armeeabteilung,[2] the Prussian 11th Brigade (Ziethen), and the Prussian Reserve Cavalry (Röder).

The second column was under GL Gorchakov. It consisted of Mezentzov's 5th Russian Division and GM Pirch's 10th Prussian Brigade. Both columns were to attack Liebertwolkwitz, one advancing from the northeast and the other to the west of the University Woods.

The third column, under Württemberg, consisted of the 2nd Russian Infantry Corps and GM Klüx's Prussian 9th Brigade. The fourth column, under GL Kleist, consisted of the Helfreich's 14th Russian Division, GM Prinz August von Preussen's 12th Prussian Brigade, a battalion from the 9th Prussian Brigade, GM Levaschoff's Russian Cuirassier Brigade, and the Lubno Hussar Regiment. These two columns were to move from Gülden-Gossa and Cröbern against Wachau. The left wing, the fourth column, was assigned to take Mark-Kleeberg. As a link between the second and third column GL Pahlen's cavalry stood before the Galgenberg Heights, between Liebertwolkwitz and Wachau.

The allied reserve, under Grand Duke Constantine, was formed from the Russian and Prussian Guard, the two Russian grenadier divisions under GM Raevsky, and the remaining two and a half Russian cuirassier divisions. It was in Rötha, where it could move to either bank of the Pleisse to support either the allied center or their right.[3]

Twice as many troops were sent against Liebertwolkwitz as against Wachau and Mark-Kleeberg. This fact alone shows the importance that Wittgenstein placed on the capture first of Liebertwolkwitz. In addition, his message to GdK Klenau written at 3:15 a.m., on 16 October, give the impression that the main objective of his attack was Liebertwolkwitz.[4]

Wittgenstein's orders for the battle of Wachau read as follows:

> At 7:00 a.m., GL Pahlen shall attack the enemy on the heights of Liebertwolkwitz and Wachau with artillery, infantry, and light cavalry, having the cuirassiers in reserve. GdK Klenau, supported by Prince Gorchakov shall attack Liebertwolkwitz and the left wing of Prince von Württemberg shall seek to turn and take the village and the woods of Wachau. GM Heifreich, supporting this attack, shall march in the direction of Leipzig, leaving Wachau to his right.
>
> The brigades of GL Kleist's Corps shall follow the Russian troops, behind which they shall form the second line. As allowed by the terrain and if the opportunity exists, they shall serve to support the first line. The grenadier corps shall march as a reserve, near the second line. Then shall come the Russian and Prussian Guard.
>
> Send forward only a few skirmishers. It is preferable to act by masses and with artillery and it is principally the latter that shall serve us to quickly capture the heights of Liebertwolkwitz and Wachau.
>
> GL Pahlen shall command all the cavalry. GdK Klenau shall command the right wing and GL Kleist shall command the left. The Prince von Württemberg shall command the center. The corps of GL Gorchakov shall form the junction between GdK Klenau and the rest of the army.
>
> The baggage shall be behind Espenhain on the road in order to later be directed towards Borna where the wounded shall also be sent, via Espenhain.
>
> I shall remain on the heights by Gülden-Gossa between the first and second lines.[5]

The infantry, cavalry, and artillery were to be formed in checkerboard pattern when advancing or withdrawing. If a retreat became necessary, Hessen-Homburg's column was to withdraw back through Pegau towards Zeitz. Wittgenstein was to move to Altenburg, Klenau was to move to Penig, and the Russian Reserve was to move either to Zeitz or Altenburg.[6]

The Allied Positions

On the morning of 16 October, that portion of the Army of Bohemia which stood on the right bank of the Pleisse, and under the command of Barclay de Tolly,[7] stood as follows:

1st Line: GdK Count Wittgenstein
  Left Wing: GL von Kleist (by Cröbern)
    Prussian 12th Brigade: Prinz August von Preussen
    Russian 14th Division: GM Helfreich
    Russian 2nd Brigade, 3rd Cuirassier Division: GM Levaschoff
    Loubny Hussar Regiment
  Center: GL Prince E. Württemberg (in Gülden-Gossa and Störmthal)
    Russian 2nd Corps: GL Württemberg
    Prussian 9th Brigade: GM Klüx (serving as 2nd Line)
    Russian Cavalry: GM Pahlen III
    Russian 1st Corps: Count Gorchakov (in Störmthal)
    Prussian 10th Brigade: GM Pirch (serving as 2nd Line)
  Right Wing: GdK Klenau (by Gross-Pösna)
    Austrian 4th Armeeabteilung: Count Klenau (by Gross-Pösna)
    Prussian 11th Brigade: GM Ziethen
    Prussian Reserve Cavalry: GM Röder
    Cossack Corps: Hetman Platov (by Seifertshain)
2nd Line: GL Raevsky (behind center of 1st Line)
    Russian Grenadier Corps: Raevsky
    Russian 2nd Cuirassier Division: GM Kretov
Reserve: Grand Duke Constantine (by Magdeborn)
    Russian Guard Infantry: GL Yermolov
    Prussian Guard Infantry: Oberstleutnant Alvensleben
  Cavalry Russian 1st Cuirassier Division: GM Depreradovich
    Prussian Guard Cavalry Brigade: Oberst Laroche von Starkenfelds
    Russian Guard Cavalry Division: GL Schivich
    Russian Reserve Artillery: General Suchosanet[8]

The allied lines in the south formed a large sweeping arc that started southeast of Leipzig, in the small village of Fuchshain. The allied right wing, GdK Klenau's Corps, was fixed in this tiny village, securing the end of the allied line. Klenau's line extended about two kilometers to the northwest to the village of Gross-Pösna.

The allied center stood to the northwest of Gross-Pösna. In the three kilometer interval to the northwest of Pösna and extending to Gülden-Gossa, stood Gorchakov's 1st Corps. Before and to the northwest of Gülden-Gossa, along a front of about 2 kilometers, stood Württemberg's 2nd Corps.

On the allied left, Kleist's Corps stood before Cröbern and extended north to Crostewitz. His left wing was anchored on the Pleisse, and the myriads of woods and swamps that lined the river's edge.

On the western bank of the Pleisse stood Merveldt's 2nd Armeeabteilung, extending to the north, until they were opposite the village of Connewitz, about 5 kilometers north of Crostewitz.

The French Positions

Facing the allies, the French were deployed as follows. Part of Poniatowski's VIII Corps defended Mark-Kleeberg, on the extreme western edge of the Wachau battlefield. The 27th Infantry Division,[9] under General Krasinski, stood in and to the east of Mark-Kleeberg. The Krakus Regiment, stood in two widely separated lines with 10-15 paces between each rider. It formed a cavalry screen extending from the left wing of the 27th Division to the IV Reserve Cavalry Corps which was deployed on the hills to the west of and beyond Wachau. The IV Reserve Cavalry was arranged in a two lines of column. Its front line consisted of the 1st (Polish) Chasseurs à Cheval Regiment on the left, a battery of 12 guns in the middle, and the 3rd Uhlan Regiment on the right. The second line, several hundred paces behind the first, had the 8th Uhlans on the left and the 6th Uhlans on the right.

Next to the Poles stood Augereau's IX Corps, which was deployed on the ridge before Dösen and behind the small branch of the Pleisse that ran to Wachau. Maréchal Victor's II Corps and Drouot's Guard Artillery were deployed behind this same stream as well as in and around Wachau. Much of the artillery was deployed on the high ground slightly to the rear and east of Wachau, on Victor's left wing. Lauriston's V Corps extended from Victor's left wing, through Liebertwolkwitz and slightly to its east. To the east of Liebertwolkwitz, behind a small stream running to the east, stood Macdonald's XI Corps, which also formed the extreme left wing of the French army.[10]

GD Lefol's forces guarded the bridges at Connewitz. The I and V Cavalry Corps were in Zwei-Naundorf and Holzhausen. The bulk of the Guard stood behind Liebertwolkwitz and the French parks stood in Schönefeld, on the left bank of the Parthe.[11] The I and V Cavalry Corps stood by Probstheida and the II Cavalry Corps stood by Zwei-Naundorf and Holzhausen.

At 9:00 a.m., the 1st Young Guard Corps, under Oudinot, arrived in Liebertwolkwitz and took up positions behind Lauriston. He was followed by the rest of the Imperial Guard. Napoleon arrived shortly later and dismounted from his coach to review the field with Murat. As he stood there, a sudden, heavy discharge of allied artillery occurred, which struck a group immediately behind the Emperor. Napoleon was not struck and he continued to stand there, surveying the field as artillery whistled round him.[12]

The First Phase: The Allies Attack in the South

The Allied Attack Between Wachau and Mark-Kleeberg

Wittgenstein had ordered his forces to be formed into four columns. At 6:00 a.m., the allies rose and began to prepare for the day's battle. The weather was dark, gloomy, and rainy. At 8:00 a.m., the allied columns began their advance. The first column (Kleist) moved against Mark-Kleeberg. The Loubny Hussars were directed to watch the empty space between Kleist's Prussians and Württemberg's Russians.

In the twilight the Russian 2nd Infantry Corps, formed in two columns, moved into the low ground by Gülden-Gossa, in order to move north of this village unobserved. Schachafskoy's 3rd Division stood to the east and Pischnitzky's 4th Division marched on the west. Two battalions of the Tobolsk and one of the Minsk Infantry Regiments, under Colonel Reibnitz, formed the advanced guard of the entire force and advanced in front of the left column. Both Württemberg and Wittgenstein marched with the left column.[13]

Wachau was strongly held by the French as Oberst Reibnitz advanced against it. Reibnitz was supported by 48 guns, which advanced before the head of the column. Victor had his artillery placed on heights to the north and northeast of Wachau, spread along the front of his massed divisions. Lauriston's batteries were by Liebertwolkwitz.

As Württemberg's column began its movement against Wachau, the third column moved out of the University Woods against Liebertwolkwitz and the fourth column moved from Neuhoff and Threna against Liebertwolkwitz.[14]

The Western Battle by Mark-Kleeberg

Soon Kleist resumed the advance. He marched in the line of Crostewitz-Auenhain. His left wing, Oberstleutnant von Löbel was detached with the 2/11th Reserve Regiment and the 2/, 3/6th Reserve Regiment[13] drawn from the 9th Brigade. He quickly occupied the village of Cröbern and then moved towards Crostewitz in order to follow the movements of the Russians on his right. Oberstleutnant Löbel was ordered to occupy this Mark-Kleeberg, which the accidents of the terrain made militarily important.

On his right, Helfreich's 2,500-man 14th Division, was ordered to take the heights between Wachau and Mark-Kleeberg. The Prussian 12th Brigade, Prinz August von Preussen, stood in the second line. Since the night before, a Prussian 12-pdr and a 6-pdr Battery had been assigned to Helfreich's 14th Division. These batteries advanced on Helfreich's right wing. The Lubno Hussar Regiment covered the interval between Württemberg's and Kleist's columns. Levaschoff's Cuirassier Brigade followed the Prussian infantry of Prinz August von Preussen.[16]

Two further Prussian battalions (1/1st West Prussian and 1/6th Reserve Regiment) advanced to support the Russians in the eastern side of Wachau and strike the Harth Woods.[17] The first shots were exchanged about 8:00 a.m.

The Poles occupied Mark-Kleeberg and the Kellerberg, a ridge to the northeast of the village, with their artillery. On the heights to the south and southwest of Dösen stood Poniatowski's VIII Corps and Kellerman's IV Cavalry Corps.

Oberstleutnant Löbel's tiny advanced guard moved against Mark-Kleeberg under the cover of Kleist's artillery. The artillery battle became more and more violent. The French were slowly pushed back to the heights behind Mark-Kleeberg, but the ravines there slowed the allied progress. The Poles held fast against the Prussian attack until they were struck in the left flank by eight battalions of Helfreich's 14th (Russian) Division. After that, Oberstleutnant von Löbel pushed into and occupied Mark-Kleeberg.

GL Kleist observed a large gap forming between the troops marching against Wachau and the 12th Brigade, and ordered Oberstleutnant von Schvichov to move into this gap with the 1/2nd Silesian, 1/11th Reserve, and the 10th Silesian Landwehr Regiments.[18]

The French started their counterattacks against Mark-Kleeberg and against the position held by the 12th Brigade, which they cannonaded in the flank with a powerful battery. Despite this, the Prussians maintained their positions. Several cavalry charges executed by the French were also thrown back. The Loubny Hussars, commanded by Colonel Davidov, distinguished itself particularly in these engagements. It was vigorously supported in these actions by the Russian 3rd Cuirassier Division. The detachment of Colonel Schvichov's infantry was subjected to murderous artillery and musketry fire, as it held its position between Mark-Kleeberg and Wachau. They held fast, however, despite their casualties.

Helfreich's 14th Division sought to take the heights to the east of Mark-Kleeberg. The French artillery on the Kellerberg and a battery by Wachau, on the allied flank, showered Helfreich's Division with shot, while to their front Helfreich's men found themselves locked in a skirmish battle.

The Allied Center Attacks Wachau

The second column, or the center, under Württemberg, marched against the Wachau heights via Gülden-Gossa. The French occupied both Wachau and the Wachau woods with infantry and their cavalry occupied, once again, the Liebertwolkwitz heights. The right wing of the allied column was preceded by 24 12-pdr cannon and followed by Pahlen's cavalry. The right was formed by GM

Schachafskoy's 3rd Division, which marched to the right of Wachau. The second line was formed by GM Pischnitzky's 4th Division, which advanced against Wachau. The first brigade of GM Pischnitzky's Division, normally commanded by Colonel Reibnitz,[19] was led by Württemberg in person. The second brigade, under Colonel Feodorov, was led by Pischnitzky. Behind them came the Prussian 9th Brigade, commanded by GM Klüx.

On the heights, southeast of Wachau and between Wachau and Liebertwolkwitz, only a few French troops and guns were noted. Wittgenstein, supposing this to be a rearguard, directed Württemberg to attack it. By that time Schachafskoy's 3rd Division had formed itself in two lines of battalions and on its left it had closed up with Feodorov's Brigade of Pischnitzky's 4th Division. The Russian artillery began to fire in support of the pending Russian assault.[20]

Most of Klüx's Brigade formed itself in two lines, with the schützen in reserve. This force then advanced behind the allied cavalry. However, two battalions from the Klüx's Prussian 9th Brigade, under Majors Haine (1/1st West Prussian) and Gayl (1/6th Reserve), advanced against Wachau supporting two Russian battalions of Reibnitz's Brigade, Pischnitzky's 4th Division. The Russians, however, did not continue their advance, but were distracted by a weak French detachment in the Harth Woods before Wachau, and the Prussians became separated from the Russians. The French quickly swooped down from Wachau against the two Russian battalions, obliging the Prussians to swing back to assist them. One of the Russian battalions lost a third of its strength as casualties in this fight. A lively battle began once the Prussians arrived, and Klüx's 9th Prussian Brigade advanced to decide the battle, sending forward the 1/, 2/7th Silesian Landwehr, 2/1st West Prussian Regiment and both companies of the Silesian Schützen Battalion.[21]

The French were, at this time, organizing a massive artillery battery on the heights above the allies. Württemberg ordered a reinforcement of his 24-gun battery and Russian Light Battery #6 and two Prussian batteries were ordered forward to join the fight.[22]

The French were not inactive, and sent forward their infantry against Wachau. The Prussians were obliged to fall back before the overwhelming numbers of French advancing against them. GM Klüx sent forward the skirmishers from his battalions and his artillery to fire on the French infantry. The French withdrew back into Wachau. However, the French artillery was very effective and dismounted 19 Russian guns and five Prussian guns. This obliged the allies to withdraw their batteries. The battle continued growing in intensity and the losses mounted on both sides. To the right of Wachau, Schachafskoy's 3rd Division stood under intense cannon fire, its casualties mounting. It was to be withdrawn back as a reserve. However, before that happened, Württemberg sent Klüx the word of this pending move. To cover the danger that was now threatening the left wing, Württemberg sent the Tchernigov Infantry Regiment and the 4th Jager Regiment, under Colonel Feodorov, to that point, where they joined the rest of Reibnitz's Brigade and held the French back. Despite this, the French prevailed and Württemberg was obliged to withdraw back to Gülden-Gossa.

Wittgenstein strove to control the rearward movement. The two Russian divisions remained south of Wachau, Klüx's Prussian 9th Brigade stood in the first line, on the sunken road south of the village. The two Prussian battalions to the east of Wachau, in the Harth woods, held off the French attack.

The Attack on Liebertwolkwitz

The third strike force of Wittgenstein's attack, under Prince Gorchakov, moved out of the University Woods towards the Liechtenwald Woods, which stood between Störmthal and Gross-Pösna, about 7:30 a.m. From there Gorchakov's Russian 1st Corps moved towards Liebertwolkwitz. Pirch's 10th Prussian Brigade had moved forward from Belgershain the night before, and at 9:00 a.m., stood by Gorchakov in the second line. On Gorchakov's right, Klenau, who was no longer united with him, advanced parallel with him.

The artillery of the French V Corps (Lauriston) was unrelenting in the pounding it gave Gorchakov. It would appear that Gorchakov's attack was not very aggressive, nor pressed forward with much vigor. Certainly, it does not appear to have ever come into close proximity with Lauriston's V Corps.

Indeed, the Austrian sources indicate a high degree of inactivity from Gorchakov that morning. They state that "Gorchakov and Pahlen passively watched the battle around Liebertwolkwitz, and contented themselves that the French artillery fire was not having any serious effect."[23] Gorchakov withdrew his troops from the heavy French artillery fire. The Russian 5th Division and the Prussian 10th Brigade retreated in good order and reestablished themselves between the University Woods and Gülden-Gossa. The University Woods were occupied by the 3/7th Reserve Regiment, under Major Winskowsky, and Mezentzov's Russian 5th Division, while Gülden-Gossa was occupied with three Prussian battalions from 10th Brigade.[24] In addition, a Russian 6-pdr battery, commanded by Captain Davidov, was positioned to protect the entrance to the village. The rest of Pirch's 10th Brigade was held in reserve and ordered to support the defense of these two points. Pirch had been ordered to hold these two points at all costs.[25]

Pahlen's cavalry was directed into the interval between Gorchakov and Württemberg's columns, on the Galgenberg Heights. The light artillery's fire against the French occupied the French for a while, but Pahlen's cavalry soon attracted the attention of the French artillery and began to suffer heavy casualties. Pahlen was eventually obliged to withdraw from the Galgenberg Heights and out of the French field of fire.

The Allied Right

The fourth column, under Klenau, moved out of Gross-Pösna about 7:30 a.m., and marched against Liebertwolkwitz. Splenyi's Brigade occupied the University Woods, defending against the French attacks. Schäffer's Brigade advanced from Threna, while FML Meyer, with Abele's entire brigade, moved forward against Köhra.[26]

Ziethen remained in his position by Belgershain and assured the communications with Wittgenstein's Corps. GM Baumgarten advanced towards Holzhausen and was supported by either Splenyi's or Schäffer's Brigade. The 1st Artillery Reserve Detachment advanced to Pomssen and the second moved to Lausigk. Ziethen's orders were soon changed and he was to move towards Gross-Pösna.

At the same time, Macdonald was reinforcing the French left wing from Sommerfeld. These reinforcements passed through the forest of the Niederholz, situated to the east of the village and took up a position on the heights situated to their right. Schäffer's Brigade occupied the Kolmberg Heights, before Gross-Pösna, with a battalion and three guns. This position flanked the French position by Liebertwolkwitz.[27]

Between 7:00 and 8:00 a.m., Klenau's forces moved forward to attack. Cannon fire from the direction of Wachau greeted the lead elements under FML Mohr. Mohr was leading the Erzherzog Karl Regiment, a battalion of the Wallachian-Illyrian Grenz Regiment, two squadrons of the Hohenzollern Chevaulégers, and four from the Palatinal Hussar Regiment, supported by eight guns.[28]

To begin the attack, Mohr's group advanced on the west of the Niederholz, along a line from Gross-Pösna to Liebertwolkwitz. His force deployed on both sides of the road. Splenyi's Brigade stood to the southwest of Gross-Pösna with the Württemberg Infantry Regiment detached into the University Woods. The Lindenau Infantry Regiment and four squadrons of the O'Reilly Chevauléger Regiment stood near the Württemberg Infantry Regiment in support.

GM Schäffer marched forward in the line from Fuchshain-Gross-Pösna with the Zach and J. Colloredo Infantry Regiments, the Kaiser Cuirassier Regiment and a half-battery. The A. Liechtenstein Regiment advanced forward from Pomssen. GM Ziethen, with his 11th Brigade, and GM Abele, with the Coburg Regiment, advanced towards Gross-Pösna from Belgershain. GM Baumgarten led forward two battalions of the Kerpen Infantry Regiment, the 1st Wallachian Regiment, and four squadrons of the Palatinal Hussar Regiment. Baumgarten was supported by 8 guns, which stood west of Naunhof, facing Fuchshain.[29]

The Erzherzog Karl Infantry Regiment, from Mohr's Group, advanced past the Niederholz, up the road to Liebertwolkwitz. On the right flank they found Kolmberg strangely unoccupied by the French.

The Erzherzog Karl Infantry Regiment encountered the infantry of Maison's 16th Division by the southeast entrance of Liebertwolkwitz and on the heights immediately east. Maison detached a battalion to the Liebertwolkwitz cemetery to hold that position. The Erzherzog Karl Infantry Regiment drove into their position and a street by street and house by house fight developed in which the two sides took heavy casualties.

The allied cavalry passed over the Kolmberg Heights and found itself quickly engaged by Sébastiani's II Cavalry Corps. At the same time, the Austrians established their artillery on the heights. The French 16th Division, under GD Maison, occupied Liebertwolkwitz. Maison's defense of the village was praiseworthy. He personally stood with a battalion in the elevated cemetery of the village.[30] Despite the vigor of the French defense of the village, it was taken by the Erzherzog Karl Regiment, which remained there as a garrison.[31] Generals Mohr and Splenyi were also wounded in this attack.

The Kolmberg Heights and Liebertwolkwitz positions were very important, because they dominated the surrounding area, as well as the road from Grimma. As soon as the French realized the Austrians had occupied these positions, they advanced in force. Macdonald's Corps moved against Liebertwolkwitz with a massively superior force. The 31st and 36th Divisions of Ledru and Charpentier pushed against the allied forces on the road from Grimma, and back towards the Kolmberg Heights. The allies held them up in the Niederholz Woods for sometime. Another tremendous cannonade began.

Gérard's 35th Division advanced along the left of the road. Gérard was wounded by one of the first musket volleys. His division, formed mostly of Italians, pushed towards the extreme left against Klein-Pösna. Marchand's weak 39th Division, formed of Hessians and Baden troops stood in reserve by Holzhausen and took little part in the day's battle.[32]

Ziethen's 11th Brigade was called forward from Belgershain and moved through Kohra and Thrana en route to Gross-Pösna, where it formed a reserve on the windmill heights behind Meyer's Division.

Around 3:00 p.m., the French artillery began pounding the allied infantry again, and this time they were more successful. Maréchal Mortier sent the 2nd and 4th Young Guard Divisions forward into the Niederholz Woods, clearing the allies out of them. They also moved against Seifertshain, obliging Klenau to withdraw to a position between Gross-Pösna and Fuchshain, near the University Woods.

The Second Phase: The French Counterattack

The Battle in the Center

Napoleon stood on a hill behind Wachau. The French defensive battle was over. Poniatowski's VIII Corps had secured his right flank along the Pleisse and the allied attacks were exhausted.

Napoleon ordered the Guard, which was formed in dense columns near Probstheida, to advance. They were to attack the allied positions in Liebertwolkwitz.

Earlier, between 10:00 and 11:00 a.m., Napoleon had shifted Curial (2nd Old Guard Division), Oudinot (I Young Guard Corps—the 1st and 3rd Young Guard Divisions), and Walther with the Guard cavalry more to the middle, in the low ground by Meusdorf Farm. As they began to advance, Piré's 9th Light Cavalry and l'Héritier's 5th Heavy Cavalry Divisions, V Cavalry Corps, followed behind. Milhaud's 6th Heavy Cavalry Division followed behind Lauriston in a "broken line."[33]

About 10:30 a.m., came Ney's announcement arrived stating that two divisions of the III Corps were moving to the south. He also reported that, in the next two and a half hours, another division of 11 French battalions would be advancing down the road from Halle and Landsberg. However, Ney had just begun his march.[34] In the best case, none of these forces would reach Napoleon before 2:00 p.m., and could not be counted on for the battle around Lindenau.

According to the official battle bulletin, which is supported by Pelet and Thiers in their writings, Napoleon realized that he would have only the forces immediately at hand, and he prepared to throw them at the weak allied line before him. However, Macdonald's version indicates that he had already begun his advance. Whatever the sequence, to cover his left wing Napoleon dispatched the XI Corps (Macdonald) from Stötteritz towards Holzhausen, with the order to refuse his left wing. That is, to form the left wing obliquely, away from the allies and extending to the northeast. This was done so that Macdonald could either turn the allied right if they should allow it, or to delay any effort to turn his own flank.

Oudinot (I Young Guard Corps) and Victor (II Corps) moved from Wachau towards Gülden-Gossa and the Auenhain Farm. Dubreton's 4th Division led the advance with a bayonet attack against the allies.[35] General Drouot, with 150 guns of the reserve artillery took up positions before Wachau. Mortier (II Young Guard Corps), Lauriston (V Corps) and Sébastiani (II Cavalry Corps)[36] advanced against Gross-Pösna via the University Woods. Their advance was supported by a two column cavalry attack. The I Cavalry Corps (Latour-Maubourg) moved east of Wachau towards Gülden-Gossa to support Victor.

Earlier, the IV Cavalry Corps had moved from its positions by the Pleisse. It was formed with Polish cavalry, which made up for its lack of numbers with equestrian skill and an aggressive nature. They were joined by part of the Empress Dragoons of the Imperial Guard. This force of Poles and guardsmen now moved forward, west of Wachau. It would appear the attack of the western cavalry column, the Polish cavalry and Guard Dragoons, was not well timed with that of the eastern column, but otherwise the attack went as planned. Napoleon's orders to his generals were as follows:

1. The "comprehensive" (all-out) attack of Macdonald's XI Corps was to be against the Kolmberg Heights and Seifertshain, while those of Mortier (II Young Guard Corps) and Lauriston (V Corps) were to be in the direction Gross-Pösna and the University woods.
2. The attacks of Victor (II Corps), Oudinot (I Young Guard Corps), and Poniatowski (VIII Corps) were to be in the area between Wachau, the Auenhain Farm, and Mark-Kleeberg, supported by the Polish cavalry (IV Cavalry Corps) and the Guard Dragoons.
3. Murat was to form the breakthrough force between Wachau and Liebertwolkwitz, then move against Gülden-Gossa when the time was right.[37]

Napoleon's plan set the scene for three major battles to be fought almost side by side during the day of 16 October. It was certainly to be one of the most complex battles fought in the history of the world to date, even ignoring the actions of the French and allies to the north of Leipzig.

Napoleon remained in his position by Wachau from the beginning of the battle until 3:00 p.m.

The Battle Around Gross-Pösna

The French still occupied the heights before Gross-Pösna. They prepared their attack with two divisions of Young Guard and Macdonald's XI Corps. On the right of the XI Corps stood part of Pajol's V Cavalry Corps, l'Héritier's 5th Heavy Cavalry Division, and Piré's 9th Light Cavalry Division. On their left stood the three divisions of Sébastiani's II Cavalry Corps.[38]

As Klenau faced the danger of Macdonald's advance on the Kolmberg, he detached the Württemberg Infantry Regiment to Liebertwolkwitz. The 1/Württemberg was inserted into the battle raging in the village. Several detachments from the Kerpen Infantry Regiment, which occupied the Kolmberg, also appear to have been sent to the fight at Liebertwolkwitz.

The Lindenau Infantry Regiment occupied the University Woods and the portion of the Niederholz Woods along the road. Schäffer's Brigade found itself between Gross-Pösna and Fuchshain. In the second line stood Abele's Brigade and in the third line, by the Windmühlenberg[39] by Gross-Pösna, was Ziethen's Prussian 11th Brigade with four squadrons of Silesian Hussars and Uhlans. The 1/Zach had been, apparently, for sometime in Seifertshain and stood on the eastern edge of the village.

In front of Schäffer's Brigade, on the left of Klenau's forces, stood the Kaiser Cuirassier Regiment, four squadrons of the O'Reilly Chevaulégers and two of the Hohenzollern Chevaulégers. Two squadrons of the Hohenzollern Chevaulégers served as the link between the Kolmberg and Seifertshain. Two hussar regiments supported the left. The Erzherzog Ferdinand Hussar Regiment stood on the left wing of the battle front of Klenau's forces as a support for his skirmisher line and to cover the artillery. The Palatinal Hussars stood east of the Seifertshain.

Macdonald's Attack Begins

Macdonald marched into the battle with two columns. Charpentier's 36th Division struck from Holzhausen towards the Kolmberg. Gérard's 35th Division and Ledru's 31st Division, supported by Sébastiani's II Cavalry Corps, moved against Seifertshain and Klein-Pösna. Sébastiani's cavalry stood on the extreme eastern flank of the French army. Marchand's 39th Division, consisting of Hessian and Baden troops, followed the Ledru's column.[40]

Toll claimed the credit for himself of advising Klenau of the danger resulting from the constant removal of reserves from the important Kolmberg position. It was, in fact, a major failure on Klenau's part to have retained only two battalions on this important point, which was about to face the assault of an entire French division.

Napoleon, now on the Galgenberg heights, reviewed the battlefield. He noted that Klenau's forces were still in control of the Kolmberg and the forest near it. Klenau's position allowed him to stop the French efforts to envelop the allies. Around 2:00 p.m., Charpentier's 36th Division stood at the foot of the Kolmberg Heights. Napoleon moved to this division and said to the first regiment he encountered "Is this the 22nd Légère that stands here with its arms crossed under the enemy's fire?"

Spurred into action, the 22nd Légère advanced with the rest of the division following it. Klenau sent his cavalry forward to strike at the flanks of the French columns, but with no success.

Charras' Brigade, which was led by the 22nd Légère Regiment, advanced after the French artillery had begun to bombard the Austrians on the Kolmberg Heights. Charras moved up the northern slope of the Kolmberg. Marching at the head of the 22nd Légère, GB Charras arrived at the crest of the plateau and threw the Austrians back, taking part of their artillery in his third assault. GB Meunier was wounded.

Before he was wounded Charras sent an infantry column to the east of the Kolmberg, with the intent of turning the position. However, this plan was foiled by a company of the Kerpen Infantry Regiment under Oberstleutnant von Finkenau. Twice Charras led his troops up the hill to strike the 1/Kerpen Infantry Regiment, supported by a division of the 2/Kerpen Infantry Regiment. They repelled the French attack with bayonets.

Oberstleutnant Irasky, of the 3rd Field Artillery Regiment, ordered his artillery forward to break the French attacks. They took three French cavalry regiments under fire with canister, driving them back.

Ledru's 31st Division advanced against Seifertshain, and Napoleon sent forward part of the Young Guard to move against the University Woods. The Young Guard was to chase the allies out of the woods and secure them for the French.[41]

Sébastiani's cavalry advanced with Exelman's 4th Light Cavalry Division in the lead. Ledru (31st Division) and Gérard (35th Division) deployed their divisions behind them, passing over the Pösgraben ditch[42] and moving into the fields between the Kolmberg and Seifertshain. At the same time Charpentier renewed his attack on the old Swedish redoubt.[43] Facing him, the Kerpen Infantry Regiment covered a front of 2,000 paces. It had dispersed itself into small groups and was struck from all sides by the French.[44] The force was overwhelming and the Austrians could not contain the French assault. They began a withdrawal to the south covered by Irasky's artillery.

The French advanced from Klein-Pösna on the left, by the road from Grimma, crossing the woods situated on the heights and the Thränengraben ditch with the intention of turning the Austrians, and taking them in the back by Fuchshain.

Klenau had FML Hohenlohe direct Schäffer's Brigade to the Kolmberg. He arrived too late to hold the hill, but his infantry could not have arrived at a more timely moment. At the same time, in the Niederholz stood the Hohenzollern Chevaulégers and O'Reilly Chevaulégers. Klenau ordered them "to have themselves a good time, by the sending a few squadrons over and riding down the French."[45]

The French cavalry attack on Schäffer's Brigade obliged them to evacuate the vicinity of the Kolmberg heights. Two squadrons of the Hohenzollern Chevaulégers and the hussars, received the next shock of the advancing French cavalry. They gave way before the overwhelming French numbers. The Kaiser Cuirassiers, under Oberst von Wibbekink, who stood by Schäffer's Brigade northwest of Seifertshain, swung forward and threw themselves against the French cavalry. They were also defeated and forced behind the infantry.

The next allied cavalry to arrive consisted of two squadrons the Silesian Uhlan Regiment, and two more the 1st Silesian Hussar Regiment. They were followed shortly later by Ziethen's Brigade and the first elements of GM Röder's Prussian reserve cavalry, Oberst von Wrangel with the East Prussian and Brandenburg Cuirassiers.

The French cavalry once again rode against the Austrian squares, until Oberst von Wrangel brought forward his brigade of Prussian cuirassiers. Von Wrangel attacked and drove back the French cavalry. However, he had attracted the punitive attention of the French artillery and was, himself, obliged to withdraw. He then pulled back to cover the right wing of Klenau's Corps by Klein-Pösna. Klenau then moved to the heights between Gross-Pösna and Fuchshain.[46]

The cavalry battle by Seifertshain ground on in its bloody fury. It was a battle of squadron against squadron, platoon against platoon, man against man, with no overall control being exercised by any general. Slowly the melee drew towards Klein-Pösna and the French attempted to go around the eastern side of this village. This threatened the 1/Zach Infantry Regiment and the two Austrian guns standing in Seifertshain.[47]

In the midst of this battle, four battalions of Schäffer's Brigade (2/, 3/Zach, 1/J. Colloredo, and one other battalion—possibly 2/J. Colloredo) moved onto the field between Kolmberg and Seifertshain. The left wing was formed by the 1/J. Colloredo Infantry Regiment.

The 2/J. Colloredo Regiment advanced at the *doublierschritt* and sought to drive Macdonald's infantry back with the shock of its attack, advancing through heavy canister and musketry fire. However, the presence of French cavalry forced it to withdraw.[48]

Splenyi's Brigade withdrew from the edge of the Niederholz along with the Erzherzog Karl and Kerpen Infantry Regiments, of Best's Brigade. They took up new positions behind Gross-Pösna.

It was about 2:00 p.m., when a pause in the battle occurred between Liebertwolkwitz and the Kolmberg. The French had set themselves right on the bloody heights, where their artillery poured a deadly fire over the Niederholz and Seifertshain.

Also, between Seifertshain and Klein-Pösna, Sebastiani's cavalry and Ledru's infantry moved to turn the right wing of Klenau's forces, but as they arrived in Konigsbach they were stopped by Platov's Cossacks.

Earlier in the morning Platov had been left the region around Hirschfeld executing orders to seek Bennigsen and to serve as the link between Bennigsen and the main army. The appearance of his mass of Cossacks on their left flank, caused the French to pull back. They dared not risk pushing their intended advance.

Napoleon felt the time for his Guard to attack had arrived. Drouot brought his Guard artillery forward and deployed. Mortier then appeared near Lauriston's V Corps with the 2nd and 4th Young Guard Divisions and soon formed four great columns on both sides of the Grimma road. Mortier advanced from Liebertwolkwitz towards Niederholz and Gross-Pösna. Lauriston moved against the University Woods and in the general direction of Störmthal. Charpentier's 36th Division closed from the Kolmberg to join Mortier's attack on the Niederholz and was to take the major role in the coming battle.[49]

The Allied Extreme Eastern Flank

The Prussian 11th Brigade (Ziethen) formed Klenau's left wing and occupied the Windmühlenberg near Gross-Pösna, as the French were attempting to capture Seifertshain. The French attacked the Niederholz Woods between Gross-Pösna and Liebertwolkwitz, which were weakly held by an Austrian force.

GM Pirch received an order to send a single battalion to Gülden-Gossa, but the situation there was so serious, that he directed that three battalions be shifted there.[50] The occupation of the western University Woods was strengthened by the addition of a few Russian battalions. Ziethen also sent two Jager companies and the 1/1st Silesian Regiment to support Klenau's Austrians and sent the 2/1st Silesian Regiment to occupy the University Woods.

The bulk of Gorchakov's Corps and the rest of Pirch's Brigade stood on the heights north of Störmthal. Pahlen and his cavalry followed Gorchakov's example, moving northeast of Gülden-Gossa.

The eastern side of the University Woods was occupied by a detachment of the Austrian Lindenau Infantry Regiment. Niederholz was occupied by other infantry from Splenyi's Brigade. As Klenau observed the advance of the French, he sent GM Abele with the Coburg Regiment into the Niederholz Woods. With this, Oberst Rothkirch found the bulk of the corps a good position between Fuchshain and Gross-Pösna.

As Abele reached the north edge of the Niederholz, Splenyi's Brigade was struck by the French. The Coburg Infantry Regiment faced an assault as Mortier turned towards the University Woods. Abele's infantry succeeded in repelling the French attack. As Charpentier's 36th Division struck anew, Ziethen sent the Austrians another half-battalion to reinforce them. This battle was to last beyond 4:00 p.m., when Abele was finally forced to pull out of the woods and back to Gross-Pösna.[51]

In the meantime Mortier sought to drive into the University Woods and to separate the east wing of the allies from the other allied units. The Austrian and Russians, through repeated bayonet charges, held their ground as best as they could. The 2/1st Silesian Infantry Regiment fought a noteworthy battle. The Russian 2nd Grenadier Division, originally moving towards Gülden-Gossa, was in the University Woods at 4:00 p.m.

The French columns advanced again towards the allied battle line. Klenau made an aggressive lunge forward with his forces and the French advance stopped. The French deployed their artillery and began to pound the Windmühlenberg until the arrival of a force of Austrian artillery forced them to withdraw.[52]

The day was beginning to end and the battle settled down to an artillery duel, though the French made one further assault against Seifertshain and the University Forest without success.

Gülden-Gossa

The French attack here began with great impetuosity. The three Prussian battalions[53] and Russian 6-pdr battery occupying Gülden-Gossa were thrown back to the center of the village. Colonel Jagow, however, brought forward the 1/2nd East Prussian Infantry Regiment, supporting the battalions already there. The beleaguered Prussians stopped the French advance and drove them back. Because of the importance of the allied position in Gülden-Gossa, GM Pirch called for reinforcements. Pirch only had two uncommitted battalions upon which to call.

Soon the French began to direct a tremendous barrage against Gülden-Gossa. Two battalions of the Russian Guard Jager Regiment arrived. They formed themselves in column behind the village. The Prussian 2/7th Reserve Regiment was posted to the right of the village and the Fus/2nd West Prussian Regiment occupied the left.

The French, despite their continued assaults with fresh troops, were unable to take Gülden-Gossa and were obliged to withdraw. The Prussian Jägers pursued them to the base of the hill, supported by the two Russian Guard Jager Battalions that came through the village at the attack pace.[54] Night was beginning to fall.

GL Pahlen, posted between the French and Gülden-Gossa, had placed his artillery on the heights which dominated the University Forest. From this position he was able to fire on the flank of the French advancing against Gülden-Gossa. In the evening the 2nd Cuirassier Division (Kretov) had been detached to support Pahlen and formed itself before Störmthal. Prince Gorchakov's forces now stood in the University Forest. GdK Klenau made every effort to hold his position by Gross-Pösna and Fuchshain.

Auenhain Farm

Since before noon, Kleist's and Württemberg's troops had struggled around by Mark-Kleeberg and Wachau, locked in a tremendous battle, as both sides sought to hold undisputed possession of the villages.

At first the French drove Württemberg's Russian 2nd Corps back in disorder towards Cröbern. Oudinot followed Victor's II Corps as it advanced. Barclay de Tolly sent the two grenadier divisions and the 2nd Cuirassier Division under GM Raevsky forward to support Württemberg. The 1st Grenadier Division formed itself behind the Auenhain farm and Levaschoff's Cuirassier Brigade marched on its flanks.[55]

In the center, around noon, Kleist's column became involved in a series of cavalry battles. Schvichov's thrust at Wachau alarmed Victor and Oudinot. More strong French columns moved

Attack of Prussian dragoons at Wachau, by Becker.

west of Wachau to strike the southern side of the village, where Württemberg stood. From there the Victor moved against Cröbern. At the same time Poniatowski attacked. He placed a brigade from Sémélé's 52nd Division in his first line and marched against Mark-Kleeberg. Kellerman's cavalry, reinforced by the Guard Dragoons under GB Letort, and as reported by the Saxons, Berkheim's 1st Light Cavalry Division, followed Oudinot's Young Guard columns.

The Prussian battalions standing in Mark-Kleeberg bravely faced the attack of the Poles and French. To support them Helfreich's decimated 14th Division and Schvichov's detachment[56] were drawn back from Crostewitz.

Sokolnicki sent the 1st (Polish) Chasseurs à Cheval Regiment against Helfreich. One squadron threatened the two Prussian batteries accompanying Helfreich while the rest attacked his infantry. One Russian square was broken and lost 600 prisoners. As the Polish cavalry attempted to reform they were rushed from the rear by a Russian cuirassier regiment from Levaschoff's Brigade. The Poles met it with carbine fire, but were dispersed. As the Chasseurs were dispersed the 3rd (Polish) Uhlan Regiment struck the Russian cuirassiers in both flanks, crushing them and throwing them back on the Loubny Hussars. The Loubny Hussars attacked the pursuing Poles and drove them back. Yet another cuirassier regiment came forward and joined the melee. They crushed a Polish grenadier company sent in support of the 1st (Polish) Chasseurs. Helfreich found himself forced to bring forward the Neumärk Dragoon Regiment and the Silesian Uhlan Regiment.[57]

The advancing Loubny Hussars were, in their turn, brought to a stop by the 6th (Polish) Uhlan Regiment, joined by the reformed 3rd (Polish) Uhlan Regiment. These two Polish regiments now totaled about 800 men and proceeded to execute seven further charges against the five allied cavalry regiments leading the allied advance.

The Poles were slowly overwhelmed by the allied numbers and began to fall back. The 8th (Polish) Uhlans executed one further attack that hit Levaschoff's Brigade in the left flank and cut it off from Mark-Kleeberg. At this critical moment Letort's Brigade of French Imperial Guard Dragoons arrived and broke the Russian cavalry.

As this battle occurred, the reformed 1st (Polish) Chasseurs and the Krakus found the Russian Guard Cossack Regiment deploying before them. The Poles moved forward quickly and struck the Cossacks before they could deploy, crushing them and driving them back.

Initially, the 1/11th Reserve Regiment advanced to support a Russian attack on Wachau, but it was drawn into the front ranks and took Wachau itself, at bayonet point, attacking a superior force of French. Oberst Schvichov's infantry, plus the 1/2nd Silesian, 1/11th Reserve, and the 10th Silesian Landwehr Regiments, suffered heavily from French fire into his flanks and was obliged to withdraw, abandoning a portion of the terrain he had captured.

About 1:00 p.m., facing a French breakthrough between his forces and those of Württemberg, Kleist ordered Oberstleutnant Schvichov, with the 1/11th Reserve Regiment, to take the western part of Wachau. This attack, supported by the Russian Krementsoug Regiment from the II Corps, was very heavily engaged by French skirmishers as they moved through the swampy terrain between them and their objective. When they arrived at their target they were so shaken by the advance that they were easily thrown back.[58]

Poniatowski's VIII Corps and a brigade of GD Sémélé's 52nd Division then advanced towards Mark-Kleeberg. Oberst Löbel and the detachment of the 12th Brigade were forced to abandon the village. Löbel's force lost three officers and 100 prisoners to the Poles. Shortly later Mark-Kleeberg was seized by French infantry. A second brigade of Sémélé's 52nd Division moved along the far bank of the Pleisse. The allied losses had so weakened them that they were unable to hold the position.

As the French moved into the village the Fus/2nd Silesian Regiment was sent forward to support Löbel's force. The Prussians pushed once again into Mark-Kleeberg. The village was recaptured for the fourth time by the 2/1st Reserve Regiment. The Prussians held Mark-Kleeberg until they were relieved by the Austrians under Bianchi that evening.[59]

The allies reorganized themselves. The Austrian reserve was ordered to form itself in several lines by Mark-Kleeberg. The Russian grenadiers moved to Wachau to support Prince Württemberg, the Russian and Prussian Guard advanced to the heights behind Gülden-Gossa, and a battery of 80 guns, drawn from the allied artillery reserve under General Suchosanet, was formed before Gülden-Gossa.

GM Schachafskoy's 3rd Division was pulled out of the line, having lost 1,100 men so far this day. It moved behind the artillery battery by Gülden-Gossa in order to give it a clear field of fire against the French. Klüx's Brigade also realigned itself and linked its left with Pischnitzky's 4th Division.[60]

Victor's II Corps continued to march forward, supported by Oudinot with the 1st and 3rd Young Guard Divisions. Klüx was unable to stand before the pressure and fell back towards Gülden-Gossa. The weak Russian battalions fell back, behind the Auenhain Farm.

Victor then moved against the Russian grenadiers, who occupied a position by Wachau. However, the grenadiers held their ground. Raevsky, who had been wounded in an earlier cavalry attack, then ordered the advance and the Russians drove the French back with the sheer weight of their bayonets, not firing a single shot. Schwarzenberg ordered the Simbschen Infantry Regiment to retake the Auenhain Farm. As it marched forward from Gülden-Gossa, however, the entire Austrian grenadier division of Graf Weissenwolf marched with it. The grenadiers marched in battalionmasses.[61]

About one hundred troopers of Levaschoff's Cuirassier Brigade drew together on the right wing of the allied cavalry. The French occupied the east of Mark-Kleeberg and Auenhain, in order to catch their breath before the next attack. The cavalry stood to the west of Auenhain, in the intervals between the infantry columns. It moved forward to fall on Kleist's infantry. Before Oudinot's front stood the remains of Württemberg's column on the heights between Wachau and Gülden-Gossa, drawn up in squares. A hole was opening up in the allied line and Napoleon had found a way into the heart of the allied army!

Victor had occupied the Auenhain Farm with a strong force and placed batteries on both flanks of it. On the right flank of Kleist's beleaguered forces trumpets were suddenly heard. The Austrian cavalry reserve had arrived.[62]

The Austrian Reserves Begin to Arrives

Prince Schwarzenberg learned that Wittgenstein's forces were being pressed by a superior force, and that Napoleon was personally directing the French action around Wachau and Liebertwolkwitz, with the intention of turning the allied left and then striking their center. Schwarzenberg responded by ordering GdK Erbprinz Hessen-Homburg's Reserve Corps to move from Zöbigker via Gautzsch and Dölsen, on the right bank of the Pleisse, and to form his forces for battle before the village of Cröbern.

Around noon Oberst Latour had met GdK Erbprinz Hessen-Homburg and passed him an order to move to the right bank of the Pleisse with his forces. Hessen-Homburg, his generals, and regiments moved in the following march order:

FML Nostitz (corps)
  FML Civalart (division)
    GM Kuttalek (brigade)
      Albert Cuirassier Regiment
      Lothringen Cuirassier Regiment
    GM Klebelsberg (division)
      GM Rothkirch (brigade)
        Erzherzog Franz Cuirassier Regiment
        Kronprinz Ferdinand Cuirassier Regiment
      Oberst Auersperg (brigade)
        Hohenzollern Cuirassier Regiment
        Sommariva Cuirassier Regiment
  FML Bianchi (division)
    GM Beck (brigade)
      Hiller Infantry Regiment
        H.Colloredo Infantry Regiment
    GM Haugwitz (brigade)
      Hessen-Homburg Infantry Regiment
      Simbschen Infantry Regiment
      Esterhazy Infantry Regiment
  FML Weissenwolf (division)
    Eight Grenadier Battalions

The column crossed the Pleisse River by Gautzsch, and galloped from Cröbern to the fields south of Auenhain, where the battle raged. Schwarzenberg and his generals moved to the old earthwork south of Gülden-Gossa where the monarchs stood, watching the battle with their staffs. Though artillery fire and musketry fell constantly around him as he stood near Cröbern, Radetzky, Schwarzenberg's chief of general staff, rode to Klüx's Brigade to get a better view of the battle. He rode over fields covered with dead and wounded soldiers and horses. He was shot in the left arm for his trouble.

Schwarzenberg struggled with the Czar Alexander's lack of military understanding and demands for success. Alexander's first question to Schwarzenberg was "Where is the Austrian reserve?" Auenhain had just been lost under the eyes of the monarchs, which explains the Czar's query about the arrival of Austrian Reserves.

From the Russian position on the slopes north of Göhren, Raevsky's 3rd Grenadier Corps and Gudovich's Brigade, Duka's 3rd Russian Cuirassier Division, marched to the battle. The allied

Foot and Horse Guard was moving from Rötha to the battlefield, and its column would be the first to cross the Pleisse.[63]

Upon Schwarzenberg's announcement of Hessen-Homburg's approach, Raevsky released his grenadiers. The 2nd Grenadier Division was posted to the southeast of Gülden-Gossa, where Jagow stood with his three battalions. However, as Lauriston's column pushed from Liebertwolkwitz ever further to the south, Raevsky's grenadiers and Gorchakov were pushed further behind the University Woods. The 1st Grenadier Division moved forward to support Kleist. The cuirassiers of GM Gudovich's Brigade[64] remained behind Gülden-Gossa as a reserve.

Bianchi and Weissenwolf advanced further to the south, in order to reach a bridge over the Pleisse controlled by the allies. Nostitz's Cuirassier Corps passed over the Pleisse at Gautzsch. The main body went over the river east of Gaschwitz. The Sommariva Regiment explored a ford by Gross-Städteln and passed over the river there.

It was 3:00 p.m.,[65] when the head of the Austrian cavalry column arrived in Cröbern, and at the same time, the Imperial Guard Dragoons, under GB Letort and Sokolnicki's IV Reserve Corps broke into Cröbern, after defeating Levaschoff's Russian 3rd Cuirassier Division. The French Guard Dragoons were supported by a force of infantry.[66] The French advance was beginning to threaten to split the allied army in half.

FML Nostitz and Civalart rode forward with the cuirassiers, in order to view the field before them. As they crossed through Cröbern, they saw the Russians and Prussians at the moment of their withdrawal. The greatest part of their forces had already pulled back to Crostewitz. The French pursued them. Large numbers of French stood by the Auenhain Farm, while thick masses of French infantry and cavalry moved against Mark-Kleeberg. The bridge over the Göselbach and the narrow village lanes of Cröbern were filled with wounded, Russian artillery, the battlewise who had abandoned their positions as soon as their ammunition were gone, and Russian trains. The nearby French artillery fired one round after another into this milling mass. Kleist was in a desperate situation when the Austrian Reserves arrived on the field.[67]

Kuttalek's Brigade of Austrian cuirassiers crossed the Pleisse River using the causeway in the village of Cröbern, despite its being broken in many places. It worked itself through the mess and into the cramped and narrow village streets. Oberst von Beierwek, commander of the Albert Cuirassier Regiment, seeing his regiment under attack, called the Oberstensdivision[68] to himself and rode with them against the attacking Polish cavalry. To be defeated by the 3rd Polish Uhlan Regiment would spell disaster, and he had to succeed to save his force. His charge stopped the Poles, giving the Majorsdivision of the regiment time to move out and deploy. They advanced into a heavy French artillery fire to join the Oberstendivision in their battle with the Poles. Both divisions threw themselves repeatedly against the Poles. At the same time the Lothringen Cuirassier Regiment, led by Oberst Prinz Ferdinand von Hessen-Homburg, arrived and the two Austrian cuirassier regiments drove back the French and Polish cavalry.

The Albert and Lothringen Cuirassiers moved against Sokolnicki's cavalry while it was engaged with Levaschoff's cuirassiers. The Austrians wore white cloaks hiding their breastplates, so the 3rd Uhlans mistook them for dragoons and charged. Unfortunately for the Poles, their lances broke against the Austrian breastplates and the Poles were forced to flee. The 1st (Polish) Chasseurs à Cheval Regiment counterattacked and dispersed the Austrians, but they were in their turn attacked by fresh Austrian regiments that eventually pushed both the Poles and French Guard Dragoons back.

The French cavalry rallied and advanced at the trot against Nostitz's Austrian cuirassiers. At that time, GM Rothkirch arrived with four squadrons of the Erzherzog Franz Cuirassier Regiment and two squadrons of the Kronprinz Ferdinand Cuirassier Regiment. A ferocious battle began as they threw themselves into the low ground between Wachau and Mark-Kleeberg.

At this point, Nostitz and his cuirassier divisions drove forward to the attack. The Albert Cuirassier Regiment struck the French first, slowing their advance. Then the Lothringen Cuirassiers struck, while Nostitz maneuvered the Prinz Ferdinand von Hessen-Homburg Cuirassiers to strike their flank, and the Albert Cuirassiers to strike them frontally again. The French Guard Cavalry found itself obliged to fallback towards Wachau.

While the cuirassiers rallied after their clash with the French Guard Cavalry, Nostitz dispatched the Erzherzog Franz and Kronprinz Cuirassiers to strike the French infantry that had been advancing after the Guard Cavalry.[69]

Fresh French infantry came forward behind the French cavalry and the Austrian cuirassiers quickly surrounded them. It was Pelet's Brigade of Young Guard, the 9th, 10th, and 1/12th Voltigeurs, which stood on Oudinot's right. The Young Guard moved to a ridge to the west of Auenhain, a few hundred paces distant, to draw together. The cuirassiers charged the Young Guard squares, which met them with concentrated musketry. Dead Austrian cuirassiers littered the ground before the squares, as the shattered remains of Nostitz's forces recoiled back to their lines.[70] GL Nostitz's cuirassiers claimed they broke some Guard squares, but this is not confirmed in the French casualty lists.[71] GL Nostitz, however, was wounded in the engagement.

The danger to the allied army had passed, because the French cavalry had failed to profit from its advantages, and was not sustained by reserve troops. They had lost precious moments, but this had not prevented Napoleon from sending a courier to the King of Saxony announcing that the battle was won.

More of the French cavalry arrived as the Albert and Lothringen Cuirassiers moved forward once again. Berkheim's 1st Light Cavalry Division pushed to the right, in order to turn the Austrian right flank.

To the north of Crostewitz, the Sommariva Cuirassier Regiment was just crossing the Pleisse. Oberstbrigadier M. Graf Auersperg, stood at the head of the regiment, and pointed out Berkheim's movement to the regiment's commander, Oberstleutnant von Seymann. Seymann immediately sent forward his first four squadrons and rode with them against the French. The cuirassiers closed ranks and formed an iron wall when they were few steps from the French. The French, surprised by the direction of the Austrian attack, fell into disorder and the attack of the Sommariva Cuirassiers threw them back against Dösen. GD Berkheim, whose helmet had been struck from his head, hurled himself furiously into the melee, but to no avail.[72]

Napoleon was by the Meusdorf Farm and could follow the battle from there. He sent orders to a line of French cavalry to the east of Wachau and directed the Saxon Zastrow Cuirassier Regiment to counterattack the Sommariva Cuirassiers.

Most of Bordesoulle's 1st Heavy Cavalry Division, including the Saxon Cuirassier Brigade, had been posted so as to cover the French artillery. As the Austrian cuirassiers were punishing the French, the Saxon Cuirassier Brigade, under Berkheim, moved to the right and joined two squadrons of the Polish 8th Uhlan Regiment. The Saxons and Poles struck and pushed the Austrian cuirassiers back, but as the they pursued them, a Young Guard square fired on them, inflicting heavy casualties on the Zastrow Cuirassier Regiment. Despite those losses, the Saxons went on to kill and capture a large number of Austrians. When the engagement was over the brave Zastrow Regiment had lost two of its four squadrons.[73]

Oberleutnant von Sternbach, of the Sommariva Cuirassier Regiment, discovered the danger in time and drew together about 100 Austrian cuirassiers, organized them and led them back against the Saxons.[74]

Though broken by the larger force, this small Austrian counterattack slowed the Saxon attack enough to give the rest of the Austrian cavalry time to prepare for the next assault. After a sharp engagement both sides fell back.

Meanwhile FML Civalart had persuaded GL Kleist to renew the infantry attack against Auenhain, and the heights east of there. Kleist's forces were, at that time, joined by the Russian

1st Grenadier Division (Pissarev). United, both formations began their attack. The Russian grenadiers, however, refused to advance with much vigor and remained on the east wing of the allies, the location where they were. Kleist's troops stood by Crostewitz and east of it, the Russian grenadiers stood behind the right wing in the second line. The village of Mark-Kleeberg remained in Prussian hands. Nostitz's Cuirassier Corps marched with their cavalry batteries northeast of Cröbern where they stood under heavy French artillery. Their attack had succeeded in stalling Poniatowski's, Oudinot's and Victor's attacking columns.[75]

In order to get to the battle sooner, FML Bianchi did not take the time to lead his division to the bridge at Ruben. Instead, he led his division by Gross-Deuben across a ford, which required his troops to wade through the three foot deep river, despite the Pleisse being greatly swollen. Bianchi's Hungarian soldiers held their bullet pouches high over their heads to keep their powder dry, as they waded across the river. The passage of his artillery required more time and could only accomplished with the assistance of his infantry.[76] Behind Bianchi's 2nd Reserve Division followed Weissenwolf's 1st Reserve Grenadier Division.

Bianchi passed straight through Cröbern. Kleist's attack, having failed, was covered by the attack of the Austrian Cuirassiers. Kleist withdrew to his original position before Crostewitz with the French in pursuit. Bianchi advanced through Crostewitz into a position behind Kleist's group, in order to close on Mark-Kleeberg and bring help to the Prussians. His main force went along the river. It stood with two battalions from both the Hiller and H. Colloredo Regiments and a battalion of the Esterhazy Infantry Regiment drawn forward. To the right GM Graf Haugwitz advanced with two battalions of the Hessen-Homburg Regiment. As a reserve there followed a battalion of the Esterhazy and two of the Simbschen Infantry Regiment. As immediate cover, the Hohenzollern Cuirassier Regiment stood on the right flank. A little further away stood the entire Nostitz Cuirassier Division. Bianchi's pending attack from MarkKleeberg against the French position by Auenhain was a hazardous undertaking and the Corps Commander, Erbprinz von Hessen-Homburg, knew that.

The Austrian division that stood south of Mark-Kleeberg was already under heavy fire and the Austrian skirmishers had already engaged the French skirmishers. Oberstleutnant Thielen, from the Army Headquarters, appeared with orders from Schwarzenberg to Bianchi. They directed that he break through the middle where the greatest danger lay. A powerful French cavalry mass stood between Wachau and Gülden-Gossa.[77]

The Austrian Grenadier Division moved forward, following Nostitz's cavalry, and replacing the Russian 1st Grenadier Division and Kleist's Corps, which now stood on the edge of the Gösel stream. The Prussian Guard relieved one of Raevsky's Divisions before Gülden-Gossa. The Guards, the reserves, the corps now arranged themselves behind these new forces. The allies relieved their fatigued troops with a fresh line.[78]

At 3:00 p.m., Napoleon felt that the time for the cavalry strike at the allies' heart had come. Murat's forces stood east of Wachau, Maison's 16th Division, V Corps, had preceded him from Liebertwolkwitz towards Gülden-Gossa escorting Drouot's reserve artillery.

The French Strike the Allied Center

The French, being unable to break the allied left, then redirected their forces against the allied center. After retaking Wachau, they began a violent pursuit of the allied forces withdrawing from the village, supported by their artillery reserve.

The French had seven divisions of cavalry formed in their center with the Guard Cavalry behind it as a reserve. Napoleon now sent Murat forward with five cavalry divisions, the four of the I Cavalry Corps, and Milhaud's 6th Heavy Cavalry Division, V Cavalry Corps. However, the actual composition of Murat's attacking force is not clear. It is certain that Bessières' Brigade, of

Bordesoulle's 1st Cuirassier Division, stood in the second rank. The Saxon Guard Cuirassiers are also known to have been assigned to him. GD Doumerc now served in the place of the seriously wounded GD Latour-Maubourg as commander of the first line, so the 3rd Cuirassier Division was also probably there as well. It is also very probable, that Piré's 9th Light Cavalry Division and l'Héritier's 5th Heavy Cavalry Division of the V Cavalry Corps took part in Murat's battle. In the beginning of the battle, GD Pajol had his horse killed out from under him, and himself received a severe wound. This indicates that the V Cavalry Corps definitely participated.

Murat's cavalry advanced east towards Wachau, swung to the right and threw themselves at the wavering battalions of Württemberg's Russian Infantry. The Russians held their ground so tenaciously that Napoleon said, "One must not only shoot the Russian soldiers but also overthrow them." Murat's cavalry did not linger long. Their goal was Gülden-Gossa and the gap to the west of there. With the French cuirassiers passing behind them, Wittgenstein also sought to withdraw his torn-up battalions in the same direction.[79]

Murat's cavalry also fell on Pahlen's cavalry, which stood between Gülden-Gossa and the Harth Woods. The Russian cuirassiers were thrown back and dispersed. Doumerc drove in the right of the allied infantry by Störmthal and captured a battery of 26 guns. The hussars and chasseurs of Chastel and Corbineau, the cuirassiers of Doumerc and Bordesoulle, and the dragoons of Milhaud thundered forward.[80]

The 2nd, 3rd, and 6th French Cuirassier Regiments (BG Sopransi's Brigade) and the Saxon Leib Cuirassier Regiment formed the first line. The second line was formed by the 1st, 9th, 11th, and 12th Cuirassier Regiments (GB Bessières' Brigade). The remainder of the cavalry formed behind them in a massive column.[81]

Prince Eugene of Württemberg at Wachau, 16 October, by Knötel.

Behind Murat's cavalry marched Victor's II Corps, supported by the assembled reserve artillery of General Drouot. The French infantry outnumbered Württemberg's infantry and Prinz Eugene had only ten squadrons to face two full French cavalry corps.

At the same time the attack of Sokolnicki's Poles and the Empress Dragoons were engaging the Austrian cuirassiers around Cröbern. The combined effect of these two attacks meant that the route to the bridges at Gautzsch and Döben was open, and once seized, the French would have a complete victory.

Having cleared the field of allied cavalry the French cavalry now moved against Gülden-Gossa. Part of the French cavalry moved across the left wing of the Russian 2nd Corps, striking it and the Prussian 9th Brigade, now formed into squares.[82]

Seeing the developments, Schwarzenberg, standing on the heights south of Gülden-Gossa, became very troubled. The Guard Light Cavalry Division, Raevsky's 3rd Grenadier Corps, Gudovich's Cuirassier Brigade, the 1st and 2nd Cuirassier Divisions, and the Russian and Prussian guards received instructions to advance towards Cröbern.[83] The Czar sent Gudovich's Cuirassier Brigade forward to counterattack the French.

GL Schivich passed straight through Göhren, leading the dragoons, hussars, and Uhlans of the Russian Guard Light Cavalry Division to the attack. Before they could form for the attack, the French struck and crushed them, killing GL Schivich and GM Davidov of the Guard Hussars in the process. The Russian Guard Light Cavalry fled to the rear, leaving Gülden-Gossa on their left.

Pahlen threw the Neumärk Dragoon Regiment and the Silesian Cuirassier Regiment into the east flank of the French cavalry, but this had little effect on the French attack. Soon Bessières' Brigade swung to the south and moved against Gülden-Gossa. The allied center was broken and the allied armies were threatened with defeat. The battle appeared to already be lost at this point by the allies.

As Bessières' Brigade moved on Gülden-Gossa, Schwarzenberg sent Bianchi's Division forward. He also learned that a few French squadrons had moved through the pond defiles west of Gülden-Gossa.[84]

Napoleon sent forward a regiment of the Gardes d'Honneur to support his cavalry in the allied center. The French V Cavalry Corps awaited the arrival of its supporting infantry, but at this time a howitzer shell struck and wounded GD Pajol, taking him from the battle. His absence had a paralyzing effect on his command. The V Cavalry Corps stood between Liebertwolkwitz and Wachau. It consisted of four divisions formed with 30 regiments. Its troops were young, but its cadres were hardened veterans. But without its leader it stopped.[85]

The French light cavalry stood only a short distance from the height where the Czar of Russia and the King of Prussia stood, watching the battle. Though a marshy pond stood between the French and the allied sovereigns, their danger was extreme. The Czar sent forward the Cossacks, under Colonel Orlov-Dennisov, to strike the French. As the Cossacks struck, Prince Schwarzenberg begged the monarchs to not expose themselves further and to withdraw to the rear.

Once relieved of the problem of the two monarchs, Schwarzenberg realized it was time for the allied commander to take his sword in hand and advance into his shaken troops to rally them.[86]

Orlov's attack stopped the French attack and recaptured 24 of the 26 guns that they had just captured. Orlov's attack drove the French cavalry back to the guns of the Imperial Guard artillery reserve. Drouot pulled back his two wings "en potence", forming a type of square with his 6-pdr and 12-pdr batteries and awaited Orlov's charge. He then pounded the Russian cavalry with canister, obliterating large numbers of them, driving them back in disorder. At the same time two squadrons of the Empress Dragoons of the Imperial Guard struck them in the right, completing the rout.

Orlov's success in stopping the French attack can only be attributed to fatigue on the part of the French, as his force only contained about 800 men, somewhat less than a full strength line cavalry regiment. His success was a matter of opportunity and timing.

Attack of the Austrian Infantry Reserve

The allies, realizing the importance of the Gülden-Gossa and Auenhain positions sent forward everything they could mass against them. At 4:00 p.m., when the Russian Guards and Raevsky's grenadiers moved against Gülden-Gossa, the Austrian grenadiers of Weissenwolf and part of Bianchi's forces marched against Auenhain. A formidable artillery force, formed of 80 guns, fired in support of both columns. Schwarzenberg, seconding Merveldt's attack, sent part of Bianchi's Division between the Gösel stream and the Pleisse, below Crostewitz. This movement, supported by Kleist, would take Oudinot and Victor in the rear.

Bianchi attacked from the west. GM Haugwitz advanced with the Hessen-Homburg Infantry Regiment in attack column northwest of the Auenhain Farm, to attack and stop the Young Guard. He attacked their right flank, capturing six cannon and fought off all their counterattacks. Under this attack the Hiller Infantry Regiment moved against Mark-Kleeberg. Two battalions of the H. Colloredo Infantry Regiment advanced as its reserve.

After a long, bloody fight with the Hungarian battalions, Augereau and Poniatowski found themselves obliged to pull back towards Dösen.

The two Austrian regiments of von Beck's Brigade rallied by Mark-Kleeberg. The 1/Esterhazy Infantry Regiment, which had followed them, was then moved into the lead. It attacked Dölitz and took this village with its bayonets. Bianchi's right wing then moved against Dösen, capturing 13 French guns.

Weissenwolf's Grenadiers crossed the Pleisse by Düben and their artillery crossed by Gaschwitz. Between 3:00 and 4:00 p.m., they arrived at Cröbern, where GdK Erbprinz von Hessen-Homburg had left part of Bianchi's Division as a garrison. These troops, the 1/, 2/Simbschen and one battalion from the Esterhazy Regiment, were replaced by the Call and Fischer Grenadier Battalions.

After being relieved of its garrison duties in Cröbern, the 2/Simbschen Regiment, under the command of Major von Ritters, attacked the Auenhain Farm, but was driven back by Dubreton's 4th Division after a bloody fight.

Weissenwolf then formed an attack column with the Call, Fischer, and Portner Grenadier Battalions and the 1/Simbschen Infantry Regiment. Even as the grenadiers began their advance, it appeared that the French were gathering their cavalry north of the Auenhain Farm to attack either Crostewitz or Bianchi's flank.[87]

The Austrian grenadier attack stalled as they advanced into a furious French artillery crossfire. The French canister tore deep holes in the ranks of the Call Grenadiers. The French battery behind the Auenhain Farm was especially galling to them.[88] The grenadiers charged forward and overran the offending battery. The position taken, Weissenwolf quickly brought his own guns forward to this position.

Seeing Sémélé's soldiers falling back, Poniatowski placed a battery of 12 guns diagonally behind his left wing and deployed his remaining infantry into a very dense skirmish screen. The combined effect of their fire and that of the Polish guns slowed the Austrian attack until more of Sémélé's infantry could arrive and stabilize the situation. The 1st (Polish) Chasseurs charged the Austrians and broke a battalion of Hungarian infantry. Oudinot's Young Guard and Victor's II Corps renewed their attacks, forcing the Austrians out of Auenhain again.

The allies assaulted Auenhain again. The Call Grenadier Battalion took the sheep pen buildings and the 1/Simbschen Regiment took the heights to the east. As night was beginning to fall, the French pulled back to their lines between Wachau. Weissenwolf garrisoned the sheep pens with the Call Grenadier Battalion. He placed the Fischer Grenadier Battalion and the 1/Simbschen Infantry Regiment behind them. Fürst Wärther was closing on their position from Cröbern.

Merveldt's artillery (2nd Armeeabteilung) responded to the initial Austrian setback by redoubling its fire and his infantry vainly sought to find a crossing on the Pleisse. Bianchi and Kleist moved to support this passage, but Lefol (Independent Division), Sémélé (52nd Division), and Poniatowski (VIII Corps) stopped them.

Napoleon directed one more effort against the allied center and sent Murat forward with his cavalry against Störmthal. Drouot was to advance his artillery in support. Macdonald, Mortier, Lauriston, Victor, Oudinot, and Poniatowski were to advance and take the last allied position. Napoleon also ordered two divisions of the III Corps to march south from Schönefeld to Liebertwolkwitz.[89]

Macdonald and Mortier renewed their attacks against Seifertshain, Gross-Pösna, and the forest. Murat moved once again to the ground before Gülden-Gossa, overthrowing everything before him. Maison and Rochambeau recaptured part of Gülden-Gossa, Lauriston stood near by with Albert's 10th Division. Victor and Oudinot stood ready to make the decisive strike against Cröbern, while Poniatowski was moving against Crostewitz.

At that time the Old Guard moved forward to support Poniatowski's attack. The artillery on the French right redoubled its efforts, when the heads of Poniatowski's columns stopped, and began to fall back. Merveldt had crossed the Pleisse and stood in the Polish rear, but not with significant forces. Napoleon had no reserve and was unwilling to use the Old Guard. He sent Curial's 2nd Old Guard Division to the right and the general French advance was stopped.

After the recapture of Cröbern, Bianchi's Division advanced in two columns from Cröbern to Mark-Kleeberg and relieved Kleist's troops, which had been in battle for nine hours against the immensely superior French force. However, despite his efforts, the French had recaptured Mark-Kleeberg and the knoll situated between Mark-Kleeberg and Wachau.

Bianchi pushed forward as hard as he could. Kleist and Weissenwolf prepared to defend Cröbern while part of the Austrian grenadiers moved into the woods by the confluence of the Pleisse and the Gösel stream. They were then behind Poniatowski and captured Mark-Kleeberg.

The Last French Attack Against the Middle

At 5:00 p.m., the rush of a new French attack struck against the allies occupying the villages of Gülden-Gossa, Gross-Pösna, and Seifertshain.

They struck Gülden-Gossa, after the great cavalry battle, with Maison's 16th Division of V Corps. The Russian Guard artillery, under GM Suchosanet, began to take the French under heavy fire. Pahlen advanced his cavalry a few times in demonstration against them, threatening the French rear, and successfully slowed the French assault against the University Woods. In the University Woods, Jagow's three battalions defended themselves tenaciously, forcing Maison to attempt to take the east part of the woods. The French were then struck by the Russian Guard, Guard Grenadiers, Pavlov Grenadiers, Guard Jagers, and the Finland Guard Regiment, which drove them back. Maison's second attack also succumbed to the resistance of the Russian and Prussian battalions. The allies moved forward in a counterattack with bayonets against the French. Maison barely escaped being taken prisoner as his division broke and fell back in confused flight towards Liebertwolkwitz.[90] The allies pursued them to the heights, but were unwilling to pursue them further. However, their success was not without cost to the allies, as Raevsky was grievously wounded.

After the Niederholz fell to the allies, GdK Klenau decided the bloody day's work was over and gave the order to settle down for the night, but that was not to happen.

The positions for the night were to be as follows. FML Mohr occupied Gross-Pösna and if possible also the adjacent forest. GM Baumgarten occupied Seifertshain. FML Fürst Hohenlohe positioned his two brigades and the O'Reilly Chevaulégers between Fuchshain and the nearby windmill. Meyer's Division and the Kaiser Cuirassier Regiment stood before Threna. Ziethen's

Brigade stood behind Hohenlohe's Division forming a second line. The 12-pdr position batteries were pulled back to Threna, while those batteries positioned between Gross-Pösna and Fuchshain remained in their positions. Oberst Stein was responsible for replacing the munition shortages that night. Stein made every effort to prepare his forces to be ready in the morning for a renewed battle.

But Klenau's troops were locked in combat and unable to follow their orders. The guns along the French front continued to fire and the strong French columns, Ledru's 31st Division, XI Corps, moved against Seifertshain, which was occupied by the 1/Zach. The French soon took the middle and the southern part of Seifertshain. Only the northern part and the ditch, which was occupied by the Regiment's 5th and 6th Companies under Hauptmann von Thierry, remained in Austrian hands.[91]

Klenau sent Hohenlohe's Division the order to throw the French out Seifertshain. GM Schäffer and Oberst Passeka placed themselves at the head of the 3/Zach Infantry Regiment and led it forward to assist the hard pressed 1/Zach Regiment. Oberstleutnant Irasky supported the attack with his artillery. Schäffer attacked from the east and threw himself into the thickest of the hand to hand fighting, risking being taken prisoner repeatedly. The battle lasted until twilight fell, ending with a limited victory for the Austrians, who still occupied only part of the village.

Any aggressive action by Sébastiani's II Cavalry Corps had been crippled by Platov's presence on the field and had prevented them from taking part in the battle. By Gross-Pösna the allies maintained a cannonade, but as night fell this came to an end.

Klenau's Corps advanced during the evening, containing Macdonald's attack. The 1/Zach Infantry Regiment remained in Seifertshain. To the east of Seifertshain stood Baumgarten's Brigade.[92]

As the action died down the various French corps assumed their positions for the night. The VIII Corps occupied Dösen with the W Cavalry Corps. Curial stood near Mark-Kleeberg, Sémélé's 52nd Division stood to the left of Mark-Kleeberg. The II Corps stood between Wachau and Auenhain. Oudinot's I Young Guard Corps stood before Wachau. The Old Guard stood between Mensdorf and Dösen. The V Corps and Ricard's 11th Division were to spend the night before Liebertwolkwitz and in Gülden-Gossa. Mortier's II Young Guard Corps spent the night in the woods. The XI Corps was spread around. Charpentier's 36th Division was in the Gross-Possnau woods, Ledru's 31st Division was behind Seifertshain, Marchand's 39th Division was on the Kolmberg heights, and Gérard's 35th Division was in Klein-Pösna with Sebastiani. The I and V Cavalry Corps were pulled back and stood behind the center of the army.[93]

Movement of III Corps

At 11:30 a.m., the III Corps arrived at the Mokau heights and was greeted by the sound of a strong cannonade to its left. GD Ricard (11th Division) was ordered to send his first brigade to Lindenau to support Bertrand. The second brigade was sent to a position below Leipzig, facing Lindenau. The 9th Division (Delmas) marched to support Fournier's 6th Light Cavalry Division and Defrance's 4th Heavy Cavalry Division at Euteritz as they covered the roads to Halle and Delitsch.

At 1:00 p.m., the 8th Division (Brayer) departed this position and marched from Schönefeld and Kohlgärten in order to move to a position to the right of the 2nd Old Guard Division standing between Dölitz and Mark-Kleeberg, where it arrived at 5:00 p.m.[94]

The 11th Division (Ricard) followed the movement of the 8th Division (Brayer). Neither division was accompanied by its artillery, because the roads along which they advanced would not permit the passage of their guns. About 4:00 p.m., they arrived near Napoleon. A heavy fire was occurring on their left. Napoleon announced to them that the battle was won and that it remained only for the III Corps to end it with the coup de grace. The III Corps accepted the invitation, and the column doubled its pace to relieve those forces which had been in combat all day and close on the enemy.

Merveldt's forces had already recrossed the river and were no longer on the right bank, except for a few skirmishers, when the III Corps arrived on the crest of the hill that lay between Dölitz and Dösen. GD Souham ordered GD Brayer to push forward a brigade of the 8th Division to take the village of Raschwitz where the allies had a large force supported by artillery. The fire of this artillery harassed the French line considerably. But the bridges were impassable and there were no fords in the immediate vicinity to allow the brigade to cross, so the brigade was obliged to take cover behind a dike. A detachment of the 6th Légère attacked a force of 150 Austrians, killing or capturing them all. At 9:00 p.m., the brigade redeployed with the 8th Division. The 8th Division took up positions with the 1st Brigade forward and the 2nd Brigade positioned behind a small woods, a half-cannon shot from the river.

The 11th Division pulled back and established its camps. The artillery of both divisions, after a very hard march, moved to the right of the main road, not far from the 11th Division. The corps light cavalry had been detached, but rejoined the corps to the left of the 11th Division, near the village of Probstheide.[95]

The 9th Division, which had left Düben at 4:00 a.m., had in its march, overtaken the III Corps park and reserves, which had been delayed by the roads and fallen back. The park and reserves were dangerously exposed because of their limited escort. GD Delmas felt it was his duty to defend the park and his division covered the march of the park in a dense column as far as Plösen. The plain over which this force marched was filled with allied light cavalry, which would have enjoyed nothing more than destroying or capturing a corps park and reserves. Delmas safely escorted his charges into the environs of Leipzig and set up his evening bivouac at Euteritz.[96]

The Night of 16/17 October

The Army of Bohemia, during the night, settled itself into positions, so as to be able to renew the battle the next day. The 3rd Austrian Armeeabteilung, the 1st Austrian Light Division, and Thielmann's Streifkorps were at Klein-Zschocher under the orders of Count Gyulai. The 2nd Austrian Light Division, under A. von Liechtenstein, stood near Connewitz, Raschwitz, and Oetzsch. The Austrian Reserve, under GdK Erbprinz von Hessen-Homburg, stood in Mark-Kleeberg. The 1st Grenadier Division was south of Auenhain, left of Nostitz's Cuirassiers. Kleist stood by Crostewitz and Cröbern with Prinz August von Preussen's 12th Brigade and Helfreich's 14th Division. In the third line stood the 2nd Grenadier Division and the 3rd Cuirassier Division.[97]

The Austrian 2nd Armeeabteilung, now commanded by FML Lederer after GdK Merveldt's capture, stood between the Dölitz castle, Gautzsch, and the bridge to Connewitz. The cavalry stood by Gautzsch. A detachment under Quallenberg stood in the low wet ground north of Gautzsch, and the Simbschen Infantry Regiment stood by Schleussig.

A brigade of the 2nd Grenadier Division and three Russian Guard Regiments stood in Gülden-Gossa. The battered Russian Guard Light Cavalry Division stood between Auenhain and Gülden-Gossa. Württemberg's Russian 2nd Corps, Klüx's 9th Prussian Brigade, Pirch's 10th Prussian Brigade, and Alvensleben's Prussian Guard Brigade stood south of Gülden-Gossa and the ponds.

The Magdeborn palace was occupied by two battalions. Two other battalions were posted on the road which cut the surrounding village along its length and a battalion of fusiliers was posted to the right. The Russian Guard Brigade[98] under GM Bistrom formed a reserve behind the village.

Prince Gorchakov had the 5th Division in the University Forest. Behind them stood a brigade of the 2nd Russian Grenadier Division. Pahlen's Cavalry Corps and the 2nd Cuirassier Division

(Kretov) stood to the right of Gülden-Gossa and the University Woods. The Austrian Reserve Corps (Hessen-Homburg), the 11th Prussian Brigade (Ziethen) and the Prussian reserve cavalry (Röder) stood between Gross-Pösna, Fuchshain, and Seifertshain. Platov's Cossacks were in Klein-Pösna.

The Prussian and Russian Guard Infantry, the Russian 1st Cuirassier Division, the Prussian Guard Cavalry Brigade, and the Russian artillery reserve stood on the heights behind Gülden-Gossa and, northeast of Magdeborn, in the middle of the bivouac of these troops, was Barclay de Tolly's headquarters.

The Austrian 1st Armeeabteilung (Colloredo) was camped in and around Borna. The Russian headquarters and that of Schwarzenberg was in Rötha. The King of Prussia's headquarters was in Borna. The Austrian emperor spent the night in Pegau.

The Army of Silesia stood in the following positions: Blücher's headquarters was established in Gross-Wiederitsch. Yorck's Corps stood on the battlefield by Möckern. Sacken's Corps stood behind him in a second line, acting as a reserve. Langeron's Corps stood in a position near Wiederitsch.

The French stood as follows: on their right wing was Lefol's Division and a brigade of the III Corps by Connewitz and Lössnig. Poniatowski's VIII Corps and Augereau's IX Corps, Curial's 2nd Old Guard Division, two brigades of Souham's III Corps, and Kellerman's (Sokolnicki's) IV Cavalry Corps stood between Dölitz and Dösen.[99]

In the middle, Victor's II Corps, Oudinot's I Young Guard Corps (1st and 3rd Young Guard Divisions), and Lauriston's V Corps stretched from Wachau east to Liebertwolkwitz.

On the French left Mortier's II Young Guard Corps (2nd and 4th Young Guard Division) stood near Niederholz, Macdonald with Charpentier's 36th Division stood behind Mortier. Ledru (31st Division) and Gérard (35th Division) stood northwest of Seifertshain and west of Klein-Pösna, Marchand (39th Division) stood on the Kolmberg, Sébastiani (II Cavalry Corps) stood behind Ledru and Gérard. Milhaud (V Cavalry Corps) was sent forward, that evening, from Baalsdorf and joined Dommagnet's Brigade by Borsdorf.

The 1st Old Guard Division, the Guard Cavalry, and the I Cavalry Corps stood as a reserve by Meusdorf.

Napoleon had five tents raised by the Meusdorf brickworks for himself and his staff. Around 9:00 p.m., he met with GdK Merveldt, who had been captured that day,[100] and spoke a while with him about the day's events.[101]

Ney's Corps

After wasting the day in marches and countermarches Souham's III Corps finally arrived aside the VI Corps, but it was too late to intervene in the battle of Möckern. The two corps passed the night by the Parthe, near Schönefeld. Maréchaux Ney and Marmont established their headquarters in the Schönefeld Palace. The villages of Gohlis, Eutritzsch, and Möckern were only lightly occupied. The III Cavalry Corps, under Arrighi, Duke of Padua, and GD Dombrowski's 27th Division, were moved to a position by Pfaffendorf and the houses near the Leipzig gate known as the Gerber-Tor.[102]

The Army of Poland

Bennigsen had been ordered to join the allies before Leipzig. At midnight, during the night of 16/17 October, Stroganov's advanced guard and Bennigsen's headquarters stood in Grimma. Docturov's Corps, after a night march would not arrive in Grimma until 6:00 a.m., the morning of 17 October. GM Kreutz had attacked the French in Wurzen and had captured it after strong resistance by the French.103

The Army of the North

On 16 October Bernadotte led his army out of Halle in the late afternoon, and after he had been assured that no French force stood in Wittenberg or Dessau. That evening his army arrived in Landsberg. It was not in a position to affect the battles of the 16th in any way, but like the Army of Poland, it would arrive on the battlefield the following day.[104]

6

The Battle to the West: Connewitz and Lindenau 16 October 1813

The Forces Gather

After nightfall on 15 October, the 2nd Armeeabteilung under GdK Merveldt left its encampments. Between 7:00 and 8:00 a.m., it marched between Gautzsch and the Harth Forest north of Zwenkau. Lederer's 1st Division formed the first line. From the right to the left his front consisted of: the two brigade batteries, two squadrons of the Erzherzog Johann Dragoon Regiment, the Strauch Infantry Regiment, the Bellegarde Infantry Regiment, and the corps artillery. A. Liechtenstein's 2nd Division formed the second line. Erbprinz Hessen-Homburg's 3rd Reserve Armeeabteilung was a general reserve. Its two infantry divisions were formed in battalionsmasse: Bianchi's 2nd Reserve marched in the first line and Weissenwolf's 1st Reserve Grenadier Division marched in the second line. Nostitz's Cuirassier Corps stood behind the right wing by GrossStädteln, facing the Pleisse River. As cover for his left flank and to maintain contact with Gyulai, Merveldt had Oberstleutnant Simbschen move the 1/Gradiscaner Grenz Regiment and 1/Kaunitz Infantry Regiment to the bank of the Elster, between Schleussig and Plagwitz. GM Quallenberg was sent, with two battalions of the Davidovich Regiment and two squadrons of the Hohenzollern Cuirassier Regiment, from Wiederau, through Knauthain, towards Klein-Zschocher with orders to move to the right and clear the French garrison out of Connewitz.[1]

It was Merveldt's goal to advance along the bank of the Pleisse, through Gautzsch towards Connewitz, in order to take the rear of the French right flank.

In order to be able to attack Connewitz without concerns for his flanks and rear, Lederer sent the Strauch Infantry Regiment to Dölitz where it could watch the left bank of the Pleisse and defend against any French push across the river. GM von Longueville was sent with the Bellegarde Infantry Regiment down the road towards Connewitz to take and hold the river crossing in that village. Lederer's cavalry remained in reserve, as Lederer soon found the region between the Pleisse and the Elster Rivers was unsuitable for cavalry. A. Liechtenstein's 2nd Division moved through Gautzsch.

About 8:00 a.m., the first shots were heard from the low wet grounds and about the same time Schwarzenberg, with Generals von Radetzky, Langenau, Jomini, and some of the general staff arrived by the Bellegarde Regiment. He rode over to the advanced posts on the Pleisse River to observe the advance. Then he rode up and down to better observe the region around Gautzsch. In addition, an observation post was established in a church tower. The view of the battlefield from this position allowed Schwarzenberg a better understanding of the action, and its observations were sent to him by dropping written notes from the tower to the ground. Schwarzenberg studied the battlefield and decided to take the right bank of the Pleisse by Connewitz.[2]

The two bridges across the Pleisse were broken and the intervening terrain covered with French posts. The village of Connewitz was occupied by Lefol's Independent Division. A frontal attack against Connewitz and the bridge was not practical, as the French defended the approaches with a large amount of artillery.

The bank of the Pleisse was quite high around Connewitz and the river itself was swollen because of the heavy rains that had fallen all month. Because of this the Austrian column could only advance along the Connewitz-Leipzig road that passed through the woods that lined the Pleisse. As the Austrians advanced along this road, seeking a crossing, they were subjected to a heavy artillery and musketry fire. The woods and swamps prevented their crossing at Lossnig as well.[3]

The Battle of Connewitz

Without waiting for the attack of the Bellegarde Infantry Regiment, Schwarzenberg ordered FML A. Liechtenstein to establish a passage over the Pleisse, by Mark-Kleeberg. The task fell to Oberst von Luxem's 2/Kaunitz Infantry Regiment.

Meanwhile GM Longueville, with two companies of the Bellegarde Infantry Regiment, crossed the Pleisse and moved against the two broken bridges. Without room to deploy and without supporting artillery fire, the assault would be bloody. They were also exposed to a heavy crossfire, which caused Longueville to forswear a direct assault.

However, Schwarzenberg personally intervened, and ordered Longueville to execute the frontal assault. The 1/W. Colloredo Infantry Regiment was ordered forward. This battalion, under the command of Oberst von Berger, moved across the Pleisse against the French. They reached the

The old castle at Dölitz, by Krause.

edge of Connewitz, where they were engaged by Lefol's garrison. Initially repulsed, Oberst Berger drove his battalion forward in a renewed attack, only to be driven back again with heavy losses.[4]

At 11:00 a.m., the attack was renewed by the Bellegarde Regiment, supported by the 3/W. Colloredo Regiment. Their assault was equally unsuccessful.

Initially, more from luck than design, the Strauch Infantry Regiment found itself by Dölitz, a village on the eastern bank of the Pleisse. On the western Pleisse bank stood a château,[5] which Poniatowski's Poles had converted into a type of fortified bridgehead and occupied strongly. In front of the château and Dölitz ran two ditches, which were crossed by two bridges, one behind the other.

Dölitz and its immediate vicinity was occupied by the 26th Polish Infantry Division, temporarily under the command of General Malachowski. It consisted of the 1st, 12th, and 15th Infantry Regiments, about 3,000 men.

Hauptmann Petzler led forward two companies of the 1/Strauch Regiment and threw the French back across both bridges.[6] At 8:00 a.m., they pushed into the village, taking about 200 Polish prisoners.

The fall of the château resulted after a terrible fight with the Poles who had occupied it, as well the village and the mill. The Austrians set the mill afire with grenades, pushing the Poles out, but the Poles had set the château afire as well, which denied the position to the Austrians.[7] The Austrians strongly occupied the buildings behind the bridge.

At 9:00 a.m., the 2/Kaunitz Regiment occupied the château in Mark-Kleeberg, on the west bank of the Pleisse. Oberst Luxem found himself facing a large French force on the far bank, but it was unlikely that they would push through the swamp to attack him. He contented himself with bringing up some artillery. The manor was strongly occupied, and the Austrian schützen spread along the right bank.

The Austrian attacks by Dölitz and Mark-Kleeberg were unwanted, but not unexpected by Prince Poniatowski, who that day was promoted to the rank of marshal. His flank was disturbed by the Prussians under Kleist attacking Mark-Kleeberg. He called Aymard's Brigade, Augereau's IX Corps, forward and ordered him to recapture the two châteaux of Dölitz and Mark-Kleeberg.

The counterattacking French battalions pushed forward to take the eastern portion of Dölitz château, as well as the main bridge, but their efforts were in vain. The four companies of the 1/Strauch Regiment held in reserve were pushed forward to drive the French back and became involved in a prolonged firefight.[8]

The 2/Strauch Infantry Regiment was, with the exception of two companies, deployed in skirmish order on both sides of the château. The southern wing reached to the manor in Mark-Kleeberg. Two companies of the 2/W. Colloredo Infantry Regiment appeared behind the left wing of the Strauch infantry, followed soon after by four more companies of the battalion.

With the exception of Meszerey's Brigade, which was marching to the north of Gautzsch, and the corps cavalry, Merveldt's entire corps found itself engaged in the battle around Connewitz and Dölitz.

Schwarzenberg could, from his observation post in the church tower, see the entire battlefield and the battle that raged across it. However, his principal attention was directed to the south and the villages of Liebertwolkwitz and Holzhausen.[9]

In the early hours of the afternoon the firefight by Dölitz raged with undiminished vehemence. The fighting was so intense that the companies of the Strauch Infantry Regiment fired almost all their ammunition. FML A. Liechtenstein supported the regiment with companies from the 2/Kaunitz Regiment, drawn from the manor in Mark-Kleeberg. The 1/,2/W. Colloredo Infantry Regiment occupied the Dölitz château.

Between 4:00 and 5:00 p.m., FML Liechtenstein observed Bianchi's advance towards Mark-Kleeberg. He immediately hurried to Merveldt and sent him forward, to renew his efforts to pass over the Pleisse. Merveldt agreed to try.

Major Volny of the Strauch Infantry Regiment was designated to execute an assault by Dölitz. A company of the Kaunitz Infantry Regiment supported Volny's bridge laying effort. GM von Ennesbruck and Generalstabsmajor von Rettenberg supervised the laying of the first beam across the river, despite the heavy French fire. Soldiers of various regiments had been formed into a detachment for the assault. They threw themselves across the beam at the French skirmishers moving at the *sturmschritt* and drove the French back.[10] As Napoleon heard the news of Bianchi's attack and of the allied troop masses gathering by Dölitz, he moved to the side of Mark-Kleeberg to observe the movements of the Austrian Infantry Reserve and his Old Guard.

Poniatowski's forces recoiled because of Merveldt's actions, as well as developments at Mark-Kleeberg. Napoleon watched Bianchi's success on the west wing and the Austrian blows against Oudinot and Victor. His generals were not only brought to a halt, but driven back.[11] Between 4:00 p.m., and 5:00 p.m., when the shakos of the Hungarian infantry appeared on the heights between Mark-Kleeberg and Dösen, he ordered Curial, to throw back the offending Hungarians with the 2nd Brigade, 2nd Old Guard Division.[12] Poniatowski's WII Corps and Sémélé's 52nd Division also appear to have participated in this attack.[13]

As Curial marched to meet the Austrians, Napoleon saw the head of a column south and east of Probstheida. Napoleon rode to see if it was friend or foe, and found it was Souham at the head of Brayer's 8th Division with a brigade of Ricard's 11th Division following. How it came to be that Souham appeared to the south of Leipzig with two divisions is not clear. Around 1:00 p.m., Brayer and Ricard received an order, whose author was not identified, to move from Mockau to the battlefield south of Leipzig.[14] Napoleon quickly ordered Souham to follow Curial and to the attack the allies east of the battlefield.

Poniatowski now found himself reinforced by Brayer's 8th Division, III Corps, but night was coming fast. The Poles pushed forward in an effort to recapture the château by Dölitz, which was now defended by a company of the W. Colloredo Regiment, under Oberstleutnant Schindler. Their efforts failed and the Austrians held their position.[15]

Merveldt's forces were continuing to advance on Bianchi's side. They were moving against the French rear, when Curial's 2nd Old Guard Division arrived at the *pas de course*,[16] and charged Merveldt with bayonets. The Polish Guard led the Velites of Turin, the Velites of Florence, and the Westphalian Guard Fusilier Battalion forward.[17] They struck the Austrians and captured 1,200 men.[18] GdK Merveldt had followed the first infantry companies across the river and urged them forward. As he spoke, he was fired on, his horse fell, and he was wounded. The Austrian solders, who held him dearly, ran to him from all sides and surrounded him. Despite their efforts, Merveldt was taken prisoner by the Curial's 2nd Old Guard Division.[19] Command then passed to FML A. von Liechtenstein.[20]

At the same time, Bianchi's Grenadiers were defeated and driven out of Mark-Kleeberg by Poniatowski's and Sémélé's forces.

Curial's Grenadiers stormed over the bridge towards the Austrian forces around Dölitz château. Major Volny made a stand with the detachments from the Kaunitz, Strauch, and W. Colloredo Infantry Regiments in hand, and stopped the French advance. As the French sought to cross to the far bank, they were met with fire and bayonets and thrown back.

Curial directed part of his division against Bianchi, in the region where the combined battalions of Poniatowski, Augereau, and Oudinot had stalled Bianchi's attack. Souham closed behind him to support the attack with his three brigades, and moved by Dösen.

One of Souham's Brigades was later directed to cross the Pleisse by Lossnig and take the Dölitz château in the flank, but it was soon obliged to give up the effort.

Bianchi could not to be sure of maintaining his position against such superior forces north of Mark-Kleeberg, but the fight for the village and the heights south of Wein pond held him locked

Polish infantry at Dölitz, 16 October, by Knötel.

tight. The 1/Esterhazy Regiment, under Oberst von Kauffman, stood at its post in Dölitz, some distance from Curial's attack, or he too would have been cut up.

As night fell, the Austrians had made little progress. They did, however, occupy the pastures between the Elster and the Pleisse with light troops from Lederer's Division. The advanced works of the sluice were held by the 1/Gradiscaner Grenz and the 1/Kaunitz Infantry, which allowed the 2nd and 3rd Austrian Abteilung to maintain liaison.[21]

The Battle Around Lindenau

At 7:00 p.m., on 15 October, Rillmeister Mareschall rode through Lützen on the way to Schwarzenberg's headquarters and made Gyulai aware of Blücher's intentions to move the Army of Silesia from Schkeuditz towards Leipzig, during the morning of 16 October. Blücher was making this move to join with St.-Priest's Corps by Günthersdorf. The timing of the planned attack he did not know. Gyulai determined to take Lindenau under fire from the left bank of the Elster, and if possible, to seize the far bank.[22]

In a later note, Blücher advised FZM Gyulai again of his determination to link up with St.-Priest, that Gyulai would not have to worry about a serious French defense of Lindenau, only slight resistance, and that the accumulation of large numbers of troops on the road would be purposeless.

At the same time, St.-Priest demanded the replacement of his posts by the advanced guard of the 3rd Armeeabteilung, because he had decided to move towards Schkeuditz. Gyulai was left to watch the Elster east of and through the north border of the Luppe by himself. During the night, he impatiently awaited dispositions of the army command for the general attack against Leipzig.

The task assigned to the 3rd Armeeabteilung, was through its attack on Lindenau, to facilitate and maintain the link with the Army of Silesia.

At 12:30 a.m., Gyulai made the following dispositions for his forces:

> The departure is to the right and shall be in two columns. The 1st column shall consist of Weigel's Brigade, which, at 3:00 a.m., shall march down the Leipzig Road to Mark-Ranstädt, turning to the left at Rückmarsdorf, then pass through Böhlitz-Ehrenberg, to the right of Barneck and Leutzsch, from where they shall, according to circumstances, strike Lindenau in the flank. This column shall obtain from Crenneville's Division a battalion of the Warasdiner Grenz Regiment, from Fürst M. Liechtenstein's Division a Jäger battalion, and from Mensdorf's Corps an officer and 30 Cossacks. These light forces shall form the advanced guard of the column. They shall be sent from their divisions that they may be in Böhlitz before day break. This column shall, so much as possible, cover the march and always advance at the same rate as Blücher's Corps advancing along the Elster and not attack earlier than does the main column with its artillery. It shall cover its left flank with side patrols. A platoon of pioneers shall march on the head of the column, behind the advanced guard. Weigel's Brigade shall leave its battery behind which shall be attached to von Czollich's column.[23]
>
> The 2nd column shall depart at 4:00 a.m., and shall follow the road to Leipzig to this side of Mark-Ranstädt. It shall march in the following order: a pioneer platoon, a battalion from Grimmer's Brigade as an advanced guard, itself followed by a battery from the brigade, then the main body of Grimmer's Brigade, and Czollich's Brigade with its batteries included. Czollich's Brigade follows, as stated with Weigel's battery, then a 12-pdr battery and two howitzers, finally the mass of infantry and artillery reserve munition caissons.
>
> Those troops belonging to the advanced guard, those from Crenneville's, M. Liechtenstein's, von Thielmann's, and Mensdorf's forces shall remain in the assigned arrangement in preparedness, to avail themselves of whatever circumstances may present.
>
> FML Fürst M. Liechtenstein shall seek to establish communication with General Graf von Merveldt, who shall be standing on the road from Pegau to Leipzig.
>
> The pontoon bridge shall follow in the artillery reserve, the ten ambulances shall move by Millen. From each brigade a well mounted officer shall be commanded there.

In the meantime the French in Lindenau did not remain idle. The defense of this suburb of Leipzig was assigned to Margaron with his eight infantry battalions, Quinette with six squadrons, and a force of one Baden and two French artillery batteries with 16 guns.[24]

Margaron had resolved, in view of his surrounded and fatigued forces, not to occupy Schönau, and to content himself with the defense of Lindenau and the plain that lay before it. The defense of the first bridge appeared to him to be questionable, and he was uncertain if he could stop any allied advance there. He strengthened this position by dispatching a sapper detachment to help defend it.

On 15 October he raised two earth works on the Lützen Road, about 600 paces west of the two rows of houses known as the "twelve apostles". The residents of the surrounding villages were pressed into service as laborers. Each of these earth works was equipped with six guns. Finally Margaron organized four batteries with breast works during the night of 15/16 October.[25]

The first battery was placed in the open field a quarter of a league from Lindenau, on the right and near the road to Klein-Zschocher. The second and third were also in the open fields, and the fourth battery was placed near the road to Mersberg. They dominated each approach to Lindenau and they were to maintain a heavy fire all day. The Austrians were unable to advance, except on the north via the Leutzsch woods.

Lindenau had been garrisoned two days earlier by two infantry battalions, Plagwitz with a battalion and 50 cavalry, Leutzsch had two companies of infantry and 50 cavalry. The remainder of Margaron's forces remained between Plagwitz and Lindenau.[26]

FZM Gyulai marched to the attack in three columns. His goal was to seize control of the six bridges that connected Lindenau with Leipzig. The first of his columns, the left column, was commanded by Prince P. von Hessen-Homburg. This column consisted of a battalion of the 1/Warasdiner-Kreuzer Grenz Regiment, Jäger Battalion #2, four battalions from Weigel's Brigade,[27] and 30 Cossacks from Mensdorf's Streifkorps. They were directed to move through Mark-Ranstädt, Rückmarsdorf, Böhlitz, and Ehrenberg and attack Leutzsch. Hessen-Homburg's column executed the prescribed march, but was unable to take its artillery, because of the bad roads. Once in Leutsch, it was to attack Lindenau in the flank, supported by the artillery of the second column.[28]

The second column which Gyulai led personally, consisted of three battalions,[29] all his cavalry, three 6-pdr brigade batteries, and a 12-pdr position battery. Gyulai led his column through Mark-Ranstädt, and down the road to Schönau, where it encountered M. Liechtenstein's Division and the streifkorps of Thielmann and Mensdorf.[30] His column was to attack Lindenau frontally down the main route, supported by a vigorous cannonade, and distract the defenders from the attacking wing columns.[31]

The third column, formed by Czollich's Brigade[32] and the remainder of M. Liechtenstein's 1st Light Division, was ordered to move through Klein-Zschocher and attack Lindenau from that flank.[33] This force was commanded by GM Quallenberg.[34]

A reserve, formed with two battalions of the Kollowrath Regiment, was held by Schönau. Gyulai took this precaution because, if he became over committed, he was very close to Bertrand's IV Corps, which could overwhelm him quickly. Bertrand had 15,000 men and could quickly receive reinforcements in the form of 4,000 cavalry.

All three columns were in position, but the attack was delayed because Blücher's army was not yet visible. This caused some concern for the rear of the first column, and a battalion of the Fröhlich Infantry Regiment was detached from Gyulai's column to Dölzig, to guard the passage over the Luppe River by Horburg and Masslau, as well as to protect the rear of the first column.

About that time, Gyulai learned that the main army was engaged between the Elster and the Pleisse, which relieved his concerns about Bertrand's potential threat. He ordered his attack.

Gyulai's Attack Begins

The 3rd Armeeabteilung advanced at the ordered time. En route to Mark-Ranstädt, where the left column under the command of FML P. Hessen-Homburg turned towards Rückmarsdorf, the main column marched in divisionsmasse. Gyulai issued further orders at that time. Liechtenstein's light infantry, Czollich's Brigade, and the two cavalry batteries led the attack through Klein-Zschocher towards Lindenau.[35]

Crenneville's 1st Division stood to the left of the road, and standing in echelon on the right, stood the Kaiser and Vincent Chevauléger Regiments, Thielmann's Streifkorps, Mensdorf's Streifkorps, Grimmer's Brigade, and the combined artillery. The orders of the front group were to advance against Lindenau, and by firing on the village, facilitate the flank attacks of the two side columns. A battalion of the Fröhlich Infantry Regiment, under Major Ackelhausen, was the cover for the advance of the left column towards Dölzig. This battalion was to occupy the passage over the Luppe by Horburg and Masslau, where it would join hands with the Army of Silesia by Schkeuditz. Gyulai revised his plans and ordered the elimination of a third column in Mark-Ranstädt, because he found the terrain between Klein-Zschocher and Lindenau would not permit

The entry of the King of Saxony with his escort onto the battlefield at Leipzig, after Syrutschöck.

Austrian artillery under Gyulai's command, 16 October.

that movement of men. It is also possible that the transfer of the army reserves from the region between the Pleisse and the Elster, caused him to worry that, as the third column, it would be isolated and subject to defeat in detail. Accordingly orders were issued that requested the exact location of GL Thielmann, and assumed it was still possible to advance from Lindenau towards Leipzig.

The main column advanced to the heights of Schönau. The main army was on the other side of the Pleisse and Elster, ready to engage in battle. Between 8:00 a.m., and 9:00 a.m., Gyulai ordered the main column to attack.

The Austrian troops moved behind the covering heights as they advanced towards the 4,000 French cavalry and infantry standing between Lindenau and Plagwitz. Quinette's cavalry[36] moved to the right flank where the Vincent and Kaiser Chevauléger stood, in order to strike them. The French attack failed and the allied cavalry drove the French dragoons back to their batteries. The Austrian cavalry was unable to overrun the French earthworks and were themselves thrown back.[37] They would appear to have been so badly hurt that Gyulai used them thereafter only as artillery cover on the right wing. Margaron's attack was little more than a spoiling attack designed to stop or slow Gyulai's advance.[38]

In the meantime the Austrian artillery began to fire on the French from the dominating Schönau heights, in an effort to suppress the French gunfire directed on the assaulting Austrian infantry. The French fire faltered and the attack of the side column moved forward with few casualties. The attacking force was formed from the 2/Fröhlich Infantry Regiment, the 1/Warasdiner-St-George Grenz, and the 1st Jäger Battalion. The Kollowrath Infantry stood in Schönau and acted as a reserve, while the cavalry deployed before the Austrian front. The cavalry on the two wings received the order to link with the flanking columns to support the attack on Lindenau. The chevaulégers from Crenneville's Division swarmed to the north, forcing back a small French detachment pushing forward from Leutzsch to Barneck.

The terrain over which the Austrian attack advanced was cut by several ditches, overgrown with bushes and broken with clumps of trees, which allowed the French to commence a heavy skirmish battle. The I. Gyulai Regiment was left behind in Leutzsch as a reserve.

The withdrawing French occupied two parallel woods and prepared their defense. The advanced guard was obliged to fight furiously for every foot of ground. This, as well as the battalions' being able to only pass through the pastures, caused them to be constantly under French musketry and artillery fire, as they closed in Divisionsmasse on Lindenau.

The French response was soon to come. Bertrand was already advancing at the head of Morand's 12th Division and Fontanelli's 15th Division, supported by four squadrons and 33 guns, which Ney had sent there. Bertrand began to form his IV Corps behind Lindenau in preparation for the coming counterattack. The French artillery stood behind the Kuhburger Stream, and their skirmishers fired on the flanks of Hessen-Homburg's column. Franquemont's Mixed (38th—Württemberg) Division, part of IV Corps, was not brought forward for the attack, but left to the rear in reserve.

The Mariassy Infantry Regiment and the 1/Warasdiner Grenz Regiment moved to the left, in the pasture accompanied by 2nd Jäger Battalion as they advanced against Lindenau. Lindenau was surrounded by walls.to its north front and these walls were pierced by only a few gates. However, on the Leipzig side, the village was open, so that the French could effectively dispute the village streets.

Major M. von Jarossy placed himself on the point of his Hungarians and led their attack against the village. Though, he was quickly wounded and struck from his horse, the Hungarians pushed into the village. The French cannon fire, however, soon made their remaining in Lindenau impossible. They quickly evacuated the front of the village. The French attacked, but the attacking I. Gyulai Infantry Regiment drew back behind the walls and forced the French back.[39]

A second attack left Lindenau in the hands of the Austrians, but again only for a short time. Two French guns taken by the 2nd Jäger Battalion, were abandoned to their former owners. Gyulai sent the 1st Jäger Battalion and the 2/Fröhlich Infantry Regiment forward as reinforcements to the left attack column, passing through the Säuberung field, the Luppe pasture, and through Leutzsch. The French artillery again forced the Austrians to abandon Lindenau. Hessen-Homburg recognized the futility in sacrificing his troops in further attacks and withdrew, leaving only the left bank of the Luppe strongly occupied. The French destroyed the bridges over the Luppe, with the exception of the Lindenau bridge.

The Austrians began an intense fire at a distance of several hundred paces, in order to support a third attack against Lindenau. The Austrians sent forward small detachments drawn from the Fröhlich Infantry Regiment and Jägers. Soon, about 4:00 p.m., they were chasing fleeing French from between the Kuhturm (Cow's Tower) and the Ratsziegelei. Then it was reported that the attack of the 2/Fröhlich Infantry Regiment had been successful. The 2/Fröhlich Regiment had struck the French standing by the right flank of Lindenau. French gendarmes, who stood on both sides of the road, were observed forcing fleeing soldiers back to the line with strong saber blows.[40]

Soon after the opening of the artillery fire, GM Czollich directed the 1/Broder Grenz Regiment and the 7th Jäger Battalion to launch their attack on Klein-Zschocher. The 1/Broder Grenz Regiment moved through the open field, on the right wing in the Elster pasture, supported by the 1/Fröhlich Infantry Regiment and advanced towards Plagwitz. The Kottulinsky and Kaiser Infantry Regiments had already occupied Klein-Zschocher. The village fell after a bloody fight. Klein-Zschocher was an important support point, for the planned capture of Plagwitz and attack against Leipzig. It was near 11:00 a.m., as the first Austrian skirmishers began to fire on Lindenau. Hessen-Homburg's column had organized itself by Böhlitz. A half-company of the 2nd Jäger Battalion was pushed forward on the meadows between Luppe and Elster Rivers to reconnoiter. A second half-company advanced under the leadership of Unterleutnant Gelber, and sought to link with the Army of Silesia.

The column then moved against Plagwitz to carry that point, but Lefol had reinforced the village with large numbers of infantry supported by artillery. The 8th Légère Regiment[41] advanced and quickly found itself in a hot fight, suffering heavy casualties. They were supported by Morand's two foot batteries, the 1/, 3/2nd Foot Artillery. Behind them stood the rest of Morand's 12th Division and the cavalry, which included four squadrons of Württemberger, Hessian, and Westphalian Chevaulégers.

Gyulai had a 12-pdr position battery drawn forward to Plagwitz under heavy fire, and Thielmann's cavalry, which had remained inactive so far, was moved to the left flank of the attack column. The Austrian artillery of the center column began to pound Lindenau. The Austrian 12-pdr battery directed its fire against the flanks of the French, placed on the Plagwitz heights. Despite the Austrian artillery fire, the French on the Plagwitz heights did not withdraw.[42] The Austrians pushed the French through the woods and across the open fields to Lindenau, foot by foot. The French withdrew behind the walls of Lindenau. They assumed a strong position, from which they were able to hold against the advancing Austrians.[43] The last four battalions held by GD Arrighi, were sent forward to defend the flanks of the road. General Morio-de-l'Isle commanded the garrison of Lindenau and defended it bravely.[44]

The French were, however, soon smothered by a murderous fire. They were initially forced to vacate the first houses on the edge of the village and a few patches of woods along the Elster, but quickly reinforced their front and went over to the attack. With effort the French drove back Czollich's forces in their effort to occupy the terrain before Klein-Zschocher. A French detachment occupied the woods along the Elster, to the north Lindenau. The 2/Fröhlich Infantry moved against the French and began a heavy fire. The 7th Jäger Battalion began to engage the French as well, but lost a large portion of its officers in the fight.[45]

The Austrians failed to take the village, and were met with a hail of musketry and canister, which repelled their every attack. Finally, assailed by French cavalry, Oberst Veyder, leading the 1/Broder Grenz Regiment and Jäger Battalion #7, found himself so cramped, that he did not have proper room to deploy into squares, so he formed his battalions by divisionsmasses. His skirmishers formed themselves into klumpen to defend themselves.[46] It was becoming desperate, when a force of Russian Cossacks arrived, attacking in dense columns, striking the French and driving them back.[47]

The French cavalry was counterattacked by Cossacks and driven back behind their own infantry. Once the field of fire was cleared of allied troops, the Austrian 12-pdr battery began to fire again. It was not, however, sufficient to break the morale of the French infantry and they held fast.[48]

Gyulai could not provide any meaningful reinforcements to the right wing column, as he had already committed his entire infantry force to the battle. Furthermore, he had received bad news from the south. Merveldt had not taken the bridge by Connewitz, and more importantly, the right flank of the main army was locked in a tremendous battle. As a result, there was no compelling reason to press the occupation of Lindenau at any price.[49]

The village of Lindenau was in flames. GD Bertrand placed a large number of guns along the edge of the ponds and directed their fire against the Austrians' flank, obliging them to withdraw. Musketry and artillery continued throughout the rest of the day, from this point near the Luppe and in the Lautsch woods.

Lindenau is Stormed

Hessen-Homburg executed an attack against Lindenau under the cover of Gyulai's artillery. The village, which was surrounded by walls on the west and offered little chance of an entrance, but the side facing Leipzig was open. However, this side was covered by the fire of the French artillery. Despite the artillery fire, Hessen-Homburg and his column advanced around to the Leipzig side of the village, braving that artillery fire, and penetrated into the village.[50]

The French had little choice but to abandon Lindenau. The Austrian Jäger Battalion #2 and the 1/Mariassy Regiment raced into Lindenau at the geschwindschritt, capturing two cannon.[51]

Bertrand then withdrew his entire corps to a position behind the Kuhturm and the tile works. There he formed his infantry into large squares, and opened a vigorous cannonade against Gyulai's troops on the left bank of the Luppe River, near Lindenau. The French batteries were placed below Luppe and the Elster, notably on the dike, so the village was showered with shot from every direction. The Austrian attempts to advance out of Lindenau were shattered by the weight of artillery. The Austrians withdrew back into the village, where they barricaded themselves behind the garden walls and in the houses.[52] At that moment, Napoleon sent the IV Corps the order to move against Lindenau. Bertrand executed those orders and quickly retook the village. More than 100 French and allied guns began firing. The losses due to the artillery were considerable, and the Austrians once again withdrew.

Twice, around 5:00 p.m., the French advanced against Klein-Zschocher, where Czollich's Brigade stood, reinforced by the 1/Fröhlich Regiment. It was also supported by Austrian artillery and a force of Russian Cossacks. However, counterattacks by the Cossacks under Orlov and Bok stopped both attacks.[53]

Attack of Austrian cuirassiers against Saxon and French cavalry, 16 October.

Liechtenstein's Advance

The third column, formed by the troops of Prince M. von Liechtenstein and GL Thielmann, maneuvered on the left flank of the village of Lindenau. It was charged with maintaining communications between Gyulai's Corps and the Army of Silesia.

The fields, which extended from Lauer to Leipzig, were covered with Austrian light troops from Lederer's Division. Everywhere, on the roads, on the banks of the Pleisse and Elster, was a huge skirmish battle. The Schleussig Farm, as well as the entire right bank of the Elster as far as Plagwitz, had been since that morning, covered by light troops, which linked the Austrian 2nd and 3rd Abteilung. These light troops had been reinforced by the 1/Gradiscaner Grenz Regiment and the 1/Kaunitz Infantry Regiment. The knowledge of the terrain by the Austrian generals was limited. They did not know that the French had not destroyed the Sauweiden Bridge across the Pleisse, which if the Heiligen Bridge was fixed, could be used to advance unhindered against the Lindenau road.[54]

As night fell the Austrian 3rd Abteilung assumed the following positions. A chain of advanced posts under Oberst Mensdorf extended from Klein-Zschocher to Leutsch.

Klein-Zschocher was occupied by the 1/Fröhlich Regiment, coming from Dölzig. Schönau was occupied the 2/Fröhlich, the 1/Warasdiner-Kreuzer Grenz Regiment, and a half-battery. Two companies of the 1/Warasdiner Saint-George Grenz Regiment were in Leutsch, and the four other companies of the same battalion were in Barneck. The other troops of the 3rd Abteilung bivouacked around Mark-Ranstädt.

The 3rd Abteilung, weakened by various detachments to guard passage over the Saale, had lost a further 2,000 casualties in the day's battle, without taking a single prisoner. Despite that, Bertrand's IV Corps had been held in position and not permitted to intervene in the main battle around Wachau, where its appearance could have been catastrophic for the allies.[55]

7

The Battle of Möckern
16 October 1813

Prelude to the Battle

On 15 October, at 8:00 a.m., Blücher's Army of Silesia stood with the lead elements of the main body of its cavalry in Lützschena and its staff to the heights lying to the north of the village. As far as the eye could see, the terrain before Blücher contained French posts and a few earth works, but no large bodies of troops. The village of Stahmeln appeared to be weakly occupied, and the heights to the north of the village was occupied by a small cavalry detachment. Where the French main body stood, could only be presumed. This forced Blücher to make a decision, for at 9:00 a.m., the thunder of cannons to the south of Leipzig grew ever stronger. Both Blücher and Langeron understood what was happening, as the increasing clouds of burnt powder fumes to the south became more noticeable. With that realization came a sense of duty, which caused Langeron to issued the order, "March forward. Go towards Leipzig and attack the enemy, where you encounter him."

Between the Lober and the Mulde, extending from Jessnitz towards Wurzen, lay a plateau, which gave the French a large advantage should they choose give battle there. Their right wing extended to the Lober and the defiles of Bitterfeld and Delitzsch, the possession of which permitted them to move to either side.

Their right wing leaned on the Parthe and the Taucha defile. The village of Radefeld, lay on the dominating terrain, from which a line of hills ran as far as the plateau. The French occupied the dominating terrain by Radefeld which controlled the roads to Leipzig on the side of Lützschena. In order to move on Leipzig the allies were obliged to take the Radefeld position.[1]

Blücher's staff was convinced that the allies had a only weakly occupied French advanced position before them, and that the main French force was to the northeast, about five kilometers from Podelwitz and Hohenossig. If the assumption was correct, then the main attack of the Army of Silesia would be by Langeron's left column over the Radefeld Heights, while his other column moved through Breitenfeld. In this case, Blücher would have to move to the north of Leipzig, to distract the French army group in order to support the attack that Schwarzenberg had already begun to the south. However, any effort to join Schwarzenberg in his battle to the south struck Blücher as highly dangerous, as it would expose his army to a flank attack as he marched past Leipzig to join Schwarzenburg.

Blücher considered his orders between 9:00 and 10:00 a.m., and finally issued the following orders: "The infantry shall begin its march: Langeron's Corps shall attack Freiroda, then Radefeld. Von Sacken's Corps shall follow this attack as a reserve. Von Yorck's Corps shall march against Leipzig, turn to the left by Lützschena to attack Lindenthal. The infantry of von Yorck's advanced guard shall remain on the road to Leipzig. When GL Count St.-Priest arrives, he shall follow Langeron's Corps. GdK Blücher shall remain on the heights between Lützschena and Radefeld."

The mistaken assumption over the French intentions also had consequences, among which was the decision for the Crown Prince of Sweden to attack Delitzsch, which was in a totally inappropriate direction. However, the decision was made, and verbal orders were sent to the Army of the North, which stood by Syblitz.[2]

Ney's Dilemma

On the French side, Ney had given his command orders, which considered neither the situation of his troops nor the known actions of the allies. Napoleon had indicated to Ney that he presumed that the bulk of the Army of Silesia and the Army of the North were on the Saale, but Ney was convinced that they were much closer, and stood on the left bank of the rivers between Halle and Merseburg. Also, the Emperor had not instructed him to take positions by Leipzig. As a result, when Ney saw the situation around Eutritzsch and Reudnitz, he abandoned his earlier ideas and resolved to move to a new position by Lindenthal. Once there he again changed his mind. Uncertainty caused Ney to abandon or surrender without a fight, one strong position after another, slowly falling back closer to Leipzig until he arrived at his final positions just to the north of Leipzig.

Ney's best chance to determine the allied moves was lost by not ordering Krukowiecki's 18th Polish Light Cavalry Brigade to probe the allied lines. This type of reconnaissance was something that the Poles performed very well. Krukowiecki, standing in Stahmeln, should have sent scouting parties against Halle and Zörbig, as well as contacting and joining with Arrighi's III Cavalry Corps. Of less importance was the reconnaissance towards Podelwitz and Eilenburg executed by Fournier's 6th Light Cavalry Division. Defrance's 4th Heavy Cavalry Division was to remain in Mockau, as well as reconnoiter and watch the Parthe passages from Schönefeld to Taucha. All in all, though the French lacked the cavalry forces they had in past years, Ney failed to use what he did have to help him make decisions that would have a critical impact on future events. As a result, the III Corps (Souham) was, as Napoleon had ordered, occupying the position by Lindenthal, while Bertrand's IV Corps stood by Eutritzsch as a reserve.[3]

Ney must have known that the relief of Marmont's VI Corps had not been completed, but he committed a major error. Souham did not arrive at the Mockau heights until shortly before noon, with the 8th and 11th Divisions. The 9th Division was far behind. Dombrowski's 28th (Polish) Division did not reach Wiederitzsch until 3:00 p.m.

In addition, Ney must have known of the lack of major allied forces in the proximity, and yet he accepted the position of the III Corps without making provision for its more useful employment.

Marmont's Actions

Marmont (VI Corps) was of the opinion that he faced a considerable allied force, and had reported the considerable line of allied bivouac fires around Schkeuditz. Camp fires at night are a common ruse de guerre and in the morning these fires were found to be the work of only 1,500 allied soldiers.

Despite that, Marmont stood under the impression that he faced a major allied threat. About 8:00 a.m., an order arrived from Napoleon to begin the march to the south and to join the battle at Wachau. Marmont vacillated, uncertain if the Emperor was not in error. Again he saw only cavalry to his front, but feared more. Marmont sought an escape and ordered one of his aides to go to Napoleon with a request for new orders. To the south, the sound of cannonfire grew in intensity, yet before Marmont's front there was still no infantry. No battle occurred by Lindenthal, but by the time Marmont realized his error, the decision on the battlefield by Wachau was made. The lack of the VI Corps caused victory to slip from Napoleon's hands. Marmont bore a heavy responsibility for the failure.

Finally, sometime around 10:00 a.m., Marmont made the decision, to permit his reserves, then standing by Breitenfeld and Lindenthal, to march to the south to join the battle around Wachau.[4] Marmont immediately informed Napoleon of this order only to learn that eight allied battalions were observed advancing on the road from Halle, and three more were advancing on the road from Landsberg. According to all estimates, Marmont faced an attack of more than 15,000 men. Marmont held fast to his decision to send troops to the south, assuming that the remaining forces would suffice for the pending battle. In addition, the III Corps was en route, in order to relieve the situation. Marmont also assumed that, in the worst case, the IV Corps, which stood by Eutritzsch, could be drawn on as a reserve.

This assumption was incorrect, for at the same time Ney received Arrighi's call for assistance and sent Bertrand (IV Corps) the order to march towards Lindenthal. The march of this column crossed the path of the VI Corps, compelling Marmont to remain in the region by Gohlis longer than he desired. In the meantime reports arrived of the advance of a strong allied column against Radefeld, and another on the road from Halle.

Marmont found himself in difficult situation. It was too late to revise his position. He needed a reinforcement of at least 10,000 men to defend against a turning movement around his left wing. The IV Corps departed, but the III Corps was not to be seen. Marmont found himself committed to a battle. The options were limited to that, or opening the way for the allies to take Leipzig, strike Napoleon's rear, or strike the rear of the defenders of Lindenau. Marmont did not have the time in which to carefully consider where to engage the allies. His choices for the site of his battle had been severely limited by his earlier decisions. The first sounds of the pending battle were already being heard by Radefeld and by Stahmeln, which were on the approaches to Leipzig, and filled with troops and vehicles of the IV Corps. Only through the fortunate misdirection of the attack columns of the Army of Silesia, was enough time gained for Marmont to draw his forces behind the Parthe River, form a battle line, and to recall the forces sent south to join Napoleon.[5]

Marmont, however, faced the very real danger that his corps would struck by the allies, before it would have a free passage to its chosen battle positions. He resolved to move his corps from the Eutritzsch plateau and ordered the advanced troops to retreat.

Marmont chose to await the development of events in his position. Until the allies arrived, the VI Corps would act as he saw fit. If faced by superior forces, he could take a position behind the Rietzschke on the Pfaffendorf plateau, or withdraw behind the Parthe. There was, however, another consideration. The VI Corps was the force by which Napoleon had sought to gain the main decision on 16 October. A gamble had to be made if victory was to be achieved. In view of the allied strength the only hopes Marmont might hold for a victory would be if he joined with the III Corps.[6] Marmont posed the question to Ney, asking Ney if he would support him in such an operation. Maréchal Ney assured Marmont that the III Corps would be ready to attack, if Marmont made the decision to engage the allies on the Eutritzsch plateau.

The Opening Shots

As Langeron and Yorck attacked, they found only weak advanced troops before them. These French forces already had the order to withdraw if threatened. The troops, which stood by Radefeld, Freiroda, and Hayna, consisted of Normann's 25th Light Cavalry Brigade, some light infantry, and the battery from Coëhorn's Brigade. Langeron's troops advanced, but after a few cannon shots, coupled with a flanking movement by GM Emanuel's Russian cavalry, the French and Württembergers withdrew to the south.[7]

Normann joined with the detachment, which had occupied the Tannenwald and Lindenthal, and engaged the Prussian cavalry, to allow the infantry an unhindered withdrawal to the French main lines. When the Prussian artillery opened fire, Normann moved to cover the left wing of the advanced troops, while the three earthworks between Lindenthal and Wahren fired their guns on the advancing Prussians. When the French saw their position compromised, they began to withdraw again.

Those detachments moving towards Stahmeln encountered the main body of Yorck's advanced guard, under Major von Hiller, but they established themselves in Wahren with little trouble.

With great quickness, Blücher perceived that his two corps had advanced without resistance into the French positions, but also that the French were not withdrawing to the main position to the west. They moved unmistakably towards the south and Blücher realized that the Army of Silesia had wasted half of the short October day striking at empty air.[8]

The Battle Around Möckern

During the morning of 16 October, as the French voluntary withdrawal before Langeron became noticeable to Blücher, he disclosed the intent of his attack dispositions. Blücher issued the following orders.

> On 16 October, at 6:00 a.m., the reserve cavalry of the three corps and the light artillery shall deploy as follows. The reserve cavalry of Yorck's Corps shall be on the grand route to Leipzig until it reaches the cavalry of the advanced guard, which shall move in the head of the column and advance on Leipzig.
>
> The reserve cavalry of Langeron's Corps shall march by Radefeld and Lindenthal and the cavalry of the advanced guard shall lead the column.
>
> Prior to the departure of this cavalry it is necessary that reports be received indicating the positions of the enemy in Düben and if they occupy Dölitz.
>
> The reserve cavalry and the advanced guard, as well as the light artillery of Sacken's Corps, following the cavalry of Yorck's Corps, shall move via Schkeuditz towards Leipzig. I shall be at the head of this cavalry.
>
> If it should be that the enemy holds no position above Parthe, Yorck's reserve cavalry shall form itself between Möckern and Gohlis, the reserve cavalry of Langeron's Corps shall form below Wiederitsch, and the advance guard shall march forward to find the enemy. I shall be advised of their position, be it behind Parthe or be it on the road to Düben.
>
> The infantry shall prepare breakfast in the very early morning and be ready to depart at 10:00 a.m. An ordnance officer (orderly) of each corps shall follow me to transmit orders to the commanders of each respective corps.

Orders for the Russian corps were sent to them as they stood on the heights by Lützschena. They were to follow the French, with the main body through the Tannenwald to Lindenthal. Previously he had sent the same orders to GM Emanuel, who commanded the cavalry of the advanced guard, on the condition that if he found French troops by Hohenossig and if they appeared to be marching from Düben to Leipzig, he too was to pursue them. Sacken's Corps had been held in Radefeld as a reserve to ensure no threat existed in the direction of Hohenossig. Upon the receipt of the report that Klein- and Gross-Wiederitzsch were occupied by the French and that French columns were moving from Düben and Eilenburg towards Leipzig, Langeron's Corps received instructions to send its cavalry and the horse artillery to stop this force and use its infantry to attack Düben and Eilenburg. Sacken's cavalry, which was following its previous orders to follow Yorck's Army Corps, received no new orders.

The village of Möckern, by Wagner.

About 8:00 a.m., Blücher arrived on the heights by Lützschena and learned that the French occupied Lindenthal with 1,200 cavalry and infantry, but that the precise French strength and dispositions were unknown because a forest masked their view.[9]

The lead elements of Yorck's advanced guard, under the command of Major von Klüx, had, after occupying Wahren, moved on the village of Möckern, in order to reconnoiter it. It was led by a combined detachment formed of a platoon of the East Prussian Jäger Battalion in the lead, followed the skirmishers drawn from two line companies, and then by the Fus/2nd East Prussian Infantry Regiment. At a distance of 300 paces behind them, marched three more East Prussian Jäger platoons and Major Wedel's 4/15th Silesian Landwehr Regiment. This group completed the link of the Army of Silesia to the Austrians, when it came into contact with the Austrian Jäger Battalion #2.[10]

The portion of the advanced guard, under the command of Major von Hiller, advanced behind von Klüx's screen, in battalion columns at a slow pace down both sides of the Leipzig road. It was not much after 1:00 p.m., when Major von Klüx encountered the weak defense of the French detachment abandoning Wahren and withdrawing towards Möckern.

The Prussian advanced guard reported to Blücher that the French had occupied the village of Möckern, on the main road to Leipzig, with infantry for several days. They also reported that every time the allies had approached the village, the French had withdrawn to Gohlis. Blücher then decided to push Langeron's cavalry forward, but Langeron reported that he could not advance, because the village of Radefeld was occupied by French infantry, cavalry, and artillery.

Between the Saale and the arc of the Mulde River, between Jessnitz and Wurzen was situated the Breitenfeld plain, where on 17 September 1631, Gustavus Adolphus defeated Tilly. This plain offered several advantages to the defender, as on the right stood the Loder River and the defiles of Bitterfeld and Dölitz. To cover the other flank stood the Parthe stream and the Taucha defile. The

Blücher at Möckern, 16 October, by Zimmer.

village of Radefeld dominated the entire plain. One could see from that village, at a great distance, the clock towers of the villages as far as Wittenberg. This height extended to the right as far as Parthe, where a small stream flowed through the fields, past Möckern and on to the Elster. This stream was crossed by three roads, the road to Eutritzsch, Lindenthal, and Möckern.

The French had occupied the terrain which dominated Radefeld, and abandoned to the Army of Silesia the road between Leipzig and Lützschena, as well as the heights running towards Lindenthal. Any significant allied movement in that direction, however, would be stopped by the French in Radefeld. GdK Blücher concluded that the principal French forces occupied this plain and would accept battle there.[11]

After all considerations, it was determined that the terrain around Radefeld was most important to the allies and that they should occupy it before accepting a general battle with the French.

The French

Marmont had drawn the VI Corps into a position such that Friederichs' 22nd Division stood on the right wing before Eutritzsch and on the Rietzschke stream. The left wing, Lagrange's 21st Division, stood on the slope of the Leipzig-Halle Road, with Möckern before its front. Between these two divisions stood Compans' 20th Division. The only reserve was Lorge's 5th Light Cavalry Division and Normann's small cavalry brigade.[12] The terrain over which the allies were to advance had little cover and favored the effect of the artillery, giving Marmont some relief. The right found slight support on the Rietzschke, but was counting on the eventual support of the III Corps. Furthermore, it was covered with marshy pastures along the Elster, which would slow any effort by the Army of Silesia to execute a flanking maneuver to advance towards Leipzig and a union with the Army of Bohemia.

It was straight at this sensitive place the allies would launch their first attack. Marmont immediately decided that the way to break the flanking movement was to hold Möckern. The skill of his troops in a village fight and the fact that village leaned on the swampy low lands of the Elster, induced the marshal to hold the village. He saw Möckern as a magnet for the allied forces, as well as the focal point of the coming battle.

Aside from taking and holding the village, Marmont realized that he would have to hold the heights from Möckern to the Gross-Wiederitzsch road, which were already in allied hands. He knew that a hot battle would soon develop.

Marmont sent the 2nd Marine Regiment, drawn from Buquet's Brigade, with some guns to assist in the defense of Möckern. In the first attack the troops of Major von Klüx were thrown out of the village, whereupon the French with accustomed skill, immediately set about preparing their defensive positions in the village.

Möckern stood on the Halle-Leipzig Road and oriented with its narrow side turned northwest, towards the allies. Between Wahren, Möckern, and Gohlis on the one hand, and Lindenthal, Wiederitzsch, and Eutritzsch on the other ran a series of gentle heights. To the south, a three-to-five-meter, steeply sloped terrace or dike, ran along the Elster from Wahren to Gohlis. This terrace overlooked Möckern, and created a flat low spot, which could not be seen from the north part of the village, when looking to the southern part of the village.[13]

Towards Wahren stood a manor house, with its solidly-built out buildings, and surrounded with gardens and a brewery. These gardens were numerous, small, and walled. Their defense would be easy. Individual buildings stood with their surrounding walls flush on the Elster, so that along the waterside only a single individual could advance. The approaches from the streets in the village were obstructed, behind the first village crossroad, such that the terrain laying before them could be swept with fire. The French quickly put a few guns in these positions, to ensure holding them as long as possible. Not far from the manor house there stood a wooden bridge over the Elster. The importance of this position was recognized and the houses around the market and gardens were manned, to bring it under fire if necessary. Also in the middle and southern portion of the village, the French positioned themselves to defend the village. In the middle of Möckern, on the crossroads of the road leading to the Elster bridge, two cannon were positioned in a massive stone tower. Here they would expose the attacking allies to flanking fire. It was especially advantageous for the French, that the allies advance along the road running from Gohlis towards Möckern, as the ridge north of the village was not occupied. As defense against a turning movement in the pastures on the other side of the Elster, the French deployed a large swarm of skirmishers and partly demolished the wooden bridge over the Elster.[14]

The Two Armies

The relationship of the two opposing armies were, in the first encounter, very favorable to the Army of Silesia. The Army of Silesia, not including St.-Priest's Corps which was detached, consisted of 84 battalions, 94 squadrons, 12 Cossack regiments, and 274 guns, or about 30,000 men, 8,000 cavalry, and 2,500 Cossacks. Blücher could, with the arrival of St.-Priest, count on having a total force of 105 battalions, 108 squadrons, 15 Cossack regiments, and 310 guns, or, in round figures, 37,000 infantry, 9,300 cavalry, and 3,200 Cossacks.

	Infantry	Cavalry	Cossack	
	Battalions	Squadrons	Regiments	Guns
Yorck's Corps	32¾	42	–	104
Sacken's Corps	19	28	10	60
Langeron's Corps	33	24	2	110
St.-Priest's Corps	20	14	3	36
Total	*104¾*	*108*	*15*	*310*

Facing Blücher was the French VI Corps, Lorge's 5th Light Cavalry Division, Fournier's 6th Light Cavalry Division, and Defrance's 4th Heavy Cavalry Division. At 11:30 a.m., the French forces were increased by the arrival of Brayer's 8th Division and Ricard's 11th Division, from the III Corps, on the heights by Mockau.

Ney again modified the details of the support the III Corps would render Maréchal Marmont, as a result of the alarming news from the defenders of Lindenau. Ney detached Charrière's Brigade, 11th Division, to support Bertrand, and sent the other half of the troops of GD Ricard to a position nearer Leipzig, so they could be deployed as reinforcements to any point of need.

At 1:00 p.m., an order arrived from Napoleon to send reinforcements to the main army around Wachau. Since Ney's forces had yet to see action, Napoleon's orders were comprehensible.

Apparently an aide-de-camp arrived by error at Souham's headquarters, instead of those of Marmont, and so enthusiastically demanded the dispatch of troops, that Souham dispatched those troops at hand, further exacerbating the situation on the northern front.[15]

The only reserve immediately available to Marmont's VI Corps was Dombrowski's 27th (Polish) Division, though Delmas' 9th Division was marching towards the battlefield. However, Delmas only arrived in Düben around 4:00 a.m.. He had been unable to move with any more rapidity, by his obligation to guard the artillery parks and train.

The French forces standing between Möckern and Mockau stood at 50 infantry battalions, 34 squadrons, and 109 guns, with about 19,500 infantry and 4,800 cavalry. With the arrival of Delmas' 9th Division this would rise to 63 battalions, 34 squadrons, and 121 guns, or 25,000 infantry and 4,800 cavalry.

	Infantry		Cavalry		
	Bns	Men	Sqns	Men	Guns
VI Corps	42	18,369	8	935	82
Dombrowski's 27th Division	8	1,380	–	–	9
Delmas' 9th Division	13	4,800	–	–	12
Fournier's 6th Lt. Cavalry Division	–	–	6	1,137	6
Defrance's 4th Hv. Cavalry Division	–	–	10	1,442	6
Lorge's 5th Lt. Cavalry Division	–	–	10	1,369	6
Total	*63*	*24,549*	*34*	*4,883*	*121*

The Army of Silesia was, as a result, about one-third stronger in infantry, and had three times more cavalry and guns than the French forces opposing them. Not only were the numbers unfavorable to the French, but they lacked the unity of command which the allies had. Blücher was the sole commander of the Army of Silesia and was in no way hindered in his freedom of action by outside influences. On the French side, Ney commanded in name only. In fact, Marmont was to command the French side in the battle, yet the French chain of command did not authorize him to give orders to GD Dombrowski, Fournier, Defrance, and Delmas. Napoleon had limited him to the command of only the VI Corps.

The consideration of all the facts relating to the battle by Möckern, led inevitably to the conclusion that Blücher was in a superior position to Marmont in every category. The attack, to which the Army of Silesia committed itself at 1:00 p.m., bespoke of victory, before the first shot was fired. However, despite the many factors stacked against the French, the French officers and men showed a bravery and tenacity in the following battle, that was to cause victory to hang by a hair throughout its course.[16]

The Assault Begins

Langeron's Corps marched against the enemy and chased them from Freiroda and Radefeld, and then moved down the main road from Landsberg to Leipzig. The French had deployed a battery near the Lindenthal woods,[17] but the superior allied artillery fire obliged it to withdraw.

Langeron's Corps marched via Breitenfeld towards Gross-Wiederitzsch, and forced the French to abandon the Lindenthal Woods. They withdrew into the village of Lindenthal. Blücher, seeing that the French did not make any serious attempt to hold Lindenthal, ordered Langeron to pursue them with all his forces through the forest, and he ordered Sacken to continue to occupy the heights of Radefeld, with the infantry of his corps, while his cavalry joined Yorck.

Fearing a force of French might appear around Podelwitz and attempt to turn the left wing of the Army of Silesia, Blücher ordered Sacken to contain any such move, and to send a reconnaissance force forward to learn what was happening around Hohenossig and Podelwitz.[18]

As Langeron's Corps advanced through Breitenfeld, the French appeared from the direction of Leipzig, and the villages of Gross- and Klein-Wiederitzsch were occupied by a large number of French infantry. Langeron ordered his cavalry and light infantry to move to contain these detachments, as well as to attack them with his infantry in the villages of Gross- and Klein-Wiederitzsch. By an incredible misunderstanding, Sacken's cavalry followed the left wing, instead of the right wing and stood with its left on Lindenthal, and the stream which ran to Wiederitzsch.

The advanced guard of the Prussian 1st Corps, commanded by Oberst von Katzeler, attacked the French advanced posts before Lindenthal along the edge of the woods. A detachment of cavalry stood before Lindenthal and a second stood to the left. Oberst von Katzeler ordered the East Prussian National Cavalry Regiment to strike them, while two squadrons of the 2nd Leib Hussars and Brandenburg Uhlan Regiment supported them.

Major Graf Lehndorf advanced the 1/, Jäger/East Prussian National Cavalry Regiment. The remaining three squadrons stood back as reserves. The Jägers moved against the left French cavalry force, while the main French force waited for the attack. Suddenly, the French cavalry withdrew, revealing a mass of infantry, which opened fire and threw the East Prussians back in disorder.

It was 1:00 p.m. The French brought their artillery forward and began to fire on both the Prussian and Russian columns. Marmont placed his 24 guns on the highest point of ground in his line. Oberst von Katzeler brought forward Horse Battery #2. The French responded to its deployment by moving 12 12-pdrs to the right of Möckern. The village of Möckern was garrisoned by the 2nd Marine Regiment.[19] Oberst von Katzeler followed with his cavalry, but Horse Battery #2 suffered two dismounted guns.[20]

In order to cover the right wing of the cavalry, Major von Hiller sent the Fus/2nd East Prussian Regiment forward against the villages of Stahmeln and Wahren. Both villages were taken and occupied. At the same time, on the far side of the Elster, a detachment of the Austrian Jäger

Battalion #2 appeared and began to fire in support of the Prussians. This battalion was part of Liechtenstein's 1st Light Division, which was engaged around Lindenau.[21]

After the exchange of a few artillery rounds, the French abandoned the village and the woods, withdrawing to the heights between Lindenthal and Wahren, where they had raised a number of earthworks. A short, vigorous cannonade caused the French to abandon this position. The French then fell back to a position between Eutritzsch and Möckern, such that Möckern covered the rear of their left wing. At the same time, Major von Hiller advanced down the main road from Lutzschena as far as Wahren, with eight battalions of the advanced guard, and after a light skirmish, the French were pushed from behind the village and back to Möckern. The French had already occupied Möckern with a large force of infantry, and used it to serve as a *point d'appui*[22] for their left wing. Behind Möckern, there were even more columns of French infantry, formed in dense columns ready to act against any important point.

In Blücher's command, the situation was very unclear. Hiller had announced that masses of infantry and artillery were visible on the heights by Möckern, so Blücher began to fear that a French attack aimed at his flank was advancing from Düben, aimed at turning his flank. He contented himself with the understanding that Hiller was advancing against Leipzig, and directed him "to strike the French." This vague order arrived as Hiller had decided to attack Möckern.

Not looking after events by Möckern, Blücher sent an order to the 1st Corps giving GL Yorck a completely free hand in the use of his force. Blücher appears to have been more concerned about the actions elsewhere, and totally neglected the decisive attack against Möckern. As a result, the Prussian 1st Corps, became an independent battle group, which according to the day's reports, consisted of 21,429 men. Various chance occurrences, acting together, had drawn Yorck's Corps away from the main body of the Army of Silesia, and made him dangerously isolated.

Yorck had quickly realized his situation and his corps, whose first line had just pushed forward into the abandoned French positions by Lindenthal, strove to turn its front to the southeast. The first line was supposed to make a pivot to the right, with the right wing of Horn's 7th Brigade forming the pivot point. Further forward movement was not to occur until Langeron's left wing was even with Yorck's Corps. Mecklenburg's 2nd Brigade had followed on the left side of the advanced guard. It was to hold the right wing of the 7th Brigade in sight. Steinmetz's 1st Brigade had to march in parallel and to retain contact, while the 2nd Brigade, acting as the reserve, was to follow. The reserve artillery was ordered to the left wing by Lindenthal, where part of it deployed, and began firing against the French artillery facing Yorck.[23]

This deployment of the Prussian 1st Army Corps, placing the reserves behind the right wing, indicates that Yorck had decided to make the decisive push with his right wing, even before he had an idea of Marmont's battle plan. It also indicates that Yorck recognized his most important task was that of marching along the shortest line possible to Leipzig. He subordinated all other considerations to this goal. Furthermore, he knew that on the left wing of the Army of Silesia stood the corps of Langeron, Sacken, and St.-Priest. He also knew that Blücher, who stood in the center of the army's line, was consequently in the position where he could support whichever side required it.

The army command risked nothing in parting with its reserve, so long as its left flank was completely untouched by French forces. It is odd, however, that Blücher had such great interest in reconnoitering in this direction, and yet he gave no orders to his Russian cavalry to take it under observation. Instead of moving against Hohenossig, GM Emanuel remained with the advanced guard, participated in the battle and fought with the French cavalry that it had pursued to Eutritzsch.[24]

Yorck Advances

Yorck's infantry marched down the main road between Schkeuditz and Leipzig. It swung off the road before the Lützschena tile works, and moving to the left, pushed towards Lindenthal. The 7th and 8th Brigades organized themselves to attack Lindenthal, while the 1st and 2nd Brigades were charged with supporting the attack. The cavalry of Katzeler's advanced guard withdrew behind the infantry, and assumed a position on the right wing of the reserve cavalry. Both formed in two lines.[25]

The Prussian infantry formed itself in battalion columns. In the first line of the 7th Brigade stood the 1/15th Silesian Landwehr, two battalions of the 4th Silesian Landwehr Regiment, and the Thuringian Battalion.[26] The Leib Regiment and 2/15th Silesian Landwehr Regiment formed the second line.

The first line of the 8th Brigade was formed by the 2/, Fus/Brandenburg Regiment and the 3/12th Reserve Regiment. The second line was formed by the 1/12th Reserve Regiment and the 4/14th Silesian Landwehr Regiment. Two batteries of 12-pdrs from the reserve followed the 8th Brigade. The Prussians had also stripped out the howitzers from the line batteries and organized them into an *ad hoc* battery. This *ad hoc* battery worked with Battery #1. The 6-pdr Foot Battery #3, from the 7th Brigade, was posted to the right of the brigade and the eight squadrons of the 1st Neumärk and 10th Silesian Landwehr Regiments covered it.

As the Prussians advanced, their movement to the right opened a large gap between the 1st Corps and Langeron's Corps, which was by Wiederitzsch. Seeing this hole in his lines, Blücher ordered forward Sacken's reserve cavalry under GL Vassil'shikov. He ordered the Russian 8th Corps, under St.-Priest, to move over the stream that ran from Lindenthal and Wiederitzsch. From there, St.-Priest was to advance down the main road from Lindenthal to Leipzig, and attack the French between Eutritzsch and the Elster with a heavy artillery barrage. The French forces there were estimated at 25,000 men and 80 guns.[27]

Yorck and an episode of the Battle of Möckern, by Knötel.

Blücher also had no success with his order to Sacken's cavalry. Apparently it was not to be found in its assigned location. Instead, they had apparently trotted across the entire front of Langeron's Corps and placed themselves on the left wing, where they joined Langeron's cavalry, nominally to ward off the feared flank attack. It would appear that Blücher's concern of an attack from the flank, had caused him expend most of his cavalry in this manner and hold back half of his army in reserve, rather than rolling forward and over Marmont's solitary corps.[28]

The confusion over the orders given to the cavalry could lead to the assumption the broad orders given by Blücher were either misinterpreted or altered by some individual on the staff, who was of a different opinion as to the proper use of the cavalry.

Strange to say, it is not entirely clear where Blücher was at this time. Blücher first appeared on the heights by Lindenthal, when the battle was in an advanced stage. Müffling reported, "The general in chief did not want to leave Radefeld sooner, than until he was certain that he had no reason to worry for his left flank." Radefeld was about seven kilometers distant from the battle line, which must explain the reason why Blücher had no influence on the course of Langeron's battle, and why he was not there to intervene when his orders were misunderstood. As a result the battle went on without the intervention of two corps because of the lack of higher guidance.

On the basis of his orders, von Yorck deployed the 8th Brigade (Hünerbein) after they had arrived at Lindenthal with their front facing Leipzig, and its right wing on the village touching the village. The 7th Brigade deployed such that its right wing lay behind Lindenthal.

Through these movements a gaping hole was formed in the center of the Prussian 1st Corps, which Yorck, for the time being, filled with the Prussian reserve cavalry. Langeron's Corps was marching against Breitenfeld, so most of Yorck's infantry remained temporarily on the heights by Lindenthal in their starting position.[29]

Maréchal Marmont noted that the main allied attack was directed against his left wing and moved to the left in echelon by brigades. The 21st Division (Lagrange) was moved in and behind the village of Möckern. The 20th Division (Compans) stood in the middle and the 22nd Division (Friederichs) stood on his right flank. Normann's 25th Light Cavalry Brigade stood behind Möckern, and Lorge's 5th Light Cavalry Division stood to the rear on the main road.[30]

The Prussian 8th Brigade was ordered to take the village of Lindenthal and the nearby forest. The 7th Brigade followed the artillery. The Prussian artillery was slowly fed forward into the battle. First 12-pdr Battery #2 moved forward and took a position to the right of 12-pdr Battery #1 in the line. Further to the right came 6-pdr Foot Battery #1, from the 1st Brigade, which was later joined by 6-pdr Battery #3 from the 7th Brigade. On the left wing of the battery stood 6-pdr Battery #15 from the 8th Brigade and between it and the two 12-pdr batteries stood Horse Batteries #1 and #3. The howitzers from these batteries had been left to the rear.[31]

At 2:00 p.m., the 12-pdr Battery #1, which was standing before the village entrance, was firing at a 20 gun French battery at a distance of 1,500 to 1,600 paces. The French round shot went, for the most part, ineffectually over the heads of the Prussians. Slowly, as the other batteries moved into position, they joined 12-pdr Battery #1 in its fire on the French gunners.

During the ensuing cannonade Hiller's advanced guard moved down the main road from Schkeuditz towards Leipzig. Major von Klüx led the attack on Möckern. According to the standing tactical doctrine of the Prussian army, any infantry attack on an enemy occupied village should be preceded by an artillery preparation. Despite that, Hiller gave his *vorhut*[32] the orders to take Möckern without careful artillery preparation.

A few Züge of Jägers and skirmishers, supported by the Fus/2nd East Prussian Infantry Regiment, made the first attack. They were followed by the three Jäger companies of the 4/15th Silesian Landwehr Regiment and the East Prussian Jägers, which were supported by the Leib-Grenadier-Battalion. The remaining five battalions of the advanced guard remained in reserve. The advance was covered by 6-pdr Battery #12.

The battle for the village became violent and bloody. The advancing skirmishers were received by heavy French fire. Major von Hiller ordered a general attack by the two formed battalions and the Jägers. One Jäger company moved to the right against the river, while the French moved over the bridge from the far bank to take the attack in the flank. The French stood behind the loopholed walls of the houses and gardens, making the attempt to capture the village on the first assault a bloody affair.

Langeron's Attack

At the same time this occurred beyond Yorck's left wing, Langeron's Corps passed through Breitenfeld. It advanced against Wiederitzsch in two columns. On the right marched Kapzevich's 10th Corps and behind him came Olsoviev's 9th Corps. To the left of the advanced guard Rudsevich, advanced the cavalry brigade of GM Emanuel, which was reinforced by the Dorpat and Lithuanian Infantry Regiments. On the left wing Korff's reserve cavalry followed in echelons.

The only French troops in Wiederitzsch were cavalry detachments from Fournier's 6th Light Cavalry Division, but at 3:00 p.m., four of Dombrowski's battalions moved into the village and established themselves in preparation for a defense of the village.[33] The Poles consisted of about 3,800 men from Zoltowski's Infantry Brigade, Krukowiecki's 18th Light Cavalry Brigade, and an artillery battery. Dombrowski also commanded Fournier's 6th Light Cavalry Division[34] and Defrance's 4th Heavy Cavalry Division.[35] The total strength of these two cavalry divisions was about 2,500 men and 12 guns.

The withdrawing screen of French and Poles soon reorganized themselves, behind the main body of Dombrowski's 27th (Polish) Division, which moved up. Dombrowski deployed his forces so that his infantry occupied both Klein- and Gross-Wiederitzsch. Twelve Polish and French cavalry squadrons were deployed on the hillocks near Plösen and Mockau facing Gross-Wiederitzsch. Krukowiecki's cavalry stood behind them as a reserve and the French 5/13th Cuirassiers stood near Seehausen.

Langeron's response was one of timidity, and covered over with gross exaggerations of the threat posed by the advancing Poles. In order to cloak the weakness of his battle leadership, he relates in his memoirs, that he had believed Napoleon himself was leading the advancing French columns. Other eyewitnesses have stated that the only forces advancing from Leipzig and the Parthe were Dombrowski's troops. Also the casualty list of the two French divisions of the III Corps, which before their march to the southern Leipzig front, had spent a long time stationary in the region between Gohlis and Eutritzsch, give no indication that any portion of their forces engaged any part of the Army of Silesia this day.

The management of the battle by Langeron was completely defective. He was quite disoriented as to the flow of the battle, and it would appear that his own batteries fired on 6-pdr Foot Battery #3 of the Prussian 7th Brigade for a while.[36]

The Prussians Strike Möckern Again

It was 3:00 p.m., when the right wing of Yorck's Corps was ordered to attack Möckern. This was supported by the Prussian artillery, which advanced in order to close to canister range. As the counter battery fight progressed, 6-pdr Foot Battery #15 moved around to the left flank of the French battery, taking it in enfilade and forcing it to withdraw.

The first attack of the *vorhut* of Hiller's advanced guard on Möckern had been unsuccessful, and the 1st Leib-Grenadier Battalion under Major Carlowitz was sent forward. Hiller resolved to send forward the remaining five battalions to attack the village. Despite the fact that the corps reserve was near enough to the battle line to reinforce the advanced guard, Yorck pulled his forces to the rear. His waiting posture was not only tactically justified, but entirely within the line of the standing general battle directions provided to the Prussian army before beginning of the fall campaign. These directions made it the duty of every commander to be as economical as possible with the troops under his command.

The first attack of the Prussian infantry succeeded solely in the front. The turning effort along the Elster failed. The narrow passage between the village and the river prevented the movement and the French detachments on the left bank of the Elster shot the advancing Prussians in the flank. No Prussian troops were sent against the left bank of the Elster.[37] Then a French column advanced from behind the village and Hiller found his forces struck by musketry and canister from all quarters. He was obliged to withdraw.[38]

At 3:00 p.m., Hiller, observing the disastrous effect of French artillery on his forces, ordered the 1/Brandenburg Infantry Regiment to advance against a French battery pushed forward to the east of the Möckern. At the same time the rallied battalions of the *vorhut*, supported by those of the main body of the advanced guard, renewed their assault against the French in Möckern. Prince K. von Mecklenburg put the Fus/1st East Prussian Regiment and the combined battalion of the 2nd East Prussian Regiment in the first line and 1/, 2/1st East Prussian Regiment in the second. The 3/6th Silesian Landwehr Regiment was deployed as skirmishers. And as the 2nd Brigade closed on Möckern, Major Hiller sent forward yet another attack.

The landwehr battalions of von Rekowsky (3/13th Silesian Landwehr) and von Thiele (2/14th Silesian Landwehr), the 1/Brandenburg, and the 2/12th Reserve Regiments, plus the detached skirmishers of the West Prussian Grenadier Battalion, were sent against the left of the village to make a bayonet attack. They drove into the village and drove back a French counterattack, but once again they were taken by heavy canister fire which disordered them.[39]

This push was successful, and half of the village was again taken. However, they were suddenly taken under fire on their right flank. A French detachment had used a narrow path and swam the Elster, to take up a position on the flank of the Prussian battalions. They were then able to inflict heavy losses on the Prussians with the resulting crossfire. All of the gains of the attack were surrendered, and the Prussians were forced to fight their way to the western edge of the village with bayonets and musket butts.[40]

In response, Marmont had moved a number of battalions from Lagrange's 21st Division, including the 37th Légère and 4th Marine Infantry,[41] supported by a 12-pdr battery, to a hill over-looking the attack. Mecklenburg advanced under the fire of this battery, taking heavy casualties. He closed to within 300 paces of it before his attack stalled. Oberstleutnant von Lobenthal took over when Mecklenburg was wounded.

A battalion of the 4th Marine Infantry counterattacked and crossed bayonets with Fus/1st East Prussian Regiment. The Prussians were thrown back. The 1/1st East Prussian Regiment was drawn forward from the second line and struck the marines, driving them back in their turn. The 2/1st East Prussian Regiment then advanced against the 12-pdr battery, while the 1/1st East Prussian Regiment captured two guns.

The French counterattacked with several more battalions. The 2/1st East Prussians found themselves facing three French battalions. Two French battalions struck it in the flank and the Prussians were driven back.

As the 2/1st East Prussian Regiment was falling back, the 1st Brigade began its attack. The two 12-pdr batteries and 6-pdr Battery #1 supported this attack with their fire. On the left wing of the artillery line stood five guns of 6-pdr Battery #15, the sixth gun of this battery had already been dismounted, then six guns of 6-pdr Battery #3 and to the right the two remaining guns of 6-pdr Battery #1.

The 1st Brigade was formed such that the 1/, 2/, 4/13th Silesian Landwehr Regiment stood in the first line. The 1/, 3/, 4/5th Silesian Landwehr Regiment stood in the second line. To the rear, as a reserve, was the Silesian Grenadier Battalion.[42]

Marmont could, from the heights occupied by his corps, observe the forward march of Yorck's Corps. He watched as his troops repelled the attack on Möckern with renewed stubbornness. He observed the continued pressure by the allied columns against Wiederitzsch and their temporary repulse. The pressure was such that he anxiously awaited the arrival of the French III Corps (Souham).

Marmont waited for the right moment to arrive in order to launch his own attack, to forestall the evacuation of Möckern because the Prussians had occupied the neighboring heights. When the time arrived, the French counterattack was by a portion of Lagrange's 21st Division. They struck the right wing of the Prussians standing outside Möckern, on the heights running to the east of Möckern. Along the entire line the French artillery also advanced, and soon 80 French guns were firing on the Prussians.

The brigades of each division swung half-left, so that they now faced front to Möckern and were formed to the right *en échelon*.

Compans' 20th Division served as a reserve and remained somewhat to the rear. Friederichs' 22nd Division closed up behind the French artillery position.

Yorck noticed that the French had not only reinforced their left wing, but also the troops holding Möckern. He realized Marmont's intentions. He perceived that Marmont intended to push forward against his right wing, and drive down the Leipzig Road against Lindenthal and Radefeld in order to hold Möckern. Yorck recognized the importance of snatching Möckern away from the French in order to thwart Marmont's battle plan.[43] An advance of his own left wing was impossible as Langeron's Corps had not won enough room to secure his flank. The battalions of the advanced guard had suffered heavy losses. Major Hiller and six battalion commanders were wounded, the battlefield was covered with dead and wounded. French artillery had inflicted heavy losses and 6-pdr Foot Battery #12 nearly lost a howitzer to an attacking French detachment.

Nevertheless the few remaining officers succeeded in rallying the shattered portions of the advanced guard and led them forward again. Yorck perceived that a failure to take the village would bring the French forward, and the battle would be lost. Yorck ordered Mecklenburg's 2nd Brigade to attack the left flank in support of the attack on Möckern. The 1st Brigade was placed in reserve behind the 2nd Brigade. The 7th and 8th Brigades were ordered to hold their right forward when advancing, and to keep themselves tied to the right wing. Oberstleutnant Schmidt stood with two 12-pdr batteries, which were posted on a ridge, from which they could strike the French positions.[44] The 2nd Prussian Brigade lowered their bayonets and advanced against the French, supported by the fire of Oberstleutnant Schmidt's 12-pdr batteries.

The intervening terrain was devoid of cover and exposed the Prussians to the fire of the French cannon. The Fus/1st East Prussian Infantry Regiment struck to its right in an effort to drive back its assailants, but failed and was thrown back. The attack of the 1/1st East Prussian Infantry Regiment fared no better. It advanced from the rear to the support of its fusilier battalion. It was repulsed, losing all of its officers and three quarters of its manpower. The two battalions could no longer maintain their positions.

The left wing of the 2nd Brigade again advanced against the French, which appeared to be only weak infantry detachments. The 1/2nd East Prussian Infantry Regiment succeeded in finding cover from the French artillery. Once positioned, it began to fire on a French battery, inflicting losses on the gunners and equipment, successfully suppressing the fire of 12 guns and advancing into their vacated position.

However, fresh French troops advanced. A rolling fire began that forced the Prussians back with heavy casualties. The weakened remains of the 2nd Brigade were in bad shape. Their commander,

GM Prinz Karl von Mecklenburg, was seriously wounded, and the situation would have been critical, had not the 1st Brigade executed an opportune attack.[45]

As the battle hung indecisively, the 7th and 8th Brigades moved forward on the left wing. However, at this point, as in others, the French were ready and responded with heavy musketry. The French then renewed their attack into Möckern, and the position of the Prussians was becoming critical. Marmont led forward the 20th and 25th Provisional Regiments, but they were stopped. The 1st Marine Infantry and the 32nd Légère then advanced.[46] All the Prussian troops, the 1st Brigade excepted, were engaged. There was no alternative but to throw the 1st Brigade into the battle or to withdraw.

The Prussian advanced guard once again sought to push into Möckern, and by using small detachments, strove to take one house and farmstead after the other. These attacks were crowned with limited success, as the Prussians did not occupy more of the village, but they could not be pushed out either. They fought as much to hold on to what they had captured, as they did to seize those portions held by the French.

It was about 4:00 p.m., when the Prussian 1st Brigade received the order to attack. GL Yorck sent the 1st Brigade, under Oberst Steinmetz, forward, but at the same time sent a plea for support to Blücher. As GM Emanuel had been unable to find any French in Podelwitz or Hohenossig, nor on the road to Düben, Blücher ordered Sacken to move against Möckern. His 6,000 cavalry swarmed around Marmont's forces.

The attack of the 1st Brigade was supported by 6-pdr Foot Batteries #1 and #2, detached from the 2nd and 1st Brigades respectively. These batteries sought to suppress the French artillery fire. Oberst Steinmetz's troops advanced at the *sturmschritt*. Two battalions attacked into the village, the remainder attacked again in the wake of the unsuccessful attack of the 2nd Brigade. That attack was also unsuccessful.

The battalions of the advanced guard, so fatigued from their fight with the French, received a few moments' rest. The balance of the battle was reestablished, but it was to begin anew with renewed ardor. The battle became a fight for each house and wall, as the 1st Brigade continued to push forward.

The attack of the Brandenburg Hussar Regiment at Möckern, 16 October, by Knötel.

Oberst Steinmetz was wounded. Major Sohr, at the head of the Brandenburg Hussars, led his regiment against the French and disordered their leading ranks. The critical moment had arrived and he did not allow the French to reorganize their lines. The battle steadily increased in intensity and vehemence. Soon, in and around Möckern, hundreds of wounded streamed to the rear from the line of struggling battalions. The Prussian line was reaching a crisis situation.

Oberst von Katzeler rode to the left wing of the corps and directed the artillery commander, Oberstleutnant Schmidt, to devote the efforts of his forces to repel the attack on Möckern.

On the left wing of the Prussian 1st Corps, which stood before Lindenthal, the battle had become an artillery battle and both sides slowly bombarded each other. As the crisis of the battle for Möckern was reached the last reserve forces arrived. These were 12-pdr Foot Batteries #1 and #2, which were assigned to the corps artillery reserve. They were ordered to the heights on the right wing.[47]

The Attack on the Left

Count Langeron had advanced to the stream that ran before the village of Klein-Wiederitzsch. The Russian 10th Corps, under GL Kapzevich, stood on the right flank. The eight battalions of the advanced guard under GL Rudsevich stood on the left. The infantry of both forces were formed in battalion columns. The cavalry of the advanced guard was reinforced by the Dorpat and Lithuanian Chasseur à Cheval Regiments, raising its strength up to three dragoon regiments, four Cossack regiments and the two weak Chasseur à Cheval Regiments. The Russian 9th Corps, which now consisted of only the 9th Division, as the 15th Division was assigned to the advanced guard, stood as a reserve behind the right wing as the battle began. GL von Korff, with the Reserve Cavalry, stood behind the left wing.

The villages of Klein- and Gross-Wiederitzsch were occupied by four Polish battalions, 800 cavalry from Fournier's 6th Light Cavalry Division,[48] and two artillery batteries of Dombrowski's 27th (Polish) Division.

GdI Langeron's cavalry vanguard moved against Seehausen first, engaged the 5/13th Cuirassier Regiment, and drove them back towards Eutritzsch. Dombrowski responded by ordering Zoltowski to form his infantry into three columns to repulse a possible cavalry attack. He then ordered Krukowiecki's 18th Light Cavalry Brigade, the 2nd Uhlan, and the 4th Chasseur à Cheval Regiments to move to the right wing.

Möckern Entered

Oberst Steinmetz ordered the right wing battalions (1/13th Silesian Landwehr and 3/5th Reserve) to strike Möckern directly, while the remainder moved against the heights occupied by the French. The 1/13th Silesian Landwehr lowered its muskets and advanced at the Sturmschritt into the murderous French defensive fire. The fire was intense and many officers and men were killed and wounded. The 1/13th Silesian Landwehr, the 3/5th Reserve, and the Silesian Grenadiers pushed into the burning village. The French were driven out.[49]

At the same time the 1/, 4/5th Silesian Regiment from the second line, the 2/, 4/13th Silesian Landwehr, and the East Prussian Grenadier Battalion attacked the hill. The French defended their position with heavy musketry and canister fire.

Immediately, the French brought forward more troops to prevent a further erosion of their position. The terribly weakened Prussian battalions holding the village were now subjected to a hail of canister, and suffered further losses from a French battery on their left that contained 50 guns.[50]

GdI Langeron struck Klein-Wiederitzsch. The outnumbered Poles fought back, contesting bitterly every foot that the Russians advanced. GM Emanuel advanced with the cavalry of the advanced guard, attacking the Polish cavalry, capturing seven guns, several caissons and taking 500 prisoners.[51] The Kiev and another Dragoon regiment, the Lithuanian Chasseurs, and the 1st and 3rd Ukrainian Cossacks, under GM de Witt and GM Obolensky, then pushed further forward.

The French cavalry, under Defrance, and the Poles under Krukowiecki counterattacked and pushed them back across the Rietzschke stream. The Polish infantry followed the attack and reoccupied the village.

The French Retake Klein- and Gross-Wiederitzsch

As GM Emanuel's cavalry was striking the Poles, the unhappy battle raged around Möckern, and the balance of the battle swung in favor of the French. The left wing of Langeron's Corps was unable to achieve a decisive advantage. Wiederitzsch was still stubbornly occupied by the Poles.

As Langeron once again ordered the infantry of the advanced guard and Kapzevich's 10th Corps to take Wiederitzsch, he saw a column of troops advancing down the Düben road towards Leipzig. It was the French 9th Division, under Delmas, which was escorting the III Corps park column. The park column had originally marched without a covering force. Delmas had seen it as his duty to ensure the safety of the column, and escorted it towards Leipzig. As it would happen the 9th Division first appeared on the battlefield around 3:00 p.m., with the III Corps train in tow.

Delmas' 9th Division, III Corps, advanced out to assist the Poles. Delmas moved against the heights of Ossig and Gobschelwitz. The 9th Division had 4,235 men, and it struck the flank and rear of the Russian position. Delmas' attack was supported by a force of cavalry as well.

Langeron responded by ordering GL Olsoviev to move to the left flank in haste, and he ordered all of Korff's reserve cavalry there as well. As a result, Langeron had no more reserves to feed into the battle around Wiederitzsch. This was a problem, for not only were Dombrowski's Poles better led, but they had bravely fought against the vastly larger Russian force. Despite the terrible odds against them, the Poles succeeded, through greater effort, in holding the village.

Olsoviev permitted the French 9th Division (Delmas) to occupy the Birkenholz, while the Russian 15th Division marched forward from the reserve. Light Battery #29, also from the reserve artillery, opened fire against Delmas' 9th Division, which had left the road and attacked a small woods occupied by the Russians. Korff's cavalry reserve positioned itself between Birkenholz and Podelwitz. In addition, four of Sacken's detached Don Cossack regiments were sent to reconnoiter towards Düben.

Delmas deployed his division and this allowed Dombrowski to reorganize his forces under their protection. Reorganized, the Poles once again drove forward, supported by Delmas, and drove Langeron's advanced guard out of both villages. Langeron's forces reeled back to their original positions by the stream. The French then occupied both villages and advanced to the stream. The French artillery pounded Langeron's forces, inflicting heavy casualties on them. GM Schenschin, Lieutenant Colonel Prigara (45th Jagers), and Major Jussofwicz (Viatka Regiment) were wounded and Lieutenant Colonel Voewodsky (Staroskol Regiment) was killed.[52]

GM Udom (9th Division, 9th Corps) advanced into a small woods with the 10th and 38th Jager Regiments, covered by the skirmishers of the Nacheburg, Apcheron, and Iakout Regiments, and set about occupying it. He was shortly after assaulted by the advancing French. An artillery duel began between Light Battery #29 (Oberst Sacedko) and the French artillery. The French renewed their assault. GL Olsoviev moved Colonel Medinzov forward with the Riajsk and Kolyvan Infantry Regiments to support Udom.

The French attack from the Birkenholz was repelled, and during the course of which, the French 145th Infantry Regiment suffered heavy losses, including their eagle. The Russians prevailed and the woods remained in their hands,[53] but the Russians could not fight long both at the Birkenholz and by Wiederitzsch. The allies needed reinforcements if they were to win the battle. Fortunately for them, Blücher still had St.-Priest's 8th Corps by Lindenthal and Sacken's 11th Corps to the rear by Radefeld. Between the crisis around Möckern, and the news from Korff's cavalry about the situation on the left flank of the Army of Silesia, Blücher decided that it was time to order forward his reserve.

GD Delmas then began to withdraw his 9th Division from Seehausen towards Neutzsch and Plösen. Korff followed him with his cavalry, capturing a few vehicles. Four regiments of Don Cossacks, which had been under von Sacken when the battle began, were sent against Düben. Here they captured six guns, which they then abandoned because of the lack of horses to draw then.

Langeron Advances Again

With the French withdrawing, Langeron once again renewed his assaults against Klein-Wiederitzsch. He personally led the Schusselburg Regiment, while GL Rudsevich stood at the head of his mounted Chasseurs. GL Kapzevich supported the attack with his 10th Corps.

A French column stood to the side of Klein-Wiederitzsch and struck the right wing of the Russian attack. GL Kapzevich sent forward 12-pdr Battery #34 (Colonel Magdenkov), supported by the Viatka and Archangel Regiments to engage them. GL St.-Priest, in the meantime, advanced and took up a position by Lindenthal awaiting orders, but supporting GM Bistrom with his Jagers.

The Russian attack proved too much and the French and Poles withdrew, abandoning Klein-Wiederitzsch to the Russians. Two Russian batteries then moved forward into the interval between the Prussian and Russian corps, supported by the 3/, 4/Brandenburg Hussar Regiment.[54]

The Battle Ends

Yorck had recognized when his last attack was repulsed the battle was at a crisis point. He directed, through an adjutant, that the 7th and 8th Brigades march forward to attack Möckern. The battalions of the second line moved into the first line. Oberst von Horn personally led the 1/Leib Regiment into the attack. Graf Reichenbach's 3/4th Silesian Landwehr Regiment found itself engaged by Normann's Württemberg cavalry, but beat off their attacks. The 8th Brigade engaged four French battalions. A battalion of the 1st Marine Infantry[55] struck the 7th Brigade.

Yorck personally ordered the cavalry forward, whose regiments stood ready in the undulating terrain behind the battle line. Major von Sohr, who stood with the 1/, 2/, Jägers/Brandenburg Hussars supporting the infantry of the right wing, stood in squadron column on the road to Leipzig. The three squadrons of the Brandenburg Hussar Regiment advanced by Möckern, close behind the infantry to prevent any further shirking in the infantry ranks. A few hundred paces from Möckern, the cavalry wheeled out and hurled themselves at the French. The hussars, closely followed by the Brandenburg Uhlan Regiment, closed quickly on the French infantry before them.

The cavalry mass roared in like a thunderstorm, a few salvos rattled over their heads, almost without effect, before they collided with the squares hastily formed by the French infantry. At the issuance of the order for a general advance, von Sohr moved to the left, with the right wing, towards the village of Möckern. Von Sohr's Brandenburg Hussars broke two French squares.

The Brandenburg Hussars at Möckern, 16 October, by Zimmer.

Fleeing French soldiers masked the fire of their batteries, screening the attacking Brandenburg Hussars as far as the French guns. Six guns were captured by the hussars in this charge.

Marmont ordered Normann's 25th Light Cavalry Brigade forward to attack the victorious Prussian cavalry, in an effort to give his shattered infantry some breathing space, and allow him to reorganize them.[56] A Württemberg cavalry regiment of this brigade threw itself on the left flank of the attacking Brandenburg Hussars. The Württembergers were countercharged by the 1/, 2/ Brandenburg Uhlan Regiment.

The Brandenburg Hussar and Uhlan Regiments pushed Normann's Brigade back, and captured a further nine guns and five caissons.[57]

After pushing Normann's Brigade aside, they struck a withdrawing battalion of the 1st Marine Infantry Regiment and shattered it completely. The 3/, 4/Brandenburg Uhlans pushed into the second line of marine infantry, "breaking further squares despite bravery and cold blooded defense of the infantry."[58] Behind the Uhlans the remaining advanced guard troops deployed and attacked in echelons.

The allies threw 6,000 cavalry against the French lines. Oberst von Jürgass led forward the 1st West Prussian Dragoon Regiment, the 1st Neumärk Landwehr Regiment and the Lithuanian Dragoon Regiment, around the right of the 7th Brigade, while the remainder of the reserve cavalry passed through the Prussian infantry lines. GL von Yorck stood at their head.

The 1st West Prussian Dragoon Regiment struck the French cavalry, drove them back and captured four cannon, then moved against Gohlis. The French infantry stood with their left wing forward, so the Lithuanian Dragoons swung with *Zügen rechtsumgekehrt*[59] and struck the French, with Brigade commander Oberst Graf Henkel, at the point, and rode over an entire battalion. They were accompanied by the 1st Landwehr Neumark Regiment.[60]

The French 1st and 3rd Marine Regiments, immediately threatened by this attack, fell back to a less exposed position and formed square. A squadron of the Mecklenburg Hussar Regiment struck a square of the 1st Marine Regiment while the remaining three squadrons passed to the left of the

The heroic death of Major von Krosigk at Möckern, 16 October, by Knötel.

squadron. Oberst von Warburg swung the Mecklenburg Hussars and took the battalion in the rear, while the infantry of the 7th Brigade struck it frontally. The Mecklenburg Hussar Regiment took a flag, an eagle and captured 700 prisoners.[61]

The 2nd Leib Hussar Regiment captured two guns with their limbers and two flags. The cavalry regiments, under Majors von Sohr (10th Silesian Landwehr) and von Osarowsky (5th Silesian Landwehr) were also fortunate in their attacks against the French. The East Prussian National Cavalry Regiment captured four cannon as well.

The French quickly fell back before this attack. Their artillery became disordered as it attempted to withdraw, and some of it was captured at Schleppthan. At the same time, the French right wing was attacked by GM Hünerbein (8th Brigade), and GM Horn (7th Brigade) and the French began to fall back. The surviving soldiers of the Marine Regiments, formed in square, held fast and slowly withdrew from the battlefield. The French retreat became general and they withdrew to the villages of Gohlis and Eutritzsch. Victory was ceded to the allies.[62]

The first victory of the Prussian cavalry joined other events that would spread panic through the rows of French infantry. The 12-pdr Batteries #1 and #2, Yorck's reserve artillery, moved forward between 500 and 800 paces from the left wing of Marmont's VI Corps, and pounded them with canister fire. Part of their fire was directed down the Möckern road, in order to stop the advancing mass of French infantry, and part of their fire was used to suppress the French artillery fire. Three Prussian batteries, 6-pdr Foot Batteries #1 and #2 and Horse Battery #2, engaged the French artillery on the left wing by Möckern.

At this moment, a Prussian howitzer shell exploded, detonating three French 12-pdr caissons into the air and silencing the battery. Marmont, who stood nearby, was not wounded. However, this explosion stilled the French artillery fire long enough for the Prussians to take advantage of the lull.

The battle took on a new character and (the French) infantry masses found themselves at times 30 paces from the (Prussians). The 20th and 25th Provisional Regiments, commanded by Colonels Maury and Durault, covered themselves with glory in this circumstance. They marched against the enemy, forcing them to withdraw, but overcome by numbers, these two regiments were obliged to stop, but continued to hold their positions. The 32nd Légère also executed prodigious acts. The troops of the 22nd Division, which formed the last echelon, took part in the combat, both to support the (French) troops which were already engaged and to resist those which the (Prussians) had marched against their left.[63]

The attack of Joubert's Brigade stabilized Marmont's lines, saving the battle for the moment.

About 5:00 p.m., the commander of the Prussian 7th Brigade understood that the battle on the right wing was becoming so doubtful, that only the quick attack of his brigade could turn the battle around. He ordered his brigade forward and they quickly advanced without firing a shot into the maelstrom of French canister fire in the middle of the field.[64] The 7th Brigade advanced against Compans' 20th Division and the French artillery position near Möckern. It swung its right wing against these and bore down on them. The Prussian cavalry stalled Marmont's attack and the 7th Brigade pushed forward, seizing ground. The remaining portion of the 7th Brigade struck the opposite artillery position and pushed it behind the French infantry. The 8th Brigade was, in the meantime, likewise advancing, yet because of the heavier French artillery fire, it suffered such heavy losses that it was not able to advance, or even retain a position as far forward into the French position as the 7th Brigade. In order to break the French left wing, which used a portion of Friederichs' 22nd Division as a flank support, Russian help was required.

St.-Priest's Russian 11th Infantry Division remained by Lindenthal, while he swung the 17th Russian Division against Marmont's right wing, that was locked in combat with the Prussian 7th Brigade. The flanking fire of two allied batteries supported this attack. However, his maneuver caused a gap to appear between the 17th Division and the Russian 10th Corps, which widened during the efforts to take Gross-Wiederitzsch. Dombrowski grasped this opportune moment and thrust forward with some of his battalions, which he had gathered behind the village. The Poles burst forward into the gap. It was only by the rapid commitment of the allied reserve that the Polish attack was repelled.

It was at this time that Olsoviev's Russian 9th Corps also went over to the offensive, and pushed back Delmas' 9th Division from Seehausen towards Neutzsch and Plösen. A part of the French park and train column was captured near Düben by Cossacks, who took six guns, 100 wagons and about 500 prisoners.[65]

The French right wing, near the Birkenholz and Wiederitzsch was pressed back, ultimately deciding the fate of the battle by Möckern in Blücher's favor. This success he credited to Yorck's determination and the bravery of his soldiers. On the north wing of the French VI Corps, an indescribable confusion reigned.

The French, struck on all sides, withdrew their right flank to Eutritzsch, with their left flank by Gohlis. In the curve of the Elster stood a few French battalions. Though dark was about to fall, they were taken under fire by 6-pdr Foot Battery #24, as the reserve advanced. Marmont advanced part of the 20th Division, forming it in echelons on the center, to support his line.

As darkness started to fall, the French executed a withdrawal to the Parthe. Marmont's withdrawing forces moved under the cover of Friederichs' 22nd Division, which had suffered the least. The Prussian cavalry struck towards Gohlis. Marmont personally rode to the Gerber gate of Leipzig, and directed GL Franquemont to watch the Rietzschkebach defile, between Gohlis and Eutritzsch, in order to cover the withdrawal of the beaten French VI Corps. Franquemont moved 300 men of the 3rd Combined Württemberg Infantry Battalion into the gap.[66]

After dusk, because of the opportunities afforded by the darkness, a French column burst forward from a woods behind Möckern. It was supported by French artillery as it drove against the Prussian lines. 6-pdr Foot Battery #24, which had not been engaged during the day, moved forward and fired canister at the French assault, repulsing this last spasmodic effort by the French.

Nightfall and the fatigue of the troops prevented further pursuit. GL St.-Priest received orders from Blücher to go forward and attack, with his left wing, the Rietzschkebach region, and Marmont's right wing. However, the order was received too late to be executed. St.-Priest would not be hurried, his troops were fatigued, and he was unable to take part in the pursuit. The greatest part of the French VI Corps pulled behind the Parthe and reorganized itself during the night. Dombrowski's 27th Division, now reduced to a few hundred men, drew itself together behind Pfaffendorf, while the 9th Division (Delmas) moved between Eutritzsch and Gohlis to cover Leipzig.[67]

The advanced posts of the Prussian 7th and 8th Brigades stood the right bank of the Rietzschke with the 2nd Leib Hussar Regiment, while the 1st and 2nd Brigades stood before Möckern. The Prussian 1st Corps cavalry bivouacked behind the village and the 1/Brandenburg Infantry Regiment occupied the bridge over the Elster by Möckern.

That night, Langeron's Corps camped between Eutritzsch and Wiederitzsch. Sacken's Corps was behind Möckern. Blücher moved his headquarters to Wiederitzsch. The allies had taken from the French two eagles, two flags, 53 guns, a large number of caissons, and over 2,000 prisoners. In addition, Marmont was wounded, as were GD Compans and Friederichs. The total French loss was estimated to be between 6,000 and 7,000 men.[68]

However, the allied army had also suffered losses that had to be set straight before the next day. Official records report 173 officers, 5,432 men, and 322 horses were lost by Yorck's Corps alone. However, a comparison of the army states from 15 and 17 October suggests that the losses were higher, 7,506 men. Langeron's losses were reported at 1,500 men. In addition, the Prussian artillery had fired 2,477 round shot, 316 howitzer bombs, and 546 canister rounds. Sacken was barely engaged and his losses were, as a result, minimal.

Immediately after the happy outcome of the battle, Blücher sent Hauptmann Knackfuss from Schkeuditz, to the headquarters of the Army of Bohemia, in order to advise them of his victory. However, the officer became lost as he tried to pass through the Elster valley, so Blücher sent his first adjutant, Oberst von der Goltz, on the morning 17 October, in order to present the captured eagle to the Prussian King. Bernadotte, crown prince of Sweden, was also advised of the victory.[69]

Napoleon was in Schönefeld around midnight, when Marmont reported his defeat. He had engaged the complete Army of Silesia with little more than a corps. Indeed, he may well have engaged even more than just the Army of Silesia, as he had taken Prussian, Austrian, and Russian prisoners. The estimated strength of his opponents stood at about 60,000 infantry and 12,000 cavalry. "I have," Marmont wrote, "done everything that is humanly possible in order to bring the battle to another conclusion. However fate chose otherwise."[70]

8

The Second Day of the Battle 17 October 1813

The Army of Bohemia

During the evening of 16 October, as Schwarzenberg stood on the battlefield, amidst the carnage and destruction of the day's struggle, he resolved to renew the battle the following morning. Under the impression that Macdonald would be striking Klenau, Schwarzenberg ordered Colloredo's 1st Armeeabteilung to support Klenau until Bennigsen's forces arrived.[1]

The reinforcement of the right wing was another indication of Schwarzenberg's vacillations. It had always been presumed that Napoleon was moving to the Saale. If Napoleon did not have a practical passage over the Pleisse by Connewitz, it was believed that he would attack down the right bank of the river to seize a suitable passage. As a result, Schwarzenberg regretted sending the 1st Armeeabteilung to the right bank. However, not having done so would have probably lost the battle of Wachau for the allies, so the lesser of two evils had been chosen.

Little is known of the influence of various messages received by the allied headquarters as it moved to Rötha, concerning the locations of the allied and French forces, or how they influenced the thinking of Schwarzenberg. The only sure thing is that Schwarzenberg, as he reached his headquarters, again issued an order to Colloredo instructing him to take a position next to the Leipzig road south of Magdeborn (Tanzberg) on 17 October at 6:00 a.m.[2]

It was soon recognized that a hasty attack before Bennigsen's arrival would have no purpose. Schwarzenberg wanted, therefore, to await Bennigsen's arrival before engaging in any action, and in the meantime await Napoleon's renewed attack or withdrawal.

Arguments over probable French actions split the allied headquarters into factions. Many advocated the French would withdraw towards the Mulde. Others argued that they would withdraw towards the Saale. Therefore Schwarzenberg pushed stronger forces to the Pleisse and found strong French forces. The transfer of the strength from the right wing to support the main battle effectively reduced the potential of surrounding the French, as well as threatening Napoleon's supposed withdrawal to the east. Only if the French should seek to break off the engagement would the allies transfer large forces to the eastern flank.

These considerations caused opinions to sway dramatically that evening in Rötha. There was no consensus as to which dispositions to make for the next morning. Indecision brought little change to the current deployments. The divisions of Bianchi and Weissenwolf stood by Cröbern, and served as a reserve for the left wing. The 1st Armeeabteilung under Colloredo, served as the reserve for the right. Bennigsen advanced from Colditz through Grimma towards Naunhof. "The army waited in these positions for the decision of the hour for the renewed attack."

This decision was made, but the order was not issued. Schwarzenberg decided that it would be superfluous, and a renewal of the attack order to Klenau was not necessary. Schwarzenberg also gave up the idea of an advance by Wittgenstein, so the existing orders were not modified.[3]

In the early morning, the Army of Bohemia formed itself for battle. The French advanced posts stood a musket shot apart from one another, and listened closely for the pending allied advance. At the break of day, the French camp sprang to life, and immediately after sunrise, large forces of infantry and cavalry appeared on the heights near Liebertwolkwitz. The allies had every reason to anticipate a general attack that morning.

In the early morning of 17 October, Klenau held the 4th Armeeabteilung ready to execute its orders, and deployed his forces as follows. Abele's Brigade stood by the Gross-Pösna windmill, from where the Erzherzog Karl Infantry Regiment closed with Paumgarten's advanced guard. Hohenlohe-Bartenstein's Division stood to the right of Abele by Fuchshain, with two battalions supporting the defenders of Seifertshain. The Prussian 11th Brigade (Ziethen) stood in the middle of the second line. Its left wing was anchored on Gross-Pösna. Röder's Cavalry Brigade and that of Desfours formed the third line by Störmthal and Gülden-Gossa. The combined artillery moved to the heights between Fuchshain and Gross-Pösna. General Kleist's headquarters were in Gülden-Gossa.

Barclay de Tolly sent the Prussian 12th Brigade to Gossa, where it joined with the battalions of the 10th Brigade, that stood to the right of the village. The 9th Brigade was placed in reserve behind the Russian 2nd Corps, between Gossa and Magdeborn.

The movements by the 4th Armeeabteilung motivated the French standing opposite them to entrench their position, and open fire with their artillery. Klenau did not advance, the guns soon fell silent, and the French limited themselves to a skirmish fight between advanced troops.

That morning Platov advanced through Naunhof towards Brandis. He sought to link with the right wing of the 4th Armeeabteilung by Albrechtshain. He was to operate against the French flank to the east of the Parthe. Oberst Illesy, accompanied the two squadrons of the Palatinal Hussars that had been with Platov, as they were dispatched back to Klenau's Corps. Platov was also requested to give up the remaining regular cavalry assigned to his Cossack corps, but he argued against it, with the justification that he needed them to cover his artillery.[4]

Despite their strength and position, surprisingly, the French did not attack. The Czar, the King of Prussia, and Prince Schwarzenberg ordered their forces not to advance until after noon, in order to allow Colloredo's 1st Corps and Bennigsen's Army of Poland time to arrive on the field. In addition, during the early morning hours, the sovereigns had no knowledge of Blücher's success at Möckern, nor of Bernadotte's approach.[5]

Late in the evening, after the original orders were issued, Schwarzenberg received word that Colloredo's arrival by Borna would be later than anticipated. The orders to advance to Frohburg were not received by Colloredo until 10:00 a.m., on 16 October.[6] Colloredo was unable to complete preparations for the advance until noon, and once ready, he advanced by forced marches in an effort to arrive on time. Despite that effort it was not to be.

In the morning, a message arrived from Hessen-Homburg's advanced posts, stating that Wachau was burning and the large numbers of French had been observed withdrawing towards Probstheida. That this news was false, soon became apparent. However, Klenau was ordered to make arrangements for the pending arrival of Bennigsen.

Gyulai sent, in the meantime, a report concerning the battle by Lindenau, and advised Schwarzenberg that Blücher had waged a battle with some success. However, he had no details or knowledge of the outcome of Blücher's battle to pass on.

At 7:00 a.m., Schwarzenberg found the Czar and King of Prussia on the battlefield. The former, who had accepted that Napoleon was withdrawing, looked upon the standing French masses with disappointment. Everyone expected that the Austrian Emperor would soon give the sign to start the battle. However, since 10:00 a.m., everything had remained immobile. Shortly later, however, the sound of cannons were heard on the north of Leipzig. The fear swept the lines of the Army of Bohemia that Napoleon had begun to settle accounts with Blücher. Schwarzenberg could not permit this to happen, but the awaited reinforcements were not at hand, and to start the battle without them was to ask for failure.[7]

Colloredo announced that the head of the 1st Armeeabteilung column, first reached Borna about 4:30 a.m., and the artillery required at least one and a half hours to arrive. As a result, the march to Magdeborn would not begin before 6:00 a.m. Subsequently, the support of the 1st Armeeabteilung was not to be strongly counted on. Schwarzenberg wanted an attack by strong forces, to strike next to the Pleisse, so there remained no option other than to draw reinforcements from the 2nd Armeeabteilung. Rittmeister Graf Schulenburg was, therefore, sent with an order for A. Liechtenstein's Division to move to Cröbern. Gyulai was to move part of the 3rd Armeeabteilung to the same place, an indication that Schwarzenberg was also of the opinion that Napoleon would be withdrawing towards the Mulde.

That morning the interim commander of the 2nd Armeeabteilung, FML Lederer, deployed his troops as follows. Facing Connewitz were two battalions with two guns. A reserve of three companies stood in the second line, and a battalion with two hussar platoons as a third line behind them. In the Dölitz château stood a battalion with two howitzers, in Raschwitz was a battalion serving as a reserve, two companies were in Lossnig, and a battalion stood facing Mark-Kleeberg. Finally Oberstleutnant Simbschen's detachment stood in the pastures facing Schleussig, and served as the link with Gyulai. Mecsery's Brigade, three brigade batteries and the bulk of the cavalry stood by Gautzsch, acting as a general reserve.

As Lederer received the order, he detached to A. Liechtenstein, a force consisting of Mecsery's Brigade, two brigade batteries, and a 12-pdr position battery. This force moved to Cröbern. It then crossed over the Pleisse by Deuben, and at 1:00 p.m., arrived in their determined positions.[8]

The Austrian 1st Abteilung (Colloredo) arrived at 11:00 a.m., and took a place in the first line between Mark-Kleeberg and Dölitz. It extended its left to the Pleisse. The Austrian grenadiers and Bianchi's Division, plus several lines of cavalry were shifted to the rear to form a reserve.

Schulenburg joined Gyulai at 1:30 p.m.. That morning the 3rd Armeeabteilung had, from French movements, concluded that an attack was imminent and prepared themselves for a

An episode of the battle of Leipzig, by Knötel.

potential movement to Schönau. However, the remaining troops stayed in their lager. Schulenburg appeared to have erroneously delivered the message that the entire 3rd Armeeabteilung would advance towards Cröbern. Gyulai placed the 1st Light Division in position opposite Lindenau with Thielmann's and Mensdorf's Streifkorps to the left rear. His troops immediately began their march.

The cannon fire of the Army of Silesia soon fell silent, the pending attack appeared to vanish. Schwarzenberg responded by stopping the process of stripping his troops from the Saale. Gyulai was once again sent an order, to only move with a part of his forces when St.-Priest's Corps of the Army of Silesia arrived at his position. He was told he should "apply everything means of inducing General St.-Priest to take over those posts, then move himself and the entire army corps to the right bank of the Pleisse in order to establish the shortest possible communication." The order, unfortunately, implicitly assumed that the purpose of the postponement of the relief of A. Liechtenstein's Division was accomplished, i.e. St.-Priest had arrived. It also erroneously allowed that the right instead of the left bank of the Pleisse, should be the objective of the directed march.

Shortly before 3:00 p.m., when Gyulai received this order, he turned back his already marching columns, because St.-Priest's Corps had not yet arrived. However, Crenneville's Division was missed by the aide carrying the message. As a result, it remained unaware of the new orders and continued its movement to Cröbern.

Towards noon, Schwarzenberg received a report from Klenau that Bennigsen's advanced guard had reached Gross-Steinberg, in the late morning hours. Colloredo's 1st Armeeabteilung had, at 9:00 a.m., marched out from Magdeborn. Around noon, Bennigsen stood by Naunhof. It was at 3:00 p.m., that the decision to attack was made.[9] Because of the continued lack of activity by the French, it was supposed that Napoleon would begin a withdrawal the next night.

Schwarzenberg issued the following order:

> The attack shall be in column after the arrival of General Bennigsen, around 2:00 p.m., and from our right wing against the enemy's left.
>
> The 1st Column of the right wing, under the command of General Bennigsen, shall consist of his army and the corps of General Klenau. The reserve of this column shall consist of an Austrian brigade and a Russian division drawn from Bennigsen's army.
>
> The 2nd Column, under the orders of General Barclay de Tolly, shall consist of the corps of Graf Wittgenstein and General Kleist. The reserve for this column shall consist of the Russian and Prussian guard.
>
> The 3rd Column, under the orders of Erbprinz Hessen-Homburg, shall consist of Bianchi's Division, Alois Liechtenstein's Division, Weissenwolf's Division, and Nostitz's cavalry. The reserve of this column shall be the 1st Army Corps under Colloredo. The Austrian reserve artillery shall march with the batteries of General Colloredo.
>
> The artillery reserve of the 2nd Armeeabteilung shall unite with the artillery of Bianchi's Division.
>
> The attack of the column of the left wing shall advance the length of the right bank of the Pleisse to the road to Leipzig.
>
> The column of the center must hold its communication to the right, as shall the left wing.
>
> The reserve shall follow the column at the distance of a cannon shot.
>
> Gyulai's Corps and Lederer Corps' shall attack at about 3:00 p.m., and demonstrate, if they are not able to force passage.
>
> I, myself, shall be between the reserve of the Russian Guard and that of Graf Colloredo.[10]
>
> In case of a withdrawal, the column of the right wing shall move over the Lausigk towards Penig. The two other columns shall move through Borna towards Altenburg, Gyulai and Lederer shall move on Zeitz.

The Austrian rally point is Rötha, the Russian is Espenhain.

The kettle horses shall stop behind Colloredo's Division where they are near the battle in such a manner that the evening meal may be cooked.

From this disposition Schwarzenberg obliged Klenau, the middle column, to displace the divided Prussian troops. Wittgenstein covered his assigned position with his army detachment on the following morning. Gorchakov's Corps stood in the University Woods in the region near Störmthal. To left of this village stood Pahlen's cavalry, which by this time had contacted the Prussian reserve cavalry. In front of this group stood the Russian 2nd Cuirassier Division. The Prussian 10th and 12th Brigades stood by Gülden-Gossa. The Russians made preparations that morning to defend against an attack, and the Prussians evacuated the village of Gülden-Gossa. The 10th Brigade took up a position behind the village, while the Russian infantry moved in to occupy the village. Württemberg's 2nd Corps stood between Gülden-Gossa and Magdeborn, with the Prussian 9th Brigade and the Russo-Prussian Guard serving as a reserve. In the region between Gülden-Gossa and Auenhain, stood a Russian light cavalry division and the Grenadier Corps. The Russian 3rd Cuirassier Division stood before Auenhain .

At 2:30 p.m., Ziethen stood with the Prussian 11th Brigade in the University Woods. The woods were occupied by three battalions, two batteries, and two squadrons on the edge of the woods, waiting for the French. A further four and a half battalions, four squadrons, and the horse battery were formed in a second line and served as a reserve. Those Austrians in positions in the woods departed to join the 4th Armeeabteilung.

The left column of Hessen-Homburg had Bianchi's Division between the Pleisse and the sheep pens of Auenhain, the Fischer Grenadier Battalion actually occupying the sheep pens. Behind this first line stood Nostitz's Cavalry Division and Weissenwolf's Division. A.Liechtenstein's Division stood on both sides of Cröbern and the 1st Armeeabteilung, under Colloredo, stood behind them serving as a reserve.[11]

The hour of 1:00 p.m., came ever closer without a report of Bennigsen's arrival reaching Schwarzenberg's headquarters. However, Oberst Goltz did arrive with news of Blücher's victory at Möckern. The news of Blücher's success was better than had hitherto had been assumed. This lowered the probability that Napoleon would use the next night in order to lead his army out of the encirclement, which would require an attack on 17 October. On the other hand, the weather was inclement, there was the uncertainty of Bennigsen's arrival, and the information from Oberst Goltz and Blücher, regarding the arrival of the Army of the North was also uncertain. Perhaps Napoleon, since he had, strangely enough, not used the day of 17 October to depart, would also remain stationary on 18 October. The combined effect of the armies on 18 October spoke of a far greater victory than could be achieved by attack with a part of the Army of Bohemia during the short October afternoon.

At the same time, a message arrived from Bennigsen announcing that his advanced guard, 4,000 men of the Army of Poland, had arrived in Fuchshain. However, Schwarzenberg also learned that the men of the Army of Poland were too fatigued to participate in any combat that day. The decision of the council was that the attack should be delayed until next morning.[12]

The number of reinforcements the allies received on 17 October exceeded 100,000 men. The arrival of these men, the day's rest, and the opportunity to replenish the munition supplies were welcomed by all. The Army of Bohemia remained in place.

The Czar and Schwarzenberg returned to Rötha that evening and were joined by the Emperor of Austria. The King of Prussia returned to Brone and Barclay de Tolly established his headquarters in Störmthal.

Schwarzenberg reported to Kaiser Franz of Austria, whose quarters were in Pegau, at 3:00 p.m., that "The dispositions humbly submitted to Your Majesty this morning for an afternoon attack

An episode of the battle of Leipzig, by Knötel.

were dependent on the premise that General Bennigsen would be united this afternoon with the corps of General Klenau. It is now past 3:00 p.m., and I have further news that there is only a slight probability that General Bennigsen will be in position for the attack. With this understanding, the hour being so far advanced, and as the enemy occupies the advantageous heights by Wachau, in the short time that remains I believe that nothing more can be undertaken. I believe it expedient that the attack be postponed until the morning. This would also permit the troops time to recuperate from the strenuous actions of yesterdays battle, as well as time to prepare their meals."[13]

Schwarzenberg related to the Austrian Emperor that Oberst von der Glotz had arrived with news of Blücher's success around Möckern, and that the situation relating to that success justified postponing the proposed attack, until the morning of 18 October. Von der Glotz was sent back with a note which advised Blücher of the revised attack plans, so that the effect of the attack by the Army of Silesia could be combined with the planned attack.

He related how he was confident that Bennigsen would also be in a position to join the battle, further improving the allied situation. It was presumed that part of Bennigsen's army would be on the field in time for the scheduled attack.

Lederer and Gyulai were unwilling to execute the attack. Gyulai reported later that afternoon: "I had again received the order, which I first received around 2:30 p.m., to merely make a demonstration and to await the principal attack of the main army, which I nevertheless did not follow. I do not consider it advisable for me to engage triple my strength."

The situation caused Gyulai considerable anguish. When the first revision of the battle plans arrived at 3:00 p.m., they advised him that he was obliged to execute what he believed to be a suicidal attack.[14]

As for the attack by the main army, nothing was to be seen or heard. Gyulai believed that a demonstration on some scale must be executed, therefore he ordered a few troops forward, as the 3rd Armeeabteilung was ordered to return to its old positions. His orders for a demonstration were weakly worded, ordering the advance of the detachment of M. Liechtenstein, Thielmann, and Mensdorf towards Lindenau. The lead brigade of the returning column, that of Czollich, was to advance towards Klein-Zschocher. They received the order they were by Knauthain and did not begin to move to their assigned positions until night began to fall. Later, they were drawn to Gross-Zschocher, where Crenneville's Division arrived the next morning from Cröbern. The remaining portions of the corps found themselves spread about in their earlier lager positions.[15]

The French to the North

During the night Marmont's VI Corps pulled back behind the Rietzschke. Delmas' 9th Division, III Corps, was withdrawn with the corps artillery park, to a position by Eutritzsch. Dombrowski remained in his position. During the morning of 17 October, Marmont pulled his corps behind the Parthe River, and watched the passes over the Parthe to Portitz. The detachment at the Gohlis and the Rietzschke bridges were covered by one and a half weak battalions. Franquemont's forces stood near Leipzig's Halle Gate. Two companies of the 10th Württemberg (Light) Infantry Regiment were posted at the gate as a garrison.[16]

Ney, who left the Württembergers dispersed, deployed them northwards along the Parthe, until their left flank reached to Gohlis and Dombrowski's forces by the bridge over the Rietzschke. Delmas stood on the right wing by Eutritzsch and Arrighi's III Cavalry Corps stood by Düben, and covered the open fields from Rietzschke and Parthe.[17]

The Army of Poland

Schwarzenberg postponed the attack as the reports of Bennigsen's arrival were received. His march from Dresden had begun during the evening of 13 October.

Unfortunately, the courier who was dispatched with the order to move forward and lift the blockade, was himself delayed 24 hours. On 14 October the army reached Nossen, on 15 October Waldheim, and on 16 October the advanced guard was in Grimma, and the main body in Colditz. Once there, Bennigsen received instructions from the Czar to quicken the advance. He marched without consideration of stragglers and hurried his troops forward in order to link with Klenau, around 2:00 p.m.[18]

The Czar ordered him to prepare for an attack at 4:00 p.m., with Klenau, Ziethen, Bubna, and Platov subordinated to him. He was to execute a turning attack against the French left wing.

Schwarzenberg did little to edify his staff of the intent of the attack. The attack, to be executed in the late afternoon hours, appeared to have little purpose. Also, with the push to the east, he contradicted his earlier stated goal of driving Napoleon away from Leipzig and the Saale. Schwarzenberg's presentation induced the Czar to sway from his earlier intent. It was around 3:30 p.m., when the order came from the army command of Kaiser Franz stating: "His Majesty the Czar of Russia has given to General Bennigsen the order to attack, even though he has stated that it is already too late for him to establish himself for the attack. The period prior to his arrival shall be used to allow the troops to cook their dinners and to distribute wine. Should Bennigsen's attack have already begun, so shall the dispositions of Your Majesty be fully set."

The Czar addressed the re-issuance of his orders in this amiable form, accepting the postponement of Bennigsen's attack. The Czar of Russia wrote him, "Tomorrow is the anniversary of Tarotino,[19] where General Bennigsen augmented his military reputation. It is a prestigious hour for the great acts of arms, which we will anticipate from him in this decisive day."[20]

Schwarzenberg remained on the battlefield, in order to await the course of events on the right wing. He faced the danger of isolated thrusts by the French occurring that day, and savored the possibility of executing, on 18 October, a powerful attack against the French from all sides. Schwarzenberg had only two thoughts. He wondered if Bennigsen, because of the Czar's orders, would stand too far to the east, and he wondered if Oberst Goltz would arrive at Blücher's head-quarters, in time to permit Blücher to participate in the simultaneous advance.[21]

Schwarzenberg ordered Oberst Latour to guide Bennigsen's decisions and dispatched him to join Bennigsen's staff. Schwarzenberg, in an effort to ensure that Blücher learned of the intent of the attack during that night, dispatched his aide-de-camp, Rittmeister Szechenyi, with orders to by the shortest ride possible way to the Army of Silesia.

Schwarzenberg moved back to Rötha, where the Czar had also established his quarters. The King of Prussia spent the night in Gruna and Göselbach.

Bubna's Actions and Arrival at Leipzig

On 8 October FML Bubna stormed the Pirna bridgehead with Zechmeister's Brigade. There they captured a French pontoon train, which they dragged off to Dresden for use in their operations against the French garrison.[22] Bubna had obtained the long sought bridging train necessary to permit his passage over the Elbe.

On 10 October Bubna drew his division together between Pirna and Helfenberg. Scherbatov separated himself from Bubna, and under Blücher's orders, moved between Meissen and Torgau on the left bank of the Elbe. As a result of an overly hurried move to Wehlen, and the presence of attacking French forces, the officers of the Erzherzog Rainer Infantry Regiment feared the French might recapture the pontoons and destroyed some of them. The remainder Bubna drew off under the cover of night to Sonnenstein and towards Pratzschwitz, where the pontoons could be installed. Once there, it was found that the number of pontoons was not sufficient and a flying bridge was built for the cavalry, while the infantry crossed the small bridge.

On 12 October, when the news of the situation at Dresden was received, Schwarzenberg sent an order to the 2nd Light Division to move as quickly as possible to the main army's position. Bennigsen was to instructed to move towards Rochlitz. Bubna began to see the crossing of the Elbe as a possibility.[23]

After strenuous day and night activity, and despite stormy weather, during the evening of 13 October, the division crossed to the left bank of the Elbe by Lockwitz and established its bivouacs. On the following day the munitions reserve and a detachment of the column maga-zine followed. The magazine detachment had a four day supply of food with it. GM Johann von Seethal remained on the eastern bank, for the time being, with four battalions of the Theresienstadt garrison and three squadrons, in order to cover the picket line of the division that ran through Neustadt.

Bubna had the intention of advancing, in conjunction with Bennigsen's army, through Nossen against the French lines of communication with Torgau. Schwarzenberg declared his agreement with Bubna's earlier decisions, and gave him free reign to act as he saw fit, writing in his own hand, "You shall seek to work with Bennigsen. At this important and decisive moment the French should not be allowed to move significant forces that could cripple our flanks. Judge the strength of the French and work so that the General Baron Bennigsen acts to the preserve the spirit of our plans. I leave myself totally in your hands."

On 14 October the division moved through Rabenau and Tharandt towards Wilsdruff. On 15 October it arrived in Nossen. Through a sudden attack by the French garrison of Dresden the divi-sion lost a part of its column magazine. This occurred because of the bad weather, the ruined road between Tharandt and Wilsdruff, which trapped the column, and as a result of having too weak a covering force to defend the column. The portion of the column which escaped capture, moved

A view of Leipzig at the beginning of the 19th Century.

as quickly as possible to a position behind the main body of the division, to escape the pursuing French troops.

Once this column and the light division were a day's march along, Bennigsen and Bubna had a war conference in Nossen. The Russian general had wished to place the Austrian division at the point of his army, and have it serve as his advanced guard. However, it was not practicable to reorganize the march order to effect this, and because of the rush to move to Leipzig.[24] Bubna pushed his forces, in keeping with Schwarzenberg's orders, forward as quickly as possible. The news that Napoleon had moved with his main body against Wittenberg arrived, and caused the two generals to the agree that the 2nd Light Division should advance on the right of Bennigsen, towards Hubertusburg, so that they could serve as the advanced guard for the Polish Reserve Army, if it was necessary to form a front facing the Elbe. A commando under the orders of Major Graf St-Quentin of the Blankenstein Hussar Regiment, was assigned to reconnoiter the right flank, moving towards Lommatzsch. They also attempted to locate a passage over the Elbe for Scherbatov's forces.

As the advanced guard, under GM Neipperg, reached Toppschadel on 16 October, the sounds of the battle raging at Leipzig reached their ears. The march rate was accelerated.

Marching through the night, Bubna's 2nd Light Division covered 42 kilometers the day before arriving at Hubertusburg.[25] Their column reached the village at 1:00 a.m. The Austrian advanced guard took a position beyond the Hubertusburg Woods by Sachsendorf. Bubna reported his arrival to Schwarzenberg and wrote that he was "marching to the sounds of the guns." Should the French retreat towards the Elbe, he and Bennigsen would move to Eilenburg, in order discommode the French retreat and inflict as much damage as possible.

During the morning of 17 October, the troops cooked their morning meal and broke camp around 9:00 a.m., moving towards Wurzen. When GM Neipperg's advanced guard reached

Wurzen, they found the bridge over the Mulde was destroyed. Bubna gathered his soldiers and the villagers together to build a bridge over the river, while a part of the Kaiser Hussar Regiment swam the river and advanced slowly down the road to Leipzig.[26]

The lack of suitable materials to rebuild the bridge only allowed the construction of a small, decrepit bridge. Despite passing his forces over the Mulde as quickly as the bridge would allow, darkness had begun to fall as his advanced guard reached Gerichshain, and the main body reached Machern. A squadron of the Kaiser Hussar Regiment and two companies of the 4/Würzburg Landwehr Regiment were left behind in Wurzen, to serve as cover for the bridge over the Mulde.

These detachments were attacked that evening by about 1,000 French infantry and a cavalry detachment, which, as Bubna presumed, belonged to the French VII Army Corps. Rittmeister Pickl, the Wurzen detachment commander, was commissioned, in this case, to fall back over the Mulde and destroy the bridge. Instead, he attacked the French and threw them back. The advanced guard by Gerichshain and a right side guard to the north of the Sorgenbergwald forest, fought back the French with the same success.

Contact was not made with Bennigsen's army that day. However, during the night, Rittmeister Farago, who stood with the Kaiser Hussars in the advanced post by Gerichshain, reported that he had contacted, in Beucha, Russian General Platov with 3,000 Cossacks, a squadron of the Klenau Chevaulégers, a squadron of the Levenher Dragoons, and six guns. Farago's advanced post then moved left to seek contact with Bennigsen, finding him with Klenau in Fuchshain.

Under orders from the Czar to bring his forces together, including moving Bubna to Grimma, Bennigsen ordered night marches to draw his forces together. Bennigsen's advanced guard had arrived in Fuchshain around 4:00 p.m. Acting in accordance with the Czar orders, Bennigsen united with Klenau for an attack, despite the fact that his main body, under GL Docturov, had not yet arrived, and would not until late that evening. GL Stroganov moved his advanced guard between Fuchshain and Seifertshain. It was reinforced with some of Klenau's detachments. The reissuance of the order to attack caused Bennigsen to issue further orders. He directed the main body to establish itself between Fuchshain and Naunhof, and prepared his dispositions for the following day, in order to comply with the Czar's orders to strike the French left wing by Klein-Pösna.

The Kolmberg was to be attacked by Stroganov's advanced guard, the cavalry of GM Kreutz, and Klenau's right wing, supported by Tschaplitz's Cavalry Division from the east side. The main body of the 4th Armeeabteilung would attack frontally and from the west. Klenau would, at the same time, strike the Niederholz. The 12th Division, under GM Chovanski, and 24 guns, were positioned by Seifertshain to support the attack. Chovanski was to push his division towards Holzhausen. The main body under Docturov, formed from half of the 13th Division and all of the 26th Division, stood behind the heights of Fuchshain and Seifertshain. It was to execute a flanking march to take Klein-Pösna by surprise. Lindfor's Brigade of the 13th Division formed the reserve for the entire army group. Platov, who had passed through Beucha, received an order to cross the Parthe by Zweenfurth and move against Hirschfeld. The 2nd Light Division (Bubna) was to cross the river by Beucha, and cover the right wing. Both groups were to strike French flank and rear, so as to fall on and cut the road from Wurzen to Leipzig.[27]

Latour arrived at Threna to see Klenau around 8:00 p.m. He gave Klenau, Schwarzenberg's orders to shift the attack more towards the middle. Klenau ordered Hohenlohe's 2nd Division to detach a single battalion to Seifertshain. Two more were ordered to occupy the Windmühlenberg, and the main body of Abele's Brigade (3rd Division) closed up to Hohenlohe's 2nd Division. Only Paumgarten (1st Brigade, 1st Division) was to remain on the left wing of Bennigsen's army and support Seifertshain.

Latour rode to Stroh, where he found Bennigsen asleep in a plundered house. He attempted to induce the General to change his disposition, but met stubborn resistance. Bennigsen referred to the Czar's orders, saw no justification in them for a move against the French middle, and related the advantages of a flanking movement. Latour realized that a change of plans at so late an hour would be impractical. Klenau, advised of Bennigsen's plans and that Bennigsen would not vary from his dispositions, advised Schwarzenberg of the situation. The next morning Klenau ordered the appropriate modifications to the dispositions his forces.

His goal was that the Polish Reserve Army would be ready to attack the French flank through Naunhof. Bennigsen wrote that the southern army group was to march "through Pösna in order to go around the enemy," while the 2nd Light Division should move through Brandis and Beucha towards Klein-Pösna before daybreak, so that it could join a general attack of the allies against Leipzig at 8:00 a.m.

In order to execute the attack as smoothly as possible, Bennigsen's and Klenau's staff officers were directed to mark the lines of march and to find the best routes possible for the maneuvering divisions.[28]

The Army of Silesia

At the break of day, Blücher went to his advanced posts closest to Leipzig. Sacken's Corps stood in the first line at Möckern. Yorck's Corps had been designated as the reserve, and withdrew to Wahren both to rest and to reorganize, after the losses of the previous day.

In many instances two battalions were reorganized into a single battalion, and the four Prussian brigades were reorganized into two divisions. The 1st and 8th Brigades became the 1st Division under the command of General Hünerbein. The 2nd and 7th Brigades became the 2nd Division under General Horn.[29]

The French still occupied the villages of Eutritzsch and Gohlis, as well as the line of the stream which ran between them. Delmas' 9th Division, III Corps, and the III Corps artillery park stood in Eutritzsch. Blücher advanced Kapzevich's 10th Corps in a frontal assault supported by 24 guns. Sacken's Corps was moved against Gohlis, and the cavalry moved over the Wiederitzsch against Parthe, while St.-Priest moved his force against Eutritzsch.[30]

The Russian frontal assault occurred at 9:00 a.m., as Kapzevich's 10th Corps struck Dombrowski's forces. Delmas found himself struck in the right, threatened by Vassil'shikov's Cavalry Corps and withdrew from Eutritzsch and moved his left wing behind Rietzschke.

Blücher then attacked Gohlis with Sacken's infantry and the Russian 2nd Hussar Division, as well as Vassil'shikov's Cossacks. As the advancing Russians began to skirmish by Gohlis, Ney assigned Dombrowski's sadly diminished 27th (Polish) Division to the defense of Gohlis and the adjacent Rietzschke passage over the river. Delmas' 9th Division was to hold the Eutritzsch heights and Quinette's Brigade of the reunified III Cavalry Corps was trusted with the defense of the right flank between the Rietzschkebach and the Parthe.

Blücher ordered Sacken's Corps forward to attack Gohlis proper, Langeron's Corps moved against the Eutritzsch heights. Vassil'shikov's Cavalry Corps took up positions between Rietzschke and Parthe. Blücher then ordered them forward. A battery began firing into Marmont's flank about 9:00 a.m., by the Parthe, and the four hussar regiments of Lanskoy's 2nd Hussar Division moved forward into the cannon fire of Delmas' and Marmont's forces. The cavalry was to follow St.-Priest's 8th Corps. However, before this the attack had advanced sufficiently, in order to prevent interference, Blücher allowed the Russian cavalry to attack. They rolled over the weak French cavalry and chased them across the Parthe. The Marioupol and Akhtyrsk Hussars, under Vassil'shikov II, advanced at the gallop and threw themselves against the right flank of Arrighi's III Corps, supported by a force of Cossacks. The attacking allied cavalry was pounded by the French artillery, but Vassil'shikov's two regiments of hussars struck the French with such fury, that the

French broke and fell behind their infantry. The Russian hussars pursued them aggressively, taking five guns.[31] The wild flight of the French cavalry shook the French troops on the other side of the river, and excitement and unrest spread far into the French lines.

Delmas' infantry stood in the middle of the field, devoid of cavalry support, and began to fire on the advancing hussars. The French infantry formed into squares, and directed its artillery against the hussars and tried to prevent them from falling back with their prisoners and captured cannons, but failed. This attack made the position of Delmas' 9th and Dombrowski's 27th (Polish) Divisions untenable, and obliged them to pull back to the advanced works by Pfaffendorf and the left bank of the Parthe.[32] The Russian attack was reasonably successful, taking five guns and 500 prisoners.[33]

Sacken's attack on Gohlis was executed by six battalions from the Kamchatka, Okhotsk, and 8th Jager Regiments. He sent the 50th Jager Regiment against the Pleisse. Sacken's attack was supported by a battery on the heights by Gohlis. The Poles defended themselves vigorously, but they were slowly pushed back. The Poles withdrew in good order, to the suburbs of the city. The attacks against Gohlis cost the Russians 192 cavalry *hors de combat*, 132 Cossacks, and about 100 infantry men.[34]

At this moment, Blücher received word that the Army of Bohemia was not going to attack until the following morning, and that the Army of the North was close at hand, but would not arrive for a while. He decided to stop his attacks and start again the following morning.

The French had evacuated the entire right bank of the Parthe, except for a few houses and earthworks raised near the Halle Gate of the city of Leipzig. An advance by Blücher would allow the French to concentrate their forces against him, should he choose to advance. It was wiser for him to remain stationary, until the resumption of combat the next morning.

The Army of the North

The magnitude of the victory by Möckern was overestimated in Blücher's headquarters. The view prevailed that on 16 October, not only had Blücher beaten the best infantry Corps in the French Army, that of Marmont, but that they had also fought and beaten the IV and VII Corps, a part of the French Guard and a Polish Corps. Aside from the fact that Blücher had faced a single corps with overwhelming forces, the magnitude of the victory was far less than it could have been, entirely due to the bungled management of the army, Blücher's unjustified fears of a flank attack, and the word that strong French armed forces were advancing down the road from Düben.

The Prussian losses were not inconsequential. Yorck's Corps had to be withdrawn from the front because of the great losses, namely in officers, for the purpose of a complete reorganization. However, Blücher's army had seized control of large sections of the Parthe, and improved its tactical situation considerably. As a result, during the evening of 16 October, the thought of a flanking movement through Taucha arose, however this would require the participation of the Army of the North if it were to be completely successful.[35]

Bernadotte was, during the morning of 16 October, aware of the movement of the Army of Silesia, but understood that Blücher was advancing towards Gross-Kugel. Bernadotte's duty was to defend the left flank, and to demonstrate towards the Mulde. During this morning, however, he decided to lead the Army of the North in a sweeping movement down the Mulde, to a position by Landsberg. The main body of the Russian cavalry under Winzingerode was to be sent to Kölsa.

The sounds of cannon to the south and the reconnaissance reports from the cavalry, indicated that Bitterfeld was unoccupied. That evening Bernadotte redeployed his army, such that at 6:30 a.m., on 17 October, it stood on both sides of Landsberg with its front facing to the south, ready to the march against Leipzig.

During the night word came of Blücher's victory at Möckern. With that word also came the concern, also held by the headquarters of the Army of Silesia, for the flank attack by a strong French corps from the direction of Düben, that Blücher had feared.[36] At 2:00 p.m., Bernadotte immediately issued orders for his troops to stand to arms and march towards Kölsa. The Russians led, followed by the Prussians.

At the same time, he issued the following statement to his army: "The commanding generals shall be made aware that the Army of Bohemia and the Army of Silesia yesterday engaged in a serious battle in the vicinity of Leipzig. The allies were victorious, but that it is indispensable that we support the Army of Silesia, which, in all probability, will be attacked by a French corps from the direction of Düben."

Bernadotte's statement clearly indicates the unmistakable and sincere desire to stand by his brothers in arms, but his sincerity was tainted by political influences. However, around 9:00 p.m., a note from Major General Stewart arrived, inviting the Army of the North to join in Blücher's proposed maneuver towards Taucha. Though Bernadotte did not know the reason for Blücher's desire for this maneuver, he did interpret from the report that, on 16 October, Napoleon had gained no victory in the south, and in the north he had suffered a setback. Surrounded by steadily growing superior forces, theoretically Napoleon had no other choice, than to remove his army from the unequal battle. The way to the Saale was difficult and blocked by allied troops, so there remained only two escape routes from Leipzig: first a march behind the Mulde, and second to move through Taucha. The Army of the North was not strong enough to stop Napoleon, should he move through Taucha. Indeed, should Bernadotte find himself facing the entire French army, as it pushed out of the Leipzig pocket, Bernadotte would find himself faced with committing the Swedish army, something that he succeeded in not doing during the course of the 1813 and 1814 campaigns. The political ramifications to Bernadotte personally, of having Napoleon smash the tiny Swedish army, were overwhelming and something Bernadotte would not accept.

Therefore Bernadotte shrank from the demands of Stewart's note, and instead, ordered the realignment of his front. Bernadotte's front originally faced Bitterfeld, but Bernadotte turned it towards Leipzig by resuming the march towards Kölsa, in order to place the Russians and Prussians in line from Breitenfeld to Podelwitz, with the Swedes serving as a reserve by Radefeld. A Prussian advanced guard was supposed to be established in Seehausen. Winzingerode, however, still had orders to detach a Cossack regiment from his cavalry corps and sent it towards Taucha, in order to destroy the bridge in the village, and to reconnoiter any possible French moves in that direction.[37]

Winzingerode advanced to Lindenthal and put himself at Blücher's disposition, who directed him to secure the passages over the Parthe by Taucha, and establish a link with the Army of Bohemia. On the morning of 17 October Blücher was already engaging the French. He still had no word of the outcome of the battle by the Army of Bohemia on 16 October, and Blücher realized that he could find himself facing the advance of the entire French army.

Ney's army group was so weakened, that it was obliged to content itself with defensive measures. Ney was strengthened by the arrival of the VII Corps coming from Eilenburg, and Souham's two divisions, which had bivouacked on the southern part of the battlefield, but during the morning hours, these troops were still not in their assigned positions, as a skirmish of pickets erupted by Gohlis. On 17 October, Marmont was chiefly occupied with reorganizing his shaken VI Corps and preparing his troops for the upcoming battle. Small French detachments secured the passages over the Parthe, upstream to Portitz.[38]

Ney was in a position of great weakness. He was also in a very difficult situation, with Napoleon warning him that he was responsible for holding Leipzig and the Parthe River line. Failure to hold his position would result in a disaster for the whole, thus saddling Ney with a burden of heavy responsibility.

Around 10:00 a.m., the battle had ended and the desultory fire of the Russian batteries quickly faded, because of the lack of sufficient targets. The engagement during the morning hours of 17 October, the battle between Eutritzsch and Gohlis, had chased the French from the right bank of the Parthe, allowing the Prussians to occupy a few houses in the outlying suburbs, and some of the earth works before the Halle Gate of Leipzig.

Blücher was overjoyed by this victory. Sacken and Yorck, about 20,000 men, now stood opposing Ney, while Langeron's and Winzingerode's cavalry could now lead the flanking movement around Taucha. Unfortunately, the way was not yet open. The arrival of significant French reinforcements had not gone unnoticed, and Blücher was disturbed that he heard no gunfire to the south. Blücher began to fear that, by being overly aggressive, he was running the danger of drawing onto himself an overwhelming force, and was courting a defeat. It was decided therefore, in view of the lack of news on the Army of Bohemia, to wait until the situation resolved itself, and push the attack no further.

Ney could now leisurely establish his position behind the Parthe for a stubborn defense. Dombrowski would defend Leipzig to the north, Bertrand's IV Corps stood to the west. Marmont's VI Corps stood in Schönefeld, Reynier's VII Corps, whose infantry first arrived at 7:00 p.m., on 17 October, stood east of Paunsdorf, and the cavalry stood by Neutzsch. The III Corps and the III Cavalry Corps were formed into a reserve. From Gohlis to Plösen, all the heights on the east of the Parthe were occupied by the French, and a shift carried out against Taucha by Blücher would have led to an interesting action, as Reynier was marching through this area and it was already occupied by an Italian brigade from Macdonald's XI Corps. The French were not showing any serious intent of crossing the Parthe. On the other hand, the whereabouts of the Army of the North was unknown to Ney, as he had been unable to obtain that information from any prisoners.[39]

Ney was very anxious for the army parks. Only a part of the artillery reserve marched with Reynier. The main portion appeared secure, but it had taken the longer way through Wurzen. Therefore, that afternoon, Ney ordered the deployment of two battalions with several squadrons on the heights to the west of the Parthe, by Taucha, to link him with GD Durrieu's forces.

Ney, who was charged with the defense of the entire northern front, the western section by Lindenau and part of the Mulde front, was facing the pending attack of two armies. That evening he found himself issuing orders to the IV Corps and Guilleminot's 13th Division, to open a line of retreat through Weissenfels. This relieved him of his immediate concern for Lindenau, and the escape to the west. The next day he prepared his dispositions, and watched with alarm the movements of the allies to the north. When he perceived that he would soon find the Army of the North before his front, he slowly began to realize that an operational accord existed between Bernadotte and Blücher.

In the early afternoon hours, as the point of the Army of the North arrived by Breitenfeld, Bernadotte realized that his premise of the withdrawal of the French was false. Winzingerode reported that the Cossacks sent to Taucha had confirmed a gathering of French in the vicinity of Leipzig. It was now understood that Napoleon had not given the game up for lost, and that a general attack was necessary in order to overthrow him.[40]

Facing the prospect of such a battle, Bernadotte chose to heal the rift between himself and Blücher. Around 4:00 p.m., Bernadotte wrote directly to Blücher, congratulating him on his victory and offering his hand in reconciliation. Meanwhile he assured Blücher that his movement against Leipzig had no other purpose than to help the neighboring army.

Bernadotte recognized that a direct thrust directly across the Parthe would not succeed, consequently the proposed attack through Taucha by one of the two armies must be executed, while the other engaged the French frontally. This placed the attacking army on Napoleon's most likely line of retreat. This could put the army by Taucha in the path of a flood of French soldiers driven as were those who struck Kleist at Kulm. The fight would be hard, but if they could hold out until the other army could arrive to strike the French in the flank and rear, a total and complete victory could be achieved. However, Bernadotte wanted to bring about a substantial reinforcement of his army. To him was this extremely important, as his grasp on the Swedish throne was weak and he was always looking over his shoulder to assure himself that Sweden was still supporting him. On the other hand, what good would it be for him to sacrifice his army to gain a great victory for the allies? It would only diminish his stature within the coalition, and he was already aspiring to greater things. He closed his letter to Blücher by stating that he sought a major role in all of the coalitions operations, but that his force had been greatly diminished by the constant necessity of detaching various forces, including Wallmoden's Corps, which had been sent to the western bank of the Elbe.[41]

In Blücher's judgement there was but one objective, but misunderstandings and bickering from various sources had caused him to grow so angry, that he did not answer those messages he received. Bernadotte's correspondence indicated to him, that the Army of the North again wished the place of honor on the right wing, as well as to take the less hazardous position behind the Parthe, while leaving the heavy fighting to the Prussians and Russians. Blücher was not willing to put the Army of Silesia in harm's way again, as these troops had already spilled enough blood by Möckern. Blücher sent a castigating response to Bernadotte, accusing the Swedes and Bernadotte of not being willing to place themselves in Taucha, and face the prospect of a fierce battle, but preferring to freely spend the lives of Prussians and Russians. Blücher then contacted Bülow directly, proposing that he and Winzingerode independently go over the Parthe, if Bernadotte ordered no advance on 18 October. Bülow allegedly answered that he would not be found lacking, where the wellbeing of the fatherland and Europe were involved. Also Winzingerode would not remain behind.

The arrival of Schwarzenberg's dispatch, delivered by Rittmeister Szechenyi, was to give the impetus to a more cordial agreement between Blücher and Bernadotte. The courier arrived in Blücher's headquarters around 10:00 a.m.[42] Schwarzenberg's invitation for the Army of Silesia to support the attack on 18 October found willing ears. Blücher had longed to know that the final settlement of accounts with Napoleon had begun, and Schwarzenberg's courier brought that word. He had, however, his concerns about the active participation of Bernadotte, when it was not directly ordered by Schwarzenberg. Szechenyi had, to be sure, brought no instruction for the Army of the North with him. Despite that, he immediately set out to Bernadotte's headquarters to give him an outline of Schwarzenberg's intentions, and an invitation to participate. Blücher gave him a fresh horse, and Szechenyi rode to the headquarters of the Army of the North. His message induced Bernadotte, despite Blücher's earlier abrupt refusal, once more to send an invitation to a personal meeting, where upon the angry Blücher finally relented.

On the morning of 17 October, both army leaders met in Breitenfeld. Major Rühle served as Blücher's interpreter, and Prinz Wilhelm of Prussia accompanied them, in case Bernadotte attempted to not cooperate. The plan was, that as a brother of the King of Prussia, Prinz Wilhelm could seize Bülow's Corps and lead it into battle without Bernadotte's cooperation.

The negotiations between the two army commanders lasted a considerable time. Blücher pushed for an attack by the Army of the North through Taucha. Bernadotte was, however, convinced that Napoleon would lead the withdrawal through this area. For this reason, he advised holding his army in echelons to the left, behind the Army of Silesia, in order to prevent a French flank attack. Arguments against this course were thrown back at Bernadotte. Napoleon's withdrawal was not certain, though it was possible. However, it was also possible that he would shift his forces, and seek to strike the Army of Bohemia with the greatest part of his forces. This possibility demanded an active attack from the north, and only an attack through Taucha gave the prospect of victory. After a long hesitation, which is very understandable from Bernadotte, as he was still convinced that the French would withdraw through Taucha, he finally accepted the proposal. However, his acceptance was tied to a condition, that the Army of the North, be reinforced by detachments drawn from the Army of Silesia.[43]

Blücher consented and sent Langeron's Corps to serve with Bernadotte's Army of the North. However, he set the condition that this corps not be committed to the movement through Taucha, but would serve on the right flank of the Army of the North and pass directly across the Parthe. Also Bülow and Winzingerode were to use the next passage over the Parthe, and the Swedes were to stand as the general reserve by Breitenfeld.

Impatient to get on with the war, Blücher did not wait for the written agreement, in which these conditions were stipulated. His mistrust was again awakened, but it was unfounded. Blücher was still uncertain that Bernadotte would carefully meet all the requirements necessary, to assure that a coordinated attack would be made.

At 2:00 a.m., on 17 October, as ordered by Bernadotte, the Army of the North departed Landsberg, in the anticipation of the battle to be given the following morning by Leipzig. When Bernadotte arrived, he set up his headquarters in Milkou.

At 8:00 a.m., the Army of the North arrived on the heights of Breitenfeld and Klein-Podelwitz, where it set up camp. A few hours earlier, General Winzingerode arrived with the advanced guard of 400-500 men, and had moved against Taucha, taking the village and capturing three French officers and 400 soldiers. A few hours later, however, part of Reynier's VII Corps counterattacked and recaptured the village. The village was then given a garrison of Saxon infantry.

In Napoleon's Headquarters

As Napoleon reviewed the battle field during the evening of 16 October, his feeling of the satisfaction had left, when he found himself unable to consider the day's actions as a decisive victory of French arms. The conditions on the north, by Leipzig and on the Parthe, were not unfavorable based on the news of 4:00 p.m., so that the high mood in the headquarters was only dampened by concern over Reynier's fate, and that of Durrieu's costly and vital park column. A report from Reynier finally arrived around midnight, stating that the VII Corps had advanced through Taucha and was moving towards Leipzig. Ney, to whom command of the VII Corps had been given, was informed and sent Reynier orders by a returning courier.

Napoleon directed the portion of Souham's III Corps, which had moved to the southern battlefield, to move back towards Leipzig, where it united with Delmas' 9th Division. This force was also placed under Ney's command. On the other hand, Dombrowski's 27th (Polish) Division was withdrawn towards Liebertwolkwitz, to serve as a reserve. Around 2:00 p.m., Gourgaud returned from Liebertwolkwitz and reported that he found the men of the II Corps very fatigued and dejected, while the allied force facing them during the battle had constantly grown in strength. The soldiers' enthusiasm had vanished, only the trust of the soldiers remained. Macdonald reported from Holzhausen, that the allied forces opposing him numbered between 40,000 and 50,000 men and that he feared that they would attack again on 17 October.[44]

Count Poniatowski portrayed his situation with little confidence. He had lost a third of his men and as many of his officers. He barely had munitions for an hour's fighting. Prisoners he had taken said that the allies awaited the arrival of Bennigsen and the Army of the North on 17 October. All this news from every side of the battlefield steadily depressed the mood in the headquarters. The truth of the situation finally broke about 3:00 a.m., as the reports from the battle around Möckern and Lindenthal arrived.

Bertrand related the significant numerical superiority of the allies marching against Lindenau, the great losses suffered by IV Corps, and that it desperately needed reinforcements and munitions, otherwise he doubted he could hold his position. Around midnight, Marmont sent only a short report from Schönefeld, stating that he faced about 60,000 men and 12,000 cavalry and that this force appeared to be growing. His own losses would not be available until he reorganized on 17 October. Ney's detailed report was even gloomier. He estimated the allied forces facing Marmont at 60,000, those facing Bertrand at 20,000. He stated that they were growing, and that they came from the armies of Blücher and Bernadotte, as well as an Austrian division. He related that his forces had captured Russians, Prussians, and Austrians, which, as there were no Swedes taken, caused Ney to believe that Bernadotte's army must be held in reserve. Marmont had lost over half of his manpower and over 30 cannon. The losses suffered by Bertrand and Dombrowski were very heavy. Ney stated that he felt he would be attacked by superior forces on 17 October, which would force him to evacuate Leipzig and withdraw to Liebertwolkwitz.[45]

With regards to Reynier, Ney related that he had received no news. Ney also stated that during the evening of 16 October, Reynier had been sent orders to march through Eilenburg and on to Leipzig, while DG Durrieu was to move through Wurzen with the grand park. Ney's pessimism evoked, in the headquarters, the impression that Ney was ready to withdraw, and so two hours later he was sent new orders stating, "It is absolutely necessary that you occupy the position by Leipzig and on the Parthe, where Reynier and his corps shall be placed. This morning we were in battle with the enemy, over which yesterday many advantages were achieved. If we are victorious and put to him to flight, then all is saved. However, if you evacuate Leipzig, everything is lost."

The movement of Dombrowski's 27th (Polish) Division, ordered earlier, was canceled. Murat found himself, on this critical Sunday morning with Napoleon, and sought, by referring to the great losses the allied forces had suffered, to console him. In case Napoleon should actually have the intent, through a renewed attack against the Army of Bohemia, to gain breathing space, preparations had to be made, otherwise catastrophe loomed.

In fearful expectation the morning hours passed. Random artillery shots echoed across the field, but the awaited allied attack did not come. The fact must have puzzled Napoleon, and perhaps awakened in him the impression that his situation was yet not so hopeless. His main concern continued to be Durrieu's column of the grand park, and its arrival in Leipzig.

Perhaps Napoleon already realized that he must withdraw to free himself from the allied encirclement. He spend much of the afternoon in dull brooding over the maps. Around 1:30 p.m., Ney's report arrived, but it gave Napoleon again little news about the situation by Leipzig and on the Parthe. Also Lefèbvre-Desnoëttes, who had an observation post in the Stötteritz church tower, reported that Reynier, with his cavalry, was coming. At this time, Napoleon had doubtless already decided to withdraw, because all reports surely indicated to him that an iron ring was closing fast around his army.

Still, he wanted to be certain before he committed himself to a withdrawal. The captive GdK Merveldt, whom Napoleon had personally known for a long time and held in esteem, was brought to him.[46] Around 2:00 p.m., Napoleon met with Merveldt and sought in a conversation with him, to gage the strength and intent of the allies. Merveldt's answers of the total situation corresponded with Napoleon's impressions and the reports sent by his generals. He questioned Merveldt if the allies would attack on 18 October. Merveldt responded that they would, and also mentioned that the Bavarian army had joined the allied cause. The conversation then took a political turn. Napoleon wished to take the opportunity of communicating with his father-in-law through Merveldt, and pass information that he was prepared to buy peace at a great personal price. It is highly unlikely, despite suggestions, that Napoleon was interviewing Merveldt with the idea of using negotiations to escape his encirclement. Speaking with a captive soldier was a questionable method of obtaining intelligence to the intentions of the allies, often fraught with deliberate misrepresentations or simple conjectures based on misinformation that could have no relation to the next decisions made by the allies. Napoleon was totally aware of this. Despite that, Napoleon

Napoleon dictates orders to Marshal Berthier during the night of 18/19 October, painting by Meunier.

spent the next few hours in conversation with Merveldt, to whom he had returned his saber. Napoleon then issued the orders for the withdrawal of the French army.[47]

It will probably never be understood why Napoleon remained inactive this day, why he did not undertake to withdraw through Weissenfels, behind the Saale, or why he did not choose to strike the principal allied army. Much of it could be tied to the need to resupply his forces with munitions. He knew that the armies of Bernadotte, Bennigsen, and Colloredo were about to join the allies, yet he remained inactive and allowed the allies to receive 100,000 reinforcements.

During the night of 17/18 October, Leipzig saw more than 500,000 soldiers camped on its plains. Never before had such a sight been seen in Europe. The skies were red with the glow of innumerable camp fires. The houses and gardens surrounding the city were destroyed, as troops on both sides gathered materials to make their bivouacs more comfortable. The night would be short and it rained.[48]

9

The Battles to the South: the Third Day of Battle 18 October 1813

The Emperor Napoleon had awaited the allied attacks during the previous day without result. In the early morning of 18 October it began raining in the French bivouacs by Dölitz, Wachau, Mark-Kleeberg, and Liebertwolkwitz. As it rained, Murat and Macdonald pulled their corps back to the positions the Emperor had ordered them to occupy around Connewitz-Probstheida-Holzhausen. The II, V, and IX Corps withdrew from Wachau and Liebertwolkwitz to a distance of a league from Leipzig.

In order to conceal their move, the French corps commanders had left detachments in Dölitz, Dösen, Wachau, the Meusdorf farm, Liebertwolkwitz, and Baalsdorf, and covered them with substantial skirmisher screens. Strong detachments were posted in front of Poniatowski's Corps in Dölitz and Dösen.

At 2:00 a.m., the entire French army was under arms and in the following positions.

The right wing, under Murat, was formed of the VIII, II, IX, and V Corps. Augereau's IX Corps had moved from Probstheida towards the west, behind the Pleisse. To their east the VIII Corps (Poniatowski) was in Connewitz and Lefol's Independent Division stood by Connewitz. Sokolnicki's IV Cavalry Corps stood to Augereau's east. The II Corps (Victor) was in Probstheida. Behind the II Corps stood the I and V Cavalry Corps. Maréchal Oudinot (I Young Guard Corps) was east of Connewitz and formed the reserve of the right wing with the 1st and 3rd Young Guard Divisions. Strong detachments were placed before the main French line in the villages of Dölitz, Dösen, Zuckelhausen, the Meusdorf farm, and the Liebertwolkwitz tile works. Overall command of this force lay with Murat.

The French center was formed by the XI Corps (Macdonald) and stood near the villages of Zuckelhausen and Holzhausen. Detachments from the corps occupied the villages of Klein-Pösna and Baalsdorf. In the second line, between Probstheida and Stötteritz, stood Lauriston's V Corps, which had detached a few battalions to Zwei-Naundorf and Mölkau. Sébastiani's II Cavalry Corps stood between Holzhausen and Zwei-Naundorf, covering Macdonald's left flank and connected Macdonald to Paunsdorf, which was occupied by Zeschau's Saxon 24th Division, part of Ney's northern group.[1]

Communications with the left wing were through Zwei-Naundorf and Mölkau. Walther's Guard Cavalry and the Old Guard stood in Thonberg, near the Quandt Tobacco Mill, where Napoleon was to spent most of the day. Maréchal Mortier held the avenues of Leipzig. GD Bertrand, in his capacity as commandant of Leipzig, watched the interior of the city.

The left wing of the French army was under Maréchal Ney. The VI Corps (Marmont) stood by Schönefeld. The III Corps (Souham) was between Meutzsch and the Thekla Church. The VII Corps (Reynier) was in Paunsdorf and Taucha.[2]

On the north side of Leipzig, in the Halle suburbs, by the Rosenthal gate to the Pfaffendorf, stood the III Cavalry Corps (Arrighi) and Dombrowski's 27th (Polish) Infantry Division and cavalry.

At 3:00 a.m., in the morning, Napoleon moved the IV Corps (Bertrand) to Lindenau and ordered him to march on the road from Lützen to Weissenfels, and to occupy the Saale River bridge near the latter village. Napoleon had decided that, in the event of a retreat, it would be necessary for him to hold this critical bridge. From there, Napoleon moved to Reudnitz, where Ney had his headquarters. As he passed through Reudnitz, Napoleon found Ney still asleep, awoke him, and had a long discussion with him. The contents of this discussion are unknown, other than it related to the hoped for arrival of GD Durrieu. Durrieu, with the imperial war chest, the engineering park, the pontoon train, and the portion of the artillery park that had not accompanied Reynier, was a major concern for both the Emperor and Marshal. Reynier was instructed to hold the way through Taucha open, without getting into a serious battle. Durutte's 32nd Division, relieved Guilleminot's 13th Division and occupied positions by the Parthe near Schönefeld. Durutte was supposed to attempt to open a passage immediately in the line Schönefeld-Paunsdorf. If this failed, Durrieu was instructed to take his trains to safety via Torgau.

In this conversation, Napoleon told Ney that he anticipated an attack in the region between Taucha and Schönefeld, from the allied forces on the opposite side of the Parthe, and that the heart of the battle would be between Paunsdorf-Schönefeld. In this region, Maréchal Ney had Reynier's VII Corps, Marmont's VI Corps by Schönefeld, and Souham's III Corps. The latter had spent the night by Reudnitz and Crottendorf, and later received the order to advance towards Sellerhausen and Paunsdorf. That movement began at 9:00 a.m.[3]

Ney deployed his cavalry in pickets before his lines, in order to contact Durrieu. Reynier's Saxon cavalry, reinforced with a battalion and a horse battery, advanced to the Parthe by Taucha. Marmont's VI Corps cavalry, the Württemberg Brigade under GM Normann, stood to their rear as a reserve behind Taucha. Reynier and Marmont were personally convinced that these troops were properly positioned and that their task was completed.

Napoleon had, in the meantime, ridden to Lindenau. It is probable he was studying whether the road through Lindenau with its numerous bridges and defiles would suffice for him to withdraw his entire army, or if he would need to secure a crossing on the Pleisse. That he did not begin a withdrawal would seem to indicate that he had consoled himself with the hope that 18 October would bring him victory over the allies, and the need for withdrawal would vanish. It may also be that he felt that a strong rearguard in Leipzig could resist any allied assault, more than long enough to withdraw his army. Napoleon also counted on his senior commanders to have the foresight to prepare for the possibility of having to move a shattered and confused army down the Lindenau road, and to make appropriate preparations.[4]

At the break of day Napoleon sent General Merveldt back to the allies on parole. Merveldt was given a letter to the Austrian Emperor in which Napoleon offered to surrender to the allies the fortresses he held along the Oder and Vistula, on the condition that the allies allow him to withdraw to a position behind the Saale. He added that, if approved, they should sign an armistice and undertake peace negotiations.[5] The offer was refused.

The Allies Prepare

On their side, the allied monarchs and Schwarzenberg moved at the break of dawn, onto the battlefield. The entire army was ready to attack and was organized into six columns. They were:

1. The column of the Erbprinze von Hessen-Homburg.
2. The column of Barclay de Tolly.
3. The column of Bennigsen.
4. The column of Bernadotte.

5. The column of Blücher.[6]
6. The column of Gyulai.

The first column, under Hessen-Homburg, consisted of a division of the Austrian 2nd Armeeabteilung under Lederer, which stood on the left bank of the Pleisse. On the right bank of the Pleisse stood the Austrian 1st Armeeabteilung (Colloredo), the reserve divisions of Bianchi and Weissenwolf, the Austrian Reserve Cavalry Corps, and the division of Prince A. von Liechtenstein. This column contained 40,000 men and was ordered to advance down the right bank of the Pleisse and along the main route from Mark-Kleeberg towards Dölitz. GML I. Lederer's 1st Division of the 2nd Armeeabteilung was to move along the left bank towards Connewitz.

The second column, under Barclay de Tolly, consisted of Wittgenstein's Russian forces, the Prussian 2nd Corps (Kleist, less Ziethen's 11th Brigade), and the Prussian and Russian Reserve Corps under the orders of Grand Duke Constantine and Miloradovich. This corps contained 55,000 men. It was to attack Wachau and Liebertwolkwitz frontally, and from there to advance against Probstheida.

The third column, under Bennigsen, was the Army of Poland. It consisted of his advanced guard (Stroganov), Docturov's Russian Corps, Tschaplitz's Cavalry Division, the Austrian 2nd Light Division (Bubna), the Austrian 4th Armeeabteilung (Klenau), the Prussian 11th Brigade (Ziethen), and Platov's Cossacks. The third column contained 50,000 men. It was to turn the French left wing and advance from Fuchshain towards Zuckelhausen, Holzhausen, and Leipzig.

Bernadotte formed the fourth column with the Prussian 3rd Corps (Bülow), the Swedish army (Stedingk), Winzingerode's Russian Corps, and Langeron's Russian Corps drawn from the Army of Silesia. Bernadotte's column contained 96,000 to 100,000 men. It had been decided that the Army of the North would pass over the Parthe at Taucha, but General Blücher observed that it would take more than a day for this to be effected, and directed Langeron to cross the Parthe at Mockau.

The fifth column, under Blücher, consisted of the 1st Prussian Corps (Yorck) and Sacken's Russian Corps. These two corps consisted of about 25,000 men after the battle of Möckern and were to move against Leipzig proper.

The sixth column, under Gyulai, was formed from the Austrian 3rd Armeeabteilung (Gyulai), the Austrian 1st Light Division (M. von Liechtenstein), and the Russian streifkorps (Thielmann). The column contained 20,000 men and was to advance from Klein Zschocher towards Lindenau.[7]

The measures the French took to conceal their movement to their new positions on the morning of 18 October were successful. The allies had just stood to arms when the word came from their advanced posts that the French had long since changed their dispositions. The generals of the Austrian left wing seemed oblivious of the changed situation. It was the lively and eager GM Langenau, who broke the news to them. In the early morning hours he had ridden towards Wachau and Dösen and had witnessed the French departure.

Between 7:00 a.m. and 8:00 a.m., the allies began their concentric advance against Leipzig.

Advance of the First Column

The first column, under the command of Hessen-Homburg, advanced down the right bank of the Pleisse and took up a position on the heights between Dösen and Lössnig. The Austrians followed their advanced guard in three columns. On the left was Bianchi's and Weissenwolf's Divisions, along the Pleisse. The middle column was formed by Haugwitz's Brigade of Bianchi's Division and six and a half battalions of A. Liechtenstein's Division, 1,000 paces to the right of Bianchi. The right column was formed by Wimpffen's and Greth's Divisions, which passed from

Auenhain through the western part of Wachau. Nostitz's cavalry marched between Bianchi and Haugwitz and was directed to hold itself ready to support either column.[8] With the first cannon shots, Napoleon moved to the Dutch Mill by Thonberg, which provided a view of the entire plain. The artillery fire ranged from Raschwitz and Dölitz to Baalsdorf. Long lines of allied infantry moved up from the south of the Galgenberg and Kolmberg Heights. To the left, towards the road to Dresden, allied corps moved against the gap between the VII and XI Corps. In contrast, nothing was to be seen on the road to Lützen or along the Elster. The allies had been, as Napoleon had predicted, obliged to concentrate their forces and to uncover the road to Erfurt. After studying the battlefield for a few minutes, Napoleon ordered Bertrand to move to Weissenfels, and for the various army corps to pull back to the line of battle to which they had been assigned.[9]

The heavy allied artillery was one of the reasons for the French withdrawal. The French cavalry withdrew behind the infantry. Sokolnicki's IV Cavalry Corps moved behind the VIII Corps, GD Doumerc's I Cavalry Corps withdrew behind Victor's II Corps, with one wing towards Poniatowski's VIII Corps and the other towards Macdonald's XI Corps.

Around 8:00 a.m., FML Ignaz Hardegg sent three squadrons of the Hessen-Homburg Hussars and two horse guns, under Oberst Simonyi, forward against Dölitz. The main body of the advanced guard, two battalions of the Deutzsch-Banat Grenz and the Reisch Dragoons, followed closely behind them.

Dölitz was strongly defended by elements of Sémélé's 52nd Division.

Although the French strongly held the village of Dölitz with guns and infantry, Simonyi resolved to march as quickly as possible to the other side of the village, so as not to lose the least time in striking the French, and get his hussars out of their menacing situation. This movement was barely begun when the French first line struck at the Austrian hussars.

Simonyi sounded the charge, and drove back not only the French infantry assault, but completely broke through the second French line and threw that back. Twice more the hussars charged forward in order to give the Austrian infantry time to arrive.

On the heights east of the village there stood a major force of French infantry and cavalry. Simonyi's squadrons were no longer a cohesive force and found themselves in a dangerous position. Before them stood the French in overwhelming numbers supported to the rear by French artillery that covered the defile. The two Austrian horse guns accompanying him had followed the hussars' rush through the village.[10] His force was soon supported by a fresh squadron of the Reisch Dragoons and the Deutzsch-Banat Grenz Regiment.

These two units joined Simonyi's cavalry and advanced against Lössnig and a French force standing to the east of Lössnig. This force consisted of number of battalions and squadrons under Poniatowski and Augereau.

FML I. Hardegg received a serious head wound in the assault and command passed to GM Karl Graf Raigecourt. This first allied assault against this French position failed.

With little effort, the Deutzsch-Banat Grenz Regiment were able seize the northern edge of Dölitz with a bayonet assault, and then occupy the eastern farmsteads.

While the advanced guard battled in and around Dölitz, the three columns of Hessen-Homburg's assault force closed on the position. Erbprinz von Hessen-Homburg led Bianchi's Division, which consisted of only six battalions. He ordered them forward to reinforce the advanced guard in Dölitz. Although Bianchi's troops had suffered tremendous losses on 16 October, they joined the Deutzsch-Banat Grenz Regiment and threw the French out of Lössnig. The French fell back to their main position to the east of the village under the strong, defensive artillery fire. At the same time as this attack began, Haugwitz's Brigade cleaned the French out of Dösen and moved north of this village. At the same time, Merczery's Brigade, of A. Liechtenstein's Division, remained to the south.

The Austrian Infantry Regiment 'Hesse Homburg' during the battle on 18 October,
painting by Neumann.

Weissenwolf's Division lingered by Mark-Kleeberg, while the Austrians advanced from the heights north of Dösen. Erbprinz von Hessen-Homburg decided not to commit Nostitz's cavalry to the battle. Nostitz's cavalry had advanced the same distance as Barclay de Tolly's column, but the terrain had been seized without using it. Though it was preferable to keep the bulk of the cavalry fresh, the Austrian reserve cavalry commander did dispatch the Lothringen and Kronprinz Ferdinand Cuirassier Regiments through the low ground between Dösen and Dölitz. The main body of the reserve cavalry remained to the south.

The Austrian right column advanced, with Wimpffen's Division in the lead, through Auenhain and into the western portion of Wachau, where it encountered only a few French skirmishers. At the same time, the Prussian schützen of Klüx's 9th Brigade moved into the village. The further advance of Wimpffen's Division took place in coordination with the Prussian movements.

Wimpffen's and Pirch's Battalions, by the Meusdorf farm, advanced one behind the other against the nearest French forces. The Austrian de Vaux Infantry Regiment and the Prussian 2nd West Prussian Infantry Regiment attacked with the Prussians circling to the right.[11]

Between the two columns advanced two brigade batteries. The allies were quickly engaged in a battle to take the farm and the surrounding woods, when suddenly, west of the farmsteads, the Austrians faced "a French Infantry column accompanied by a cavalry regiment." Strong detachments occupied the farm, the French cavalry went forward against the Austrian artillery in order to push between the Austrians and Prussians. The attack threatened to capture Austrian Brigade Battery #2. The allies responded with heavy canister fire, while two companies of the Prussian 7th Reserve Infantry Regiment and the 1/de Vaux Infantry Regiment moved into the interval between the columns and fired on the French cavalry, throwing them back. The allied infantry advanced against the farm, forcing the French to abandon the Meusdorf farm and the adjacent woods. The French pulled back to Probstheida. The occupation of the farm, however, cost the life of GM von Giffing.

Wimpffen reported that the French fighting in Meusdorf were reinforced by forces coming from Liebertwolkwitz, forcing Mayer's Division into the fight. However, the Prussian reports make no mention of such a French movement, which would have had to pass in front of them. The French that Wimpffen reported were probably a detachment sent forward from Probstheida.

The Prussian 12th Brigade (Prinz August von Preussen), advancing to the right of the Prussian 10th Brigade (Pirch), and Platov's cavalry, moved into contact with the Prussian 11th Brigade (Ziethen), advancing from Liebertwolkwitz. Because the area into which the allies advanced was growing ever more narrow, the two Russian infantry corps of Gorchakov and Württemberg were withdrawn from the 1st line and now followed behind the right wing.[12]

The Advance of the Second Column

Barclay de Tolly's attack column had organized itself on the other side of the Borna-Wachau-Leipzig road. It formed itself on the Gülden-Gossa-University Forest line, while Hessen-Homburg had formed his Austrians in the region around the Auenhain Farm, Mark-Kleeberg, and Cröbern. It was planned that the left column would remain on the defensive until Barclay de Tolly's troops reached Wachau, then both would be on the offensive.

Barclay de Tolly directed his force in two columns down the road from Gülden-Gossa. Wittgenstein moved through Liebertwolkwitz and Kleist moved through Wachau. The French, as mentioned earlier, had abandoned the heights of Gossa and left only a few cavalry outposts on them.

As Barclay de Tolly's forces moved forward as prescribed, these pickets withdrew, leaving the terrain open for the advancing allies. The Russian and Prussian Guard infantry, the Russian grenadiers, and the Russian guard cavalry moved to the right of Gülden-Gossa and Wachau, towards the Meusdorf Farm. The Czar, the King of Prussia, and Prince Schwarzenberg found themselves with this column, between the first line and the reserve. The sovereigns charged themselves personally with maintaining the communications between the various advancing columns and with holding the reserve within good supporting distance of the first line.[13]

Kleist's 2nd Prussian Corps advanced on and to the right of the Wachau road. They went slowly forward as a solid mass, but Kleist decided to pull Klüx's 9th Brigade back and move forward Prinz August von Preussen's 12th Brigade. This shifting of brigades occurred immediately northeast of Wachau. When the evolution was complete the 10th and 12th Brigade moved into the first line, while Klüx's 9th Brigade moved back with the reserve cavalry in the second line. The Prussian reserve cavalry followed behind the middle. Gorchakov's (1st) and Württemberg's (2nd) Russian Corps, neither being stronger than a Prussian brigade, were grouped together in the University Forest to form the second line. On their flank, linking them with Klenau, stood Kretov's 2nd Cuirassier Division reinforced by Pahlen's Cavalry Corps.

Barclay de Tolly's column had, as a reserve, the Russian 2nd Grenadier and the 3rd Cuirassier Divisions. These two divisions were followed at a great distance by the Russian 1st Grenadier Division and the Russian and Prussian Guard infantry and cavalry.

The advance of Barclay de Tolly's middle column was apparently delayed as a result of Klenau's battle. As the last infantry and artillery moved from the Steinberg heights, Kleist's Prussians, Wittgenstein's Russians, and Wimpffen's Austrians began their movement towards Probstheida. The Prussian skirmishers pushed up to the clay village walls bristling with French bayonets. Greeted by devastating volleys of musketry, they turned back as quickly as they had arrived, thrown back on their supporting troops much battered for the effort.

Oudinot's Attack by Dölitz and Lössnig

Napoleon turned back from Lindenau towards the Quandt Tobacco Mill around 8:00 a.m. From there he watched the advance of the allies, and ordered Bertrand to move his corps from Lindenthal and attack Weissenfels. From Murat's front came the report of the heavy blows by the allies from the south and southeast. Napoleon was not very disturbed by these messages. More forces deployed against Murat, meant fewer allied troops remained available on the far side of the Pleisse, to hinder the planned breakthrough. Of more concern was the danger which threatened from the east.

At 9:00 a.m., the Old Guard marched from its positions by Strassenhäusern past Napoleon. The Guard artillery advanced and moved to a position to the west of Probstheida. Napoleon lingered a short time in the gun line, then moved back to the mill, and issued some more orders. He then lay down on the ground, apparently lost in thought.

First Murat shocked him from his thoughtful torpor. The King of Naples came in highly agitated, leapt from his horse, and gave the Emperor a quick, breathless report. He was highly concerned about his position, especially his right wing under Poniatowski, who faced assaults by Hardegg, Bianchi, and Haugwitz. Poniatowski's VIII Corps had already suffered huge losses in the battles of 16 October, and had little fight left in it. Murat's report impressed the Emperor with the gravity of the situation.[14] A successful assault by the allies along the Pleisse threatened the army with a catastrophe. Maréchal Oudinot detached Decouz's 3rd Young Guard Division, to a position behind Poniatowski's feeble battle line.

Murat led his reinforcement to the flat heights east of Connewitz, and ordered Decouz's Young Guard to immediately attack the allies in Lössnig and the adjacent heights. This attack was preceded by a murderous artillery bombardment and Sokolnicki's cavalry moved on its left flank. Facing them was Bianchi's Division and the Deutzsch-Banat Grenz Regiment, which occupied Lössnig and the eastern farmsteads of Dölitz.

The French cavalry moved forward from Probstheida. Bordesoulle's 1st Cuirassier Division on the left and Doumerc's 3rd Cuirassier Division on the right. These two divisions charged repeatedly, throwing back the Russian cuirassiers, as well as the Prussian and Austrian cavalry that was thrown against it. The allies found themselves on the defensive at the most important point in the line.

The overwhelming power of the combined forces of Poniatowski and the Guard Division was too much. Bianchi's Division steadily crumbled and one weak battalion after another fell away. The losses of the division grew, as Bianchi's troops struggled to resist the Young Guard. Bianchi's forces were finally compelled to fall back towards Dölitz, where they were struck by the French cavalry. The Austrian battalions withdrawing southwards from Lössnig took the blow in the flank.

The infantry of the II Corps followed behind the victorious cavalry and Decouz's 3rd Young Guard Division moved out from Probstheida. However, Napoleon grew concerned about the advanced salient and ordered the forward movement stopped.[15]

The Austrian Major Wernhardt appeared at the head of part of the reserve cavalry, northwest of Dösen. He led a division of the Lothringen Cuirassier Regiment forward into the French cavalry, threw them back, and took one officer and 20 men prisoner. The confusion in the French ranks grew, when a division of the Kronprinz Ferdinand Cuirassier Regiment, under Major von Bolza, struck two French battalions and them threw back. This quick attack gave Bianchi and Raigecourt's Advanced Guard Division time to drag their artillery back to safety. Decouz quickly recovered and sent his attack forward once again. After a short, violent fight, in which GdK Hessen-Homburg was wounded and disabled,[16] the French pushed into Dölitz. At the same time another French column struck Haugwitz's Brigade in its position north of Dösen. The French blow was irresistible, throwing Haugwitz back.[17]

Schwarzenberg had ridden to the heights to the south of Wachau with the monarchs, to observe the action around Lössnig, Dölitz, Dösen, and the Meusdorf farm. The French counterattack appears to have made a deep impression upon him and his companions. This assault had the appearance of the feared eleventh hour, all out assault, by which Napoleon would mass his army against the allies and attempt to break through to the south. Overreacting, Schwarzenberg ordered Gyulai's 3rd Armeeabteilung to move from the left bank of the Elster towards Cröbern.

Schwarzenberg, with his staff, moved towards Mark-Kleeberg and Weissenwolf's 1st Reserve Division, which was not then engaged in combat. Schwarzenberg ordered Weissenwolf to move towards Dölitz. In consequence of Schwarzenberg's order, the 1st Brigade (Fürstenwärther) organized itself in three battalionsmassen, one behind the other on the heights to the right of the road. The second brigade battery moved up to the front, and skirmishers were sent forward. The 2nd Brigade moved to the road, and the position batteries took up a position on the Kellerberg northeast of Mark-Kleeberg. At this moment, Bianchi's Battalions came tumbling back, out of Dölitz. Weissenwolf immediately ordered a grenadier battalion forward to retake the village.

These grenadiers advanced in two groups in a bayonet assault that succeeded in gaining a lodgment, but at the cost of heavy casualties. FML Weissenwolf reinforced the first battalion of grenadiers with Fischer's Grenadier Battalion and later sent in Czartoryski's Division of the Portner Grenadier Battalion. The French and their allies were slowly pushed out of the village.

Weissenwolf later wrote that while the Austrian grenadiers moved into the burning village of Dölitz, the village was found to be filled with dead and wounded French and Poles, a large quantity of discarded weapons and countless corpses covering both sides of the field.[18]

At the same time, by Dösen, there was a heavy battle underway. According to battle reports, Haugwitz's Brigade stood in a ring around a wooded strip occupied by French soldiers to the north of Dösen. FML A. Liechtenstein drew the Reuss-Greiz Regiment into the first line and sent it forward. Major von Karlstein led the first battalion forward to clear the woods of French. Shortly later, von Karlstein was reinforced by a division of the 2nd Battalion. Slowly the Austrians succeeded in clearing the woods, but only with further reinforcement, in the form of the main body of the 2/Reuss-Greiz Infantry Regiment. Around noon, the French were finally thrown out of the wooded strip.

With battles taking place around Dölitz and Lössnig, since 9:00 a.m., the 2nd Armeeabteilung under FML Lederer, which stood on the left bank of the Pleisse, was eager to join the fray. The Bellegarde Regiment, facing Connewitz, and the W. Colloredo Regiment were detached from the left bank to take the Dölitz Palace, while the 2/Kaunitz and the Strauch Infantry Regiments remained as reserves. As Hardegg's battle by Dölitz slowed down, Lederer had the village shelled by four howitzers. After the capture of the village by the Austrian advanced guard Lederer moved to the Connewitz bridges in order to make preparations for the next move. Lederer personally reconnoitered the situation along the river, to evaluate his ability to seize a passage. The observations which he made of the French defensive preparations, convinced him that it was highly unlikely that he could, with the weak detachments available to him, force a passage over the river. He therefore chose to shell Lössnig in the hope that he the might have occasion to pass over the Pleisse there. Soon Lederer's attention was again drawn towards Dölitz, which the French had just reoccupied. The W. Colloredo Infantry Regiment formed on the river bank and engaged the French on the far side of the Pleisse with its musketry fire when possible.

As the Austrian grenadiers recaptured Dölitz, Lederer received an order from Schwarzenberg to send troops. In response he sent two battalions, one from the Kaunitz and the other from the W. Colloredo Infantry Regiment to support Weissenwolf on the right bank of the Pleisse.

By 1:00 a.m., Schwarzenberg had turned back the French threat to Wachau. He and the Czar stood on the heights halfway between Liebertwolkwitz and Probstheida, on the *Monarchenhügel*.[19] From there Schwarzenberg watched Macdonald's withdrawing troops abandoning Zuckelhausen and Holzhausen and moving towards Stötteritz, as well as Klenau's subsequent actions. Pahlen's cavalry was swinging west of Zuckelhausen, in order to increase the confusion in Macdonald's withdrawing columns.

In the first hours after noon, the sun came out of the clouds, illuminating the entire battlefield. The observers, who stood in the church tower in the occupied village, found themselves with an outstanding view of the action. Their reports were subjected to doubtful interpretations by the allied headquarters. These reports held Gyulai's Corps in suspension, even drawing his forces to the east. Unfortunately Schwarzenberg was tied up in the critical battle around Dölitz and could not provide overall battle administration.[20]

Wittgenstein's Column

Wittgenstein's column contained Gorchakov's men. They occupied the edge of the University Forest and marched forward with the Russian 2nd Corps from Gülden-Gossa towards Liebertwolkwitz while Pahlen's cavalry, reinforced by the Russian 2nd Cuirassier Division, maintained junction between the troops. The French formed on the Liebertwolkwitz heights, but they were chased off with a heavy cannonade. The French then reformed on the heights by the tile works between Liebertwolkwitz and Probstheida. However, once again heavy artillery fire forced them to retire. The allied infantry, preceded by its artillery, marched forward at the *geschwindschritt*.[21] Their musicians played military marches to encourage them and add to the martial air of the assault.

The village of Probstheida was occupied by the French II Corps (Victor) and by a large number of French cavalry. The French artillery was situated on the Windmill Heights in great force. This ridge was to the right of Probstheida and the artillery there directed its fire on Zuckelhausen. There was also a large force of French infantry and cavalry in Stateritz and on the left wing a cuirassier division was held in reserve. However, Drouot's artillery was the heart of the French resistance.

Napoleon, in response to Drouot's request, sent forward Curial's 2nd Old Guard Division and a number of dragoons to Probstheida, to support Drouot's batteries and the II Corps. Curial's second brigade, formed of the Velites of Turin and Velites of Florence, was positioned slightly to the rear of Decouz's 3rd Young Guard Division where they supported the left.

At around the same time, 2:00 p.m., Pahlen was ordered to pass between Zuckethausen and Stötteritz, so as to fall on the French, who withdrew from Holzhausen in the greatest disorder. To do this the allied cavalry passed through a hail of canister, but were unable to catch the withdrawing French. Two squadrons of the Grodno Hussars attacked the French artillery and seized a couple of guns. The Grodno and Soum Hussars then moved to the right of Holzhausen, while the infantry and artillery advanced towards Probstheida, followed by the Russian 2nd Cuirassier Division and by two squadrons of the Loubno Hussars.

Unfortunately for the allies, the Russian light troops became too advanced and were outside of supporting distance of the formed infantry behind them. The French cuirassiers charged forward and did a great execution amongst them, until Pahlen intervened. The Russian cavalry threw the French cuirassiers back behind their artillery. For his efforts, Pahlen had his horse killed underneath him and received two bad contusions in the resulting fall.[22]

Kleist's column advanced towards Wachau with the Prussian 9th, 10th, and 12th Brigades and the Prussian reserve cavalry. In front of them advanced 50 guns. The 9th and 10th Brigades formed the first line and the 12th Brigade acted as a reserve. The 10th Brigade was ordered to advance against the heights before Gülden-Gossa. They found those heights and the Wachau heights abandoned by the French. They continued forward.

The 9th Brigade, left Gülden-Gossa to the right, followed the other two brigades as a reserve, and occupied Wachau. Three battalions of the 7th Reserve Regiment were posted in the woods behind Wachau. The 10th Brigade found the Meusdorf Farm occupied by the French.

The Fus/2nd West Prussian Infantry Regiment advanced and engaged the French with its sharpshooters. At the same time, two French columns came out of the farm on the right, while two squadrons of French cavalry suddenly swung out of the left of the farm. Major Hundt wished to turn the French and to take them in the back, while engaging them with the Russian Uhlans, who seconded his attack. The French perceived his project and withdrew rapidly.[23]

The 10th Brigade joined on the left with the Austrian troops of the de Vaux Infantry Regiment. The 10th Brigade advanced towards Probstheida with the 12th Brigade at its side and the 9th following them. However, Kleist's Corps, like that of Wittgenstein, was forced to stop by heavy French resistance. He waited for the allied left wing to attack as well as the arrival of Bennigsen's column, which had a much longer route to take.

The Course of the Battle Pondered

The orders which Schwarzenberg sent FZM Gyulai around 2:00 p.m., and his order to the Austrian left wing that initially directed it to content itself with occupation of Dölitz, causes me to believe that Schwarzenberg already felt the battle was finished. It would also appear that he had renounced to Napoleon a clear path to the west by his orders to Gyulai. For Gyulai to achieve any type of success with certainty, he would have needed significantly stronger forces than the 3rd Armeeabteilung possessed. To achieve this strength, Schwarzenberg would have had to strip forces from the south and send them across the Elster, with no guarantee that they would arrive in time to influence the battle. Orders in hand, Gyulai knew what to do, to simply reconnoiter and identify the French line of withdrawal.[24]

To Schwarzenberg the pursuit was of decisive significance, and it was of greater importance than the continued efforts to encircle the remaining French forces still in Leipzig.

Leipzig would fall into the hands of the allies. This was certain and acknowledged ever since Napoleon had begun his withdrawal. This tactical victory caused the allied armies to eschew a renewed sacrifice of men, when they knew that in an hour or a half-day the city would be theirs. For Schwarzenberg the Leipzig campaign was settled. The question of the pursuit demanded a quick solution and Schwarzenberg's attention was fully occupied.

As Schwarzenberg turned back to the Monarchs, he wished to discuss the necessity of the battle against Probstheida. Kleist, after seeing the failure of his skirmishers, spoke strongly against sending his troops against the village, which would obviously be defended ferociously by the French.

Schwarzenberg's opinion on the attack was not recorded. However, his earlier directions vis-à-vis Weissenwolf's column, indicated an inclination to content himself with the terrain gained. Schwarzenberg knew the heavy sacrifice that would be demanded by an attack against the main strong point of the French southern front. In addition, it is highly probable that he did not wish to push large portions of the allied army into the narrow confines of the region around Leipzig. Such a balling together of the army as it flowed into Leipzig, would only complicate the beginning of an effective pursuit.[25] For several reasons therefore, it is probable that Schwarzenberg was against the attack, but was too intimidated to protest the needless assault when confronted by the will of the three monarchs.

The Czar intervened in the conversation with a lust for battle that had not heretofore motivated him, urging that Probstheida must be taken. Württemberg's Corps had been mangled and only had 1,800 effectives. Gorchakov's Corps had been reduced to at most 2,500 effectives, so it was fell to the Prussians to take the village.

The village of Probstheida stood in the center and was the key to the French position. As a result, it was strongly held. It was decided to carry it with a frontal assault, which would be difficult because of the houses and gardens. The garden walls were quite high and thick, and the village was defended with several batteries. In addition, there was a strong infantry garrison, and a large infantry reserve standing in dense columns behind the village.[26]

The Russian and Prussian Guards, as well as the Russian grenadiers, advanced to the ridge on the right of the tile works on the Liebertwolkwitz road. Not far from the tile works to the right of the main road, the three monarchs and Schwarzenberg stood watching the battle. It was 2:00 p.m.

The Futile Attack on Probstheida

The Prussian 10th Brigade was to attack the western side of the village, and the Prussian 12th Brigade the eastern side. The Prussian 9th Brigade stood behind the 10th Brigade. To the left of the 10th Brigade stood a Russian 12-pdr battery. The artillery of Wimpffen's Division moved up to the same heights. To the right, more Russian batteries moved down the road. The artillery fire from both sides was tremendous, but the French batteries under Drouot's guidance finally gained the upper hand.

In the first assault wave, GM Pirch sent the 10th Silesian Landwehr Regiment forward to attack, while Prinz August von Preussen sent forward the Fus/2nd Silesian Regiment and the 11th Reserve Regiment. The Prussians advanced at the geschwindschritt and the sharpshooters of the fusilier battalions penetrated into the village, seizing a battery, before superior forces obliged them to withdraw and abandon their prize.

The storming of Probstheida, Leipzig, 18 October, by Knötel.

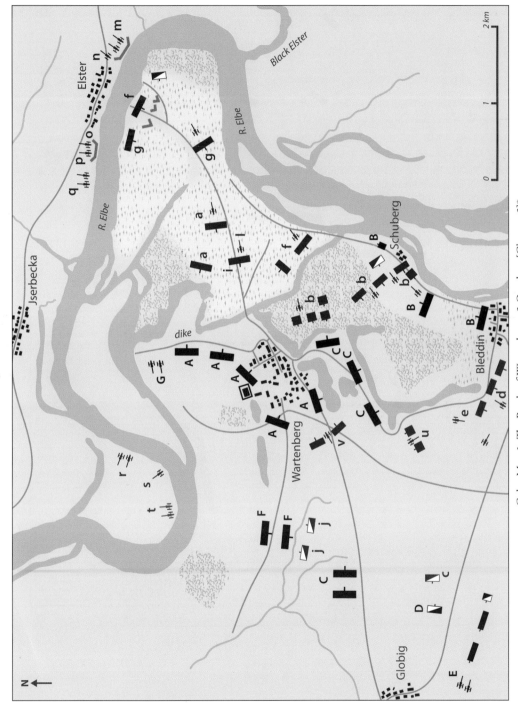

Color Map 1 The Battle of Wartenburg, 3 October. [Chapter 3]*

i

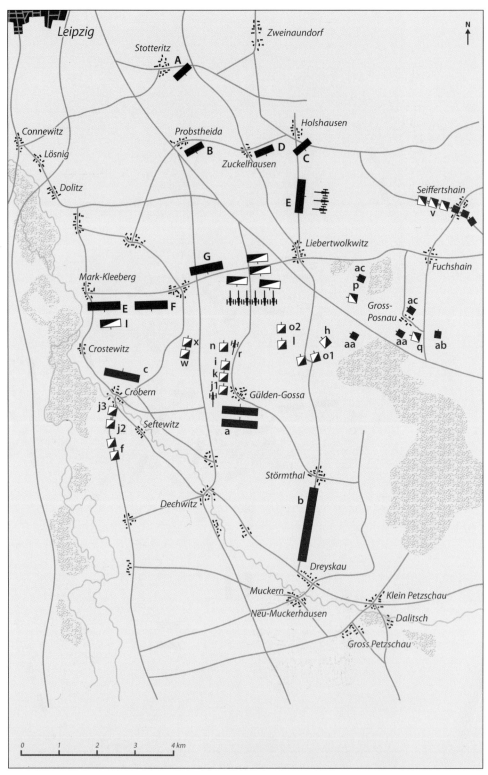

Color Map 2 The Battle of Liebertwolkwitz, 14 October, 11 A.M., between the French cavalry under Murat and the Allied cavalry under Wittgenstein. [Chapter 4]*

ii

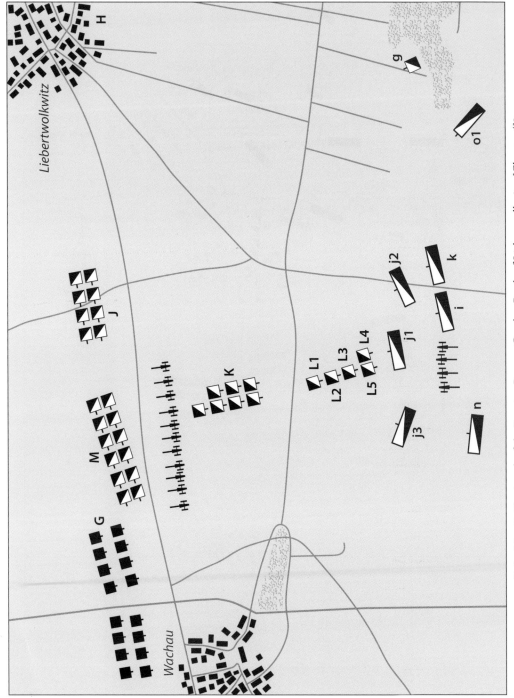

Color Map 3 The Attack of the Prussian Reserve Cavalry, Battle of Liebertwolkwitz. [Chapter 4]*

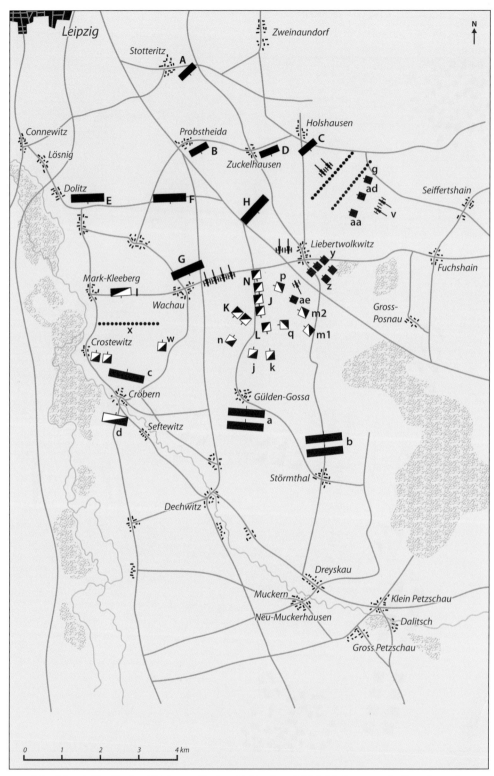

Color Map 4 The Battle of Liebertwolkwitz, 14 October, 2.30 P.M., between the French cavalry under Murat and the Allied cavalry under Wittgenstein. [Chapter 4]*

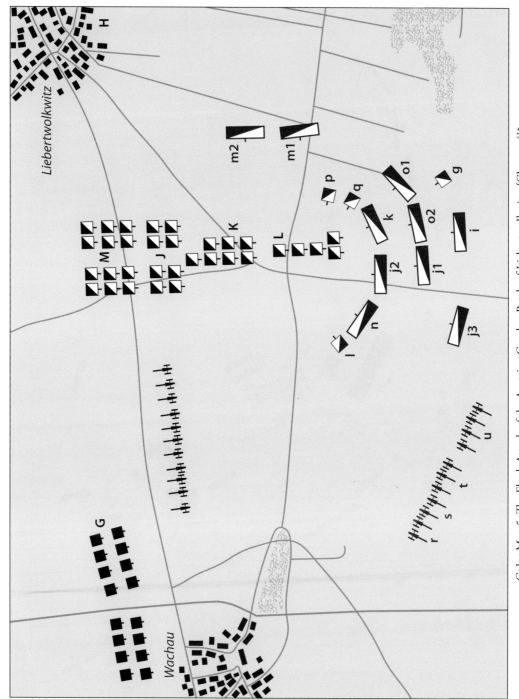

Color Map 5 The Flank Attack of the Austrian Cavalry, Battle of Liebertwolkwitz. [Chapter 4]*

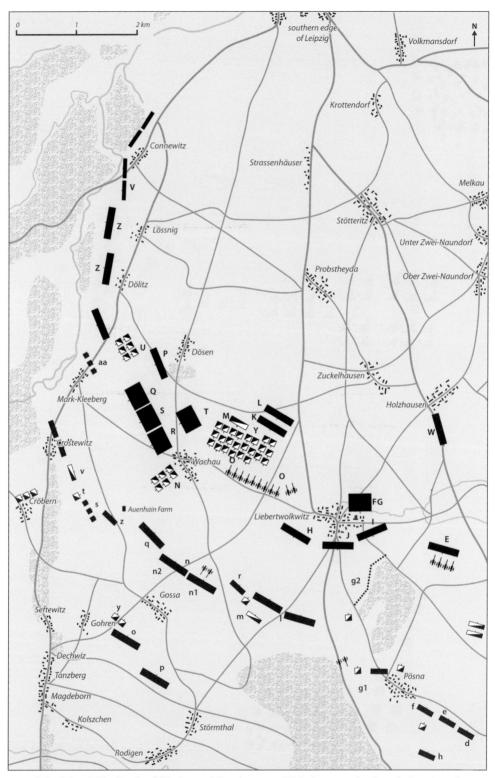

Color Map 6 The Battle of Wachau, 16 October, 2.00 P.M., between the Grande Armée under
Napoleon and the Army of Bohemia under Schwarzenberg. [Chapter 5]*

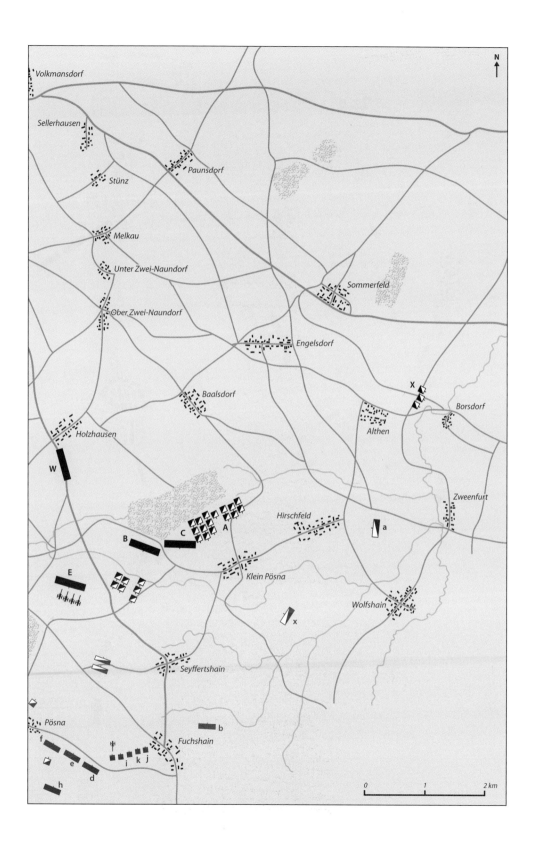

N

Volkmansdorf

Sellerhausen

Stünz

Paunsdorf

Melkau

Unter Zwei-Naundorf

Ober Zwei-Naundorf

Sommerfeld

Engelsdorf

Baalsdorf

X

Borsdorf

Holzhausen

Althen

W

Zweenfurt

C   A

Hirschfeld

a

B

E

Klein Pösna

Wolfshain

x

Seyffertshain

Pösna

b

f

Fuchshain

e   d

i   k   j

h

0   1   2 km

vii

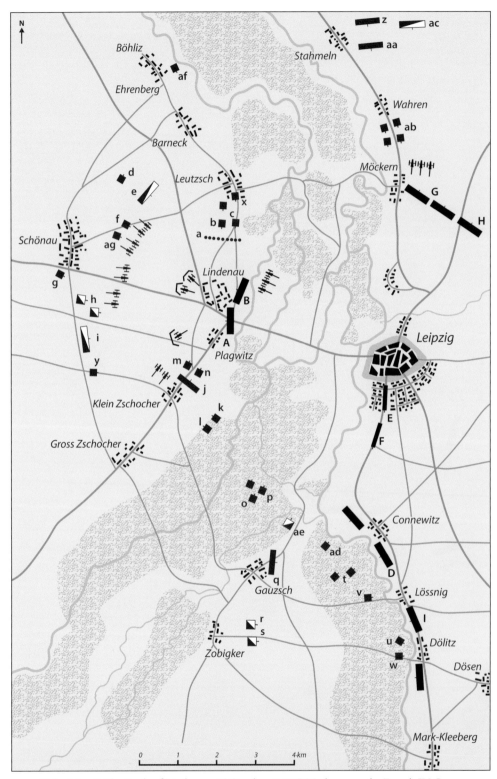

Color Map 7 The Battle of Lindenau, 16 October, 2.00 P.M., between the French IV Corps
under Bertrand and the Austrian 3rd Armeeabteilung under Gyulai. [Chapter 6]*

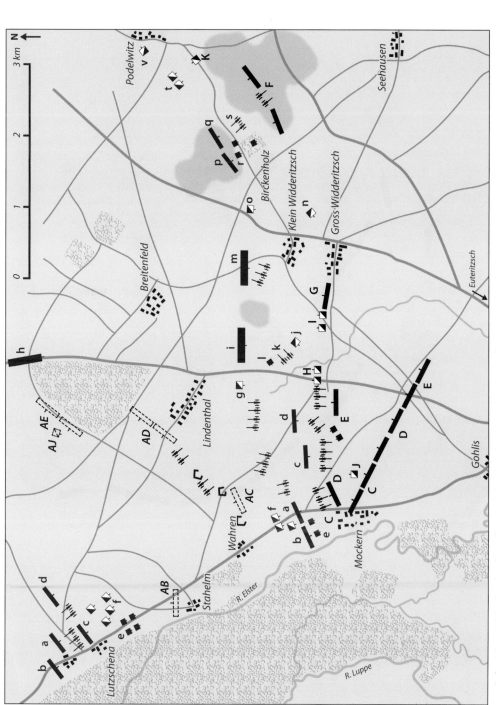

Color Map 8 The Battle of Möckern, 16 October, between the Army of Silesia under Blücher and the French VI Corps under Marmont. The Flank Attack of the Austrian Cavalry, Battle of Lieberwolkwitz. [Chapter 7]*

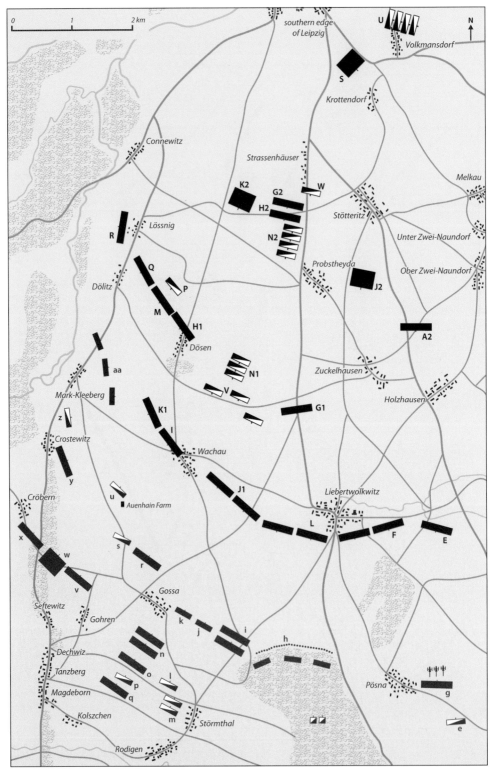

Color Map 9 The Battle of Wachau, Night of 17-18 October, between the Grande Armée under Napoleon and the Army of Bohemia under Schwarzenberg. [Chapter 8]*

x

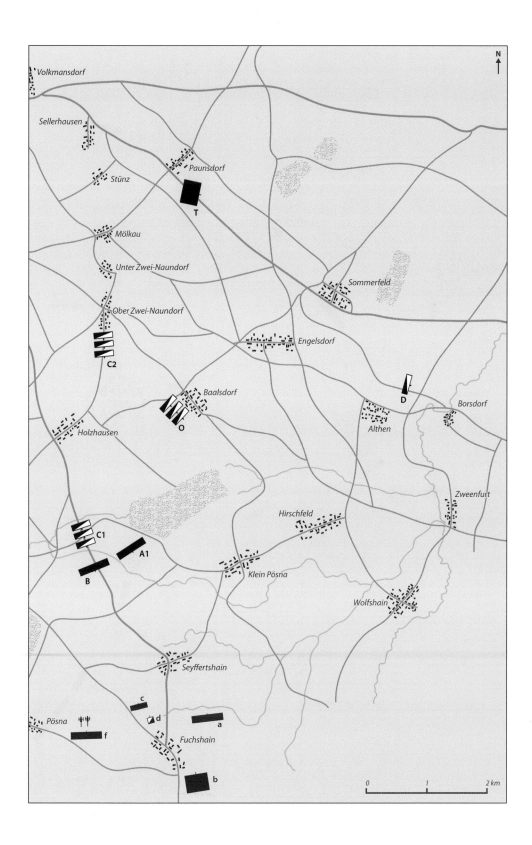

N

Volkmansdorf

Sellerhausen

Stünz

Paunsdorf

T

Mölkau

Unter Zwei-Naundorf

Ober Zwei-Naundorf

Sommerfeld

C2

Engelsdorf

Baalsdorf

D

Borsdorf

O

Holzhausen

Althen

Zweenfurt

Hirschfeld

C1

A1

B

Klein Pösna

Wolfshain

Seyffertshain

c

Pösna

d

a

f

Fuchshain

b

0   1   2 km

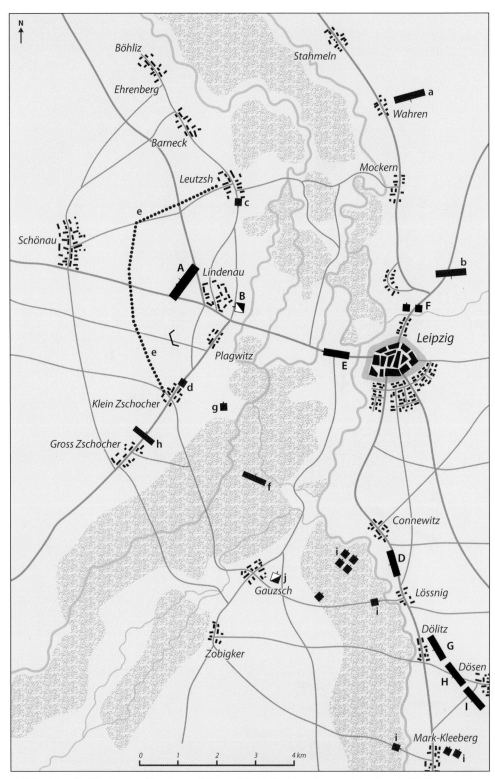

Color Map 10 The Battle of Lindenau, Night of 17-18 October, between the French IV Corps under
Bertrand and the Austrian 2nd Armeeabteilung under Lederer. [Chapter 8]*

xii

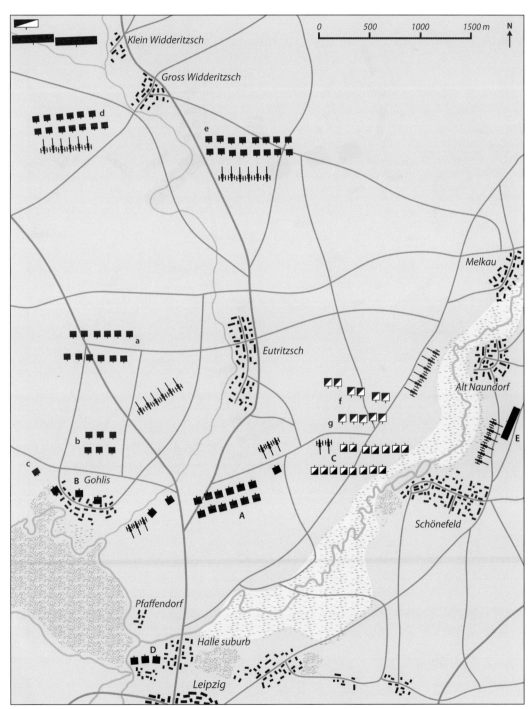

Color Map 11 The Battle of Gohlis, 17 October, between the Army of Silesia under Blücher and the French 9th and 27th Infantry Divisions and III Cavalry Corps. [Chapter 8]*

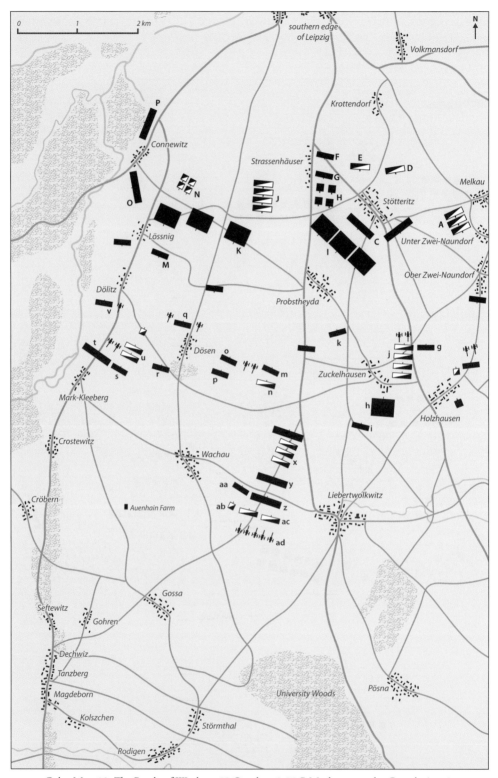

Color Map 12 The Battle of Wachau, 18 October, 2.00 P.M., between the Grande Armée
under Napoleon and the Army of Bohemia under Schwarzenberg. [Chapter 9]*

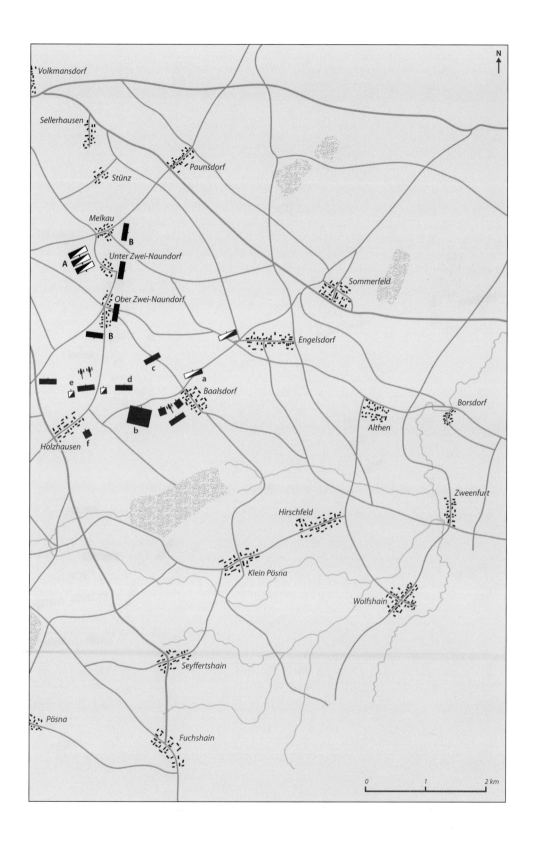

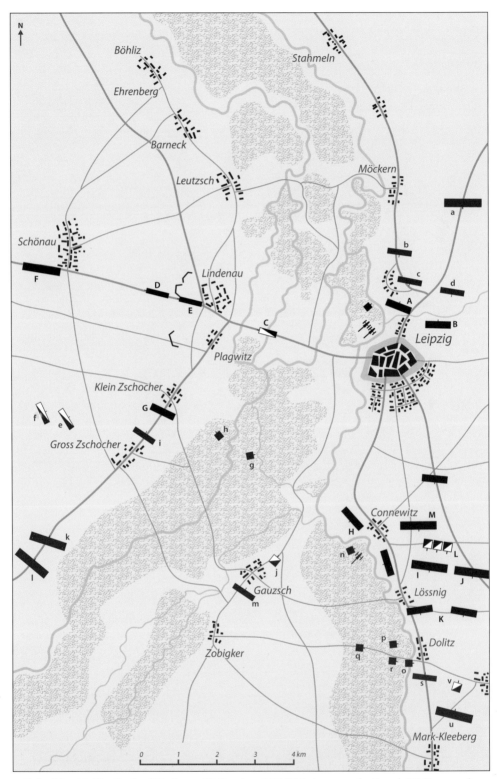

N

Böhliz

Stahmeln

Ehrenberg

Barneck

Leutzsch

Möckern

a

Schönau

b

c

d

F

Lindenau

A

D

B

E

Leipzig

C

Plagwitz

Klein Zschocher

G

f

e

h

Gross Zschocher

i

g

Connewitz

M

k

H

L

n

I

I

J

j

Lössnig

Gauzsch

m

K

Zobigker

p

Dolitz

q

r

o

s

v

u

Mark-Kleeberg

0   1   2   3   4 km

Color Map 13 The Battle of Lindenau, 18 October, 2.00 P.M., between the French IV Corps under
Bertrand and the Austrian 2nd Armeeabteilung under Lederer. [Chapter 9]*

xvi

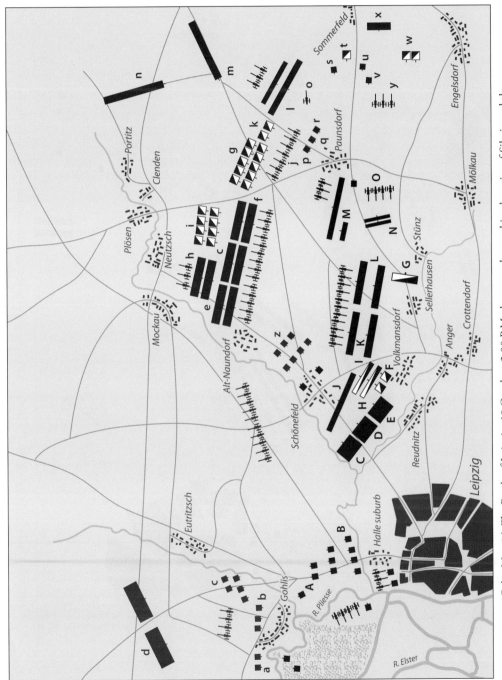

Color Map 14 The Battle of Leipzig, 18 October, 2.00 P.M., between the combined armies of Silesia and the North and the French Grande Armée. [Chapter 10]*

xvii

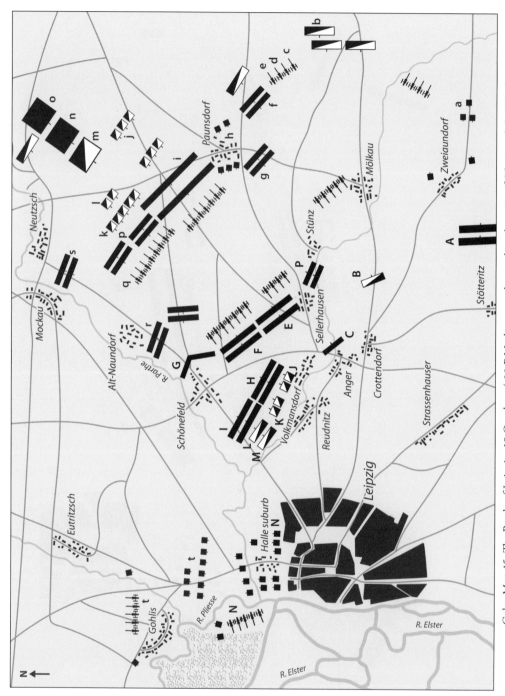

Color Map 15 The Battle of Leipzig, 18 October, 4.00 P.M., between the combined armies of Silesia and the North and the French Grande Armée. [Chapter 10]*

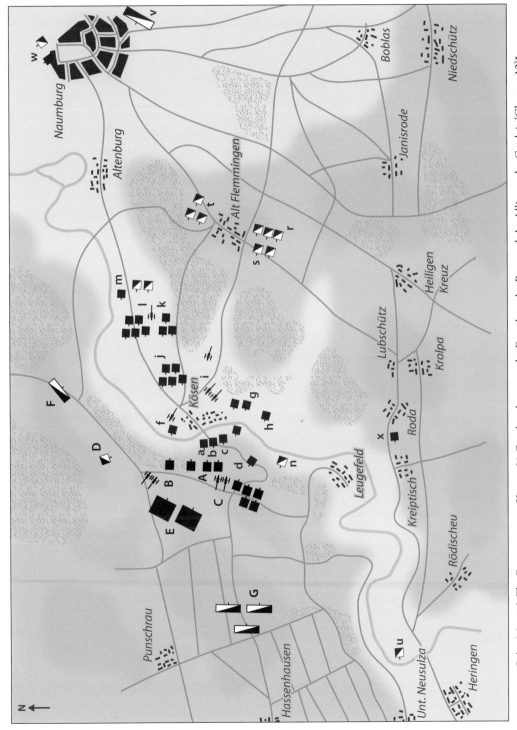

Color Map 16 The Engagement at Kösen, 21 October, between the French under Bertrand the Allies under Gyulai. [Chapter 12]*

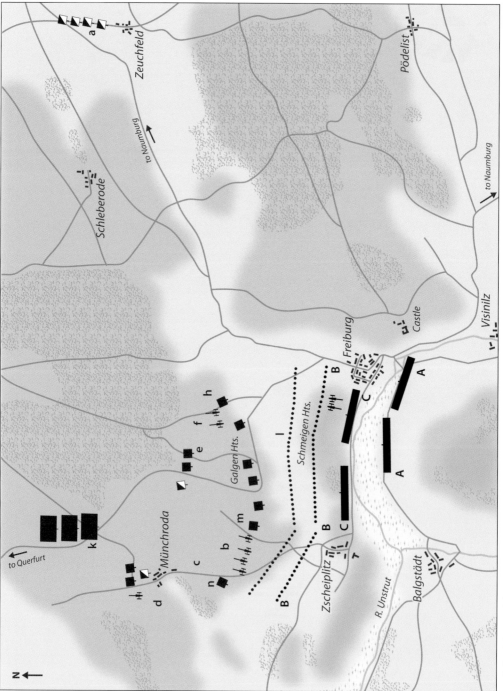

to Querfurt

to Naumburg

to Naumburg

Zeuchfeld

Schleberode

Pödelist

N

a

k

d

Münchroda

c

n

b

m

e

f

h

Galgen Hts.

Schmeigen Hts.

l

B

B

B

C

Zscheiplitz

T

Freiburg

Castle

Visiniz

A

C

B

A

C

A

R. Unstrut

Balgstädt

Color Map 17 The Engagement at Freiburg, 21 October, between the Grand Armée under Napoleon and the Army of Silesia. [Chapter 12]*

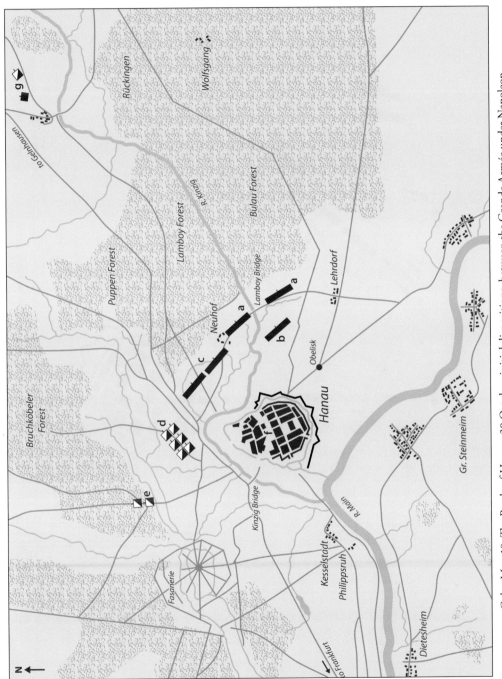

Color Map 18 The Battle of Hanau, 30 October, initial dispositions, between the Grande Armée under Napoleon and the Austro-Bavarian Corps under Wrede. [Chapter 13]*

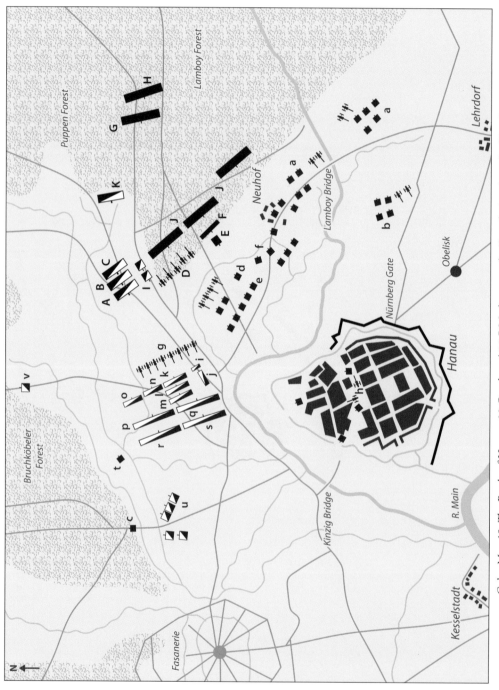

Color Map 19 The Battle of Hanau, 30 October, 4.00 P.M., between the Grande Armée under Napoleon and the Austro-Bavarian Corps under Wrede. [Chapter 13]*

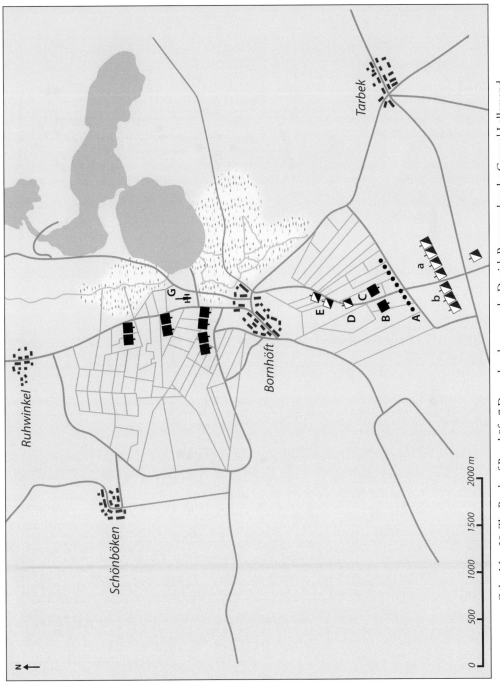

Color Map 20 The Battle of Bornhöft, 7 December, between the Danish Rearguard under General Lallemand and the Pursuing Swedes under General Skjölderbrand. [Chapter 14]*

Tarbek

Ruhwinkel

Schönböken

Bornhöft

G
H

E
D
C
B
A

a
b

N

0   500   1000   1500   2000 m

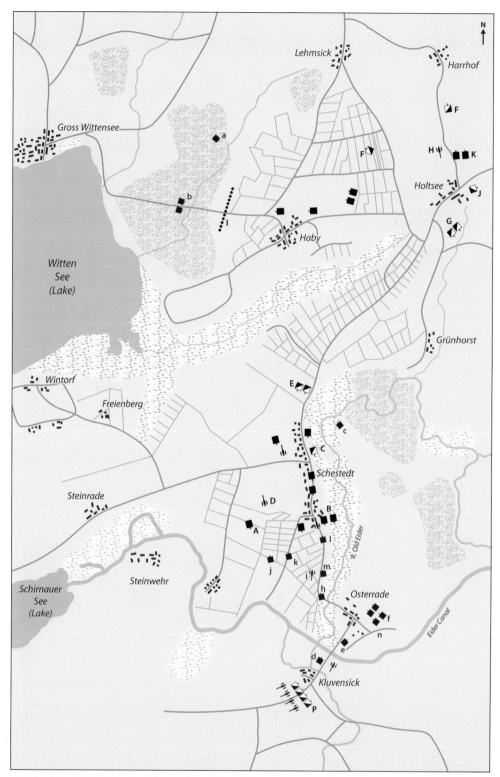

Color Map 21 The Battle of Schestedt, 10 December, 11.00 A.M., between the Danish Corps under Prince Frederick von Hessen and the Pursuing Allies under General Wallmoden. [Chapter 14]*

List of Map Keys

Color Map 1 – The Battle of Wartenburg, 3 October 1813

French
A   12th Division (Morand)
B   38th Division (Franquemont)
C   1st & 2nd positions of 15th Division (Fontanelli)
D   29th Light Cavalry Brigade (Beaumont)
E   Withdrawal of 38th Division
F   Withdrawal of 12th & 15th Divisions
G   French Battery by Wartenburg
H   French Battery

Prussians
a   1st Brigade (Steinmetz)
b   2nd Brigade (Mecklenberg) attack on Bleddin
c   2nd Brigade cavalry attack on Beaumont
d   von Lobenthal's facing Torgau
e   ½ 6-pdr Foot Battery #1 facing Beaumont
e   Captain Ziegler with 5 guns
f   7th Brigade attack on Bleddin
g   8th Brigade during Bleddin attack
h   7th Brigade attack on the dike by Sauanger
i   1st Brigade attack
j   7th Brigade cavalry attack on French 15th Division
l   Positions of 1st Brigade's artillery
m   12-pdr Foot Battery #2
n   ½ 12-pdr Foot Battery #4
o   ½ 6-pdr Foot Battery #19
p   ½ 12-pdr Foot Battery #4
q   12-pdr Foot Battery #1
r   4 guns of l2-pdr Foot Battery #1 pursuing the French 15th Division
s   ¼ 12-pdr Foot Battery #4
t   ½ 6-pdr Horse Battery #6
u-v 2nd Brigade attack beyond Bleddin

Color Maps 2–5 – The Battle of Liebertwolkwitz, 14 October 1813

French
A   2nd Brigade (Aymard), 51st Division, IX Corps
B   1st Brigade (Lagarde), 51st Division, IX Corps
C   Unknown Young Guard Division
D   52nd Division (Sémélé), IX Corps
E   VIII Corps—Poniatowski
F   II Corps—Victor
G   10th Division (Albert), V Corps—Lauriston
H   16th Division (Maison), V Corps—Lauriston
I   IV Cavalry Corps—Sokolnicki
J   9th Light Cavalry Division (Subervie), V Cavalry Corps—Pajol
K   5th Heavy Cavalry Division (l'Héritier), V Cavalry Corps—Pajol
L   6th Heavy Cavalry Division (Milhaud), V Cavalry Corps—Pajol
L1 18th Dragoon Regiment
L2 19th Dragoon Regiment
L3 20th Dragoon Regiment
L4 22nd Dragoon Regiment
L5 25th Dragoon Regiment
J   1st Light Cavalry Division (Berkheim), I Cavalry Corps—Latour-Maubourg

Allies
a   Russian 2nd Corps—Württemberg
b   Russian 1st Corps—Gorchakov
c   Russian 14th Division—Helfreich
d   Russian 3rd Cuirassier Division
e   7th & 8th Landwehr Cavalry Regiments—Mutius' Brigade
g   Kerpen Infantry Regiment
h   Grekov #8 Cossack Regiment
i   Neumärk Dragoon Regiment
j   Wrangel's Brigade, Prussian CavalryReserve—von Röder
j1 East Prussian Cuirassier Regiment
j2 Brandenburg Cuirassier Regiment
j3 Silesian Cuirassier Regiment
k   Silesian Uhlan Regiment
l   Olviopol Hussar Regiment
m   Cavalry Brigade (Desfour), 3rd Austrian Division
m1 Kaiser Cuirassier Regiment
m2 O'Reilly Chevauléger Regiment
n   Soum Hussar Regiment
o   Cavalry Brigade (Lissanevich), Pahlen's Cavalry Corps
o1 Tchougouiev Uhlan Regiment
o2 Loubny Hussar Regiment
p   Erherzog Ferdinand Hussar Regiment
q   Hohenzollern Chevauléger Regiment
r   Prussian Horse Battery #7
s   Prussian Horse Battery #8
t   Prussian Horse Battery #10
u   Russian Horse Battery #7
v   Baumgarten's Brigade, 1st Division, 4th Army Abteilung
w   Grodno Hussar Regiment
x   Illowaiski #12 Don Cossack Regiment

Color Map 6 – The Battle of Wachau, 2:00 p.m. 16 October 1813

French

A   II Cavalry Corps—Sébastiani
B   31st Division—Ledru
C   35th Division—Gérard
D   4th Light Cavalry Division—Exelmans
E   36th Division—Charpentier
F   3rd Young Guard Division—Decouz
G   4th Young Guard Division—Roguet
H   16th Division—Maison
I   I 10th Division—Albert
J   19th Division—Rochambeau
K   2nd Old Guard Division—Curial
L   1st Old Guard Division—Friant
M   3rd Guard Cavalry Division—Walther
N   IV Cavalry Corps (reinforced with Empress Dragoons)—Sokolnicki
O   Artillery Reserve—Drouot
P   2nd Young Guard Division—Barrois
Q   VIII Corps—Poniatowski
R   4th Division (Dubreton), II Corps—Victor
S   5th Division (Dufour), II Corps—Victor
T   6th Division (Vial), II Corps—Victor -
U   1st Light Cavalry Division—Berkheim
V   Independent Division—Lefol
W   39th Division—Marchand
X   8th Light Cavalry Division—Dommanget
Y   I Cavalry Corps—Latour-Maubourg
Z   IX Corps—Augereau

Allies

a   Platov's Cossacks
b   Baumgarten's Brigade
c   Klenau's Cavalry
d   Mayer's Brigade
e   Abele's Brigade
f   Prussian 11th Brigade—Ziethen
g1 Splenyi's Brigade
g2 Splenyi's Brigade Grenz
h   de Best's Brigade-Erzherzog and Kerpen Regiments
i   2/J. Colloredo Infantry Regiment
j   2/Zach Infantry Regiment
k   3/Zack Infantry Regiment
l   Russian 1st Corps—Gorschakov
m   Russian Cavalry Corps—Pahlen
n   Russian 2nd Corps—Württemberg
n1 Russian 3rd Division—Schachafskoy
n2 Russian 4th Division—Pychnitzki
o   Russian lst Grenadier Division—Pissarev
p   Russian 2nd Grenadier Division— Tchoglokov
q   Prussian 9th Brigade—Klüx
r   Prussian 10th Brigade—Pirch
s   1/11th Resrve Regiment, Krementsoug Infantry Regiment—Schvichov
t   Loubny Hussar Regiment

u   Russian 14th Division—Helfreich
v   Russian Cuirassier Brigade (Levaschoff), 3rd Cuirassier Division—Duka
w   Austrian Cuirassier Brigades (Rothkirch, Kuttalek, Auersperg)—Nostitz's Corps
x   Prussian Reserve Cavalry—Röder
y   Gudovich's Brigade, 3rd Cuirassier Division
z   Prussian 12th Brigade—Prinz August
aa Prussian 2/11th Reserve Regiment and 6th Reserve Regiment—Löbel

Color Map 7 – The Battle of Lindenau, 2:00 p.m. 16 October 1813

French

A   12th Division—Morand
B   15th Division—Fontanelli
C   "C" Division, Leipzig Garrison—Margaron
D   Independent Division—Lefol
E   11th Division—Ricard
F   8th Division—Brayer
G   21st Division—Lagrange
H   20th Division—Compans
I   VIII Corps—Poniatowski

Allies

a   Warasdiner Kreuzer Grenz Regiment
b   Mariassy Infantry Regiment
c   Jager Battalion #2
d   Jager Battalion #1
e   Mensdorf's Streifkorps
f   1/Warasdiner St-Georg Grenz Regiment
g   Kolowrath Infantry Regiment
h   Levenehr Dragoon Regiment and Vincent Chevauléger Regiment
i   Thielemann's Streifkorps
j   Czollich's Brigade—Kottulinsky and Kaiser Infantry Regiments
k   1/Gradiscaner Grenz Regiment
l   1/Kaunitz Infantry Regiment
m   Broder Grenz Regiment
n   Jager Battalion #7
o   1/Esterhazy Infantry Regiment
p   Davidovich Infantry Regiment
q   Meszerey's Brigade—Reuss-Greiz and Vogelsang Infantry Regiments
r   Kienmayer Hussar Regiment
s   Erherzog Johann Dragoon Regiment
t   Longueville's Brigade—Strauch and Bellegarde Infantry Regiments
u   1/W. Colloredo Infantry Regiment
v   2/W. Colloredo Infantry Regiment
w   2/Kaunitz Infantry Regiment
x   Ignaz Gyulai Infantry Regiment
y   1/Fröhlich Infantry Regiment
z   Prussian 1st Brigade—Steinmetz
aa Prussian 2nd Brigade—Mecklenberg

ab Prussian Advanced Guard—Katzeler
ac Army of Silesia Reserve Cavalry—Jürgass
ad 3/W. Colloredo Infantry Regiment
ae Hohenzollern Cuirassier Regiment (two squadrons)
af 3/Fröhlich Infantry Regiment
ag 2/Fröhlich Infantry Regiment

Color Map 8 – The Battle of Möckern, 16 October 1813

French

A Initial French Positions
B Buquet's Brigade, 21st Division
C 21st Division—Lagrange
D 20th Division—Compans
E 22nd Division—Friederichs
F 9th Division—Delmas
G 27th (Polish) Division—Dombrowski
H 5th Light Cavalry Division—Lorge
I 6th Light Cavalry Division—Fournier
J 25th Light Cavalry Brigade—Normann (A—withdrawing from Radefeld before Langeron's advance)
K 1 Cavalry Regiment

Allies

a Prussian 1st Brigade—Steinmetz
b Prussian 2nd Brigade—Mecklenberg
c Prussian 7th Brigade—Horn
d Prussian 8th Brigade—Hünerbein
e Prussian Advanced Guard—Katzeler
f Prussian Reserve Cavalry—Jürgass
g Russian 2nd Hussar Division
h Russian 11th Corps—Sacken
i Russian 8th Corps—St.-Priest
j Brandenburg Hussars (two sqns.)
k Two Russian batteries
l Wilmanstrand Infantry Regiment
m Russian 8th Division, 10th Corps—Kapsevich
n Cavalry Advanced Guard—Rudsevich
o Emanuel's Cavalry (10 sqns.)
p 9th Corps—Olsoviev
q Russian 15th Division (Kornilov), 9th Corps—Olsoviev
r Russian 9th Division (Udom), 9th Corps—Olsoviev
s 12 Russian guns
t Korff's Cavalry
v Four Cavalry Regiments

Color Map 9 – The Battle of Wachau, Night of 17–18 October 1813

French

A1 35th Division—Gérard (Initial Position)
A2 35th Division—Gérard (Morning Position)
B 31st Division—Ledru
C1 II Cavalry Corps—Sébastiani (Initial Position)
C2 II Cavalry Corps—Sébastiani (Morning Position)
D 8th Light Cavalry Division—Dommanget
E 39th Division—Marchand F 36th Division—Charpentier
G1 1st Old Guard Division—Friant (Initial Position)
G2 1st Old Guard Division—Friant (Morning Position)
H1 2nd Old Guard Division—Curial (Initial Position)
H2 2nd Old Guard Division—Curial (Morning Position)
I II Corps—Victor
J1 V Corps—Lauriston (Initial Position)
J2 V Corps—Lauriston (Morning Position)
K1 1st Young Guard Corps—Oudinot (Initial Position)
K2 1st Young Guard Corps—Oudinot (Morning Position)
L 2nd Young Guard Corps—Mortier
M IX Corps—Augereau
N1 I Cavalry Corps—Latour-Maubourg (Initial Position)
N2 I Cavalry Corps—Latour-Maubourg (Morning Position)
O V Cavalry Corps—Milhaud
P IV Cavalry Corps—Sokolnicki
Q VIII Corps—Poniatowski
R Independent Division—Lefol
S HI Corps—Souham
T VII Corps—Reynier
U III Cavalry Corps—Arrighi
V Guard Cavalry Corps
W 3rd Guard Cavalry Division—Walther

Allies

a Advanced Guard Division, Polish Reserve Army—Stroganov
b Main Body Polish Reserve Army—Bennigsen
c Baumgarten's Brigade, 1st Division, 4th Armeeabteilung
d 2/Palatinal Hussar Regiment
e Hohenzollern Chevauléger, Palatinal and Erherzog Ferdinand Hussar Regiments
f 2nd Division (Hohenlohe-Bartenstein), 4th Armeeabteilung
g 3rd Division (Mayer), 4th Armeeabteilung
h Prussian 11th Brigade—Ziethen
i Russian 1st Corps—Gorschakov
j Prussian 10th Brigade—Pirch
k Prussian 12th Brigade—Prinz August

l   Russian 2nd Cuirassier Division
m   Russian Cavalry Corps—Pahlen
n   Russian 2nd Corps—Württemberg
o   Prussian 9th Brigade—Klüx
p   Russian 1st Cuirassier Division— Depreradovich
q   5th (Russo-Prussian Guard) Corps—Yermolov
r   Russian 3rd (Grenadier) Corps—Raevsky
s   Russian Guard Light Cavalry Division— Chevich
t   Fischer Grenadier Battalion (In Auenhain Farm)
u   Russian 2nd Cuirassier Division—Duka
v   2nd Division (A. Liechtenstein), 2nd
    Armeeabteilung
w   1st Armeeabteilung—Colloredo
x   1st Division (Crenneville), 3rd Armeeabteilung
y   1st (Grenadier) Division (Weissenwolf), Austrian
    Army Reserve
z   Austrian Cuirassier Corps—Nostitz
aa 2nd Division (Bianchi), Austrian Army Reserve

Color Map 10 – The Battle of Lindenau, Night of 17–18 October 1813

French
A   IV Corps—Bertrand
    12th Division—Morand
    15th Division—Fontanelli
    Mixed Division—Franquemont
B   Quinette's Dragoon Brigade, 4th Heavy Cavalry
    Division
C   "C" Division, Leipzig Garrison— Margaron
D   Independent Division—Lefol
E   13th Division—Guilleminot
F   27th Division—Dombrowski
G   VIII Corps—Poniatowski
H   IX Corps—Augereau
I   2nd Old Guard Division—Curial

Allies
a   Prussian 1st Corps—Yorck
b   Russian Corps—Sacken
c   Jager Battalion #2
d   Jager Battalion #1
e   Mensdorf's Streifkorps
f   Quallenberg's Brigade—Esterhazy and
    Davidovich Infantry Regiments
g   Simbischen Infantry Regiment
h   Czollich'sBrigade—Kottulinsky and Kaiser
    Infantry Regiments
i   Detachments of 2nd Armeeabteilung—Lederer
j   Sorenberg's Brigade—Kienmayer Hussars and
    Erherzog Johann Dragoons

Color Map 11 – The Battle of Gohlis, 17 October 1813

French
A   9th Division—Delmas
B   27th (Polish) Division—Dombrowski
C   III Cavalry Corps—Arrighi
D   38th (Württemberg) Division—Franquemont
E   21st Division—Lagrange

Allies
a   11th Corps—Sacken
b   Assault on Gohlis: Kamchatka and Okhotsk
    Regiments (16th Division) and 8th Jager Regiment
    (10th Division)
c   Move against the Pleisse: 50th Jager Regiment
    (27th Division)
d   10th Corps (Kapsevich) from Langeron's Wing
e   8th Corps—St. Priest
f   Line Cavalry of Vassil'shikov's 11th Corps Cavalry
g   Cossacks of Vassil'shikov's 11th Corps Cavalry

Color Map 12 – The Battle of Wachau, 2:00 p.m. 18 October 1813

French
A   II Cavalry Corps—Sébastiani
B   Part of XI and V Corps
C   XI Corps—Macdonald
D   1st and 2nd Guard Cavalry Divisions— Nansouty
E   3rd Guard Cavalry Division—Walther
F   1st Old Guard Division—Friant
G   Rothembourg's Brigade, 2nd Old Guard Division
H   Rousseau's Brigade, 2nd Old Guard Division
I   V Corps—Lauriston
J   I Cavalry Corps—Latour-Maubourg
K   1st Young Guard Corps—Oudinot
L   VIII Corps—Poniatowski
M   51st Division—Sémélé
N   IV Cavalry Corps—Sokolnicki
O   IX Corps—Augereau
P   Independent Division—Lefol

Allies
a   Russian Advanced Guard Division (Stroganov),
    Polish Reserve Army
b   Main Body (Docturov), Polish Reserve Army
c   Baumgarten's Brigade, 1st Division, 4th
    Armeeabteilung
d   Austrian 2nd Division (Hohenlohe-Bartenstein),
    4th Armeeabteilung
e   Austrian 3rd Division (Mayer), 4th
    Armeeabteilung
f   2/43rd Austrian Regiment
g   Prussian 11th Brigade—Ziethern
h   Russian 1st Corps—Gorschakov

i   Russian 2nd Corps—Württemberg
j   Russian Cavalry Corps—Pahlen
k   Prussian 12th Brigade—Prinz August
l   Prussian 10th Brigade—Pirch
m   Prussian 9th Brigade—Klüx
n   Prussian Reserve Cavalry—Röder
o   Austrian 2nd Division (Wimpffen), 1st
    Armeeabteilung
p   Austrian 3rd Division (Greth), 1st Armeeabteilung
q   Austrian 2nd Division (A. Liechtenstein), 2nd
    Armeeabteilung
r   Haugwitz's Brigade, 2nd Division, Austrian Army
    Reserve
s   Raigecourt's Brigade, 1st Division, 1st
    Armeeabteilung
t   Austrian 2nd Division (Bianchi). Austrian Army
    Reserve
u   Austrian Cuirassier Corps—Nostitz
v   Austrian 1st Division (Weissenwolf), Austrian
    Army Reserve
w   Russian 1st Grenadier Division—Pissarev
x   Russian 3rd Cuirassier Division—Duka
y   Russian 1st Guard Division—Rosen
z   Russian 2nd Guard Division—Udom
aa Prussian Guard Infantry—Albensleben
ab Prussian Guard Cavalry
ac Russian Guard Cavalry Corps—Gallitzin
ad Allied Reserve Artillery

Color Map 13 – The Battle of Lindenau, 2:00 p.m. 18 October 1813

French
A   1st Young Guard Division—Pacthod
B   27th Division—Dombrowski
C   6th Heavy Cavalry Division—Milhaud
    1st Guard Cavalry Division—Ornano
    2nd Guard Cavalry
    Division— Lefèbvre-Desnoëttes
D   13th Division—Guilleminot
E   II Young Guard Corps—Mortier
F   IV Corps—Bertrand
G   12th Division—Morand
H   Independent Division—Lefol
I   VIII Corps—Poniatowski
J   I Young Guard Corps—Oudinot
K   52nd Division—Sémélé
L   IV Cavalry Corps—Sokolnicki
M   IX Corps—Augereau
N   Rothenbourg's Brigade, 2nd Old Guard Division

Allies
a   Prussian 1st Corps—Yorck
b   Rachmanov's Brigade, Russian 16th t Division
    (Repninsky)
c   Russian 27th Division—Neverovsky
d   Russian 10th Division—Lieven

e   Mensdorf's Streifkorps
f   Thielemann's Streifkorps
g   Quallenberg's Brigade (Esterhazy and Davidovich
    Infantry Regiments)
h   Simbischen Infantry Regiment
i   Czollich's Brigade (Kottulinsky and Kaiser
    Infantry Regiments)
j   Sorenberg's Brigade (Kienmayer Hussar Regiment
    and Erherzog Johann Dragoon Regiment)
k   Austrian 1st Light Division—M. Liechtenstein
l   2nd and 3rd Divisions, 3rd Armeeabteilung
    —Gyulai
m   1st Division (Crenneville), 3rd Armeeabteilung
n   Bellegarde Infantry Regiment
o   1/W. Colloredo Infantry Regiment
p   3/W. Colloredo Infantry Regiment
q   Strauch Infantry Regiment
r   1/Kaunitz Infantry Regiment
s   1st Division (Weissenwolf), Austrian Army
    Reserve
t   2nd Division (Bianchi), Austrian Army Reserve
u   Raigecourt's Brigade, 1st Division, 1st
    Armeeabteilung
v   Austrian Cuirassier Corps—Nostitz

Color Map 14 – The Battle of Leipzig, 2:00 p.m. 18 October 1813

French
A   1st Young Guard Division—Pacthod
B   27th (Polish) Division—Dombrowski
C   11th Division—Ricard
D   8th Division—Brayer
E   9th Division—Delmas
F   23rd Light Cavalry Brigade—Beurmann
G   4th Heavy Cavalry Division—Defrance
H   5th Light Cavalry Division—Lorge
I   6th Light Cavalry Division—Fournier
J   21st Division—Lagrange
K   22nd Division—Friederichs
L   20th Division—Compans
M   32nd Division—Durutte
N   24th (Saxon) Division—Zeschau
O   Saxon Artillery

Allies
a   Rachmanov's Brigade, 16th Division
b   27th Division—Neverovsky
c   10th Division—Lieven
d   Prussian 1st Corps—Yorck
e   Russian 8th Corps—St.-Priest
f   Advanced Guard (Rudsevich), Langeron's Corps
g   Manteufel, Pahlen, and Zagriajski's Cavalry
    Brigades, and Illowaiski IV's Cossack Brigade,
    Winzingerode's Corps
h   Russian 9th Corps—Olsoviev
i   Korff's Cavalry Division, Langeron's Corps

j   Prussian Artillery Reserve—Holtzendorff
k   Emanuel's Cavalry Brigade (Kharkov and Kiev Dragoons)
l   Prussian 3rd Brigade—Hessen-Homburg
m Prussian 5th Brigade—von Schoon
n   Advanced Guard (Voronzov), Winzingerode's Corps
o   British Rocket Battery
p   Prussian 1/4th Reserve Regiment
q   Prussian 2/4th Reserve Regiment
r   2/3rd East Prussian Regiment
s   5th Jäger Battalion
t   Liechtenstein Hussar Regiment
u   1/Peterwardeiner Grenz Regiment
v   6th Jäger Battalion
w Kaiser Hussar Regiment
x   Weiland's Brigade, Austrian 2nd Light Division
y   Horse Artillery, Austrian 2nd Light Division
z   Russian 10th Corps—Kapzevich

Color Map 15 – The Battle of Leipzig, 4:00 p.m. 18 October 1813

French
A XI Corps—Macdonald
B 4th Heavy Cavalry Division—Defrance
C 1st Brigade, 1st Old Guard Division—Christiani
D Guard Heavy Cavalry Division—Nansouty
E 9th Division—Delmas
F 20th Division—Compans
G 22nd Division—Friederichs
H 8th Division—Brayer
I 11th Division—Ricard
J 3rd Brigade, 3rd Guard Cavalry Division— Laferrière
K 23rd Light Cavalry Brigade—Beurmann
L 6th Light Cavalry Division—Fournier
M 5th Light Cavalry Division—Lorge
N 1st Division—Pacthod
O 27th (Polish) Division—Dombrowski
P 32nd Division—Durutte

Allies
a   Advanced Guard Division, Polish Reserve Army—Stroganov
b   1st and 3rd Ukrainian Cossacks—Witt
c   Russian Battery
d   Birnbaum's Saxon Battery
e   Austrian Horse Battery
f   Austrian 2nd Light Division—Bubna
g   Prussian 3rd Brigade—Hessen-Homburg
h   Prussian 6th Brigade—Krafft
i   Prussian 5th Brigade—von Schoon
j   Prussian Reserve Cavalry—Oppen
k   Cavalry, Winzingerode's Corps
l   Kharkov & Moscow Dragoon Regiments —Emanuel

m Korff's Cavalry Division, Langeron's Corps
n   Advanced Guard Infantry, Winzingerode's Corps—Voronzov
o   Swedish Army—Stedingk
p   Advanced Guard, Langeron's Corps— Rudsevich

Color Map 16 – The Engagement at Kösen, 21 October 1813

French
A 12th Division—Morand (13 bns)
     Mixed (Württemberg) Division—Franquemont (3 bns)
     14th Division—Guilleminot (11 bns)
     1 Bavarian company
B French battery of 20 guns
C French battery of 12-14 howitzers and 12-pdrs
D French Cavalry (2-3 squadrons)
E 15th Division—Fontinelli
F 2nd Guard Cavalry Division— Lefèbvre-Desnoëttes
G V Cavalry Corps—L'Héritier

Allies
a   3/Erherzog Ludwig Infantry Regiment
b   Jäger Battalion #7
c   1/1st Warasdiner Kreutzer Grenz Regiment (2 companies)
d   2/Erherzog Ludwig Infantry Regiment
e   Würzburg Infantry Regiment
f   Jäger Battalion #1
g   1/Broder Grenz Regiment (2 companies)
h   Prussian Guard Jäger (1 company-Boltenstern Company)
i   Liechtenstein's Cavalry Battery *and* Brigade Battery
j   1 Grimmer's Brigade (5 battalions)
k   Weigel's Brigade en route (4 battalions)
l   2 6-pdr batteries from Corps Reserve
m 1/Warasdiner St-Georger Grenz, Rosenberg Chevauléger (5 sqns), and Klenau Chevauléger (5 sqns)
n   Detachment of 100 cavalry from Liechtenstein's Division
r   Vincent Chevauléger Regiment (8 sqns)
s   Mensdorf's Streifkorps (3 Austrian sqns & 2 Cossack Regiments)
t   Thielmann's Streifkorps (3 sqns & 1 detachment Austrian Cavalry, 4½ Prussian sqns, 2 Cossack Regiments, and 4 howitzers)
u   ½ Squadron from Thielmann's Streifkorps
v   Austrian Cuirassier Reserve (28 sqns)— Nostitz
w Warasdiner Kreutzer Grenz Regiment (4 cos) and Klenau Chevauléger (1 sqn)
x   Gyulai Infantry Regiment

Color Map 17 – The Engagement at Freiburg, 21 October 1813

French
A   Main Body of French Army
B   Skirmish line
C   Main Position
D   French Battery of 8 guns

Allies
a   Mecklenberg Hussar Regiment
b   Horse Battery #2 and (later) ½ Foot Battery #2
c   Advanced Guard—Henkel von Donnermark
d   Combined Cavalry, 2 Landwehr Battalions, and Foot Battery #8
e   7th Brigade—von Horn
f   ½ Foot Battery #3
g   Von Rummel Combined Battalion (Fusiliers of 1st and 2nd East Prussian Infantry Regiments)
h   Fusilier/Leib Infantry Regiment
i   Combined Infantry Regiment
k   8th Brigade—Hünerbein
l   Skirmish line with East Prussian Jäger Battalion & 2 Austrian Jäger Battalions
m   Silesian Grenadier Battalion
n   Thuringian Battalion

Color Map 18 – The Battle of Hanau, 30 October 1813: Initial Dispositions

Austro-Bavarian Corps
a   2nd Bavarian Division—Becker
b   Klenau's Austrian Brigade
c   3rd Bavarian Division—Lamotte Volkmann's Bavarian Brigade

Bach's Austrian Division
d   Allied Cavalry
e   Allied Reserves and Grenadiers—Diemar
f   Schützen Co./5th. Bavarian Line and ½ sqn 2nd Bavarian Chevauléger Regiment

Color Map 19 – The Battle of Hanau, 30 October 1813, About 4:00 p.m.

French
A   Guard Chasseurs à Cheval and Grenadiers à Cheval—Laferrière-Levesque
B   St-Germain's Cavalry Division (1st, 5th, 8th, 10th Cuirassiers, and 1st and 2nd Carabiniers)
C   1st, 2nd, 3rd, and 4th Gardes d'Honneur
D   Guard Artillery
E   Old Guard Infantry and skirmishers from the 36th Division
F   36th Division—Charpentier

G   VI Corps—Marmont
H   Young Guard Corps—Oudinot
I   Old Guard Dragoon and Lancer Regiments
J   V and XI Corps and 4th Division—Macdonald
K   II Cavalry Corps—Sébastiani

Austro-Bavarian Corps
a   2nd Bavarian Division—Becker
b   Klenau's Grenadier Brigade
c   Jäger Battalion #3 from Volkmann's Brigade
d   Stocky's Brigade, Lamotte's 3rd Division
e   Deroy's Brigade, Lamotte's 3rd Division
f   Erherzog Rudolph and Jordis Infantry v Regiments—Bach
     Szekler Grenz Regiment—Hardegg
g   Light Battery #3 "Haider"
     6-pdr Foot Battery #9 "Achner"
     3 Austrian 12-pdr Batteries (18 guns) and a 6-pdr Battery
h   4 Grenadier Battalions—Diemar
i   4/5th Bavarian Chevauléger Regiment
j   4th Bavarian Chevauléger Regiment
k   1st Bavarian Chevauléger Regiment
l   2nd Bavarian Chevauléger Regiment
m   7th Bavarian Chevauléger Regiment
n   3rd Bavarian Chevauléger Regiment
0   6th Bavarian Chevauléger Regiment
p   Liechtenstein (Austrian) Cuirassier Regiment
q   Knesevich (Austrian) Dragoon Regiment
r   Erherzog Joseph (Austrian) Hussar Regiment
s   Schwarzenberg (Austrian) Uhlan Regiment
t   1/Erherzog Rudolph Infantry Regiment
u   Mensdorf's Streifkorps (2 Cossack Regiments and 3 squadrons Austrian Szekler Hussar Regiment)
v   Freiwillige Jäger squadron/3rd Prussian Dragoon Regiment

Color Map 20 – The Battle of Bornhöft, 7 December 1813

Danes
A   Schleswig Jäger Comapny
B   2/Holstein Infantry Regiment
C   1/Holstein Infantry Regiment
D   17th Lithuanian Uhlan Regiment
E   Holstein Cavalry Regiment
F   1/, 3/Jutland Infantry Regiment
G   Conner Artillery Battery

Allies
a Mörner Hussar Regiment (4 squadrons)
b Schonen Hussars (1 squadron) & von Schill Hussars (2 squadrons)

Color Map 21 – The Battle Schestedt, 11:00 a.m. 10 December 1813

Danes

A   1/Fünen Infantry Regiment
B   Oldenburg Infantry Regiment
C   2/, 3/, 4/Fünen Dragoons and 6/Jutland Hussars
D   6-pdr Foot Battery Friis
E   2/, 3/Holstein Cavalry Regiment
F   17th Lithuanian Uhlans
G   2/Jutland Hussars
H   2 Danish Guns
I   4 Jäger Companies
J   1/Fünen Dragoons
K   3/, 4/Holstein Infantry Regiment

Allies

a   Kielmansegge Jäger Battalion#
b   Wardenburg (3rd and 4th RGL Battalions)
c   Mecklenburg Jägers
d   Bennigsen Battalion
e   Langrehr Battalion
f   Mecklenburg Jägers
g   Lauenburg Battalion
h   Anhalt-Dessau Battalion
i   2 guns of Wiering's Battery
j   1st RGL Battalion
k   2nd RGL Battalion
l   5th RGL Battalion
m   6th RGL Battalion
n   7th RGL Battalion
o   "Holtzermann" KGL Light Brigade
p   1st RGL Hussars, Bremen-Verden Hussars, and Mecklenburg Mounted Jägers

The 10th Brigade threw out the skirmishers of its fusilier battalions and advanced behind them towards the French. The skirmishers marched forward into the middle of the fire, went over the parapets of the high walls and penetrated into the village. However, the French quickly responded and sent out a large force to strike the left wing of the brigade. General Pirch then ordered the 2/2nd West Prussian Regiment to execute a conversion to the left, and then to attack with bayonets. This attack was supported by the fire of a Prussian battery, and the French were forced back into the village. Then the two brigades of Prince August von Preussen and Pirch renewed their attack on Probstheida.[27]

The 12th Brigade, following the example of their commander, penetrated once again into the village and engaged in a bloody house to house battle.

Yet the French were on the alert. Lauriston's attack columns stood to the north of Probstheida, ready to strike the Prussians in the embattled village. The infantry of the French V Corps took in detachments of Victor's II Corps and rolled forward. Some of the attacking French moved around either side of the village. The French artillery redoubled its fire, and played especially hard on the forces of Prinz August. Some regiments of the I and II Cavalry Corps[28] formed a large attack column to turn the position. After taking heavy casualties, the Prussians were thrown back. A force of Russian cavalry advanced against the French, but was also thrown back. It fell back behind the Prussian 11th Reserve Regiment for support. The Prussians then held off an assault by a force of French cuirassiers.

The Prussians did not stop with their single failed attempt, but pushed forward a second and third time. Prinz August von Preussen placed himself, and the officers of his staff, at the head of one attacking column and led it forward only to be repelled.

Defeated, the two Prussian brigades pulled back and formed in the second line, while Eugene von Württemberg prepared his sadly weakened battalions to storm the village. Schachafskoy's 3rd Division advanced, its lead elements pushing over the clay wall which surrounded the village.

The French defensive fire was too much and a further push forward was impossible. Disordered and having lost 600 men, the Russians fell back to the cover of their artillery, pursued by French infantry and cavalry. Its withdrawal was covered by its skirmishers and it formed line once again further back.

Napoleon had watched each episode of the battle around Probstheida from his position at the Quandt Tobacco Mill, and initially was quite concerned when the Prussians appeared to the north of the village. He ordered Curial's 2nd Old Guard Division forward. Rousseau's Brigade moved immediately north of Probstheida, while Rottembourg was sent to support Oudinot with the Saxon, Polish and Westphalian Guard. Napoleon himself directed the artillery forward, and with a cold blooded disregard for his personal safety, stood under the growing allied artillery fire. As the battle progressed, he recovered his trust in the ability of Victor and Lauriston's troops to resist the allies. However, actions on the eastern portion of the battle field soon drew his interest.[29]

Schwarzenberg was also able to witness the battle around Probstheida from his position on the *Monarchenhügel*. Schwarzenberg spoke to the Czar, stating that if further attacks were to be made, it was necessary to send the Russian Guard into combat. The Czar demurred. His guard had been savaged at Kulm and Dresden. Now it had only slightly over 400 men per battalion, when its normal strength should have been over 670 men. At 4:00 p.m., it was decided that no further assaults would be made against Probstheida. It was also decided that the French were to be pounded into submission with artillery. Adjutants then dashed in all directions in order to bring forward artillery.

The reserve cavalry of Röder placed itself on the left wing of the second column, to maintain communications with Colloredo. The line reformed with the 9th, 10th, and 12th Prussian Brigades and the 1st and 2nd Russian Corps. On the right stood Pahlen's cavalry and the Russian 2nd Cuirassier Division. The artillery was placed on a dominant point, where it could inflict great

The attack of Curial's Division of the Guard against Probstheida, from the panorama painting originally at Leipzig.

losses on the French. From that point until nightfall, the battle was carried on principally by the artillery. Each time the French attempted a sortie from Probstheida, they were forced back.

The actions around Probstheida this day brought glory and honor to several units, among them the Prussian 10th Silesian Landwehr, the 11th Reserve, and the 2nd Silesian Infantry Regiments especially. In addition, the French troops of Vial's Division, the 2nd, 4th, and 18th Line Regiments earned a special place in the military histories of their country. Generals Vial and Rochambeau died bravely in this engagement.

The actions of Wimpffen's Austrian Division at Probstheida should not be overlooked either. The division's artillery supported the assault, and the division itself stood in support, performing no less bravely than the assaulting battalions. They were formed in battalionsmasse and stood for hours without moving from their positions while under a heavy cannonade. Their skirmishers repeatedly drove back French skirmishers. The two brigade batteries and two position batteries of Wimpffen's Division also displayed incredible endurance under fire. Six Austrian guns were dismounted, and the caissons of Oberstleutnant Teleki's battery fell victim to French artillery fire.

When darkness fell, the allies withdrew a further 600 paces from Probstheida. The French fire ceased and they remained masters of Probstheida. During the night a strong chain of infantry pickets was established before the allied lines.

The Advance of the Third Column

General Bennigsen issued the following instructions to his column in preparation for the attack on 18 October.

> My intention is to turn the enemy's left flank, to second as soon as possible the general attack, and as the village of Klein-Pösna is still occupied by the French, the left wing shall extend below it. The advanced guard of General Stroganov and the Austrian troops of Mohr's Division

shall attack by the left the fortified heights known as the Swedish Redoubts, while Klenau's Corps shall attack it from the front and right. The University woods shall, at the same time, be attacked and occupied. Two companies of Russian heavy artillery, under the protection of the 13th Division shall be placed in Seifertshain and bombard the Swedish Redoubts. If the attack achieves the desired success, the artillery shall advance down the Holzhausen road. The cavalry division of General Tschaplitz shall form a second line behind the advanced guard and in case of attack shall support it. The 12th and 26th Divisions shall move by a flank march against the village of Klein-Pösna, and permit the Austrian 2nd Light Division of General Bubna and Platov's Corps to turn the French. Count Bubna shall pass over the Parthe by the village of Beucha and General Platov shall cross at Zweenfurth.

Platov's streifkorps departed Zweenfurth at 3:00 a.m., and begun its movement through Hirschfeld. Bubna's troops also found themselves marching in the early hours of the morning. The bridges over the swollen and swamp lined Parthe were broken, forcing the infantry to wade through water up to their chests in order to cross. The artillery was able to cross with the greatest effort. The munition reserve was obliged to turn back and pass through the road to Gerichshain. At 9:00 a.m., the light division crossed over the Parthe and formed in two lines by Klein-Pösna, where it encountered French skirmishers and patrols.

Bennigsen united his army behind Fuchshain at 6:00 a.m. To his left, between Fuchshain and Gross-Pösna, stood Klenau's 4th Armeeabteilung. Ziethen's Prussian 11th Brigade stood between Klenau's Armeeabteilung and Barclay de Tolly's advancing columns.

Bennigsen was still worried about his right flank. As a result, he ordered Platov to move between Althen and Engelsdorf, across the Wurzen road from where he was to pass around Paunsdorf, and to link with Blücher and Bernadotte. Bubna, on the other hand, was instructed to occupy Engelsdorf.

Bennigsen divided his forces into three principal columns. The first column, formed with Kreutz's detachment, Stroganov's advanced guard and Tschaplitz's cavalry advanced from Klein-Pösna through Baalsdorf. Docturov's column moved from Klein-Pösna into the region north of Holzhausen, with half of the 13th Division and the 26th Division. The third column, formed from the Russian 12th Division (Chovansky), Klenau's 4th Armeeabteilung, and the rest of Lindfor's 13th Division, reinforced by some Russian cavalry regiments, were to pass over the Kolmberg and through Liebertwolkwitz, then move against Holzhausen.[30]

At 6:00 a.m. the 3rd principal column was under arms and the 12th and 26th Divisions marched against Klein-Pösna. As they arrived they found the French had abandoned the village the day before, moving their battle line further to the rear. This movement did not upset the dispositions made for the attack of the right wing, other than its first goals had been abandoned and the enemy's line shortened.[31]

Bennigsen ordered his forces to attack in four columns and a heavy cannonade began. The first column, on the extreme left, consisted of the 11th Prussian Brigade (Ziethen). As the French had abandoned the Gross-Pösna woods at the break of dawn, this brigade occupied it with its skirmishers and Ziethen was ordered to maintain, during the general movement, the corps' communications with Klenau's 4th Armeeabteilung and those of Wittgenstein, leaving Liebertwolkwitz to the left. The general advanced his forces to attack the village of Zuckelhausen, and took it after a heavy fight. The French were then observed in Stötteritz and Ziethen moved to chase them out, however Probstheida was situated on his flank and heavily defended. This prevented him executing his attack on Stötteritz. The French were in great strength in Stötteritz, and had a large force of artillery to support their position. To counter them a battery of the Prussian 11th Brigade was brought forward, and the village was taken under fire. Towards evening, the 11th Brigade withdrew to Zuckelhausen.

The second column, or 4th Austrian Armeeabteilung (Klenau) marched against Holzhausen. As GdK Klenau's forces advanced, they encountered only a few French patrols on the Kolmberg, so he permitted Paumgarten's advanced guard to move in.[32] Artillery Oberleutnant Irasky's battery still stood by the old Swedish earth work and he directed his fire against the few French detachments around Liebertwolkwitz. A view towards Wachau revealed that Barclay de Tolly's and Hessen-Homburg's troops were advancing to the attack. The Corps commander immediately directed Paumgarten to attack Holzhausen, and ordered FML Mayer, whose division advanced from the Kolmberg, with the Coburg Regiment, to occupy the heights to the left with the bulk of his division, then to swing towards Liebertwolkwitz and seize the village. The storming of the village required no special effort by GM Abele's troops. The French skirmish screen recoiled back towards Holzhausen and Zuckelhausen.

As Mayer's Division stood in battle before Liebertwolkwitz, Hohenlohe's Division passed over the Kolmberg. Löderer's Cavalry Brigade[33] and the Hohenzollern Chevaulégers marched behind at the appropriate distance, and were assigned to support Mayer's Division. The Russian reserve brigade, part of Lindfors 13th Division, followed on Hohenlohe's right wing.

Paumgarten's Brigade had moved to the north after the abandonment of the Kolmberg in order to execute a comprehensive movement towards Holzhausen. Advancing before Docturov's main Russian column, they cleaned the Zauchgehölz woods of French skirmishers, and placed themselves on the western edge of the forest in battalionsmassen, ready to attack Holzhausen. At the same time Kreutz and Stroganov occupied Baalsdorf without exceptional effort.

A far harder piece work waited for Klenau's troops in their pending attack on the villages of Holzhausen and Zuckelhausen, which were strongly defended by Macdonald's XI Corps. Charpentier's 36th Division stood in Holzhausen, while the Baden and Hessian battalions of Marchand's 39th Division formed the second line. Macdonald's artillery and Gérard's 35th Division stood on the Steinberg, which dominated the two villages. Further to the north, by Zwei-Naundorf, stood the concentrated battalions of Ledru's 31st Division.

Klenau advanced between 10:00 and 11:00 a.m., in an effort to take the two villages. Several brigade batteries and the corps reserve artillery occupied the heights to the southwest of Zuckelhausen. GM Paumgarten led the Kerpen Regiment from the west against Holzhausen, while de Best led the 2/Württemberg Infantry Regiment against it from the south. Zuckelhausen was attacked by the A. Liechtenstein Infantry Regiment under the command of GM Abele. Klenau's main body marched forward on both sides of the main artillery position. Chovansky's 12th Russian Division and Lindfors' 13th Russian Division followed behind the middle. Docturov's column passed its lead elements through the Zauchgehölz Woods at the same time.[34]

After a short artillery bombardment the allies advanced. The French responded by punishing Paumgarten's massed Austrian infantry as well as that of de Best and Abele, as they marched forward to the attack. As the battalions of the Kerpen Infantry Regiment pushed to within 200 paces of Holzhausen, they were greeted with heavy musketry fire. The regiment's skirmishers pushed back the French advanced detachments, only to quickly encounter new forces. Paumgarten had drawn forward two horse guns with him, whose canister fire visibly shook the defenders. Oberst O'Brien placed himself at the head of the regiment's Fifth Division[35] and advanced into the village. They quickly seized the first house in the village, but he was struck in the jaw by a musket shot. Soon the bulk of the division's officers were wounded. Paumgarten sent forward, in succession, the remaining four companies of the 2/Kerpen, the 1/, 3/Wallachian-Illyrian Grenz, and the 1/1st Wallachian Grenz Regiments into the village, but without success. Macdonald countered with several of Gérard's Battalions, to throw back the intruders in a bloody battle.

To the south and southwest the 1/Württemberg Infantry Regiment attacked the village, which was defended with desperate tenacity. It was also thrown back.

In the meantime the Russian 12th Division (Chovansky) approached. The division commander ordered the Narva Regiment and Light Battery #45 forward to reinforce Paumgarten. The Narva Infantry Regiment charged the French with bayonets, supported by Colonel Begunov's Light Battery #45. With the combination of the attack of the 12th Division, the maneuvers of the 26th Division on the left flank, and the fire of the allied infantry the French were not only thrown out of Holzhausen, but chased to the heights just beyond the village. The 26th Division took up a position on the right of Holzhausen, and the 12th Division took a position to the left. The 13th Division and two artillery companies stood in front of the village.[36]

The French began to bombard the Russians with their artillery. Sébastiani's II Cavalry Corps made several attacks against the Russian 12th Division, with little to show for the effort. The Smolensk and Narva Infantry Regiments distinguished themselves in this battle by taking two guns.

At the same time GM Lindfors placed his 30 reserve guns under Klenau's reserve artillery. At 1:00 p.m., the French abandoned their attempts to retake Holzhausen and withdrew back to the Steinberg.

Various Russian reports state that the French battalions of Ledru's 31st Division and the defenders of Zwei-Naundorf, during the battles around Holzhausen, were engaged by the Russian columns of Kreutz and Stroganov.[37]

After Zwei-Naundorf fell to the Russians, a terrible musketry battle began, but it did not prevent Kreutz's Cavalry Division from advancing from Zwei-Naundorf. Six Russian Uhlan squadrons and six Russian Hussar squadrons struck Sébastiani's cavalry and threw them back. However, once the French cavalry had left the field, the victorious Russian cavalry found itself subjected to the undivided attention of the French artillery. This situation continued until Colonel Taube directed the fire of his own artillery against the French artillery. Two batteries of Russian artillery were brought onto a ridge that allowed them to take the French in the flank. This artillery also prevented the French from attacking Docturov's Corps.

Soon after the capture of Holzhausen, Zuckelhausen also fell. The 3rd Baden Infantry Regiment occupied the gardens and houses of the village facing Meusdorf, covering four Baden cannon. The von Stockhorn (1st Baden) Regiment occupied the south as well as the portion facing Holzhausen. The Hessians occupied the northern part of the village.[38] The Baden and Hessian troops held to the last moment. Abele attacked the village from the south and Ziethen, whose 11th Brigade moving west towards Liebertwolkwitz, detached a few battalions to strike the Baden and Hessian flank from the west. As their position deteriorated the Hessian and Baden troops sent their artillery out of the burning village towards the Steinberg heights. In their withdrawal they met clumps of French troops withdrawing from Holzhausen, and their pursuing Austrian skirmishers. The Baden and Hessian infantry withdrew in closed battalion columns under the cover of a battery on the Steinberg heights, and followed by a heavy screen of skirmishers. The Hessian Leib-Regiment stood as a reserve and struck back at the Austrians, stopping their pursuit long enough to permit the French and their German allies to reach the Steinberg heights. However, their new position also proved untenable.

While the Austrians and the Russian 12th Division advanced through Zuckelhausen and Holzhausen, Paskievich went around Holzhausen in order to attack Steinberg from the northeast. The French cavalry, under Sébastiani, seized this opportune moment to execute a flank attack against Russian 12th Division, as the 26th Division was passing through Holzhausen. The French cavalry attack struck the rows of the Russians, spreading confusion and breaking several units, but the French attack broke on the closed squares of the Narva and Smolensk Regiments. Klenau placed himself at the head of the O'Reilly Chevauléger Regiment and led them forward to help the Russians, but he came too late. He was obliged to content himself with sabering some of the withdrawing French infantry.

In the meantime the movement of Paskievich's 26th Division forced Macdonald's Battalions to once again withdraw, this time towards Stötteritz. The Austrian and Russian artillery quickly followed, moving to the heights and firing on the withdrawing French.

Around 2:00 p.m., Bennigsen's and Klenau's troops stood on the Baalsdorf-Steinberg line. Ziethen's Prussian 11th Brigade stood southwest in contact with Kleist's II Corps, which at this moment was advancing over the heights between Zuckelhausen and the Meusdorf farm.[39]

The third column, formed of Stroganov's troops and supported by Tschaplitz's cavalry, moved from Klein-Pösna towards Baalsdorf. It had the mission of maintaining the communications between Docturov and Bubna's 2nd Light Division. As the battle developed they overran the villages of Baalsdorf and Zwei-Naundorf. They also overran the forest to the right of the first village, which was occupied by the brigade of Jagers under Glebow. At the same time Tschaplitz's cavalry found itself engaging Walther's cavalry, forcing it to retire before it was able to strike the Russian artillery.

Colonel Klebeck, at the head of a regiment of dragoons, attacked the French cavalry, which was menacing Captain Schischkin's Light Battery #1. General Sébastiani was wounded in the encounter and the French cavalry withdrew.[40]

The Army of the North was to intervene in a decisive manner on the eastern side of Leipzig. Langeron's cavalry commanders, GM Rudsevich and GM Emanuel, had passed over a quickly improvised flying bridge by Mockau and moved towards the French. Emanuel's cavalry swarmed towards the Eilenburg road, where he soon linked with Platov's Cossacks, between Mockau and the earth works of Heiterblick, a mound on the road between Leipzig and Taucha. Shortly later part of Winzingerode's cavalry joined Emanuel's forces. Count Platov's movement meant all the terrain between Zuckelhausen, Zwei-Naundorf, Mölkau, and Paunsdorf was occupied by the forces of General Bennigsen. The Cossack regiments that had spent the previous evening by Taucha had been, by daybreak, chased out by the French, but an attack by the cavalry brigade of GM Baron von der Pahlen soon overran the village and it was again occupied by the Russians.

The sudden appearance of allied cavalry on both of their flanks and rear motivated the Saxon and Württemberg Cavalry advancing against Taucha to defect to the allies. When he defected, GM Normann, commander of the Württemberg Cavalry Brigade, stated that without orders from their King they could not fight against the French.[41] The Württemberg Brigade consisted of two weak regiments.

Bennigsen remained quiescent until about 3:00 p.m. when he moved to his right wing to speak with Bernadotte relative to the dispositions they were to make. All the danger which had menaced the right flank of Bennigsen's column had vanished with the arrival of the Army of the North. Bennigsen now found himself able to reconcentrate his overly extended forces and reform what was to become the allied center. His forces were quickly supported by the cavalry and the artillery of the Army of the North as he attacked the village of Sellerhausen.

As night was beginning to fall, Bennigsen sent the Russian 26th Division (Paskievich) via Ober-Zwei-Naundorf to the Windmill Heights. By this maneuver he would strike the French fighting Klenau and those in the village of Stötteritz in the flank and oblige them to abandon the village that night. After that, all it would take for a decisive allied victory, would be for the Army of Poland to climb the walls of Leipzig.

During the night the Army of Poland was redeployed as follows. The Prussian 11th Brigade (Ziethen) moved into Zuckelhausen. The Austrian 4th Corps (Klenau) stood before Holzhausen, towards Stötteritz. Docturov's Corps stood before Ober- and Unter-Zwei-Naundorf. The 26th Division (Paskievich) stood before the Windmill Heights, towards Stötteritz. Stroganov's advanced guard stood in Mölkau. Tschaplitz's Cavalry Division was to the rear. Kreutz's cavalry detachment stood before Mölkau towards Stötteritz. The Austrian 2nd Division (Bubna) and Platov's Cossacks stood by Paunsdorf. Bennigsen's headquarters were in Baalsdorf.[42]

Bennigsen was moved to action by the allied capture of Holzhausen and Steinberg. The main body of the Russian forces moved towards the north, behind Stroganov's column, shifted to the region around Baalsdorf. Klenau took up a position on the Steinberg. The A. Liechtenstein Regiment and several guns occupied the heights. The Erzherzog Karl Regiment formed a second line. The Löderer Cavalry Brigade stood to the left, with the O'Reilly Chevauléger Regiment closed up on the right. In view of the fact that Zwei-Naundorf was not occupied by the Russians, Hohenlohe's Division marched immediately west from Holzhausen, Schäffer's Brigade to the right, the Württemberg Infantry Regiment on the left flank. The 1/Kerpen Regiment was detached to Holzhausen, while the 2/Kerpen Regiment, which had suffered heavily in earlier battles around that village, stood behind Holzhausen. The 1/1st Wallachian Grenz and 1/, 3/Wallachian-Illyrian Grenz Regiments of Paumgarten's Brigade appeared before the French in Zwei-Naundorf, with the Palatinal and Erzherzog Ferdinand Hussar Regiments standing behind them in support.

Klenau's instructions were to storm Stötteritz. A view of the map shows that the execution of these orders was impossible, so long as the French held Zwei-Naundorf and Mölkau. The Austrian 4th Armeeabteilung limited itself therefore to a cannonade. Their further advance depended on events on the Wurzen Road and on Bennigsen's actions.

Around 3:00 p.m., Grand Duke Constantine came with a great retinue to Klenau. He then rode to Bernadotte's headquarters, in order to greet him in the name of the monarchs.[43]

The Sixth Column

At daybreak on 18 October, the advanced posts of Bertrand's IV Corps began skirmishing with Mensdorf's Streifkorps, which was facing them. The condition of the Austrian 3rd Armeeabteilung was not in the least enviable. The 1st Jäger Battalion stood in the first line by Klein-Zschocher and the 2nd Jäger Battalion stood by Leutzsch. Czollich's Brigade stood behind the right flank, near Gross-Zschocher. Czollich had passed over the Pleisse during the twilight of 17 October, advancing towards Plagwitz in order to demonstrate against the French as ordered by Schwarzenberg. Weigel's Brigade stood by Mark-Ranstädt, as did the 1st Light Division and Thielmann's Streifkorps. Grimmer's Brigade stood by Alt-Ranstädt forming the left flank. Crenneville's 1st Division was ordered to pull back to the main position of the 3rd Armeeabteilung, but had not received the order and still found itself marching for Cröbern.

Because of the magnitude of the casualties suffered in the attacks on Lindenau on 16 October the Austrian forces facing Lindenau had no thought of attempting to renew their assault. They were too weakened to consider such an attempt, and had assumed passive defensive positions.

Gyulai's few battalions facing the French were covered by pickets during the night, but they failed to notice the steady massing of French forces across the Elster. This force, under Bertrand's leadership, was preparing to push down the road towards Naumburg, and open the way for the withdrawal of the Grande Armée. Around 7:00 a.m., the French columns pushed out of Lindenau leading the advance of the IV Corps. Following Bertrand were Guilleminot's 13th Division, the II Young Guard Corps under Mortier, the V Cavalry Corps, Lefèbvre-Desnoëttes' 2nd Guard Cavalry Division and Ornano's 1st Guard Cavalry Division. The movement was visible about a half-hour later, but to the Austrians them everything remained calm until 10:00 a.m.

At 10:00 a.m., a French force of infantry, cavalry and artillery suddenly lunged against Klein-Zschocher, as other columns moved down the road that ran to Merseburg and Lützen, rousing the Austrians from their stupor.

In view of Gyulai's lack of familiarity of the general area and his greatly weakened forces, there remained for Gyulai nothing else to do but to evacuate Mark-Ranstädt. Because of the open land on all sides, any defense of Mark-Ranstädt would be difficult, if not impossible. He drew his forces together, forming them on his right wing, which leaned on the Elster. This move precluded the possibility of the French columns striking his flank, and kept him in contact with his headquarters. He immediately ordered the brigades by Alt- and Mark-Ranstädt to begin movement. His reserve artillery, standing by Lützen, was ordered to move to Eythra, where when circumstance permitted, they were to pass over the Elster and to await further instructions in Zwenkau. It was hoped that they might be able to join the pending attack by Blücher and St.-Priest on the French rear and flank. FML Murray was instructed to draw back towards Zeitz as was GM Salins. General staff chief Oberstleutnant Kinsky galloped to the threatened Klein-Zschocher in order to quickly bring the Austrians into a state of readiness. However, as he arrived there, he saw the right was already in a bad way.

The prerequisite for the secure withdrawal of the French, was the occupation of the allied positions in Leutzsch and Klein-Zschocher, which were thorns in their flesh. At 1:00 p.m., Bertrand directed an assault by two overwhelming forces against Leutzsch and Klein-Zschocher. In Leutzsch the French found the job quite easy and quickly dealt with the isolated 2nd Jäger Battalion. The Austrians quickly fell back to the Luppe River and later, being completely cut off from their command, attached themselves to Blücher's army.

However, a heated battle erupted by Klein-Zschocher as Morand's Division attacked, with GB Belair again leading the 13th Line Regiment forward, supported by the Württemberg infantry. Klein-Zschocher was brought into a state of defense. Each entrance to the village was blocked with wagons and other materials. It was weakly occupied by the 1st Jäger Battalion and a few detachments from the Kottulinsky Infantry Regiment. They were unable to hold back the overwhelming assault, and soon withdrew to the southeast, where they joined other Austrian forces standing by the Elster.[44] The edge of the village was evacuated by the Jägers and the greater part of them moved to the far side of the Elster where they joined the Austrian forces standing there. The French and Württembergers captured 18 officers and 700 men.[45]

From a nearby ridge, Oberstleutnant Simbschen, who had commanded, since 16 October, the 1/Gradiscaner Grenz and the 1/Kaunitz Regiments and occupied the village of Klein-Zschocher, looked around to survey the situation as the French thundered into and through Klein-Zschocher. He had, despite repeated orders to draw back, continued to hold a number of small posts, that protected the flank of the Main Army and the 3rd Armeeabteilung. As the French infantry now advanced towards the passage through Schleussig, and at the same time moved past the right flank of Klein-Zschocher, he threw forward two companies of the 1/Gradiscaner Grenz Regiment. They engaged in a substantial engagement with the French and covered the burning of a bridge. Because they were so far forward and heavily engaged, the Jägers were the last forces withdrawn. With the Elster against their back they despaired of their fate at the hands of the overwhelming French forces facing them. They had no alternative but to surrender.

The 13th Company of the von Kottulinsky Infantry Regiment, commanded by Oberstleutnant Cron, pushed forward on the west edge of Klein-Zschocher. It was cut off from the rest of the battalion and not wishing to move into the open where they would be quickly overwhelmed, they threw themselves inside the village. Unfortunately they quickly encountered the advancing French as they penetrated into the village. In the next moment, the company was surrounded and crushed. Six Austrian officers and 292 men surrendered to the French.

Klein-Zschocher fell to the French. The Kottulinsky and the 3/Kaiser Infantry Regiments could no longer hold their positions near the village and were pulled back for the defense of Gross-Zschocher. The defense of this village, whose edge was barricaded by pioneers, was to be most significant to the outcome of the day's fighting. While Czollich's Brigade and a brigade battery held back the attack of the French, in response to Schwarzenberg's verbal order, the 3rd Armeeabteilung had moved to the support of Hieronymus Colloredo's 1st column, as it advanced towards Cröbern. The allied cavalry standing on the Austrian left wing was driven further backwards.[46]

Gyulai ordered the march of the corps towards Knauthain in echelons from the left wing, the 1st Light Division and Mensdorf's and Thielmann's Streifkorps had relieved the front line, while Czollich's Brigade was reinforced by a brigade battery and sent to hold Gross-Zschocher, the Austrian base of operations. On the left bank of the Elster there stood six weak Austrian battalions, 23½ squadrons, four Cossack regiments, and 26 guns. This force had little hope of delaying the advance of Bertrand's Corps and those that followed. If they were to be of use, it would be more to observe the French movements, and screen any allied countermove by major forces from the south. Nevertheless they were a not insignificant worry to the French as they moved past, even in their relatively inactive role. The French detached forces to Gautzsch and Schleussig to watch the Austrians while they passed through. In addition, until the evening, the French were forced to cover the stretch Schönau-Mark-Ranstädt with a considerable side guard. The French lead elements reached Lützen, after 2½ hours of marching, around 5:30 p.m.

Czollich's Brigade stopped the French between Gross-Zschocher and the Elster, and also strongly occupied the passage by Knauthain. The main body of Gyulai's Corps had barely arrived by Gautzsch, when Simbschen and GM Scheither reported movements of large French forces from Schleussig and the region between Gross-Zschocher-Knauthain-Rehbach. Their reports indicated that at least two French corps had crossed over the Elster. Simbschen's report described a massive retreat of troops, oxen and wagons, all mixed up, hurriedly advancing down the road.[47]

Around 2:00 p.m., Gyulai received Schwarzenberg's order to remain on the left bank of the Elster and to explore the French line of retreat.

This order was immediately sent to Murray, who, around 5:00 p.m., found himself facing Bertrand's IV Corps and was obliged to evacuate Weissenfels.

Gyulai sent his light infantry and cavalry against Bertrand's IV Corps as it moved from Lindenau to Lützen. Bertrand left Guilleminot in Lützen. Mortier's II Young Guard Corps was to advance into Lindenau and occupy it, holding open the road west for Napoleon.[48]

On the left bank of the Elster, Gyulai's cavalry remained in contact with the French. It had one further success, breaking into a French column, seizing 10 caissons, numerous baggage wagons of all kinds, more than 100 prisoners, and a large number of horses. The Cossacks of Thielmann's Corps shared in the booty.

The immediate observation of the French was passed to the two streifkorps, which immediately began the march towards Naumburg, and clung to the heels of the withdrawing French. Gyulai, on the basis of reports that Bertrand's main body was already in march towards Lützen, believed the best way to execute Schwarzenberg's order was through preliminary convergence of his forces by Pegau. He, therefore, dispatched P. Hessen-Homburg's Division towards Pegau. A battalion moved to Zwenkau to garrison the village and seize the bridges. The main body prepared dinner, rested and then moved towards Pegau.

At 6:00 p.m. the Emperor of Austria departed the battlefield to return to Rötha. Generals Gyulai and Scheither sent word at different times to him, that the French IV Corps had departed that morning towards Weissenfels and that its baggage took the same road.

It was easy to believe that if the French defended the points of Connewitz, Probstheida, Stötteritz, and Schönefeld with such vigor, it was not to gain a victory, but to assure a line of retreat.

At the same time, Prince Schwarzenberg moved to the heights where the Czar and the King of Prussia and all their lieutenants stood, in order to communicate to them that the battle would be decided in the morning.

The sovereigns ordered that their armies should hold themselves ready to recommence the battle at the break of dawn, and to act in a decisive manner so as to end the battle. In case of a French retreat, it was agreed to march towards Leipzig in five columns, and to take the city by assault. The Czar also stated that he wanted the Russian and Prussian Guard and the Russian grenadiers to cross the Elster at Pegau, and to fall on the flank of the French during their retreat, as he perceived the French as greatly fatigued and lacking provisions. It was also ordered that during the day, the Austrian 3rd Armeeabteilung (Gyulai), the Austrian 1st Light Division and Thielmann's Streifkorps would also move to Pegau, that the Prussian 1st Corps would move against Merseburg, that Platov's Cossacks would cross the Pleisse at Dölitz or Gaschwitz to pursue the French, and that the remaining forces would advance to pursue the French. The conference broke up at 8:00 p.m.[49]

The Czar and Schwarzenberg spent the night in Rötha. The King of Prussia spent the night in Gruna, on the road to Borna, and Barclay de Tolly slept in Liebertwolkwitz.

During the night Gyulai advanced from Knauthain to Pegau, in preparation for his attack on the flank of the retreating French the next day.

Yorck's Corps, with its reserve cavalry in the lead, supported by two of Sacken's Cossack Regiments and the Austrian Jäger Battalion #2, moved out at 7:00 p.m. with its mission of assuring the passage over the Saale near Merseburg and Halle. After a forced march, the reserve cavalry and Horn's Division arrived at the break of dawn in Halle. Hünerbein's Division arrived at the same time Bruckdorf and Liebenau.

Napoleon, realizing that he could not win or maintain himself resolved to withdraw the following day. He lacked the munitions necessary to engage in yet another day of battle. According to the reports of his artillery generals, Sorbier and Dulauloy, the French artillery had fired 84,000 cannon rounds on 16 October and another 85,000 rounds on 18 October.

As the escaping French passed across the Elster the Württemberg Division was placed to the rear to act as a rearguard with three dragoon regiments. As Marmont's park passed through Mark-Ranstädt it came under Austrian artillery fire, but the French continued down the road to Lützen via Röcken, where they arrived ad midnight.

That evening Napoleon returned to the suburbs of Leipzig and spent the night with Murat. During the evening a steady stream of equipment, and some artillery and cavalry, began to move out towards Weissenfels, the single line of retreat left to the French.[50]

10

The Battles to the North and West 18 October 1813

The Advance of the Fourth Column

During the morning Bernadotte and Blücher held a conference in Breitenfeld. It was agreed that the Army of the North would pass the Parthe at Taucha with a reinforcement of 30,000 men drawn from the Army of Silesia. Blücher agreed to dispatch Langeron's Corps, and to renounce his rank and his rights as army commander, putting himself at the head of his Prussians. After the dispositions were made, the Army of the North was to pass over the Parthe, join its left flank to the Army of Poland and march against Leipzig from the northeast.

The Army of the North left is bivouac about 8:00 a.m. and passed over the Parthe in the following order.

1. The Prussian 3rd Corps (Bülow) and Winzingerode's cavalry, which served as the extreme left wing near Taucha.
2. Winzingerode's Corps and Voronzov's advanced guard crossed near Grassdorf.
3. The Swedish Army (Stedingk) crossed near Plaussig.
4. Langeron's Russian Corps, detached from Blücher's command, crossed at Mockau.[1]

The Swedes Arrive

The advance of the Swedish army towards Leipzig had been slow, purportedly because Bernadotte had received word that Napoleon planned a renewed attack towards Berlin. This slowness would result in only the Swedish artillery taking a serious part in the battle at Leipzig. On 4 October the Swedish reserve artillery had crossed the Elbe and by 12 October it was in Bernberg. It was not until 18 October that it was on the field at Leipzig. When it broke camp that morning it attempted to cross the Parthe River near Plaussig, but found the river impossible to cross and moved further north, away from the field, to seek a ford. In Plaussig, von Cardell, commander of the Swedish artillery, met GM Charles de Suremain, who informed him that Bernadotte wished him to cross as quickly as possible. Bernadotte knew that the French would offer a strong resistance to the planned movement of the Army of the North over the Parthe. Von Cardell then marched on Plösen seeking a crossing.

As the Army of the North advanced, Bülow's Corps stood at the head and Winzingerode's Corps, now under by Voronzov, came behind him. Langeron had, at the same time as Voronzov crossed, placed more pontoon bridges over the Parthe and begun his own passage. He followed Stedingk's Swedes, in order to insert himself in the line where he was assigned.[2]

At 9:00 a.m., Bülow marched, always ready, from Podelwitz in two columns towards Leipzig to be able to attack the French on the Mulde with his strong right wing. As his forces moved past Taucha they found it filled with Russian vehicles. This press was so great that the Swedes would not be able to begin their passage by Plaussig until around 4:00 p.m.

Langeron was ordered by Bernadotte to cover the flank march of the Army of the North as it moved to a position on the right bank of the Parthe by Plösen-Mockau. At 9:00 a.m., to facilitate the passage over the Parthe between Mockau and Alt-Naundorf, Langeron's Corps pulled up 36 Russian 12-pdr guns[3] to silence the French artillery positioned near Nautzsch. The passage then occurred without interruption, the infantry finding the water reaching up to their waist.[4]

The French reformed their forces in Schönefeld and began a skirmish battle until the Prussian 3rd Corps entered the line of battle and opened communications with the Army of Poland near Paunsdorf.

Langeron's cavalry commanders, GM Rudsevich and GM Emanuel, had passed over a flying bridge by Mockau and moved towards the French. Emanuel's cavalry swarmed towards the Eilenburg road, where he soon linked up with Platov's Cossacks, between Mockau and the earth works at Heiterblick, a mound on the road between Leipzig and Taucha. Shortly later part of Winzingerode's cavalry joined Emanuel's forces. The Cossack regiments, that had spent the previous evening by Taucha, had been chased out by the French by daybreak, but an attack by the cavalry brigade of GM Baron von der Pahlen soon overran the village and it was again occupied by the Russians.[5]

The French position behind the Parthe was now pierced at several points and Maréchal Ney was obliged to withdraw his advanced forces in order to save them from the advancing allies. He reorganized the three corps under his command in a line running between Schönefeld, Sellerhausen, and Stünz.

At the same time Platov's Cossacks and Bubna's Austrian 2nd Light Division advanced against Paunsdorf. An insignificant skirmish developed between Rudsevich's advanced guard (Langeron's Corps) and the French near Mockau, while Emanuel's (Korff's) cavalry moved through Plösen. Langeron's Corps stood between Mockau and Alt-Naundorf. Pontoon bridges were thrown over the Parthe and by 11:00 a.m., three infantry corps and the reserve cavalry had moved to the east bank of the Parthe River. Only the three heavy batteries remained in their original positions on the west bank.[6]

As the battle was developing Reynier had a small garrison in Taucha. At 9:00 a.m., he sent his cavalry brigade with one battalion of the von Sahr 2nd Light Regiment and a horse battery to the left against the Parthe and sent Zeschau's 24th (Saxon) Division behind Paunsdorf, where it stretched its left wing towards Schönefeld, occupied by Durutte's 32nd Division.[7]

The VIII Corps (Reynier) was formed around Paunsdorf in two lines. Detachments of cavalry and artillery, the weak brigades of the VI and VIII Corps, stood by Blick, Cleuden and Taucha. The von Sahr 2nd Light Regiment and Normann's Württemberg Cavalry Brigade stood between Paunsdorf and Taucha. As the Russian cavalry approached them, Normann's cavalry and the von Sahr Regiment quickly defected to them.[9]

Marmont looked across the fields and saw a large force of light cavalry heading in his direction. He called his corps to arms and assumed that Normann's Brigade had been attacked and was withdrawing in disorder. It turned out to be Cossacks, as Normann and his brigade had defected to the allies.[9]

It was about 10:00 a.m. that Major von Fabrice, with the Saxon cavalry, found himself faced with Emanuel's Russian cavalry (part of Korff's force). The engagement was very one-sided and the Saxon cavalry may not have attempted any resistance. According to Marmont it simply defected, passing into the allied lines. Adding insult to injury, the Saxon battery with them promptly unlimbered and began firing on the French.[10]

At the same time Platov moved his forces forward from Zweenfurth and moved to the south, by Baalsdorf. Platov's artillery began to fire on the Saxons around Paunsdorf and Reynier responded by detaching his reserve artillery to engage them, a 12-pdr battery and Horse Battery #2 "Groshain".

The French began reorganizing their forces and at 10:00 a.m. Marmont advanced his corps to the Schönefeld-Paunsdorf line. Lagrange's 21st Division stood adjacent to Schönefeld, with Friederich's 22nd Division to the east and Compans' 20th Division stood on Friederich's right. Durutte's 32nd Division, of Reynier's VII Corps, held the gap between Compans and Paunsdorf. Behind and to the rear of Durutte was Zeschau's 24th Division which stood between Paunsdorf and Stünz. Paunsdorf, itself, was occupied by two companies of the Lecoq 1st Light (Saxon) Infantry Regiment. Arrighi's III Cavalry Corps was divided and stood behind both flanks. Fournier (6th Light Cavalry Division) and Lorge (5th Light Cavalry Division) stood behind Schönefeld and Defrance stood by Stünz.[11]

The III Corps stood behind Marmont, by Volksmarsdorf. The 9th Division stood in reserve behind Schönefeld, forming a number of small posts that stretched from the left of Parthe to Leipzig. The 11th Division was by Reudnitz; the 8th Division stood by the gardens, between Reudnitz and Paunsdorf, contacting the VII Corps, which was behind Paunsdorf.

The 8th and 11th Divisions had begun moving at 9:00 a.m. to occupy their new positions, followed by the III Corps park, reserves, and light cavalry. The 8th Division formed the head of the column. It was ordered to pass to the right of the village kitchen gardens and to move towards Pfaffendorf.[12]

The allies slowly advanced across the plain between the Parthe and Taucha, driving out the French and Saxon advanced posts. The small village of Taucha continued to be occupied by the Saxons who defended their position with great courage. General Pahlen turned the village, seconded by Colonel Arnoldi, who lost an arm in supporting this attack with his artillery. As the village fell, about 11:00 a.m., the Saxon Prince Friedrich August Regiment, its garrison, was forced to lower its arms and surrender.

Polish infantry 1813, by Raffet.

At noon, the 2nd Brigade, 8th Division, left its position near Dombrowski's 27th (Polish) Division and moved down the main road between the village's kitchen gardens and towards Schönefeld, where it took up a new position before the windmill, with its left on the tree lined road and its right in the village of Reidniz.[13]

Once there it found itself in contact with the 11th Division, which had received orders to form a second line behind the VI Corps. Six guns of its divisional artillery fired for over an hour on the allied forces attempting to move towards the Schönefeld bridge. The 9th Division formed the extreme right of the III Corps. The light cavalry stood in reserve, 600 paces from the 11th Division, where it covered the III Corps artillery reserve.

Bubna's 2nd Light Division

Bennigsen's fourth column, formed with Bubna's Austrian 2nd Light Division, advanced despite the heavy French resistance from Zweenfurth on the main road from Wurzen to Leipzig, taking the village of Mölkau. Bubna's 2nd Light Division had, around 10:00 a.m., reached the Wurzen road. It stood in the great open zone on both sizes of the Wurzen Road where Bennigsen had sent it to await the arrival of the Army of the North.

It soon engaged the French defending around Paunsdorf, and despite its small size, did not permit the French to shake it off until decisive forces of the Army of the North arrived from Walplatz.

Upon his arrival before Paunsdorf, Bubna was joined by the Platov's Cossacks, who had engaged the French XI Corps around Sommerfeld as it fought its way in great chaos towards Leipzig. Bubna's appearance moving towards a union with Langeron's forces, as they passed over the Parthe, forced Marmont to swing his right flank around the pivot of Schönefeld, back towards Paunsdorf. Lagrange's 21st Division occupied Schönefeld.

Initially, a battery of six Saxon 6-pdrs faced the Austrians. Birnbaum (Horse Battery #1) sent three of his horse guns to reinforce them and the Saxon battery eventually rose to 21 guns before Paunsdorf. They directed their fire down the road against Bubna's advancing division. Bubna responded by detaching his two horse batteries, a total of 12 guns. He held back his battery of six 3-pdrs, which he did not want to face the greater weight of the French and Saxon 8-pdr and 6-pdr batteries.

The Austrian artillerists served their guns better than the French and Saxons, despite their fewer numbers and lighter guns. After a half-hour of uninterrupted fire the Austrians succeeded in suppressing the French batteries. Seven French guns were dismounted, whereupon the remaining guns withdrew behind the village. However, half of the Austrian guns were also destroyed, 30 horses from their teams were killed, and they had fired off all of their ammunition. The Austrian horse artillery was also obliged to pull back and stayed out of the rest of the battle.[14]

The artillery duel was decided by noon. With the departure of the Saxon artillery, the way was cleared for the Austrian infantry assault. Bubna ordered Zechmeister to attack the French and Saxon forces occupying Paunsdorf. Zechmeister's Brigade led the assault with Neipperg's Brigade to his right, while Platov's Cossacks held the attention of Durutte's 32nd Division. Jäger Battalion #6 advanced into the edge of the village. The 1/Peterwardeiner Grenz Regiment, also part of Zechmeister's Brigade, pushed in to support the Jägers.

The Austrians eventually broke into Paunsdorf, but with heavy casualties on both sides. As the Austrian Jägers passed over each village wall, the French directed a heavy canister fire against them and threw fresh infantry forward to throw them back. In the meantime the Saxon artillery began to fire on the village with its howitzers and the village began to burn. The dense smoke and the heat of the flames, coupled with the fire of the Saxon and French infantry, were more than the Austrians could bear. The Jägers pulled back out of the village.

Zechmeister had positioned six squadrons of the Liechtenstein Hussars, supported by the 1/ Peterwardeiner Grenz Regiment, so that they could strike the French as they pursued the Jager Battalion #6 out of Paunsdorf. As they drove the French back, the hussars and grenzers pushed into Paunsdorf, renewing the battle. As the battle in the village raged, Bubna learned from Platov that the French were forming to strike Paunsdorf from the north. He swung Neipperg's Brigade to the right. Soon the entire light division was drawn into the battle, except for two battalions from Weiland's Brigade, which were held back as the division's last reserve. The battle had already lasted two hours.[15]

It was around 1:00 p.m., that cannon fire was heard in the direction of Schönefeld. Langeron's attack on the left wing of Ney's army group had begun. At the same time, the first advance of the columns of the Army of the North appeared moving from Taucha towards Leipzig. Ney hurried to his right wing and found the Saxon 24th Division, under Zeschau, behind Sellerhausen, which was occupied by a part of Durutte's 32nd Division. He ordered the Saxons to counterattack. Because of their unreliability, however Reynier had held the Saxons back as reserve. Reynier launched into an immediate and vehement exchange of words with Ney, but Ney again ordered the Saxons to attack Paunsdorf, so that he could once again gain possession of it. Ney also ordered the Saxons to hold the village as long as possible, despite the overwhelming force facing them.

The Austrian foothold became stronger and the battle continued. Reynier threw in Ryssel's Saxon Brigade, 24th Division, supporting it with Brause's Saxon Brigade, which stood by Sellerhausen. The Saxon Jägers advanced into Paunsdorf and supported the left of the Saxon artillery line to the south of the village.

The battle over Paunsdorf remained undecided, so Ney directed Durutte to sent one of his battalions into the village. It advanced into the village, with the support of its entire division, and quickly became embroiled in the street fighting. At the same time, Neipperg's Brigade moved to the north and began to engage Durutte's 32nd Division.[16] This assault succeeded in throwing the Austrians out of Paunsdorf, doing so shortly before the arrival of Bülow's Corps.

When Durutte had engaged part of his six battalions in his attack against Paunsdorf, Zechmeister found himself in a difficult situation. A partial envelopment of the village by the French actually placed two companies in the greatest danger of being cut off and the 6th Jägers suffered heavy losses as they tried to escape. The Jägers lost 20 dead, five officers and 62 men wounded, and 49 prisoners during Durutte's attack. Bubna's Division engaged the French on the east side of Leipzig until 2:00 p.m.[17]

Shortly after Blücher noted that the French were sending reinforcements from Leipzig to Schönefeld, and directed Sacken's Corps towards the Halle Gate of Leipzig to face them. At the same time, he attacked the entrenchments on the right bank of the Parthe. The effect of these two moves was to stop the advance of the French reinforcements.

The French at 2:00 p.m.

The allied advance had obliged the French to redeploy their forces. Pacthod's 1st Young Guard Division had been pushed back from Gohlis and stood between it and the Halle suburb of Leipzig. Behind him stood Dombrowski's infantry. The plains to the east of the Eutritzsch-Leipzig road were empty with the first French forces to the east being Lagrange's 21st Division which occupied Schönefeld. The rest of Marmont's IV Corps stood to Lagrange's right at Schönefeld, with Friederich's 22nd Division being adjacent to Schönefeld and Compans' 20th Division to its right. Across their front was a large battery of artillery. Reynier's VII Corps occupied Paunsdorf with Durutte's 32nd Division Behind Durutte stood Zeschau's 24th (Saxon) Division and a large battery of Saxon artillery faced due east, south of Paunsdorf.

French troops in the environs of Leipzig, 18 October.

Behind Friederichs stood Fournier's 6th and Lorge's 5th Light Cavalry Divisions in two lines. Behind them, extending from the Schönefeld-Leipzig road stood the divisions of Ricard, Brayer, and Delmas (11th, 8th, and 9th). Beurmann's 25th Light Cavalry Brigade (III Corps) stood on Delmas' right. Nansouty's Guard Cavalry Corps stood to the south, between Stünz and Stötteritz. Defrance's 4th Heavy Cavalry Division stood just north of Stünz, behind Zeschau's 24th Division.

The Army of the North

At about 2:00 p.m. the Army of the North found itself level with Blücher's forces. Sacken's forces had just occupied Gohlis. Lieven's 10th Division stood to the east of Gohlis, Neverovsky's 27th Division occupied Gohlis, and Yorck's Corps was advancing south towards Gohlis.

To the east, between Eutritzsch and Schönefeld stood a large allied battery whose fire was directed across the Parthe River against Schönefeld. On the east of the Parthe, Kapzevich's 10th Corps was attacking Schönefeld. The rest of Langeron's Corps stood to the north of Schönefeld, deployed behind a massive line of artillery that extended across their entire front. Behind this artillery stood St.-Priest's 8th Corps, with its flank against Alt-Naundorf. To the east of St.-Priest stood Rudsevich's advanced guard (Langeron's Corps). Then stood Winzingerode's cavalry, Emanuel's (Korff's) Cavalry, and Hessen-Homburg's Austrian light infantry.

Behind St.-Priest stood Olsoviev's 9th Corps, and behind that an artillery reserve. To Olsoviev's left rear stood Korff's reserve cavalry. Advancing down the Grassdorf-Leipzig Road was Borstell's 5th Brigade. Behind him, parallel with Taucha, was Voronzov's advanced guard.

The Battle at 2:00 p.m.

The village of Schönefeld was 1,000 paces long on its northern side and about 500 paces long on its southern side. To its left (west) flowed the Parthe river. It was occupied by Lagrange's 21st Division, about 3,000 men.

As Hessen-Homburg's Division of Bülow's Corps made junction with the left of Langeron's Corps around Blick, Langeron commenced his attack against Schönefeld. The attack was preceded with a heavy cannonade. At 2:00 p.m., Kapzevich's 10th Corps assaulted the village.

Kapzevich's 10th Corps formed two lines. At about 2:00 p.m. it moved to the attack with 7 battalions (29th, 37th, 45th Jagers, and the Staroskol Infantry Regiment). These seven battalions, whose normal strength would have been nearly 6,000 men, now numbered barely between 1,800 to 2,200 men.[18]

It pushed into the village, moving down the main street only to be driven back out of the village, occupying and holding only the last house.

In the attack, Kapzevich lost his horse, killed under him. The Staroskol Infantry Regiment attacked the manor farm, killing or capturing the garrison of 200 men. However, the French succeeded in stopping the assault and by 3:00 p.m. the was fight was stabilized. The Staroskol Infantry Regiment suffered heavily, losing a great number of staff and senior officers.[19]

The assault on Schönefeld was renewed as Paunsdorf fell and Durutte's 32nd Division fell back to Sellerhausen. In order to renew the fight Langeron sent forward the 9th Corps under Olsoviev. GL Kapzevich sent forward the Viatka Infantry Regiment (two battalions—700 men), part of GM Schkapski's Brigade, to renew his assault on the village. At the same time, from the left of Schönefeld, St.-Priest's 8th Corps and Rudsevich's advanced guard, supported by the artillery line, advanced to the attack Friedrich's 22nd Division. Olsoviev's 9th Corps stood back as a reserve. The Russian artillery advanced and St.-Priest's Corps moved to strike the eastern side of Schönefeld.

As Kapzevich attacked, St.-Priest turned his 17th Division (Pillar) and struck the side of the village. General Kern, with 2 battalions of the Riazan and Bieloserk Infantry Regiment (1,375 men), moved down the main street, while General Pillar moved with the two battalions of the Brest and Wilmanstrand Infantry Regiments (1,375 men) through the village's gardens. They were followed by two battalions of the 11th Division (Jeletz and Polotsk—1,097 men), which formed a second line.

About 4,600 Russians moved into the attack against Lagrange and Friederichs.

Three times Kapzevich assaulted the village and three times he was repelled. Schönefeld was set afire during all these assaults and made the battle in its streets all the more ferocious.

Von Cardell's Swedish artillery slowly began arriving on the field as St.-Priest was engaged. First came the horse artillery, which had force marched onto the field and advanced to within canister range of the French. Two heavy batteries soon arrived "with a speed until then unknown for 12-pdrs." These three batteries, totaling 20 guns, quickly joined the fight.

In the middle of the field, before Langeron's main body, was a clear and open plain. Facing Langeron across that plain were the massed forces of Marmont's VI Corps. Langeron organized a battery of 100 guns from his corps, adding to that 60 guns from Winzingerode's Corps and 20 Swedish guns under von Cardell before his line. To the east a second battery was formed with 36 of Bülow's guns, though this figure later rose to 40 guns.[20]

The combined effect of the French artillery deployed before Friederichs' line on the Russians and the Russian artillery firing back on the French was devastating. Marmont responded with his own artillery, which may not have exceeded 49 guns, though he had 82 at his disposal. To his left Reynier faced 27 guns north. Reynier already had 21 of his guns deployed to defend Paunsdorf from the east and could not move them to counter this threat. Eventually the French gun line rose by another 61 guns which were sent forward from the III Corps, which stood in reserve. A total of 137 French guns faced 220 allied guns. The artillery roared and the field between the two lines of guns was swept clean of the living. Both sides lost heavily, the French losing no fewer than six generals. Friederichs was obliged to pull his division back.[21]

The Battle of Paunsdorf

Bubna's 2nd Light Division faced it from the left on the Wurzen Road. Bülow and Hessen-Homburg advanced south against this important corner of the French line. When Bülow received a report that Paunsdorf was occupied by the French, he directed his artillery to take the village under fire and at the same time ordered Hessen-Homburg's Prussian 3rd Brigade to turn off the road. The Prussian Horse Battery #6 and the Russian Position Battery #7 of Colonel Dietrichs' Artillery Brigade fired on the northern portion of the village, Captain Bogue's British rocket battery[22] fired on the south side of the village, while on the right wing, Prussian 12-pdr Battery #5 and Horse Battery #11 engaged the French artillery by the village.[23]

These guns, however, directed their fire against Marmont's right, while the British rocket battery began firing into Paunsdorf from a position between Bubna's Division and Hessen-Homburg's Division.[24]

With the beginning of this bombardment, Bülow ordered his forces to attack Paunsdorf. Three battalions from his left wing advanced, the 2/3rd East Prussian Regiment and the 1/, 2/4th Reserve Regiment. As the attack developed these three battalions sent their schützen forward. To the left of the Prussian attack advanced the Austrian Jäger Battalion #6 of Bubna's Division. The advancing schützen took heavy fire from Durutte's Battalion facing them, littering the field with their dead and wounded.

The defenders were supported by the remainder of Durutte's 32nd Division, which stood to the west of the village, behind a substantial battery. Despite this, the attacking Prussians advanced their own batteries firing canister to support their advance. The Prussian 4th Reserve Regiment was joined by the Austrian 1/Peterwardeiner Grenz Regiment and supported by the British rockets. Durutte's forces defending Paunsdorf were driven back towards Sellerhausen. Three field pieces were abandoned on the Wurzen road because their teams had been killed.

In their enthusiasm, the 1/, 2/4th Reserve Infantry Regiment and the British rocket battery pursued the French back as far as Sellerhausen and united there, but quickly found themselves facing superior organized French forces. Captain Bogue was shot dead and the two Prussian battalions were driven back. The Prussian casualties were so heavy that they were unable to take further part in the battle on 18 October.[25]

It was the moment for the French counterattack. Reynier, with the Saxon 24th Division, stood south of Sellerhausen and made ready. However, a most unanticipated incident thwarted his intent. It was about 3:00 p.m. GD Reynier, who stood by the Saxons, ordered the withdrawal of the Saxon 12-pdr battery behind the 2nd Brigade. When this order reached the artillery, instead it limbered up and moved in the opposite direction. It advanced in a column by sections towards the allies. The French cavalry behind it accompanied this evolution, which they took for an attack, and cried *Vive l'empereur.* Then the entire Saxon division began to roll forward. The Saxon flags flew and their drums pounded a military staccato. The cries of Durutte's troops encouraged them forward in their seeming counterattack.

The Saxons were defecting to the allies. Both Saxon infantry brigades and the greatly weakened hussar regiment[26] followed the artillery, and in an ever quickening pace, moved into the area between Bubna's 2nd Light Division and Docturov's column. In vain GL von Zeschau and Reynier sought to stop the movement. Mounted Saxon officers hurried ahead of their advancing columns and announced their intentions to the allies, who opened their lines and allowed the Saxons to enter. It was 3:00 p.m. and the French were stunned by the betrayal of the Saxons.[27]

However, the defection was not complete. Parts of the Anton and Friedrich August Infantry Regiments were unable to defect with the rest of the division, because they were in too close contact with Durutte's forces. In addition four guns of Birnbaum's 1st Horse Battery did not escape.

The Saxon forces were marched to the allied rear and distributed amongst the various allied corps. The Saxon cavalry went to Yorck's Corps, the von Sahr Light Regiment was assigned to the Swedish Army Corps. The Saxon artillery[28] under Birnbaum also provided ammunition to the two Austrian batteries that had earlier shot off their ammunition, permitting them to rejoin the battle.[29]

During the Saxon defection Durutte's forces pulled back to Sellerhausen and reestablished their line. The defection of the Saxons had an effect on the course of the battle, but not a major one. They had nine and a quarter battalions, totaling only 2,635 men, and 12 squadrons with a total of 630 men. In addition, they had 19 guns. This force totaled slightly more than the strength of three full strength infantry battalions and a weak cavalry regiment. The impact on the French was more one of morale, than that of the loss of significant forces. It was also ill timed, for at the same moment the Army of the North came into full view.

Defrance's 4th Heavy Cavalry Division was quickly thrown forward to fill the gap left by the Saxon defection. The Baden battery galloped forward, deployed and began to fire on the allies.

Durutte's forces defended their positions in Sellerhausen and extended their right wing to occupy the village of Stünz. From here they continued to exchange musketry and artillery with Bülow's forces.

As Durutte withdrew, Marmont's right wing had no choice, but to maintain its link with Durutte. To do so, Compans' 20th Division fell back. However, the gap was too large and Ney dispatched Delmas' 9th Division, III Corps, forward to fill the gap between Durutte and Compans. There were, apparently, some counterattacks by the French, but they were unsuccessful in stemming the allied advance.

During the withdrawal Manteuffel's Cavalry Brigade, part of Winzingerode's Corps advanced along the left of Bülow's forces and executed a few charges against Durutte's forces as they withdrew. These charges helped to encourage the French withdrawal to Sellerhausen, but the Russian General Manteuffel was killed during these charges.

As the French established themselves in new positions between Sellerhausen and Schönefeld, the victorious allied left took up positions by Paunsdorf. In front of and to the west of Paunsdorf, extending westwards from Paunsdorf, were Prussian 6-pdr Battery #6, Russian 12-pdr Battery #7, and Prussian 6-pdr Battery #10. Behind them stood Hessen-Homburg's Prussian 3rd Brigade,[30] consisting of the 2/, 1/3rd East Prussian Infantry Regiment, the 2nd East Prussian Grenadiers, and the 3/4th Reserve Regiment. Behind them stood the 3/3rd East Prussian Regiment and the 2/, 3/, 4/3rd East Prussian Landwehr Regiment. Borstell's 5th Brigade stood to the west of Hessen-Homburg and Winzingerode stood to his right. In front of Borstell's 5th Brigade stood the 2nd Kurmärk Landwehr Regiment.[31]

The French Positions

At 4:30 p.m., Dombrowski's infantry stood just north of the Halle suburbs, between the Rosenthal gate and Pfaffendorf. A small detachment stood further to the west in the Rosenthal. Pacthod's 1st Young Guard Division stood in the Halle suburbs. Lagrange's 21st Division occupied the village of Schönefeld. The divisions of Friederichs, Compans, and Delmas (22nd, 20th, and 9th) were deployed between Schönefeld and Sellerhausen with their infantry deployed before them. In a second line behind them stood Ricard's 11th and Brayer's 8th Divisions. Forming a third line, also west to east, was Fournier's 6th Light Cavalry Division with Lorge's 5th Light Cavalry Division behind it. To their right was Beurmann's Brigade (III Corps) and Laferrière's Guard Cavalry Brigade, part of the 3rd Guard Cavalry Division.

Durutte's 32nd Division occupied Sellerhausen and Stünz. An artillery battery stood before Mölkau, facing northeast, and Nansouty's Guard Cavalry Corps faced Stroganov's advanced guard, which stood due east of Mölkau.

Defrance's 4th Heavy Cavalry Division stood behind Stünz in a second line. To Defrance's left stood the Imperial Guard Chasseur a pied Regiments of Christiani's Old Guard Brigade.

The Army of the North

At 4:30 p.m. Sacken stood south of Gohlis, facing Dombrowski and the Halle suburbs. Kapzevich was assaulting Schönefeld frontally, from the north, while St.-Priest struck it from the east. Rudsevich's advanced guard stood in the interval between Schönefeld and Paunsdorf with a massive battery before him and to his left, extending to Paunsdorf. Behind him stood Winzingerode. To his left rear, with its left flank against Paunsdorf stood Borstell's 5th Prussian Brigade. Hessen-Homburg's 3rd Prussian Brigade was deployed by Paunsdorf and Bubna stood to the southeast of Paunsdorf. Paunsdorf itself was occupied by Krafft's 6th Prussian Brigade. Oppen and Emanuel's cavalry stood behind Borstell's 5th Brigade. Olsoviev's 9th Corps stood by Alt-Naundorf, south of Mockau. Further to the rear stood Korff and Voronzov, while still further back were the Swedes under Stedingk. Stroganov's advanced guard stood on the extreme southeastern end of the allied line facing Mölkau.

Ney's Reserve Advances

Ney was had held two divisions and the artillery of the III Corps by Volkmarsdorf. As Marmont fell back, Ney threw them forward. Delmas' 9th Division and Beurmann's 32nd Light Cavalry Brigade, as mentioned earlier, moved to the right of the French line by Sellerhausen. Ricard's 11th Division moved to the left, towards Schönefeld. Brayer's 8th Division remained behind the middle.

As Delmas' 9th Division arrived on the heights by the Sellerhausen's kitchen gardens it was greeted by a heavy artillery barrage. It responded in kind. General Delmas ordered General Estève to move against the village of Sellerhausen and to take it. The 2nd Provisional Légère Regiment pushed into the village at the *pas de charge*, supported by the 43rd and 136th Line Regiments. Mataly de Maran's Brigade stood in reserve, behind the houses, covered by a low ridge. The allies were thrown out of the village and the 136th, as a result of a successful effort, recaptured five guns and three caissons that had earlier been lost by Durutte's 32nd Division.[32]

The 9th Division in the village's kitchen gardens soon found itself faced by far superior forces. Allied light forces pushed into the village and large numbers of allied cavalry appeared before its position. General Beurmann vainly sought to distract the allied cavalry with four successive charges of his tiny brigade, but he was always thrown back behind the squares formed by the 9th Division. Delmas soon realized he could no longer hold his position, since the French on both flanks were falling back, and ordered the retreat. The village's kitchen gardens were evacuated, but as the 9th Division withdrew, Delmas was mortally wounded. The 136th Regiment was also obliged, because of the lack of draft horses, to abandon the guns it had recaptured.[33]

After the loss of Delmas, the 9th Division assumed a position before Reudnitz, where the enemy artillery continued to fire on it. The 9th Division was unable to respond because its guns had fired all their ammunition.

Langeron's massive artillery battery had, for the most part, fired off its ammunition and had retired behind his lines to reload its caissons. The canister fire of Souham's III Corps inflicted severe casualties on St.-Priest's Corps, as they moved across the east side of Schönefeld.

The allied threat to Schönefeld had become so great that Ricard's 11th Division had been moved to defend the village. He prepared his advance with two battalions of the 142nd and one of the 50th Line Regiment in echelon, supported by the remainder of the battalions of these two regiments. Their advance into the village was abrupt and the marines of Marmont's VI Corps, holding the village, thought their fire was that of the allies and returned the fire. The 50th Line Regiment suffered from this fire and broke. The 142nd, seeing the 50th break, fell back precipitously, but with slightly more order, until it was able to reform itself 100 paces behind the village.[34]

Ricard's arrival obliged Kapzevich to commit his last forces, two battalions of the Archangel Regiment and two battalions of the Old Ingermannland Regiment (a total of 1,273 men). Langeron sent two further battalions from Olsoviev's 9th Corps, the Nacheburg and Iakout Regiments (a total of 1,156 men), to support Kapzevich. During the ensuing attack, both Ney and Souham were wounded and obliged to leave the field.[35]

Brayer's 8th Division stood to the east of the village, covered by a line of skirmishers which fired on some allied cavalry that got too close. The 2nd Brigade, 8th Division, advanced to drive them away, supported by the 11th Division and the fire of the corps reserve artillery.

As Kapzevich committed his last reserves, Winzingerode brought forward 60 guns (24 12-pdrs and 36 horse guns) and placed them in line. Shortly later there arrived a further 20 Swedish guns (one horse and two foot batteries with 12 6-pdrs and eight 12-pdr guns) under Colonel Cardell. These 80 guns began to bombard the corps of Souham and Marmont.

The allies had evacuated part of Schönefeld and General Bony, who had replaced the now-wounded General Brayer as commander of the 8th Division, felt the moment was opportune to attack. The 2nd Brigade, 8th Division marched forward and took up a position 200 paces in front of the village. They quickly came under a heavy musketry fire, to which General Bony chose not to respond. The allied infantry facing him advanced at the charge, but the 59th Line turned their right flank. Only the 40th Line remained in reserve. The allies were driven back, but they still held the foot of the bridge in the village. A violent battle raged and after a half-hour of melee, firing off their last cartridges, the French of the 59th Line fell back behind the 40th.[36]

With a renewal of the allied artillery bombardment, Langeron sent forward his 9th Corps (Olsoviev), in a third attack on Schönefeld. Six battalions of the 9th Division (Riajsk and Apcheron Infantry, 10th and 38th Jagers—2,166 men) were led into the battle by Olsoviev personally. A further three battalions of the 15th Division, under General Kornilov (Kolyvan and Kourin—1,004 men) quickly followed them into the battle. A further reinforcement arrived from St.-Priest's Corps which also sent three battalions of the 30th and 48th Jagers (1,385 men) into the attack. A reserve was established with two battalions from the Vitebsk and Koslov Regiments (895 men) behind Schönefeld.

The attack was supported by the Polish Uhlan Regiment and the Iakhontov Opolochenie Cavalry Regiment, which overran and captured four cannon.[37]

The allied assault was successful. Ricard's 11th Division and the entire French line was obliged to fall back. Langeron then pressed forward against Reudnitz, which he nearly took, when Napoleon appeared in person and pushed Langeron back. It was 6:00 p.m.

Napoleon's Counterattack by Zwei-Naundorf

Around 3:00 p.m., Napoleon, standing by the Quandt Tobacco Mill, learned of the Saxon desertion. He soon left his position and rode in his usual quick trot across the fields to Reudnitz, where he met with Ney and Reynier. Before this, Napoleon had been very calm and relaxed as the battle progressed, but now he was visibly rattled.

He quickly ordered the organization of an attack column formed from Christiani's Old Guard Brigade, supported by the Grenadiers à Cheval and the Empress Dragoons from Nansouty's Guard

Cavalry Corps. In addition, he attached to them Daugeranville's Brigade[38] and 20 guns. This force was then dispatched towards Stünz and Mölkau.

In the meantime Bülow's 3rd Corps formed itself for battle. Paunsdorf was occupied by the 2/3rd East Prussian Infantry Regiment and the Austrian 6th Jäger Battalion. To the right, in the first line was the 1/, Fus/3rd East Prussian Infantry Regiment, a battalion of the 4th Reserve Regiment and the 2nd East Prussian Grenadier Battalion. Behind them, in the second line stood two battalions of the 3rd East Prussian Landwehr Regiment. Behind the advancing columns of Borstell's 5th and Krafft's 6th Brigades was Bubna's 2nd Light Division which stood between Bülow and Bennigsen's Corps. French forces were observed moving from Stötteritz, towards this portion of the French battle line, causing the allies to surmise that Napoleon would soon seek to break through at this point.

Bülow immediately ordered a shift to the left of the second line of Hessen-Homburg's 3rd Brigade to fill a gap that appeared between that brigade and Borstell's 5th Brigade. Krafft's 6th Brigade was to move into the gap formed by this movement.

At about 4:00 p.m. Bülow advanced his artillery against the withdrawing French forces. His artillery formed a single large battery of 76 guns.[39] Facing this were the 21 guns of the divisions of Delmas (9th) and Durutte (32nd), supported by 16 guns from Compans 20th Division. A massive, one sided artillery duel began, in which the allied guns inflicted considerable casualties on the French.[40]

At about 4:30 p.m. the French advanced once again in columns and pushed a large force between the villages of Mölkau and Engelsdorf. It was their intention to attack Bernadotte's left wing and then fall on the flank and rear of the allies. Their advance was aimed at the junction of Bubna's 2nd Light Division and that of Hessen-Homburg's 3rd Brigade.

The Imperial Guard cavalry, under Nansouty, advanced at the trot with 20 horse guns, which fired into Bülow's flanks, while a Guard infantry division was sent forward in a frontal assault. The allies directed nearly all of the artillery on their left against the advancing French.

The French cavalry roared forward. Neipperg's Austrian Brigade, the advanced guard of Bennigsen's army, almost rode into captivity, and found itself east of Zwei-Naundorf bearing the brunt of the main French assault. The 5th Jäger Battalion formed square at a run, delivered a volley, and waited its fate with bayonets at the ready.[41]

Count Bubna, seeing this movement, advanced his troops and charged the French frontally. The Prussian 3rd Brigade (Hessen-Homburg) joined Bubna's attack.[42] The Austrian horse artillery, four guns of Birnbaum's recently-defected 1st Saxon Horse Battery, the British Congreve rocket battery, and a battery from Docturov's Corps fired on the ranks of French cavalry. At the same time the Kaiser Hussars and a force of Russian cavalry under GM Tschaplitz struck the French in both flanks and threw them back.

Bülow's Attack on Stünz and Sellerhausen

General Bülow was then ordered to lead his corps against the villages of Stünz and Sellerhausen, cutting off the French advance from their base. He advanced his forces at the *geschwindschritt*.[43]

It was 5:30 p.m. as Hessen-Homburg sent forward the 1/3rd East Prussian Infantry Regiment and the 3/3rd East Prussian Landwehr Regiment moved against Stünz and the 2nd East Prussian Grenadiers and the 1/3rd East Prussian Infantry Regiment advanced against Sellerhausen. The assault on Stünz was supported on the left by the East Prussian Jäger Battalion and a horse battery reinforced by a Saxon howitzer. The assault on Sellerhausen was supported by the 2/, Fus/3rd East Prussian Regiment. In addition, Glasenapp's 6-pdr Foot Battery #5 and the jägers and schützen detachments of the 2/3rd East Prussian Landwehr Regiment supported this attack.[44]

Prussian cuirassiers under artillery fire at Leipzig, 18 October, by Knötel.

The battle over Sellerhausen bogged down, so four battalions from Krafft's 6th Brigade were sent forward to break the impasse. They were covered by their skirmishers and advanced on the west of the attack of the 1/3rd East Prussian Infantry and 2nd East Prussian Grenadiers. The 2/ Colberg advanced on the western side of the assault against Sellerhausen. To its left was the 1/9th Reserve Regiment, and the 3/, 4/1st Neumark Regiment.

The Prussians pushed into the villages and established strong lodgments and finally pushing the French out. As night was falling the battle died down quickly. The French fell back from the two villages, and the Prussians pulled most of their assault forces out of the villages. At 8:00 p.m. only the battalions of Müllenheim (2/3rd East Prussian Regiment) and Friccius (Fus/3rd East Prussian Regiment) remained in Stünz.[45]

The success of this attack had forced the assault by Nansouty's Guard cavalry and the Old Guard infantry, between the villages of Mölkau and Engelsdorf, to stop. With their line punctured at Sellerhausen and Stun the French had little choice but to withdraw.

It was questionable if everything would be ready for Bernadotte's attack before twilight, which in the second half of October arrived around 5:30 p.m. Any assault against Ney would have to succeed before dark. In addition, the question of munition and resupply had a great roll to play, as both sides had shot off most of their ammunition. Vainly the French sent for new ammunition, but those munitions were cut off in Eilenburg and resupply was an impossibility. The munition reserves of the Army of the North were, however, largely unconsumed and close at hand.

When Bernadotte was convinced that the infantry attack on the two flank strong points of the French had not succeeded, he ordered a new artillery bombardment. Winzingerode's approximately 80 guns advanced to the side of Langeron's batteries, which had completely shot off their ammunition. They were joined by 20 of Cardell's Swedish guns. No other troops from Stedingk's Swedish army corps took part in the battle of 18 October. The Swedish corps remained on the left bank of the Parthe as a reserve.[46]

Bülow's Corps deployed 76 guns before Sellerhausen and Stünz and began bombarding the French positions. Soon the entire line before the French consisted of artillery that proceeded to blast the French artillery into submission. Between 5:00 and 6:00 p.m., everything was ready to begin the assault and Bernadotte gave the order to GL Bülow to take Sellerhausen and Stünz. Both attacks were covered by skirmishers of all three divisions, supported by formed units. The Austrian 6th Jager Battalion and the 1/Peterwardeiner Grenz Regiment also joined in the attack, which was successful and drove the French back.

The arrival of night hindered a pursuit of the French, who pulled back down the fork in the road east of Volkmarsdorf. It was during this withdrawal that GD Delmas was fatally wounded.

That night the chain of advanced posts stood 100 paces apart. The Peterwardeiner Regiment remained in Sellerhausen during the night.

Heavy fighting that cost many casualties was required to take Schönefeld. To take it Langeron had sent forward the entire corps of Olsoviev and Rudsevich's advanced guard infantry, but they were only able to slowly drive the French back, and by 6:00 p.m., the French had been pushed back only as far as the windmill heights between Schönefeld and Reudnitz. Around 9:00 p.m., however, the French evacuated this area and moved behind the Rietzschkebach. Around 11:00 p.m., the French attempted another, unsuccessful assault against Schönefeld.

The Advance of the Fifth Column

On the morning of 18 October, Franquemont's 38th (Mixed) Division moved to Weissenfels, leaving the Halle suburb defended only by Dombrowski's tiny division. Dombrowski's 27th (Polish) Division now totaled between 1,000 and 1,500 infantry and eight guns. Behind him, in Leipzig, stood the Italian Milan Guard Battalion and Hochberg's Baden Brigade. To watch the Halle Gate there was only a single Baden company, as the two divisions of Young Guard under Mortier marched to the west towards Lindenau.[47]

Dombrowski's forces stood in the small village of Pfaffendorf, which was a short distance from the Halle suburb. At 9:00 a.m., as Blücher ordered Langeron across the Parthe, he also ordered Sacken to move against Pfaffendorf and the Halle Gate. The Prussian 1st Corps (Yorck) had been in position to act since 10:00 a.m. as a reserve in the second line on the heights between Eutritzsch and Gohlis. Horn's Division, formed the right wing and that of Hünerbein formed the left wing.[48] Later in the day, General Blücher placed the Saxon Hussar and Uhlan Regiments under the orders of Yorck, after they deserted to the allies.

At 10:00 a.m. Neverovsky's 27th Division (about 3,000 men), supported by its artillery, moved to the attack. Dombrowski knew that his tiny force could not hope to hold back over twice its numbers, and withdrew behind the Parthe River taking up positions to defend the bridge and the suburb's gate. He was supported by the Baden company that manned the gate.

Everything depended on the endurance of the weak 27th (Polish) Division. The loss of the Halle suburb meant disaster to Napoleon, because the Ranstädt Gate was the choke point through which Napoleon's entire army must pass as it withdrew from Leipzig.[49]

Gourgaud, one of Napoleon's aides-de-camp, recognized the danger, and reassured by Dombrowski that he would die before abandoning his position, hurried to advise Napoleon of the threat. Pacthod's 1st Young Division (12 battalions—6,000 men and three batteries) was sent from Thonberg at the double, to support Dombrowski. Pacthod moved his division forward and deployed his artillery in the Rosenthal Woods, on the west bank of the Pleisse.

The battle for the Halle Gate at Leipzig, 18 October, by Knötel.

At 11:00 a.m. the 1st Brigade, 8th Division, moved into Pfaffendorf and reinforced Dombrowski's Division, which was under attack on the right. The 2nd Brigade, with all the artillery of the 8th Division, took up a position on the plain to the right of the village to prevent the allies from turning the suburb and Pfaffendorf.

At noon, the allies appeared to withdraw, and the 2nd Brigade, 8th Division, left the artillery in the position it had occupied and moved down the main road between the village kitchen gardens and towards Schönefeld, where it took up a new position before the windmill, with its left on the tree lined road and its right in the village of Reudnitz.[50] Sacken's attack with Neverovsky's 27th Division was now supported by Lieven's 10th Division, which was posted to Neverovsky's left rear. Neverovsky sent forward five battalions, supported by Position Battery #13 and Light Battery #35, to attack the French. However, the flanking fire from Pacthod's artillery and infantry, standing behind the Pleisse in the Rosenthal Woods, was devastating and broke the attack. Rachmanov's four battalions of the Okhotsk and Kamchatka Infantry Regiments, already terribly under strength, were severely punished and forced to withdraw back to Gohlis.[51]

So successful was the breaking the Russian attack by Pacthod's Young Guard that they went over to the attack and threatened to take Gohlis. At 1:00 p.m., however, with Gohlis being threatened, Yorck sent forward four battalions. Two battalions, the Fus/Leib Regiment and a combined battalion formed from the fusilier battalions of the 1st and 2nd East Prussian Regiments, moved into Gohlis. Yorck then moved his forces forward, writing Blücher to advise him that Sacken's attack had failed and was falling back in disarray. He also advised Blücher that he was sending two infantry battalions and a cavalry regiment to Schkeuditz and that two battalions were sent into Gohlis.[51]

About that time, the first Young Guard battalion actually made an assault on Gohlis, but it was pushed back. By 3:00 p.m. Sacken's forces were once again pushing forward towards Pfaffendorf, where the French Young Guard batteries in the Rosenthal Woods once again showered them with shot and shell. The battle degenerated into a skirmish fight with one Jager battalion pushing across the Pleisse, in an attempt to strike the Guard artillery there. However, this effort was inconclusive and the battle for the Halle suburb ended with the coming of night.[52]

The Russian soldiers had fought with incredible tenacity and many Russian officers and men fell in this battle. Neverovsky (27th Division commander), Artillery General Huene, and brigade commander Colonel Rachmanov all fell as did many staff officers. All their sacrifices were in vain.

11

The French Retreat 19 October 1813

After Yorck's 1st Prussian Corps departed for Halle on 18 October, Blücher threw a few more bridges over the Parthe, in order to be able to cover the terrain between that river and the Pleisse. He recalled Langeron's Corps to the right bank of the Pleisse and united it, between the two rivers, with that of Sacken. He was then able to either follow Yorck's 1st Corps or cross over the Pleisse and the Elster.

During the night the French army had been ordered to withdraw without a noise from Connewitz, Probstheida, Stötteritz, Volkmarsdorf, and Reudnitz, towards Leipzig. Those in Lindenau were to move to Weissenfels. Weak rearguards occupied the villages in order to conceal the retreat, and support troops were placed in the outer suburbs by the windmills and near the walls of Leipzig. The garden and cemetery walls by the gate of the village of Grimma were pierced with loopholes as well as the gates themselves. Skirmishers were posted in the farm houses, in the brush, in the parks, and everywhere possible. Leipzig was to be occupied by the VII Corps (Reynier), the VIII Corps (Poniatowski), and the XI Corps (Macdonald). They were ordered to hold it for 24 hours or to the last extremity, in order to allow the rest of the army, its artillery, and its equipment sufficient time to effect its retreat.[1]

The allied cavalry advanced posts were ordered to attack without relief the French advanced posts during the night to determine whether or not the French were attempting to withdraw. However, they failed to discover that the French were, in fact, pulling out.

At the break of dawn all doubts about the French withdrawal vanished. The allies commenced their maneuvers as prescribed. The French detachments attempted to slow the allied advance, and had some success. The allies occupied all the villages and took several prisoners. Everywhere they found abandoned equipment and broken caissons.

Durutte had been charged with occupying the Halle suburb. He placed most of his forces behind the Halle Gate and behind the Parthe in order to slow the allied movement against Lindenau. Ricard's 11th Division was charged with holding the "*Hinter*" or Rear Gate and had the VI Corps to his right, defending the Blinden and outer Grimma Gates. The bulk of the III Corps was deployed in the wooded area between the Hinter Gate and the Halle Gate.[2]

The allied armies marched immediately towards Leipzig, and between 8:00 and 9:00 a.m., the last remaining French forces were thrown into the city. The fog, which had appeared at dawn, finally dispersed. After riding over the battlefield of the previous day, the Czar and King of Prussia arrived behind Probstheida.

They ordered an assault on Leipzig. As soon as all the batteries, mortars and howitzers could be prepared, a general bombardment of the city of Leipzig began. The Army of Bohemia marched against the Peters Gate. The Army of Poland marched against the Spital Gate, the Sand Gate, and the Windmill Gate. The Army of the North marched for the Hinter and the Grimma Gates. The Army of Silesia attacked the Halle Gate. Each of the four armies formed a single attack column and moved against the city.[3]

Platov's Cossacks passed across the Pleisse and the Russian reserve corps marched on Pegau. Blücher sent the cavalry of the Army of Silesia across the Elster at Schkeuditz in order to advance

Attack of the East Prussian Landwehr in the area of the Grimma Gate, Leipzig,
19 October, by Neumann.

against Lützen and attack the French rear. During this time, the Austrian 2nd Light Division crossed the Pleisse and the Elster to harass the French flank.

The sovereigns and Schwarzenberg stood by the houses which bordered the road. Shortly after this Saxon and French officers, including Maréchal Macdonald, arrived and presented themselves to begin negotiations for the surrender of the city. They proposed to surrender the city, if the troops in the city were allowed to depart freely, and they asked that, in any case, the city be spared. The sovereigns responded that the French were not to be allowed to escape, and that the city would be carried by assault. It would be unfortunate for the city's inhabitants, but no exception was to be made. This response was taken into the city by General Toll and his aide, Oberst Natzmer.[4]

Before abandoning the village of Probstheida, the French burned 50 caissons and spiked 12 cannon. Kleist's 2nd Prussian Corps followed the French, and formed itself by the tobacco mill, where the King of Prussia arrived at 8:00 a.m.

The other allied corps were equally advanced and the bombardment of the city was begun by the Russian artillery commander, General Nikitin. The corps of Colloredo, Wittgenstein, and Kleist were prepared for the assault.

The Army of Poland

At 7:00 a.m., the Army of Poland moved through Stötteritz against Leipzig and formed itself a cannon shot's distance from the city. General Klenau took up a position by the houses that lined the road and awaited the arrival of the reserve artillery, because the French artillery on the Galgenberg had begun to fire on his troops.

General Bennigsen brought forward four companies of heavy guns (48 guns) and they began firing. They quickly silenced the French artillery, destroying several caissons. The French artillery withdrew and their skirmishers occupied the gardens, the walls, and all houses in the area.

The allied artillery advanced and was followed by the Russian 12th and 13th Divisions, who marched in columns at an accelerated pace. The Russian 26th Division and a light artillery company advanced further to the left, towards the houses along the road. At 300 paces from the garden walls, the artillery company began to bombard the suburbs and the city walls, but caused no damage to the city's walls, which were made of brick.

About 10:00 a.m., Macdonald moved Stockhorn's Baden Brigade to the Peters Gate to support the hard pressed Poles. The 1st Baden Regiment was moved to garrison the Grimma Gate, supported by a force of Polish Uhlans.[5]

The troops of the Army of the North attacked to their right, and at the same time, General Bennigsen ordered the 13th and 26th Divisions to carry the Grimma suburb. A sapper company, under Colonel Afanassiev, was charged with destroying the garden walls, to facilitate the entry of the Russian 13th Division. The weak French forces were unable to prevent the Russians from penetrating into the city. The Ladoga Regiment captured seven guns, the Poltava captured 11, the Orel captured three, and the 5th Jagers captured eight. The Polish forces lost General Malachowski prisoner, with 15 officers and 300 men, plus 17 guns and 27 caissons. General Bennigsen sent a battalion into the city to serve as a guard for the King of Saxony. This battalion obliged the 2/ Saxon Guard Grenadier Regiment to surrender their arms, and provided interior and exterior security to the King of Saxony.[6]

The Army of the North

Bernadotte advanced his forces with the Prussian 3rd Brigade (Hessen-Homburg) leading the advance, supported by the 5th Brigade (Borstell) and several Swedish battalions. The village of Reudnitz was carried and the Army of the North advanced to the left down the road from Wurzen. The 3/3rd East Prussian Landwehr Regiment led the advance, followed by the 2/, Fus/3rd East Prussian Regiment. They quickly encountered French skirmishers behind every garden wall and house. The Prussians lost heavily, but pressed forward and finally reached the palisaded Hinter Gate and the gardens. During this battle, which was indecisive for a long time, Prince Ludwig von Hessen-Homburg was wounded and replaced by General Borstell.

General Borstell advanced his brigade and Bernadotte advanced six Russian battalions and a Swedish battalion to support them. Soon French resistance collapsed and the Prussians penetrated into the city.

At the same time General Voronzov directed his advanced guard of five Jager battalions, led by the 14th Jagers, under Colonel Krassovsky, towards the Spital Gate supported by several cannon.

After the capture of the Hinter Gate and the Spital Gate the other gates were menaced from the rear. The French and Poles, who still possessed a large number of guns, began a heavy bombardment against all of the points being attacked. But gradually every one of the French batteries were overrun and captured.[7]

The Army of Silesia

Blücher directed Sacken to attack the Halle Gate of Leipzig and placed a 12-pdr battery to fire on the city and the village of Reudnitz. This battery strongly supported Bülow's attack and forced the French back into the suburbs. At the same time, Langeron's Corps arrived on the right bank of the Parthe, before Leipzig, and began to attempt to cross it in order to take the Halle Gate in the rear. Sacken captured the houses and entrenchments by the gate.

Marmont had occupied a large house outside the wall with a detachment of the 70th Line Regiment and placed it under the command of Major Roguet. Supporting it, a carabinier company of the 25th Légère counterattacked out of its barricades and inflicted heavy losses on the advancing allies. However, Ricard's 11th Division, by the Hinter Gate, was under heavy pressure and the VI Corps was sent back to help extricate him.[8]

At one point the allies drove into the city between the VI and XI Corps. Marmont led forward the 142nd Line and 23rd Légère in a counterattack that cleared the allies out of the streets.[9]

Around noon, the French defensive fire on the bridge over the Parthe slowed up and the allied infantry captured the gate and three guns. They pursued Durutte's French (32nd Division) and overran their artillery park, baggage train, and munition dump. The French defense was feeble and they withdrew towards the Ranstädt Gate.[10]

About 10:00 a.m., Napoleon departed the city after visiting the King of Saxony. He wished to move through the Ranstädt Gate, but that was impossible because of the heavy congestion of troops and equipment, so he detoured through the Peters Gate, moving around the west side of the city, and across the bridge.

There are numerous stories about the destruction of the bridge over the Elster. If indeed Colonel Montfort did abandon his post to a corporal, who then panicked and prematurely destroyed the bridge, it is immaterial. What is relevant is that the bridge was destroyed while it was packed with hundreds of men. It was also destroyed with a large part of the French army still inside Leipzig. Macdonald and his corps arrived three minutes too late to move across the bridge.[11]

The departure of Napoleon from the battlefield, 18 October, by Knötel.

When the bridge was destroyed, the remaining French sought another route out of the city. A second bridge had been raised in the Richter Garden, but it broke under the weight of the traffic. Many attempted to swim the Elster; Macdonald made it across, but Poniatowski drowned in his effort to escape. The remainder, trapped in the city, milled about. Some fought, others threw away their arms and attempted to escape in any way the could. Others simply waited for the allies to take them into custody.

Marmont's forces had crossed the main bridge. He moved Durutte's 32nd Division, VII Corps, into the plains to the west of Leipzig to hold off the Austrians, while the remainder of his forces marched west. The rearguard was organized with the 1st and 3rd Young Guard Divisions under Oudinot.

Napoleon began leading those forces that found themselves on the western bank of the Elster back to France. They were, for the most part, his guard, part of the cavalry, which had passed through Lindenau during the afternoon of 18 October and the evening of 18/19 October, Bertrand's IV Corps, Marmont's VI Corps, Victor's II Corps, and the remnants of several others.[12]

Victory and its Price

The losses of both sides in the battle were immense. The French losses were estimated at 15,000 killed and 30,000 wounded, including 23,000 sick and wounded abandoned during the withdrawal. About 15,000 prisoners, 300 guns, 900 caissons, and hundreds of other pieces of military equipment were captured. Among the dead or mortally were Maréchal Poniatowski and Generals Rochambeau, Delmas, Vial, Aubry, and Friederichs. Among the wounded were Ney and Marmont and Generals Souham, Compans, Latour-Maubourg, Sébastiani, Maison, Pajol, and 57 others.[13] Among the prisoners were Prince Emil von Hessen-Darmstadt, and Generals Lauriston, Reynier, Schaefer, and others.

The marketplace at Leipzig, after a drawing by Täubert.

The death of Prince Poniatowski, 19 October.

The capture of General Lauriston at Leipzig, 19 October.

The allied losses were not light either. The Austrian army lost one general, 57 officers, and 2,000 men killed, Erbprinz Hessen-Homburg, and Generals Hardegg, Nostitz, Mohr, and Splenyi, 3,303 officers and 5,000 men wounded, one general, 39 officers, and 1,000 men captured.

The Russians under Barclay de Tolly lost Generals Schevich, Neverovsky, Manteufel, and Prince Kudaschov killed, and Generals Raevsky, Duka, Kryschanovski, Karatiev, Levaschoff, and Pissarev wounded. They also lost 110 officers and 2,960 men killed, 670 officers and 13,017 men wounded, and 15 officers and 2,763 men prisoners of war.

The Army of Poland lost General Lindfors killed, and 123 officers and 3,000 men killed and wounded.

The Prussian army lost Prince Ludwig von Hessen-Homburg and Prince Karl von Mecklenburg wounded. Yorck's Corps lost 176 officers and 5,568 men killed and wounded. Kleist lost 244 officers and 7,882 men killed and wounded. Bülow was estimated to have lost 100 officers and 1,500 men killed and wounded. The Swedes lost about 100 officers and 300 men killed and wounded. The total allied losses were 21 generals, 1,793 officers, and 44,990 men killed, wounded, or captured.[14]

Though neither side fought a perfect battle, Napoleon obviously fought less effectively than the allies. He had the advantages of interior lines of communication and should have been able to act as he chose, concentrated and ready for battle against any of the individual converging elements of the allied army. However, instead of maneuvering free from fixed positions, Napoleon felt compelled to tie himself to the defense of Leipzig. Using hindsight, Napoleon would have been more successful if he had played Leipzig as he had played the Dresden campaign in late August.

The Allied commanders at Leipzig, 18 October, by Neumann.

In August Napoleon had left a garrison in Dresden and acted with his field armies against three converging allied armies. When two of the allied armies were withdrawing from Dresden, he turned with the best portion of his armies against the Army of Bohemia and achieved both the tactical interior position and numerical superiority of forces on the battlefield. The result was a significant victory.

At Leipzig, Napoleon did not maneuver, but surrendered the initiative to the allies. He remained immobile and not only permitted the allies to concentrate all their forces against him, achieving numerical superiority, but he also permitted them to surround him and sit astride his lines of communication with France.

It is true that his concentration was late. If all his forces had been on the field a day earlier the results of the battle could have been different. However, even so Napoleon was in a position to select any of the four converging armies as his target and move to engage it.

French General Officers Killed or Wounded at Leipzig

GD Compans, wounded 10/16 and 10/18	GD Aubry, wounded 10/18, captured, dead 11/10
GB Montéléger, wounded 10/18	GB Grabowski, wounded 10/18, captured
GD Lefol, wounded 10/16	GD Delmas, wounded 10/18, captured, dead 10/20
GB Pelleport, wounded 10/18	GD Rochambeau, wounded 10/19, captured, dead 10/20
GD Latour-Maubourg, wounded 10/16, amputated	GD Friederichs, wounded 10/18, captured, dead 10/20
GB Pouchelon, wounded 10/18	GD Brayer, wounded 10/19
GD Maison, wounded 10/16	GD Belliard, wounded 10/18
GB Sopransi, wounded 10/18	GB Boyer, wounded 10/19, captured, dead 10/30 .
GD Pajol, wounded 10./16	GD Gérard, wounded 10/18
GB Aymar, wounded 10/18	GB Pelletier de Montmarie, wounded 10/19, captured, dead 11/1
GB Bachelet 'd'Amville, killed, 10/16	GD Charbonnel, wounded 10/18
GB Baillo, wounded 10/18	GB Kwasniewski, wounded 10/19, dead 12/8
GB Camus, killed, 10/16	GD Souham, wounded 10/18
GB Tolinski, wounded 10/18	GB Pellegrin, wounded 10/19
GB Ferrière, killed, 10/16	GD Sébastiani, wounded 10/18
GB Mongenet, wounded 10/18	GB Valory, wounded 10/19, captured
GB Ménard, wounded 10/16	GD Ledru des Essarts, wounded 10/18
GB de Coëtlosquet, wounded 10/18	GB Bertrand, wounded 10/19
GB Meunier, wounded 10/16	GD Rozniecki, wounded 10/18
GB Bessières, wounded 10/18	GB Lafitte, wounded 10/19, captured
GB St-André, wounded 10/16	GD Kamieniecki, wounded 10/18
GB d'Avrange d'Augeranville, wounded 10/18, captured	GB Maneville, wounded 10/19, captured
GB Filrol de Caman, wounded 10/16	GB Coëhorn, wounded 10/18, dead 10/29
GB Bony, wounded 10/18, captured	GB Brun, wounded 10/19, captured
GB Choisy, wounded 10/16 and 10/18	GB d'Estko, wounded 10/18, dead 10/30
GB Bronikowski, wounded 10/18, captured	GB Uminski, wounded 10/19, captured
GB Laferrière-Levesque, wounded 10/16	GB Maury, killed, 10/18
GB Siérawski, wounded 10/18, captured	GB Malachowski, wounded 10/19, captured
GB Gros, wounded 10/17	GB Maran, wounded 10/18
GB Gruyer, wounded 10/18	GB Rautenstrauch, wounded 10/19, captured
GD Vial, killed 10/18	
GB Zoltowski, wounded 10/18	

One can argue that the allied victory at Leipzig would have been avoided if either the Army of the North or the Army of Silesia had been pushed away from Leipzig by either a battle or the advance of Napoleon against them. But merely pushing them back would not have provide Napoleon with the opportunity for the decisive victory that had evaded him so far in 1813.

Military parade of the Allied armies in the marketplace at Leipzig, 19 October.

The Allied monarchs and leading generals arrive in the marketplace at Leipzig
on 19 October, by Knötel.

An attack against the Allied Polish Reserve Army would not have been an acceptable alternative. The destruction of the Polish Reserve Army would have been simple as it was largely formed of second line troops and it would have broken the siege of Dresden, but neither success would have been a decisive blow against the allies. On the other hand, it would have put a concentrated allied army in his rear and on his lines of communication. This would have had two results. The first would be the probable collapse of the readiness of his German allies to remain with him. The second would have been a concentrated target against which he could then act. The latter had some possibilities, but there were significant risks and the desirability of this situation is, at best, uncertain.

The preferable target would have been the Army of Bohemia. The advantages of a victory over this army would have been as follows: having defeated it, he would have been able to push it back against the mountain passes and the congestion would have permitted the devastating victory that his lack of cavalry would have denied him in the open plains. By crushing the largest single army, he could have then turned on his remaining antagonists and dealt with them individually with relative success.

A second advantage was that a decisive victory over the Army of Bohemia would have probably pushed Austria out of the war, as the Army of Bohemia contained nearly all the Austrian troops participating in the war. In every campaign since 1792, the destruction of the main Austrian army in a major battle had resulted it the collapse of. Austria's will to continue the fight. With Austria out of the battle, Russia and Prussia could have handled far more easily and might even have been persuaded to a negotiated peace before their armies were cornered. Such a victory would have definitely caused Bernadotte to panic and fear for his throne. There is no doubt that Sweden would have extricated itself as expeditiously as possible from the situation.

The third advantage to striking and defeating the Army of Bohemia was that the King of Prussia and the Czar of Russia were with the Army of Bohemia and the capture or death of both or either would have been politically sensational.

Napoleon did attempt this third option, but he did not permit himself sufficient space and time to execute this maneuver. He should have advanced out of Leipzig and engaged the Army of Bohemia as far south of the city as possible. During the first day, he came within a breath of breaking the Austrian center and of the victory he sought. The presence of Marmont's VI Corps during the engagements of 16 October would have given Napoleon the depth and reserves he needed to finish the Army of Bohemia.

Napoleon was too fixed on the defense of a geographical feature and had lost sight of the maxim that it is the destruction of the enemy's army that brings victory, not the holding of terrain.

12

The Fox and Hounds 20 October–
29 October 1813

As Napoleon and his entourage moved westwards, he passed through Lindenau in a stream of shattered soldiery. While in Lindenau he heard that Bertrand's IV Corps had occupied Weissenfels. Oudinot's I Young Guard Corps stood in Lindenau as a rearguard.

The next morning, 20 October, Napoleon once again moved west, to Weissenfels with his Old Guard as an escort. Bertrand moved the remains of the IV Corps to Freiburg, because Gyulai had seized Kösen and forced the detour. Blücher moved the Army of Silesia to Lützen. Yorck moved to threaten the French flank and Schwarzenberg stood near Naumburg and Zeitz.[1]

Napoleon was particularly concerned because of the allied occupation of Kösen. On 20 October he wrote to Bertrand, ordering him to raise three bridges and to send reconnaissance forces in the directions of Merseburg and Naumburg, along the right bank of the Saale. Bertrand was to seize Naumburg and Merseburg if possible. He directed that the passage over the Saale be assured, by occupying strong houses between Lützen and Weissenfels and by placing a rearguard in earthworks with artillery in the defile by Weissenfels, where Bessières had been killed in the spring.[2]

Napoleon's proposed line of march westwards was through Merseburg, Lützen, Weissenfels, Naumburg, Auerstädt, Erfurt, Gotha, Eisenach, Fulda, Frankfurt, and Mainz.

Napoleon at Lindenau, 19 October.

Skirmish at Kösen

On 21 October Napoleon sent General Bertrand, with a strong force, to the left bank of the Saale to attack and destroy the bridge by Kösen, in an effort to cover the French withdrawal from attack by the allies via that avenue. On the left bank, where Neu-Kösen lay, the road crossed a nearly unclimbable ridge, an important tactical position to seize so as to stop the allies, who were advancing through Naumburg in their pursuit of the French.

The main portion of the Austrian 3rd Armeeabteilung, under FZM Gyulai, had, at daybreak of 21 October, moved into Alt-Kösen, on the right bank of the Saale. An allied aide-de-camp arrived with news that a strong French column was moving against Kösen. Further reports from the advanced posts on that side of the Saale stated that the French were advancing in overwhelming strength. Gyulai ordered M. Liechtenstein's 1st Light Division and Salin's Brigade to advance at a "gallop" towards Kösen, in order to establish their defense. Once there, they found that the French had taken advantage of the fog to seize the critical heights, chased off the Austrian advanced posts and occupied a few of the houses in Neu-Kösen. However, most importantly, the bridge remained in the hands of a company of Warasdiner Kreuzer Grenz, which was supported by Mensdorf's nearby streifkorps.

Immediately after receiving word of the French advance, four companies of the Erzherzog Ludwig Infantry Regiment, Oberst Beyder's Jäger Battalion #7, and the Broder Grenz Battalion were sent from the village of Schulps and Saale-Altenburg to reinforce the position. Part of the Jägers quickly drove the lead elements of the advancing French forces back across the Saale. FZM Gyulai arrived on the field about the same time and immediately dispatched Oberst Beyder and the rest of Jäger Battalion #7, plus the Broder Battalion, across the Saale to support them.[3]

In the meantime, the French brought ever more forces onto the field. They occupied the largest portion of Neu-Kösen and struck at the bridge. It was at that moment when GM Graf Salin's Brigade arrived. A battalion of the Erzherzog Ludwig Infantry Regiment counterattacked and drove the French back to the heights. A second battalion of the regiment moved against the French in Neu-Kösen. The Austrians were unable to deploy their forces and the terrain was to the French advantage. The left bank of the Saale controlled the right bank; the bridge, Neu-Kösen, and Alt-Kösen were dominated and surrounded by a the semi-circular heights.

The French deployed along the heights, in order to destroy the bridge, to delay the allied advance and assure the withdrawal of the main French armies. The French had advantageously posted their heavy guns to sweep the narrow entrances of Kösen and formed their infantry on the crest of the heights.

The reserve of Graf Salin's Brigade was sent forward and it worked to establish itself more strongly in Kösen. Gyulai placed the rest of his infantry at the foot of the heights on the right bank, on both sides of the road, out of the field of fire of the French artillery. Grimmer's Brigade moved into the defile to serve as a reserve. The corps cavalry was, because of the nature of the ground, not usable and was left to the rear. M. Liechtenstein's 1st Light Division stood in front of Flemmingen, facing the French occupied ridge.

In the meantime, the battle on the left bank continued with great bitterness. The Austrian skirmishers occupied more terrain as the French withdrew more forces. More Austrian detachments from the right wing pushed their way onto the heights. On this side alone, did the French suffer from heavy Austrian artillery fire. However, they soon brought forward their own artillery to respond in kind, as well as prevent any effort by the Austrians to turn that flank.

On the left wing, the Austrians occupied a deep ditch, into which the French on the heights fired. Suddenly, the French redoubled their artillery fire and large infantry columns, in overwhelming numbers, moved forward towards Neu-Kösen. The French assault was successful and the bridge was quickly seized. Gyulai placed himself at the head of a battalion of the Würzburg

The withdrawal of the French army from Leipzig, by Knötel.

Infantry Regiment and led it forward at the *sturmschritt*. Despite suffering heavy losses, the bridge was recaptured before it could be destroyed. The French withdrew their forces back behind their guns, into their original positions, abandoning the defile to Gyulai's victorious troops.[4]

Night fell, bringing the battle to an end. After a few hours, the French abandoned the Neu-Kösen heights, with the Austrian cavalry following them in a cautious pursuit. Allied sources indicate that the French lost about 1,000 men in their attack. In contrast, Gyulai's forces lost 800 dead and wounded in Salin's Brigade alone.

As the French withdrew, they were followed by Platov's Cossacks and Thielmann's Streifkorps. The allies organized a new advanced guard with four battalions, four guns, and the Prussian Guard Light Cavalry Regiment, under the command of General Bistrom. This force moved through Kösen to the far side of the defile. The Russian and Prussian Guard, as well as the headquarters of General Barclay de Tolly, were in Naumburg with Wittgenstein's Corps. The Russian 4th Division, General Pschinski and the Lubny Hussars were in Weissenfels. Kleist's 2nd Prussian Corps arrived on the Elster by Prödel and passed over it, on 21 October moving towards Pega4.[5]

The important outcome of the battle was that the French had not been able to seize the defiles at Kösen, and had failed to destroy the bridge, but they were able to stop a tentative attack by Gyulai's forces. Bertrand received a rebuke from Napoleon for opening up the French army's flank to a possible attack by the allies, if they had been more aggressive.

Forces converged on Freiburg and its bridge above the Unstrut. On the heights over Freiburg stood an old castle. Two bad roads passed through the tiny village, which were surrounded by walled gardens and houses. The road was so narrow as to preclude any possibility of marching a platoon or section in line through the village. It was through this funnel that the Grande Armée sought to move, along with is baggage and train. As the French arrived, they discovered that four days prior the Austrians had burnt the bridge, and a tremendous traffic jam resulted. However, it was learned that only a 15 minute march away stood a second bridge, below a mill. Napoleon arrived, driving the milling mass forward, issuing orders, forcing movement and enforcing discipline in the hapless mass that was beginning to disintegrate, as it had a year earlier on the Berezina.[6] The spurs were applied to the French anxieties, as they listened to the sound of cannon fire coming from Kösen, but the strength of Napoleon's will restored order to the disintegrating army.

Efforts immediately began to repair the bridge, and soon a structure was in place that would permit cavalry to pass. The troops began to pass over the river. Between 2:00 and 3:00 p.m., the sound of cannon fire was heard from the direction of Hassenhausen, where Bertrand was again in battle. At that time, Napoleon and his general staff passed over to the right bank of the Unstrut. There was no more time to lose. Napoleon turned right and moved down a small road towards the castle and behind the mill by the second bridge. From the hills unoccupied by the French, there suddenly erupted a volley of allied musketry. A few minutes later the French light infantry moved forward against the allied position. At the same time, a cannon shot and a pair of howitzer shells landed near the Emperor without causing him harm. The attack was successful, but very costly.[7]

With both bridges firmly in French control, the French army once again began to move towards the west. However, Yorck still had a chance to catch the French army in its confused crossing of the Unstrut.

Their flank covered, the Grande Armée marched across the Unstrut at Freiburg. It was not clear of danger yet, as Blücher had built a bridge at Weissenfels and was pushing westwards as fast as he could. Schwarzenberg, however, did not advance so aggressively and moved only slowly towards Kösen.

The second column of the Army of Bohemia contained the 1st and 2nd Armeeabteilung, and the infantry reserve. It moved towards Eisenberg. The 4th Armeeabteilung under Klenau bivouacked in Grossen. Schwarzenberg's headquarters were in Eisenberg. The Camburg pass was occupied by GL Raevsky's 2nd Grenadier Division and a brigade of the Russian 3rd Cuirassier Division.

The withdrawal of the French through Erfurt, 24/25 October.

During the morning of 21 October, General Illowaiski XII and three Cossack regiments moved into Weimar. That evening Bertrand's leading elements approached Weimar, only to be attacked by Illowaiski's forces and those of Oberstleutnant Krapowski. However, Bertrand's forces were not to be stopped by the Cossacks.

The Army of Poland marched into Weissenfels with General Kreutz commanding its advanced guard. The French rearguard had crossed the Saale that morning and destroyed the bridge behind it. They abandoned a hospital with 1,500 sick and wounded, as well as a considerable quantity of baggage. Kreutz passed over the Saale and set up his bivouacs in Bussendorf and Reichardtswerben. The advanced troops of General Stroganov marched to Merseburg, Tschaplitz's cavalry moved to Göhren, Docturov's infantry moved into Mühlig, and Bennigsen set up his headquarters in Lützen.[8]

Napoleon realized that the allied pursuit was aggressive enough to prevent him reorganizing his army and turning on them, until he had once again crossed into France. The march westwards had to continue. On 22 October the French army arrived in Buttelstedt, where it encountered a small force of Cossacks. On 23 October Napoleon and the Old Guard arrived in Erfurt.

The allies lacked the aggressiveness that the French had shown after their defeat of the Prussians in 1806, and paused at this time. The allied leaders, savoring their victory, stayed in Leipzig until 22 October, planning their future moves. Klenau was to be ordered to advance against Dresden, Bernadotte and Bennigsen were to move against Hamburg. Rather than concentrating their forces against the shattered French army, they were dispersing their forces and chasing secondary objectives.[9]

The Allied Army

Yorck's Prussian 1st Corps of the Army of Silesia had moved into Halle on 18 October, following the withdrawing French, and occupied the bridge over the Saale. In Halle, Yorck learned that Napoleon's army had moved towards Weissenfels. Yorck hoped to intercept the French at Freiburg, as they attempted to cross the river there.

On 20 October the 1st Prussian Corps moved towards Mücheln. There was a possibility that a French force might be moving through Querfurt, in order to reach Magdeburg, so a force of allied cavalry was sent in that direction, to reconnoiter the region. Yorck marched with the cavalry reserve through Lauchsädt and Frankenleben towards Reichardtswerben. Horn's 7th Brigade marched to Frankleben and Hünerbein's 8th Brigade moved through Merseburg to Lauchsädt.

About 10:00 a.m., Yorck and the Reserve Cavalry arrived in Grosskayna. Here they discovered a French column, which was moving from Luftschif and Mark-Röslitz towards Freiburg. It was part of the French rearguard. When word came of the presence of this column, a detachment of the Prussian reserve cavalry was quickly moved forward towards Reichardtswerben.

The French column stopped, occupied Reichardtswerben with infantry, and took a position on the heights, sending its skirmishers and Polish cavalry forward. The Prussian horse artillery opened fire and the French answered with their own. The cannonade lasted until night with little results. Oberst Jürgass' reserve cavalry remained by Reichardtswerben, facing the French.

It was not known if the French were heading towards Laucha or Freiburg, so on 21 October General Yorck dispatched forces towards both points. He built a new advanced detachment, placing it under the command of Oberst and Flügeladjutant Graf Henkel von Donnersmark. The infantry force of this advanced guard consisted of seven and two-thirds battalions of infantry under Major Burghof—the Silesian Grenadier Battalion and a combined Fusilier Battalion of the 8th Brigade, the Thuringian Battalion, the 1/Leib Infantry Regiment, two landwehr battalions, three companies of East Prussian Jägers, and two Austrian Jäger battalions. The cavalry portion consisted of sixteen squadrons from the 1st and 2nd Leib Hussars, the Brandenburg Hussars, and the Saxon Prinz Clements Uhlan Regiment. In addition, it had a foot and a horse battery.

At 7:00 a.m., the Prussian brigades of Horn (7th) and Hünerbein (8th) and the advanced guard of Graf Henkel stood by Petschkendorf. Oberst Jürgass was ordered to leave only the pickets and a single cavalry regiment by Reichardtswerben to watch the French column, while the rest moved towards Freiburg.

In Petschkendorf, Henkel's detachment separated from the main body and moved through Baumesroda towards Laucha. In Baumesroda they encountered a French prisoner transport column with 4,000 allied prisoners and a not much larger infantry guard. The 2nd Leib Hussar Regiment and the Saxon Prinz Clemens Uhlans stopped the column by Gleina, and attacked the covering force, releasing part of the prisoners. When they arrived in Laucha, they found that a French cavalry detachment had burned the bridge and stood behind the city. Graf Henkel moved to the left bank of the Unstrut River, to rejoin the main body of his parent column.[10]

In the meantime General Yorck moved to Zeuchfeld and received news about the direction of the French withdrawal. He left four squadrons by Zeuchfeld, to observe the French troops locked inside the village, and ordered the advance through Schleberoda and Müncheroda where he joined with Graf Henkel's advanced guard detachment.

Yorck soon found himself facing the French rearguard, under Oudinot, outside of Freiburg. Yorck ordered an attack, issuing the following orders: "The advanced guard shall form the right wing and advance against Zscheiplitz and against the French before the village. Horn's 7th Brigade shall form the left wing and clean the left of Zscheiplitz and the adjacent woods of French skirmishers. Hünerbein's 8th Brigade shall remain behind Horn's Brigade and serve as a reserve."

The French had occupied Zscheiplitz in order to cover their passage over the Unstrut. They fought hard and defeated the assaults of the Prussian skirmishers. Behind the Prussian skirmishers, however, General Horn cleared the brush and vineyards of French skirmishers. The heights were surmounted with numerous French guns and they soon began a heavy cannonade. In contrast to their normal practice of attacking under heavy artillery barrages, the French rapidly withdrew to Freiburg. The Prussian guns fired as fast as they could, in order to inflict as much damage as they could, before the French withdrew out of range.

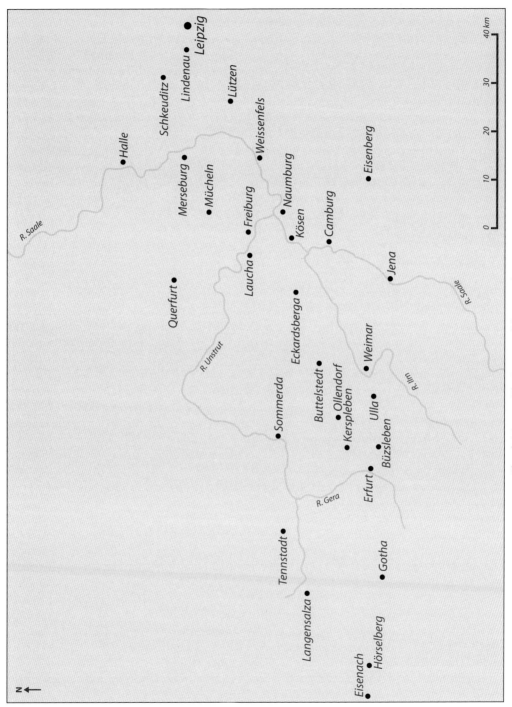

Sketch Map 10 The Retreat of the Grande Armée.

The reserve cavalry, under Oberst Jürgass, followed the withdrawing French since day break and pushed as far as Mark-Röslitz. Behind this village, the French occupied another village, from which they could control the Naumburg and Freiburg roads. They were attacked by the Saxon Hussar Regiment, which led the reserve cavalry, capturing 170 prisoners and clearing the wood. The 1st West Prussian Dragoon Regiment undertook an attack and threw the French off an adjacent height.[11] Oberst Jürgass then sent forward his artillery. The French rearguard held fast, and Oberst Jürgass led forward his entire cavalry force. The French infantry threw itself into the woods and took shelter there. The supporting French cavalry, however, was thrown back. The French cavalry then withdrew behind the French infantry. Nightfall brought an end to the battle before it developed further. The Prussian reserve cavalry withdrew back to Gleina. Henkel's advanced guard remained in Zscheiplitz and Freiburg facing the French.

Yorck's Prussian 1st Corps, including Jürgass' reserve cavalry, lost 17 officers and 823 men. Further losses were suffered by Henkel's advanced guard. The French casualties were not known, but Jürgass and the Mecklenburg Hussar Regiment captured about 1,000 French stragglers. A further 18 cannon and many caissons were captured. In order to prevent their capture, the French destroyed several caissons of powder.[12]

The Russian Pursuit

On 19 October the two Russian Corps of the Army of Silesia, those of Langeron and Sacken, were sent by Blücher to Schkeuditz, where they bivouacked that evening. Langeron and Sacken had passed over the Elster and pursued the withdrawing French during the next two days. The days of 18 and 19 October had been spent allowing the troops to recover from the battles around Leipzig. On 20 October their pursuit was not very fast. This permitted Napoleon to pass through Weissenfels and destroy the bridge. The French rearguard was also very well led and fought fiercely to defend its charges. The cavalry of Sacken's Corps, led by Vassil'shikov, joined with that of General Kreutz of the Polish Reserve Army. Near Lützen they engaged a force of French cavalry under Murat in a nasty rearguard action, while the Grande Armée passed over the Saale by Weissenfels. General Vassil'shikov captured 2,000 prisoners and pursued the withdrawing French through Lützen. Blücher moved his headquarters to Lützen after the French were cleared out and brought forward the corps of Langeron and Sacken.

On 21 October, the Army of Silesia moved out of Lützen towards Weissenfels. During this march the brigade of Prinz Wilhelm von Preussen joined the march.[13]

Towards noon, the Army of Silesia arrived in Weissenfels. The French rearguard abandoned the city as they arrived. Blücher directed a battery of 12-pdr guns to the heights that overlooked the withdrawing French and it began to bombard them. The bridge over the Saale was in flames and the French rearguard prevented Blücher's troops from extinguishing the fire. The bridge gone, Blücher found himself obliged to move to another intact bridge, moving through Naumburg towards Kösen, or to build his own bridge. Blücher drew together the carpenters of the city and his army, and had construction of a pontoon bridge begun immediately. One of the carpenters, it would turn out, had built for Frederick the Great a pontoon bridge by Weissenfels for the battle of Rossbach. The bridge was quickly completed and by that evening the entire army had passed over the Saale. The advanced guard moved quickly towards Freiburg.

During the following day the Army of Silesia drew together around Freiburg and Yorck was sent further orders. However, since the bridge over the Unstrut was destroyed, the army was obliged to remain on the eastern bank of the Unstrut all of 22 October.

The allied armies renewed their pursuit, passing through the Thuringian Forest, their light cavalry scouting the way. The main army did not reach Erfurt until 26 October. Blücher had arrived in Freiburg on 22 October, but the damage to the Unstrut bridge had forced him to divert through Sömmerda, Langensalza, and Eisenach, to turn the French flank at Erfurt, where he supposed Napoleon would stand. However, knowing the Bavarians had betrayed him, and were marching on Ansbach in an effort to reach Mainz first, Napoleon pressed his march westward through Gotha towards Eisenach.

The French Withdrawal

During the two days march on 20 and 21 October, the French had placed the Saale river between themselves and the pursuing allies. The bridges along the main line of retreat were destroyed. Bertrand's forces had fought one battle around the bridge and defile at Kösen, in an effort to further delay the allied pursuit. During the day of 21 October Napoleon repeated his orders to move on Freiburg. That evening he established his headquarters in the Heszler Cloister. All night his forces filed past him in their movement west, Napoleon renewing his own movement at 9:00 a.m., the following morning. The French rearguard and baggage passed over the Unstrut. The road behind them was littered with abandoned and broken down equipment.

There were two roads open to the French in their movement towards Erfurt. One road ran through Buttelstedt and the second ran through Weimar. Weimar had, however, been occupied by allied cavalry, mostly Cossacks, during the night, so Napoleon moved through Buttelstedt. En route, near Ollendorf, a force of Cossacks appeared and threatened Napoleon's person, but they were driven off.[14]

On 22 October the French rearguard moved out of Freiburg towards Eckardsberga and took up positions there. There was, however, no further rearguard action, as FZM Gyulai had advanced only as far as Popplitz, where he sent the Russian 3rd Cuirassier Division.

GD Lefèbvre-Desnoëttes maneuvered his cavalry on the left flank of the French army. He moved towards Weimar, and the Russian light cavalry, mostly Cossacks, was cleared from the town. Platov did not surrender Weimar easily, and it required effort and casualties on the part of the French before they finally recovered possession of Weimar.

Gyulai's column of the Army of Bohemia, moved from Popping towards Eckardsberga, while the Prussian and Russian guard moved towards Hassenhausen, where Barclay de Tolly established his headquarters. Kleist also moved towards Eckardsberga, but only reached Naumburg.

The second column marched parallel to the first, moving on Jena with the 1st and 2nd Austrian Armeeabteilung, Bianchi's Infantry Reserve, and Schwarzenberg's headquarters. The Austrian 2nd Light Division of General Bubna marched towards Weimar and the Austrian 4th Armeeabteilung under Klenau received orders to break its bivouac before Dresden and move forward.

The Army of Poland followed the Army of Silesia across the Unstrut, where the bridge was rebuilt. General Kreutz marched towards Freiburg, while the advanced troops of Stroganov and Tschaplitz's Cavalry Division moved towards Mücheln. Docturov's infantry marched through Weissenfels. Bennigsen, the army commander, arrived in Weissenfels on 22 October, and ordered the erection of two permanent bridges.

On 23 October, Czar Alexander grew unhappy with the slow pace of FZM Gyulai's advance and organized an advanced guard from Wittgenstein's forces, and placed it under the command of Count Pahlen III. It consisted of the Russian light cavalry, the Russian 3rd Cuirassier Division, Röder's Prussian cavalry reserve, and one Russian and two Prussian horse batteries. It was ordered to pass Gyulai's Corps on the Eckardsberga-Buttelstedt Road and pursue the French down the road to Erfurt. General Osaroffski was to move with his column through Auerstädt towards Buttelstedt, maintaining himself on the allied left flank.

The French rearguard departed Eckardsberga during the night and moved through Buttstedt. In their march, the Russians overran a large number of stragglers, abandoned wagons, destroyed caissons, and dead horses. Buttelstedt was occupied by French infantry, who camped on the far side of the city in large numbers. Count Pahlen sent a detachment of Osaroffski's forces through Weiden and Daasdorf, sent three Cossack regiments from Kreutz's forces to the right flank and moved to strike the French. The Tchougouiev Uhlan Regiment advanced with four horse guns. Their advance proved enough to cause the French garrison to withdraw. As the remainder of the allied cavalry moved through the gorge, the French cavalry attacked the Tchougouiev Uhlans, driving them back. Kreutz's Cossacks moved forward from Schwerstedt, reinforcing the Tchougouiev Uhlans, stabilizing the situation. The French then withdrew in two columns. One moved through Heichelheim and the other moved through Ettersburg. The Russians resumed their pursuit, but night fell, ending any hope of further action.[15]

As the French withdrew they were beset by Cossacks and Russian light cavalry under Colonel Krapovitski. This force, ranging ahead of the main allied armies, moved into Gotha and captured General Baron St-Aignan, 73 other officers, and 900 men, as well as destroying 30 powder wagons. The first column of the Army of Bohemia advanced behind an advanced guard under Count Pahlen. The Russian Guard, Prussian Guard and reserves marched towards Oberreussen, where Barclay de Tolly established his headquarters. The Austrian 3rd Armeeabteilung, under Gyulai

French troops on the march, Autumn 1813, by Beyer.

moved to Dernsdorf, while Wittgenstein's Corps moved to Trensdorf. Kleist's 2nd Prussian Corps moved through Eckardsberga and advanced towards Buttelstedt. The allied artillery reserve moved into Eckardsberga.

Bubna's Austrian 2nd Light Division arrived before Weimar on 23 October. The remaining troops of the second Austrian column, the 1st and 2nd Armeeabteilung and the Infantry Reserve, bivouacked between Nohra and Ulla, on the road to Erfurt. The second column marched parallel to the first.

On 23 October, the Army of Silesia, formed in three columns, passed over the Unstrut. The advanced troops crossed just after midnight by Laucha and at 6:00 a.m., Yorck's 1st Prussian Corps followed them. Henkel's advanced guard advanced to Sömmern. Langeron's and Sacken's Russian Corps bivouacked by the Vippach Castle and Blücher established his headquarters in Gross-Benhausen.

Schwarzenberg feared that Napoleon might turn and strike, so he arranged the advance of his armies such that, though dispersed, they could concentrate in very short order. Despite the crippling blows dealt the French at Leipzig, the allies were still very conscious of the military genius of Bonaparte, and feared to push too hard and suddenly discover the French army still had enough teeth to destroy an isolated corps.

On 24 October Barclay de Tolly reinforced Pahlen's advanced guard with an infantry division and sent them through Gross-Mühlhausen, throwing the French back across the Gramme.[16] Gyulai's Corps, Kleist's 2nd Prussian Corps, and the Russian and Prussian Guard and reserve cavalry moved to a position by Ollendorf and Ballstädt. Schwarzenberg, worried the first Austrian column might find itself in a major battle with the French, redeployed his assets and directed Kleist and Wittgenstein, with the Russian and Prussian Guard and reserve, to move to Ulla. At the same time, he ordered the Army of Silesia to move through Tennstädt towards Langensalza, in order to pass around the French position in Erfurt. This was done, so that if Napoleon felt himself strong enough to turn on his pursuers, the allies could strike him from several directions.

Pahlen's advanced guard continued to harass the French rearguard and was reinforced by GM Mezentzov's Russian 5th Division and Pirch's Prussian 10th Brigade. Once formed, the first order to this force was to assault Erfurt. The Prussian light cavalry led the advance. However, the advance stopped in Ollendorf, when it received word to await the arrival of Gyulai's Corps. They were to merge and form a new advanced guard for the Army of Bohemia.

After Gyulai's arrival, General Pahlen and the Russian light cavalry was to move into Utzberg, while the Prussians under Kleist moved into Ulla. GM Sesslawin, commanding the Isoum Hussars and two horse guns, advanced from Ollenberg to join Pahlen. However, on a hill behind the stream by Kerpsleben, they encountered about 15,000 French in a strong defensive position.

Pahlen moved to the left, to a position behind Utzberg and Hopfgarten, on the right side of the Weimar-Jena road. Gyulai's advanced troops moved towards Gross-Mössen and established a line of pickets to Udstädt. In front of Udstädt and on the right flank, stood General Kreutz's Cossacks. Further to the right, by Eckstädt, stood a detachment of Gyulai's Corps to serve as a link to the Army of Silesia.

The Army of Silesia had orders to fall on the flank and rear of the Grande Armée, should Napoleon attempt to hold Erfurt. Sacken's and Langeron's Corps moved through Tennstädt and Yorck marched through Cölleda, Leublingen, and Weissensee towards Gangloff-Sömmen. The cavalry reserve moved to Gross- and Klein-Urleben. The Army of Poland moved towards Wiehe, with Stroganov's infantry and Tschaplitz's cavalry in the lead. Docturov's Corps moved to Bibra, where Bennigsen established his headquarters.

However, Napoleon was not to turn on the allies. Indeed, only six of his 14 corps had moved through Erfurt. What the allies did encounter were the corps of Maréchaux Macdonald (XI) and Victor (II), Sébastiani's II Cavalry Corps, and two divisions of I Young Guard Corps under Oudinot.[17]

On 24 October the French advanced guard reached Gotha. Its forces consisted of those assigned Macdonald (XI), Victor (II), and Sébastiani (II Cavalry). Oudinot's I Young Guard Corps was assigned to support them. Marmont's VI Corps and Bertrand's IX Corps followed them. In the center marched the old Guard under the orders of Friant and Curial, the Guard cavalry under Nansouty, the cuirassiers of the I Cavalry Corps, and the artillery park under Generals Sorbier, Neigre, and Dulauloy. Behind them came Ney's III Corps and Augereau's IX Corps. The rear-guard was formed of the II Young Guard Corps under Mortier.

The Bavarians

Wrede, commander of the Bavarian army, had left Braunau on 15 October and crossed the Danube at Donauwörth on 19 October. With Bavarian's defection its army was quickly incorporated into that of the allies and was joined by an Austrian force to form a small corps. Wrede acted with such swiftness in his taking the field against the French that one would have to believe he had a personal score to settle with the French.

On 21 October, during negotiations with the neighboring state of Württemberg, a Bavarian officer arrived in Wrede's headquarters in Dinkelsbühl, with a handwritten letter from Metternich for Wrede, which had been written on the Leipzig battlefield at 9:00 a.m., the morning of 18 October. This letter informed Wrede of the great events that were happening. Though it took several days, this was a rather rapid transit. The letter prompted Wrede to divide his forces in two parts. On 22 October, the 1st Division moved through Ansbach to Uffenheim and then moved towards the right column. On the same day, the two Austrian Divisions of Bach and Fresnel arrived in Ansbach from Gunzenhausen, and the 2nd (Bavarian) Division also arrived in Ansbach. Wrede decided that the right column, with four divisions, would attack the city of Würzburg. The artillery reserve of his corps, which should have followed the right column, stood in Dinkelsbühl on 22 October. On the same day two field mortars from the Würzburg Fortress, joined Wrede's forces.[18]

The left column no longer contained the 3rd Bavarian Division (Becker), the 1st Cavalry Brigade, Trautenberg's Austrian Grenadier Division, and Splenyi's Reserve Cavalry Division. They had been detached to blockade the Mergentheim Fortress, but now operated against the main line Hanau-Frankfurt and the Rhine River, in an effort to clear that area of French troops. Those forces, which were standing on the soil of the state of Baden, were also applying pressure on the still wavering courts at Karlsruhe and Darmstadt.[19]

In Ansbach Graf Wrede received a letter from Schwarzenberg, carried by Hauptmann Freiherr von Greifenklau, dated 19 October, with definitive news of the outcome of the battle of Leipzig. Indeed, the high command had, the evening after the battle's end, no full overview over the actual results of the battle, for in the letter Wrede found, directing his future actions, only the phrase: "Your Excellency, I must ask that your attention be directed in denying the enemy all munitions and reinforcement." This invitation caused Wrede to strongly suspect that Schwarzenberg anticipated another battle against the French army in the near future, as confirmed by the slow and careful advance he was to execute.

Wrede's response to this letter must be viewed in the perspective of his location and the indefinite nature of the order. What was asked of him was clear, but Wrede had no cause to believe that the French would march so precipitously towards the French frontier, and that he did not have sufficient time to execute other plans that he had already made.

The further inference which the leader of the Austro-Bavarian Southern Army drew from this letter, was that he had time in which to actually carry out the seizure of Würzburg. A reinforcement of this interpretation lay, no doubt, in a further letter received from Schwarzenberg, dated 22

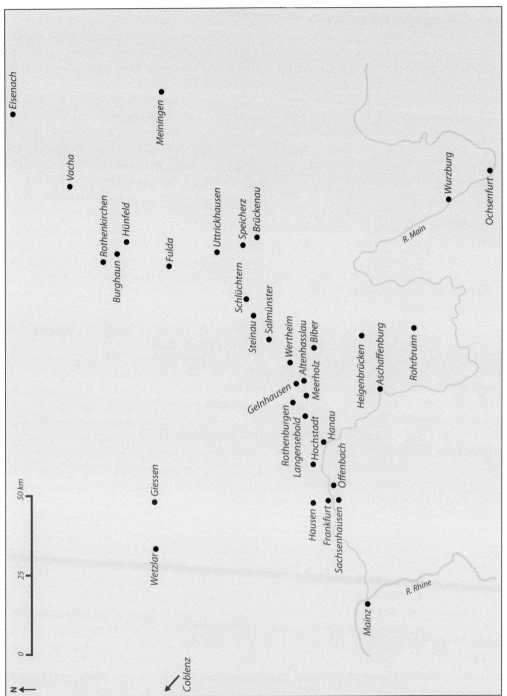

Sketch Map 11   The Passage to the Rhine.

October, from Naumburg, wherein he advised Wrede of Napoleon's hasty withdrawal to Erfurt. Wrede's task was laid forth as: "Meanwhile, I figured that on 24 October Your Excellency would arrive in Würzburg, I request you immediately dispatch strong strike force to effect the total inter-ruption of the communication between Erfurt and Frankfurt. General Thielmann's Streifkorps and that of Platov have been sent off to assist in the execution of that order. According to news, which I cannot completely guarantee, the Duke of Valmy [Kellerman] who is marching to Erfurt, has turned towards Würzburg. I believe that the direction of his march from Würzburg should be determined."[20]

Kellerman's movements were also to play an important role in Wrede's decisions, even though Kellerman himself remained in Mainz with his hands full holding together a 1,000-man depot and replacement pool in this important fortress. In any case, Wrede considered himself obliged to carry through his first instructions, though no justification was given for those orders by his commander. Wrede was ordered to the move away from Napoleon's line of retreat and hurry to the Main River line. Besides, in attacking Würzburg, Wrede saw an important opportunity to strike a blow that would speed up the end of the war, a blow that should be struck while the opportunity was present.

The fortress of Würzburg was not strongly held. Wrede knew that the garrison of the fortress consisted of only about 3,000 men.[21] Part of these forces had earlier served as the garrison of Spandau, and because of the capitulation of that place were obliged, by terms of their capitulation, not to engage in combat with the allies until properly exchanged. Consequently, Wrede felt that he could reasonably expect that if he appeared before the fortress with a sizable force, the garrison might well capitulate.[22]

The orders for the move against the fortress were issued in Wrede's headquarters in Uffenheim on the 23 October 1813, "March Disposition."

During the morning of 24 October, at 6:00 a.m., the advanced guard of Rechberg's Bavarian Division passed over the Main on the Ochsenfurt bridge, which it had taken the night before. The Austrian divisions of Fresnel and Bach followed behind them. A few French hussar pickets by Randersacker were encountered and encouraged to withdraw to the fortress. In this position, the right wing leaned on the Rottendorf Würzburg road and waited there for the two Austrians divisions to arrive. Bach's Line Division moved forward and to the right of the 1st Bavarian Division, where it occupied the area by the Rottendorf-Bergtheim Road. The main portion of Fresnel's Light Division, under GM Volkmann, stood on the Rottendorf-Bergtheim Road in the region of Neumühle. Three companies of the Austrian Jäger Battalion #3 took up positions in the adjacent mountains covered with vineyards. Towards the Schenkenschloss, two more Jäger companies and a squadron of the Schwarzenberg Uhlan Regiment were placed in an observation post. The sixth company of this jäger battalion stood with another squadron in Veitshöchheim. Two Austrian 12-pdr batteries stood in positions on the heights to the south of Unterdürrbach. At the same time the two Bavarian divisions, which came from Aub, closed the allied lines on the west side of the fortress. They held one battalion as a reserve in Heidingsfeld, while two battalions and two squadrons stood on the Leistenberg. A skirmish line stood between the Tauberbischofsheim road and Zell.[23]

The rest of the division's cavalry and infantry stood in the region between the Himmelspforte Cloister and closed the ring around Würzburg. On the left bank of the Main, stood the two Bavarian 12-pdr batteries and a 30-pdr mortar battery. Wrede hoped to close and protect the northwest with strong patrols by Schleiber's Streifkorps.

Austrian Oberst Scheibler had orders not to engage his streifkorps in any skirmishes, and on 20 October, he drew his forces together in Neumärkt, in order to watch over the Nürnberg-Bamberg road, and the activity on the French line of communications down the Frankfurt-Leipzig road. In addition to his commanding various detachments of Bavarian troops, he also commanded two squadrons of the Austrian Szekler Grenz Hussar Regiment.

At 9:00 a.m., General Graf Rechberg sent forward Major Graf von Seyboltstorff to summon the fortress commander to surrender. The Austro-Bavarian force had completed its envelopment of Würzburg on the eastern surrounding heights around 1:00 p.m. They then pushed their skirmish line to within a cannon shot of the fortress on the edge of the glacis.[24]

However, the French commander sought only to win time in order, if possible, to gain news from Napoleon, for he had no information on the outcome of the battle of Leipzig. Also he sought to avoid problems with his forces, many of whom, including himself, were covered by the Spandau Capitulation. Negotiations began and Graf Seyboltstorff, Austrian Oberstleutnant de l'Ort, and Austrian GM Freiherr von Geppert were offered as Wrede's negotiators, but their entreaties were refused by Turreau. Wrede ordered, therefore, that at 6:00 p.m., that evening, the city was to be fired on by 20 guns from Steinberg. In fact, only six 7-pdr howitzers and 12 6-pdr cannon actually opened fire and each fired 20 rounds. The French answer was limited to a few cannon shots from the bastions by the Pleicher Gate, which wounded a few schützen from the 1st and 3rd Line Regiments. It did, however, convince Turreau to accept a fourth parliamentary. Though negotiations were held, Turreau negotiated unsuccessfully for an armistice, and the right to dispatch an officer to Napoleon for instructions.

Wrede refused and ordered the city bombarded again between 12:00 p.m., and 1:00 a.m., but this time 82 guns bombarded the city and each gun fired 40 rounds. However, the only heavy caliber guns to fire were eight Austrian 12-pdrs.[25] The mortar battery and the Bavarian 12-pdr batteries were stuck on the bad roads and unable to reach their firing position by the Mariahilfkapelle for the bombardment. During the two bombardments, Wrede had ordered his gunners to minimize damage on the city itself, by concentrating their fire on the roofs. The second nocturnal attack did give Turreau a far lasting impression, not the least result of which was his moving to the Marienberg fortress to assure his personal safety.

The divisions of Bach and Rechberg had pulled their skirmishers back under the cover of the glacis during the night bombardment. They also began gathering material with which to fill the Marienberg fortress's ditch, which they felt was too shallow and too narrow to resist an assault. Guns were brought forward to make a breach in the city's defenses on the southwest face of the city. In addition, during the evening of 25 October, Wrede finally succeeded in obtaining an order from the Grand Duke of Würzburg, which absolved the Würzburg troops of the need for further obedience to the French.[26]

That same evening, Wrede resolved to make one further attempt on the city. However, at 8:00 a.m., on 26 October, before that, he sent forward a fifth parliamentary to seek a resolution on the blockade of the city. Turreau capitulated the city to Wrede, but not the Marienberg fortress. By 1:00 p.m., the Rennweger Gate was occupied by a half-company of the 1st Bavarian Infantry Regiment and a half-company of Austrian infantry. By 4:00 p.m., Wrede had occupied the entire city. However, Turreau and his garrison had withdrawn back into the Marienberg fortress.

By 24 October, Wrede stood in Würzburg and three days later he was in Aschaffenburg. He detached a force of 10,000 men to Frankfurt and marched to Hanau in an effort to block the French army as it moved through the Main valley. On 27 October he stood in Hanau.

The French Army

The French departure from Leipzig occurred after the near total destruction of the VII and XI Army Corps, the Poles of the VIII Corps, and the desertion of most of the troops from the Confederation of the Rhine. The Rhenish troops knew that they would soon stand in the ranks of their enemies, facing their former allies, the French. On 17 October, the weak Bavarian brigade under Maillot, the remains of Raglovich's Division, found itself in Eilenburg, serving as the guard for the main French wagon park.[27] They declared themselves neutral on 18 October, and as soon as the park was safely inside Torgau, they slipped through the loose French lines, as the defeated French army withdrew from Leipzig.

In the battles by Kösen and by Freiburg on 21 October, Bertrand and Oudinot thwarted the attempts by Gyulai and Yorck to cut off a considerable portion of the withdrawing French army. Now Napoleon had the Saale and Unstrut Rivers between himself and his pursuers. On 23 October his lead elements reached the protection of the Erfurt walls.

The fortress at Erfurt gave Napoleon an advantage he was to use as much as possible. Also, the appearance of strong French forces on the Büszleben-Kerspleben line east of Erfurt, threw the Austrians immediately on the defensive, and motivated Schwarzenberg to draw together his forces. On 26 October Schwarzenberg wrote to Wrede, he believed that Napoleon would engage in a battle here, but in a later letter written on the same day, he wrote that the French had remained passive around their bivouac fires. He also reported that it was rumored that Napoleon was in Vacha on 26 October, two hard day's march from Erfurt, so it appeared that Napoleon had 30-40 hours in this fortress, with which to direct the reorganization of his army.

Erfurt's supplies were inadequate for the needs of army. In an effort to ensure as much benefit as was possible, Napoleon made his marshals responsible for the condition of the weapons, clothes and equipment, and above all also, the shoes of their soldiers. A more efficient food supply system was organized. In order to prevent any slowing of the military columns by those that could not maintain the marching rate, the sick and wounded remained in the fortress, and the numerous superfluous officials and officers were, as much as possible, dispatched on 23 October, down the great army road to Mainz, passing under the control of Kellerman. On 25 October Napoleon departed Gotha and shortly after received news of the arrival of 100,000 French infantry and 30,000 cavalry in Hanau, Frankfurt, and surroundings.[28]

Kellerman had dispatched to Napoleon two columns with replacement troops under the command of Generals Grouvel and Guérin.[29] They were mostly young recruits with little military experience or training. In addition, in Erfurt, Napoleon found 6,000 recruits and depot personnel, which were absorbed into the field army almost immediately.

While in Erfurt, Napoleon paid considerable attention to the reorganization of his artillery. He had suffered heavy losses in his own artillery and correctly assumed that if these weapons were not absorbed by his army, they would be turned over to the armies of his former German allies, now in his enemy's ranks. Accordingly, on his arrival in Erfurt, General Sorbier, Napoleon's artillery commander, began an immediate reorganization and equipping of the French artillery, drawing from stocks held in the fortress of guns and equipment, to replace the guns and wheeled equipment which had been lost, as well as issues of ammunition to replace what had been expended. The army was to thank him for his farseeing concern for their welfare, when they found themselves facing the Austro-Bavarian Corps a few days later.

On 24 October, Napoleon's tireless enemy, Blücher, stood 30 kilometers north of Erfurt. He had intercepted a message from General Turreau. From that dispatch, he learned of the Bavarian defection to the allies, and the march of Wrede's army against the French.[30]

The Main Allied Armies

As Napoleon reorganized in Erfurt, Pahlen stood in Kerpsleben and deployed a line of pickets against Erfurt. These Cossacks, under General Kreutz, moved close enough to Erfurt to be fired on by the fortress's artillery.

On the allied left flank, Bubna's 2nd Light Division moved across the Gera, as did the three Austrian Armeeabteilungs. As the Austrians bivouacked in Ulla, they learned of Napoleon's departure from Erfurt.

During the same day the streifkorps of General Illowaiski XII found itself engaged in battle with Fournier's 6th Light Cavalry Division as it moved towards Fulda. The Russian light cavalry found itself obliged to maintain more of a harassing role, because of the superior force of French cavalry.[31]

On 25 October the Army of Silesia continued its effort to turn the French flank, as it marched on Langensalza. Blücher received a report that the French had left Erfurt in three columns, moving through Gotha and Eisenach. The first had already passed through Eisenach, while the second would arrive that day and the third would arrive on 26 October. Blücher realized that there was the Fulda gorge through which the French must pass, and offered the allies an opportunity to punish the French, if they could only reach it. He pulled together his reserve cavalry and horse artillery, dispatching it to take advantage of the opportunity. He also remembered that Yorck and Sacken had been detached to the main allied advanced guard, so his corps was cut in half.

The French Retreat Continues

On 25 October, at 3:00 a.m., Napoleon ordered his army westwards once again, in order to reach the passes by Eisenach, before the advanced guard of the Army of Silesia. This effort was yet another inevitable forced march. To the young infantry that just joined the army, however, this march proved a shock. On 26 October, in yet another rearguard action, Oudinot and Mortier engaged Yorck's Corps around Hörselberg. Their four weak divisions of Young Guard, totaled about 14,000 men, and suffered about 2,000 casualties.

Don Cossacks and French prisoners in front of the town hall in Artern, 26 October, after a lithograph by Hoffmann.

A deluded Blücher wrote that he would be within a day's distance of Napoleon on 30 October, the day of the battle at Hanau. However, on 30 October, Yorck, Langeron and Sacken had only moved their corps to the line of Rothenkirchen-Burghaun-Hünfeld. They were 75 kilometers from Hanau and 60 kilometers from Mortier's rearguard. Napoleon had won a two day lead over the allies. Contact was lost and the reconnaissance efforts of the Army of Silesia failed. Napoleon once again had recovered his freedom of movement, but this advantage was achieved by surrendering a degree of the French army's battle readiness.[32]

The streifkorps of Orlov, Czernichev, Kaisarov, and the Austrian Oberst von Mensdorf were well suited to inflict heavy losses on the withdrawing French army, and proceeded to pursue and harass the French.[33]

Once in Eisenach, Napoleon moved through Vacha, Fulda, and Schlüchtern, towards Mainz in an effort to avoid the Thuringian Forest. Blücher, operating in concert with Wrede, moved through Giessen and Wetzlar to catch the French at Coblenz, should they move away from Wrede's columns.

Napoleon, however, had no intention of turning away from Wrede. Quite possibly, he knew the condition of the newly reorganized Bavarian army would be too poor to stop his Guard and battle-hardened veterans.

The Skirmish at Hörselberg

On 27 October Czernichev's Streifkorps arrived in Fulda only to encounter Sébastiani with three cavalry divisions leading the French withdrawal. This was far more than Czernichev's small force could hope to engage and the Cossacks wisely vanished before the overwhelming numbers of French cavalry. On 28 October Sébastiani reported, "Four thousand horse precede me daily and joined a detachment of infantry, formed of the infantry moving from Meiningen towards Brückenau." Doubtlessly Sébastiani was referring to the infantry under Oberst Scheibler, which had moved during the night through Speicherz-Ulrichshausen, in an effort to reach Fulda. Czernichev renounced attacking the French cavalry advanced guard, and turned against a French column with an artillery park of 20 guns, reported to be a half-day's march away from the French advanced guard Scheibler moved quickly forward in an effort to occupy the Fulda gorge, but he lost considerable time when he gave his troops a rest and failed to occupy the gorge in time. Then he came into contact with Sébastiani's forces. Scheibler's small force was quickly driven back, out of the gorge and the French now held the critical pass.[34]

As Exelman's 4th Light Cavalry Division spent the night in the Wertheim Pass, Napoleon responded to his messages with the comment, "The way to France is open."

During the morning of 28 October, General von Volkmann was ordered by Wrede to send part of his light division to move against the Fulda-Frankfurt road, in order to harass the French columns on that road, and if possible, to stop them. This detachment, led by Oberst Freiherr von Mengen, commander of the Schwarzenberg Uhlan Regiment, consisted of his own regiment, Jäger Battalion #3, and a company of the Szekler Grenz (Infantry) Regiment. They departed for their gathering point at Rohrbrunn at 11:00 a.m., and passed through Rothenbuch at 5:00 p.m., en route to Heigenbrücken. Once there, Mengen separated from his force a company of Jägers, the Szekler Grenzers, and a squadron of Uhlans under Major Graf Hadik and sent them to reconnoiter in the direction of the gorge. Oberstleutnant Alberti was sent through Biber with two squadrons of Uhlans and two Jäger companies, to serve as an observation post on the Ausenau-Wertheim-Saalmünster Road. Mengen moved the rest of his forces over the Unterschneppenbach River to Altenhasslau and waited for events.[35]

Snow mixed with rain was falling and made the advance of these detachments more strenuous. It was not until between 6:00 a.m., and 7:00 a.m., on 29 October, that they reached the French line of retreat. Once there, they found signs that indicated that a large body of troops had already passed down the road.

Oberstleutnant Alberti soon encountered a force of French, the 23rd and 24th Chasseur à Cheval Regiments of Marbot's Brigade.[36] According to statements of the officers of von Colomb's Prussian Streifkorps, this surprise attack was crowned with success. They stated that the French were thrown into an unbelievable confusion. The Franco-Dutch General, Dedem van Guelder, who withdrew with Macdonald's staff, also spoke of panic breaking out in the French ranks. Fortunately for the French, von Colomb's force was unable to join the attack. The volunteer Jager detachment of the von Ziethen Hussars was too exhausted to attack. On the other hand, Marbot recounts quite the opposite and suggests that it was the Prussians who lost the engagement.

Sébastiani reorganized his cavalry and sent it southwest of Wirkheim. The main body of the Schwarzenberg Uhlan Regiment pulled back to Altenhasslau. Oberst Mengen waited for the French with three squadrons by the Altenhasslau stone bridge. Four companies of Austrian Jäger Battalion #3 stood to the west of the village. Gelnhausen was occupied by one Jäger company, its bridge was broken down, and the city gate was barred. Forrestier's squadron of the Schwarzenberg Uhlans stood before the Hanau Gate, ready to move to the Jägers' assistance if necessary.

In addition, the beams from the bridge were removed, in case the French advanced guard arrived at the bridge. However, the French executed a quick assault and the allied cavalry detachment between Wertheim and Gelnhausen was driven back. Macdonald sent four guns and three attack columns to attack Gelnhausen's northern wall.[37] In the subsequent street fight, Captain Saintenoi vacated the city. He joined Forrestier's squadron of Uhlans by the Hanau gate and then Mengen's force, which then withdrew nearly unmolested down the road to Meerholz.

It was 3:00 p.m., as Saintenoi's small group, hotly pursued by Sébastiani's cavalry, reached the edge of the woods between Rothenburgen and Langenselbold. The Erzherzog Joseph Hussar Regiment, which stood there, rode forward, counterattacked and drove back the pursing French towards Rothenburgen. This drove the French back in another panic, as even Macdonald reported.

In the meantime General Volkmann, at Wrede's direction, sent the remainder of his light division forward from Hanau, to support his advanced forces. Because of the forces involved, Volkmann was not to get into an decisive battle. His only goal was to delay the French retreat.

Supported by two guns from the cavalry battery, Oberst Freiherr von Geramb and his Erzherzog Joseph Hussars forced the French once again to deploy their infantry and broke up the closed column, which stood on the heights to the north of the forest edge. Now Volkmann vacated Langenselbold and moved his Szekler Battalion back. The grenzers took up a new position 500 meters west of Riedmühle. The greatly fatigued Schwarzenberg Uhlans were drawn back over the Niederrodenbach River to Hanau. Twilight had long since begun, when Volkmann received Wrede's 6:00 p.m. order to pull his light division back to the main army's position. The French had the not passed the western edge of Langenselbold. North of Rückingen and on the Kinzig River Bridge south of the village, there stood two hussar pickets. The defense of these two positions was left to Deroy's Brigade, which stood near the Lamboy forest.

Hadik's detachment was passed to Orlov-Denisov's Streifkorps and would remain with him during the course of the battle around Hanau.

Volkmann's Light Division had suffered about 60 casualties during the day's affair. It had engaged and slowed the advance of the French advanced guard for more than nine hours and covered a distance of 15 kilometers.[38]

On 29 October the French army stood in Langenselbold. The Old Guard led the march with Macdonald following with the V and XI Corps. Victor (II Corps) and Augereau (IX Corps) were in Gelnhausen. Marmont (VI Crops) was in Salmünster and Bertrand (IV Corps) stood behind him. Oudinot's I Young Guard Corps and Mortier's II Young Guard Corps were in Steinau and Flieden. Napoleon knew of Wrede's maneuver and had sent his baggage through Coblenz. His army was in "light marching order," ready for combat.[39] During the night of 29 October, the Baden Dragons, who were brigaded with the French 10th Hussars and served with the III Corps, quietly saddled up and defected to the allies.

When the French advanced guard arrived in Schlüchtern, Napoleon learned of Wrede's position. The allied armies were marching parallel to his flanks and pressing his rear. Napoleon could not maneuver to avoid this obstacle and he did not have time to fight a protracted battle. He had about 25,000 men with him and the remainder of his army was strung out to the rear as far as Fulda.

13

The French Fall Back on the Rhine 28 October-31 December 1813: The Battle of Hanau

Hanau: The First Day of Battle

During the night of 27/28 October, the 3rd Bavarian Division reached Aschaffenburg and its advanced posts stood in Klein-Ostheim. There Wrede learned from prisoners that Hanau lay in the path of the withdrawing French.[1] In the early morning, at 4:00 a.m., Wrede had sent Vieregg's 1st Cavalry Brigade and the "Halder" Cavalry Battery #3 towards Dettingen and sent the 3/7th Chevaulégers forward to serve as a communications link between Vieregg and himself.

Around 7:00 a.m., the Bavarian advanced guard moved forward. They quickly encountered and overthrew a French cavalry picket, before the town of Neuwirthaus. Once in the village they found and captured about 40 French officers and 100 men, including General Santa Andrea. The 4/1st Bavarian Chevauléger Regiment advanced towards the Lamboy bridge, while the rest of the regiment sought a ford across the Kinzig River. As his horses were in poor shape, Oberst von Kracht led a single squadron towards the houses of the suburb that stood north of the Kinzig, on both sides of the Fulda-Frankfurt military road. They encountered French skirmishers deployed in the gardens around those houses, quickly engaged and drove them back. Shortly after, around 10:00 a.m., a Young Guard cavalry column of 500-600 men arrived, escorting Napoleon's personal baggage. The Young Guard cavalry assumed an offensive posture and pushed forward across the Lamboy bridge, in order to open a pass.[2]

The attacks were simultaneous against the two Kinzig bridges. The Guard cavalry placed the wagons in their middle and charged, plowing irresistibly through the Bavarian Chevaulégers, and then moving towards Frankfurt. The stream of refugees on the line of retreat, which had been blocked by the Bavarian cavalry, now flowed into the village, now that it was clear of Bavarian cavalry. The Bavarian move against the Lamboy bridge failed as well.

The receipt of a message from Kracht caused Wrede to send the 3/7th Chevaulégers forward to support Kracht. As the regiment pulled back to the town, it found itself obliged to release the French prisoners it had taken. Oberst von Kracht found himself obliged to detach the 4/7th Chevaulégers to assist the 3/7th Chevaulégers, when they found themselves in trouble.

Shortly before the arrival of Podewils' (3/7th) squadron, Kracht learned of the cavalry battle by the Kinzig bridge and forwarded the word to Wrede. Kracht then divided his force into two columns. The right column consisted of the 3/7th and 4/1st Chevaulégers. They passed through the Nürnberg Gate, while the rest of the two regiments moved through the Steinheimer and Canal Gates. They pushed into the town, and after a short fight, captured the French they found there, a detachment of the French 128th Line Regiment.[3]

Around the suburbs and the Kinzig Bridge Gate the French defense was tenacious and bloody. The right column at first was able to overrun the French defenders, but the defense quickly stiffened. The Bavarian left column was more successful. It cleared the vicinity of the Frankfurt Gate of French troops and seized the important bridge. They drove the French back into the walled gardens, who these skirmishers then emptied many Bavarian saddles from the safety of their walls.

In the meantime Podewils' squadron, 3/7th Chevaulégers, pursued a wagon column.[4] Although the covering force of Young Guard infantry offered strong resistance, several equipment wagons were cut off and carried away. The squadron lost two officers and several troopers in this attack.

Gradually Podewils withdrew his fatigued squadron from the street battle to the entrance of the city. The advancing French shut the portcullis of the inner Frankfurt Gate and set themselves up defensively behind it. As his forces pulled back and reformed by the bridge, Oberst von Kracht realized that he was in danger of being cut off from Wrede, by forces at the Lamboy bridge.

In his report, immediately after his engagement with the guard cavalry, Oberst von Kracht also mentioned that Napoleon was alleged to personally be in Gelnhausen, moving towards Hanau. Similar rumors were also heard by Wrede from other sources. As Wrede learned of the cavalry battle north of Hanau and the rumor of Napoleon's approach, he sent his chief of staff, GM Graf von Rechberg, with orders to General Vieregg, directing that he take his cavalry brigade down the road towards Gelnhausen and Hanau and drive the French back.[5] Vieregg, however, had already carried out this order.

Somewhat later, around 1:00 p.m., Wrede's chief of staff rode forward with the main portion of Vieregg's 1st Cavalry Brigade and the Light Battery #3. The 7th Bavarian Chevaulégers and two guns formed the advanced guard. These guns quickly forced the opening of the portcullis and the evacuation of the suburb. With the support of the 1st Bavarian Chevauléger Regiment, Oberleutnant Feuerlein, with two guns, moved to the Lamboy bridge and began to fire on it with canister. The 2nd Bavarian Chevaulégers formed themselves as a reserve behind the Nürnberg Gate.

Podewils came forward with his fresh half-squadron and requested permission from Oberst Winkler, commander of the 7th Chevaulégers, to strike against the Military road by Gelnhausen and the Lamboy forest, with the support of Hauptmann Halder and two of his guns.

At the same time La Motte's 3rd Division was ordered to move on Hanau. General La Motte moved out of Aschaffenburg about 11:00 a.m. The road was bottomless mud, which with a cutting wind and driven snow, made the march fatiguing and slow.

In the city of Hanau the allied forces stood to arms, both by the Kinzig River bridges and in the surrounding terrain extending to the forest. Rittmeister Freiherr von Podewils was not pleased that so many French skirmishers had penetrated into this area. The advanced half-squadron of the 7th Bavarian Chevaulégers was moved to the south of the main road. Hauptmann Halder and his two guns took up position with them. It was 4:00 p.m., when a reformed French column arrived on the main road, with its weapons ready for instant action. General Grouvel, leader of the reinforcement column that had earlier turned back from Vacha, advanced with from 4,000 to 5,000 infantry, 5 squadrons and eight guns.[6] His force quickly collided with Rittmeister von Podewils and Hauptman Halder's tiny force. Immediately an artillery duel began

between the French artillery and two Austrian guns from Hauptman Halder's Light Battery #3. The 7th Bavarian Chevaulégers, which had bravely withstood the French artillery fire, were forced to withdraw through Hanau. They rejoined General Vieregg's Brigade by Lehrhof, south of the town, to await the assault of the advancing French infantry.

General Grouvel stopped by Hanau only for a moment and quickly made an agreement with the city's authorities for the feeding of his troops, on the condition that they not enter the city. He had threatened to leave the city to the mercy of the swarm of freebooters, which deserted in ever larger numbers from the Grande Armée. Despite this, there was still rioting and ,quarrels, especially between the French and the few remaining soldiers of small Rhenish states that had belonged to what used to be the Confederation of the Rhine.[7]

That evening, while his division hurried forward, GM La Motte consulted in Lehrhof with Rechberg, Vieregg, and Deroy, whose brigade was in a forward position with already schützen companies pushed forward into the fight. A general staff officer of Freiherr von Horn's Division deplored General de La Motte's earlier decision to dispatch a force of infantry north of Dettingen at 8:00 p.m., the prior evening. The only requirement was that the main portion of Deroy's Brigade march forward at the first cannon shots, yet from 4:00 p.m., it had remained stationary. To be sure, even when it arrived before Hanau, it "stood for hours, before the troops were permitted to move forward."

Shortly after 8:00 p.m., the schützen of the 5th and 9th Bavarian Line Infantry Regiments, and those of the 1st Isar and 2nd Iller Kreis Battalions, pushed into Hanau and seized the town without resistance. Once in control, Horn secured all the gates and found himself in control of a considerable number of prisoners. Between 9:00 and 10:00 p.m., the main portion of Deroy's Brigade finally arrived and scoured the gardens to the north of the Kinzig, taking 20 French officers and 800 soldiers prisoner.

The 1/5th Bavarian Line Regiment, which belonged to Deroy's Brigade, arrived later with von der Stocky's Brigade. Slowly La Motte's entire division began to concentrate in the city of Hanau. The Bavarian troops deployed for their evening bivouacs. The 1/9th Line Regiment and 2/Iller Kreis Battalion placed themselves facing the east, on the eastern edge of the group of houses to the north of the Kinzig, along both sides of the Gelnhausen road. The 1/8th Line faced west on the west side of the same group of houses. The reserve for these two groups was formed by the 1/Isar Kreis Battalion, which stood in the Kinzig bridgehead. The 1/7th Line and Achner's 6-pdr Battery #9 served as the guard for the Nürnberg Gate.[8] The remaining five battalions of the division positioned themselves in the various squares in the city, as did the 2nd Chevauléger Regiment and a third of Halder's Light Battery #3. The rest of Halder's Light Battery #3 stood with the 1st Cavalry Brigade by Grossauheim. Part of the 1st Chevauléger Regiment stood on the Lamboy bridge. In case of a French attack, General Deroy also had at his disposal the 2nd Chevauléger Regiment as well as one and a third batteries in and immediately around Hanau.

The night passed calmly. Only occasional shots from the pickets disturbed the night, as French soldiers sought to slip out of Hanau, and small groups cleaned out stray French soldiers.

Prelude to Hanau

Czernichev had been joined on 28 October by more than six Cossack regiments and several horse guns, under the command of Austrian Oberst Graf Mensdorf. With this force he attacked Guérin's 55th Colonne de Marche (3-4,000 men), some of whom lacked weapons. Guérin had mostly infantry supported by a weak force of cavalry and two guns. The engagement was typical of this type of action. During the night of 28/29 October, it had found itself beset by the Cossacks of Czernichev and Kaisarov to the east of Langenselbold. General Guérin's heavily pounded column pulled back towards Langenselbold.

During the morning of 29 October, Wrede's main army prepared for what was coming. The 1/9th Line Regiment and 2/Iller Kreis Battalion took up their weapons and moved out of Hanau. Hauptmann Achner brought his six guns into line with the infantry and began to fire on Guérin's column, at a range of 650-800 yards. Soon, after three or four shots, the artillery accompanying Guérin broke and withdrew to the rear taking up position on a height by a point of woods.[9] The 1/9th Bavarian Line deployed to the south and the 1/5th Bavarian Line deployed to the north of the road, while the I/Isar Kreis Battalion advanced to a position by the 1/5th, and the II/Isar Kreis Battalion remained behind on the road, serving as a reserve.

The Bavarian battalions advanced in a line of columns, covered by their schützen in skirmish order. The unequal artillery duel quickly ended when a French caisson was destroyed and several horses were killed. The two French guns fired barely five or six more times before the 1/9th Bavarian Line overran them in a bayonet attack. The 2nd Chevaulégers, with half of Halder's Light Battery #3, moved forward to pursue the withdrawing French down the military road, capturing several caissons and wagons as they advanced.

The schützen pursued the French infantry into the woods and soon found themselves engaged in a hot little fight. The schützen of the 5th Bavarian Line Regiment and those of the I/Isar Kreis Battalion particularly distinguished themselves in this fight. The French infantry was soon surrounded by Kaisarov's and Czernichev's Cossacks. The situation being hopeless, the French surrendered with over 100 officers and 3,000 men being taken prisoner. Of them, 20 officers and 800 men were taken prisoner by the Bavarians.[10]

To support the schützen companies, Deroy had dispatched the 1/5th Bavarian Line Regiment to the western part of the Lamboy Forest. The remaining battalions were with the 2nd Bavarian Chevaulégers on the heights west of Rückingen. General La Motte ordered the mixed brigade, with three battalions, four squadrons, and one and a third batteries (Achner's 6-pdr Foot Battery #9 and a third of Halder's Light Battery #3) to form the advanced post on that position.[11]

Von der Stocky's 1st Brigade, La Motte's Division, drew the 1/5th Bavarian Line Regiment to itself and replaced it with the 1/Unterdonau Kreis Battalion, which had been en route to Bischofsheim.[12] The 1/8th Bavarian Line was, at Wrede's direction, on the road to Frankfurt, and stood north of the Kesselstadt castle. Czernichev was supported by two companies of the 11th Bavarian Line Regiment, that stood by the bridge over the Krehsbach near Freiberg. The 1st Brigade now had a total of only four battalions, four companies, and half of Achner's 6-pdr Battery #9. At Wrede's order, this force was sent into Hanau at 2:00 p.m. The 1st Chevaulégers, accompanied by the other half of Halder's Light Battery #3, were sent towards Niederrödenbach and were to take no further part in the battle. The rest of the 1st Cavalry Brigade, the 2nd and 7th Chevaulégers, remained south of the Lamboy bridge. The green 7th Chevauléger Regiment, however, had need of careful treatment after the strenuous activities of the previous day.

Since noon, to the east, had been heard sporadic musketry and cannon fire. Towards 4:00 p.m., Austrian General von Volkmann sent out forces to assist Stocky's heavily engaged brigade. However, by 6:00 p.m., Volkmann had pulled all of his forces back to their bivouacs by Lehrhof for the night.

Although the French advanced guard no longer had the Bavarian advanced posts under artillery fire, no effort was made by the Bavarians to reconnoiter further afield. The Bavarian advanced posts simply returned reports stating that that a large and growing number of bivouac fires were observed behind Langenselbold. The Bavarian generals failed to explore the situation, and further more, ignored the possibility that the rumored presence of Napoleon was true.

30 October: The Battle of Hanau

General Wrede did not judge himself strong enough to close the road to Frankfurt to the entire Grande Armée, but he had decided, nonetheless, to use his 36,000 to 40,000 man corps to harass the retreating French. He decided to use his cavalry on the plains of Hanau, where he could use them to advantage, and under the cover of a heavy cannonade, inflict damage on the French, as they came out of the forests to the east of Hanau.[13]

When Wrede arrived in Hanau at 1:30 p.m., on 29 October, he was convinced that at that time he faced only a small column and not the main body of the Grande Armée.[14] He estimated the force facing him had no more than 20,000 men.

On 29 October, after the engagements at Gelnhausen and Langenselbold were over, the French realized that they had finally encountered Wrede's Bavarians and began to prepare for the battle. Macdonald observed that the "morning would seal their (the Bavarians) fate." Oudinot's Young Guard had stood as a rearguard, but was ordered forward to the point of the main body, closed up with the Old Guard.[15]

The French army organized itself for the assault during the night of 29/30 October. Macdonald led the column with the V and XI Corps. Behind him came the Old Guard. Lefèbvre-Desnoëttes stood to the north of the Old Guard, with Milhaud and the Polish cavalry behind him. Arrighi's III Cavalry Corps formed to the south of the Old Guard. Behind the Guard came Victor's II Corps, Sorbier with three artillery parks, Oudinot's I Young Guard Corps, and Bertrand's IV Corps. The rearguard was formed by Mortier's II Young Guard Corps with Berkheim's cavalry to his south and Latour-Maubourg's I Cavalry Corps to his north. To their rear, Blücher's Army of Silesia was just exiting the Thuringian Forest, 30 miles behind Mortier. Only Platov was near Mortier and stood about five miles from him.

When day broke, Macdonald had been with the advanced guard since 4:00 a.m., and Napoleon was himself mounted and about the day's tasks since 7:15 a.m.

A gloomy morning greeted the Austro-Bavarian forces, as their pickets began to stir under the cover of the edge of the forest west of Rückingen. A light snow covered the ground and by 9:00 a.m., flurries began to fall.[16]

The main part of the Bavarian infantry remained united south of the Kinzig River. Bach's Austrian Division, eight line infantry battalions, and the four grenadier battalions of Klenau's Brigade stood in Lehrhof. The tiny Prussian streifkorps of Rittmeister von Colomb stood on the Rodenbach road and served to link Deroy's advanced posts near Rückingen with the main body. The allied cavalry stood on both sides of the Gelnhausen-Frankfurt road and was divided into two groups. Their right wing stood on the road and the leading edge of the first line stood two thirds of

French and Bavarian cavalry at the Battle of Hanau, by Kobell.

a mile to the west at the forest edge. The left wing was covered by the marshland by the Fallbach stream, which was cut by several ditches. During the night, von der Stocky's Brigade had bivouacked to the right. The Szekler Grenz Regiment served as the link between the two groups north and south of the Kinzig. It was posted in the forest by Neuhof. The Austrian grenadier battalions of Diemar's Brigade occupied Hanau. The 2nd Bavarian Division (under Becker) and the Austrian 12-pdr batteries were still en route.

During the early hours of the morning, around 3:00 a.m., GM Deroy sent word back from the advanced guard that a very large French force stood before Rückingen, and that he awaited an attack. Wrede responded by ordering forward three squadrons of the Szekler Hussar Regiment on a reconnaissance towards Langenselbold. However, at 6:00 a.m., the hussars encountered the front of the French lines by Riedmühle and were chased back without completing their mission.

Wrede deployed his forces as follows. The right, consisting of the 2nd Bavarian Division (Becker), was posted on both banks of the Kinzig River, between the Neuhof farm to the Bulau woods, in a line even with the Rodebacher House, situated on the road. Klenau's Austrian Brigade was placed behind the Lamboy bridge as a reinforcement for the 2nd Bavarian Division.

The center was formed by Bach's Austrian Division. It was planned that if it was pushed back it was to unite with the 3rd Bavarian Division (Lamotte) and Volkmann's Austrian Brigade. Once united infantry would cover the entire right bank of the Kinzig along the grand route to Gelnhausen, facing the Lamboy Forest.[17]

The left wing was formed by the Bavarian and Austrian cavalry. It was formed in several lines and stood to the left of the Gelnhausen Road, towards the Bruchköbel and Puppen Forests. The Cossacks and partisans, under Czernichev and Orlov-Denisov, were posted behind the left wing and on the main road to Friedberg. The reserve stood behind the left bank of the Kinzig, in the Rodenbach ravine, with a brigade of Austrian grenadiers.[18] The Bavarian pickets stood to the east and north of Rückingen and were formed from the schützen company of the 5th Bavarian Line Regiment and a half-squadron from the 2nd Bavarian Chevauléger Regiment.

In the early morning, Rittmeister von Colomb observed the deployment of the French army and admired the calm and order of their movements. General Ruty, who did not leave the Emperor Napoleon's side this day, also spoke repeatedly of his astonishment over the conspicuous order of the French troops. Napoleon watched the battle for the Rückingen bridge from Metzeloh.

The engagement began, but at a low level, as the French advanced very slowly. General Deroy sent forward the 1/8th Line Regiment and a half-battery. He faced the French with four battalions, four squadrons, two guns of Halder's Light Battery #3, and half of Achner's 6-pdr Battery #9.[19] Later Deroy sent forward the grenadier companies of the 1/9th Line Regiment and somewhat later the rest of regiment, while the I/Isar Kreis Battalion moved to Langendiebach where it served as a reserve.

The two guns of Halder's Light Battery #3 moved to the east edge of the town to fire on the cloud of French skirmishers. Macdonald did not, however, press hard against the Bavarians, as he was waiting for the arrival of Sébastiani's II Cavalry Corps. He contented himself with engaging the Bavarians with skirmish fire which soon forced Hauptmann Halder's battery to withdraw under the cover of Achner's 6-pdr Battery #9, and eventually back to Hanau.

Wrede witnessed the first engagements and was comforted by the excellent attitude of his young troops. Shortly before 8:00 a.m., he returned to his main force, where he conferred with FML Graf Fresnel as to how best to deal with the French. Meanwhile, the 1/9th Bavarian Infantry Regiment calmly pulled back under the mounting pressure of the French. The Bavarian brigade on the plateau west of Rückingen was unable to resist much longer, as the French deployed artillery and pushed forward a large force of cavalry on the left. The 1/9th Line formed column, and with half of Achner's 6-pdr Battery #9, began to withdraw. Ledru's 31st Division, Macdonald's XI Corps, struck at the Bavarians while Sébastiani's and Exelman's cavalry supported his advance. Soon the

IX Corps and part of the II Corps, under General Dubreton, pushed to the south in order to cut off the retreat of the 1/9th Bavarian Line.[20]

French light cavalry struck with a swarming attack of a few small detachments, while formed bodies of cavalry advanced to strike the Bavarian cavalry brigade in an effort to stop its withdrawal and permit the French infantry to come to grips with it. Achner's half-6-pdr Battery #9 responded with salvo after salvo of canister, keeping the skirmishers at bay. The French advanced continued, causing the Bavarians around the Lamboy Forest to sound the alarm and prepare for battle.

At 8:00 a.m., the French vigorously attacked the 3rd Bavarian Division's advanced posts. These posts were very weak and were only able to hold their position until about 10:00 a.m., though they repelled several attacks before being obliged to retire. Then Charpentier's 36th Division, Friant's Old Guard Division, Sébastiani's II Cavalry Corps, and a force of artillery under the command of Maréchal Macdonald, advanced towards Rückingen.

The 1/8th Bavarian Line Regiment was deployed and sent forward to support the advanced posts, but despite the reinforcement, the Bavarians were driven back. They retreated, covered by Deroy's 2nd Brigade of La Motte's Division and the 2nd Bavarian Chevauléger Regiment.[21]

At 10:00 a.m., Deroy's Brigade vacated its position by the Diebach Forest and was pursued by the French.[22] It reached the western edge of the Lamboy Forest about 11:00 a.m., followed by a cloud of French skirmishers, cavalry and several of Macdonald's batteries. The French encountered the schützen from von der Stocky's Brigade and the two battalion strong Szekler Grenz Regiment. The French advance forced them back as well. A general Bavarian withdrawal had begun.

Macdonald let loose his forces and deployed them into a long thin line to sweep the Austro-Bavarian skirmishers from the edge of the forest before him.

La Motte concentrated and organized his division. Von der Stocky's Brigade stood in the first line and Deroy's Brigade formed behind them. The cavalry and artillery of the advanced Guard moved through gaps.

The allied cavalry stood in three lines on the left wing. The Bavarian cavalry stood in the first line. The right wing was formed with the four squadrons of the 3rd Cavalry Brigade. The 4/5th Chevauléger Regiment stood in line across the Sandweg Road, the three squadrons of the 4th Chevaulégers were in a closed regimental column behind the road. On the left of the 4/5th Chevauléger stood the 1st Cavalry Brigade, with the 1st, 2nd, and 7th Chevauléger Regiments, each with four squadrons, lined up behind one another. The six squadrons of the 2nd Cavalry Brigade were on the outermost left wing. The 3rd Chevaulégers stood on the right. To the west, left, was the 6th Chevauléger Regiment. In the second line stood the Austrian heavy cavalry. To the left were the four squadrons of the Liechtenstein Cuirassier Regiment and on the right were the five squadrons of the Knesevich Dragoon Regiment. In the third line stood the Erzherzog Joseph Hussar Regiment, with six squadrons, and the Schwarzenberg Uhlans, with five squadrons.[23]

On the left flank of the allied cavalry stood the 1/Erzherzog Rudolph Infantry Regiment. Mensdorf's Streifkorps waited further to the left and to the rear by the Friedberger Road. Mensdorf was joined by two weak Cossack regiments and three squadrons of Austrian hussars. The freiwillige Jäger squadron of the Prussian Lithuanian Dragoon Regiment was posted in Bruchköbel Forest facing the north. Two Prussian squadrons, the von Rohr's freiwillige Jägers and von Colomb's freiwillige Jägers, held the advanced post on both flanks of the army serving as feelers. On the southern edge of the Bruchköbel Forest, by the Freiberg road, stood the Austrian Jäger Battalion #3.

The strong streifkorps of Czernichev and Kaisarov were still in their bivouacs. As their supporting reserve, two companies, were detached from the 11th Bavarian Line Regiment. Soon Cossacks brought word of the approach of a very large baggage train, moving from the north towards Bruchköbel. The lust for booty quickly drew Czernichev to the north and the train. However, near Friedberg he encountered Lefèbvre-Desnoëttes' cavalry and Milhaud's veteran dragoons and received a "bloody head" for his efforts. Mensdorf's Austrian hussars and the Prussian freiwillige Jägers, not wishing a decisive battle against overwhelming odds, remained in their positions.

About 300 paces before the cavalry of Generalfeldmarschal Splenyi, Austrian GM von Strotnik deployed an artillery line to receive the French. Halder's Light Battery #3 was deployed on the right wing, across the road. To its left was Achner's 6-pdr Foot Battery #9. These 12 Bavarian guns were joined by the 18 12-pdrs from three Austrian batteries and an Austrian 6-pdr battery from the general reserves.[24] On the far left wing, alone and in echelon, stood a squadron of the Knesevich Dragoon Regiment and a horse battery.

Shortly before 11:00 a.m., 44 allied guns, commanded by GM Strotnik, stood ready to greet the French. The 2/Erzherzog Rudolph Infantry Regiment covered them from the edge of the Puppen Woods stood. The rest of the regiment with two divisions from the 1/, 3/Erzherzog Rudolph Regiment and its landwehr battalion stood in the middle of the position, to the south of the Frankfurt-Gelnhausen road.

To the right forward of these regiments, and in an extension of the artillery line, stood von der Stocky's Brigade. His schützen deployed along the edge of the woods, with the closed companies 200-300 paces behind them in an open field. From left to right they were arranged as follows: the 1/7th Line Regiment, 2/11th Line Regiment, 1/11th Line Regiment, and 1/Iller Kreis Battalion. The Iller Battalion stood on the right wing, 300 paces from Neuhof. To the rear of the brigade were two guns of "Aign" Light Battery #2. They had moved both 7-pdr howitzers behind a small ridge on the edge of the woods. Deroy's Brigade, behind von der Stocky's Brigade, was arranged in two lines. On the left, by the road stood the 1/5th Line. To their right were the 1/9th, 1/8th Line Regiments, 2/Iller Kreis Battalion, and 1/Isar Kreis Battalion.

On the southern portion of the western edge of the Lamboy Forest, the two battalions of the Szekler Grenz Regiment deployed in skirmish order. The forest was thicker here than in the northern portion, with thick underbrush cut by ditches and old water courses. As the Szekler Regiment began to run out of ammunition its commander resolved to cross over the Kinzig River in the afternoon.

After its march from Aschaffenburg, between 7:00 and 8:00 a.m., Becker's 2nd Division stood on the southern bank of the flowing stream. Four battalions of Zoller's Brigade, with about 1,450 men, arrived about 10:00 a.m.[25] Graf Pappenheim's Brigade stood to their right and Zoller's Brigade stood somewhat farther to the rear and left of the Lehrhof-Neuhof road. The Austrian Jordis Infantry Regiment and Klenau's Brigade stood in Lehrhof.

Around noon, one of Wrede's adjutants carried an order to Pappenheim's Brigade, directing it to pass over the bridge and occupy the woods, where the Szekler Grenz Regiment was heavily engaged with French skirmishers. Graf Pappenheim advanced with the 4th Combined Light Battalion leading his brigade. The remaining battalions, the 1/4th Line, the 1/Regen Kreis Battalion, and the Salzach Kreis Combined Battalion followed behind. The edge of the forest was occupied by the light battalion, replacing the slowly crumbling Szeklers.

Half of the "Danner" 6-pdr Foot Battery #7 stood to the south of the Lamboy bridge and supported the fight in that area. Zoller's Brigade, moving on the Kinzig, occupied the far side of the Lamboy bridge and the Neumühle (new mill) with the 1st Schützen Company of the 6th Line Regiment. The rest of the 1/6th Line remained on the left bank of the Kinzig River. The 1/Jordis Infantry Regiment moved further to the right and occupied the Bulauwald Forest. This detachment was to slow the passage of the French over the Kinzig, but to no purpose.[26]

At noon, the French army, about 60,000 men including 12,000 cavalry, moved in dense masses out of the Lamboy Forest. Napoleon's advanced guard consisted of Charpentier's 36th Division and Dubreton's 4th Division, about 5,000 infantry, which pushed through the woods in skirmish formation. On the right were 4,000 men from the commands of Lefèbvre-Desnoëttes, Arrighi, and Dombrowski.[27]

The Bavarian 4th Light Battalion was forced to pull back from its position in the woods south-east of Neuhof, where it had fought alongside the Szekler Grenzers. Its schützen and karabinier companies were deployed in skirmish order and the four center companies remained closed up behind them, only to find themselves showered with canister, howitzer shells, and small arms fire. Their losses were such that they were forced back, out of range.[28]

The French II Corps deployed its artillery in the edge of the woods, and by 11:00 a.m., its fire had set Neuhof ablaze. Danner's 6-pdr Battery #7 had detached one gun and a howitzer under Oberleutnant von Bridoul, to a position where the Neuhof-Gelnhausen road exited Neuhof. Under the cover of their fire, the rest of Pappenheim's Brigade passed over the Lamboy bridge in order to assist the 4th Light Infantry Battalion. According to the general's report of 17 November, the brigade moved six battalions, two cavalry regiments, and several guns across the river. In addition, the 2/, 3/Jordis and its landwehr battalion passed over the Kinzig behind Pappenheim and took up a position to the southwest of Neuhof.[29]

At 1:00 p.m., an order from Wrede arrived stating, "The brigade shall steadfastly repel further assaults by the French, in order to assure that possibility that, as reported in many reports, only a part of the Grande Armée stands before us, and to permit us to maneuver around the French Corps facing us and permit us to capture it lock, stock, and barrel." This order makes it painfully clear that Wrede had no idea what he faced. Shortly there after, Bavarian illusions were shattered as at least some staff officers heard, echoing from deep in the woods, the Old Guard greeting Napoleon with their cry, *Vive l'Empereur!* Wrede's hour of reckoning had arrived, and Bavarian duplicity was about to receive a down payment from the head cashier.[30]

Wrede moved to the northern group of his army and reviewed the situation along the forest edge before him. Before him he saw only scattered skirmishers and cavalry supported by the fire of a few guns. The rising and falling sound of cannon fire to the south was of so little concern to him that he deployed the 12-pdr Batteries of Dietrich (#11) and Ulmer (#8) to support Danner's 6-pdr Foot Battery #7 on the northern half of the battlefield. The detachment of these two Bavarian batteries left only 18 guns in the artillery line the Bavarians had established earlier, and of those guns, only eight were 12-pdrs.

Though Deroy's infantry was occupied with the skirmishers facing it, the allied cavalry had so little to do that the regimental band of the Liechtenstein Cuirassier Regiment serenaded the lines of cavalry, as they waited for action that was ominously near.

The musical interlude lasted only until 1:00 p.m., when the pace of the battle picked up. Macdonald's artillery, under General Baron Nourry, began to deploy before the forest's edge. The Bavarian batteries to the north began to fire on the French artillery, in an effort to nip the French move in the bud.[31]

Macdonald soon executed his attack, leading forward about 8,000 men of the V and IX Corps, plus 3,000 men of Dubreton's 4th Division of the II Corps. The attack, however, had no more success than the others and the French were thrown back into the forest. The battle continued until 3:00 p.m. The artillery fire became more and more intense. Every French move out of the forest was driven back.

Napoleon had not, so far, been involved in the battle, but spent his time on overseeing the rear-guard of his army. He now turned his attention to the battle and sent forward his forces in dense columns. At the head marched Curial's Old Guard Division and the Guard Cavalry.

Napoleon recognized the impossibility of forcing the center and moved to attack the right flank.[32] Shortly before 4:00 p.m., he gave the order for the artillery and cavalry to be the main effort of the French attack, while the infantry remained idle. Marmont's VI Corps and the 1st and 3rd Young Guard Divisions under Oudinot were closing fast. The Old Guard, the last untouched body of French infantry, were finally ordered to attack. General Curial received the order to clear the edge of the forest south of the road with the 1st and 2nd Chasseurs à Pied Regiment. The Old

Guard began to roll forward irresistibly at the *pas de charge*.[33] The artillery, under GD Drouot, deployed before the woods where it could enfilade the allied left, and GD Nansouty's Guard cavalry swung out behind it, deploying to attack.

Curial's two regiments advanced down the road in closed columns at a quick pace, with drums and music announcing their advance, Charpentier's skirmishers covered their front. The rush of the Old Guard swept von der Stocky's skirmishers from the forest edge. General von der Stocky, at the head of the 1/7th Bavarian Line, was struck dead, and the commander of the 1st Iller Kreis Battalion was taken prisoner, as his legionnaires fought their way out of an encirclement.

The French artillery moved forward to renew the bombardment, but the Old Guard Horse Artillery pushed even further forward. Covered by the Old Guard Dragoons and Lancers, two Guard Horse Batteries under Colonel Griois moved down the road at the gallop. They deployed and began a devastating bombardment of the right wing of the first Bavarian cavalry line, while covered by the Guard cavalry.[34]

According to its commander, the 1st (Polish) Chevauléger-lancier Guard Regiment, were struck by a heavy artillery fire from the northwest. The Poles began to take heavy losses, as they moved to the right of the Guard Dragoons. The second line of French cavalry, the 10th Cuirassier Regiment and the 2nd Carabinier Regiment, moved forward. The Empress Dragoons then advanced forward to strike La Motte's 3rd Division as Deroy's Brigade, in the second line, moved forward to support Stocky's Brigade.

The French flankers began to take a toll on the four squadrons of the 3rd Cavalry Brigade. Without waiting for orders, their leader, Oberst Diez, drew his forces forward and led them against the French. This was a relief for his young troopers standing behind the artillery line. The two French Guard Cavalry Regiments were forced to yield, but the action of the 3rd Bavarian Cavalry Brigade was not to be crowned with complete success, for French infantry and artillery in the woods poured out onto the field and broke their advance. As the Bavarian horse was concentrating on the Guard horse artillery and their covering cavalry, Drouot had, under the cover of the edge the woods, drawn forward five Old Guard foot batteries, with 20 12-pdr cannon, deployed them, and pushed them out of the edge of the woods.

The second artillery battle was very brief and quite one-sided. The Bavarian artillery was short of ammunition and completely outclassed by the finest gunners in the world.[35] Wrede instructed the Austrians to provide the Bavarians with ammunition and 12-pdr shot was provided, but there was nothing for the Bavarian 6-pdr guns: the Bavarian artillery reserve was 60 miles away in Ussenheim! Wrede had no choice but to withdraw his guns.

The Cavalry Battle

In an effort to stabilize the situation, Wrede ordered the seven Chevauléger regiments to attack the French artillery line. They passed forward, through their withdrawing artillery line and threw themselves at the French, overwhelming the two heavy French cavalry regiments and pushing them into the woods.

Drouot's artillery stood waiting the charging lines of green clad Bavarian cavalry. The French held their fire until the Bavarians were within musketry range and unleashed a whirlwind of canister that shredded their ranks. Despite their losses, the Bavarian cavalry broke into the line of artillery, the gunners diving under their guns. As their shattered and broken ranks moved through the guns and equipment they found themselves facing fresh French cavalry.[36]

Nansouty's Guard cavalry charged them frontally, while Curial's Chasseurs fired on their flank. Behind the Guard cavalry, two more lines of French cavalry moved out of the woods and began

The Grenadiers à Cheval of the Guard at Hanau, by Knötel.

to deploy. The impact of Nansouty and the prospect of further French reinforcements was more than the Bavarians could hope to withstand. Beaten, the allied cavalry fell back and joined the retreating artillery.

Nansouty reformed his cavalry into three lines. The Guard Chasseurs à Cheval and Grenadiers à Cheval, under General Laferrière-Levesque,[37] formed the first line. The second line consisted of the four cuirassier and two carabinier regiments of St-Germain's 2nd Heavy Cavalry Division. The third line contained the four regiments of Gardes d'Honneur, who were about to committed to battle for the first time, and under Napoleon's eyes![38]

Nansouty dispatched the cuirassiers of the second line to the east to maneuver and strike La Motte's left flank. The Gardes d'Honneur handled themselves well, and Exelmans combined the 3rd Garde d'Honneur Regiment with the Grenadiers à Cheval and maneuvered them to strike the Austrian cavalry in the left flank.[39] The impact was terrible. Oberst von Flachnfeld, commander of the Liechtenstein Cuirassiers, was killed and Oberst von Olay, commander of the Knesevich Dragoons, was wounded. The Erzherzog Joseph Hussars and Schwarzenberg Uhlans were drawn into the battle, as was Sébastiani's entire II Cavalry Corps. Shortly after, Graf Mensdorf arrived with his two Cossack regiments and three Austrian hussar squadrons, which he threw without hesitation into the French right flank. Though surrounded by French cavalry, the Erzherzog Joseph Hussars succeeded in forming column and punching back through the French lines, as Mensdorf's attack broke the French concentration.

As soon as the allied cavalry was chased back by the French cavalry, the allied battery renewed its firing. At 4:00 p.m., Wrede attempted once again to use his cavalry to force Drouot's battery back, but failed again.[40] The allied artillery on the left wing, lacking ammunition, could not respond and remained exposed to a murderous fire.[41]

As they pulled back, the Schwarzenberg Uhlans and a fresh 6-pdr battery were moved back across the Kinzig, to the south bank. The Schwarzenberg Uhlans, supported by the 1/Erzherzog Rudolph Infantry Regiment and its landwehr battalion, repeatedly charged the French as they attempted to cross the Kinzig, and assisted the rest of the allied cavalry to break out. However, the allied cavalry was severely handled and soon its actions began to assume the character of panic, as casualties mounted and one unit after another sought to save itself.[42] The seven Bavarian regiments had lost a third of their officers and a fifth of their manpower.

Curial's Infantry Attack

La Motte's 3rd Division found itself facing the advance of Curial's Old Guard Chasseurs à Pied. Wrede had dispatched the 1/9th Bavarian Line to the edge of the forest to face the French and supported them with artillery. Shortly after, the artillery duel began on their right, followed quickly by the 1/9th Bavarian Line exhausting its ammunition. At this moment, St-Germain's cuirassiers struck the flank of La Motte's 3rd Division. The 1/5th Bavarian Line Regiment and 2/Iller Kreis Battalion rallied around their flags, in a desperate bid to stay alive in the mass of thundering cavalry. The 2/Iller Kreis Battalion shot off all its ammunition and found itself depending on its bayonets to survive.[43] The 1/8th Bavarian Line Regiment and 1/Iller Kreis Battalion formed squares with cannon placed between them. A volley from the 1/Iller Kreis Battalion, coupled with an attack by the Erzherzog Joseph Hussars, stalled the attacking French cuirassiers and permitted the 2/Iller Kreis Battalion to move to the assistance of the 1/9th Line Regiment. The 1/9th found itself alone, facing Curial's Old Guard Chasseurs à Pied, supported by the 2nd Old Guard Grenadier à Pied Regiment under Cambronne.[44]

Surrounded by French cavalry and facing the advance of Napoleon's best infantry, La Motte's 3rd Division began to pull back in an effort to break off contact. They withdrew down the main road towards the bridge over the Kinzig, where Drouot's artillery began to pound them furiously.[45]

The punishment and threat of the advancing Old Guard was more than Wrede's troops could handle. "At the sight of the advancing bearskins (of the Old Guard), the Bavarian infantry was seized with terror, and recoiled in panic." With the Bavarian lines crumbling, the French cavalry thundered forward again. Sébastiani's cavalry and all of the Imperial Guard Cavalry—the grenadiers, the Chasseurs, the mamelukes, the lancers, and the dragoons—rode against the Bavarians, striking them with a fury. Several squares were literally ridden down and the Bavarians suffered heavy losses.[46]

The withdrawal and passage over the Kinzig were effected with much disorder, and many soldiers drowned in the river as they tried to ford elsewhere.[47] In Hanau, by the Frankfurt Gate, Diemar's Brigade of Austrian Grenadiers and the "Dietrich" Bavarian 12-pdr Foot Battery #11 waited in reserve. The grenadiers joined the army's gendarmes with their bayonets, in an effort to stop the flood of refugees. The flood of beaten Bavarians, however, moved around them, pushing through the Kinzig and into the city.

The dam of the Herrenmühle, a grist mill on the Kinzig, was full to the top with water from the constant rain and snow of the previous few days. The sluice gates had not been opened. Those that could, slipped across the top of the dam, while others simply threw away their equipment and swam the Kinzig. The 1/5th and 1/9th Line Regiments and the 2/Iller Kreis Battalion disintegrated as they escaped across the Kinzig, losing about 300 prisoners.[48]

On the left flank Wrede stood with the Schwarzenberg Uhlans covering the withdrawal of that flank. Von Mengen's forces were covered by two squadrons of the 1st Chevauléger Regiment. Part of Halder's Light Battery #3 fired off its last canister rounds at the advancing French cavalry. Oberst Mensdorf had withdrawn from the battlefield after his one attack.[49] Part of the Erzherzog

Rudolph Infantry Regiment and Jäger Battalion #3 withdrew towards Frankfurt and crossed over to the left bank of the Main River, but stopped and took up a post to defend the bridge. The 2/11th Line Regiment pulled its two companies on the Krebsbach back. The Prussian freiwillige Jäger squadrons were ordered back to watch the Friedberg Road. However, they found themselves cut off by the *Fasanerie* (animal gardens), and were obliged to withdraw in a different direction.

At 5:00 p.m., north of Neuhof the engagement was definitively concluded. The Bavarian left wing was thrown back across the Kinzig and the center ruptured. The Bavarian right wing had also been pushed back to the west. In an ironic gesture, Wrede's 3:00 p.m. order for a divisional attack arrived. Wrede hoped that a strike by his right wing could stop the French torrent through his lines.

To the south, by the Lamboy Bridge, Zoller's Bavarian Brigade suffered a few losses to French artillery and was itself supported by the greatly fatigued Pappenheim Brigade. Zoller had deployed the 6th Bavarian Line Regiment on his western flank. The 1st Reizat Kreis Battalion stood on the road with two guns of Bridoul's battery, and on its left was the 1st Light Battalion. Further to the left stood the Austrian Jordis Infantry Regiment.[50] The schützen companies and two more companies of the 1st Light Battalion were deployed before them in skirmish line, engaging Dubreton's French skirmishers in the forest edge. The French breakthrough left the 6th Bavarian Infantry Regiment hanging in the air, exposed to the French. The 1st Light Battalion and the Jordis Infantry Regiment, however, stood by the Ihmhäuschen and faced little of the wrath of the Old Guard as it advanced.

However, this did not last long. Four more battalions of the Old Guard were given the order to "blow the powder from the pans of their muskets and advance directly against the (Bavarian) skirmishers." This assault was, in fact, executed by the 1st Grenadiers à Pied, the Fusilier-Chasseurs, the Fusilier-Grenadiers, the Velites of Turin, and the Velites of Florence. Instead of four battalions, eight advanced.[51]

With a terrible momentum, these elite troops thundered forward into the flank of Becker's 3rd Division, crushing and obliterating the 1st Light Battalion and the Jordis Infantry Regiment. The losses of the 6th Bavarian Line Regiment were even worse. The survivors of the allied brigade fled to the rear, towards the Herrenmühle Mill and into the woods. The 1st Reizat Kreis Battalion had one of its detachments cut off in Neuhof as the rest of the battalion withdrew. It dug itself in for a long defense. Its sole hope for survival was if the French ignored Neuhof and passed to the north.

As Zoller's Brigade disintegrated and fled into the woods, Pappenheim's Brigade advanced, only to be struck in the left flank by the squadrons of St-Germain and Sébastiani. The Bavarians hastily formed square. The schützen of the 6th Bavarian Line Regiment that formed in front of the 4th Bavarian Line Regiment, quickly pulled aside so that the 4th Line could defend itself with volley fire against the attacking cavalry, only to witness the Old Guard move around Neuhof and against the hapless Jordis Infantry Regiment.[52] According to Pappenheim's report, this regiment and its flanker line were bowled over by the overwhelming force and vehemence of the Guard attack. The regiment broke and its soldiers fled to the rear, across the Kinzig River. Much of the regiment and several hundred Bavarians were pushed towards the Herrenmühle Mill.[53]

The attack of the Old Guard was seconded by Marmont's advanced guard, driving the rest of the Bavarians across the Lamboy bridge. The Bavarian officers desperately attempted to stem the flow of their fleeing soldiers. Pappenheim had two horses killed under him in the effort. Fortunately, Pappenheim encountered Hauptmann Zurnieden's Battalion, with about 1,800 marching convalescents, and led them forward to the Lamboy bridge.

Oberleutnant Bridoul and his two guns had pulled back to the Lamboy bridge and defended this position with canister fired on the French at ranges of 50-60 paces. A few surviving companies of the 6th Bavarian Line Regiment occupied the Neumühle, while the bridge itself was defended by a number of schützen from the 6th Line under Oberstleutnant Fick, which built an impenetrable barrier of bayonets.[54] They found themselves covered by the concentrated fire of the three Bavarian batteries, Danner (#7), Dietrich (#11), and Ulmer (#8), and an Austrian 6-pdr battery.

The Bavarians occupied the strong points on the south of the battlefield, and with the swampy nature of the land, the French attack stalled, allowing the survivors of the shattered allied right wing to fall back and regroup.

Once that occurred, the Bavarians attempted to renew their assault, pushing across the bridge and throwing the French back into the woods.

The 1st Light Battalion advanced, with Zurnieden's Battalion behind them, under the command of General Freiherr von Zoller. They were followed by the two brigades of Becker's 3rd Division, and supported by the fire of the Bavarian right wing artillery. The Bavarians succeeded in throwing the French back and securing the region between the Kinzig and the Lamboy Forest by 7:00 p.m.

As night fell, the two bridges over the river were still in allied hands. The Lamboy Bridge was held by Klenau's Grenadier Brigade and Jager Battalion #3, which stood in the gardens by the Wasenmeisterei. Diemar's Grenadier Brigade occupied Hanau and the bridgehead before the Margaret Tower. Though they had suffered heavy losses, the spirit of the Bavarian conscripts was good. However, they knew that in the morning, they would once again face the advance of Napoleon's Old Guard.[55] The arrival of night finally ended the battle.

The night of 30/31 October was not without incident. A large portion of the French army marched in haste towards Frankfurt. On 31 October Marmont was left behind with the III, IV, and VI Corps to hold Wrede, while the rest of the army passed through the Hanau.[56]

October 31st at Hanau

Napoleon spent the night in the Lamboy Forest, surrounded by his Guard. However, the movements and actions of his army did not end. That evening the Guard Lancers probed the northern suburb of Hanau, only to be driven back with losses. GB Charrière's 8th Division, III Corps, passed over the weir by the Herrenmühle Mill and found themselves in a bayonet duel with the Austrian Hromada Grenadier Battalion.[57]

Napoleon set out at 1:00 a.m., with the Guard. His troops did not pass through Hanau, but took the roads through Wilhelmsbad and Höchstadt, so that they rejoined the main road around Mainnankers.

During the night, Napoleon reorganized his forces for what he anticipated would be a second day of battle. He was in a difficult situation, despite his victory, and had to clear the road to France. To his rear and on his left flank, however, the Cossacks of Platov and Orlov continued their harassing tactics. During the day of 30 October, Platov's Cossacks had twice broken through Bertrand's and Mortier's forces, while Orlov's Streifkorps, supported by the Hohenzollern Chevaulégers, had broken into the village of Rothenbergen at 4:00 p.m., spreading havoc and mayhem. His horse battery had also taken a French column under fire on the road to Gelnhausen.[58]

At 3:00 a.m., Macdonald's artillery began firing on the bend in the river and Marmont's forces pushed out of Neuhof. Marmont detached a portion of this force to bombard Hanau. The houses by the Kinzig bridge soon began to burn and the French attacked the allies defending the Lamboy bridge. The Austrian grenadiers repelled several attacks, but the French efforts were more than the allies could bear and at 8:00 a.m., Wrede gave the order to evacuate Hanau. Marmont's forces made a quick rush at the Lamboy bridge. They were stalled by the Austrian grenadier battalion posted there long enough for the allies to burn the bridge, denying its use to the French.

At 10:00 a.m., as Napoleon ordered his forces forward once again, a dragoon officer brought him the report that the Bavarians had evacuated Frankfurt. Oudinot moved his Young Guard forward once again, to assume the function of the army's advanced guard. Behind him, Macdonald formed his troops. Then followed Victor's II Corps. Marmont's VI Corps occupied Hanau while the Old Guard, the Poles, and the remainder of Marmont's troops passed through in rapid order. The Lamboy bridge was watched by Guilleminot's 13th Division, III Corps, and Morand's 12th Division stood north of Lamboy as a reserve by the paper mill. The II Young Guard Corps and the I Cavalry Corps remained by Gelnhausen under Mortier.[59]

Around 11:00 a.m., Ulmer's 12-pdr Battery #8, in Bavarian General Colonge's position north of Lehrhof, and a French battery at the forest edge south of Neuhof engaged in a heavy artillery duel. The 1/Regen Kreis Battalion was allocated to support the battery.[60] Soon another battery southeast of the Herrenmühle, probably belonging to Morand's 12th Division, opened fire on the Bavarian battery. Dietrich's 12-pdr Battery #11 joined the fight, though it only had 3 usable guns. After several minutes of firing, the Bavarians destroyed two French caissons, forcing the French 8 gun 12-pdr battery to withdraw. A second French battery then withdrew at General Colonge's order after having shot off all its ammunition.[61]

During the morning, the Austro-Bavarian corps moved into a position not far from Hanau. Its right wing stood by the Lamboy bridge. The allied line was attacked by the IV Corps (Bertrand) on the right and thrown back to the banks of the Main River. However, allied reinforcements arrived about then and stabilized the situation. A quick counterattack by the reduced Jordis and Erzherzog Rudolph Regiments pushed the French back to their original positions.

Below the gates of Aschaffenburg and Steinheim, the allied and French cavalry engaged in several skirmishes, but the French found little success. The casualties on both sides were considerable and the artillery fire was heavy.

During the previous day's cavalry battle the allied artillery had suffered heavily. Only half of Dietrich's 12-pdr Battery #11, which had left much of its ammunition near Aschaffenburg, Ulmer's 12-pdr Battery #8, and a combined battery formed from Achner's and Danner's 6-pdr Batteries #9 and #7, remained operational. At 4:00 p.m., they took up position to support a renewed Bavarian assault.

At 4:00 p.m., three Bavarian columns advanced on the right flank. The 6th Bavarian Line Regiment, now a single combined battalion, supported by a battalion of the Erzherzog Rudolph Regiment, advanced under the command of Oberst Palm.[62]

Wrede advanced at the head of the Frisch Grenadier Battalion and Jager Battalion #3 against the Nürnberg Gate, crossed the ditch and climbed the wall. Behind them came Diemar's Grenadier Brigade and part of the Erzherzog Rudolph Infantry Regiment. A total of six battalions made the attack, supported by a hussar regiment.[63] However, Fontanelli's 15th Division threw them out of Hanau, after a short engagement.

Wrede then led a small force of cavalry forward in an effort to seize the suburb and the Kinzig bridge, and encountered a French battalion in the bend of the river. The skirmish screen of this battalion opened fire on the Bavarian cavalry and seriously wounded Wrede. FML Graf Fresnel took over command of the allied corps. A battalion of the Erzherzog Rudolph Regiment cleared the barricade at the gate. Once the gate was cleared, the Szekler Hussars raced through the city at a gallop, followed by dense columns of Austrians and Bavarians moving to the Kinzig bridge.[64]

Shortly after 4:00 p.m., Bertrand led his corps out of Hanau, followed by a detachment from the Szekler Hussars. Mortier still stood in Gelnhausen, acting as a rearguard. He listened apprehensively to the renewed cannon fire around Hanau, as he moved down the Langenselbold-Bruchköbel road to link with Bertrand.

Initially the bridge remained in French hands, with their infantry formed behind it in dense columns and supported by heavy artillery fire. Though the bridge was heavily defended and covered with the dead and wounded of both sides, it was finally carried.

The Bavarians and Austrians watched as Bertrand's IV Corps filed across the Kinzig bridge and passed down the road, with cavalry on both sides of the road, screening the infantry and wagon train.

On 31 October, none of the Army of Bohemia appeared around Hanau in pursuit of the French, except for Orlov-Denisov's Cossacks, which had united with the small detachment of Major Graf Hadik near Somborn, seven kilometers southeast of Langenselbold. The French had broken down all the bridges over the Kinzig to cover their withdrawal. The Cossacks moved forward and encountered three French guns on the far side of the river, set up to slow any pursuit. Hadik had his Jägers hang onto the saddles of his Uhlans, as they swam the river and took these guns in the rear. Orlov also passed over the river quickly and took 20 officers and 1,500 French soldiers prisoner.[65]

The Skirmishes at the Sachsenhausen Bridge

As the Grande Armée pushed through Hanau, another French force fought against a Bavarian contingent to cross the bridge across the Main River by the Old City of Frankfurt.

On 30 October the 1st Bavarian Division stood in Offenbach, with its 1st Brigade moving towards Frankfurt at 7:00 a.m. They were led by two squadrons of the 5th Chevaulégers under Major von Karwinski.

At 10:00 a.m., Leutnant Graf Saporta with 60 men of the 1st Bavarian Line Regiment occupied the bridge over the Main, while Hauptmann Winther led his two schützen companies through Bockenheim towards Rödelheim. In Bockenheim Major von Karwinski learned from prisoners that the advanced guard of General Préval had orders to burn the bridges by Rödelheim, Hausen, and Praunheim. Karwinski moved his two squadrons forward quickly in an effort to save the bridges. They charged across the burning bridge at Hausen, taking 10 prisoners. He detached one squadron to fight the fire and led the other forward towards Rödelheim, where he encountered two squadrons of French Guard organized from the Mainz depots. He attacked and drove the French back.[66]

Winther's schützen moved into Rödelheim and occupied the gardens on the western edge of the village. Karwinski came forward with both of his squadrons, the fire being under control, and 50 schützen. This advanced position was soon reinforced by the arrival of two grenadier companies from the 1st Bavarian Line Regiment.

The bridges secured, Oberst Freiherr von Hertling led the 1st Brigade into Frankfurt about 2:30 p.m. General Rechberg had an attack of gout and was obliged to ride in the wagon train, so command passed to Prinz Karl. The two battalions of the 1st Bavarian Line Regiment bivouacked by the Mainz Gate, while the 1/3rd Line stood by the Hanau Gate. Light Battalion #3 and the "Rudersheim" 6-pdr Light Battery #4 stood as a reserve inside the city. Later that evening Mensdorf arrived with part of his forces and informed Prinz Karl of the battle around Hanau. At the same time, the lead elements of the Grande Armée arrived before the Hanau Gate and grabbed a few prisoners from the startled Bavarians.

Prinz Karl had received orders from Wrede not to engage Napoleon in a battle, and quickly withdrew his 1st Brigade to Sachsenhausen. The security of the bridge had been assigned to Oberst Theobald at 7:00 a.m., that morning.

The head of the French army arrived in Frankfurt at 11:00 a.m. on the 31st. Its light cavalry and Chasseurs occupied the roads from the Main Bridge, but the 1st Bavarian Division, which had retired to Sachsenhausen on the left bank of the Main and had partially destroyed the bridge, attempted to dispute the French passage with its artillery.[67]

The French cavalry began a desultory skirmishing with the few Bavarian Chevaulégers left in the city while the Bavarian pontoon train was drawn to the left bank of the Main. Control of the Bockenheim Gate was left to Leutnant von der Mark of the 1st Bavarian Line Regiment with orders to delay the French.[68]

Oberst Theobald moved the major portion of his brigade east from the Darmstadt road to the south edge of Sachsenhausen, and placed detachments in the woods on both sides of the bridge, while barricading the road itself in front of two mills. The area between the two mills was occupied by some of the schützen of the 10th Bavarian Line Regiment, while the rest of the schützen and the grenadiers occupied the houses on both sides of the bridge. Two guns of Rudersheim's battery, under Leutnant Bruckner, stood on the south side of the bridge. Pickets watched the stream below Sachsenhausen, Light Battalion #3 stood in Oberrad on the Oberrad-Sachsenhausen road with the "Finkenauer I" 6-pdr Battery #5, and the 1st Brigade stood to the south of Sachsenhausen.[69]

The first French infantry attack on the bridge was supported by the fire of a French battery by the Obermain Gate. It began firing on Finkenauer's battery. The Bavarians responded and added the fire of two howitzers posted east of Sachsenhausen. The French responded by bringing out howitzers of their own. Soon the French fire began to set the houses in Sachsenhausen afire, but no major conflagration erupted. The French attacked by moving skirmishers into the buildings along the river, who began to fire on the Bavarians defending the bridge.

Casualties began to mount in the schützen and grenadiers of the 10th Bavarian Line Regiment, and they were relieved around 2:00 p.m., by the 5th Fusilier Company, 10th Line Regiment.

At 10:30 p.m., the French rushed the bridge in an effort to take it by storm. The 2nd Schützen Company of the 1st Bavarian Line Regiment fell back behind the two guns. The 5th Fusilier Company, 10th Line, also fell back. Canister and musketry then swept the bridge clear of the Imperial Guard who rushed the bridge.[70] Two officers of the Young Guard and GD Pacthod were wounded as they personally led the assault. As the night deepened the engagement ended.

After Hanau

The battle of Hanau might properly be compared to the battle of Kulm. In both instances, Wrede and Vandamme did what a good general should do. In both instances neither general made any significant strategic errors. And in both instances, these two generals found themselves outgeneraled.

At Kulm an accident put Kleist in Vandamme's rear and ended the battle. At Kulm Wrede's troops, fighting as valiantly as they did, simply were no match for the finest infantry in the world under the command of the greatest general of the age. Wrede's situation was worsened by his poor choice of a battlefield, fighting with a river to his back.

Wrede recognized the potential outcome if he could delay the French retreat long enough for the allied armies to catchup. A victory from such a battle would have ended the Napoleonic Wars right then. Bonaparte's later comment about Wrede, "I could make him a Baron, but I could not make him a general," is an unfair evaluation of Wrede's generalship. His comprehension of the strategic value of his effort requires that Wrede be recognized as a good general who gambled and lost.

It is suggested the Bavarian army ceased to be a viable force after this battle, but that is not true either. It was to form a corps in the allied army and fought at the battle of Arcis-sur-Aube in 1814.

The Grande Armée moved through Frankfurt and on to the Rhine. It arrived in Mainz on 2 November, where it crossed. Guilleminot's 14th Division was assigned to serve as the rearguard and suffered heavily in the covering operation.

Napoleon had slipped past the allies, and now that he was in France again, they grew fearful. The allies were uncertain of how to deal with the series of frontier fortresses that lined the French border, and they seemed intent on a series of political secondary objectives. Once again Napoleon found himself in the position of having to rebuild his shattered armies. This time, however, he did not face an equally shattered enemy.

French soldiers suffering from typhus in Mainz, by Raffet.

On 12 November Napoleon ordered the dissolution of the III Corps. The 8th Division of the III Corps was incorporated into the VI Corps, which now consisted of two divisions, the 8th and the 20th.

In order to form the 8th Division, all the regiments of the former III Corps, except for the 2nd Provisional Regiment, were reduced to a single battalion. Those regiments which had more than one battalion absorbed those battalions into the one battalion that remained, except for the cadres, which were sent back to the depots. The 8th Division now consisted of 18 battalions under the command of General Ricard.

The 136th, 138th, 142nd, 144th, and 145th Regiments, which were formed of National Guard Cohorts, were reduced to two battalions by this reorganization.

Twelve hundred Dutch conscripts in the four battalions of that nation were near Mainz and were incorporated into the battalions of the 22nd, 40th, 59th, 69th, 43rd, 138th, 145th, 142nd, 144th, 50th, and 65th Line Regiments.[71]

For Napoleon, the 1813 fall campaign in Germany was finished. Now he prepared to fight for his life and his empire in what would be his hardest and most desperate campaign.

14

Operations on the Lower Elbe: Mecklenburg and Holstein October-December 1813

The Mecklenburg Campaign

After the French check at Göhrde, the allies found themselves in control of the territory between the Weser and the Elbe, and they sent Cossacks as far as Harburg. Wallmoden, however, moved his main force behind the Ietzel between Dannenberg and Dömitz on 19 September. He was still seriously outnumbered, and if Davout were to turn on him, he could be smashed.[1] Davout responded by organizing a mobile column of 500 men and two guns, under Major Hug, to escort provision convoys from Bremen and Stade.

On the other side, to contend with the allied forces before Harburg, Davout directed Major of Engineers Vinache to raise a strong bridgehead at Hope, on the left bank of the Elbe, and to reestablish the old fort there.[2]

Davout's forces had always occupied a position on the Stecknitz. Davout made frequent reconnaissances along that line and moved to Hamburg to oversee and hasten the efforts to fortify that city.

A large wooden bridge was raised completing communications with the island of Wilhelmsburg, which was established as a fortified larder for the city. Large numbers of cattle grazed within its protected boundaries. Numerous other fortification work continued night and day as Davout prepared for the possible investment. In addition, the old square fort "Sternschanz," on the Altona front, and the entrenched camp at Harburg, were high on his list of projects requiring attention.

General Lauberdière was charged with overseeing the preparations for putting the city of Bremen in a state of defense. He gathered the boats along the Weser and destroyed the bridge at Hoya.[3]

At Lübeck, Davout constructed 20 prefabricated blockhouses that were eventually moved to Hamburg where they became part of the city's defenses. Ten further blockhouses were built with larger dimensions and able to mount cannon. In addition, Major Vinache organized a bridgehead at Kronsforde and was charged with the preparation of works at Lübeck.

During the first half of October, military operations amounted to little more than reconnaissance efforts and tentative probes by both the allies and the French.[4] Before the village of Mölln, General Rome briefly engaged the allies, losing 40 men, while taking 150 prisoners and capturing a large number of cattle.

The French undertook a similar reconnaissance from the Hope bridgehead against Winsen. Wallmoden responded, committing parts of the Russo-German Legion (RGL) and the Hanoverian Brigade, supported by two batteries.[5] These found themselves facing by two voltigeur companies of the 30th Line Regiment in an earthwork in a swamp by Stecknitz. The French lost 30 men, but held the allies at bay.[6]

Wallmoden next sent a reconnaissance probe against Ratzeburg, and became engaged in a fight with a Danish advanced post at Kogel on 7 October. When Wallmoden's forces pushed through Seedorf and Sterley towards Kogel, the Danes abandoned their posts in Seedorf and their fleche by the Kogler windmill. Some Jägers and the skirmishers of the 1st Battalion, von Lützow Freikorps, then occupied a small woods with the intention of using those woods as a jumping-off point for an attack on Kogel. The Danish Major Späth responded by dispatching two Danish infantry companies to attack them. The Danish attack was successful, but the 1st Battalion, von Lützow Freikorps quickly counterattacked, supported by the 2nd Battalion, von Lützow Freikorps, and some Cossacks. The woods were cleared of the Danish infantry and the von Lützow Freikorps pursued them up to the main Danish position. Here the Germans were thrown back in confusion by heavy Danish musketry and were then attacked by a troop of Danish hussars. The allied forces fled the field with the Danish cavalry in pursuit. The Danes suffered six wounded; Wallmoden's forces lost about 70.[7]

During the same period, the French found themselves daily receiving deserters from the Russian army, whom they incorporated into the Lithuanian 17th Lancer Regiment.

Wallmoden's army was threatening a general attack. Davout responded by sending his main park to Mölln, behind the Stecknitz. He then reinforced his easternmost position with a few battalions and the cavalry of General Watier St-Alphonse. Watier was to patrol the region as far as Büchen; the responsibility for general defense was assigned to General Delcambre.[8]

On 12 October, the 2nd RGL Hussar Regiment stood in the advanced posts facing Mölln. The same day, GB Vichery dispatched the Danish Jutland Dragoon Regiment on a reconnaissance towards Gluckow. Between Segran and Rosengarten, the Danes encountered some Cossacks and hussars in green uniforms. The allied cavalry quickly withdrew with the 1/,2/Jutland Dragoons in pursuit. About 6:00 p.m., the noise of this engagement drew the attention of the 2nd RGL Hussars under von Dohna at Gallin.

The RGL Hussars advanced and threatened to move between the 1/,2/Jutland Dragoon Regiment and the 3/, 4/Jutland Dragoon Regiment. The Danes responded with a charge by the 3rd & 4th Squadrons, which the RGL Hussars accepted by standing and trying to stop it with carbine fire.

Their musketry failed to stop the Danish attack. Their discomfort was completed when the 1/, 2/Jutland Dragoon Regiment struck them in the flank. The RGL Hussars were routed from the field.

This skirmish was in the Danes' favor, as they lost five *hors de combat* for the 107 lost by Wallmoden's forces.[9]

The second half of October consisted of the same type of military operations. Throughout the month of October, the French were able to communicate with Bremen, Nienburg, and Minden. Provisions were regularly gathered in the area between Eutin and Lübeck, as well as all of the other territories they occupied. The French also held the two bridgeheads, one in Hope and the other in Harburg, giving them the ability to maneuver against Wallmoden as they might find fit.

After with Leipzig and the advance of the main allied armies, communications with France were quickly cut. This brought on, among other things, a financial crisis. Hard currency grew scarce and Davout found himself acting as a financier, arranging paper currency, bonds, and forced loans to support his army.

On 2 November, Hamburg finally found itself completely isolated from France by the allied advance into western Germany. Davout then began to shorten his lines by pulling his outlying forces back towards Hamburg. The Danes occupied Lübeck and Kronsforde, resting their right on the entrenched camp at Mölln. The French positions at Ratzeburg were destroyed. On 12 November, Loison moved his forces into reserve by Schwartzembeck.[10]

As the French destroyed the works at Ratzeburg, the allies decided to attack. On 13 November the 111th Line Regiment found itself under attack, successfully fought off its attackers, while

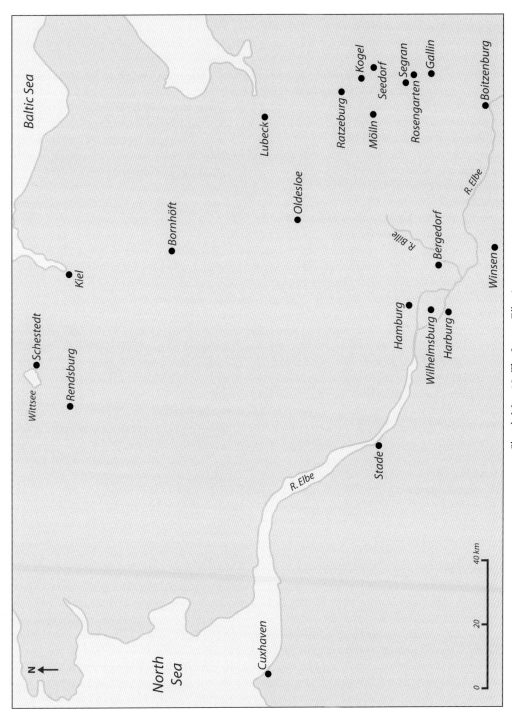

Sketch Map 12 The Lower Elbe Area.

inflicting heavy losses on the allies, because it was in fortified positions. The French pursuit after the battle was limited to a small cavalry affair.

As the month wore on, the French abandoned Carlsburg, Blexen, and Cuxhaven. On 27 November a large force of allies, about 4,000 men and 10 guns, moved against Stade, which was garrisoned by about 400 men of the 29th Line Regiment, a few customs officials, some dismounted cavalry, and some sailors.[11]

The allies advanced a column under the cover of their artillery and struck at the Bremervörde Gate. It was manned by 25 voltigeurs in an entrenchment. Three times the allies attacked and were thrown back by the French voltigeurs and their supporting artillery. The allies abandoned the fight and left 200 dead and wounded on the field. The allies then withdrew a short distance and began to bombard the tiny force of Frenchmen. After seven hours, and losing two guns dismounted by counterbattery fire, the allies gave up their attack and withdrew. None of the engagements in this period were conclusive.

Two days later the French abandoned Stade and withdrew all their supplies and material. The French, however, remained before Stecknitz, and Wallmoden ceased any further activities until Bernadotte and Bennigsen arrived with their corps. He sent a division to Harburg, 2,000 men to Winsen, and a force to face Zollenspicker. The remainder of his corps remained in his main line.

Davout profited by this period of allied inactivity by sending part of the 3rd Division to Hamburg and preparing palisade sections that were used as rafts and floated to Hamburg with tiny crews drawn from the 61st Line Regiment.[12]

Bernadotte and Bennigsen crossed the Elbe at Boitzenburg in boats and moved against Mölln, causing the French to pull back to Hamburg.

On 2 December all the sluices on the Stecknitz were destroyed, as well as the bridgehead at Mölln and the batteries on both banks of the Elbe. The French then withdrew behind the Bille River. The works at Hope were destroyed after its garrison fell back behind Bergedorf.

The allies then moved the bulk of their forces north, against Lübeck and Oldesloe, in an effort to cut the communications between the Danes and the French. Davout wrote to Prince Friedrich von Hessen, the Danish commander, offering to cooperate militarily with him, if the Prince was not already in negotiations with the allies. The situation of the Danish army prevented any cooperation.[13]

Davout pulled his forces back to a defensive position. Because the Prince von Hessen was unable to cooperate, Davout allowed the allies to pass to the north relatively unmolested. Wallmoden's Corps moved aggressively northwards, pursuing the Danish corps as it withdrew.

The Skirmish at Bornhöft

On 7 December Wallmoden's lead elements caught up with the retreating Danes near Bornhöft.[14] The French general Lallemand, with the advanced guard and a small force of cavalry stood three-quarters of a mile from Daldorf. The 1/, 3/Jutland Regiment led the march with a battery and was covered by the battalion of sharpshooters. They were followed by four squadrons of the Holstein Heavy Cavalry Regiment, advancing in two columns, and a force of the 17th Lithuanian Uhlan Regiment. Prince Friedrich had posted his 1st Brigade by Bornhöft. The 3/, 4/Holstein Regiment and two guns from the Gönner Battery were deployed in echelons on the hills to the north of the village. A Jäger company from the 4/Oldenburg and a second Jäger company from the Slesvigske Jägerkorps, plus Spath's 6th Hussar Squadron stood in the village. The remainder of the 1st Brigade stood in reserve and the 2nd Brigade waited in march columns further to the rear.

It is at Bornhöft that the terrain changes from the open plains of Holstein and Mecklenburg into the closed terrain so common in Schleswig. As a result, much of the land is broken by diked roads and fenced fields. It was in the broken and enclosed fields around Bornhöft that the Danes chose to fight.

The Swedish general Skjöldebrand began the engagement by sending forward two squadrons of the von Schill Hussars under Major von der Lancken to hold the Danes in position. The Swedish cavalry engaged the Poles in a skirmish fight with their carbines. About 3:00 p.m., the supporting force of approximately 900 Swedish cavalry arrived at the trot and moved towards Daldorf. Four squadrons of the Mörner Hussars moved to the right, while one of the Schonen and two of the von Schill Hussar squadrons moved to the left and formed by half-squadrons. A second line was formed by two squadrons of the Schonen-Karabiniers and three squadrons of the Schonen Hussars. The remainder of the Swedish cavalry remained too far to the rear to intervene in the battle.

Faced with a larger enemy cavalry force, Lallemand withdrew his forces into the village of Bornhöft and took up the strongest positions he could. The 1/3rd Jutland Infantry Regiment occupied the churchyard in the center of the village while the 1/Holstein Skarpskytterkorps[15] (253 rank and file) deployed to the west of the road and the 2/Holstein Skarpskytterkorps (483 rank and file) deployed to the east.

The light troops of the 2nd Brigade pushed into the village and formed a skirmish line in front of these two battalions while two guns from the Gerstenberg battery positioned themselves close to the southern entrance of the village.

Having deployed his rearguard, Lallemand's Brigade lead, followed by the Danish artillery, then the Holstein Regiment, and finally the Poles through the village.

The Swedish cavalry moved to the attack, charging the Danes in the village. Skjöldebrand took one and a half squadrons into the pass leading into Bornhöft and his two wings attacked the Danish formations to the east and west of the road. The Danish guns were quickly overrun because the limber drivers fled, taking their limbers with them. The gunners, left with only ball shot and no canister, were unable to hold their positions.

With the guns in Swedish hands, the hussars attacked the Poles. The Polish cavalry, however, could not deploy because of the narrow village streets. Instead they lowered their lances and tried to force their way through the Holstein cavalry, who were in turn blocked by the guns in front of them.

The Swedish hussars forced their way into the confused mass only to discover there was no room for them to use their weapons, and the fight became a tangled mass.

To the west the Prussians report that the 2/Holstein Regiment met the Swedes with musketry and inflicted heavy losses on them, while standing its ground bravely. The Danes contend that it was ridden down while trying to form square. By Danish accounts this force of Swedish hussars then forced their way into the confused mass in the streets of Bornhöft, adding to the confusion.

Quistorp goes on to relate that the 1/Holstein Regiment stood in closed column before the village, covered by the Schleswig Jäger Company. The 2/Holstein Regiment fell back beside its sister battalion and together they waited for the Swedes. The Swedes attacked and were greeted with concentrated musketry at a range of 12-20 paces. The Swedish cavalry lost badly and Skjöldebrand quickly realized that he stood little chance and withdrew his forces. The Danes lost a total of about 66 men and three cannon, while the allies lost four officers and 96 men.[16]

In contrast, Danish records relate that the 1/Holstein Regiment withstood two attacks and then collapsed. It withdrew and then reformed on the Neumunster road.

The 3rd Jutland Regiment had remained in the churchyard during the first phase of the battle. However, after receiving an order from one of Lallemand's aides it moved into the swirling mass of confusion in the streets of Bornhöft.

As the tangled mass of fighting humanity flowed out of the village it was greeted by the fire of the 2nd Danish Brigade. The Danes and Poles quickly separated themselves from their attackers and pulled clear. The remaining Swedish hussars received volley after volley from the Danish squares and withdrew to the rear.

The Danes give their losses at 11 killed, 45 wounded, and 75 missing, while claiming 80 Swedes *hors de combat*.[17]

As the Swedes withdrew, the Danish brigade began its withdrawal, withdrawing to the north, towards Denmark. The Danish army was not concentrated when the battle at Bornhöft occurred, but Prince Friedrich von Hessen realized that the allies were close and pulled his forces together as quickly as he could, while continuing to retire north. The next engagement was to occur at Schestedt on 10 December.

The Battle at Schestedt

The Prince of Hessen decided to withdraw to the Rendsburg Fortress instead of continuing north. Wallmoden, pursuing the Danes, assumed that they would continue their withdrawal northwards and advanced his forces along a parallel course. These two movements resulted in the Danes turning into Wallmoden's Corps as it was spread along the road north and catching it widely dispersed. As the Danes rammed their train through Schestedt, Wallmoden tried to fix them there while he hoped Skjöldebrand would strike them in the rear and Dörnberg (Wallmoden's advanced guard) would turn around and attack the Danish northern flank.

Schestedt straddles the road from Gettorf to Rendsburg, at the intersection of the road from Cluvensick. It lies on the northern side of the Eider River, where two large ox-bow bends almost meet. However, by Steinwehr, to the west of Schestedt, the Eider River had been artificially rerouted through a man-made canal. This canal runs approximately southeast through the villages of Osterrade and Cluvensick. Just north of Osterrade, the old Eider River bed swings almost due north to Schestedt. From there it swings to the east again, only to swing due south in about a mile. Once moving south, it rejoins the new canal. Slightly south of Osterrade, the Eider canal swings northeast and runs towards the Baltic Sea. Northwest of Schestedt lies the massive Wittensee Lake. The lake is connected to the Eider through a canal that runs from Bünsdorf, on the western edge of the lake, south to Schrinau, on another of the many lakes on the Eider's course. Another stream feeds into the Wittensee due north of Schestedt and runs northeast and disappears near Holtsee, about two miles from Wittensee.

The roads through the region cross in Schestedt. The main east-west road runs along the north side of the Eider River and passes through Schestedt, where it meets the major north-south road. From Schestedt this road moves south, along the western bank of the old Eider River bed, crosses it at Osterrade, then goes across the new Eider Canal to Cluvensick. As a result, any force wishing to cross the Eider and interdict the east-west road must pass through Osterrade and across the old Eider.

Schestedt lies near the highest point of ground in the immediate vicinity, and as a result, dominates the surrounding territory. To the north, between the road and the old Eider, stood a noble's house with stout walls, suitable for a strong defense. The remaining houses were nothing particularly significant.

The Danes began their march at 1:00 a.m. Lallemand led the 1st Brigade in the advanced guard, followed by the 2nd Brigade with the headquarters, and finally the train covered by the 1/Schleswig, two companies of the 2/Oldenburg, the Jägers of the 2/Fünen, and a squadron of Fünen light dragoons.

The first engagement occurred when Lallemand captured Wardenburg's train just outside of Haby. This forced Wardenburg to stop his advance and turn around to face the threat. The Danes deployed the 1/Dronningen, the Jägers of the 2/Dronningen, the 3/, 4/Holstein, and the 2/Danish Hussar Regiment to counter Wardenburg's and Dörnberg's forces in Haby.

The Danish 2nd Brigade drove three companies of their Jägers into Schestedt, where they encountered von der Goltz's dismounted 1st RGL Hussar Regiment. Rittmeisters von Simolin and von der

Horst each detached a Zug from their squadrons and sent them forward as skirmishers, to occupy the hedges before Schestedt and one of the houses. The remaining hussars were withdrawn behind the village, to hold the horses of the dismounted hussars. Despite the fact that the hussars were armed only with carbines, they were able to discourage the Danish Jägers from rushing the village.

While the skirmish fight in Schestedt continued, Wallmoden brought forward the rest of his infantry. The first to arrive were small numbers of men from the 1st and 2nd RGL Battalions, detached as skirmishers, and totaling no more than 60 to 80 men. They were immediately sent into the village to support the hussars, bringing the total allied strength holding the village to about 200 men.[18]

The Danish Jägers withdrew to Holtsee and deployed, covering the rest of the Danish corps as it formed for an attack. South of the Holtsee Mill marched the 2/Schleswig Jäger and 2/Holstein Sharpshooters of General Lallemand. Behind them the 3rd Jutland Regiment formed in line. Further to the rear the Oldenburg Regiment stood in column on the road, the 1/Schleswig and the 1/Fünen Regiments stood to their right. Further to the rear the 2/Fünen Regiment remained on the road with the Koye, Friis, and Gönner Batteries. The Danish cavalry, 6th Hussar Squadron, 2/, 3/, 4/Fünen Light Dragoons, 2/, 3/Holstein Cavalry, were held in reserve behind the 1/Schleswig and 1/Fünen.

Gerstenberg's Battery was covered by a line battalion next to the mill. The 1st Brigade sent the 1/Dronningen and 3/, 4/Holstein Infantry Regiments and the 2/Jutland Hussars to the heights northwest of Holtsee, to cover their right flank against a move by Oberstleutnant Wardenburg and General von Dörnberg through the heights by Gross-Wittensee. Two guns of Gerstenberg's battery were posted on those heights.

The remaining forces[19] moved down the highway in line with the advanced guard and formed an attack column. Two battalions of the 2nd Brigade[20] marched, in the same manner, down the right side of the road supporting a skirmish line. Their cavalry and artillery remained on the road as a reserve, and their wagon train followed them at some distance. The defiles through Holtsee were being held by two squadrons of the 17th Lithuanian Uhlans and the Holstein Cavalry Regiment. These two cavalry formations also watched the rear of the wagon train.[21]

The next allied forces to arrive were the Anhalt-Dessau Battalion and the 6th and 7th RGL Battalions, plus Wiering's Battery. Oberstleutnant von der Goltz took command of the Anhalt-Dessau and 6th RGL Battalions and two howitzers from Wiering's Battery. The 6th RGL Battalion was immediately sent forward in column through the village, with its schützen division 500 paces in front of it. The schützen moved down the road to Haby. The Anhalt-Dessau Battalion and the two guns were placed in the church to hold that point, while the 7th RGL Battalion was sent to Osterrade on the left bank of the northern ox-bow of the old Eider, to prevent the Danes from using that passage.[22]

About 9:00 a.m., the skirmishers of the two Danish light battalions split and moved to the right to Haby Moor, and to the left to the Eider, where they encountered the 6th RGL Battalion. A lively musketry fight began between them. The detachments of Lieutenants Boden and Schleiter held the woods on the banks of the Eider with the 6th RGL Battalion. The Danes struck them with two companies detached from the 4/Oldenburg Regiment, supported by the Gerstenberg battery. The 7th RGL Battalion found itself stuck on the other side of the Eider, behind a swamp, and was unable to join the battle.[23]

The Danish skirmishers engaged those of the 6th RGL Battalion and drove them and their parent battalion back. Twelve Danish guns were brought up to join the battle and the two guns of Wiering's Battery, standing to the left of a hedge, dismounted one of the Danish guns. The Anhalt-Dessau Battalion was drawn into the battle as the defense of the village began in earnest.

Prince Friedrich von Hessen felt it was time for his main assault on the village and organized the 1/, 4/Oldenburg Regiment[24] into an attack column, covered by skirmishers at a distance of 100 paces. The column advanced to attack the village. The light battalion of the advanced guard was slowly whittled down by allied musketry, and soon the Oldenburg Regiment began to suffer heavy casualties from the defensive fire of the 6th RGL Battalion. The grenadier company, which led the attack, suffered 28 casualties from a total strength of 95 men.[25]

Nonetheless, Danish attack was successful enough to force the allies to withdraw to the south side of the village, though not to throw them out of the village altogether. The Danes had, however, opened the way through Schestedt by 10:30 a.m., and were beginning to move through the village.

Schestedt was occupied by three companies of the Oldenburg Regiment, supported by seven guns, and various light troops. Behind the Oldenburg Regiment stood the Fünen Light Dragoon Regiments, the Fünen and the 1/3rd Jutland Infantry Regiments, three companies from the 1/ Schleswig Regiment, and four guns. To the north of Schestedt stood the Holstein Cavalry Regiment, the Gönner Battery, and guns detached from other batteries.

Wallmoden was still unable to trap the Danes. By 11:00 a.m., he did not have all of his force in position. Vegesack's Advanced Guard was closing and consisted of 10½ battalions, 10 squadrons, and 18 guns. A detachment from this force was placed by Cluvensick, in case the Danes sought to escape through that defile.

The 1st Infantry Brigade of Wallmoden's Corps was sent forward. The 1st RGL Hussar Regiment withdrew over the Osterrade Bridge, where it encountered a strong force of Danes. The 1st and 2nd RGL Battalions were sent to the left in the hedgerows in an effort to cut the Rendsburg Road, but quickly encountered the 1/Fünen Regiment of the 2nd Danish Brigade.

The 5th RGL Battalion, supported by two guns of the Wiering Battery, was stopped as it attempted to advance through the defile filled with wagons and Danish 1st Hussars. General von Arentschildt ordered it to move against Schestedt with bayonets. The battalion was organized in a column by sections and sent forward. As the last section of the column advanced over the bridge into the village, it began to take artillery fire from a Danish battery to the west of Schestedt. The fire of the battery and the advance up the hill with heavy packs was more than the 5th RGL Battalion could handle and it came apart, though its men continued advancing as a disorganized mob. On either side of the collapsing column, small groups of schützen advanced to engage the Danes. The two guns of the Wiering Battery fired from the left of the road in support of the advance.

On the southern side of Schestedt part of the Danish Oldenburg Regiment faced the 5th RGL Battalion. A Danish howitzer discharged two rounds of canister into the 5th RGL Battalion. The Danes fell back to the next ditch and continued their defense of the village. The continued Danish defense was left to a few skirmishers under Lieutenant von Grandville and a veteran sergeant from the 3rd Company, 1st Battalion.[26]

The 2/, 3/, 4/Fünen Dragoon Regiment, 2nd Danish Brigade, came up in their long red capes and charged the advancing RGL column, driving it back. Part of the 1st and 2nd Companies of the 5th RGL clumped together in the open field in a tight knot,[27] while the remainder of the battalion was scattered by the charging dragoons. The Danish infantry then reorganized itself and advanced against the remaining RGL infantry, capturing many of them. A small force of RGL infantry, however, found shelter in a house, and under the command of Captain von Uslar-Gleichen, defended themselves against the Danes. The two howitzers of Wiering's battery were overrun as their gunners either abandoned their guns or were sabered where they stood.

The Danish cavalry pushed to the Osterrade bridge, where they were engaged by the 6th RGL Battalion and the Dessau Battalion. The Danes pushed back these two battalions, badly cutting up the Dessau Battalion in the process, and drove into the enclosures where the 1st and 2nd RGL Battalions stood. Here the Danes were met with a heavy skirmish fire and lost many men.

When the attack was over the Danes had annihilated the 5th RGL Battalion and savaged the Dessau Battalion. The Danish dragoons broke the allied advance, but at a high cost to themselves and they required the help of the 1/Fünen and 1/Schleswig Regiments, which advanced to assist their withdrawal with the two guns of the Wiering Battery and the 300 prisoners they had taken.[28]

About noon Rittmeister von Simolin, of the 1st RGL Hussar Regiment, brought his force to the Cluvensick defile. As his regiment arrived at the Osterrade bridge, the road became so narrow that he could only advance his regiment in a column four men wide. It was in that formation that he led his men forward in an attack against the Danes. The 1st RGL Hussars quickly came under fire and swerved to the side, moving through the village gardens and over hedges. They captured one Danish dragoon and 20-30 draft horses, before they withdrew to their original position. As they withdrew, so did the shattered remains of the 5th RGL and 6th Battalions, and the Dessau Battalion.[29]

Around 11:00 a.m., the last forces of General von Vegesack's advanced guard were thrown into the battle. The Bennigsen Battalion and both RGL Horse Batteries were posted in Cluvensick, on the left bank of the Eider canal. Behind them stood the three squadrons of Mecklenburg Mounted Jägers and the Bremen-Verden Hussars, in reserve behind the 1st RGL Hussar Regiment.

The two other battalions of Halkett's Brigade, the Lauenburg (3rd) and Langrehr (5th) Battalions, as well as Holtzermann's detachment of the King's German Legion (KGL), the 7th RGL Battalion, and the Mecklenburg Fussjägers stood by Osterrade. Behind them the remains of the 5th RGL Battalion, as well as the 6th RGL and Dessau Battalions, rallied and reorganized themselves.[30]

The allies prepared a second assault into Schestedt. The Lauenburg (3rd) Battalion and Holtzermann's KGL Detachment advanced over the bridge. They advanced in doubled squads across the bridge to be met by a hail of canister from two Danish guns sitting in the village. The Danish battery to the west of Schestedt also joined in, and forced the entire battalion to deploy into skirmish order behind the hedges at the edge of the village. Holtzermann moved to the right wing of the battalion and a lively skirmish battle began.

The 7th RGL Battalion and a company of Mecklenburg Fussjäagers advanced across the bridge to join the fray. As they advanced, Prince Friedrich von Hessen sent forward yet another Danish cavalry assault with the 2/, 3/, 4/Fünen Dragoons and 6/Jutland Hussar Regiment.

The Fünen Dragoons plunged through the Lauenburg (3rd) Battalion's position, and before them stood the battalion's flag, unprotected. Lieutenant Colonel Halkett, an Englishman, cried out that the flag was in danger and led forward a small force of mounted officers. Also a small force of infantry, responding to Halkett's German cries, rushed forward to protect their standard. Quickly 40-50 men gathered around the flag, defending it. They then quickly withdrew towards the bridge to escape the Danish cavalry.[31]

The Danish dragoons drove down the street again and struck the 7th RGL Battalion, disordering it and throwing it back. The Mecklenburg Fussjägers under Hauptmann von Brandt, had moved out of the dragoons' path, now began to pepper the Danes with fire.

Then Wallmoden sent the three squadrons of the Mecklenburg Mounted Jägers over the bridge. Under the command of Prince Gustav von Mecklenburg, they passed over the bridge, then quickened their pace to the gallop. They drove the Danish hussars and dragoons before them, pushed through the skirmish line formed by the Oldenburg Infantry Regiment, and advanced against the Danish guns on the southern end of the village.

Despite that success, the Mecklenburg Mounted Jägers quickly found themselves under fire from the Fünen and Schleswig Infantry Regiments and the various Danish cannon that could be brought to bear. The Danish resistance was too much. Prince Gustav fell, struck by four musket balls, and was bayoneted. The Mecklenburgers sounded the recall and withdrew back across the bridge. The Danish fire, however, was so intense that many chose to ride back through the fields and over the hedges, rather than attempt to pass through the village streets. As they rallied, it was found that nearly all the horses in the regiment were either killed or wounded.

This unsuccessful attack Mecklenburg Mounted Jägers resulted in heavy casualties in the 7th RGL Battalion, the Lauenburg (3rd) Battalion, and the Mecklenburg Mounted Jäger Regiment. Holtzermann's KGL Detachment lost its commander and a small number of men. The Mecklenburg Fussjägers also lost a small number of dead and wounded in the various skirmish fighting. Despite losses of the attack, the Lauenburg and 7th RGL Battalions gained from it by reforming their shattered ranks.

The 1st and 2nd RGL Battalions found themselves facing part of the 2nd Danish Brigade, supported by a battery in the village and a four-gun battery on the right. The advance of the 1st and 2nd RGL Battalions had quickly degenerated into a skirmish fight, at a range of 200 paces. They, too, found themselves attacked by the Fünen Dragoons, who inflicted a few casualties on them, but not the level of damage suffered by the other units the Fünen. Dragoons had struck earlier in the engagement.[32]

About 1:00 p.m., Natzmer's 1st Brigade was ordered forward in a bayonet attack against the village of Schestedt. They advanced forward to find themselves faced by the two companies of the Danish 2/Fünen Infantry Regiment. Though these Danish companies had nearly exhausted their ammunition; a musketry battle erupted.

Prince Friedrich von Hessen responded by sending forward the 1/Dronningen and 3/, 4/Holstein Infantry Regiments, as well as the 2/, 3/Holstein Cavalry, in an attack like those executed against the other RGL battalions. The Danish cavalry attack was too much, and Natzmer pulled his 1st Brigade back across the Eider bridge.[33]

The Danes followed Natzmer in two columns, one down the main street and the other on the canal, in the direction of the upper fields. The 1st Brigade moved to the Eider, with Danish artillery fire pounding them as they withdrew. Earlier, the 1st RGL Horse Battery had assumed a position to the south of the canal, to cover the allied advance. Two guns under Lieutenant von Schwerin stood by Culvensick to cover the bridge, and two others stood on the heights to the left, under Premier-leutnant Ramaer. They were able to cover the Eider, and the ground as far as Schestedt. However, there was not sufficient clear space to allow the deployment of the remaining two guns, so they were held in reserve. At 2:00 p.m., when Natzmer's 1st Brigade withdrew back over the bridge, the two guns under Ramaer began to fire on the pursuing Danish columns. RGL skirmishers and the Mecklenburg Jägers in Osterrade moved up to the river and fired at the Danes, until darkness fell. Two Danish batteries moved forward and exchanged fire with Ramaer's two guns, but the result was limited to two dead horses and one wounded gunner.[34]

While the Danes were pushing Natzmer back, their wagon train poured through Schestedt and down the road to Rendsburg, led by the line brigade and with Lallemand's forces acting as a rearguard. By 5:00 p.m., the wagon train was in Mühlberg, where it stayed until midnight.

At 4:00 p.m., Vegesack moved his division to the windmill heights by Bovenau. The Mecklenburg Jägers stood in the advanced posts and the remainder of Wallmoden's forces pulled back behind Bovenau. Only the Bennigsen (4th) Battalion remained immediately behind Cluvensick.

The Fighting by Haby

During the battle of Schestedt the 2nd RGL Brigade found itself engaged with the Danish flanking forces around the village of Haby. In order to reach Schestedt, Oberstleutnant Wardenburg had to pass through Haby. In addition to the Danish forces facing him, Wardenburg had to pass through a marshy woods and cross a small stream, before he reached Haby. Even, if he were to take Haby, he would have to cross yet another stream to be able to move against the Danish line of retreat through Holtsee.

As the RGL moved forward, it encountered two squadrons of the 17th Lithuanian Uhlan Regiment, which were defending the flank of the wagon train. Having no cavalry, Wardenburg was at a distinct disadvantage. The Danes, however, chose to use the Uhlans to usher the wagon train forward, while replacing them in the line facing Wardenburg, with four companies of lagers.[35]

Once in place, the Jägers began a skirmish battle with Wardenburg's two battalions, pinning them in place. Meanwhile, Prince Friedrich von Hessen detached the 1/Dronningen, 3/, 4/ Holstein Regiment, the lager company of the 2/Dronningen Regiment, the 2/Jutland Hussars, and two cannon from Schulenburg's Brigade and sent them to a ridge northwest of Holtsee, where they could face any threat from that direction.

His advance stymied, Wardenburg called for assistance from Dörnberg's forces to the north. Dörnberg responded by sending only the Kielmansegge Jägers forward to assist him. The skirmish battle intensified, with the two sides separated by a distance of about 200 paces.

Combat continued like this until about noon, when the Danes chose to break off the engagement and withdraw their forces. The first to go were the three line battalions. Once they were safely away, the Jägers also withdrew. Wardenburg encouraged them on their way with a quick rush of bayonets, but that attack amounted to little but window dressing. The battle was already over and the Danes had accomplished what they wanted.

The cost of the battle of Schestedt had not been too frightful. According to Quistorp the Danes lost about 17 officers and 531 men *hors de combat*. The allies lost 25 officers and 543 killed and wounded, plus 598 taken prisoners.[36] The allies also lost two guns to the Danes, but the Danes did abandon one dismounted gun to the allies as they withdrew.

Pursuit and Armistice

The Danish corps continued its withdrawal northward, with Wallmoden in a leisurely pursuit. On 11 December Wallmoden's forces found themselves on the road from Rendsburg to Kiel. Arentschildt's Division stood around the Westensee, with its divisional headquarters in Nienhof. Lyon's Division stood between the lake and Nortorf. The Hanseatic forces watched Rendsburg from Cluvensick to Ievenstedt.

On 12 December Wallmoden's advanced guard moved from Marienthal to a position between Eckernförde and the Wittensee Lake. Schestedt was occupied by the 3rd and 4th RGL Battalions. The allies remained in this position until 16 December, when they learned of the signing of the armistice between Denmark and the allies. Wallmoden's Corps settled down into its bivouacs until a definitive peace was signed. On 18 January 1814, they marched south to join in the siege of Hamburg and Harburg.[37]

15

The Siege of Danzig 15 August-31 December 1813

Spring in Danzig

In January 1813 the French had fallen back from Russia and the shattered remains of several divisions fell back to Danzig, seeking shelter from the weather and the Cossacks. On 12 January, the Cossacks were in Marienburg, ready to cross the Vistula and move on Danzig. Platov had quickly begun to press the French forces under General Rapp. Rapp withdrew into Danzig and by 21 January, found himself under siege by Platov's forces. Once in Danzig, he found himself commanding Destrées' 33rd Division (Neapolitans), Grandjean's 7th Division of the X Corps, and the 30th Division and 34th Division of the XI Corps.[1] Though summoned to surrender, Rapp refused.

On 5 January, Wittgenstein's Corps detached a corps under the command of GL Steingel and sent it to assist in the blockade of Danzig. Steingel's force consisted of the 5,000 men forming the 25th Infantry Division, reinforced with militia and Cossacks. GL Steingel was shortly relieved of command of the blockade force by GL Lewis. Wittgenstein established himself in a provisional position at Dirschau, with 11-12,000 to screen the siege of Danzig. In addition Platov's Corps was dissolved, part of it being sent to join the Danzig blockade operation.

GD Rapp began preparing for what was to become a year long siege. During the spring the garrison was reorganized into three divisions in Danzig, which kept their designations as the 7th, 30th, and 33rd Divisions. The remains of the old 34th Division were incorporated into the 30th Division.

Rapp set about preparing the defense of the city, improving its fortifications, flooding approaches to the city, and setting about the classical defenses for a protracted siege, that would be fought much as sieges had been fought for the previous 100 years.

Because of the political and economic importance of Danzig, as well as his desire to recover the thousands of veteran troops locked up there, during the spring Napoleon had developed elaborate plans to relieve Danzig. In a letter dated 11 March, Napoleon explained to Eugène his thoughts. He counted on converging at the beginning of May, Ney's Armée du Mein at Würzburg, Erfurt, and Leipzig. The Armée de l'Elbe, under Eugène, would be at Magdeburg, holding Havelberg and Wittenberg. Napoleon presumed that at the same time the allied army would be still to the east of the Elbe, stretched between Danzig and Glogau.[2]

If these conditions existed, the goal of the French army would be to march immediately to the succor of the garrison of Danzig. The entire Armée de l'Elbe, followed by the Armée du Mein, would march by Havelberg on Stettin. After having made feints to cause the allies to believe that he was moving on Dresden and into Silesia, he intended to move through Havelberg and on to Stettin with a force of 300,000 men, using the Thuringian mountains as a screen. Once there he would continue his march on Danzig, where he estimated this force would arrive in 15 days, 20 days after crossing the Elbe. Once there he would break the siege of Danzig, take Marienburg, the

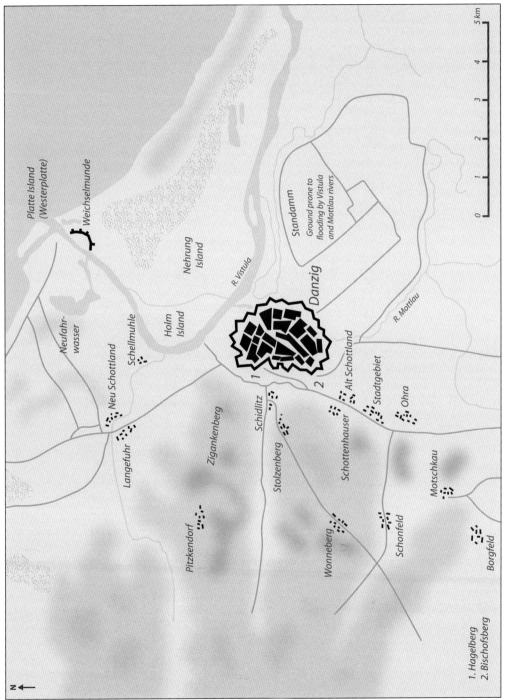

Platte Island
(Westerplatte)

Weichselmunde

Neufahr-
wasser

Neu Schottland

Schellmuhle

Holm
Island

Nehrung
Island

R. Vistula

Standamm

Ground prone to
flooding by Vistula
and Mottlau rivers

Danzig

R. Mottlau

Alt Schottland

Stadtgebiet

Ohra

1

2

Langefuhr

Zigankenberg

Schidlitz

Stolzenberg

Schottenhauser

Motschkau

Pitzkendorf

Wonneberg

Schonfeld

Borgfeld

1. Hagelberg
2. Bischofsberg

N

0   1   2   3   4   5 km

Sketch Map 13 Danzig in 1813.

island of Nogat, and all the bridges on the lower Vistula. This would free 50,000 veteran soldiers that were trapped in various garrisons and provide a tremendous reinforcement for his army, as well as making good the losses of the long march.[3]

However, this was not to come about and the near term fate of Danzig was covered in the armistice of Plesswitz signed on 4 June 1813. Article Five addressed Danzig and several other cities. It stated that "the cities of Danzig, Modlin, Zamosc, Stettin, and Cüstrin shall be reprovisioned every five days, according to the strength of their garrisons, by the efforts of the commander of the besieging forces." Formal contacts were to be arranged between the garrison and the besieging allied forces, to ensure conformance to that and other regulations. Couriers were allowed to pass between Napoleon and Rapp.

The summer passed with Rapp preparing his positions even more strongly, including several redoubts, earthworks and forts. At the same time, the allies erected a string of redoubts across his front. His forces were drilled and organized to meet the coming battles.

The Resumption of Hostilities

On 6 August, GL Prince Wolkonski sent Rapp a letter advising him that the armistice was broken and that hostilities were about to resume.[4] No doubt this was a professional courtesy and not an officially required action. It did not matter that hostilities on the main front were not to resume until 16 August, war had returned to Danzig.

As the blockade resumed, Danzig stood as a large, entrenched camp. Three works were built behind Zigankenberg, which were to protect the French advanced posts and stood on the left of the camp. Three others stood to the left of the road to Langfuhr. Another line of defenses ran to the Vistula River, where there were two more mutually supporting works.

An old brick works standing on the left bank of the Vistula was demolished and converted into a redoubt. The various works around the front of the camp were Battery Kirgener, Isteria Lunette, Battery Caulaincourt, Battery Romeuf, Battery Grabowsky, Battery Deroy, Battery Montbrun, Battery Fiszer (on the Langfuhr road), and Battery Gudin.

With the exception of the Isteria Lunette, which stood a bit forward, by the Kirgener and Caulaincourt Batteries, the first seven of these works were placed on the hills that offered any approaching enemy the greatest difficulties possible.

Their forms were basically those of lunettes or detached redans, but they were modified to meet the particular requirements of the terrain, so as to make them more defensible. Kirgener and Caulaincourt were surrounded by a covered way, to ensure their communications with the Isteria Lunette. The others remained detached to permit the X Corps to sally forward in columns and act against the allies as necessary. Later other works were raised on the Holm Island, to flank the right of the entrenched camp. The left was equally defended against surprise by the construction by several barracks behind the Kirgener Battery.[5]

The entrenched camp covered Hagelsberg as well, and through the Isteria Lunette and Kirgener Battery, extended its control across the Stolzenberg plateau. Those two works would, by virtue of their position, enfilade any allied entrenchments by Bischofsberg or oblige the allies to move to the left, which was covered by the two bastions Medloch and Gertrude, the demi-lune on the front of the fortress and the Lasalle Redoubt. And so it went, around the city of Danzig, one bastion or redoubt after another, crossing fields of fire, entrenchments, abatis, and every trick of the craft of siege warfare was deployed to defend the city.

With the resumption of hostilities Rapp set up his advanced posts as follows:

Ohra, Alt-Schottland, and vicinity	600 men
Schidlitz and Stolzenberg	250
Fort Napoleon	82
Heubude	103
Weichselmünde	387[6]

The First Attack

Despite the strength of the French position, the allies were not to leave it alone and content themselves with a blockade. On 28 August, at 8:00 a.m., the Russians gathered 400 men[7] behind their redoubt (No. 2) near Ohra, to assault the French post in a small woods before Ohra.

Major Legros, with 200 men forming two grenadier companies[8] of the 7th Demi-brigade, stood in reserve by Alt-Schottland. As the Russian attack advanced, Major Legros led his men forward and drove the Russians back. However, a strong Prussian support group advanced. At 10:00 a.m., they had pushed Major Legros' force and the original defenders back and were on the verge of seizing the woods.

The French reserves, under Capitaine Capgran, then moved against the allied right along the main road, while another part of the reserves, under Major Legros moved forward against the woods. The Russians and Prussians were unable to withstand the assault and fell back.

The French resumed their positions in the woods, only to find themselves assaulted a third and a fourth time by the allied forces. The fight, however, was little more than a small skirmish, and despite its ferocity and often hand to hand combat, the French lost only six dead and one officer and 22 soldiers wounded. The French estimated the allied losses at 30 dead and wounded, but the allies had recovered their casualties, so a count was impossible.[9]

On 29 August, on a day that was marked by heavy rain, the allies probed a second time. They formed four regiments of Russian infantry and a Cossack regiment into two columns, which attacked Langfuhr. One column advanced through the village towards Stries, while the other moved against the Heiligenbrun heights.

The small French posts in Langfuhr and the surrounding fields withdrew into two blockhouses,[10] where they took up positions. The Russians assaulted both houses, but the defensive fire of the grenadiers of the 11th Polish Infantry Regiment held them at bay. After heavy losses, they began to withdraw as Capitaine Kmita, of the 11th Polish Regiment, pushed them with a bayonet attack.

The Russians withdrew back to the heights that overlooked Langfuhr and brought forward two guns. The Russian artillery began to fire down the road and stopped the Polish counterattack. Prince Radziwill advanced his reserves to Aller-Engel and Kabrun, with four guns, to face this new allied threat. However, the allied position was too strong and he was forced to withdraw back to his original positions.

It was 7:00 a.m., when the Russians once again advanced and occupied Grand Belvedere (a high point of ground) where the French maintained a post only during the day. Rapp arrived and directed Chef de bataillon Szembeck's Battalion of the 11th Polish Regiment to take the position. The attack was successful and the Russians fell back before the superior Polish forces.

The Russians then gathered their forces to make a more serious attempt on Langfuhr. They organized a large force of infantry and cavalry supported by 15 guns, and sent it forward between Pitzkendorf and Brentau. The Russians had serious intentions of taking Langfuhr and Rapp, determined to anticipate them, prepared to march out and meet their attacks with his main force.[11]

Colonel Kamienski, 10th Polish Regiment, moved forward with part of his regiment to support the 11th Polish Regiment, which was engaging the Russians behind Langfuhr, in the gorge of the Jeschkenthal Valley and before the Petit Belvedere (high point of ground).

At the same instant, the Russians sent forward two columns by Stries, supporting them with a battery behind the village. A lively firefight began all along the line and it continued to be intense until about 11:00 a.m., when it began to slacken.[12]

The Russians began to indicate, through their movements, that they were making a serious attempt to take Langfuhr. Rapp decided not to surrender this piece of ground, and ordered the Poles not to begin their attack on the Grand Belvedere (high point) and Johannisberg, until they were specifically ordered to do so.

In an effort to embarrass the Russian attack, Rapp decided to attack himself from the side of Pitzkendorf. He decided to strike the center of the allied forces on the Pitzkendorf plateau and those in the Königsthal Valley.

He deployed his forces as follows. Colonel Kamienski, with two battalions of the 10th Polish Regiment and two of the 11th Polish, was to remain before Langfuhr. The rest of the 7th Division, under General Grandjean, was placed in the ravines by Zigankenberg, with the cavalry supported on its left by the 34th Division, which was under General Bachelu. General Destrées with the 33rd Division covered the right and observed Langfuhr. Finally, the 30th Division, under General Heudelet, occupied Schidlitz and Stolzenberg and served as a reserve.[13]

Twenty-four guns, commanded by General Lepin were placed in the middle and between the two wings. Two six gun batteries took positions on the Zigankenberg plateau and began firing on the allied redoubts, on the Pitzkendorf camp, and on their massed infantry. The two Russian batteries before Wonnenberg and the Russian artillery standing to the right and left of Pitzkendorf, responded with little success against the French artillery. The fire served to cover the advance of the French infantry into their assigned positions. The Russians lost two guns dismounted by the French artillery fire.[14]

A battalion of the 11th Polish Regiment, under Chef de bataillon Szembeck moved rapidly against Diwelkau and chased the Russians out of the village, but not before they put it to the torch. Two other battalions of the 10th Polish Regiment, led by Major Krasyn, supported by the 13th Bavarian Regiment and the 1st Westphalian Regiment, moved forward from the left of the French artillery.

The cavalry in the first line, under General Farine, consisted of 250 hussars, Chasseurs, and lancers.[15] It moved in parallel with the infantry to support their attack on the Russian Redoubts Nos. 9, 10, 11, and 12 standing before Pitzkendorf. These redoubts were now manned solely with infantry, the artillery having been withdrawn.

The fall of Diwelkau had forced the Russians to withdraw hastily from a small earthwork covering that position. The Poles and the light cavalry, seeing the Russian hesitation, moved quickly against the four redoubts. As they burst over the front of the redoubts, they caught the Russian and Prussian garrisons in the act of withdrawing through the back of the redoubts and plunged pell-mell into the mass of milling soldiers. The allies lost many dead and prisoners to the attack. The commander of the redoubts was taken prisoner.

The Russian Cossacks attempted a counterattack to restore the situation, but General Caveignac led forward the reserve cavalry and threw them back into the large ravine which lies by Pitzkendorf. The French and Poles remained the masters of the Russian position.

The artillery battle continued and the allies remained in Johannisberg and the Königsthal Valley. To respond to this Rapp directed that four guns be detached from the principal French battery, and that they move to the crest of the hill that forms the back of the Königsthal Valley and extends to Langsfuhr. The position was quite favorable to the French move and the first rounds put the allies into a rapid withdrawal.[16]

The allies fell back to the crest of a hill occupied by a large force of cavalry and a battery of five guns. Rapp ordered a battalion of the 11th Polish Regiment[17] and two platoons of dragoons to attack this position.

The 5th, 6th, and 7th Neapolitan Regiments, led by General Destrées, advanced behind the Poles. General Bachelu, with some of his troops, advanced behind the Neapolitans as a further reserve. The Neapolitans acted with surprising vigor and military ardor led on by General Pépé and Colonel Lebon.[18]

This column moved through the Königsthal Valley at the *pas de charge,* against the flanks of the allied position. Colonel Kamienski, by Langfuhr, saw this movement and knew it was his signal to execute his advance. He ordered the drums to sound the charge and his force began to roll forward irresistibly. The two columns succeeded in taking Johannisberg, despite the vigorous resistance of the allies.

The allied infantry and guns on the plateau withdrew hastily from their positions around Pitzkendorf. Their withdrawal was hastened by fire from the two large French batteries by Zigankenberg. The rain had been heavy enough that at times muskets failed, as at Dresden, but despite this, the French and their allies were able to take the position at Langfuhr and inflict a heavy blow to the allies.

The allies withdrew to a strong position behind Pitzkendorf, where they had a larger force. Rapp, having no desire to hold the ground he had captured, began to slowly withdraw back to his original positions. The allies, seeing his retrograde movement, slowly advanced at a respectable distance. Rapp's goal was to keep the allies as far as he could from the walls of Danzig. If he did not contest their advance into this terrain it would have allowed them to establish batteries and begin digging their saps that much closer to their final goal.

The advancing allies then encountered Colonel Kamienski, who occupied the heights of the Petit Belvedere (high point) and took them under a heavy fusillade. This did not last long and finally Kamienski was ordered to withdraw.

While the allies fell back before the fury of the French artillery, and the impetuosity of the French infantry by Pitzkendorf, they attempted a diversion and attacked the French advanced posts between Schidlitz and Niederfeld.

The engagement at Schidlitz and at Stolzenberg was a small affair, with about 300 allied infantry attacking the French lines. Major Treny, commanding the 8th Provisional Demi-brigade,[19] repulsed them with ease. However, the attack at Ohra was more serious. Two allied battalions advanced from Niederfeld and four more moved from the nearby heights. Major Schneider was in command of that part of the line. The rapid movement of the Russians obliged him to withdraw his advanced posts quickly. The Russians and Prussians advanced in good order, slowed briefly by a small woods and the village of Ohra itself. They were quickly engaged in a lively fusillade.

A Russian column cautiously advanced into the village where it was showered with canister and routed. General Husson arrived at that moment with his reserve, an elite battalion formed from the 9th Provisional Demi-brigade, and the French passed over to the offensive.[20] When the elite battalion of the 9th Provisional Demi-brigade arrived it joined the forces of Major Schneider, formed behind the Stadgebiet, where all the advanced posts had rallied after being driven back. The elite battalion formed column and Major Gleize led the it in a bayonet against the woods occupied by the Russians. Major Schneider[21] led the 17th Provisional Demi-brigade[22] against the head of the village. They advanced on the flank of Major Gleize's elite battalion.[23]

The allies fell back with little or no resistance, before the advancing French columns. Their losses in the woods were heavy, especially when they found themselves obliged to fall back across a ravine. The village fell with equal rapidity. The allies lost 40 dead and 62 prisoners, with a large number of wounded. The French losses were one officer and seven soldiers dead and 44 wounded.[24]

Between Langfuhr and Pitzkendorf, the engagement lasted from the early morning until 6:00 p.m. The allied losses were heavy because of the superiority of the French artillery placed near Zigankenberg, which took their columns in the flanks. The engagement around and the fall of the four redoubts before Pitzkendorf by French infantry, and the annihilation of a battalion of 300-400 men in the Jeschkenthal Valley by the 11th Polish Regiment, cost the allies heavily.

Despite the success of the day's engagement, it became clear to the French command that they would be unable to maintain themselves indefinitely on the Johannisberg heights, so they withdrew and the heights were occupied by the allies. Their loss to the allies did not portend any serious impact on the French position in Danzig.

However, Langfuhr and Ohra were two positions that the allies had to occupy, if they intended to begin formal siege operations against Danzig. They would not be able to open trenches except before Hagelsberg or Bischofsberg, the two assailable fronts of the fortress. And these trenches could not be opened, until they had secured their right and left flanks.

Though these two posts were important to the besiegers, they did not have the same importance to the defenders of Danzig. The batteries at Frioul and the palisade prevented an occupation of the Star plateau, and the French fortification of Jesuitenberg and the occupation of the Ohra suburb, helped by the inundation, would make any allied move on the Ohra front difficult at best.

On the other hand, the French position by Langfuhr was separated by a distance of 2,000 to 2,400 meters from the fortress.[25] It was dominated by the Johannisberg heights on its right, and could be enveloped from all sides, and isolated easily by a few batteries established on the high points facing the position.

Because of this, the garrison could not hope to occupy and hold Langfuhr, so strong forces were held by Pitzkendorf, ready to strike at any attempt by the allies from Langfuhr. Rapp chose to abandon the position to the allies, but contented himself with occupying Johannisberg, and with fortifying the two high points opposing it. Once in possession of Langfuhr, the allies still found themselves a considerable distance from the main wall of Danzig. Their sacrifices in taking the village, were not compensated by the advantages gained.[26]

Naval Actions

On 1 September, a few days after the allies occupied the Grand and Petit Belvedere (high points), the Russo-British fleet appeared off Danzig. Though menacing, it stood out of cannon range. On 2 September, the allied fleet appeared and formed again. It consisted of a corvette and 40 gunboats. At 10:30 a.m., it began to fire on the Weichselmünde Fort (mouth of the Vistula) and Neufahrwasser. The French batteries replied with sufficient success, that by 2:00 p.m., the allied fleet was obliged to withdraw. Four of their gunboats were heavily damaged. For their efforts, the allies succeeded in dismounting one howitzer in Battery #4 on the Platte Island, as well as destroying a small magazine, which killed two and wounded three.[27]

The second allied line, with 27 gunboats, which formed up as the first attacked, did not advance to attack the fortifications. However, later in the evening, around 5:00 p.m., a force of 76 gunboats advanced to renew the bombardment of Neufahrwasser. This attack was renewed in the morning, and after three hours of combat the flotilla was obliged to withdraw. Their effect on the French was one man wounded. During the two days engagements, the allies fired 3,500 rounds and the French responded with 1,500 of their own.

During the second day of the naval engagement the Russians advanced two infantry columns and a force of cavalry from the Königsthal Valley and the village of Stries, moving rapidly against the gorge of Langfuhr and Neu-Schottland.[28] They quickly passed Schellmühle and turned the Kabrun redoubt.

The advanced posts by Langfuhr retired in haste to their blockhouses. Those before Neu-Schottland withdrew to Schellmühle, and from there to the redoubt by Kabrun, to find refuge from the overwhelming allied forces.

A large force of allied cavalry covered the plains and the heights before the entrenched camp of Zigankenberg. It advanced to the foot of the Montbrun Battery. The engagement quickly became general and a lively fusillade began and stretched from Schellmühle to Ohra.

Major Poyeck, of the 13th Bavarian Regiment, commanded the post at Kabrun. He fought off the allied attacks with the assistance of the two guns in the redoubt. On several occasions his redoubt was surrounded by the allies.

The Bavarians and Westphalians, who had taken refuge in the redoubt, executed a quick sortie against their assailants, but their numbers were too small and they quickly fell back to their loop-holed buildings.

After several fruitless assaults against the Bavarian and Westphalian positions, the Russians decided to set them afire. They set fire to several adjoining buildings in the hope that the fires would spread to the Bavarian and Westphalian positions. Even this effort failed, as the flames were extinguished before they threatened the positions.

In Ohra, Lieutenant Mayon, of the 21st Légère (6th Provisional Demi-brigade) held his post as long as possible, then withdrew to a position behind Ohra commanded by Major Dauger. From there the French garrison of Ohra engaged the Russians, inflicting heavy casualties on them while suffering none themselves.[29]

At the same time a strong detachment of Cossacks, supported by infantry, moved on Zigankenberg and occupied it. A little later fires appeared in Schellmühle, Zigankenberg, and in Ohra, where the allies had also penetrated.

General Rapp, the governor of Danzig, sent two strong columns forward in a sortie against the allies. One moved towards Schellmühle and the other moved against Langfuhr.

The allies, already suffering from the French artillery fire from all of the batteries that overlooked the battlefield, as well as from a Polish light battery[30] that had moved forward to engage them, were quickly dislodged. A Neapolitan battalion advanced at the *pas de charge* down the avenue to the palace, while a company of Polish voltigeurs turned the village. The allied incendiaries were caught and struck down. It is estimated that the allies lost 200 men in this action. The fire, however, was not put out until after a major portion of the palace, the mill, and several other buildings had been severely damaged. The allied troops chased from Schellmühle, rallied by the screen of trees before Neu-Schottland.

Moments of Courage and Resolution

The French second column was unable to push its movement, because the day was already well advanced. It encountered considerable forces in the Königsthal Valley, and between there and Neu-Schottland. It was unable to advance to the Westphalian and Bavarian position in Langfuhr. A small detachment of Neapolitans, forming the advanced guard of the column, was cut off by an allied cavalry charge. They were presumed to have been cut down and captured, but they had succeeded in throwing themselves in the blockhouses and were trapped with the troops they had been sent to rescue.[31]

The smoke from the constant musketry blocked the French view of the two loopholed houses, so that they were no longer able to ascertain who held them. However, a soldier who had been made prisoner at Langfuhr, and who escaped back to the French lines, advised them that Captain Fahrbeck and his entire detachment had been either killed or taken prisoner. One further attempt was made to reach the buildings by a small force of Neapolitan soldiers, but a hail of musketry convinced the French that they were no longer held by their comrades.[32]

At 10:00 p.m., Zigankendorf was retaken and part was saved from the flames. By Ohra several houses had been entirely burned to the ground, as well as a post known as "*de la barrière*," established in the extreme end of the suburb.

Though night fell there was a continuous musketry and cannon fire. Observations indicated to the French that musketry had ceased from their blockhouses, that were now behind the allied lines. It was presumed that the garrisons had fallen.

The Russians had been chased from Schellmühle and Zigankendorf, but Rapp began to consider a new attack against Langfuhr. However, the night did not promise success, so he ordered General Grandjean to withdraw to Aller-Engel, and to establish a new line of posts between Schellmühle and Zigankendorf.

As they withdrew to their new lines, the French reinforced the garrisons of the various redoubts and strong points. A strong reserve was left at Aller-Engel, to support Kabrun. The artillery withdrew. That which had stood by Aller-Engel pulled back to the glacis of the fortress, with orders to resume its positions after dawn.

During the night frequent patrols were sent forward to observe the troops now occupying the loopholed buildings. These troops were deployed all night, but these night patrols proved to be a very boring experience.

Captain Fahrbeck, with his 80 Bavarians, Westphalians and Neapolitans, however, had not been taken. His force had ceased firing because they were all required to fight the flames threatening to consume their position. They fought the flames without access to water and under constant enemy fire, but they succeeded in saving themselves.

The Russians, seeing their efforts failed, tried once again to penetrate the palisades surrounding Fahrbeck's position, but that too failed. Despite that, the Russian efforts continued. Fahrbeck's garrison, thirsty, hungry, and fatigued by constant allied attacks and their fire fighting efforts, continued to resist every attack. Their position became desperate as their ammunition began to run low. They then hit upon the desperate idea of attempting to gather the cartridges from their fallen enemies around the second rampart.

At the same time Captain Marnier, followed by eight of his braver troops, slipped out of the Kabrun Redoubt. Running from house to house, they moved to within pistol shot of the blockhouse.[33] To their delight the door opened and out stepped the garrison that everyone had presumed massacred. A few brave Cossacks moved forward to prevent the contact, but they were quickly driven off. Unfortunately, the other loopholed house had fallen and there was no one left to save.

The word of the escape of Captain Fahrbeck's tiny force spread quickly, despite the continual musketry and cannon fire. As they returned to the main French lines, they were received as victors and their wounded sent quickly to the rear for treatment. Their ordeal had lasted twelve hours and stands as one of the finer moments of the defense of Danzig.

On the other points along the line the French fought with equal tenacity. Chef de bataillon Bauer, 1st Westphalian Regiment, was mentioned in dispatches for his efforts against Langfuhr. The Bavarian Lieutenant Muck's efforts to hold the blockhouse on the left, and Captain Ostrowski, who commanded the Polish light battery, and several officers of the 5th and 6th Neapolitan Regiments were also recognized. Maréchal-des-logis Dargot, of the 5th Dragoon Regiment, commanded a small cavalry detachment by Heubude and was commended for his conduct during the engagement.

Later that night the alarm was sounded again. The garrison took arms and General Husson, with the 8th Provisional Demi-brigade and the Imperial Guard detachment moved to Schidlitz. The 17th Provisional Demi-brigade moved to a reserve position near Bischofsberg.[34]

The establishment of the allies in the throat of Neu-Schottland and in Langfuhr, delayed the French from continuing their establishment of a line between the Vistula and Kabrun, with two new earthworks. They gave up on that effort and contended themselves with a palisade on the road to Langfuhr, another on the Aller-Engel heights, and elongating the Zigankenberg entrenched camp.

The French Dig In

The siege settled down again. The French continued their entrenching activities and the allies licked their wounds for a while. The works of the French line ran, left to right, Caulaincourt, Romeuf Redoubts, Grabowsky Battery, Deroy Redoubt, and Montbrun Battery. To complete this line of fortifications and to extend it to the Vistula, two more batteries were established. One, called Fiszer, stood across the road from Langfuhr, and the other, known as Gudin, a little farther distant. The Gudin Battery rested in an artificial inundation that extended to the dike on the left of the Vistula and formed the right of the line, which still included two batteries that were placed on the other side of the river. All of the works were palisaded, provided with barracks and magazines. Rapp also ordered two entrenched camps to be erected. One was to hold 400 men and stood on the extreme left behind the Kirgener Battery. The other held 150 men and stood behind Montbrun.[35] The section of the works that extended from Montbrun to Gudin was connected by a covered way. That section of the line, which extended to the left, was sufficiently protected by the poor nature of the ground. The following guns were in the various redoubts since 26 August:

Redoubt	Guns
Kirgener	2 12-pdrs and 1 6.4" howitzer
Caulaincourt	2 12-pdrs and 16.4" howitzer
Montbrun	4 8-pdrs and 1 6.4" howitzer
Kabrun	2 6-pdrs
d'Istrie	2 12-pdrs and 1 Russian licorne

Ohra was also fortified. It was a mass of houses, which communicated with each other, with the doors and windows walled up with parapets and palisades. It had no other outlet but a tongue of land bounded by two rather deep, water-filled trenches and formed an advanced retrenchment known as the "first entrenchment" of Ohra. The second, situated 400 yards to its rear, consisted of the same material and was supported by the large Jesuit convent, which had been fortified. The heights and defiles, which approach the suburb, were fortified. The redoubt that stood atop those heights, prevented the allies from turning the French and became known as the batteries and lines of Frioul.[36]

In addition, these redoubts and many of the small blockhouses were improved by the addition of a defensive brick guardhouse, to house their garrisons. This work, however, was not left undisturbed by the allies, who constantly cannonaded the French laborers working in Ohra from their batteries on the heights.

During the night of 4/5 September, the Russians attempted to seize the Kabrun redoubt. At the same time a strong party of Cossacks penetrated into Schellmühle and forced the French garrison to withdraw. However, the overall assault failed and the status quo was resumed.

To defend the banks of the Vistula a brig named the *Nymphe de la Vistule* was placed up the Schellmühle canal. In addition, a house between Schellmühle and Neufahrwasser was loopholed, palisaded, and occupied by a strong detachment. This was done to ensure constant communications with Weichselmünde by the left bank of the river.

The Russians had, at this time, considerable forces before Stolzenberg, Schidlitz, and Ohra, but they were held back by the French cannons at Bischofsberg. At the same time they renewed their seaward attacks and bombarded for a third time Weichselmünde and Neufahrwasser, during the day of 3 September.

On 4 September, the allied flotilla deployed their forces again and at 10:00 a.m., they engaged the French batteries with three bomb ketches and two frigates, while 80 gunboats formed their line of battle by the mouth of the Vistula. These vessels began a bombardment that lasted until 3:00 p.m. The allies reported to have fired 8,500 rounds of all types. This hail of shot and bombs pounded the batteries and houses along the beach, dismounting two French guns, killing two, and wounding six.

The French, however, claimed to have sunk two gunboats and severely damaged nine others, putting them out of commission. The two frigates were struck by two bombs and ten shot from the batteries at the Möwenschanze.[37] A deserter from the allied flotilla reported that they had suffered 150 men killed and wounded.[38]

On the landward side, around 11:00 a.m., an allied force of approximately 600 infantry and 100 cavalry moved against Schidlitz and overran the position. The French garrison escaped without loss. Chef de bataillon Bellanger, who commanded the garrisons of Schidlitz and Stolzenberg, quickly counterattacked with a force of 100 men and recaptured the French positions. Unfortunately, the French pushed too far, were ambushed and fell back.

Two hours later the allies renewed their assault, took the position and were, once again, driven out. This time they succeeded in burning some of the houses.[39] These attacks were coordinated with an effort on the part of the allies to fortify their position in the Langfuhr gorge and Neu-Schottland. New batteries were observed in both villages on 6 September.

During the night of 7 September, an officer in charge of part of the Kabrun position panicked during a small shelling. Part of the position had been packed with combustibles, so that the position could be destroyed if the allies were to attack in overwhelming numbers, before reinforcements could arrive. In his panic this officer set the building afire, when he saw columns advancing from Neu-Schottland. He quickly realized he had reacted too hastily, but was unable to put out the fire. The allies, seeing the fire, thought it had been caused by one of their howitzer bombs, but did not perceive that the work had been evacuated. The French took up new positions during the night.

Shortly after a supply ship broke its moorings and exploded on the boom across the Vistula. When it exploded, it severely damaged Fort Napoleon and the adjacent works.

In addition, the explosion broke an earthen dike, flooding some of the interiors of the Mottlau Bastion with 20 to 25 feet of water. The explosion also raised a wave that pushed into the plain by Schellmühle, by the canals that connected with the river, and caused a temporary inundation. This water, however, was rather easily drawn off by the canals by which it entered.

By 12 September, the allies had established seven batteries, each with three or four guns. On 13 September, a new battery was established in Neu-Schottland and began firing on the Gudin Battery. This effort continued with further batteries being organized and established. On 15 September, two further batteries were unmasked. One stood by the Grand Belvedere and Pitzkendorf, and the other stood to the left of Pitzkendorf. They were equipped with heavy caliber guns and were intended to slow the French work on the entrenched camp at Zigankenberg.

By Ohra, where the incendiary attacks continued, but with only slow progress being made by the allies. The French simply withdrew from one building to the next as the allies set it afire.

Another Naval Bombardment

On 16 September a fifth naval bombardment was executed. Forty gunboats and three bomb ketches advanced with their right towards Brösen, and their left in line with Redoubt #3 of the

Platte Island, in a manner so as to cross their fire on all the batteries on the coast, and by the Neufahrwasser entrenched camp.[40]

At 6:30 a.m., these vessels began to fire. Masses of infantry were soon observed massing behind Brösen and Saspe, preparing to move forward in a general assault against the French earthworks around Neufahrwasser after the naval artillery had knocked down the palisades and opened some practical breaches.

The numerous allied artillery fired without cease, obscuring the sky with clouds of smoke. The bombardment continued with the screech of shot slamming into the ramparts and knocking down the palisades.

The French counterbattery was equally effective, striking many of the gunboats and forcing them to withdraw from the fight. Those losses did not slow down the allied attack, each damaged vessel being replaced by another. The divisions rotated every three hours, bringing forward a refreshed crew of gunners on each rotation. By 2:00 p.m., much of the palisade around Neufahrwasser had been knocked down, and the allied columns began their assault.

As the attack occurred around Neufahrwasser, another attack struck the French advanced posts at Ohra. Rapp perceived this attack as a diversion and it soon faded into nothing.

On the side of the ocean, under the hail of allied projectiles, the French continued to bring forward munition and supplies to support their gunners. A fortunate shot from a French gun penetrated into a gunboat's magazine and it exploded, leaving nothing but a swirl of debris on the ocean's surface.

By the end of the day, the flotilla had been in combat twelve hours, inflicting little permanent damage on the French, but suffering serious losses, including the one vessel totally obliterated and eight more heavily damaged. The flotilla withdrew at dusk to Pulzig Bay, to repair its many wounds.

The Russian admiral had sworn to destroy the French magazines, houses in the ports, and their fortifications, as well as to silence their batteries and level their earthworks. He had, however, failed miserably in his attempt. Despite the firing of 20,000 rounds, the total damage to the French was minimal.

The French reported losing two dead and three wounded. Three gun carriages were damaged, several hundred feet of palisade were knocked down, and most of the houses in Neufahrwasser were ruined. The naval effort to date had fired over 35,000 rounds, costing them an estimated 1,470,000 francs. Hardly a reasonable return for the effort expended.

With the failure of the flotilla to effect anything significant, it drew into Zoppot and Koliebke, where many of the guns were dismounted from the gunboats and sent forward to the various earthworks being raised around Danzig.

Coupled with the naval bombardment the allied army executed a general attack on the French advanced posts. Major Schneider stood in Ohra with the 17th Provisional Demi-brigade. He led his forces forward and recaptured the positions overrun by the allies in their initial attack, with the exception of the *Étoile*.

On 16 September, the allies received Prussian reinforcements and a large force of artillery, which formed a new camp behind Redoubts #2 and #3 on the line by Matschkau. The Prussian force was significantly smaller than the Russian, and came to be considered a minor partner.

The Prussians occupied Niederfeld, St-Albrecht, Schweinsköpf, Matschkau, Borgfeld, and Schönfeld. The Russian camps stood to the right and left of Wonneberg, in Tempelburg, Miggau, Pitzkendorf, on the Divelkau Heights, on those before Brentau, Pelonken, Stries, and around the Neu-Schottland forest. Nehrung was occupied by the Russians camped in Neufähr and Bohnsack, behind redoubts and entrenchments raised by them during the month of May.[41] In addition there was a force of British artillery, recognized by their Congreve rockets, which were aimed principally at the villages and fortifications.

Despite their numbers, estimated to be about 50,000 men, the allies remained rather timid in their actions against Danzig. They perfected their batteries with infinite care. All of the batteries were reveted with fascines and gabions, with palisades in their throats and ditches. They were all prepared to defend themselves against assaults.

To protect their works by Langfuhr and Neu-Schottland, as well as to distract the French attention, they often sent forward several guns onto the Schellmühle plain, to disquiet the French in Neufahrwasser, as well as to fire on the vessels anchored in the Vistula.

On 17 September the siege forces aimed their fire principally on the brig *la Nymphe de la Vistule,* standing near Schellmühle. A howitzer shell pierced its powder magazine, destroying it. Fortunately, the greatest portion of its equipment had been transported ashore, so the loss was minimal—30 men killed and wounded.[42]

The *Nymphe* had served to support Kabrun and Schellmühle. Its destruction caused the allies to move that night against those two posts and take them. The French garrisons fell back to their second line at Legau and Aller-Engel, where they reestablished themselves.

The next dawn the batteries of Montbrun, Grabowsky, and all the batteries of Danzig, Holm, and Hagelsberg, opened a sustained fire with 30 cannon and three howitzers, on Kabrun and Schellmühle, as the allies attempted to entrench themselves in those positions.

Under the cover of their guns at Neu-Schottland and Johannisberg, the allies had begun to raise palisades in Kabrun, and to establish a communication trench to the other nearby works. The first trench ran from Kabrun to the Böttchler House, Klein-Schellmühle. Five more zig-zags carried the trench from there to Neu-Schottland.

At 7:00 p.m., on 18 September, Major Legros lead forward the elite battalions of the 6th and 7th Demi-brigades in a combined assault against the *Étoile*. Captains Aubry and Vallard each led forward 200 picked men in a surprise assault that threw the allies out of the earthwork and sent them back to their main lines in a hail of French musketry fire.

The allies recovered quickly and returned with about 800 men in a counterattack. The French waited until they were within a half-pistol shot of the earthwork before they opened a devastating fire that sent the shattered allies back in great disorder.

During the night of 18/19 September, the allies perfected their position in Kabrun, Schellmühle, and Langfuhr. During the night they also continued the preparation of their works in the Königsthal Valley and began work on a battery with eight gun ports behind Schellmühle.

On 21 September another battery was raised near Schellmühle, barely 300 meters from the Vistula. On 24 September yet another battery was raised by the Böttchler House. All of these fortifications were aimed at the Gudin Battery.[43]

The progress of the allies obliged GD Rapp to abandon the left bank of the Vistula. The three posts, the first and second in Legau, as well as the fortified house, were insufficient to assure communication with Neufahrwasser and were abandoned. However, in order not to leave a position from which the Russian sharpshooters could shoot at the French labor gangs, all three posts were burned.

Once the allies were established in Schellmühle, they raised a new work by Holm, which was to cover the rear of their works and to provide counterbattery fire. There was also a new work raised on the edge of the river and near the mill. This work became known as the "*batterie du Moulin*" or "Mill Battery". On both sides the process of a formal siege were now well under way, and the engineering rules established in the previous century began to take effect. Battery and sap were prepared and pushed forward. Counterbattery and sortie were the order of the day for the defenders.

During the night of 16/17 September, the allies attacked the post of *Étoile*. They succeeded in overrunning it. General Rapp, however, decided not to simply surrender claim to it once it was lost, and the next night, at 7:00 p.m., he sent forward a bayonet attack.

Four elite companies under the commands of Captains Vallard and Aubry marched to the attack, forcing the position through the breeches made by the allies the previous night. The Russians were sent reeling backwards, with the French firing on them, inflicting numerous casualties. A large number of the casualties were captured because they were unable to cross a ravine that blocked their way.[44]

The Russians received a reinforcement of 800 men and they advanced with bayonets lowered. When they arrived at the crest of the hill where the *Étoile* stood, the French infantry cried *"en avant"* and pushed forward themselves, striking and driving the Russians backwards again.

Despite that check, the Russians launched a third assault. It too was defeated and the Russians lost as many casualties, as in the first two attacks. The French took up strong positions and a fusillade continued until 11:00 p.m.

Two allied companies were placed in reserve in the Schottenhäuser ravine, before the Stadtgebiet blockhouse, to support the right flank of those attacking the French on the ridge. They advanced into point-blank range with 150 infantry and cavalry, but the French volleys broke their advance.

Major Legros directed the attack. He had under his command the 6th and 7th Provisional Demi-brigades of the 30th Division. His maneuvers forced the allies to withdraw backwards into a small woods by Ohra, where they occupied an entrenched position, ending the battle.

Six days later, during the night of 23/24 September, the Russians once again attacked the *Étoile* and received such heavy musketry that they withdrew without launching their assault. They probed the position at 4:00 a.m., the following night, received the same treatment and withdrew again.

The siege again fell into a period of quiet that lasted until 5 October, when the allies cut down several trees in the garden by Kabrun and unmasked a new mortar battery. On 6 October, a new trench was run across the crest of the Königsthal ridge and before the Zigankenberg plateau. A strong redoubt was also raised on the Zigankendorf-Dreilinden road. In front of it was traced part of a trench to cover advanced pickets.

Fearing a coming bombardment, Rapp had the part of the Old City closest to Kabrun evacuated, as well as several military posts, magazines, hospitals and other unnecessary personnel. The French troops also evacuated the barracks at Holz-Raum. Some were sent to Hagelsberg, while the rest were pulled further back into the city. Rapp ordered granaries organized in the Wallhof and Jacobsthor towers as well as in the Poggenfuhl and Lang-Garten churches.

These precautions were none too soon, for on 8 October, the Russian batteries by Kabrun began firing on Fort Napoleon, between the two walls. On 9 October, at 10:00 a.m., the Russians began firing all their batteries, principally directing their fire on the Gudin Redoubt and the works around Holm. The following morning a few shells were fired, but the major bombardment began that evening at 7:30 p.m., when they once again began to fire all their batteries on the city, Holm and the entrenched camp at Zigankenberg. Four mortars and about 40 cannon and howitzers fired, uninterrupted, throughout the night.[45] In addition French accounts relate that the British battery fired over 6,000 rockets. However, only 10 rockets struck in the interior of the village. Part exploded in the air and the major portion exploded on the glacis and in the ditches. One rocket struck the Dominican convent, which had been converted into a hospital, at 8:30 p.m. The resulting fire did severe damage, but most of the sick and wounded, as well as the prisoners of war, were rescued.

Between that rocket and other bombs, a major fire erupted. As the garrison was occupied with controlling the fire, the Russians made a push to seize the French positions in Ohra.

The allies planned a major attack for 10 October. A diversionary attack was to be made from Langfuhr against the Oliva Gate. While the main attack came from the right bank of the Radaune, where the allies formed an attack with three columns, under the command of the Prussian Oberst Graf von Dohna. One column was designated for the attack and the other two were to serve as reserves. The first being under Prussian Major Graf von Eilenberg. It was to move to the left while

Pitzkendorf, Langfuhr, and Tempelburg were cannonaded. The second column, under Prussian Major Julius, stood as a reserve to the left of the Kosakenberg batteries. The third column, under the Russian GM Kolubakin, stood as a reserve for both columns and was ordered to take a position between Kosakenberg and Wonneberg.[46]

Assault on the Frioul Batteries

At 7:00 p.m., on 10 October, the attack began. First came a heavy bombardment with mortars and Congreve rockets, which shortly succeeded in starting three separate fires in the city. One of the fires soon engulfed the Dominican Cloister, which housed Russian wounded. The attack on the Oliva Gate distracted Rapp, who then sent out a force to strike at the allied batteries by Langfuhr and suffered heavy losses for his efforts.

As Rapp was distracted, the allied attack columns moved forward. They contained about 4,000 infantry under the command of General Kouloubakin. Major Legros saw the impossibility of facing them with the 600 men under his command and withdrew his advanced posts behind the palisades and into the various blockhouses while the Frioul redoubts bombarded the advancing allies.[47]

The Russians threw themselves into the ditches of the smallest work near the Frioul battery and began a heavy fusillade. They were supported by the allied batteries by Ohra and Schottenhäuser. Their fire was responded to by the artillery in the Frioul Battery and the two guns by Ohra. At 11:00 p.m., reinforcements arrived and Rapp issued the order to attack. Major Dauger, with the elite battalion of the 7th Provisional Demi-brigade was ordered to move to the right of the road, capture the heights occupied by the allies, and recapture the posts known as "The Sergeant" and "The Officer." Four hundred Poles were to follow his movement and form a second line. Their objective was to prevent the forces of Major Dauger from being turned and to assure their retreat if it became necessary.

Chef de bataillon Charton, leading 500 men of the 6th Provisional Demi-brigade, advanced to the left of the city and moved against the post known as "The Capitaine" and subsequently against the *Étoile*. He detached 40 men as skirmishers and directed that they close the defiles that lead from the *Étoile* as well as to suppress the fire of the two blockhouses in the cemetery and Wemberg. Three hundred more men from the 8th Provisional Demi-brigade formed before the Petershagen Gate, where they served as a reserve.

The attacks of Major Dauger and Chef de bataillon Charton were successful and the positions they assaulted were retaken with the bayonet. In the dark of the night, the Russian forces in the *Étoile* decided to pull back. They encountered a "French" column moving as if to cut them off and began a fifteen minute fire fight with it, only to discover that it was a battalion of Prussians. The French reported losing five officers and 15 men killed, eight officers and 114 men wounded. The Russians left 153 dead behind on the field.[48]

The next morning, 11 October, the allies once again resumed their probes against the *Étoile* plateau. They attacked the barricaded houses occupied by the French, marching directly at them, while others moved to circle them. They attacked twice and were repulsed. A detachment of the 8th Provisional Demi-brigade drove them back, but the Russians returned a third time and set fire to the houses. The burning of the houses stopped the fight and forced the French to withdraw. The flames began to spread to the houses on the left of the French position, but the marine artisans deployed and fought the fires under an almost constant sniping by Russian sharpshooters, who had moved forward.[49]

Just as night fell, the Russians sent forward a force of 400 men against the 50 Frenchmen guarding the *Étoile* and took it. Seeing the situation, the commanding officer of the *Étoile* had withdrawn his forces, before they were crushed. In addition, several other positions in the area were also quickly abandoned.

After a battle of 24 hours and enormous losses, the Russians finally had become masters of this position. During the night of 11/12 October, they began digging their positions on the plateau, which were completed on 12 October.

It was also on 12 October that three boats carrying French sappers, under the command of captain Neunnez, slipped out of Fort Lacoste and arrived at the mill, unobserved by the allies. They quickly moved into the mill, part holding the allies at bay, while the other part quickly disassembled the important parts of the machinery and loaded them back aboard their boats. This precious[50] cargo was then hauled back to the Ochs bastion, and a new windmill was erected inside Danzig, at a point farthest from the allied guns. The same type of operation was executed against Plönendorf, where another mill was stripped of pieces. The Holm mill was disassembled and moved to the interior as well.[51]

The siege was not without its effects inside the city walls. Aside from fire, disease was rampant, and food was becoming in short supply. Many of the citizens found means to slip away. Some succeeded in passing through the allied lines, while others took boats and slipped across the river and the inundations to safety.

The Bombardment Resumes

On 18 October, at 7:00 a.m., another major bombardment began, with rockets, howitzer shells, bombs and heated shot being fired in immense quantities, from the four batteries on the *Étoile* plateau, and those at Kabrun, Schellmühle, Johannisberg, and others. At noon, the rockets ceased to be fired, but the bombs and heated shot continued. Some of the rounds went as far as 3,300 meters, reaching the Lang-Garten Church.

The bombardment continued throughout the night and the following day. At 6:30 p.m., the bombardment reached a violent crescendo. A violent fire began. The flames were fought by the sappers, marine artisans, and artillerists, but the French were unable to master it until 22 magazines and barracks were reduced to cinders. The losses to the citizens of Danzig were estimated at 9,000,000 francs. Eventually, the greater portion of the garrison was sent to fight the fire. By 5:00 a.m., the French had controlled the fire, and saved their provisions magazines. The bombardment was still not over.

A group of citizens came to Rapp the following day, begging him to allow them to send a deputation to the allies and ask them not to begin such a bombardment again, that it was simply destroying their homes and that the fortifications were almost unscathed by the effort, but Rapp refused. Instead, he allowed a note to be sent out requesting that the allies allow those citizens who wished to depart, be allowed to do so. The Russian general chose to ignore the note and continued to bombard the city as suited him.

The allied fire did not go unopposed. The French batteries responded in kind, causing considerable damage in return. They fired on average 1,000 rounds per day, back at the allies.[52] Despite that, the city of Danzig continued to be bombarded and to burn, first here, then there.

Slowly the French and citizens abandoned the outer portions of the city, withdrawing further into it. The privations continued to take their toll as well. The cavalry horses were ruined and no longer serviceable as cavalry mounts. As they faltered and failed, they were taken to the butchers and fed to the garrison.

Dissent in the Garrison

These hardships, and newspapers from Berlin slipped into the city discussing Napoleon's defeat at Leipzig, caused considerable dissent amongst the allied forces, and confusion among the French.[53]

The German portions of the garrison were most affected and began to desert. The first deserters came from the French regiments formed in Hamburg and Bremen, followed by the Saxons and Dutch.

Rapp began to put the least reliable troops further inside the city than the reliable troops. He found the Bavarians and the Poles as reliable as native French and continued to place them on the advanced posts.

The garrison was deployed with Heudelet's 30th Division between the Ochs Bastion and the Neugarten Gate, including the Bischofsberg. Bachelu's 34th Division extended from the Ochs Bastion to the Mottlau. The 11th Polish and 1st Westphalian Regiments extended from Mottlau to the Jacob Bastion. The 10th Polish and 13th Bavarian Regiments extended from the Tardivelle Lunette to the Neugarten Gate, including Hagelsberg and Holm. The 5th Polish Regiment was in the entrenched camp of Hagelsberg and by Oliva. Fort Desaix was manned by 300 cavalry and dragoons. Another 120 occupied Fort Lacoste. The 6th and 7th Neapolitans were lodged in the city proper. The reserve consisted of the Imperial Guard, the miners and sappers. It was posted in the Lang-Garten. The sailors and naval artisans were in the city. In Weichselmünde and Neufahrwasser stood the 1/29th French Regiment, some dragoons, and a company of Polish sappers. The artillery was spread all along the French position, manning the various batteries.[54]

The siege continued with almost mathematical precision. Saps were dug, batteries erected, sorties and raids executed against both the positions of both sides. The siege was also marching towards its inevitable conclusion.

In late October, Rapp decided to evacuate the French positions at Stadtgebiet. As winter closed, the various flooded areas would cease to be protection and would be completely passable to the allies. The probability of an assault grew as the weather chilled. Adequate grain supplies remained to feed the garrison and population for another six months. Rapp was resolved to hold the city until all the supplies and means of defense were gone.

On 31 October, the inclement weather forced a vessel close to Danzig. A quick naval sortie captured it, and though chased by three or four allied gunboats, the French sailors succeeded in bring it and its much needed supplies into the city.

As his resources began to fail Rapp organized a special force of the strongest men, a *compagnie franche* designated to serve as a shock force to handle all special tasks. It was formed of 70 volunteers and consisted almost entirely of French. The exception was a few Poles, who knew Russian and would be needed. They were each armed with a short carbine, a long bayonet, a saber, and a pair of pistols.

Frioul Attacked Again

On 1 November, the cry of alarm rose as the Russians and Prussians advanced against the French advanced posts at Schidlitz, Stolzenberg, and Ohra. The defensive fire from the French line and batteries threw them back. Part of the Frioul works was attacked by a battalion supported by a second battalion and 200 sappers. This work contained 50 French soldiers from the 23rd Légère Regiment.

The Russians poured into the ditch and knocked down the weak palisades. The tiny garrison was quickly overrun, before reserves could be brought forward.

The Russians moved with the same abruptness against other French posts, but were beaten back with some loss. Twelve dead Russians were found on the main street of Stadtgebiet after they withdrew.

The Russians now held the outworks of the Frioul fortress, but not the main fortress. These Russian troops began to fire their muskets at the French in the main works, as well as the French troops in Alt-Schottland. The two weak garrisons were reinforced by a force of Young Guard,

French Line Infantry, Autumn 1813, by Bombléd.

because it was feared that the allies would strike again. In addition, efforts were made quickly to repair the damage to the ditch and palisade to prevent such an attack.[55]

Every precaution was taken to ensure a sound defense of the French positions. The troops deployed in the ditches behind the palisades, in the various works and along the parapets were prepared to repel any assault with bayonets. Sixty men were also placed in the Weimberg Valley, near a loopholed house, to support the Frioul batteries. A further 50 Imperial Guard were sent to another house on the Stolzenberg heights.

The Russians, seeing this build up, attacked. They drove the French back to the cover of their blockhouses and the Cafarelli Lunette. In addition, the 7th Division, under GD Grandjean, was also forced to withdraw, abandoning the post known as "chef de division" to the right of Schidlitz.[56]

The French guns on Bischofsberg, the Lasalle Redoubt, and those of the Frioul fortress began to pound the Russians in Redoubt #3 and their supporting reserves, inflicting numerous casualties.

As the battered allies staggered from the weight of artillery brought to bear on them, the French counterattack was prepared. Chef de bataillon Carré was ordered by GD Heudelet to move from Bischofsberg with the 1st Provisional Demi-brigade, leaving only a reserve of 100 men in the fort and 100 others at the Neugarten Gate. He organized his forces as quickly as possible, including everyone he could draw from the 30th Division.

Unfortunately, the night was too dark to allow the French to judge the strength of the Russians and to maneuver to advantage, so it was decided to wait until morning.

As dawn arrived General Devilliers attacked the Chef de Bataillon post and General Breissand marched against Schidlitz and Stolzenberg with detachments from the 6th and 10th Provisional Demi-brigades from Bischofsberg.

The attack on the right was slowed by the terrain, but General Breissand finally began his movement and executed it at the *pas de charge.* The Russians were pushed back 400 yards and the French reoccupied their posts. General Breissand was wounded during these assaults.[57]

The Russians responded by advancing a significant reserve force. At the same moment Devilliers attacked and carried the positions on the right. Major Treny, of the 17th Provisional Demi-brigade, led forward a detachment of the 5th Polish Infantry Regiment, into the Russian held work from the left while Captain Chambure led an independent company in from the right. The redoubt was recaptured, after about 100 casualties were inflicted on the Russians. The French and Poles were motivated by a desire for revenge and only one Russian officer and 20 men survived the French assault.[58] The French then executed a general assault and drove the Russians off the Stolzenberg plateau.

The Russian efforts to turn the redoubt against the French were quickly undone, but a Russian counterstroke occurred on the French left. Towards midnight, the Russians advanced against the French posts in Schidlitz and Stolzenberg, driving them back and tracing a new trench behind the latter village, that was 300 meters long and 700 meters from the Cafarelli Lunette.

Below Schidlitz, they drew another trench and began to raise palisades along the crest of the small plateau, which dominated Schidlitz.

The French posts in the ruins of Stolzenberg were obliged to withdraw, covered by a sortie under Adjutant-Major Rivet. Rivet's small force was obliged to withdraw into a small blockhouse, which the Russians struck at three times without success.

Rapp moved to this front and prepared a counterblow for the break of dawn. Two columns, one under General Breissand composed of troops of the 30th Division, and a second formed from Polish and Bavarian troops under General Devilliers, attacked the Stolzenberg plateau, and the Russian positions before Kirgener.

Though heavily outnumbering the French, the Russians were unable to repel their assault and were thrown back, leaving numerous dead and 80 prisoners among the recaptured positions. The ardor of the French allies, the Poles and Bavarians, calmed concerns about their continued loyalty.

Shortages in the Garrison

During the night of 1/2 November, the Russians renewed their artillery barrage, firing 4,000 rounds. In addition to destroying houses and other private property, they also succeeded in setting 132 warehouses afire on Speicher Island. The losses to the defenders of Danzig were enormous, aside from losing various commercial properties, large quantities of food and war material were also lost.[59]

Bischofsberg became the renewed point of Russian interest and attacks.[60] The Russians chose to destroy the brick work on the face of the Scharffenord bastion and began to bombard it. An emplacement for two 24-pdr cannon was established.

The French were actively attempting to silence the Russian batteries with their counterfire, but they were finding themselves running short of large caliber munitions. They began to search through the ruins of Neufahrwasser and found many allied rounds that were suitable. These were then transported by water to the French batteries, who promptly returned them to the allies. It was rather humorous that rounds fired by the English Fleet were transported to the batteries by Russian prisoners and fired back at the allies with Prussian guns.[61]

An auxiliary force of 500 men was organized to transport munitions to the batteries and 350 gunners were attached to the guns at Bischofsberg. The command of the artillery was given to Chef d'escadron Farjon. The engineering work was supervised by Chef de bataillon Michaux and the overall command remained with Colonel Cabrié.

Stolzenberg Falls

During the day of 2 November, the Russians remained quiet until about 10:30 p.m., when 800 Russians advanced, pushing back all but one of the French posts before Stolzenberg.

A new parallel was dug 700 meters from the Leclerc and Cafarelli Lunettes and extended across the plateau to a point near Schidlitz. At the break of dawn on 3 November, General Husson, with the first demi-brigade of the 30th Division attempted to recapture the Stolzenberg plateau, but was repelled.[62]

A dense fog, which did not disperse until noon, assisted the allies in the establishment of this parallel. As a result, it was only the French artillery that was able to, in any way, disturb the efforts of the allied engineers as they worked. The new works were completed around midnight.

The French established a new line of advanced posts. along the ravine before the Cafarelli Lunette, through the village of Schidlitz. The plateau provided a good position from which they could enfilade and take the rear of the Stolzenberg parallel. Two guns were also established in the Istria Lunette, which could dominate Stolzenberg, without being taken in the flank by the old allied batteries. The other positions facing a potential attack were reinforced as much as possible and the works were strengthened.

The allied attack came at the end of the day on 5 November. They quickly overran the advanced posts at Kirgener. They reestablished their trenches, which had been begun during the nights of 1 and 2 November, and connected the two batteries by Zigankenberg with their redoubt. At the same time they abandoned the bulk of Schidlitz, which they set afire, as well as all the houses placed in the valleys between Schidlitz and Zigankenberg.[63]

From 5 to 16 November, the allies made no progress in their siege efforts. The consolidated their positions, strengthened their earthworks, and brought forward munitions to their batteries. They also established a new battery directed at the Neugarten Gate, the Kool Battery.

During the evening of 8/9 November, they renewed their attack against the Frioul Redoubts. It was an attack of siege warfare, rather than a rush of troops. They pushed forward their trenches to within pistol range of the French positions and prepared explosive charges in the counterscarps. They also placed howitzers to fire on the Frioul Redoubts.

The Garrison Strikes Back

During the night of 5 November, Captain Chambure embarked his company at Neufahrwasser and rowed to Nehrung, behind the allied lines, where he disembarked. He fell on the headquarters of the allies' chief of staff, burnt the village of Bohnsack and a number of caissons loaded with munitions, destroyed several magazines and generally brought confusion and chaos to the allied lines.

Captain Chambure then pulled his small force together and pushed over land, towards the rear of the allies trenches and the French posts at Weichselmünde, which he reached at dawn. Aside from the destruction of materials and supplies, his sortie killed or wounded more than 150 allied soldiers.[64]

Fearing a repeat of the action, the commander of Bohnsack alerted his garrison on the following night (5/6 November). Around 10:30 p.m., he advanced five field guns and several Congreve rocket launchers onto the plain of Heubude. They began fire on Fort Desaix and the Lang-Garten portion of the village. He hoped to set fire to those positions, including the grain magazine in the Lang-Garten Church and the powder magazine there. The French responded with the battery at Holm and the guns in Fort Desaix. The exchange of artillery fire lasted until 2:00 p.m.

A few days later Chambure's company departed from Neufahrwasser during the night, to surprise the post at Brösen. It left in two detachments. One was embarked in boats and the second advanced by foot. The two units attacked simultaneously, killing 8-10 allies and wounding about 30 more. After burning the boats at the small camp at Brösen, they withdrew back to their original positions, taking with them, the horses of several Cossacks.[65]

As if two successful raids weren't enough, yet another blow was struck by Chambure's free company during the night of 11/12 November. It passed from the Frioul batteries and crossed the Wemberg ravine. It ambushed an allied force 400 to 500 paces from the trench, and killed 120 allied troops with bayonets, wounded many more, and returned to its original positions with little losses.

Captain Chambure's name became well known amongst the besieging allies, when they could no longer count on the security of their trenches because of his actions. He continued his efforts and during the night of 16/17 November, his company once again slipped into the night. They passed through Oliva Gate, towards Langfuhr. They advanced in the shadows, until they arrived at an allied trench. The dropped into the trench killing many Russians and pursuing the Russians pell-mell into the Kabrun Redoubt. The battery was taken, 70 to 80 Russians were killed, for the loss of two dead and five wounded Frenchmen. After destroying what he could of the redoubt, Chambure's tiny force quickly withdrew back to the French lines, before the Russians could respond.[66]

Aside from that, there were no major military operations by the French in early November. The rest of their efforts were expended in expanding and improving their defenses. On 15 November, the French began a barrage against the allied entrenchments that lasted for a few hours.

At this time, the garrison of Danzig consisted of 17,597 men. There were 1,182 in hospital and 2,915 sick in their chambers. The gendarmes and various artisans had another 600 men, and there were 12,900 combatants. The combatants broke down as follows:

Artillery	
French	900
German and Polish	700
Engineers	
French	240
Polish	80
Imperial Guard Depot	250
Navy	480
Cavalry	
French	700
Polish	250
Infantry	
French	3,500
Polish	3,300
Neapolitan	1,300
German	1,200

The situation in the garrison was difficult. The Bavarians had received an order from their sovereign, which they were attempting to authenticate. The rest of the German allies were ready to desert in mass. The allies brought proclamations forward daily, and directed them principally, at the German troops in the garrison. Rapp ordered the proclamations burnt, but their propaganda still found its way into the hands of the various national troops. They learned of the defections of Bavaria and Saxony, of the battle at Leipzig and of the withdrawal of the French to the line of the Rhine.

A parliamentary, accompanied by a trumpeter, came forward on 6 November, with a letter from Alexander, Duke of Württemberg, to Rapp. In it he swore on his honor, the truth of the French disaster at Leipzig, Napoleon's abandonment of Saxony and Erfurt, and that he was in full retreat to the Rhine.

Rapp responded that he believed the Duke's word, but that his duty was to hold Danzig, until ordered by his Emperor to leave it, and that he would do so as long as he was able. In response, the next day the Duke of Württemberg sent forward public papers, gazettes and other documents, including the Courier of London, which repeated and reinforced the news that he had provided in his earlier letter.[67]

After praising the valor of the French garrison, the Duke of Württemberg, finished his letter with the following:

His Majesty, the King of Bavaria, having made an offensive and defensive alliance with the allied powers, I have the honor to officially present to your excellency (to Rapp), that he wishes permission for the Bavarian troops, which find themselves in Danzig, be permitted to leave that place. At the same time I give you my word of honor, my General, that these troops shall not be employed by me, but sent directly to Germany. I shall, in a few days, make the same request relative to the Polish and Saxon troops, after the arrival of news that we await momentarily, of the conclusion of peace and a treaty of alliance between the allied powers and the King of Saxony, who is in Berlin.

The series of letters between Rapp and the Duke of Württemberg continued, as Rapp played for time and the Duke sought to minimize his casualties.

Rapp's situation was becoming grave. The desertion rate among his allied troops was growing, and the fire of 1 November, which had destroyed two thirds of his supplies, leaving him sufficient supplies to last only until May 1814. It became urgent to contact Napoleon and advise him of the situation in Danzig.

Captain Marnier, commanding officer of the corsair *Heureuse Tonton,* was selected to carry dispatches to Napoleon. He carried with him Captain Dumoutier and eight men of proven reliability and bravery. During the night of 8 November, they quietly slipped out of Danzig and set sail for France, with dispatches for the Emperor.[68]

As correspondence passed between Rapp and the Duke of Württemberg, both the French and allies continued improving their positions. The allies began preparing a large number of batteries, the last of which was not complete until 17 November. Once completed, the allies began to fire all of their batteries on Danzig, in another tremendous bombardment. This time, instead of firing on the city, the allies concentrated their fire on the French Frioul batteries, the works at Zigankenberg, and on Bischofsberg. The number of allied shots fired was beyond count, but the French fired 3,400 rounds back in response.

The allies needed to destroy the three redoubts at Frioul, which enfiladed the extreme left of their newest parallel. Above all, they needed to destroy the howitzer that could fire effectively against their Batteries #1 and #2. As a result, they concentrated the fire of six mortars *à la Coehorn* and their batteries at the *Étoile*, against the French redoubts. The artillery battle continued through the following days, not ending until 21 November.[69]

Assault on the Gudin Battery

During the night of 18/19 November, 200 Russian workers, supported by two full battalions, advanced with picks and shovels, to destroy the Gudin Battery. Captain Razumsky commanded the battery and spotted them during their advance. He received them with canister fire and a heavy fusillade of musketry.[70] Despite that, the Russians advanced into the ditch and began to climb the palisades. Major Deskur led forward 100 French infantry from his reserve, in a bayonet charge so impetuous it shocked the Russians into flight, abandoning their tools and weapons.

That same night, the Russians attempted to surprise the Fiszer Battery, under the command of Colonel Plessman, without success. Three times they rushed this battery and three times they were repelled with heavy musketry and a large quantity of grenades. However, during the days that followed, the French found themselves obliged to abandon several fortified houses, the Yellow House, and the Weimberg house because of the artillery fire.

Rapp had hoped to preserve his corps as long as possible. However, the allied proclamations, false and true, that the various German monarchs had deserted Napoleon, were having a terrible effect on the morale of his German allies, the Dutch, and the others. Even the Spanish pioneers, who had rendered most valuable services, deserted whenever the opportunity presented itself. Only the French and the Poles were truly reliable in this regard and were the only troops used to garrison or labor on the exterior works. The Bavarians also remained quite loyal. They had a long history of alliance with France dating back to the War of the Spanish Succession, and were loath to betray the French, their honor and their sensibilities.

The commander of the Bavarians, Oberst Buttler, learned of the Duke of Württemberg's statements, and his word of honor regarding the defection of Bavaria. However, he had no direct orders from his sovereign and would not abandon General Rapp. At the same time, he also felt that he could no longer continue to engage in combat with the allies. He then requested that Rapp not oblige him or his troops to work or serve outside the main fortress. Rapp granted his request, but regretted losing the service of such a fine body of men.

Frioul is Abandoned

On 21 November, Rapp found himself obliged to evacuate Alt-Schottland and the three Frioul batteries. The withdrawal of the garrisons and artillery was effected without major mishap by 9:00 p.m. Once evacuated their former positions were set afire and rendered useless to the allies.

The Petershagen Gate was sealed and armed with six guns taken from the Frioul batteries. The Bischofsberg artillery was spread among the abandoned works and the Legethor front. The floating batteries descended down the Mottlau, to assume new positions, and ten small mortars were emplaced in support of Bischofsberg.

The allies occupied the ruined works shortly afterwards and began to turn them against the fortress of Danzig. They raised new batteries at the "poste du sergent," and in the throat of the Frioul Redoubts #1 and #2, which were aimed at Bischofsberg, the Petershagen Gate, and the Lasalle Redoubt. They raised a new battery near Niederfeld, on the edge of the inundation, a second on the Mottlau dike, and a third one on the Radaune dikes, to serve as a counterbattery force.[71]

On 23 November the order was received to reorganize the garrisons of the various French positions. The new garrisons were as follows:

Lasalle Lunette	1 officer	25 men
Dehouse Lunette	1	25
Between Lasalle and Dehouse Lunettes	6	200 skirmishers
Petershagen Gate	1	30
Neugarten Gate	1	30
Vigilance Bastion	1	25
Saugeube Bastion	1	25
Bischofsberg Fort	3	120 men and 200 workers
Cafarelli Lunette	2	40
Leclerc Lunette	2	40
Fort Holm	2	50
Fort Napoleon	3	100
Fort Weichselmünde	15	200[72]

Once ready, the allies could have renewed the bombardment on 25 November, with 150 guns, without counting those on the Étoile, Kabrun, Schellmühle, and Johannisberg. This bombardment could have spelt the end of the garrison.

The Surrender is Negotiated

Rapp had earlier called a council to discuss the continuation of the siege. It decided to seek terms with the allies and on 25 November, General Heudelet and Colonel Richemont went to the Russian headquarters to negotiate a surrender. The bombardment began on 25 November and lasted for two days until the convention was concluded. The noise of the roaring cannons was followed by a profound silence.

The convention that was concluded permitted the garrison the honors of war[73] on 1 January 1814, and would turn the fortress over to the allies, if not relieved. Rapp had made arrangements for the inhabitants to move in and out of the fortress, to buy food from the countryside and they promptly did so.

On 4 December, in conformance with the convention, Rapp sent a courier to Napoleon. Colonel Richemont was selected for this duty. In addition, a few days later, Rapp returned to the allies, the 800 prisoners he still held. Many others had succumbed to their wounds, sickness and to the allied bombardments. This was done earlier than required, because Rapp thought it preferable to not be burdened with feeding and caring for them and knew that, without arms, they would be useless to the allies.

On 12 December, the Bavarian, Württemberg, and other German troops departed the fortress. During 24 December, Rapp made preparations to turn over the Weichselmünde and Holm works, as well as the fortress's magazines. However, in a most sinister turn of events, the Russian commissaries did not appear to assume control of them.

Treachery

At noon, Rapp received a note from the Duke of Württemberg stating that Czar Alexander had accepted the convention, with the exception of the clause allowing the garrison to return to France. The Czar ordered him to take the French garrison as prisoners of war into Russia until they were

The French garrison of Danzig marches into captivity, by Röchling.

exchanged. The Polish and German troops could, now the Confederation of the Rhine no longer existed, return to their homes.

Colonel Richemont, en route to Napoleon, had been stopped on 13 December, in Frankfurt on Main and not permitted to continue. He was sent to Fulda and finally to Dresden, where he spent his captivity.

Indignation replaced joy in the French garrison. The perfidious allied behavior displayed earlier at the capitulation of Dresden, was about to be reenacted. Rapp protested this strange infraction of the traditional method of handling such conventions, but to no avail. The allies now knew the exact quantities and locations of his supplies. They knew the strengths and weaknesses of his positions. The situation was grave, but all was not yet lost.[74]

A new council of war was held and Rapp and his staff began to work on the situation. It was, however, felt impossible to resume the defense of the city. Though the Duke of Württemberg offered to put things in their former condition, Rapp felt that this "was a mockery. What could we do? We had no more provisions."[75] A new capitulation was to be negotiated. It did not differ, except regarding the articles regarding the return to France, as well as the Poles and Westphalians, who were to be returned to their countries.

The second capitulation was signed on 29 December. On 30 December, the German members of the garrison and the Poles left Danzig. On 2 January 1814, at 10:00 a.m., the rest of the garrison marched out of the city. The officers retained their swords and those non-commissioned officers and soldiers with the Légion d'Honneur were permitted to retain their sabers.

The Spanish Pioneers and the Dutch were absorbed into the French regiments, but abandoned the French ranks as soon as they left the city. Some were to take service with the Russians and Prussians, while others returned to their homes. Those that became prisoners consisted solely of French and Neapolitans. The French sick and wounded totaled about 1,500 men. They remained in the hospitals in Danzig. Along with Rapp, Généraux de Division Heudelet, Grandjean, Bachelu,

Franceschi, Cavaignac, Lepin, and Campredon, and Généraux de Brigade Bazancourt, Husson, Destrées, Gault, Breissand, and Devilliers passed into captivity.

The French prisoners were divided into four columns and sent to nearby cantonments marching at two day intervals. The siege, which had begun on 21 January 1813, had lasted until 2 January 1814. Of the 35,934 in the initial garrison, only about 10,000 remained on 2 January.[76]

It had been an honorable and valiant defense, adding to the glory of French arms, and to the shame of those of the allies, for their treacherous and shameful treatment of the initial capitulation.

16

The Other Sieges 15 August–
31 December 1813

The Siege of Glogau

Glogau stands on the German-Polish border on the main road from Dresden to Posen, in the heart of the Silesian provinces of Prussia. It is actually considerably east of Berlin and, as such, sat on the major east-west lines of communication. It had been provisioned and garrisoned in the spring of 1812, prior to the invasion of Russia, and in August stood miles behind the allied lines, an isolated souvenir of times when the unbeaten French armies roamed freely across the Polish plains.

After the withdrawal of the French from Russia, on 28 February 1813, the garrison found the first Russians at its doors. The debris of the IV Corps had sought refuge within its walls and from that force, plus a few limited reinforcements, a garrison was established. The formal investment began on 1 March 1813.[1]

This first investment ended with the summer armistice and communications were allowed between the garrison and the main French armies. Men and material were brought into the garrison, the fortress' walls and defenses were substantially improved, and its larders were filled.

In August, when the war renewed, the city's defenses consisted of 73 cannon with 506,500 pounds of powder, 78,735 projectiles, and 15,000 howitzer shells. The garrison consisted of 2,565 men of the 1/, 2/, 3/151st Line Regiment, 1,168 men of the 1/1st Croatian Provisional Regiment, and 499 of the 1/, 2/2nd Croatian Provisional Regiment, the 2/, 3/Frankfurt Regiment with 1,034 men, a company of Spanish with 144 men, four companies of artillery with a total of 370 men, a company of miners, a company of sappers, and a few naval artisans. In addition, there were 619 men from various depots, 93 train personnel, and a number of sick and wounded left behind by the retreating French armies for a total of over 6,500 men.[2]

The siege, once it resumed, was not particularly active. The garrison sent out reconnaissance forces regularly until mid-October. The routine of the siege was broken on 28 September when the allies issued bulletins announcing that the French armies were beaten and dispersed, that the allied armies were converging on Leipzig, that the French convoys and hospitals had been captured, that the British had taken San Sebastian in Spain, and were menacing Bayonne.

Despite the efforts of the garrison governor, the gazettes were brought into the city by the pickets and circulated amongst the citizens. The immediate result was that a post of 19 Croatians deserted on 1 October. Severe measures were taken to prevent recurrences, bounties were offered to those who informed on desertion plots and harsh punishment threatened to captured deserters.

On 28 October, a triple discharge of blank rounds by the allied siege forces announced the French defeat at Leipzig to the garrison. An emissary brought copies of the newspapers to the garrison announcing the decisive battle and the capture of 80,000 men and 100 cannon.

The newspapers cited ample details of the disaster, listing the names of generals killed and wounded. It also announced the defection of all of Napoleon's German allies, Suchet's retreat to Barcelona, and the invasion of Italy by the Austrians.[3]

Though the governor burned every copy he found, copies still circulated throughout the city. The damage was done and the Croatians and Frankfurters no longer showed quite the same zeal as they went about their duties. With the potential for a fifth column within the city walls, the governor had the entire population disarmed.

During the night of 7/8 November, the first trenches were opened by the siege forces. During the day of 8 November, a force of 2,400 men in four columns sallied out of the garrison to attack the new works. Despite the fire of the allied battery in Brostau, the French sappers under Nempde destroyed a significant length of trench.

In the morning of 10 November, a similar operation was executed against trenches below Fort l'Étoile. The 151st Line Regiment penetrated into the enemy trenches at the pas de charge, chased the Prussians out, and allowed the French workers to destroy the trenches. Major Sellier, not content with this success, led two battalions forward against Fort l'Étoile. The Prussians were advancing out of the fort to strike the French, but the 3/151st, hidden in a fold of the earth, struck them in the flank. According to French accounts the Prussians lost 300 *hors de combat*, 80 prisoners, and 400-500 drowned in the Oder. The French lost 60 dead and 300 wounded.[4]

The prisoners informed their captors that Fort l'Étoile was armed with three guns. They also stated that the siege force was commanded by General Heister, who had 10,000 Prussians on the left bank and 3,000 Russians, under General Rosen, on the right bank. The allied engineering officer directing the siege was Colonel Blumenstein.

Through the end of November the French garrison constantly made small sorties to disquiet the allied operations. There was, however, a constant attrition through desertion and between 15 and 30 November, 54 Croatians, 12 Belgians of the 151st, 29 Frankfurters, and one Spaniard deserted. French soldiers were now posted in the moats to guard against desertion and further measures were taken to control the discontented Croatians.

French prisoners guarded by Bashkirs and Kalmucks, by Knötel.

During the siege there was a constant stream of letters from the siege force to the garrison, calling on them to surrender. These documents contained the same sort of propaganda as the earlier newspapers circulated throughout the city, that the French had collapsed, that Napoleon had been arrested in Strasbourg, etc. They were invariably ignored and no response made.

The siege of Glogau continued on a low scale. There were few assaults made by the allies during the siege other than the constant barrage of propaganda issued in an effort to convince the garrison to capitulate. Food became scarce in late January, and on 16 January, all non-essential and untrustworthy individuals were put outside the walls. On 10 February, the Russians executed the only assault against part of the fortress, the Zerbau Redoubt. The work was overrun and a mine placed, but the dampness prevented the mine from exploding. The following day a French counterattack recaptured the work and it was destroyed. The allies lost 30 dead, 50 wounded, and 32 prisoners.

On 27 March, 640 of the city's inhabitants were let outside the walls due to the lack of food, but there were no further assaults on the city. The siege was to last until 17 April 1814, and the end of the war, when 1,700 French marched back to France.[5]

The Siege of Dresden

Napoleon left Dresden for the last time on 7 October, as the maneuvers for the battle of Leipzig began in earnest. When he departed, Napoleon left Maréchal St-Cyr as garrison commander, and as commander of the reorganized I and XIV Corps. He had hoped to destroy Blücher, take Berlin, and then reunite with St-Cyr on the right bank of the Elbe. Unfortunately for the French, Napoleon's hopes were dashed at Leipzig.

On 7 October, Bubna's Austrian 2nd Light Division, which had been skirmishing with the 43rd Division around Lohmen and Fischbach, moved against the Pirna bridgehead and attacked. Its successes during the day began with the capturing of a small redoubt on the left of the bridgehead, by the village of Copitz. On 8 October Bubna's forces continued their attack, moving out of Copitz and firing all day on the troops of the I Corps, which had relieved the 43rd Division.

That same day the Russian 6th Corps under Scherbatov, detached from the Army of Silesia, arrived and took up positions on the left bank of the Elbe, near Dresden. About noon, they moved against the position occupied by the 44th Division. General Berthezène moved to support the battalion he had deployed before his positions. However, he was shortly obliged to withdraw his entire division behind the redoubts to prevent the Russians from turning his right. In addition Schetal's Austrian column was moving down the right bank of the river and could soon be in position to turn his flank. However, the Austrian column stopped near Zschokwitz and the Russian attacks were stopped by fire from Redoubts #6, #7, and #8.[6]

Bennigsen moved out of Bohemia, and on the morning of 8 October, chased the French cavalry out of its camps by Giesshübel and Borna. This occurred as Bonnet was preparing to reoccupy the redoubts he had previously abandoned. Faced with a serious engagement with a superior enemy force, Bonnet withdrew. On 10 October, the I Corps was at Grüna, the 42nd Division was in Strehlen, and the 44th Division was on the heights by Räcknitz.

During the afternoon of 11 October, the allies deployed a force of about 40,000 men before St-Cyr's position. They engaged in an exchange of musketry and artillery with the 44th Division, but made no serious effort to attack the French.

The next morning all of the outlying French detachments were summoned and ordered to return to Dresden. Efforts were then made to send the sick and wounded in Dresden by ship north, up the Elbe to Torgau. The chaos that resulted as the panic-stricken invalids pushed to get aboard the ship, limited the effectiveness of the effort.[7]

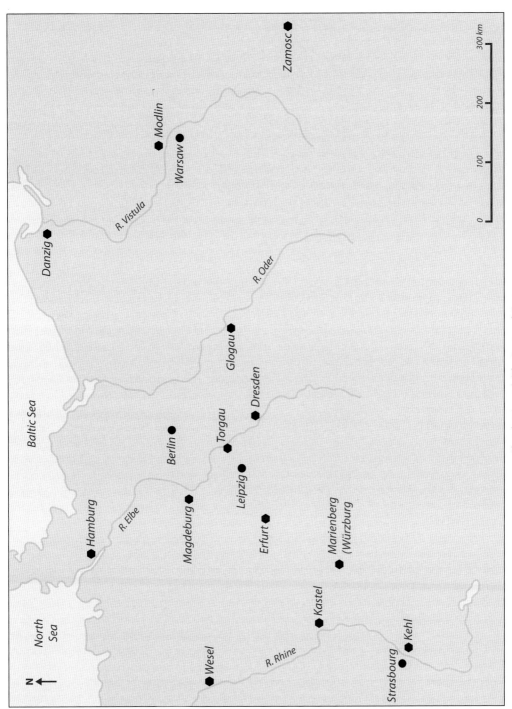

Sketch Map 14   The Besieged Fortresses.

On 12 October the expected battle did not occur, but St-Cyr found himself faced by part of General Bennigsen's Russian Reserve Army.[8] This force was led by FZM Colloredo, commanding his division and the 2nd Light Division of FML Bubna en route to the battle of Leipzig. As Bennigsen's forces arrived at Dresden, the Austrians marched off to Leipzig, leaving behind a Russian corps under GL Count Ostermann-Tolstoy and a force of Austrians. Tolstoy commanded a militia corps, three regiments[9] and a few cavalry under General Markoff.[10]

Tolstoy moved towards Dresden from Plauen, crossing the Elbe and taking up positions. At the same time, the Austrian GM Seethal, with four battalions, one each from the Kaiser, Vogelsang, Czartorsky, and Kollowrath Infantry Regiments, moved against Neustadt, the eastern suburbs of Dresden. At the same time, the Austro-Russian force also had to watch Sonnenstein. The allies had a total of about 20,000 troops, most of whom were second line, facing St-Cyr's 27,000 men.

Shut up in Dresden, St-Cyr learned little of what was happening to the west around Leipzig. He knew he was enclosed by a strong force that threatened his ability to sustain himself and his forces. On 17 October he decided to send out four columns in a reconnaissance in force, as well as to attempt to break the siege. The divisions of Berthezène (44th), Teste (23rd), and Dumonceau remained behind. Berthezène's 44th Division occupied the various French positions and redoubts on the right bank of the Elbe facing General Seethal. Teste's 23rd Division occupied the French positions between the Dohna suburb and the Elbe. Dumonceau's 2nd Division was distributed between the Grossen-Garten and Strehla.

The remaining four divisions, Cassagne (1st), Mouton-Duvernet (42nd), Claparède (43rd), and Razout (45th), supported by F. Gérard's (formerly Pajol's) 10th Light Cavalry Division, were to attack. Count Lobau sent forward Cassagne's 1st Division from the Grossen-Garten past Strehla and against Zschertnitz. General Claparède marched, with the 43rd Division, from the Moczinskischen Garden against the village of Räcknitz. The eight battalions of Mouton-Duvernet's 42nd Division advanced at 10:00 a.m., from the Plauen suburbs against the village of Plauen[11] and joined there with the eight battalions of General Razout's 45th Division. The French cavalry, under General F. Gérard, marched between the divisions of Claparède and Mouton-Duvernet. Mouton-Duvernet's 42nd Division attacked the Russians between Plauen and Räcknitz, supported by Claparède's 43rd Division and F. Gérard's cavalry. The position was taken, as were three redoubts the Russians had built there.

The French attack between the Grossen-Garten and the Elbe struck Ostermann-Tolstoy's forces. Tolstoy's troops were brave, but his infantry was formed from drafts from the Asian borders of the Russian empire and his cavalry consisted only of bashkirs and Cossacks. By 11:00 a.m., St-Cyr's attack had advanced quite far, driving the Russians back over the Gittersee Lake, and Tolstoy ordered a retreat.[12]

The Russians were hotly pursued through Mockritz and Nöthnitz. As the French pushed into Nöthnitz, F. Gérard unleashed his 7th (Vistula) Lancers, under General Gobrecht (who had led the French cavalry at Kulm), and captured four cannon in addition to inflicting heavy losses on the Russians.

At the same time, Durosnel (commandant of Dresden) and Bonnet were crushing Tolstoy's left flank and advancing against Bannewitz, forcing Tolstoy's irregular cavalry to withdraw. The Cossacks redeployed and covered the withdrawal of the fleeing Russian militia. Even though the Russian cavalry was all irregular cavalry, St-Cyr's cavalry was too weak to engage it and push the destruction of Tolstoy's army. Tolstoy withdrew to Dohna, leaving six guns and 300 prisoners to St-Cyr.

With the allied forces driven off, St-Cyr settled down to gathering in supplies necessary to support his forces and provisioning the garrison of Dresden.

The allies, however, were not idle and waited only for the arrival of Chasteler's Corps from the Army of Bohemia.[13] Chasteler arrived on 19 October and on 20 October the combined forces of Chasteler and Ostermann-Tolstoy drove forward in strength against the French. The Austrians attacked from Sporbitz and Seidnitz and the Russians from Lockwitz and Räcknitz. St-Cyr's forces were forced back to the outskirts of Dresden.

However, the forces were still closely matched, and though the French were back in the outskirts of Dresden, Chasteler called for more reinforcements. As the battle of Leipzig was over and the French were falling back towards the Rhine, there were troops available. The required reinforcements came in the form of the Austrian 4th Army Corps under GdK Klenau, who arrived on 26 October.[14]

On 26 and 27 October, the Austro-Russian forces pushed against St-Cyr again and drove him out of Gorbitz, Pennerich, Döltzchen, and Briesnitz. The Austrian divisions of Mayer and Hohenlohe-Bartenstein, which arrived with Klenau, remained on the left bank of the Elbe, while Weid-Runkel's Division took up positions on the right bank by Weinsdorf to allow contact to be maintained with Torgau.

The combined force of Austrians and Russians, some 43,000 men, was then placed under the overall command of General der Kavallerie Klenau.

The situation for St-Cyr was not good. He had not succeeded in fully provisioning the city. The shortage of food, salt, and firewood was such that the city had no more than a two month supply. After that time St-Cyr would either have to fight his way out or surrender. All of the city's provisions were gathered together and placed under the control of Intendant Dumas, in an effort to control the situation. About the same time, official word of the French defeat at Leipzig was received.

The siege settled down to a level of inactivity where both sides stared at one another, but neither took any aggressive action. The siege languished at this low level until the morning of 6 November, when the I Corps, reinforced by two divisions of the XIV Corps and all of the cavalry available in the city of Dresden, about 15,000 men, marched down the Grossenhain Road. They advanced with over 100 wagons in their wake in an effort to capture more supplies to support the garrison.

They quickly ran into a force of Austrian sharpshooters[15] by a vineyard wall. The Austrians and Russians under FML Fürst Weid-Runkel counterattacked and inflicted 800 casualties on the French before they withdrew back into Dresden.[16]

St-Cyr then called his generals together and reviewed the French situation. The council must have been a difficult one, not because of dissent, but because of the options available to the French. Eventually they was decided to enter into negotiations with the allies, and attempt to negotiate an exchange, whereby they would be allowed to march to France in return for abandoning Dresden.

On 11 November, Oberst Rothkirch, Austrian Chief of Staff, and Colonel Muraviev, Russian Chief of Staff, entered into negotiations with Colonels Morion and Perrin. A capitulation was quickly negotiated whereby the French garrison of Dresden would, with weapons and baggage, leave the city in six columns and lay down their arms before the city's redoubts. The officers would be allowed to retain their swords. The officers and men were to be made prisoners and returned to France. They would then be exchanged for an equal number of allied prisoners of war. The sick and wounded were to be returned to France immediately and all munitions, supplies, material, and equipment would be surrendered to the allies intact.[17]

On 17 November the French surrendered to the allies. Maréchal St-Cyr; GD Count Lobau, Claparède, Bonnet, Mouton-Duvernet, Berthezène, Razout, Dumonceau, Gérard, Cassagne, Gomez-Freyre, and Teste; GB Schramm, Borcelli, Peroletti, Bertrand, Couture, Godard, Le Telier, Goguel, Estevin, Jacquet, Doucet, Chartrand, Gobrecht, Stedmann, Baldus, O'Meara,[18] Potocky, Weissenhof, Bernard; 1,759 officers and 33,744 non-commissioned officers and men surrendered. A total of 25 howitzers and 69 field cannon, plus eight mortars, 26 howitzers, and 117 guns from various fortifications were handed over to the allies.[19]

However, instead of keeping their oath and conforming to the agreement they had made, the allies marched the French off to prisoner of war camps and made no effort whatsoever to exchange

The garrison of Dresden surrenders on 12 November.

them as guaranteed. St-Cyr states that Chasteler, who had succeeded Klenau, wrote him that Prince Schwarzenberg would under no condition allow the return of the garrison to France. St-Cyr was offered the opportunity to negotiate another capitulation or to reenter Dresden and resume the siege.[20] The French passed into captivity rather than return to the city. It was a sad end for this gallant force and a tragic loss of 35,000 men who could have made a significant contribution to Napoleon's desperate 1814 campaign.

The Siege of Torgau

In contrast to Dresden, which was an open city, whose medieval walls had decayed and had no significant fortifications, Torgau was a fortress of the first order. As such it had played a significant role in the 1813 spring campaign, as well as serving as a base of operations and a supporting position for Oudinot and Ney in the 1813 fall campaign.

Since 1812, the Torgau defenses had been repaired and strengthened with a strong wall, fosses and open exterior works. The wall consisted of seven bastioned fronts and was open to the east, except for a parapet which covered part of the opening. However, the east was completely covered by the Elbe. On the far side of the Elbe was a bridgehead of considerable strength. The wall fronts were 370 to 380 yards long.

The fortress was defended by a number of exterior works, Fort Zinna, Fort Mahla, and the Repitz and Losswig Lunettes on the left bank. On the right bank stood the bridgehead and the Zwethau and Werda Lunettes.

To the northwest of Torgau proper, there was a significant ridge on which stood Fort Zinna and Fort Mahla. It was 1,100 yards from Bastion #6 and was a squared bastion some 270 yards on a face. The fort was defended by a ditch, had a covered way and two fronts were covered by demi-lunes. Fort Mahla was 550 yards from Bastion #6 and 815 yards from Fort Zinna and was shaped like a priest's hat. It was 260 yards long and 65 yards deep. It was surrounded by a covered way, its throat was bastioned and it had a ditch, but it did not have a parapet.

The bridgehead was a crown work covered by three bastioned fronts and a gorge somewhat separated from the Elbe. Its exit was covered by a ravelin or small demi-lune. The ditches were deep enough to be flooded from the Elbe. The bridgehead was connected to the main fortress by a covered, wooden bridge.[21]

The population of Torgau was about 5,000. With the exception of one public square, most of the interior of the city was occupied by its 557 houses.

On 14 September, Count de Narbonne, formerly a minister under Louis XVI, became governor. He published a decree from Napoleon indicating that Torgau was to become the central depot for the army and was to render those services necessary to accomplish this goal. General Lauer was nominated to command the depots of the Grande Armée established in Torgau and General Brun was to command the service troops, the artillery, and the engineers. In addition, a major hospital was established in Torgau which housed 6,000 sick and wounded.[22]

On 10 October, the inhabitants had to evacuate 82 houses that were requisitioned as barracks and hospitals. Earlier, granaries, provision magazines, and other necessary facilities had been established.

Soon afterwards, as Ney withdrew from the area, he took with him all of the men who were fit for combat and could march, nonetheless there remained within the walls of Torgau a large number of men from the I, II, III, IV, V, VI, VII, XI, XIII, and XIV Corps, as well as the Imperial Guard.

As the fall campaign progressed, the bridge over the Elbe was covered to protect it from enemy artillery fire. In addition, defenses were built to protect the bridge from fire ships and other water born attacks that the allies might make it. A fire brigade was organized from among the city's inhabitants.

After the battle of Dennewitz, a Prussian observation corps, under Wobeser, had established itself on the eastern bank of the Elbe, facing the bridgehead. His presence made water communications with Dresden difficult, but the village of Kreyschau masked his position from the guns of the bridgehead.

On 1 October, Narbonne ordered the bridgehead and Bastion #8 to fire on Kreyschau, but a ruse was played, where the French pretended that their powder was of such poor quality that the village was out of range. General Brun de Villeret then executed a sortie and burned the major portion of the village about 1:00 p.m. On 3 October, the Army of Silesia crossed the Elbe at two positions below Wittenberg, near Wartenburg, and pushed forward towards Torgau.[23]

On 4 October, the allies destroyed the abandoned blockhouses in Neiden and Süptitz. The next day the allies occupied the villages of Welsau and Zinna. The fodder and the best horses of the Royal Saxon stables in Repitz were drawn into the fortress, and the Saxon Justice Tribunal moved its seat to Belgern.

On 8 October, Narbonne wrote to the city's magistrates that he judged it in the best interest of the public that he assume the powers of a governor of a besieged city and declared the city invested. With that accomplished, he began to issue the various orders to control life in the city. He ordered that all public cafes, cabarets and restaurants be closed by 7:00 p.m., and that no one walk about the city after 8:00 P.NI., without a lantern. The inhabitants were to remove all trash within 24 hours or it would be removed by soldiers and the inhabitants involved would be taxed 60 centimes.[24]

The last convoys from Dresden arrived on 10 October. On 13 October Napoleon left Dresden for his rendezvous with the allies at Leipzig. On 19 October General Durrieu moved his forces into a position between Fort Zinna and the Grosser Teich Lake. He commanded 6,700 men, 2,560 horses, and 540 vehicles. In addition, in Torgau, including 7,400 sick and wounded, there were a total of 19,425 men; this included a small Saxon brigade under General Mellenthin, 1,475 men, who were to shortly leave the city. The total force defending Torgau came to 24,650 men.

General Durrieu brought in a reinforcement of artillery and engineering troops, the 2nd and 8th Naval Military Artisan Battalions, two battalion cadres of the 42nd Line, the 6th and 17th

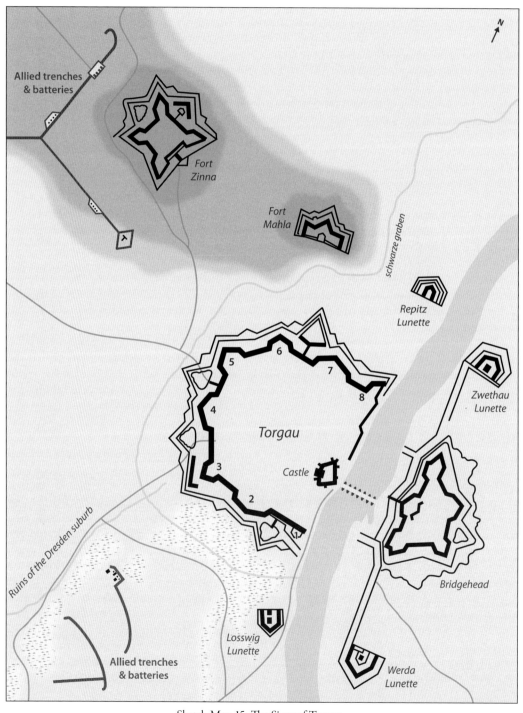

Sketch Map 15 The Siege of Torgau.

Military Equipage Battalions, and a number of men employed in the various military administrations. The artillery park was placed under General Bouchu and the engineering park was under Major Finot.

Narbonne began to organize the men at his disposal. His first action was to organize eight provisional battalions. The first was formed from men of the Imperial Guard. The 2nd, 3rd, 4th, 5th, and 6th Battalions were formed from the men in the various depots. The 7th and 8th were formed from men from three companies of the 131st, 132nd, and 133rd Line and the cadres of battalions of the 42nd and 65th Line. The first of these eight provisional battalions served as an independent formation, but the remaining seven were organized into three Régiments Provisoires de Torgau. The 1st and 3rd Torgau Provisional Regiments contained only two battalions, while the 2nd had three. After receiving instruction in the manual of arms and other infantry drill, the two military equipage battalions were organized into the 4th Provisional Regiment, but it rendered almost no service. The commanders of the three regiments were Majors Charrière, Deschanges, and Jamin.[25]

In addition, Narbonne had a company of Polish Cossacks organized to serve as scouts and an elite reserve company, under Capitaine Catel, to be used in a last, desperate contingency.

The infantry was organized into three brigades, the Fortress Brigade, the Exterior or Entrenched Camp Brigade, and the Bridgehead Brigade. General Brun, who commanded the Fortress Brigade, led the 8th Marine Artisan Battalion, the Guard Battalion, the 2nd Torgau Regiment, and the Würzburgers. The Exterior Brigade consisted of the 2nd Marine Artisan Battalion (715 men), the 1st Torgau Regiment (1,100 men), and a Hessian battalion (320 men). General Durrieu, commanding the Exterior Brigade, also had an artillery company (190 men), a sapper company (140 men), and the Polish Cossack company.

General Devaux, who commanded the Bridgehead Brigade, was charged with defending the bridgehead and the Werda and Zwelhau Lunettes. He commanded the 3rd Torgau Regiment, a Hessian battalion, an artillery company, and Capitaine Lenoir's miner company.

Prussian infantry and Landwehr in action during the autumn of 1813, by Knötel.

The fortress was defended by 199 guns, including eight 24-pdrs, 30 howitzers, six mortars, and a large number of 8-pdrs. The powder supply was good, but theoretically less than necessary to defend the fortress. The number of infantry cartridges, 700,000, was considered to be insufficient for a long siege.

Artillery assignments	No. of Guns
Main Fortress	85
Bridgehead	50
Fort Zinna	31
Fort Mahla	8
4 Lunettes	12
Mobile Battery	6 6-pdrs and 4 24-pdr howitzers

There were more artillerists than necessary to man these guns, so the excess was placed at the disposition of the engineering staff. The relations between the engineers and the artillerists were most harmonious, and as a result, the sappers, pontooneers, artisans, and train worked together without distinction between their branches of service.[26]

The fortress was provisioned with 360,000 rations for 4,000 men and 400 sick for a period of three months. This duty had been left to the Saxons prior to their defection, and the required materials were nearly all in place, except for the wood rations, which would prove hard on the sick.

On 22 October Narbonne chased out the Saxon troops that had formed part of the garrison. They were deemed to be a liability and they were given the transport necessary to evacuate themselves and their baggage. The Würzburgers and Hessians were authorized to dispatch couriers to their sovereigns, so that they could receive orders as to how they were to acquit themselves.

On 22 October the Bavarian General Maillot withdrew before the allied forces facing him and joined the French garrison in Torgau.

On 20 October Tauentzien's forces advanced from Potsdam and joined Wobeser. On 29 October GM Graf Lindenau's Brigade moved across the Elbe at Coswig and took up positions by Dommitsch.[27] Tauentzien deployed his own forces between the village of Staupitz and Mockrehna, where he was slowly being joined by the Saxon forces that had defected at Leipzig.

On 2 November Tauentzien's troops arranged themselves with their left wing on the Elbe and their right wing on the Eilenburg-Düben road. The small Saxon corps advanced towards Torgau and positioned itself with its right wing on the Elbe, extended its line through Staupitz and Melpitz, and secured its left on the Eilenburger road. During this march, the second brigade under Oberst Brause stopped by the village of Bennewitz in order to reconnoiter the area between the Elbe, the ponds, and the road to Torgau. There they encountered a wagon train hauling supplies into Torgau, which they attacked, seizing several wagons and making a few prisoners.[28]

On 3 November the French struck at Losswig and the blockhouse near it as well as seeking to destroy the palisades, which had been raised in the woods. The French column consisted of 1,000 men supported by a single battery of four guns. They encountered the von Sahr/von Rechten Infantry Battalion,[29] supported by a single battery. The allies drew in three battalions that were posted in Beckwitz to reinforce the fight. One of these battalions, the Saxon von Anger Grenadier Battalion, executed a bayonet attack. A sharp fight ensued and the French withdrew back into Torgau after accomplishing their mission.[30]

On 5 November there was another sortie under General Durrieu. He led 1,200 infantry, 40 cavalry, a battery of six guns, and all of the wagons of the engineering park, the artillery park, and the equipage park in an effort to gather supplies and material. He pushed the Prussians out of Losswig and advanced his infantry down the road to Schildau, where he took up a position in the forest and covered the 8th Marine Artisan Battalion as it gathered supplies.[31]

The Prussians drew together several battalions and attacked from Beckwitz. General Durrieu's infantry was not yet well trained, and in executing a bayonet attack against the Saxon von Anger Battalion, suffered heavy losses—80 men. Fortunately, the forest prevented the allied artillery from reaching the battle.

The provisions of fodder had run short. They had been established before the arrival of the various park detachments and were now terribly insufficient to support the demands made on them by the numbers of horses present. The artillery was ordered to be reduced to 150 horses, the engineers 100, the equipage 100, officers of all grades were to reduce to the least number possible, and all the rest, except for 200 reserved for the Polish Cossacks, were slaughtered. Most of them were then thrown into the Elbe, though some were salted down to serve as food for the garrison.[32]

Prior to this time, the Dresden suburb had not been demolished, as was the normal practice. This had been done to spare the inhabitants, as well as to provide better lodging for the garrison. However, now the time had come for the suburb to be evacuated and the demolition begun.

Major Finot, commander of the engineers, raised a dam between Fort Mahla and the Wittenberg Gate to capture the waters of the Schwarz-Wasser before the walls of the fortress to the northwest. The governor then ordered the rest of the inundations to be raised to their maximum depth.

On 8 November Narbonne fell from his horse during a review and suffered a severe blow on his head. Though unconscious for a while, he recovered and resumed work until 17 November, when he succumbed to a typhus fever. On 18 November he was given the last rites and was buried at the base of Bastion #8, which received his name.

Command of the garrison then fell to Count Dutaillis. However, General Lauer felt that this was an improper usurpation of power, quoting the Decrees of 24 December 1811, which stated that senior officers closed in a besieged fortress could not take command until they are authorized by their letters of service. However, his protestations in the defense council went unheeded and unsupported.

On 14 November the garrison had 743 officers and 12,775 non-commissioned officers and men. In addition, there were 5,808 infirm, giving a total of 19,326 men. Of this number, 2560 men, mostly the officers without troops, all those employed in the various administrations and the sick were reduced to half-rations.[33]

On 22 November the Prussians opened fire against the post at Scierie with two howitzers and two 12-pdr cannon. During the night their movement had been masked by two dikes and the roads which run to Losswig. After a prolonged fire, these guns began to cause some damage to the works and blockhouse that they took in the flank. By the end of the day they had set the Scierie work, which was made of wood, afire. As the French abandoned the position, the Prussians then occupied it after a quick fight. The attacking Prussian force consisted of 200 volunteers from the Fus/3rd Reserve Regiment and the 3/Neumark Landwehr Regiment. The Prussians lost 20 men in the action.[34] The work of destroying the Dresden suburb continued with increased vigor, and that evening what had not been knocked down was set afire.

During the night of 24 November, the Prussians ranged their howitzers against the bridgehead, in an effort to show the residents the type of attack they could expect. That day the French set off the mines, destroying the bridges by the Schwarz-Graben.

The resulting inundations were deepest before the walls running between Bastions #1, #2, and #3, stretching across the southern face of the fortress west from the Elbe. The Schwarz-Graben (ditch) was filled where it ran between Bastions #3, #4, and #5 and an inundation was made between Bastions #5 and #6.

On 24 November the Grand Duchies of Würzburg and Hesse-Darmstadt directed their troops to leave the fortress, but with the stipulation that they would not be obliged to serve against France for one year. An epidemic of typhus had raged in the fortress for sometime and as these Germans walked out of the fortress their illness became quickly apparent to the allies.[35]

The covered way of Fort Zinna was weakly palisaded and the slopes of the ditch were in a sandy soil which drained easily. This had prevented the completion of the gorge of the work, and it appeared to be open to a coup de main, as a result of its separation from the main works of Torgau. Though other defenses existed, the garrison slept with its weapons at hand, so as to allow a quick defense. The three blockhouses had 60 man garrisons and the Polish Cossacks constantly patrolled the plain before and around the fortress.

The Exterior Brigade now consisted of 955 men. Of them, 654 were in Fort Zinna, 230 were in Fort Mahla with a sapper company, and 71 were in the Repitz Lunette. During the first night and during all of those remaining before the outwork capitulated, the governor sent 250 men from the main fortress and a detachment of artillery train into Fort Zinna, as an evening reinforcement.

During the night of 26/27 November, the Prussians opened a trench before the wall between Bastions #2 and #3. A parallel was established and armed with two batteries. The darkness and the sandy nature of the soil had permitted them to erect their work without alarming the garrison. The sentinels on the covered way heard absolutely nothing.

The right of their work was 480 yards from the covered way of Bastion #2. One of the batteries, armed with three 12-pdrs and two mortars, was facing the right face of demi-lune 2-3. The other stood on the point of this work and contained two mortars.[36]

At 9:00 a.m., these batteries opened fire and dismounted one of the guns in the fortress. The French gunners, under Chef de bataillon Forgeot, responded by firing 600 rounds back at the Prussians.

The same night the Prussians executed a diversionary attack against the Zwethau Lunette and the bridgehead. They built a battery behind the dike, which united the villages of Werda and Kreyschau. This road, raised high enough to cover a man mounted on a horse, favored the Prussians. The battery consisted of a howitzer and three mortars.

During the night of 27/28 November, the allies fired about 350 bombs and 600 rounds against the fortress. In the morning the French found they had constructed a redoubt on the right of their parallel, and that they had commenced work on two new batteries. One was to have five guns and face the left face of the attack demi-lune. The other was to have four mortars.

As this active assault was beginning, the high death rate in the fortress was growing further. Deaths were running slightly over 330 a day. Cadavers lay in the hospitals, in the streets, and on the ramparts. Fortunately, a hard frost froze the bodies and prevented the significant spread of any disease from this. The governor was obliged to renounce any efforts to use the external cemeteries and accorded to the inhabitants part of the castle's gardens, and other land was set aside for the garrison's burials.[37]

During the night of 28/29 November, the Prussians ran a communications parallel in front of the village of Zinna. The work was done under the supervision of Oberst Plauzen, the engineering officer for Tauentzien's Corps. The trench moved from the right flank through the ruins of the Ziegelei and Coswig suburbs to the old Elbe channel.[38] The French responded by moving their heavy caliber guns around to the faces of the fortress where they could best support Fort Zinna.

At 10:00 p.m., on the night of 29/30 November, Colonel Jamin led a sortie from the bridgehead and advanced as far as Kreyschau, before returning to its garrison.

The artillery in Fort Zinna consisted of 31 guns. Seven were directed against the Prussian battery on the left, nine against their center, and four against the Prussian redoubt. Though the Prussians were subjected to intense fire, they were able to continue to discommode the garrison, dismounting a gun and setting a barracks afire.

This night the left wing of the Prussian parallel was advanced and a howitzer battery was erected. Though five batteries were to be organized, only three existed. The first stood on the left bank of the Elbe with two howitzers. The second had four 10-pdr mortars and faced the hospital, while the third, to the right of the mortar battery, had four 12-pdrs.[39]

The next day the French fired 1,070 rounds from Zinna and 100 from Mahla. The Prussian batteries were silenced. During the nights of 1 and 3 December the actions continued. Zinna's forces were reduced to 600 men, not including artillery. Mahla fell to 204 men, including 60 sappers, and Repitz had 50 men.

During the night of 3/4 December, the Prussians bombarded the city heavily. Several resulting fires were extinguished by the soldiers, but the civilians did not assist them. They preferred to hide in their bomb cellars.[40]

The governor of Torgau decided to use four Prussian officers taken prisoner earlier as emissaries to carry a proposal of surrender to the allies. However, Tauentzien declared that the proposal to surrender the fortress in exchange for being allowed to march back to France was unacceptable. These negotiations lasted from 4 to 7 December, and the bombardment of the city stopped during that period. Though the firing stopped, the Prussians continued working on their works, perfecting communications between the village of Zinna and their redoubt on the right.

The French too continued their work, but the typhus epidemic further ravaged the garrison. The strength of the garrison was slowly fading. Food continued to be in short supply and the lack of firewood was beginning to be sorely felt. Vehicles and other non-essential wooden objects rapidly vanished into the various fireplaces around the fortress.

On 8 December the Prussian bombardment was renewed. Several fires were set and seven houses were burned to the ground. The French batteries in the Losswig Lunette and Bastions #1, #2, and #3 fired on the Prussian batteries, but were unable to silence them. However, the gun fire from the bridgehead batteries was more successful and succeeded in silencing the batteries firing on its positions.[41]

The allied bombardment continued and by the night of 10/11 December, Fort Zinna was scheduled for evacuation and destruction by its French garrison. At 10:00 p.m., that night, all the artillery except four field pieces was withdrawn. At 2:00 a.m., the blockhouses were set afire and the garrison slipped off to Fort Mahla. The mines in the gorge were detonated at 2:30 a.m.

In order to assure the complete destruction of the fort a force of 50 gendarmes was sent forward. They discovered that parts of the work were still intact. A force of miners ran forward and began the demolition, discovering the explosive charge that had failed to detonate. The second attempt to detonate the charge failed, so the miner Dereins, fearing a third failure and for the honor of his company, chose to detonate it by hand, dying in the process. The remainder of the forces holding the now destroyed fort withdrew, leaving the ruins to the Prussians, but reentered the work at 4:00 a.m., with the marine artisans. The Prussians occupied Fort Zinna at 8:00 a.m.[42] General Durrieu still had 400 men in Fort Mahla and 80 in Repitz.

For the next two nights, the allies bombarded the fortress. Several fires were started and the garrison fought them bravely. The bombardment ceased on 17 December. Rations were cut once again.

The Prussians, now established in Fort Zinna, established another battery with two 12-pdrs and two howitzers and began to fire on Fort Mahla. The French batteries in the main fortress began to direct their fire against this new battery, but started to receive the attention of the Prussian batteries in the Dresden suburb in turn.

On 15 December, a third parliamentary was sent to Tauentzien. General Brun conducted these negotiations and a capitulation was considered, which would have the French surrender the fortress on 5 January 1814, if they were not relieved before that. That date was selected based on calculations of food supplies, etc.

Again the bombardment ceased, but work continued on the Prussian earth works. The Prussians opened ten embrasures in the demi-lune at Zinna, facing Fort Mahla. Negotiations continued.

On 20 December negotiations terms of the capitulation were reached on 25 December. During the time since the siege had begun, the garrison had shrunk from 24,650 men to 9,500 men. It had lost 15,150 men during the two months of the siege.[43]

The capitulation, signed on 26 December, turned the fortress and all of its equipment and material over to the Prussians. The garrison was to depart on 10 January, with the honors of war. Their arms were to be surrendered on the glacis of the fortress and they were to become prisoners of war until exchanged. The fit soldiers were to be taken to Silesia and the sick and wounded were to remain in Torgau. As usual, the officers were to retain their swords, baggage and horses. The soldiers were to be allowed to retain their haversacks. All members of the Légion d'Honneur were to be allowed to retain their sabers. Those officers and men who had lost limbs were not to be made prisoners, but were to be returned to France.

With the capitulation signed, Fort Mahla and the Repitz Lunette were turned over to the Prussians on 27 December. Once that was done Tauentzien dispatched his siege artillery and part of his corps to support the siege of Wittenberg.[44]

Despite the capitulation, no provisions were provided to the fortress and on 10 January, the rations were cut again. The garrison then moved out of the fortress and surrendered its arms. The men were then subjected to the medical inspection required by Article 8 of the capitulation, and were sent to Döhlen. Of them, 197 were sent back to Torgau.

However, the remaining articles of the capitulation were not executed. Tauentzien chose to recant on the agreement. Finding only 8,000 to 9,000 muskets in the fortress, which had held 20,000 men, he contended that they had been destroyed or thrown into the Elbe. The non-combatants who had begun the march to France were stopped and became prisoners of war. None of the promised exchanges were ever to be made. Tauentzien's violation of his agreement was based solely on the issue of the number of muskets taken and his presumption that they had all been deliberately thrown into the Elbe, in violation that article of the capitulation.[45]

Though some weapons were thrown into the Elbe from the bridgehead, because they had belonged to dead soldiers, those were isolated instances, but the Saxon population of Torgau had reported them to Tauentzien. It is most probable that this was looked upon by Tauentzien as a convenient excuse to tear up the capitulation, much in the same manner as St-Cyr was treated by the Austrians at Dresden.

The Siege of Magdeburg

The Imperial Decree of 2 February 1812, directed that Magdeburg be provisioned and garrisoned in preparation for a siege. The fortress had served as a major supply center during the 1812 campaign. In the 1813 spring campaign, Eugène had used it as the fulcrum for his operations. It was outside its gates that, on 5 April, he had fought and lost the inconclusive battle of Möckern/Danigkow. During the summer armistice the city had been further strengthened and GD Lemarrois was sent to be its commander.[46]

Girard had operated out of the fortress from August through September. After he lost the battle of Hagelberg, his forces had fallen back to the fortress and engaged in few aggressive activities.

At the beginning of September, the Prussian Major Grollman was charged with watching the fortress. His forces consisted of two infantry companies, 50 cavalry, and a single gun. His forces took up positions by Körbelitz and Waltersdorf. After the battle of Dennewitz, on 8 September, Oberst Boguslavsky assumed the duties of observing Magdeburg. His force consisted of two battalions, a squadron, and two 6-pdr half-batteries.[47]

On 14 September, General Puttlitz recovered from his illness and resumed overall command of his brigade and of the blockade of Magdeburg. Shortly after, Oberstleutnant Marwitz arrived with his detachment, the 3rd Kurmark Landwehr Infantry Regiment and the 3rd Kurmark Landwehr Cavalry Regiment. Initially Marwitz was posted by Ferchland, but later he moved Major Lavière's Battalion (3/3rd Kurmark Landwehr Regiment) to the left bank of the Elbe. Major Grollman established his headquarters in Waltersdorf and occupied the villages of Gerwisch, Biederitz, Alt- and Neu-Königsborn, Menz, Gübs, Pechau, and Randau. General Puttlitz had his headquarters in Möckern.

During the night of 16/17 September, two companies of Spanish from the Joseph Napoleon Regiment deserted to the Prussians from Friedrichstadt. On 19 September, a force of 30 Kurmark Landwehr cavalry and 50 Cossacks moved across the Elbe to attack the French lines of communications. Their first target was a voltigeur company of the 3/93rd Line Regiment garrisoned in Rogätz, which they destroyed.

Bernadotte ordered a bridge raised in Ferchland and the 3/3rd Kurmark Landwehr Infantry was assigned there permanently as a guard force. Oberstleutnant Marwitz then led the rest of his force across the Elbe and marched into Altmark as a partisan force. Schramm's Landwehr Battalion was detached and sent to the lower Elbe to support the Landsturm, but it returned to Möckern on 26 September.

On 8 October, Bernadotte advised General Puttlitz that he was going to attack General Lanusse's forces. In order to support this attack, Puttlitz dispatched two battalions, one squadron, a cannon, and a howitzer, which struck at the French posts by Prester. This attack brought out all the French forces on the right bank of the Elbe. Puttlitz's Cossacks moved to Ranies, where they swam the Elbe and passed between Lanusse's Division and Magdeburg. They rampaged behind Lanusse's lines, wreaking havoc before they withdrew. Ultimately, however, Bernadotte's proposed attack never occurred.[48]

The Prussian activity around Magdeburg consisted of a very loose blockade. The forces present were far too inadequate to begin a formal investment and the French, with sufficient escort, could and did move about as they wished. However, after the battle of Leipzig, this was to change. Lanusse was driven back into Magdeburg and Bennigsen took over command of the blockade operations on the left bank of the Elbe. Magdeburg was now totally surrounded.

That brought about a flurry of activity on the French part, as they began to gather in all the materials they could to support what they knew would be a long siege. French foraging columns moved out of the fortress regularly, gathering what they could.

However, no formal siege began. On 10 December, General Bennigsen led his Army of Poland to Hamburg to begin the siege of that city. He detached the Russian General Rossy with seven battalions, the Tartar Uhlan Regiment, and 18 guns. The Prussian General Hirschfeld and his corps, remained behind and took over operations on both banks. He established his headquarters in Schönebeck.[49]

On 16 December, the French General Jolly sortied from Magdeburg's Kröken Gate with four battalions, a number of squadrons, and four guns, and advanced against Wolmirstedt. The Prussian garrison of Wolmirstedt consisted of a single squadron and a single company. Oberstleutnant Marwitz drew his forces together between Ranstedt and Coblitz and sent his cavalry through Ohra, to take the French in the flank and rear. Jolly, however, escaped Marwitz and brought back 200 cattle, 70 horses, 180 pigs, and about 1,000 sheep, plus 35 Landwehr prisoners.

On the same day, GD Lemoine sortied with five battalions, seven guns, and a number of cavalry against the right bank of the Elbe, striking the Prussian posts in Pechau and Gübs. In contrast to the other raid, Lemoine found himself quickly facing the Landwehr battalions of Grollman, Schwerin, Lavière, and Ozarowsky,[50] supported by two guns and a number of cavalry. The French withdrew back into the fortress after suffering a number of casualties.

When 1814 arrived, the allies stood with Generals Hirschfeld and Rossy guarding the left bank of the Elbe and General Puttlitz responsible for the right bank. Hirschfeld's forces consisted of the 5th, 6th, and 7th Kurmark, and the 1st Silesian Landwehr Infantry Regiments, four squadrons of the 5th, and two of the 6th Kurmark Landwehr Cavalry Regiments, and one and a half 6-pdr batteries. General Rossy commanded eight battalions with six heavy guns (probably 12-pdrs) and

12 6-pdr guns. General Puttlitz commanded the 1st, 3rd, and 4th Kurmark Landwehr Infantry Regiments, four squadrons of the 3rd, and two squadrons of the 6th Kurmark Landwehr Cavalry Regiments, and a 6-pdr foot battery.[51]

As the new year progressed, the French continually sortied to gather in supplies while the allies rotated troops through the blockade force, but a formal siege with entrenchments and bombardments never began. When Napoleon abdicated, arrangements were made for the French to return home. On 16 May, the 4,000 strong garrison of Magdeburg marched out of the fortress. The Italians, Dutch, Spanish, and Croatians were sent to their homes, and the French marched back to France. When the fortress was turned over to the allies, it contained 841 guns, 32,000 muskets, over 1,000 sabers, 8,445 centner of powder, 4,000 centner of meal, 6,000 centner of salt flesh, and a massive quantity of unprocessed wheat.[52]

The Siege of Erfurt

As Napoleon's beaten armies marched westwards back to France, they passed through Erfurt. On 25 October at 3:00 a.m., the corps of Wittgenstein and Kleist, hot in pursuit of Napoleon, appeared before the city, and began the formal siege. The defense of the two citadels of Erfurt had been left in the hands of GD d'Alton and a garrison of 5,000 men. Of these men, 2,000 were under arms. He also had 18 of the most prominent burgers of the city as hostage, to ensure the behavior of the city.

On 30 October the formal investment began. The Prussian 9th Brigade, under General Klüx, occupied positions in Viselbach and by the Galgenberg Heights. Pirch's 10th Brigade took up positions by Gispersleben, Ilversgehofen, and in Marbach. The Prussian 11th Brigade occupied positions by Alach, Hungerbach, and Hochheim. The Prussian 12th Brigade, of Prince August von Preussen, occupied positions by Egstedt, Dittelstedt, and by the Steiger. Kleist's headquarters were in Büssleben.[53]

During the morning of 5 November, the French sent two battalions out in a sortie against Ilversgehofen in an effort to burn some houses of the village, that allowed the Prussians to approach the fortress under cover. A short fight began and the French withdrew after setting a few houses afire.

That same day Kleist received artillery reinforcements from the Austrian siege train that were to assist him in his assault on the city.

The bombardment of Erfurt began at 6:00 a.m., on 6 November, announcing the beginning of the formal siege. The allied fire was directed at the Petersberg Citadel. The allies had erected batteries at three points: the Napoleonshöhe (Napoleon's Heights) by Steiger, from the Hungerbach by Marbach, and from the Eispersleber Way. The bombardment soon began to set fires in the city proper and lasted for two days and a night. When it was over 117 houses were destroyed by the flames.[54]

On 7 November an armistice was arranged. Initially it was to be a 48 hour armistice, but it was stretched to 12 November and finally to 20 November. Food, however, became scarce, and a fever raged in the city before the armistice ended.

When the armistice ended, the siege resumed, but the bombardment did not. The month of December saw continued siege efforts. On 6 January 1814, another armistice was arranged and the French, finding the city was impossible to control, withdrew into the two fortresses, Petersberg and Cyriaksburg, with 1,800 to 2,000 soldiers.

Shortly there after the Prussian 2nd Corps marched out, leaving a blockade corps of Russians under General Jagov to continue holding the French in their fortresses. Once Wittenberg fell, Dobschütz moved to Erfurt to assume responsibility for this siege. The siege was to continue as a quiet blockade until 9 April, when 700 French soldiers sortied in a final desperate effort. The results were minimal and only six Prussians were wounded.

The siege finally ended when a commission from Louis XVIII arrived with dispatches for d'Alton. On 6 May, a white flag was hoisted and negotiations began again. On 16 May, the French garrison, 250 officers and officials and 1,884 soldiers, marched out with six field guns. In the fortress they left 180 guns and several hundredweight of powder and shot. The siege was over.[55]

The Siege of Marienberg

The siege of Marienberg began with movements by the Austro-Bavarian Corps under Wrede and his efforts to take the city of Würzburg. The siege of Marienberg, the citadel of Würzburg, amounted to little more than a blockade of the fortress. General Turreau manned the fortress with 2,000 men. After two short bombardments with field artillery and a number of negotiation sessions the French garrison commander withdrew into the Marienberg Fortress, and allowed the allies to occupy the city.

With the city occupied, the bulk of the Austro-Bavarian force marched on to its next operation, while a force under GM Graf Spreti consisting of the 2/2nd and 2/4th Bavarian Infantry Regiments and the 1/Inn Kreis (Bavarian) Mobile Legion remained behind to observe the fortress. The Würzburg depot and reserve forces in the city were placed under his command as well.

The Bavarian blockade corps on 18 December consisted of 59 officers, 1,774 men, and 11 horses. From the city of Würzburg itself came 29 officers, 502 men, and 71 horses. On 22 December the 2/2nd Bavarian Infantry Regiment rejoined the field army and in its place stood the 2nd National-Feldbatallion Ansbach. On 10 January 1814 one officer and 65 men from the Reserve Division of the 2nd Chevauléger Regiment arrived.[56]

No active siege was pursued and the French garrison quietly went about its business. The Bavarians were relieved by a force of three Austrian battalions and 60 Chevaulégers. On 21 May 1814, orders arrived from Paris directing Turreau to release the Italians and Hanseatic citizens in his command and for the remainder to return to France. The remaining 600 French soldiers and a battery of six guns marched out of Germany and into Strasbourg.[57]

Other Sieges

Wesel was in the province of Lippe, and stood on the Rhine. The French garrison was commanded by GD Bourke and consisted of 10,000 men. Once news of Leipzig arrived, Bourke had prepared his fortress for a long siege, destroying the suburbs outside the fortress and bringing in all the supplies he could. On 16 November, the first Cossacks appeared at the city gates and the blockade began.

During December the Prussian 5th Brigade, under General Borstell, arrived before the gates of the city and the formal siege began. In January, Borstell's Brigade was dispatched to Holland to join Bülow and the siege was taken over by the Russian General Orurk with the advanced guard of Winzingerode's Corps. Orurk's forces, however, were insufficient, and Prussian forces under Puttlitz were sent to strengthen the blockade force.

On 20 March 1814, a French sortie of 1,500 men supported by 80 cavalry and four guns occurred, exiting from the Berlin Gate. The results were minimal and the French gained nothing by it, other than to let the allies know that they were still a force with which to be reckoned.

The order to surrender arrived on 23 April. It was delivered to the fortress on 25 April, but Bourke did not believe the order and continued to resist. Eventually Bourke was convinced that the war was over, and between 8 and 10 May, the garrison marched out of the fortress and back to France.[58]

The siege of the Kastel Fortress was quite different. The fortress stood on the right bank of the Rhine opposite the city of Mainz on the left bank. The Prussian 1st Corps blockaded the city and fortress through November and December. In January, the Prussians advanced over the Rhine and Winzingerode's Corps assumed responsibility for the blockade. In February, the 5th German Bundescorps, under GdK Herzog von Sachsen-Coburg, arrived and the blockade of the right bank of the Rhine was assumed by the Prussian General Hünerbein. When the order came from Louis XVIII to surrender the city and fortress, GD Morand did so, and the fortress was occupied by the 1st and 3rd Berg Infantry Regiments, then in Prussian service.

The Fortress of Kehl stood on the right bank of the Rhine across from Strasbourg. It was block-aded by the Bavarians through November and December. General Deroy commanded the siege forces initially, but he was relieved by Prince Karl. When the Bavarians left, they were relieved by the Russians under Wittgenstein, and in the middle of January, the Baden forces under Graf von Hochberg served as the blockade force. The fortress surrendered on 19 April 1814.[59]

Siege of Modlin

The siege of Modlin was not without its forays and sallies, but, for the most part, it consisted of the slow process of starving out the garrison. The garrison consisted of the 1/33rd (French) Regiment, the 4/1st Würzburg Regiment, the Saxon 2/Prinz Friedrich and 2/von Niesemeuschel Regiments, the Polish 1/3rd and 1/17th Regiments, and the 18th, 20th, and 21st (Lithuanian) Regiments. The signing of the armistice in June 1813 brought no relief or resupply. Conditions were so bad that Daendels and the various German regimental commanders wished to surrender during the armistice period, but the French, Polish, and Lithuanian commanders prevented this from happening.

As the fall campaign ground on the garrison of the fortress hung on doggedly, but eventually hunger, disease, and the news of the French defeat at Leipzig proved too much. A preliminary act of capitulation was signed on 2 November, and on 1 December 1813 the garrison marched out of the fortress. As with the many other such capitulations, Czar Alexander refused to grant the garrison the honors of war. The Poles and Lithuanians returned to their homes, but the Germans and French went into captivity.

Siege of Zamosc

During the armistice Zamosc was subjected to the same conditions of reprovisioning as was Danzig. The Russian commander of the siege forces, General Rath, made every effort to hinder the gathering of supplies by the garrison. The Czar also added to this by forbidding any deliveries.

After the renewal of hostilities, the penury of the garrison obliged the garrison commander, General Hauke, to confiscate the silver from the Franciscan church. He used it to mint his own coinage which was then used to feed his troops. All the horses were quickly slaughtered, followed by cats, dogs, mice, rats, and crows. All forms of rations quickly vanished and scurvy became rampant. Soon half of the garrison could only walk with the aid of crutches and the sick were standing front line duty.

Through all of this 48 Russian heavy siege guns pounded the fortress. After Leipzig the garrison called a meeting of the siege council. In this meeting General Hauke reviewed the inventory of provisions and found that they had five days supplies. The decision was made to capitulate.

Hauke sent word to the Russian General Rath and demanded the "honors of war." Rath refused to even consider such a request, threatening a mass assault, and the request was quickly dropped. The final capitulation was signed on 23 November. On 25 November the garrison marched out receiving full military honors.[60] After surrendering their arms and eagles, the defenders went into captivity. The soldiers were to keep their equipment and other possessions, while the officers were to retain their swords. The fortification guns were returned to the Count Zamoyski, who was the owner of the fortress. Furthermore, the garrison was to remain in the Grand Duchy until exchanged, though everyone who wished to return home could receive permission to do so. Soldiers from the veteran company were allowed to join the veteran corps in Warsaw.

Hamburg

Hamburg stands on Elbe River, on the northwestern coast of Germany. During the 1813 campaign it was garrisoned by Davout's XIII Corps. Because it is in western Germany it did not come under siege by the allies until long after Napoleon's defeat at Leipzig. Davout had, aside from his various maneuvers in Mecklenburg and Holstein, spent his time strengthening the city's defenses so when the allies once again arrived before Hamburg, the city was well prepared to withstand the siege. Davout's 42,000 man garrison was to hold 60,000 allied soldiers before him until after Napoleon capitulated in April 1814, but, as the first allies didn't appear before Hamburg until 4 January 1814, the siege is truly part of the 1814 campaign.[61]

17

Italy and Spain, the Political Situation, and Retrospective September-December 1813

Political Situation

When news of the battle of Dresden arrived in France, *Te Deums* were sung and the bells sounded once again for one of Napoleon's many victories. The Empress, an Austrian princess, celebrated her husband's victories in Cherbourg, amidst the people of her father's enemy.

To the east her father, the Austrian Emperor, celebrated the allied victories at Hagelberg, Löwenberg, Gross-Beeren, Katzbach, and Kulm. Though the allies were unable to defeat Napoleon himself, as shown at Dresden, they had learned they could defeat his generals and they had begun to do so.

On the Spanish frontier, Wellington pushed King Joseph's defeated army northwards, back towards the French frontiers. The victory at Vitoria on 21 June 1813 had all but ended the French control of Spain. Wellington advanced northwards only to be stopped by the fortresses of Pamplona and St-Sebastian. Once Wellington's armies reached these two cities, there began a series of maneuvers, sieges, and assaults as both sides attempted to take or hold these two vital fortresses.

Wellington had to embroil himself in discussions with the Spanish Cortes, attempting to control the course of the war despite the meddling of the Spanish government. When St-Sebastian finally fell, he refused to allow the Spanish army to plant its flag in the ruins.

Soult's army stood at St-Jean-de-Luz. Snows would soon come and block the mountain passages. If the month of October passed without further reverses, the French frontier would be secure for another season.

This, however, was not to be. Wellington began a slow, steady advance through the Pyrenees. Soult tried to stop it at several fortified, but in a series of victories the British broke through, and slowly and relentlessly crossed the mountains and pushed into France.

On the Italian frontier the Austrians had also begun hostilities. On 17 August they crossed the Save by Zagreb and quickly overran all of Croatia. Soon Dalmatia was also back in Austrian control.

Prince Eugène reacted by moving his army from Goritz to a position where he could face the Austrians under General Hiller. His left extended to the mountainous source of the Save River and his right reached to Trieste. On his extreme left he guarded the passes through the Tyrol Mountains with a detached corps under the command of General Gifflenga.

Fiume and Trieste were occupied by the Austrians under General Nugent, but General Pino quickly pushed them out. The city of Villach was also occupied by the Austrians, but was taken back as well. The only vigorous operation undertaken was the capture of the Austrian camp at Feltriz by General Grenier.

The Austrians had begun a major propaganda effort in Italy and soon the Germanic inhabitants of northern Italy declared for them. The Italian troops did not show the same ardor as they had in the past and General Pino quit the army. In view of the weakened morale of the army, Eugène ordered it to withdraw to the Isonzo, effectively surrendering the Illyrian provinces to Austria.

The campaign in Italy was not a successful one for the French. Eugène could not count on any support from Napoleon or France and was left to call on only those resources available to him in the Kingdom of Northern Italy. The kingdom was slowly disintegrating, and his troops were equally unstable. He had little choice but to fight a delaying action, holding as much as long as possible before finally being forced, by superior numbers, to withdraw again.

Bavaria was also unstable. When Vandamme was defeated at Kulm the Bavarian General Wrede had entered into secret conversations with the Austrian General Prince von Reuss. On 20 September Wrede then had a long and mysterious interview with the King of Bavaria after which he departed in haste to his headquarters in Braunau. In fact, the seeds of the pending defection of Bavaria had been planted and were beginning to grow.

The King of Bavaria, not wishing to keep Napoleon ignorant of the difficult position in which he stood, wrote a series of letters through an intermediary, the Prince of Neufchâtel, Maréchal Berthier. They conveyed the anticipated justification for what he felt he would be forced to cede to the allies. The King's protestations were, however, soon made clear by the indiscretions of his minister, von Pfeffel.

Further meetings were held between Wrede and Prince von Reuss, and word of these meetings did reach Napoleon. It soon became apparent that the defection of Bavaria was inevitable. Napoleon's reaction, however, was to ignore this threat. Seeing nothing that would divert or discommode his next military maneuvers, Napoleon did nothing to prevent Bavaria's eventual defection. "Bavaria cannot march seriously against us. It will lose too much in Austria's victory and France's disaster. It knows well that Austria is its natural enemy and that France is its necessary support. If it cedes to the needs of the moment, its political life shall be destroyed by the blows which shall fall on it."[1] In October the great surprise was Napoleon's discovery that his logic was not shared by the King of Bavaria.

On 8 October Bavaria formally signed a convention at Braunau. It was between General Wrede, commanding the Bavarian troops, and Prince von Reuss, who commanded those of Austria. In this convention the two parties agreed to join in the "good cause" and unite their troops with those of the allies. Their combined forces, which consisted of 60,000 to 70,000 troops, immediately moved to Bamberg on the Main, where they could act in Bavaria's and the allies' best interest.

Despite his apparent lack of concern about Bavaria, Napoleon's German allies were a source of continual concern. The coalition of German allies was beginning to crack at every level. The Westphalian and Cleve-Berg troops deserted at every opportunity. The Hanseatic cities rose in revolt and were only held in line by Davout's iron hand. Bavaria was still superficially cooperating, but its army had not taken part in any major action and would not until the battle of Hanau, when it fought against the French.

On the other hand, allied actions had driven Denmark firmly into Napoleon's camp. Their refusal to deal with the King of Denmark and their acknowledged intention to give Norway to Sweden had provided Napoleon with a 35,000 man corps that would operate with Davout in his campaign in Mecklenburg.

Saxony remained the political key of Germany and Napoleon's maneuvers from 15 August to 15 October were aimed solely at keeping Saxony allied to France. Napoleon felt that once it fell, so too would the rest of the Confederation he had formed in 1806-7.

His perception proved all too accurate and Germany had slowly run between Napoleon's fingers like so much sand. What he had once held so firmly in his grasp slipped away to the camp of his enemies as each individual German state sought to make its own accommodation with the victorious allies. After Leipzig the Württemberg Army, Baden, and Hesse-Darmstadt formations marched back to their home provinces where they would refit, fill out their ranks, and join the allies as full partners.

The story of Württemberg was one of success. The father of the ruler, King Friedrich II of Württemberg, had married Sophie Dorothee, a niece of Friedrich the Great of Prussia. King Friedrich II had Czar Paul of Russia as his brother-in-law and his wife was the daughter of George III of England.

On 23 October 1813, after the French disaster at Leipzig and the overrunning of Germany by the allies at the end of the 1813 campaign, Württemberg signed a military convention with Austria. Friedrich's marital and family ties to England and Russia ensured him that he not only retained his title, but all of the territories that had been transferred to him during his alliance with France. Württemberg was one of the few states to retain everything that it had obtained during the period of the Confederation of the Rhine.

The Duchy of Baden was not as fortunate as Württemberg. The Baden contingent had fought to the last at Leipzig. Elements of the light regiment threw themselves into the Pleisse and swam to the far bank to escape the surrounding Russians and Prussians. Others were approached by the Count de Noailles, an émigré sent by Bernadotte as a parliamentarian to the King of Saxony, who offered a ceasefire to General Hochberg. This was accepted and the Baden forces passed into captivity. Hochberg arranged with the allies that the Baden weapons, equipment and standards be held such that, should the Grand Duke of Baden cast his lot with the allies, they might be easily returned to the Baden forces.[2] Their action was not a desertion of the French cause, as the Baden soldiers had fought to the last for the French. However, Hochberg realistically approached the prospects for a future accommodation with the victorious allies.

Baden was given three weeks to determine its next actions and its troops were held as prisoners of war until such time as Baden chose to join the allies. After three weeks had passed, no word arrived and on 16 November General Tauentzien announced that the Baden troops had the choice of either joining the Prussian army or being taken into Russia as prisoners of war. The Baden general, Hochberg, protested and a further delay was granted. On 25 November word arrived that the Grand Duke of Baden had acceded to the allied demand that he join the allied cause.[3] The Baden troops were then released, given their equipment and standards, and allowed to return to Baden.

The story of Hesse-Darmstadt was different. Much of the Hesse-Darmstadt contingent had succeeded in escaping with the French army as Leipzig was overrun by the allies. It retreated with the French to Freiburg, arriving on 21 October, then continued on to Hanau, which it reached on 28 October. It took no part in the battle against the AustroBavarian Corps which tried to stop the French escape.

The Grand Duke of Hesse-Darmstadt announced his withdrawal from the Confederation of the Rhine on 29 October, and on 30 October those few Hessians still with the Grande Armée left it and arrived in Darmstadt. Only the 2nd Battalion of Fusiliers remained in French service because they were locked in the fortress of Torgau, then under siege by the allies.[4] The Hesse-Darmstadt army was rebuilt and also joined the allies in the 1814 campaign.

The major defection of Napoleon's German allies had been the defection of the Saxons during the battle of Leipzig. Regiment after regiment passed over to the allies, with only the Garde Grenadiers remaining loyal. They formed in front of the Royal Palace to guard the King of Saxony as the French withdrew.

After its defection, the Saxon army remained at Leipzig where it reorganized. Many regiments were disbanded and others were reorganized into provisional regiments. These provisional regiments were quickly pressed into action. On 19 October 1813 Generalmajor von Ryssel assumed command of the Saxon division and was sent to operate with the Prussian General Tauentzien's

Corps blockading Torgau, where the Saxons engaged their former allies, the French, in a number of sharp skirmishes. Though the records are not overflowing with details, the indications are that the Saxons were not overly aggressive in these actions and tended to be thrashed by the French when they met. This force operated with the allies, but more on the basis of a prisoner than as a full ally. Torgau fell, and on 14 November the remaining Saxon forces were taken to Merseburg where they were reorganized.

For Saxony, Napoleon's fall and the liberation of Germany did not spell the end of its agony. As a result of the Congress of Vienna, Saxony found many of its soldiers drafted into the Prussian army and much of its northern provinces were seized by Prussia as an indemnity for losses Prussia had suffered. Saxony would eventually lose half of its territory and inhabitants to Prussia as a result of the Congress of Vienna.

The states of Westphalia and Cleve-Berg found themselves reoccupied their former rulers. As individual entities they were rapidly torn apart and their territories redistributed to their pre-1805 owners. Their armies had dwindled steadily throughout the 1813 fall campaign. The Westphalians had deserted at every opportunity, and the reputation of the Cleve-Berg infantry was so bad that Napoleon had exiled them to garrison duty on the French coasts where desertion would be almost impossible. Only the Cleve-Berg Chevauléger-lanciers had shown any significant level of loyalty. The Westphalian Jérôme Hussar Regiment had also remained loyal, but as it was formed of Alsatians and other German speaking Frenchmen, it hardly qualified as being a truly Westphalian regiment.

The soldiers of those states returned to their homes as the allies entered their homelands. Those shattered remnants that still remained under arms were quickly absorbed into the Prussian and Hesse-Cassel armies and would march against the French in the 1814 campaign.

Despite the collapse of his German empire Napoleon's name still invoked respect and even fear in the allies. His escape across the Rhine was remarkably uneventful. The French army, however, left a sorrowful trail of misery, suffering, destruction, and death in its wake as abandoned equipment and sick and dying soldiers littered its line of march.

Napoleon still displayed much of the genius he had in his previous campaigns, but he was slow in recognizing that the tools with which he had to work were not as supple and strong as they had been in his previous campaigns. Despite that he had marched and fought his *Marie-Louises* successfully in many pitched battles and taught the allies that he was still to be respected.

Aside from the caliber of his army, Napoleon too was older. He could no longer march and fight as he had in previous campaigns and he was beginning to show signs of exhaustion. He was also beginning to miss opportunities and make errors, which allowed complete victory to evade his grasp. His marshals were beginning to crack and doubt him as they aged and began to long for the comfort and pleasures of their rank and station.

The allies made their errors too. They had stood on the edge of disaster on several occasions. They were not a unified body, as can be seen by the dissension between Blücher and Bernadotte before and during the battle of Leipzig. National and personal interests constantly tore at the fabric of their alliance. It can be argued that they were their own worst enemies and that it was only by a strange twist of fate that they were able to agree at Trachtenberg upon the one strategy that would allow them to defeat Napoleon. In the end, this one strategy and the sheer weight of numbers spelled the end of Napoleon's empire in Germany.

Napoleon's biggest failings in the 1813 campaign were not military, but political and diplomatic. He gravely underestimated the resolve of all his opponents. He presumed that his Austrian father-in-law would, in the worst case, be neutral. He badly misjudged the Prussian thirst for revenge, the Russian desire to exploit their successes of 1812, and their resolve to obtain it. He had discounted the resentment of the German states against his policies and assumed that their obedience would be unquestionable. The only one of his opponents he truly understood and justifiably despised was Bernadotte, whose every maneuver and action was aimed solely keeping him perched on his tottering throne and reinforcing his sham emulation of Napoleon's military greatness.

Above all, Napoleon failed to recognize that the spirit of the French Revolution and nationalism had been firmly planted in the German states and was slowly building a national spirit that sought its own place in the sun. This spirit was not only to collect its accumulated debts at France's expense in 1814 and 1815, but was to ultimately take its revenge in 1870 during the Franco-Prussian war as the modern German state was born.

It was gone. The empire was shattered. The conquests of a lifetime had fallen away one by one like the lights of a great city slowly being snuffed out one by one. Croatia and Illyria were lost. Northern Italy, where his star had shown brightly on the fields by Marengo, was gone. The bevy of cowering German states that once scampered to and fro to avoid his terrible stare now glared back at him with an armed fury. The satellite states he'd built for his family, Westphalia, Cleve-Berg, and Spain were lost. His trusted lieutenant and brother-in-law, Murat, had deserted him. The "natural borders" of France were lost as the Netherlands fell and the allies poured across the Rhine and the Pyrenees. All that remained was the core of his empire and he sat upon it, husbanding his resources and preparing, like a wild animal, to fight for his life in the last corner of his empire.

Retrospective on the Campaign

Napoleon's biggest failure of the Leipzig campaign was his failure to assume the offensive. For an unknown reason he ceded the initiative to the allies and stood idle in Saxony, waiting to see what the allies would do. This reached its climax at the battle of Leipzig when he did little more than concentrate his troops and circle the wagons while the allies gathered about him and finally closed on him in a concentric attack from all directions.

All of the peripheral actions were just that—peripheral. They are, for the most part, symbolic of Napoleon's abandonment of the initiative. They were side shows in the extreme and most of them had little impact on the campaign other than the continuing allied effort to bleed the French army with the death of a thousand cuts.

Ideally, Napoleon should have abandoned Leipzig and marched westwards to destroy the Austrian army marching from that direction and reopened his communications with France. Barring that, the next solution would have been to strike north and engage the Army of Silesia in a decisive battle. If Blücher were to avoid the blow, then Napoleon could have marched on Berlin and forced Blücher to come after him, then turned and engaged in the decisive battle. Of course, this would entail abandoning his lines of communication, but as the campaign stood Merveldt's army had already cut those lines. What was there to lose?

A third choice would have been to march against Bernadotte seeking the decisive battle, but it is most probable that Bernadotte would have turned yet again and fled north before any resolution could have been reached.

If Napoleon had once again turned south against the Army of Bohemia, seeking a decisive battle, his advance would probably have resulted in the Austrians simply pulling back into the mountains and escaping before Napoleon could catch them. To have struck eastwards would have been to strike at an army of little significance, the Polish Reserve Army, but it might have allowed Napoleon to gather up the garrison of Dresden and then permitted other action. On the negative side, that would have put the entire allied army astride his lines of communications and shoved his head further into the lion's mouth.

A 19th Century English proverb of, "If you're doing nothing, you're obviously doing something wrong" was never truer.

Admittedly, abandoning Saxony would have resulted in the loss of the bulk of the Confederation of the Rhine. What loss would this have been? Westphalia was in near revolt and Saxony was loyal only because the entire French army was camped there. Bavaria barely concealed its desire to abandon him. The smaller states of the Confederation varied in their loyalties, but would quickly fall into line with a major victory. There was nothing to lose that wasn't already lost, and everything to gain. The only possible explanation is Napoleon's ability to understand the political situation and the proper military actions had been lost along with Napoleon's grasp on political realities.

As the campaign unfolded, when Napoleon did finally engage the allies, he did so in such a manner as to not permit him any opportunity to concentrate his forces against one allied army. Ideally this battle would have been far enough from the other allied armies that he would have the time necessary to defeat them by using the distance from the other allied armies to protect his rear. A day or two's march should have been sufficient. Certainly his troops' morale would have been boosted by the idea of being on the attack, rather than sitting and waiting to be attacked. He came so close to victory that any boost might have been enough to tip the scales. And, if he had succeeded in crushing the Army of Silesia, Bernadotte would have most assuredly fled. After such a victory, when Napoleon turned south against the Army of Bohemia, it would have most certainly withdrawn to digest Blücher's defeat.

As it was, the effect of the loss at Leipzig was the destruction and loss of a major portion of the French army, both physical and moral. Though a large number of men did escape the closing jaws of the allies' victory, they quietly disappeared from their units, taking "French leave" as the army marched westwards and melted away.

Ideally, the allies should have launched a massive pursuit, but they were probably incapable of it, both from the fatigue of the battle as well as the administrative and managerial efforts necessary to launch such a pursuit. It was simply beyond their ability to execute such a pursuit, the first major pursuit they would have attempted in 21 years of warfare.

So, the allied machinery slowly lumbered into motion. The pampered and self-serving staffs celebrated their victory, counted the spoils of Leipzig, and only then thought about the pursuit. It is possible that they were still somewhat afraid of Napoleon, but that is unlikely. The magnitude of their victory should have erased any such thoughts.

The withdrawal was a classic and highly successful withdrawal. Though Wrede's treacherous attack at Hanau held the potential for the total destruction of Napoleon, it failed because of the difference in the quality of the troops engaged. It certainly showed that the core of the Grande Armée was as sharp and deadly a sword as ever.

The disaster at Leipzig, the collapse of his German empire, and the disintegration of his army splashed cold water in his face and brought Napoleon back to an increased awareness of his situation, though still far short of seeing how serious was his predicament.

Napoleon's intellectual resiliency brought back a sense of optimism and the aggressive spirit of old. Though his military actions in the 1814 campaign would show a renewed vigor and aggressiveness, an understanding of the changed political reality was still beyond Napoleon's grasp.

Orders of Battle

THE ARMIES IN THE NORTH

French XIII and the Hamburg Garrison 15 September 1813

Commanding General: Maréchal Davout
Chief of staff: Général de brigade Baron César de Laville
Adjudant-Commandant: Chef de bataillon Zadera, Major Brosset
Adjunct Captains: Laloy, Chaupin, d'Houdetot, Lieutenant aide-major de Villeneuve
Danish Adjudant: Captain Count Dannstjold Löwendal
Artillery Commander: Colonel Ourie
Engineering Cmdr: Chef de Bataillon Vinache

3rd Division: Général de division Loison
(Total infantry—7,166 men)
Brigade: Général de brigade Rome
1/, 2/, 3/, 4/15th Line Regiment
3/, 4/44th Line Regiment
Brigade: Général de brigade Leclerc
1/, 2/, 3/, 4/48th Line Regiment
1/, 2/, 3/, 4/108th Line Regiment
Artillery: Mathis
3/8th Foot Artillery Company
17/8th Foot Artillery Company
14 guns—257 men
4/5th Horse Artillery (95)
Det. 1/6th Principal Artillery Train
Det. 5/7th Principal Artillery Train
(Total Train—263 men)

40th Division: Général de division Thiébault
(Total infantry—8,517 men)
Brigade: Général de brigade Delcambre
1/, 2/, 3/, 4/30th Line Regiment
3/, 4/33rd Légère Regiment
Brigade: Général de brigade Gengoult
1/, 2/, 3/, 4/61st Line Regiment
1/, 2/, 3/, 4/111th Line Regiment
Artillery: Grosjean
12/2nd Foot Artillery Company
18/8th Foot Artillery Company
14 guns—288 men
Det. 7/2nd (bis) Artillery Train
Det. 3/8th (bis) Artillery Train
Total Train—220

50th Division (Mobile): Général de division Pécheux
Brigade: Général de brigade Pietrowsky (Total—3,589 men)
2/, 3/, 4/, 6/3rd Line Regiment
3/, 6/105th Line Regiment
Artillery Foot Battery (92)
4/1st Horse Battery (6 guns) (86)
Train (171 men)

Danish Auxiliary Corps: General Prinz Friedrich von Hessen
Chief of staff: Major Karl von Bardensleth
Asst-CoS: Major Lövenörn von Bardensleth
Artillery Commander: Lieutenant Colonel d'Aubert
(Total—10,478 men)
Advanced Guard: Colonel von Waldeck
2/Schleswig Jagerkorps
1/, 2/Holstein Sharpshooter Corps
2/, 6/Hussar Regiment
Von Gertsenberg Horse Battery (10 3-pdrs)
1st Brigade: Generalmajor Graf von der Schulenberg
3/Oldenburg Regiment (Detached to Rendsburg Garrison)
1/, 2/, 4/, Lt. Co 3/Oldenburg Regiment
1/, and Lt Co. of 2/Dronningen Guard Regiment
1/, 2/, 3/, 4/Holstein Cavalry Regiment (4)
Kove Foot Battery (10 6-pdrs)
2nd Brigade: Generalmajor Lasson
1/, Jäger Co of 2/Fünen Infantry Regiment
1/, 2/Schleswig Infantry Regiment
3/, 4/Holstein Infantry Regiment
1/, 2/, 3/, 4/Jutland Light Dragoon Regiment
Von Conner Horse Battery (10 3-pdrs)
Von Lohse Foot Battery (10 6-pdrs)

Cavalry: Général de division Watier de St-Alphonse
30th Light Cavalry Brigade: Général de brigade Lallemand
1/, 2/28th Chasseurs à Cheval Regiment (258)
1/, 2/, 3/17th Polish (Lithuanian) Uhlan Regiment (286)
1st and 2nd Hamburg Régiment de Marche (362)

Reserve and Grand Park
Pontooneers (122)
8/4th Sapper Battalion (98)
Artillery Artisan Det. (22)
Det. 4/5th (bis) Artillery Train
Det. 1/6th (bis) Artillery Train
Det. 3/6th (bis) Artillery Train
Det. 1/6th Principal Artillery Train
Artillery Train Total (147)
12th Equipage Train Battalion (4 coys)
Total Military Equipage (610 men)

Garrison of Hamburg 50th Division (Immobile): Général de brigade Avril
Brigade: Général de brigade Osten
1/, 2/33rd Légère Regiment (797)
2/, 3/, 4/, 5/29th Line Regiment (2,123)
Brigade: Général de brigade Avril
5/3rd Line Regiment (546)
4/, 5/105th Line Regiment (1,512)

Cavalry: Général de division Watier de St-Alphonse
Brigade: Général de brigade Guiton
Régiment de Marche (415)
2 Sqn Lt Coy
1 Sqn Dragoons
1 Sqn Cuirassiers
Dismounted Régiment de Marche (888)

Brigade: Général de brigade Dubois
  1st Provisional Cuirassier Regiment (633)
    4/1st, 4/2nd, 4/3rd, 4/4th Cuirassier Regiments
  2nd Provisional Cuirassier Regiment (663)
    4/5th, 4/6th, 4/7th, 4/8th Cuirassier Regiments
  3rd Provisional Cuirassier Regiment (609)
    4/9th, 4/10th, 4/11th, 4/12th Cuirassier Regiments
  3/, 4/, 5/28th Chasseurs à Cheval Regiment (3) (537)
    (dismounted)
  Depot/17th Polish Lancer Regiment (89)
Other Troops
  13th Veteran Battalion (472)
  Transient Depot Battalion (1,070)
  Foot and Horse Customs Soldiers (279)
  Foot and Horse Gendarmes (171)
  Garrison Artillery (765)
  Foot Artillery (50)
  Train (409)
  Artisans (47)
  Military Equipage (23)
  Engineers Sappers (1 co) (152)
  Miners (?)
  5th Equipage de Flotille and 25 gunboats (1,142)
  Naval Artisans (246)
  Various Detachments (646)

Quistorp, *Geschichte der Nordarmee im Jahr 1813;*
Danish Archives and French Archives, Carton X -3

BATTLE OF GÖHRDE 16 SEPTEMBER 1813

FRENCH FORCES
50th Division (Mobile): Général de division Pécheux
Brigade: Général de brigade Osten
  2/, 3/, 4/, 6/3rd Line Regiment (4)
  ?/29th Line Regiment (1)
  ?/105th Line Regiment (1)
  (Total—about 4,000 men)
Attached 28th Chasseurs à Cheval Regiment (1) (80 men)
Foot Battery (6 6-pdrs and 2 how.)

ALLIED FORCES
Generallieutenant Count Wallmoden-Gimborn
Left (1st) Division: Oberst Friedrich von Arentschildt
1st Brigade: Major von Natzmer
  1st Battalion, Russo-German Legion (14/663)
  2nd Battalion, Russo-German Legion (1.9/662)
  5th Battalion, Russo-German Legion (17/661)
2nd Brigade: Oberstleutnant von Wardenburg
  3rd Battalion, Russo-German Legion (11/483)
  4th Battalion, Russo-German Legion (16/772)
  6th Battalion, Russo-German Legion (16/506)
  1st Hussar Regiment, Russo-German Legion
    (23/575)

1st RGL Horse Battery (8 guns)—Scheele
Erlenbusch Foot Battery (8 guns)
Total Artillery (9/337)
Center (2nd) Division: Generalmajor von Tettenborn
  Combined Jäger Battalion
  Kielmansegg's Hanoverian Battalion (2 coys) (157)
  Jäger Company, Russo-German Legion (2/100)
  Reiche Jäger Battalion **
  Staalts Foot Battalion von Lützow Freikorps **
    ** (Total 1,470 for von Lützow infantry)
  Von Lützow Freikorps Cavalry (5) (427)
  Komissarov #1 Cossack Regiment (394)
  Sulima #9 Cossack Regiment ***
  Denisov #7 Cossack Regiment ***
    *** (602 men)
  Hanseatic Horse Battery, Cpt. Spoorman (4 guns)
    (115)
Right (3rd) Division: Major General Lyon
Light Brigade: Lt. Colonel Martin
  Bremen and Verden Battalion (8 coys)*
  73rd Highland Foot Regiment (500)
  Anhalt-Dessau Battalion (534)
Line Brigade: Lt. Col. Halkett
  Von Langsohr Battalion (8 coys)*
  Von Bennigsen Battalion (6 coys)*
  Lauenberg Battalion (8 coys)*
    * (Total 2,554)
  KGL Composite Battalion von Holtzermann
    (16/200)
    (Dets from 1st and 2nd Light Bns and 5th Line
    Bn)
  Foot Battery von Wiering, (6 guns) (161)
4th (Cavalry) Division: Generalmajor von Dörnberg
  3rd KGL Hussar Regiment (5 sqns) (805)
  Luneburg Hussar Regiment (2 sqns) (240)
  Bremen and Verden Hussar Regiment (1) (180)
Horse Artillery Brigade: Major Brockman
  2nd KGL Horse Battery, von Kuhlmann (6 guns)
  1st KGL Horse Battery, von Sympher (6 guns)
  British Rocket Battery (Half-Troop), Lt. Strangways
    (16 rocket launchers)
  Total Artillery (390)

Schwertfeger, *Geschichte der Königlich Deutschen Legion 1803-1816*, Hanover and Leipzig, 1907.

BATTLE OF WARTENBERG 3 OCTOBER 1813

PRUSSIAN FORCES
1st Corps:
Advanced Guard: Oberst von Katzeler
  1/, 2/, 3/, 4/Jäger/Brandenburg Hussar Regiment
  3/, Jäger, 2nd Leib Hussar Regiment
  1/, 2/, 3/, 4/Brandenburg Uhlan Regiment
  1/, 2/, 3/, 4/East Prussian National Cavalry
    Regiment

1/, 2/, 3/, 4/5th Silesian Landwehr Cavalry Regiment
Horse Battery #2 (8 guns)
Infantry: Major Hiller von Gartringen
Leib-Grenadier Battalion
West Prussian Grenadier Battalion
2/12th Reserve Infantry Regiment
1/Brandenburg Infantry Regiment
Fus/2nd East Prussian Infantry Regiment
3/13th Silesian Landwehr Regiment *Rekowsky*
2/14th Silesian Landwehr Battalion *Thiele*
4/15th Silesian Landwehr Battalion *Wedell*
East Prussian Jäger Battalion (2 companies)
Guard Jäger Battalion (1 coy)
1st Brigade: Oberst von Steinmetz
1st East Prussian Grenadier Battalion
1/2nd East Prussian Infantry Regiment
2/6th Silesian Landwehr Regiment *Fischer*
1/5th Silesian Landwehr Regiment *Mumm*
3/5th Silesian Landwehr Regiment *Seidlitz*
1/13th Silesian Landwehr Regiment *Walter*
2/13th Silesian Landwehr Regiment *Larisch*
4/13th Silesian Landwehr Regiment *Martitz*
6-pdr Foot Battery #2
2nd Brigade: Generalmajor Prinz Karl von Mecklenburg
Silesian Grenadier Battalion
1/, 2/, Fus/1st East Prussian Infantry Regiment
2/2nd East Prussian Infantry Regiment
4/5th Silesian Landwehr Regiment *Kosecky*
1/, 2/, 3/, 4/Mecklenburg Strelitz Hussar Regiment
1/, 2/, 4/2nd Leib Hussar Regiment
6-pdr Foot Battery #1 (8 guns)
6-pdr Foot Battery #3 (5 guns)
7th Brigade: Generalmajor von Horn
1/, 2/, Fus/Leib-Infantry Regiment
Thuringian Battalion
1/15th Silesian Landwehr Regiment *Sommerfeld*
2/15th Silesian Landwehr Regiment *Pettingkofer*
3/4th Silesian Landwehr Regiment *Reichenbach*
Combined 2 and 4/4th Silesian Landwehr Regiment *KnorrKottulinski*
6-pdr Foot Battery #3 (3 guns)
8th Brigade: Generalmajor von Hünerbein
2/, Fus/Brandenburg Infantry Regiment
1/, Fus/12th Reserve Infantry Regiment
4/14th Silesian Landwehr Regiment *Brixen*
6-pdr Foot Battery #15 (8 guns)
Reserve Cavalry: Oberst Freiherr von Wahlen-Jürgass
1/, 2/, 3/, 4/Jäger/Lithuanian Dragoon Regiment
1/, 2/, 3/, 4/West Prussian Dragoon Regiment
1/, 2/, 3/, 4/10th Silesian Landwehr Cavalry Regiment
1/, 2/, 3/, 4/1st Neumärk Landwehr Cavalry Regiment
Horse Battery #1 (8 guns)
Horse Battery #3 (8 guns)

FRENCH FORCES
IV Corps: Général de division Bertrand
Chief of Staff: Général de division Taviel
12th Division: Général de division Count Morand
Brigade: Général de brigade Ligier-Belair
1/, 2/, 3/, 4/8th Légère Regiment
Brigade: Général de brigade Toussaint
1/, 2/, 3/, 4/13th Line Regiment
Brigade: Général de brigade Hulot
1/, 2/, 4/23rd Line Regiment
15th Division: Général de division Fontanelli
Brigade: Général de brigade Martel
1st Italian Line Regiment (1)
4th Italian Line Regiment (1)
Brigade: Général de brigade St-Andrea
1st Italian Light Regiment (1)
6th Italian Line Regiment (1)
Brigade: Général de brigade Moroni
Milan Guard Battalion (1)
7th Italian Line Regiment (1)
38th Division: Generallieutenant Graf Franquemont
Brigade: Général de brigade Stockmayer
Combined Württemberg Light Battalion
1st Combined Württemberg Line Battalion
Brigade: Général de brigade von airing
2nd Combined Württemberg Line Battalion
3rd Combined Württemberg Line Battalion
24th Light Cavalry Brigade: Generalmajor von Jett (100 total)
1/1st Württemberg Chevauleger Regiment
1/3rd Württemberg Chevauleger Regiment
Cavalry Division: Général de division Beaumont
29th Light Cavalry Brigade: Generalmajor Wolff
Westphalian Guard Chevauléger Regiment (1)
Hessian Chevauléger Regiment (1)
Artillery: 32 guns

Mirus, R., *Das Treffen bei Wartenburg am 3. Oktober 1813*; Prussian General Staff *Plane der Schlachten und Treffen welche von der preussischen Armee in den feldzügen der Jahre 1813, 14, und 15 geliefert worden*, G.Reimer, Berlin, 1821.

THE FORCES THAT DID NOT MAKE IT TO LEIPZIG

FRENCH GARRISON OF DRESDEN 15 SEPTEMBER 1813

Dresden Garrison: Général de division Durosnel
Brigade: Général de brigade Gros
1/, 2/11th (Young Guard) Tirailleur Regiment (1,362)

1/, 2/11th (Young Guard) Voltigeur Regiment
  (1,341)
Brigade: Général de brigade Bernard
  1/, 2/2nd Westphalian Line Regiment (unknown)
  1/, 2/3rd Westphalian Line Regiment (1,179)
  2nd Westphalian Light Infantry Battalion
    (unknown)
Brigade
  2/Saxon Grenadier Guard Regiment (717)
Depots
  Infantry Depots (1,595)
  Polish Depot (867)
  Imperial Guard Depot (965)
  Saxon Cavalry (19)
Artillery: Colonel Lafout
  French Foot Artillery (738)
  French Train (900)
  Polish Artillery (30)
  Saxon Artillery: Oberst von Hoyen
  Saxon Artillery (277)
  Saxon Train (89)
Engineers: Colonel Marion
  French Sappers (816)
  Saxon Sappers (44)

French Archives, Carton X—3D

FRENCH I CORPS 25 SEPTEMBER 1813

I Corps: Général de Division Count de Lobau
  Chief of Staff: Général de brigade Revest
  Artillery Commander: Général de brigade Baltus
1st Division: Général de division Cassagne
1st Brigade:
  1/, 2/7th Légère Regiment (41/602)
  1/, 2/12th Line Regiment (43/933)
2nd Brigade: Général de brigade Fezensac
  1/, 2/17th Line Regiment (45/691)
  3/36th Line Regiment (19/394)
Artillery
  8/2nd Foot Artillery (1/63)
  23/3rd Foot Artillery 2/79)
  Det. 1/1st Principal Train Battalion (0/45)
  Det. 14th Principal Artillery Train (0/7)
  Det. 1/1st (bis) Principal Artillery Train (1/80)
2nd Division: Général de division Dumonceau
1st Brigade: Général de brigade Chartrand
  1/, 2/13th Légère Regiment (41/599)
  1/, 2/25th Line Regiment (42/542)
2nd Brigade: Général de brigade Doucet
  1/, 2/, 3/57th Line Regiment (63/1,421)
  3/51th Line Regiment (20/363)
Artillery
  5/4th Foot Artillery (2/71)
  Det. 1/1st (bis) Train Battalion (1/80)
  Det. 5/8th (bis) Train Battalion (1/52)

23nd Division: Général de division Teste
1st Brigade: Général de brigade O'Meara
  1/, 2/, 3/, 4/21st Line Regiment (59/1,068)
  1/, 2/33rd Line Regiment (40/955)
2nd Brigade:
  1/, 2/85th Line Regiment (54/1,056)
  4/55th Line Regiment (22/389)
Artillery
  21/4th Foot Artillery Company (1/68)
  Detachment 1/1st (bis) Artillery Train (1/80)
21st Light Cavalry Brigade: Général de brigade Gobrecht
  1/9th Chevaulégers-lanciers Regiment
    (14/103/20/103)
20th Light Cavalry Brigade: GB Weissenwolf
  13th Polish Hussar Regiment (16/199/20/199)
  16th Polish Uhlan Regiment (33/239/38/399)
Reserve and Park: Major Gargant
  2/6th Foot Artillery (2/74)
  15/9th Foot Artillery (1/68)
  2/4th Horse Artillery (2/40)
  5/6th Horse Artillery (2/81)
  4/1st Horse Artillery (2/45)
  Det. 3/, 5/9th Principal Train Battalion (4/360)
  Det. 6th Principal Train Battalion (2/28)
  5/3rd Sapper Battalion (3/118)
  7/3rd Sapper Battalion (3/98)
  1/10th Equipage Battalion (2/135)
  2/10th Equipage Battalion (1/69)
  3/10th Equipage Battalion (1/70)

French Archives, Carton C2-538.

FRENCH XIV CORPS 15 SEPTEMBER 1813

XIV Corps: Maréchal Count St-Cyr
  Chief of Staff: Général de brigade Borelli
  Artillery Commander: Général de brigade Pernety
42nd Division: GD Mouton-Duvernet (6,106)
1st Brigade:
  22nd Provisional Demi-brigade
    2/4th Légère Regiment
    4/12th Légère Regiment
  4th Provisional Demi-brigade
    6/9th Légère Regiment
    3/28th Légère Regiment
  32nd Provisional Demi-brigade
    4/10th Légère Regiment
    3/21st Légère Regiment
2nd Brigade: Général de brigade Creutzer
  17th Provisional Demi-brigade
    3/27th Line Regiment
    3/63rd Line Regiment
  16th Provisional Demi-brigade
    4/40th Line Regiment
    3/43rd Line Regiment

2/, 3/76th Line Regiment
3/96th Line Regiment
Artillery
1/7th Foot Artillery
9/7th Foot Artillery
Det. 6/1st (bis) Train Battalion
Det. 7/1st (bis) Train Battalion
Det. 5/11th Principal Train Battalion
43rd Division: Général de division Claparède (5,219)
1st Brigade: Général de brigade Godard
2/, 3/27th Légère Regiment
3/29th Légère Regiment
2/, 3/, 4/100th Line Regiment
2nd Brigade: Général de brigade Butrand
2/, 3/45th Line Regiment
3/65th Line Regiment
4/103rd Line Regiment
21st Provisional Demi-brigade
2/59th Line Regiment (1)
3/94th Line Regiment (1)
Artillery
2/7th Foot Artillery
4/6th Foot Artillery
Det. 4/10th Principal Train Battalion
Det. 6/12th Principal Train Battalion
Det. 6/1st (bis) Train Battalion
Det. 7/1st (bis) Train Battalion
44th Division: Général de division Berthezène (5,443)
1st Brigade:
1/, 3/8th Légère Regiment
3/, 4/64th Line Regiment
Provisional Demi-brigade
2/16th Légère Regiment
1/18th Légère Regiment
2nd Brigade: Général de brigade Letellier
19th Provisional Demi-brigade
2/50th Line Regiment
2/75th Line Regiment
Provisional Demi-brigade
3/24th Line Regiment
3/39th Line Regiment
Provisional Demi-brigade
3/54th Line Regiment
3/95th Line Regiment
Artillery
4/1st Foot Artillery
15/7tn Foot Artillery
Det. 7/1st (bis) Train Battalion
Det. 3/11th Principal Train Battalion
Det. 5/11th Principal Train Battalion
Det. 6/12th Principal Train Battalion
45th Division: Général de division Razout (7,100)
1st Brigade: Général de brigade Goguet
3/6th Légère Regiment
26th Provisional Demi-brigade
3/5th Line Regiment
3/11th Line Regiment

Provisional Demi-brigade
3/8th Line Regiment
2/28th Line Regiment
2nd Brigade: Général de brigade d'Esclevin
Provisional Demi-brigade
4/32nd Line Regiment
4/58th Line Regiment
18th Provisional Demi-brigade
3/34th Line Regiment
3/69th Line Regiment
27th Provisional Demi-brigade
4/60th Line Regiment
3/79th Line Regiment
6/81st Line Regiment
Artillery
21/5th Foot Artillery
Det. 5/12th Principal Train Battalion
Det. 4/11th (bis) Train Battalion
10th Light Cavalry Division: Général de division Pajol
16th Brigade: Général de brigade Jacquet
1/, 2/, 3/, 4/2nd Italian Chasseurs à Cheval Regiment (510)
1/, 2/, 3/, 4/7th Chevaulégers-lancier Regiment (522)
31st Brigade: Général de brigade Stedmann
1/, 2/, 3/, 4/14th Hussar Regiment (343)
Reserves and Grand Park: (721 men)
5/7th Foot Artillery
10/7th Foot Artillery
5/6th Foot Artillery
5/2nd Horse Artillery
3/6th Horse Artillery
1 Pontooneer Company
4 Sapper Companies
4/10th (bis) Train Battalion
Det. 3/4th Principal Train Battalion
Det. 6/4th Principal Train Battalion
Det. 3/1st (bis) Train Battalion
Engineering Train Det.
Equipage Train Det.

French Archives, Carton XP-3.

THE BATTLE OF LEIPZIG
16-19 OCTOBER 1813

FRENCH ARMY

COMMANDING GENERAL: EMPEROR NAPOLEON I
Chief of Staff: Maréchal Berthier, Prince of Neuchatel
Artillery Commander: Général de division Count Sorbier
Adjutant General: Général de division Count d'Erlon

Engineering Commander: General Rogniat
Commander of HQ: General Durrieu
Southern Front Cdr: Maréchal Murat, King of
  Naples
Northern Front Cdr: Maréchal Ney, Prince de la
  Moskowa

Imperial Guard:
1st Division Old Guard: Général de division Friant
(6,255)
Brigade: Général de brigade Christiani
  1/, 2/1st Chasseurs à Pied Regiment
  1/, 2/2nd Chasseurs à Pied Regiment
Brigade: Général de brigade Michel
  1/, 2/1st Grenadier à Pied Regiment
  1/, 2/2nd Grenadier à Pied Regiment
Artillery:
  1st Old Guard Foot Battery (4/105) (6 6-pdrs and 2
    5-7" how.)
  2nd Old Guard Foot Battery (3/118) (6 12-pdrs and
    2 6" how.)
  6/1st Guard Train Battalion
  ? Guard Train Company
**2nd Division Old Guard: Général de division
Curial (4,664)**
Brigade: Général de brigade Rousseau
  1/, 2/Fusilier Chasseur Regiment
  1/, 2/Fusilier Grenadier Regiment
  Velites of Turin (1)
  Velites of Florence (1)
Brigade: Général de brigade Rottembourg
  1/Saxon Guard Regiment
  Polish Guard Battalion
  2/Westphalian Guard Fusilier Battalion
Artillery:
  10th Young Guard Foot Battery (4/99) (6 6-pdrs and
    2 5-7" how.)
  14th Young Guard Foot Battery (3/91) (6 6-pdrs and
    2 5-7" how.)
  2 Guard Train Companies
I Corps Young Guard: Maréchal Oudinot
1st Division: Général de division Pacthod (6,044)
Brigade: Général de brigade Lacoste
  1/, 2/1st Voltigeur Regiment
  1/, 2/2nd Voltigeur Regiment
  1/, 2/3rd Voltigeur Regiment
Brigade: Général de brigade Couloumy
  1/, 2/7th Voltigeur Regiment
  1/, 2/11th Voltigeur Regiment
  1/, 2/11th Tirailleur Regiment
Artillery:
  1st Young Guard Foot Battery (3/110) (6 6-pdrs and
    2 5-7" how.)
  2nd Young Guard Foot Battery (3/109) (6 6-pdrs
    and 2 5-7" how.)
  8th Young Guard Foot Battery (3/90) (6 6-pdrs and
    2 5-7" how.)
  4/1st Guard Train Battalion
  3/2nd Guard Train Battalion

? Guard Train Company
2/5th Sapper Battalion
1st Guard Equipage Train Company
3rd Division: Général de division Decouz (4,731)
Brigade: Général de brigade Boyer de Rébeval
  1/, 2/5th Voltigeur Regiment
  1/, 2/6th Voltigeur Regiment
  1/, 2/7th Voltigeur Regiment
  1/, 2/8th Voltigeur Regiment
Brigade: Général de brigade Pelet
  1/, 2/9th Voltigeur Regiment
  1/, 2/10th Voltigeur Regiment
  1/, 2/12th Voltigeur Regiment
Artillery:
  9th Young Guard Foot Battery (3/86) (6 6-pdrs and
    2 5-7" how.)
  11th Young Guard Foot Battery (3/87) (6 6-pdrs and
    2 5-7" how.)
  13th Young Guard Foot Battery (3/84) (6 6-pdrs and
    2 5-7" how.)
  4/Guard Train Battalion
  5/Guard Train Battalion

II Corps Young Guard: Maréchal Mortier
2nd Division: Général de division Barrois (5,470)
Brigade: Général de brigade Poret de Morvan
  1/, 2/1st Tirailleur Regiment
  1/, 2/2nd Tirailleur Regiment
  1/, 2/3rd Tirailleur Regiment
Brigade: Général de brigade
  1/, 2/4th Tirailleur Regiment
  1/, 2/5th Tirailleur Regiment
  1/, 2/6th Tirailleur Regiment
Artillery:
  3rd Young Guard Foot Battery (2/85) (6 6-pdrs and
    2 5-7" how.)
  4th Young Guard Foot Battery (3/92) (6 6-pdrs and
    2 5-7" how.)
  12th Young Guard Foot Battery (3/96) (6 6-pdrs
    and 2 5-7" how.)
  9/1st Guard Train Battalion
  9/2nd Guard Train Battalion
  ? Guard Train Company
  3/7th Sapper Battalion
  7th Guard Equipage Train Company
4th Division: Général de division Roguet (5,521)
Brigade: Général de brigade Flamand
  1/, 2/Flanquer-Chasseur Regiment
  1/, 2/Flanquer-Grenadier Regiment
  1/, 2/7th Tirailleur Regiment
Brigade: Général de brigade Marguet
  1/, 2/8th Tirailleur Regiment
  1/, 2/9th Tirailleur Regiment
  1/, 2/10th Tirailleur Regiment
Artillery:
  5th Young Guard Foot Battery (3/88) (6 6-pdrs and
    2 5-7" how.)
  6th Young Guard Foot Battery (3/86) (6 6-pdrs and
    2 5-7" how.)

7th Young Guard Foot Battery (3/89) (6 6-pdrs and
2 5-7" how.) 1/2nd Guard Train Battalion
2/2nd Guard Train Battalion
Guard Artillery: General Dulauloy (3,911)
3/Old Guard Foot Battery (3/83) (6 6-pdrs and 2
5-7" how.)
4/Old Guard Foot Battery (4/106) (6 6-pdrs and 2
5-7" how.)
5/Old Guard Foot Battery (3/118) (6 6-pdrs and 2
5-7" how.)
6/Old Guard Foot Battery (3/98) (6 6-pdrs and 2
5-7" how.)
1/, 2/Old Guard Horse Battery (4 6-pdrs and 2 5-7"
how. ea.)
Berg Horse Battery (4 6-pdrs and 2 5-7" how.)
2 Guard Sapper Companies
12 Gendarme Companies
1 Pontooneer Company
3/Guard Marine Battalion
1 Neapolitan Guard Marine Company
14 Guard Artillery Train Companies
1 Berg Artillery Train Company
1 Guard Engineering Train Company
1 Guard Equipage Train Company
3 Administrative Ouvrier Companies
Guard Cavalry Corps: Général de division
Nansouty
(Strength as of 15 October 1813)
1st Division: Général de division d'Ornano
Brigade: Général de brigade Colbert
1/, 2/, 3/, 4/, 5/, 6, Berg Lancer Regiment (39/409)
2eme Chevauléger-lancier Régiment de la Garde
(Dutch Lancers) (10) (63/731)
Brigade: Colonel Pinteville
5/, 6/Empress Dragoon Regiment (Young Guard)
(18/223)
Artillery:
6th Old Guard Horse Battery (3/84)
(4 6-pdrs and 2 5.7" how.)
5/11th Train Battalion (2/71)
2nd Division: Général de division
Lefèbvre-Desnoëttes
Brigade: Général de brigade Krasinski
4/, 5/, 6/, 7/1st Chevauléger-lancier Régiment de la
Garde
(Polish Lancers) (Young Guard) (43/535)
6/, 7/, 8/, 9/Chasseurs à Cheval de la Garde
(Young Guard) (38/628)
Brigade: Général de brigade Castex
5/, 6/Grenadiers à Cheval de la Garde
(Young Guard) (17/290)
Artillery:
5th Old Guard Horse Battery (3/86)
(4 6-pdrs and 2 5.7" how.)
6/10th Train Battalion (1/79)
3rd Division: Général de division Walther
Brigade: Général de brigade Lyon
1/, 2/, 3/1er Chevauléger-lancier Régiment de la
Garde

(Polish Lancers) (Old Guard) (42/530)
4th Gardes d'Honneur Regiment (10/192)
1/, 2/, 3/, 4/, 5/, 10/Chasseurs à Cheval de la Garde
(Old Guard) (51/871)
1/, 2/1st Gardes d'Honneur Regiment (15/269)
Brigade: Général de brigade Letort
1/, 2/, 3/, 4/Empress Dragoon Regiment
(Old Guard) (45/747)
1/, 2/2nd Gardes d'Honneur Regiment (15/246)
Brigade: Général de brigade Laferrière
1/, 2/, 3/, 4/Grenadiers à Cheval de la Garde
(Old Guard) (57/881)
1/3rd Gardes d'Honneur Regiment (8/146)
Artillery:
4th Old Guard Horse Battery (2/83) (4 6-pdrs and 2
5.7" how.)
3/, 4/12th Train Battalion (1/144)
Artillery:
3rd Old Guard Horse Battery (4/85) (4 6-pdrs and 2
5.7" how.)

II Corps: Maréchal Victor (Strengths as of 1
October)
4th Division: Général de division Dubreton
Brigade: Général de brigade Ferrière
Staff/24th Légère Regiment (11/23)
1/24th Légère Regiment (13/529)
2/24th Légère Regiment (15/435)
4/24th Légère Regiment (16/398)
Staff/19th Line Regiment (12/23)
1/19th Line Regiment (14/401)
2/19th Line Regiment (13/430)
4/19th Line Regiment (12/353)
Brigade: Général de brigade Brun
Staff/37th Line Regiment (13/24)
1/37th Line Regiment (13/329)
2/37th Line Regiment (17/385)
4/37th Line Regiment (17/342)
Staff/56th Line Regiment (4/19)
1/56th Line Regiment (22/463)
2/56th Line Regiment (21/467)
4/56th Line Regiment (18/379)
Artillery: Chef de bataillon Reisser
7/2nd Foot Artillery (3/93) (6 6-pdrs and 2 24-pdr
how.)
11/4th Foot Artillery (2/92) (6 6-pdrs and 2 24-pdr
how.)
Det. 3/12th Principal Train Battalion (1/103)
Det. 2/3th (bis) Train Battalion (1/92)
1/14th Military Equipage Battalion (0/11)
5th Division: Général de division Dufour
Brigade: Général de brigade Estko
1/26th Légère Regiment (18/515)
2/26th Légère Regiment (17/515)
4/26th Légère Regiment (17/514)
1/93rd Line Regiment (29/386)
2/93rd Line Regiment (17/413)
4/93rd Line Regiment (24/408)

Brigade:
  1/46th Line Regiment (29/540)
  1/72nd Line Regiment (29/578)
Artillery: Chef de bataillon Grosset
  13/5th Foot Artillery (2/86)
  12/8th Foot Artillery (1/85)
  Total (6 6-pdrs and 2 24-pdr how.)
  Det. 3/12th Principal Train Battalion (0/12)
6th Division: Général de division Vial
Brigade: Général de brigade Valory
  Staff/11th Légère Regiment (14/21)
  1/11th Légère Regiment (16/500)
  2/11th Légère Regiment (19/421)
  4/11th Légère Regiment (18/394)
  Staff/4th Line Regiment (15/26)
  1/4th Line Regiment (16/412)
  2/4th Line Regiment (15/521)
  4/4th Line Regiment (18/358)
Brigade: Général de brigade Bronikowski
  Staff/2nd Line Regiment (14/26),
  1/2nd Line Regiment (17/435)
  2/2nd Line Regiment (17/500)
  4/2nd Line Regiment (18/402)
  Staff/18th Line Regiment (10/24)
  1/18th Line Regiment (18/510)
  2/18th Line Regiment (17/526)
  4/18th Line Regiment (17/483)
Artillery:
  25/3rd Foot Artillery (3/100) (6 6-pdrs and 2 24-pdr
    how.)
  26/3rd Foot Artillery (3/103) (6 6-pdrs and 2 24-pdr
    how.)
  3/14th Principal Train Battalion (1/102)
  3/3rd (bis) Train Battalion (1/90)
  Ambulance (0/14)
Reserve: Général de brigade Mongenet
  10/6th Foot Artillery (3/97) (8 12-pdrs)
  Det. 2/9th Principal Train Battalion (1/49)
  2/14th Principal Train Battalion (1/103)
  1/2nd Horse Artillery (3/99) (4 6-pdrs and 2 24-pdr
    how.)
  Det. 2/11th (bis) Train Battalion (1/40)
  Det. 3/11th (bis) Train Battalion (0/19)
  Det. 4/11th (bis) Train Battalion (0/4)
  Det. 4th Principal Train Battalion (0/7)
  Equipage Train Detachment
Park:
  9/2nd Foot Artillery (3/84) (1 6-pdr)
  15th Artisans Company (1/22)
  2/4th Principal Train Battalion (1/50)
  Det. 4th Principal Train Battalion (0/27)
  4/8th Principal Train Battalion (1/64)
  2/9th Principal Train Battalion (0/6)
  Staff/12th Principal Train Battalion (1/2)
  Det. 12th Principal Train Battalion (0/40)
  3/3rd (bis) Train Battalion (0/16)
  7/11th Principal Train Battalion (0/22)
  4/11th Principal Train Battalion (0/17)
  2/2nd Sapper Battalion (3/137)

  3/3rd Sapper Battalion (3/113)
  3/5th Sapper Battalion (3/120)

III Corps: Général de division Souham
8th Division: Général de division Brayer (4,442)
Brigade: Général de brigade Fournier
  2/, 3/6th Légère Regiment
  1/, 3/28th Légère Regiment
  2/3/16th Légère Regiment
  2/, 3/40th Line Regiment
Brigade: Général de brigade Bony
  1/, 3/, 4/22nd Line Regiment
  2/, 3/59th Line Regiment
  3/, 4/69th Line Regiment
Artillery:
  10/2nd Foot Artillery
  5/9th Foot Artillery
  Det. 3/9th Principal Train Battalion
  Det. 4/3rd (bis) Train Battalion
9th Division: Général de division Delmas (4,235)
Brigade: Général de brigade Estève
  2nd Provisional Regiment
  3/2nd Légère Regiment (1)
  3/4th Légère Regiment (1)
  1/, 2/, 3/136th Line Regiment
Brigade:
  1/, 2/, 3/138th Line Regiment
  1/, 2/, 3/145th Line Regiment
Artillery:
  2/9th Foot Artillery
  11/9th Foot Artillery
  Det. 4/3rd (bis) Train Battalion
  Det. 4/6th Principal Train Battalion
  Det. 7/10th Principal Train Battalion
11th Division: Général de division Ricard (4,357)
Brigade: Général de brigade Charrière
  3/, 4/, 6/9th Légère Regiment
  2/, 3/, 4/50th Line Regiment
  3/, 4/65th Line Regiment
Brigade: Général de brigade Vergez
  1/, 2/, 3/142rid Line Regiment
  1/, 2/, 3/144th Line Regiment
Artillery:
  19/7th Foot Artillery
  5/9th Foot Artillery
  Det. 7/10th Principal Train Battalion
  Det. 7/11th Principal Train Battalion
  Det. 4/13th (bis) Train Battalion
23rd Light Cavalry Brigade GB Beurmann (1,065)
  1/, 2/, 3/, 4/, 5/, 6/10th Hussar Regiment
  1/, 2/, 3/, 4/, 5/Baden Dragoon Regiment
Park: (3,069)
  2 Foot Batteries
  1 Horse Battery
  Artillery Train (3 coys)
  Spanish Sappers (3 coys)
  Gendarmes (1 coy)
  Equipage Train Detachment

6th Light Cavalry Division: Général de division Fournier
14th Light Cavalry Brigade: Général de brigade Mouriez
  4/29th Chasseurs à Cheval Regiment (9/112/21/109)[1]
  4/31st Chasseurs à Cheval Regiment (9/168/15/171)
  4/1st Hussar Regiment (1) (17/237/25/233)
15th Light Cavalry Brigade: Général de brigade Ameil
  3/, 4/2nd Hussar Regiment (16/337/26/337)
  5/4th Hussar Regiment (4/29/11/27)
  4/12th Hussar Regiment (7/195/28/198)
Artillery:
  ½ Horse Battery
Brigade: Général de brigade Axamitowski
  4/4th Dragoon Regiment (4/102/14/8)
  3/5th Dragoon Regiment (12/204/21/211)
  3/14th Dragoon Regiment (10/129/16/129)
  3/12th Dragoon Regiment (8/229/13/109)
  24th Dragoon Regiment (0/58/0/57)

IV Corps: Général de division Bertrand
12th Division: Général de division Morand (5,705)
Brigade: Général de brigade Belair
  1/, 2/, 3/, 4/8th Légère Regiment
Brigade: Général de brigade Toussaint
  1/, 2/, 3/, 4/13th Line Regiment
Brigade: Général de brigade Hulot
  1/, 2/, 4/23rd Line Regiment
  1/, 2/, 3/137th Line Regiment
Artillery:
  1/2nd Foot Artillery
  3/2nd Foot Artillery
  1/7th (bis) Train Battalion
  2/7th (bis) Train Battalion
15th Division: Général de division Fontanelli (1,859)
Brigade: Général de brigade St-Andrea
  1st Italian Légère Regiment (2)
  6th Italian Line Regiment (1)
Brigade: Général de brigade Martel
  1st Italian Line Regiment (1)
  4th Italian Line Regiment (1)
Brigade: Général de brigade Moroni
  Milan Guard (1)
  7th Italian Line Regiment (1)
Artillery:
  1 Italian Foot Battery
  1 Italian Train Company
Mixed Division: Generalleutnant Graf Franquemont (1,168)
Brigade: Generalmajor Stockmayer
  1st Württemberg Combined Light Battalion
  1st Württemberg Combined Line Battalion
  2nd Württemberg Combined Line Battalion
  3rd Württemberg Combined Line Battalion

24th Light Cavalry Brigade: Generalmajor von Jett
  1/1st Württemberg Chevauleger Regiment *Prinz Adam*
  1/3rd Württemberg Chevauleger Regiment *Herzog Ludwig*
  Württemberg Horse Battery
29th Light Cavalry Brigade: Général de brigade Wolff (221)
  1/Westphalian Chevauléger Regiment
  1/Hesse-Darmstadt Chevauléger Regiment
Reserve Artillery (871)
  1 Foot Battery
  Train
  Sapper Company
  Gendarmerie
4th Heavy Cavalry Division Général de division Defrance
Brigade: Général de brigade Axamitowski (with III Corps)
Brigade: Général de brigade Quinette
  4/16th Dragoon Regiment (5/111/9/111)
  3/17th Dragoon Regiment (15/185/44/187)
  4/21st Dragoon Regiment (8/118/17/119)
  4/26th Dragoon Regiment (4/66/7/65)
  5/27th Dragoon Regiment (6/114/16/112)
  5/13th Cuirassier Regiment (5/147/11/149)
Artillery:
  ½ Horse Battery

V Corps: Général de division Lauriston
(Strengths as of 1 October 1813)
10th Division: Général de division Albert
Brigade: Général de brigade Bachelet
  4th Provisional Regiment
    4/5th Légère Regiment (17/320)
    4/12th Légère Regiment (22/175)[2]
  1/139th Line Regiment (23/463)
  2/139th Line Regiment (19/430)
  3/139th Line Regiment (21/483)
Brigade: Général de brigade Bertrand
  1/140th Line Regiment (26/216)
  2/140th Line Regiment (14/214)
  3/140th Line Regiment (14/201)
  1/141st Line Regiment (23/309)
  2/141st Line Regiment (16/297)
  3/141st Line Regiment (18/314)
Artillery:
  3/7th Foot Artillery (4/63) (4 6-pdrs and 1 how.)
  4/7th Foot Artillery (3/59) (4 6-pdrs and 1 how.)
  4/1st Principal Train Battalion (2/177)
16th Division: Général de division Maison
Brigade: Général de brigade Mandeville
  1/152nd Line Regiment (19/410)
  2/152nd Line Regiment (8/459)

---

1   Numbers are officers, men, officer's horses, and men's horses.

2   Joined parent regiment in 42nd Division on 10/10/13.

3/152nd Line Regiment (7/393)
1/153rd Line Regiment (23/428)
2/153rd Line Regiment (11/431)
3/153rd Line Regiment (11/429)
Brigade:
1/154th Line Regiment (23/340)
2/154th Line Regiment (5/365)
3/154th Line Regiment (9/376)
Artillery:
1/1st Foot Artillery (3/68) (4 6-pdrs and 1 how.)
3/1st Foot Artillery (3/88) (4 6-pdrs and 1 how.)
4/8th (bis) Train Battalion (1/141)
19th Division: Général de division Rochambeau
Brigade: Général de brigade Lafitte
1/135th Line Regiment (26/250)
2/135th Line Regiment (9/245)
3/135th Line Regiment (12/252)
1/149th Line Regiment (27/270)
2/149th Line Regiment (9/210)
3/149th Line Regiment (10/236)
Brigade: Général de brigade Harlet
1/150th Line Regiment (13/160)
2/150th Line Regiment (10/311)
3/150th Line Regiment (10/407)
1/155th Line Regiment (35/418)
2/155th Line Regiment (12/384)
3/155th Line Regiment (16/364)
Artillery:
12/5th Foot Artillery (2/82) (4 6-pdrs and 1 how.)
17/5th Foot Artillery (3/78) (4 6-pdrs and 1 how.)
4/4th Principal Train Battalion (1/134)
6th Light Cavalry Brigade: Général de brigade Dermoncourt
1/2nd Chasseurs à Cheval Regiment (14/58/44/53)
2/2nd Chasseurs à Cheval Regiment (8/61/14/57)
3/2nd Chasseurs à Cheval Regiment (3/65/6/68)
1/3rd Chasseurs à Cheval Regiment (12/110/34/107)
2/3rd Chasseurs à Cheval Regiment (5/9711/95)
1/6th Chasseurs à Cheval Regiment (11/121/33/103)
2/6th Chasseurs à Cheval Regiment (5/141/12/131)
3/6th Chasseurs à Cheval Regiment (6/47/13/42)
Reserve:
16/1st Foot Artillery (2/78) (5 12-pdrs and 1 how.)
17/1st Foot Artillery (3/56) (5 12-pdrs and 1 how.)
2/5th Horse Artillery (3/87) (3 6-pdrs and 1 how.)
7/6th Horse Artillery (2/68) (3 6-pdrs and 1 how.)
7/3rd Principal Train Battalion (1/116)
4/9th (bis) Train Battalion (1/173)
Park
15/1st Foot Artillery (5/66)
(1 12-pdr and 1-24-pdr how., 1-6/4" how.)
15th Artillery Artisan Company (1/18)
1/6th Sapper Battalion (5/45)
2/6th Sapper Battalion (2/84)
3/6th Sapper Battalion (3/81)

VI Corps: Maréchal Marmont
(Strength as of 1 October 1813)
20th Division: Général de division Compans

Brigade: Général de brigade Pelleport
2/32nd Légère Regiment (19/231)
3/32nd Légère Regiment (15/313)
Staff/1st Marine Infantry Regiment (8/14)
1/1st Marine Infantry Regiment (16/333)
2/1st Marine Infantry Regiment (16/335)
3/1st Marine Infantry Regiment (14/358)
4/1st Marine Infantry Regiment (16/344)
5/1st Marine Infantry Regiment (15/364)
Brigade: Général de brigade Joubert
Staff/3rd Marine Regiment (8/13)
1/3rd Marine Regiment (11/487)
2/3rd Marine Regiment (1/186)
3/3rd Marine Regiment (13/447)
20th Provisional Regiment
5/66th Line Regiment (21/319)
3/122nd Line Regiment (19/300)
25th Provisional Regiment
3/47th Line Regiment (20/445)
3/86th Line Regiment (21/357)
Artillery:
16/5th Foot Battery (2/112) (6 6-pdrs and 2 how.)
10/8th Foot Battery (3/102) (6 6-pdrs and 2 how.)
3/8th Principal Train Battalion (1/168)
5/8th Principal Train Battalion (2/119)
21st Division: Général de division Lagrange
Brigade: Général de brigade Jamin
Staff/37th Légère Regiment (8/21)
1/37th Légère Regiment (16/339)
2/37th Légère Regiment (18/382)
3/37th Légère Regiment (–) (not reported)
4/37th Légère Regiment (16/322)
Staff/4th Marine Regiment (11/27)
1/4th Marine Regiment (15/414)
2/4th Marine Regiment (12/456)
3/4th Marine Regiment (17/431)
1/Joseph Napoleon Regiment (14/316)
Brigade: Général de brigade Buquet
Staff/2nd Marine Regiment (21/34)
1/2nd Marine Regiment (18/436)
2/2nd Marine Regiment (10/426)
3/2nd Marine Regiment (14/397)
4/2nd Marine Regiment (17/446)
5/2nd Marine Regiment (14/404)
6/2nd Marine Regiment (18/453)
Artillery:
10/4th Foot Artillery (2/117) (6 6-pdrs and 2 how.)
18/5th Foot Artillery (3/108) (6 6-pdrs and 2 how.)
Det. 1/10th (bis) Train Battalion (1/77)
7/12th (bis) Train Battalion (1/110)
2/8th Principal Train Battalion (2/167)
22nd Division: Général de division Friederichs
Brigade: Général de brigade Coehorn
3/23rd Légère Regiment (22/228)
4/23rd Légère Regiment (17/280)
11th Provisional Regiment
4/1st Line Regiment (21/276)
2/62nd Line Regiment (17/335)
13th Provisional Regiment

3/14th Line Regiment (24/668)
4/16th Line Regiment (19/416)
3/15th Line Regiment (21/319)
4/15th Line Regiment (20/291)
Brigade: Général de brigade Choisy
16th Provisional Regiment
6/26th Line Regiment (18/308)
6/82nd Line Regiment (19/221)
3/70th Line Regiment (20/308)
4/70th Line Regiment (18/293)
3/121st Line Regiment (21/285)
4/121st Line Regiment (19/266)
Artillery:
14/4th Foot Artillery (2/107) (6 6-pdrs and 2 how.)
22/9th Foot Artillery (3/87) (6 6-pdrs and 2 how.)
3/8th Principal Train Battalion (1/167)
2/10th (bis) Train Battalion (1/96)
25th Light Cavalry Brigade: Generalmajor Normann
1/2nd Württemberg Chevauleger Regiment (8/112/8/112)
2/2nd Württemberg Chevauleger Regiment (4/117/4/117)
3/2nd Württemberg Chevauleger Regiment (3/105/3/104)
4/2nd Württemberg Chevauleger Regiment (4/116/4/116)
1/4th Württemberg Chevauleger Regiment (7/112/7/112)
2/4th Württemberg Chevauleger Regiment (4/113/4/113)
3/4th Württemberg Chevauleger Regiment (3/115/3/115)
4/4th Württemberg Chevauleger Regiment (4/108/4/108)
Reserve and Park: Général de division Foucher
26/5th Foot Artillery (3/127) (6 12-pdrs and 2 6" how.)
7/9th Foot Artillery (3/100) (6 12-pdrs and 2 6" how.)
1/1st Horse Artillery (3/92) (4 6-pdrs and 2 24-pdr how.)
3/4th Horse Artillery (2/77) (4 6-pdrs and 2 24-pdr how.)
3/5th Foot Artillery (3/92) (park coy)
Park guns—4 6-pdrs and 2 24-pdr how.
Det. 7/10th (bis) Train Battalion (2/94)
4/12th Principal Train Battalion (2/108)
4/6th (bis) Train Battalion (2/93)
6/6th (bis) Train Battalion (2/119)
7/6th (bis) Train Battalion (1/114)
18th Artillery Artisan Company (1/22)
6/2nd Sapper Battalion (3/103)
2/4th Sapper Battalion (3/102)
9/4th Sapper Battalion (3/110)
4/7th Sapper Battalion (4/04)
5th Light Cavalry Division: Général de division Lorge
12th Light Cavalry Brigade: Colonel Shea
3/, 4/5th Chasseurs à Cheval Regiment (20/373/47/358)

3/, 4/10th Chasseurs à Cheval Regiment (11/215/26/211)
5/, 6/13th Chasseurs à Cheval Regiment (17/253/40/244)
13th Light Cavalry Brigade: Général de brigade Merlin
4/15th Chasseurs à Cheval Regiment (8/126/14/133)
3/21st Chasseurs à Cheval Regiment (7/110/14/111)
3/, 4/22nd Chasseurs à Cheval Regiment (8/212/22/210)

VII Corps: Général de division Reynier (12,637)
13th Division: Général de division Guilleminot
Brigade: Général de brigade Gruyer
4/1st Légère Regiment
1/, 2/18th Légère Regiment
3/7th Line Regiment
1/156th Line Regiment
Brigade: Général de brigade Lejeune
2/Illyrian Regiment
3/52nd Line Regiment
3/67th Line Regiment
2/, 3/101st Line Regiment
Artillery: 1 Foot Battery
32nd Division: Général de division Durutte
Brigade: Général de brigade Devaux
1/35th Légère Regiment
3/131st Line Regiment
3/132nd Line Regiment
Brigade: Général de brigade Jarry
1/36th Légère Regiment
3/133rd Line Regiment
3/Würzburg Line Regiment
Artillery: 1 Foot Battery
24th Division: General von Zeschau (3,679)
Brigade: General Brause
1st (Lecoq) Light Battalion (9/468)
Von Spiegel Grenadier Battalion (6/215)
Von Steindel Infantry Regiment (1) (14/332)
Prinz Friedrich Infantry Regiment (1) (14/557)
2/von Rechten Infantry Regiment (1) (10/149)
Brigade: General Ryssel
2nd (von Sahr) Light Battalion (13/705)
Von Anger Grenadier Battalion (5/176)
1/Niesemeuschel Infantry Regiment (1) (8/292)
Saxon Jäger Company
Saxon Sapper Company (3/42)
Artillery:
1 Saxon 6-pdr Foot Battery (5/188)
1 Saxon 12-pdr Foot Battery (4/140)
Saxon Train Detachment
26th Light Cavalry Brigade: Oberst von Lindenau (32/652)
1/, 2/, 3/, 4/, 5/Prinz Clement Uhlan Regiment
Saxon Hussar Regiment (3 to 8 sqns) (sources vary)
Artillery: Total (6/178)
1st Saxon Horse Battery
2nd Saxon Horse Battery

VIII Corps: Général de division Poniatowski
26th Division: Général de division Kamieniecki (5,000)
Brigade: Général de brigade Sierawski
  1/, 2/Vistula Legion Regiment
  1/, 2/1st Polish Line Regiment
  1/, 2/16th Polish Line Regiment
Brigade: Général de brigade Malachowski
  1/, 2/8th Polish Line Regiment
  1/, 2/15th Polish Line Regiment
  1st Polish Foot Battery
  2nd Polish Foot Battery
  3rd Polish Foot Battery
Brigade: Général de brigade Grabowski
  1/, 2/12th Polish Line Regiment
  1/, 2/14th Polish Line Regiment
  4th Polish Foot Battery
  1/2 unknown Polish Foot Battery
27th Light Cavalry Brigade: Général de brigade Uminski
  1/, 2/14th Polish Cuirassier Regiment
  1/, 2/, 3/, 4/Krakus Regiment
  5th Polish Foot Battery
  6th Polish Foot Battery
  1 Polish Sapper Company
  Polish Equipage Train Detachment

XI Corps: Maréchal Macdonald
31st Division: Général de division Ledru (5,023)
Brigade: Général de brigade Fressinet
  11th Provisional Demi-brigade
    4/27th Line Regiment
    6/20th Line Regiment
    4/102nd Line Regiment
  13th Provisional Demi-brigade
    4/5th Line Regiment
    4/11th Line Regiment
    4/79th Line Regiment
Brigade:
  1/, 2/8th Westphalian Line Regiment
  4th Westphalian Light Battalion
Brigade: Général de brigade Macdonald
  Neapolitan Elite Regiment (1)
  1/, 2/4th Neapolitan Light Regiment
Artillery:
  5/1st Foot Artillery
  2 Westphalian Batteries
35th Division: Général de division Gerard (3,551)
Brigade: Général de brigade d'Henin
  3/, 4/, 7/6th Line Regiment
  1/, 2/, 3/, 4/112nd Line Regiment
Brigade: Général de brigade Zucchi
  3/, 4/2nd Italian Légère Regiment
  1/, 2/, 3/, 4/5th Italian Line Regiment
Artillery:
  6/1st Foot Artillery
  3rd Italian Horse Battery
  Det. 1/11th (bis) Train Battalion
  3rd Italian Train Battalion
  4th Italian Train Battalion

36th Division: Général de division Charpentier (4,229)
Brigade: Général de brigade Simmer
  1/, 2/, 3/, 4/22nd Légère Regiment
  4/, 6/10th Line Regiment
Brigade: Général de brigade Meunier
  3/, 4/3rd Légère Regiment
  3/, 4/, 7/14th Légère Regiment
Artillery:
  5/1st Foot Artillery
  19/2nd Foot Artillery
  Det. 1/7th Principal Train Battalion
  Det. 2/12th Principal Train Battalion
39th Division: Général de division Marchand (4,602)
Brigade: General Stockhorn
  1/, 2/1st Baden Line Regiment
  1/, 2/3rd Baden Line Regiment
Brigade: General Prince Emil von Hesse
  1/Hesse-Darmstadt Guard Fusilier Regiment
  1/, 2/Hesse-Darmstadt Leibgarde Regiment
  1/, 2/Hesse-Darmstadt Leib Infantry Regiment
Artillery:
  1 Baden Foot Battery
  1 Hessian Foot Battery
28th Light Cavalry Brigade: GB Montbrun (446)
  1/, 2/4th Italian Chasseurs à Cheval Regiment
  1/Würzburg Chasseurs à Cheval Regiment
    (detached)
  1/, 2/, 3/, 4/2nd Neapolitan Chasseurs à Cheval
    Regiment
Park: (2,613)
  2 French 12-pdr Foot Batteries
  1 Neapolitan or French Battery
  3 Train Companies

IX Corps: Maréchal Augereau
51st Division: unknown (4,350)
Brigade: Général de brigade Lagarde
  32nd Provisional Demi-brigade
    2/25th Légère Regiment
    4/32nd Légère Regiment
    2/63rd Line Regiment
Brigade: Général de brigade Aymard
  34th Provisional Demi-brigade
    3/10th Légère Regiment
    2/21st Légère Regiment
  35th Provisional Demi-brigade
    3/32nd Line Regiment
    2/58th Line Regiment
Artillery:
  22/1st Foot Artillery
  5/2nd Foot Artillery
  21/2nd Foot Artillery
  Artillery Train Detachment
52nd Division: Général de division Sémélé (4,297)
Brigade: Général de brigade Bagneris
  37th Provisional Demi-brigade
    2/17th Légère Regiment

4/29th Légère Regiment
2/39th Line Regiment
Brigade: Général de brigade Godard
6/121st Line Regiment
6/122nd Line Regiment
2/86th Line Regiment
Artillery: (539)
2 Foot Batteries
2 Train Companies 1 Sapper Company
1 Engineering Train Company

Independent Divisions
Division: Général de division Lefol (2,229)
1st Erfurt Battalion
2nd Erfurt Battalion
2/54th Line Regiment (detached)
1 ½ Bataillon de Marche (Dets. 29th Légère, 25th,
and 33rd
Line Regiments)
27th (Polish) Division: GD Dombrowski (2,350)
Brigade: Général de brigade Zoltowski
1/, 2/2nd Polish Line Regiment
1/, 2/4th Polish Line Regiment
18th Light Cavalry Brigade: Général de brigade
Krukowiecki
1/, 2/, 3/, 4/2nd Polish Uhlan Regiment
1/, 2/, 3/, 4/4th Polish Chasseurs à Cheval Regiment
Artillery:
1 Foot Battery
1st Polish Horse Battery
Polish Artillery Train
1 Sapper Company
Division (Leipzig Garrison): GD Margaron (4,320)
Brigade: Général de brigade Bertrand
Gendarmes (19)
4/35th Légère Regiment (605)
1/132nd Line Regiment (730)
138th Line Regiment (352)
1st Provisional Infantry Regiment (1,942)
(probably consisted of)
2/96th Line Regiment
2/103rd Line Regiment
1st Provisional Cavalry Regiment (4) (855)
2nd Provisional Cavalry Regiment (4) (819)
Artillery:
1 Horse Battery (93)
Train (81)
Artisans (16)
Baden Brigade: Generalleutnant von Hochberg
Baden Lingg Jager Battalion (826)
1/, 2/2nd Baden Line Regiment (1,597)
Baden Artillery (54)
Baden Train (55)

I Cavalry Corps: GD Latour-Maubourg (6,480)
**1st Light Cavalry Division: Général de division
Berkheim**
2nd Light Cavalry Brigade: Général de brigade
Montmarie

1/, 2/16th Chasseurs à Cheval Regiment
1/, 2/1st Chevauléger-lancier Regiment
1/, 2/3rd Chevauléger-lancier Regiment
3rd Light Cavalry Brigade: Général de brigade Piquet
1/, 2/, 5th Chevauléger-lancier Regiment
1/, 2/8th Chevauléger-lancier Regiment
1/, 2/, 3/, 4/1st Italian Chasseurs à Cheval Regiment
**2nd Light Cavalry Division: Général de division
Corbineau**
1st Light Cavalry Brigade: Général de brigade
Coëtlosquet
1/, 2/6th Hussar Regiment
1/, 2/, 3/7th Hussar Regiment
1/, 2/, 3/8th Hussar Regiment
**3rd Light Cavalry Division: Général de division
Chastel**
4th Light Cavalry Brigade: Général de brigade Vallin
1/, 2/8th Chasseurs à Cheval Regiment
1/, 2/9th Chasseurs à Cheval Regiment
1/, 2/25th Chasseurs à Cheval Regiment
5th Light Cavalry Brigade: Général de brigade Vial
1/, 2/, 3/1st Chasseurs à Cheval Regiment
1/, 2/, 3/, 4/19th Chasseurs à Cheval Regiment
**1st Cuirassier Division: Général de division
Bordesoulle**
Brigade: Général de brigade Sopransi
1/, 2/2nd Cuirassier Regiment
1/, 2/, 3/3rd Cuirassier Regiment
1/, 2/, 3/6th Cuirassier Regiment
Brigade: Général de brigade Bessières
1/, 2/, 3/9th Cuirassier Regiment
1/, 2/, 3/11th Cuirassier Regiment
1/, 2/12th Cuirassier Regiment
Brigade: Général de brigade Lessing
1/, 2/, 3/, 4/Saxon Garde Cuirassier Regiment
1/, 2/, 3/, 4/Saxon Zastrow Cuirassier Regiment
3rd Heavy Division: Général de division Doumerc
Brigade: Général de brigade Audenarde
1/, 2/, 3/4th Cuirassier Regiment
1/, 2/, 3/7th Cuirassier Regiment
1/, 2/14th Cuirassier Regiment
1/, 2/, 3/, 4/Italian Napoleon Dragoon Regiment
Brigade: Général de brigade Reiset
1/, 2/7th Dragoon Regiment
1/, 2/, 3/23rd Dragoon Regiment
1/, 2/28th Dragoon Regiment
1/, 2/30th Dragoon Regiment
Corps Artillery:
6/3rd Horse Artillery
3/1st Horse Artillery
1/6th Horse Artillery
1/4th Horse Artillery
3rd Saxon Horse Artillery
Det. 1/16th Principal Artillery Train
Det. 2/16th Principal Artillery Train
Det. 2/8th (bis) Artillery Train
Det. 5/8th (bis) Artillery Train
1st Saxon Artillery Train

II Cavalry Corps: GD Sébastiani (5,679)
2nd Light Cavalry Division: GD Roussel d'Hurbal
7th Light Cavalry Brigade: Général de brigade Lagrange
  1/, 2/, 3/2nd Chevauléger-lancier Regiment
  1/, 2/, 3/11th Chasseurs à Cheval Regiment
  1/, 2/, 3/12th Chasseurs à Cheval Regiment
8th Light Cavalry Brigade: Général de brigade Dommanget
  1/, 2/, 3/4th Chevauléger-lancier Regiment
  1/, 2/, 3/5th Hussar Regiment
  1/, 2/, 3/, 4/9th Hussar Regiment
Artillery:
  7/1st Horse Battery (½ coy)
  Det. 2/11th (bis) Artillery Train
4th Light Cavalry Division: Général de division Exelmann
9th Light Cavalry Brigade: Général de brigade Maurin
  1/, 2/, 3/6th Chevauléger-lancier Regiment
  1/, 2/, 3/4th Chasseurs à Cheval Regiment
  1/, 2/, 3/, 4/7th Chasseurs à Cheval Regiment
  1/, 2/, 3/, 4/20th Chasseurs à Cheval Regiment
10th Light Cavalry Brigade: Général de brigade Wathier
  1/, 2/, 3/, 4/23rd Chasseurs à Cheval Regiment
  1/, 2/, 3/24th Chasseurs à Cheval Regiment
  1/, 2/, 3/11th Hussar Regiment
Artillery:
  7/4th Horse Battery (½ coy)
  Det. 4/11th (bis) Artillery Train
2nd Heavy Division: Général de division St-Germain
Brigade: Général de brigade Daugeranville
  1/, 2/, 3/1st Carabinier Regiment
  1/, 2/, 3/2nd Carabinier Regiment
  1/, 2/, 3/1st Cuirassier Regiment
Brigade: Général de brigade Thiry
  1/, 2/, 3/5th Cuirassier Regiment
  1/, 2/8th Cuirassier Regiment
  1/, 2/10th Cuirassier Regiment
Artillery:
  8/6th Horse Battery
  Det. 3/13th (bis) Artillery Train

III Reserve Cavalry Corps: GD Arrighi
  (Strength Figures as of 1 October 1813—distributed to various corps as indicated above)
5th Light Cavalry Division: Général de division Lorge
12th Light Cavalry Brigade: Colonel Shea
  1/, 3/, 4/5th Chasseurs à Cheval Regiment (20/373)
  1/, 3/, 4/10th Chasseurs à Cheval Regiment (11/215)
  5/, 6/13th Chasseurs à Cheval Regiment (17/253)
13th Light Cavalry Brigade: Général de brigade Merlin
  4/15th Chasseurs à Cheval Regiment (8/126)
  3/21st Chasseurs à Cheval Regiment (7/110)
  3/, 4/22nd Chasseurs à Cheval Regiment (8/212)

6th Light Cavalry Division: Général de division Fournier
14th Brigade: Général de brigade Mouriez
  4/29th Chasseurs à Cheval Regiment (9/112/21/109)
  4/31st Chasseurs à Cheval Regiment (9/168/15/171)
  4/1st Hussar Regiment (17/237/25/233)
15th Brigade: Général de brigade Amiel
  3/, 4/2nd Hussar Regiment (16/337/26/337)
  5/4th Hussar Regiment (4/29/11/27)
  4/12th Hussar Regiment (7/195/18/198)
4th Heavy Cavalry Division Général de division Defrance[3]
Corps Artillery: Colonel Chauvian
  4/6th Horse Artillery (2/85)
  1/5th Horse Artillery (2/85)5/5th Horse Artillery (3/96)
  Total 4 6-pdrs and 2 24-pdr how.
  5/1st Principal Train Battalion (2/131)
  5/4th Principal Train Battalion (1/72)

IV Cavalry Corps: GD Sokolnicki (3,000)[4]
7th Light Cavalry Division:
17th Light Cavalry Brigade: Général de brigade Tolinski
  1/, 2/, 3/, 4/1st Polish Chasseurs à Cheval Regiment
  1/, 2/, 3/, 4/3rd Polish Uhlan Regiment
  1 Polish Horse Battery
8th Light Cavalry Division: Général de division Sulkowski
19th Light Cavalry Brigade: Général de brigade Krukowski
  1/, 2/, 3/, 4/6th Polish Uhlan Regiment
  1/, 2/, 3/, 4/8th Polish Uhlan Regiment
  1st Polish Horse Battery
Artillery:
  4/2nd Horse Artillery
  2/6th Horse Artillery
  Det. 5/11th Principal Train Battalion
  Det. 5/4th Principal Train Battalion

V Cavalry Corps: Général de division Pajol
9th Light Cavalry Division: Général de brigade Pire
  (Strength as of 10 October 1813)
32nd Light Cavalry Brigade: Général de brigade Klicki
  1/, 3/, 4/3rd Hussar Regiment (26/268/58/237)
  1/, 2/, 3/, 4/27th Chasseurs à Cheval Regt (38/357/71/348)
33rd Light Cavalry Brigade: Général de brigade Vial
  1/, 3/, 4/14th Chasseurs à Cheval Regt (18/223/68/331)

---

3 Detached to III and IV Corps.
4 Général de division Kellerman served as a wing commander, directing both the IV and V Cavalry Corps.

1/, 3/, 4/26th Chasseurs à Cheval Regt
(20/170/58/158)

5th Heavy Cavalry Division: Général de division l'Héritier
Brigade: Général de brigade Quennet
1/, 2/, 3/2nd Dragoon Regiment (27/323/68/321)
1/, 3/, 4/6th Dragoon Regiment (24/290/55/264)
1/, 2/, 3/, 4/11th Dragoon Regiment (28/355/72/342)
Brigade: Général de brigade Collard
1/, 3/13th Dragoon Regiment (19/221/50/202)
1/, 2/, 3/15th Dragoon Regiment (28/303/74/292)

6th Heavy Cavalry Division: Général de division Milhaud
Brigade: Général de brigade Lamotte
1/, 3/18th Dragoon Regiment (15/205/43/206)
1/, 3/19th Dragoon Regiment (22/231/59/218)
1/, 3/20th Dragoon Regiment (14/464/35/168)
Brigade: Général de brigade Montelegier
1/, 2/, 3/22nd Dragoon Regiment (18/245/50/217)
1/, 2/, 3/25th Dragoon Regiment (27/239/65/198)
Artillery:
5/3rd Horse Battery (1/72)
Det. 11th Artillery Train Battalion (1/83)

Quistorp, *Geschichte der Nord Armee;*
Spectateur Militaire, 1827; Rousset, *La Grande Armée de 1813;* French Archives, Cartons 02-536, 537, 538, 539, 540, 541, 542, 543, 544, and XP-3

ALLIED ARMIES

ARMY OF BOHEMIA: GENERAL PRINZ SCHWARZENBERG
Headquarters Guard and Escort: (4,000)
Ingermannland Dragoon Regiment (3)
Kireva Don Cossack Regiment
Platov #4 Don Cossack Regiment
Popov #3 Don Cossack Regiment
Tabounetchikov Don Cossack Regiment
2nd Bug Cossack Regiment
3rd Bug Cossack Regiment
1st Ural Cossack Regiment
2 Little Russian Cossack Regiments
Vologda, Olonetz, and Tula Opolochenie

RUSSIANS: GENERAL OF CAVALRY BARCLAY DE TOLLY
Wing: General of Cavalry Wittgenstein
1st Corps: Generallieutenant Prince Gorchakov
5th Division: Generalmajor Mezentzov (4,100)
Brigade:
Sievesk Infantry Regiment (t)
Kaluga Infantry Regiment (2)
Brigade: Generalmajor Prince of Siberia
Penn Infantry Regiment (2)
Mohilev Infantry Regiment (2)
Guard Battalion Grand Duchess Catherine Pavlovna
(1)

Brigade:
23rd Jager Regiment (2)
24th Jager Regiment (2)
14th Division: Generalmajor Helfreich (1,600)
Brigade:
Tenguinsk Infantry Regiment (2)
Estonia Infantry Regiment (2)
Brigade: Generalmajor Winstoff
25th Jager Regiment (2)
26th Jager Regiment (2)
Corps Artillery Brigade:
Position Battery #3 (12 guns)
Light Battery #6 and #7 (12 guns ea.)
2nd Corps: Prince Eugene of Württemberg (5,200)
3rd Division: Generalmajor Schachafskoy
Brigade:
Mourman Infantry Regiment (2)
Revel Infantry Regiment (2)
Brigade:
Tchernigov Infantry Regiment (2)
Selenguinsk Infantry Regiment (2)
Brigade:
20th Jager Regiment (2)
21st Jager Regiment (2)
4th Division: Generalmajor Puschnitzki
Brigade: Colonel Reibnitz
Kremenchug Infantry Regiment (2)
Minsk Infantry Regiment (2)
4th Jager Regiment (2)
Brigade: Colonel Feodoroff
Tobolsk Infantry Regiment (2)
Volhynie Infantry Regiment (2)
34th Jager Regiment (2)
Artillery:
Position Batteries #5 and #13 (12 guns ea.)
Light Battery #27 (12 guns)
2 Horse Batteries (12 guns ea.)
Reserve: Grand Duke Constantine
3rd "Grenadier" Corps: GL Raevsky (9,100)
1st Grenadier Division: Generalmajor Pissarev
Brigade: Generalmajor Kniasnin
Ekaterinoslav Grenadier Regiment (2)
Arakcheyev Grenadier Regiment (2)
Brigade: Colonel Ocht
St-Petersburg Grenadier Regiment (2)
Tauride Grenadier Regiment (1)
Brigade: Colonel Yemelianov
Pernau Grenadier Regiment (2)
Kexholm Grenadier Regiment (2)
2nd Grenadier Division: Generalmajor Tchoglokov
Brigade: Generalmajor Levin
Kiev Grenadier Regiment (2)
Moscow Grenadier Regiment (2)
Brigade: Colonel Damas
Astrakhan Grenadier Regiment (1)
Fangoria Grenadier Regiment (1)
Brigade:
Siberia Grenadier Regiment (2)
Little Russia Grenadier Regiment (2)

Corps Artillery:
Position Batteries #30 and #33 (12 guns ea.)
Light Battery #14 (12 guns)

5th (Guard) Corps: GL Yermolov (8,070)

1st Guard Division: Generalmajor Baron Rosen
Brigade: Generalmajor Potemkin
Preobragenski Guard Infantry Regiment (3)
Semenovski Guard Infantry Regiment (3)
Brigade: Generalmajor Bistrom
Ismailov Guard Infantry Regiment (2)
Guard Jager Infantry Regiment (2)

2nd Guard Division: Generalmajor Udom
Brigade: Generalmajor Kryschanovski
Lithuania Guard Infantry Regiment (2)
Guard Grenadier Regiment (2)
Brigade: Generalmajor Scheltuchin II
Finland Guard Infantry Regiment (2)
Pavlov Guard Grenadier Regiment (2)
Artillery:
Guard Sapper Battalion
1st Guard Position Battery (12 guns)
1st and 2nd Guard Light Batteries (8 6-pdrs and 4
Licornes)

**Prussian Guard Infantry Brigade: Oberstleutnant
von Alvensleben**
(Strength as of 1 October)
1/1st Garde zu Fuss (727)
2/1st Garde zu Fuss (685)
Fus/1st Garde zu Fuss (728)
Jäger/1st Garde zu Fuss (398)
1/2nd Garde zu Fuss (690)
2/2nd Garde zu Fuss (652)
Fus/2nd Garde zu Fuss (707)
Jäger/2nd Garde zu Fuss (281)
Garde Jäger Battalion (2) (425)
Guard 6-pdr Foot Battery #4 (8 guns) (162)

Guard Cavalry: GL Prinz Gallitzin (6,800)

**1st Cuirassier Division: Generallieutenant
Depreradovich**
Brigade: Generalmajor Arseniev
Chevalier Guard Regiment (6)
Horse Guard Regiment (6)
Brigade:
Emperor Guard Cuirassier Regiment (4)
Empress Guard Cuirassier Regiment (4)

2nd Cuirassier Division: Generallieutenant Kretov
1st Brigade: Generalmajor Karatiev
Astrakhan Cuirassier Regiment (4)
Ekaterinoslav Cuirassier Regiment (4)
2nd Brigade: Generalmajor Leontiev
Gluchov Cuirassier Regiment (5)
Astrakhan Cuirassier Regiment

3rd Cuirassier Division: Generallieutenant Duka
Brigade: Generalmajor Gudovich
Military Order Cuirassier Regiment (4)
Little Russia Cuirassier Regiment (4)
Brigade: Generalmajor Levaschoff
Novgorod Cuirassier Regiment (4)
Starodoub Cuirassier Regiment (4)

**Guard Cavalry Division: Generallieutenant
Schevich**
Brigade:
Guard Hussar Regiment (6)
Guard Dragoon Regiment (6)
Guard Uhlan Regiment (6)
Guard Cossack Regiment (4)
Black Sea Cossack Squadron
Artillery:
1st and 2nd Guard Horse Batteries (12 guns ea.)
Unknown Line Horse Battery (12 guns)

Prussian Guard Cavalry Brigade
(Strengths as of 1 September)
Garde du Corps (4) (497)
Jägers/Garde du Corps (101)
Guard Light Cavalry Regiment (4) (656)
Jägers/Guard Light Cavalry Regiment (128)
Guard Horse Battery #4 (8 guns) (121)

Corps Cavalry: GL Count Pahlen III (2,600)

Brigade: Generalmajor Rudinger
Grodno Hussar Regiment (6)
Soum Hussar Regiment (6)
Brigade: Generalmajor Lissanevich
Tchougouiev Uhlan Regiment (6)
Loubny Hussar Regiment (4)
Brigade: Generalmajor Illowaiski XII
Grekov #8 Cossack Regiment
Illowaiski #12 Don Cossack Regiment (457)
Rodinov #2 Don Cossack Regiment (396)
Eupatoria Tartar Regiment

Cossacks: Generallieutenant Count Platov (3,464)

Brigade: Lt. Colonel Bergmann
Tchamusubov #5 (Kostina) Cossack Regiment (308)
Black Sea Cossack Regiment #1
Sluysarev Cossack Regiment (260)
Schaltanovka Don Cossack Regiment
Brigade:
Ataman Don Cossack Regiment (796)
Illowaiski #10 Don Cossack Regiment (443)
Rebrejev #2 Cossack Regiment (382)
Grekov #21 Don Cossack Regiment (286)
Grekov #1 Don Cossack Regiment (179)

Reserve Artillery:

2nd Guard Position Battery (12 guns)
Count Arakcheyev Position Battery (12 guns)
Position Battery #1 (12 guns)
Position Battery #2 (12 guns)
Position Battery #10 (12 guns)
Position Battery #29 (12 guns)
Horse Battery #1 (12 guns)
Horse Battery #3 (12 guns)
Horse Battery #10 (12 guns)
Horse Battery #16 (12 guns)
Horse Battery #23 (12 guns)
Guard Marine Equipage Artillery (2 guns)

AUSTRIAN ARMY: GENERAL PRINZ SCHWARZENBERG

1st Eintheilung

1st Light Division: FML Fürst Moritz Liechtenstein
Brigade: Generalmajor von Hessen-Homburg
Jäger Battalion #1 (850)
Jäger Battalion #2 (527)
Kaiser Chevauléger Regiment No. 1 (6) (705)
3-pdr Brigade Battery (6 guns)
Brigade: Generalmajor Scheither
1/Broder Grenz Regiment No. 7 (1,043)
Jäger Battalion #7 (532)
Levenehr Dragoon Regiment No. 4 (4) (613)
St-Vincent Chevauléger Regiment No. 4 (4) (718)
6-pdr Cavalry Battery (6 guns)

2nd Light Division: FML Bubna
Brigade: Generalmajor Zechmeister von Rheinau
1/Peterswardeiner Grenz Regiment (1) (1,229)
Jäger Battalion #6 (848)
Liechtenstein Hussar Regiment (6) (825)
6-pdr Cavalry Battery (6 guns)
Brigade: Oberst Weiland
3/Rainer Infantry Regiment (857)
4/Würzburg (Landwehr) Regiment (1,109)
Blankenstein Hussar Regiment (6) (710)
3-pdr Brigade Battery (6 guns)
Brigade: Generalmajor Graf Neipperg
Jäger Battalion #5 (846)
Kaiser Hussar Regiment (6) (838)
6-pdr Cavalry Brigade (6 guns)

1st Army Abteilung: FZM Graf H. Colloredo

1st Division: Generalmajor Feldmarschal-leutnant Hardegg
Brigade: Generalmajor Count Raigencourt
Deutsch-Banat Grenz Regiment (2) (1,714)
Hesse-Homburg Hussar Regiment (6) (723)[5]
Riesch Dragoon Regiment (6) (868)
6-pdr Brigade Battery (8 guns)

2nd Division: Feldmarschal-leutnant Wimpfen
Brigade: Generalmajor Gifting
Froon Infantry Regiment (3) (2,457)
De Vaux Infantry Regiment (3) (2,469)
Brigade Battery (8 guns)
Brigade: Generalmajor Czerwenka
Argenteau Infantry Regiment (2) (2,601)
4/Argenteau Infantry (Landwehr) Regiment[6]
Erbach Infantry Regiment (2) (1,762)
6-pdr Brigade Battery (8 guns)

3rd Division: Feldmarschal-leutnant Greth
Brigade: Generalmajor von Mumb
Prinz de Ligne Infantry Regiment (3) (2,445)
Czartorisky Infantry Regiment (2) (1,816)
6-pdr Brigade Battery (8 guns)

Brigade: Generalmajor Quasdannovich
Albert Gyulai Infantry Regiment (2) (1,828)
Reuss-Plauen Infantry Regiment (3) (2,631)
6-pdr Brigade Battery (6 guns)
Artillery Reserve:
1 12-pdr Position Battery (6 guns)
2 6-pdr Brigade Batteries (6 guns ea.)

2nd Army Abteilung: GdK Graf Meeifeldt

1st Division: Feldmarschal-leutnant Ignaz Lederer
Brigade: Generalmajor Sorenberg
1/Gradiscaner Grenz Regiment (1) (997)
Kienmeyer Hussar Regiment (6) (568)
Erzherzog Johann Dragoon Regiment (4) (524)[7]
6-pdr Brigade Battery (8 guns)
Brigade: Generalmajor Longueville
Stauch Infantry Regiment (2) (1,085)
Graf Bellegarde Infantry Regiment (2) (1,592)
6-pdr Brigade Battery (8 guns)

2nd Division: FML Fürst Liechtenstein
Brigade: Generalmajor Ennsbruck
Kaunitz Infantry Regiment (3) (2,137)
W. Colloredo Infantry Regiment (3) (1,924)
6-pdr Brigade Battery (8 guns)
Brigade: Generalmajor Meszerey
Vogelsang Infantry Regiment (2) (2,492)
4/Vogelsang (Landwehr) Infantry Regiment[8]
Reuss Greitz Infantry Regiment (2) (1,651)
4/Erzherzog Rayner (Landwehr) Regiment (1,159)
6-pdr Brigade Battery (8 guns)
Artillery Reserve:
1 12-pdr Position Battery (6 guns ea.)
2 6-pdr Foot Batteries (6 guns ea.)

3rd Army Abteilung: Feldzeugmeister Graf I. Gyulai

1st Division: Feldmarschal-leutnant Crenneville
Brigade: Generalmajor Hecht
1/Warasdiner Kreuzer Grenz Regiment (899)
1/St-George Grenz Regiment (1,004)
Klenau Chevauléger Regiment (7) (903)[9]
Rosenberg Chevauléger Regiment (6) (804)
6-pdr Cavalry Battery (6 guns)

2nd Division: Feldmarschal-leutnant Murray
Brigade: Generalmajor Lamezan-Salins
Erzherzog Ludwig Infantry Regiment (3) (2,845)
Würzburg Infantry Regiment (3) (2,722)
6-pdr Brigade Battery (8 guns)
Brigade: Generalmajor Weigel von Lowenwarth
Mariassy Infantry Regiment (2) (1,503)
Ignatz Gyulai Infantry Regiment (2) (1,652)
6-pdr Brigade Battery (8 guns)

---

5   One squadron detached to Mensdorffs streifkorps.
6   The landwehr battalion is included in regimental total.

7   One squadron detached to Thielmann's Streifkorps.
8   The landwehr battalion is included in regimental total.
9   One squadron detached to Thielmann's Streifkorps.

3rd Division: FML P. von Hessen-Homburg
Brigade: Generalmajor Czollich
  Kottulinsky Infantry Regiment (3) (2,214)
  Kaiser Franz Infantry Regiment (2) (1,588)
  6-pdr Brigade Battery (8 guns)
Brigade: Generalmajor Grimmer
  Kollowrath Infantry Regiment (2) (1,602)
  Fröhlich Infantry Regiment (3) (2,790)
  6-pdr Brigade Battery (8 guns)
Artillery Reserve
  1 12-pdr Position Battery
  2 6-pdr Foot Batteries

4th Army Abteilung: GdK Graf I. Klenau
1st Division: Feldmarschal-leutnant Freiherr Mohr
Brigade: Generalmajor Baumgarten
  1/1st Wallachen Grenz Regiment (986)
  Wallachen-Illyrian Grenz Regiment (2) (1,628)
  Hohenzollern Chevauléger Regiment (6) (690)[10]
  Palatinal Hussar Regiment (6) (778)
  Erzherzog Ferdinand Hussar Regiment (6) (626)[11]
  2—6-pdr Cavalry Battery (10 guns)
2nd Division: FML Fürst Hohenlohe-Bartenstein
Brigade: Generalmajor Schäffer
  J. Colloredo Infantry Regiment (2) (2,014)
  Zach Infantry Regiment (3) (2,721)
  6-pdr Brigade Battery (8 guns)
Brigade: Generalmajor Splenyi
  Württemberg Infantry Regiment (3) (2,631)
  Lindenau Infantry Regiment (3) (2,512)
  6-pdr Brigade Battery (8 guns)
3rd Division: Feldmarschal-leutnant Mayer
Brigade: Generalmajor Abele
  Alois Lichtenstein Infantry Regiment (3) (2,725)
  Koburg Infantry Regiment (3) (2,681)
  6-pdr Brigade Battery (8 guns)
Brigade: Generalmajor von Best
  Erzherzog Karl Infantry Regiment (2) (1,805)
  Kerpen Infantry Regiment (2) (1,566)
  6-pdr Brigade Battery (8 guns)
Brigade: Generalmajor Desfours
  Kaiser Cuirassier Regiment (6) (614)
  O'Reilly Chevauléger Regiment (6) (577)
Artillery Reserve
  1 3-pdr Brigade Battery (8 guns)
  1 12-pdr Foot Battery (6 guns)
Army Abteilung Reserve:
GDK Erbprinz F. von Hessen-Homburg
1st Division: Feldmarschal-leutnant Graf Weissenwolf
Brigade: Generalmajor Fürstenwarther
  Grenadier Battalion Czarnotzky (779)
  Grenadier Battalion Obermeyer (792)
  Grenadier Battalion Berger (762)
  Grenadier Battalion Oklopsia (736)
  6-pdr Brigade Battery (8 guns)

Brigade: Generalmajor Weissenwolff
  Grenadier Battalion Habinay (558)
  Grenadier Battalion Fortner (752)
  Grenadier Battalion Fischer (705)
  Grenadier Battalion Rüber (710)
  6-pdr Brigade Battery (8 guns)
2nd Division: Feldmarschal-leutnant Bianchi
Brigade: Generalmajor Beck
  Hiller Infantry Regiment (2) (1,904)
  H. Colloredo-Mansfield Infantry Regiment(2)
    (1,824)
  6-pdr Brigade Battery (8 guns)
Brigade: Generalmajor Haugwitz
  Hesse-Homburg Infantry Regiment (2) (1,626)
  Simbischen Infantry Regiment (2) (1,475)
  6-pdr Brigade Battery (8 guns)
Brigade: Generalmajor Quallenberg
  Esterhazy Infantry Regiment (2) (1,596)
  Davidovich Infantry Regiment (2) (2,078)
  6-pdr Brigade Battery (8 guns)
Cuirassier Corps: Feldmarschal-leutnant Graf Nostitz
Division: Generalmajor Graf Klebelsberg
Brigade: Generalmajor von Rothkirch
  Erzherzog Franz Cuirassier Regiment (4) (497)
  Kronprinz Ferdinand Cuirassier Regiment (4) (443)
Brigade: Generalmajor Aürsberg
  Hohenzollern Cuirassier Regiment (6) (626)
  Sommariva Cuirassier Regiment (6) (752)
Division: Feldmarschal-leutnant Civalart
Brigade: Generalmajor Kuttalck
  Herzog Albert Cuirassier Regiment (4) (537)
  Lothringen Cuirassier Regiment (4) (562)
Extra Corps:
  2—3-pdr Batteries (8 guns ea.)
  2—6-pdr Position Batteries (6 guns ea.)
  8—12-pdr Position Batteries (6 guns ea.)
  2—18-pdr Position Batteries (6 guns ea.)
  4—6-pdr Cavalry Batteries (6 guns ea.)
    Artillery (2,029)
  21 Artillery Handlanger Companies (3,331)
  31/2 Pioneer Companies (762)
  Pontooneer Companies (340)
  1 Sanitats-Abtheilung (Medical corps) Battalion
    (689)
  Staff Infantry Battalion (139)
  Landwehr Dragoon Squadron (129)
  Staff Dragoons (2) (15)
Army Commando: Feldmarschal-leutnant von Prohaska
  4/de Vaux Landwehr Battalion (79)
  4/Froon Landwehr Battalion (387)
Mobile Column: Generalmajor August von Herzogenberg
  4/Erbach Landwehr Battalion (1,152)
  3/, 4/2nd Silesian Landwehr Cavalry Regt
    (unknown)

2nd Prussian Corps: Generallieutenant von Kleist

---

10   Two squadrons detached to Thielmann's Streifkorps.
11   Two squadrons detached to Mensdorffs Streifkorps.

9th Brigade: Generalmajor von Klüx (5,833)
Infantry: Oberst von Schmalensee
  1/, 2/, Fus/1st West Prussian Infantry Regiment
  1/, 2/, 3/6th Reserve Infantry Regiment
  Silesian Schützen Battalion (2 coy)
  1/, 2/7th Silesian Landwehr Infantry Regiment
  1/1st Silesian Landwehr Cavalry Regiment
  6-pdr Horse Battery #10
10th Brigade: Generalmajor Pirch I (4,551)
Infantry: Oberst von Jagow
  1/, 2/, Fus/2nd West Prussian Infantry Regiment
  1/7th Reserve Infantry Regiment
  Combined 2 and 3/7th Reserve Infantry Regiment
  Combined 1,3, and 4/9th Silesian Landwehr
    Infantry Regt
  2/9th Silesian Landwehr Infantry Regiment
  3/, 4/Silesian Landwehr Cavalry Regiment
  6-pdr Foot Battery #8
11th Brigade: Generalmajor Ziethen (5,363)
Infantry: Oberst von Carnall
  1/, 2/, Fus/1st Silesian Infantry Regiment
  1/10th Reserve Infantry Regiment
  Combined 2 and 3/10th Reserve Infantry Regiment
  Silesian Schützen Battalion (2 coy)
  Combined 1 and 3/8th Silesian Landwehr Infantry
    Regiment
  Combined 2 and4/8th Silesian Landwehr Infantry
    Regiment
  1/, 2/, 3/, 4/Neumärk Dragoon Regiment
  1/1st Silesian Landwehr Cavalry Regiment
  6-pdr Foot Battery #11
12th Brigade: Generalmajor August von Preussen (5,419)
Infantry: Oberst von Funk
  1/, 2/, Fus/2rtd Silesian Infantry Regiment
  1/, 2/, 3/11th Reserve Infantry Regiment
  10th Silesian Landwehr Infantry Regiment (2)
  1/, 2/, 3/, 4/Silesian Uhlan Regiment
  2/1st Silesian Landwehr Cavalry Regiment
  6-pdr Foot Battery #13 *Held*
Reserve Cavalry: Generalmajor von Röder
Brigade: Oberst von Wrangel
  1/, 2/, 3/, 4/East Prussian Cuirassier Regiment
  1/, 2/, 3/, 4/Silesian Cuirassier Regiment
  1/, 2/, 3/, 4/Brandenburg Cuirassier Regiment
Brigade: Oberst von Mutius (2,350)
  1/, 2/7th Silesian Landwehr Cavalry Regiment
  1/, 2/8th Silesian Landwehr Cavalry Regiment
Artillery:
  Horse Battery #7
  Horse Battery #8
Reserve Artillery: Oberst von Braun (735)
  12-pdr Foot Batteries #3 and #6
  6-pdr Foot Batteries #7, #14, and #21
  7-pdr Howitzer Battery #1
  Horse Battery #9
  2 Field Pioneer Companies

Streifkorps von Thielmann:
Brigade: Oberstleutnant von Gasser
  Hohenzollern Chevauléger Regiment (2) (210)
  Klenau Chevauléger Regiment (1) (140)
  Kienmayer Hussar Regiment (1) (100)
Brigade: Generalmajor Prinz von Kurland
  1/, 2/2nd Silesian Hussar Regiment (200)
  1/, 2/Silesian National Cavalry Regiment (250)
Brigade: Oberst Graf Orlov-Denissov
  Jagodin #2 Cossack Regiment (362)
  Gorin #2 Cossack Regiment (399)
Artillery:
  2 Austrian Horse Howitzers
  2 Russian Cossack guns

ARMY OF SILESIA: GENERAL DER KAVALLERIE BLÜCHER
Prussian 1st Army Corps: GL von Yorck
Advanced Guard: Colonel von Katzeler
  Leib-Grenadier Battalion (682)
  West Prussian Grenadier Battalion (582)
  East Prussian Jäger Battalion (2 coys) (288)
  4/Guard Jäger Battalion (1 co) (70)
  Fus/2nd East Prussian Infantry Regiment (377)
  1/Brandenburg Infantry Regiment (530)
  2/12th Reserve Infantry Regiment (530)
  3/13th Silesian Landwehr Regiment (403)
  2/14th Silesian Landwehr Regiment (299)
  4/15th Silesian Landwehr Regiment (408)
  2nd Leib Hussar Regiment (1 and Jägers) (183)
  1/, 2/Jag/Brandenburg Hussar Regiment (308)
  1/, 2/, 3/, 4/Brandenburg Uhlan Regiment (342)
  1/, 2/, 3/, 4/East Prussian National Cavalry
    Regiment (421)
  1/, 2/, 3/, 4/5th Silesian Landwehr Cavalry Regiment
    (201)
  6-pdr Foot Battery #12 (110)
  Horse Battery #2 (125)
1st Brigade; Colonel von Steinmetz
  1st East Prussian Grenadier Battalion (364)
  Silesian Grenadier Battalion (650)
  1/, 3/, 4/5th Silesian Landwehr Regiment (960)
  1/, 2/, 4/13th Silesian Landwehr Regiment (996)
  1/, 2/, 4/2nd Leib Hussar Regiment (375)
  6-pdr Foot Battery #2 (117)
2nd Brigade: GM Prinz Carl von Mecklenburg-Strelitz
  1/, 2/, Fus/1st East Prussian Regiment (1,840)
  Comb 1 and 2/2nd East Prussian Regiment (614)
  2/6th Silesian Landwehr Regiment (680)
  1/, 2/, 3/, 4/4th Mecklenburg-Strelitz Hussar
    Regiment (321)
  6-pdr Foot Battery #1 (107)
7th Brigade: Generalmajor von Horn (3,325)
  1/, 2/, Fus/Leib Infantry Regiment (1,597)
  Thuringian Battalion (368)
  2/, 3/, 4/4th Silesian Landwehr Regiment (925)
  1/, 2/15th Silesian Landwehr Regiment (772)
  3/, 4/3rd Silesian Landwehr Cavalry Regiment (94)

1/, 2/, 3/, 4/10th Silesian Landwehr Cavalry
Regiment (132)
6-pdr Foot Battery #3 (102)

8th Brigade: Generalmajor von Hünerbein
2/, Fus/Brandenburg Infantry Regiment (1,433)
1/, 3/12th Reserve Infantry Regiment (1,004)
4/14th Silesian Landwehr Regiment (646)
3/, 4/Brandenburg Hussar Regiment (190)
6-pdr Foot Battery #15 (109)

Cavalry Reserve: Generalmajor Jürgass
1/, 2/, 3/, 4/1st West Prussian Dragoon Regiment (294)
1/, 2/, 3/, 4/Lithuanian Dragoon Regiment (439)
1/, 2/, 3/, 4/1st Neumärk Landwehr Cavalry
Regiment (219)
Horse Battery #1 (121)
Horse Battery #3 (129)

Reserve Artillery: Oberstleutnant Schmidt
12-pdr Foot Battery #1 (194)
12-pdr Foot Battery #2 (170)
6-pdr Foot Battery #24 (116)
3-pdr Foot Battery #1 (92)
Horse Battery #12 (111)

Park Column
Park Column #1
Park Column #3
Park Column #5
Park Column #13
Artisan Column #1
Field Pioneer Company #1
Field Pioneer Company #2

11th Corps: Generallieutenant Osten-Sacken
10th Division: Generalmajor Lieven
Brigade:
Jaroslav Infantry Regiment (2) (745)
Brigade: Colonel Sass
Crimea Infantry Regiment (1) (463)[12]
Bieloserk Infantry Regiment (2) (848)
Brigade: Colonel Achlestischev
8th Jager Regiment (2) (620)
39th Jager Regiment (1) (583)
27th Division: Generalmajor Neverovsky
Brigade: Colonel Stawicki
Vilna Infantry Regiment (1) (576)
Simbrisk Infantry Regiment (1) (516)
Brigade: Colonel Alexejev
Odessa Infantry Regiment (1) (503)
Tarnopol Infantry Regiment (1) (430)[13]
Brigade: Colonel Kollogribov
49th Jager Regiment (2) (623)
50th Jager Regiment (1) (445)
16th Division: Generalmajor Repninsky
Brigade: Colonel Rachmanov
Okhotsk Infantry Regiment (2) (372)

Kamchatka Infantry Regiment (2) (415)
Corps Artillery:
Position Battery #10 (12 guns) (240)
Position Battery #13 (12 guns) (226)
Light Battery #24 (12 guns) (143)
Light Battery #35 (12 guns) (161)
Horse Battery #18 (12 guns) (215)
Pioneers (87)

Corps Cavalry: Generallieutenant Vassil'shikov
3rd Dragoon Division
Brigade: Generalmajor Uschakov
Smolensk Dragoon Regiment (2) (233)
Kourland Dragoon Regiment (5) (268)
2nd Hussar Division
Brigade: Generalmajor Yurkowski
White Russia Hussar Regiment (4) (565)
Akhtyrsk Hussar Regiment (6) (786)
Brigade: Colonel Vassil'shikov
Marioupol Hussar Regiment (6) (638)
Alexandria Hussar Regiment (5) (648)

Cossacks: Generalmajor Karpov II
Karpov #2 Cossack Regiment (226)
Loukoffkin Cossack Regiment (233)
Kutainikov #4 Cossack Regiment (264)
Grekov Cossack Regiment (284)
Semencikov #4 Cossack Regiment (292)
Illowaiski #9 Cossack Regiment (264)
2nd Bashkir Regiment (295)
2nd Kalmuck Regiment (179)
Baron Bode (St-Petersburg) Volunteer Regiment (193)
4th Ukrainian Cossack Regiment (3 sotnias) (219)

Army Corps: General of Infantry Count Langeron
Advanced Guard: Generallieutenant Rudsevich
Cavalry Corps: Generallieutenant Korff
Kargopol Dragoon Regiment (4) (484)
Kiev Dragoon Regiment (4) (474)
Kinbum Dragoon Regiment (2) (253)
Lithuania Chasseurs à Cheval Regiment (2) (197)
Dorpat Chasseurs à Cheval Regiment (2) (266)
Kutainikov #8 Cossack Regiment (297)
Selivanov #2 Don Cossack Regiment (231)
1st Ukrainian Cossack Regiments (3) (473)
3rd Ukrainian Cossack Regiments (3) (610)
9th Division/9th Corps: Generalmajor Udom II
Brigade: Colonel Poltaratzky
Nacheburg Infantry Regiment (1) (638)
Apcheron Infantry Regiment (2) (714)
Brigade: Generalmajor Juskov II
Riajsk Infantry Regiment (1) (535)
Iakoutsk Infantry Regiment (1) (518)
Brigade: Colonel Grimbladt
10th Jager Regiment (1) (463)
38th Jager Regiment (1) (454)
Artillery:
Position Battery #15 (12 guns) (123)
Horse Battery #8 (12 guns) (243)
Pioneer Company (78)

---

12   Detachment from above sent to Halle.
13   Detachment from above sent to Halle—General
Rauch.

9th Corps: Generallieutenant Olsoviev
15th Division: Generalmajor Kornilov
Brigade: Lt. Colonel Anensur
  Kourin Infantry Regiment (2) (478)
  Kolyvan Infantry Regiment (1) (526)
Brigade: Colonel Tern
  Koslov Infantry Regiment (1) (514)
  Vitebsk Infantry Regiment (1) (381)
Brigade: Colonel Tichanowski I (993)
  12th Jager Regiment (2) (505)
  22nd Jager Regiment (1) (481)
10th Corps: Generallieutenant Kapzevich
8th Division: Generalmajor Count Ourousov
Brigade: Colonel Schenschin
  Archangel Infantry Regiment (2) (550)
  Schusselburg Infantry Regiment (1) (645)
Brigade: Colonel Rehren
  Old Ingremannland Infantry Regiment (2) (723)
  7th Jager Regiment (2) (489)
  38th Jager Regiment (1) (514)
22nd Division: Generalmajor Tourchaninov
Brigade: Generalmajor Schkapski
  Viatka Infantry Regiment (2) (850)
  Staroskol Infantry Regiment (2) (751)
  Olonetz Infantry Regiment (1) (459)
Brigade: Colonel Durnov
  29th Jager Regiment (2) (558)
  45th Jager Regiment (2) (418)
Corps Artillery:
  Position Battery #2 (7 guns) (218)
  Position Battery #18 (12 guns) (256)
  Position Battery #34 (12 guns) (242)
  Position Battery #39 (12 guns) (261)
  Light Battery #3 (12 guns) (189)
  Light Battery #19 (12 guns) (175)
  Light Battery #29 (12 guns) (143)
  Don Cossack Battery #2 (7 guns) (125)
  Pontooneer Company #4 (162)
  Pontooneer Company #5 (164)
  Pioneer Company Gresser (123)
  Pioneer Company Helwig (135)
  75th Marine Equipage Battalion (126)
Det. 1st Cavalry Corps:
  Arasmass Chasseurs à Cheval Regiment (149)
  Sievesk Chasseurs à Cheval Regiment (234)
8th Corps: Generallieutenant Count St.-Priest
11th Division: Generalmajor Prince Gourialov
Brigade: Colonel Turgenev
  Ekaterinburg Infantry Regiment (2) (936)
  Rilsk Infantry Regiment (1) (564)
Brigade: Generalmajor Karpenko
  Jeletz Infantry Regiment (1) (526)
  Polotsk Infantry Regiment (1) (571)
Brigade: Generalmajor Bistrom H
  1st Jager Regiment (1) (478)
  33rd Jager Regiment (2) (527)
17th Division: Generalmajor Pillar
Brigade: Colonel Kern
  Riazan Infantry Regiment (2) (670)

  Bieloserk Infantry Regiment (2) (705)
Brigade: Colonel Tscherioff
  Wilmanstrand Infantry Regiment (2) (566)
  Brest Infantry Regiment (2) (746)
Brigade: Major Charitanov
  30th Jager Regiment (2) (472)
  48th Jager Regiment (2) (913)
Corps Artillery:
  Position Battery #32 (12 guns) (270)
  Light Battery #32 (12 guns) (176)
  Light Battery #33 (12 guns) (155)
Corps Cavalry:
Brigade: Generalmajor Borozdin II
  Mitau Dragoon Regiment (4) (458)
  New Russia Dragoon Regiment (4) (377)
Brigade: Generalmajor Emanuel
  Kharkov Dragoon Regiment (4) (484)
  Moscow Dragoon Regiment (2) (250)[14]
Cossacks: Generalmajor Kaisarov
  Grov #2 Cossack Regiment (194)
  Stavrapol Kalmuck Regiment (298)
  Grekov #21 Cossack Regiment (317)

ARMY OF THE NORTH:
BERNADOTTE, CROWN PRINCE OF SWEDEN
Prussian 3rd Army Corps: Generallieutenant
Bülow
3rd Brigade: Generalmajor Hessen-Homberg
(7,168)
  2nd East Prussian Grenadier Battalion (w/Jägers)
  2/, Fus/3rd East Prussian Infantry Regiment (w/
    Jägers)
  1/, 2/, 3/4th Reserve Infantry Regiment
  1/, 2/, 3/, 4/4th East Prussian Landwehr Regiment
  1/, 2/, 3/, 4/1st Leib Hussar Regiment (w/Jägers)
  6-pdr Foot Battery #5 (8 guns)
5th Brigade: Oberstleutnant von Schoon (7,767)
  Pomeranian Grenadier Battalion (w/Jägers)
  1/, 2/, Fus/1st Pomeranian Infantry Regiment
  1/, 2/, 3/2nd Reserve Infantry Regiment
  1/, 2/, 3/, 4/2nd Kurmark Landwehr Regiment
Cavalry: Oberst von Hobe
  1/, 2/, 3/, 4/Pomeranian Hussar Regiment (w/Jägers)
  1/, 2/, 3/, 4/East Prussian Uhlan Regiment (w/Jägers)
  6-pdr Foot Battery #10 (8 guns)
6th Brigade: Generalmajor Krafft
  1/, 2/, Colberg Infantry Regiment (w/Jägers)
  1/, 2/, 3/9th Reserve Infantry Regiment
  1/, 2/, 3/, 4/1st Neumärk Landwehr Regiment
  1st Pomeranian Landwehr Cavalry Regiment (3)
  East Prussian Jäger Battalion (2 coys) (322)
  6-pdr Foot Battery #16 (8 guns)
Reserve Cavalry: Generalmajor Oppen
1st Brigade: Oberst Treskow
  1/, 2/, 3/, 4/Konigin Dragoon Regiment (w/Jägers)

---

14   Above detached to Mersberg, not present.

1/, 2/, 3/, 4/Brandenburg Dragoon Regiment (w/ Jägers)
1/, 2/, 3/, 4/2nd West Prussian Dragoon Regt (w/ Jägers)
2nd Brigade: Oberstleutnant Sydow
  1/, 2/, 3/, 4/2nd Kurmark Landwehr Cavalry Regiment
  1/, 2/, 3/, 4/4th Kurmark Landwehr Cavalry Regiment
  2nd Pomeranian Landwehr Cavalry (1)
Artillery:
  Horse Battery #5 (8 6-pdr guns)
  Horse Battery #6 (8 6-pdr guns)
Artillery Reserve: Oberstleutnant Holtzendorf (753)
  12-pdr Foot Battery #4 (8 guns)
  12-pdr Foot Battery #5 (8 guns)
  6-pdr Horse Battery #11 (8 guns)
  6-pdr Foot Battery #19 (8 guns)
Pioneers:
  Prussian Pioneer Companies #4 and #5 (153)
Russian Troops:
  Position Battery #7 (10 12-pdr guns)
  Position Battery #21 (12 12-pdr guns)
  Illowaiski #5 Cossack Regiment (440)
  Bihalov #1 Cossack Regiment
Russian Corps: GL Baron Winzingerode
Advanced Guard: Generallieutenant Count Voronzov
Brigade: Generalmajor Kniper
  2nd Jager Regiment (1) (487)
  13th Jager Regiment (2) (751)
  14th Jager Regiment (2) (1,026)
Cavalry: Generalmajor Orurk
Cavalry Brigade: Generalmajor Bekendorf
  Volhynie Uhlan Regiment (3) (495)
  Pavlovgrad Hussar Regiment (6) (1,002)
  Diatchkin Cossack Regiment (417)
  Artillery: Horse Battery #11 (12 6-pdr guns)
Cossack Brigade: Colonel Melnikov IV
  Melnikov #4 Cossack Regiment (368)
  Melnikov #5 Cossack Regiment (297)
Cossack Brigade: Generalmajor Stael
  Andreinov #2 Cossack Regiment (382)
  1st Bashkir Regiment (343)
Cossack Brigade: Colonel Brandel
  1st Bug Cossack Regiment (455)
  3rd Ural Cossack Regiment (275)
21st Division: Generalmajor Laptiev
Brigade: Colonel Rosen
  Petrovsk Infantry Regiment (1) (812)
  Podolsk Infantry Regiment (1) (693)
  Lithuania Infantry Regiment (1) (728)
Brigade: Colonel Rudinger
  Neva Infantry Regiment (1) (681)
  44th Jager Regiment (2)1,135)
Artillery:
  Light Battery #42 (12 6-pdr guns)
  Position Battery #31 (12 12-pdr guns)

24th Division: Generalmajor Vuich
Brigade: Colonel Zwarikin
  Chirvan Infantry Regiment (2) (940)
  Oufa Infantry Regiment (2) (860)
Brigade: Colonel Maznew
  Bourtirki Infantry Regiment (2) (841)
  19th Jager Regiment (2) (886)
Brigade: Colonel Bulinski
  Tomsk Infantry Regiment (1) (461)
  40th Jager Regiment (1) (367)[15]
Artillery:
  Light Battery #46 (12 6-pdr guns)
Temporary Division: Generalmajor Harpe
  Tula Infantry Regiment (2) (1,230)
  Navaguinsk Infantry Regiment (2) (1,227)
  Converged Grenadiers of the 9th Division (1) (639)
  Converged Grenadiers of the 15th Division (1) (692)
  Converged Grenadiers of the 18th Division (1) (718)
Artillery:
  Position Battery #21 (2 12-pdr guns)
  Position Battery #26 (10 12-pdr guns)
  Horse Battery #13 (12 6-pdr guns)
Cavalry Brigade: Generalmajor Manteufel
  St-Petersburg Dragoon Regiment (4) (459)
  Elisabethgrad Hussar Regiment (6) (900)
  Iakhontov Opolochenie Cavalry Regiment (2) (217)
  Horse Battery #4 (8 6-pdr guns)
Cavalry Brigade: Generalmajor M. Pahlen
  Riga Dragoon Regiment (3) (382)
  Finland Dragoon Regiment (2) (353)
  Isoum Hussar Regiment (4) (547)
  Horse Battery #1 (4 6-pdr guns)
  Horse Battery #5 (2 6-pdr guns)
Cavalry Brigade: Generalmajor Zagriajski
  Nijine Chasseurs à Cheval Regiment (2) (221)
  Polish Uhlan Regiment (6) (704)
Cossack Brigade: Generalmajor Illowaiski IV
  Illowaiski #4 Cossack Regiment (455)
  Grekov #9 Cossack Regiment (449)
  Barabanchtchikov #2 Cossack Regiment (390)
  Lotchilin Cossack Regiment (454)
Swedish Army: Field Marshal Stedingk
1st Division: Generallieutenant Skjoldebrand
  (1st and 2nd Brigade—6,557)
1st Brigade: Generalmajor Schützenheirn
  Svea Life Guard Regiment (1)
  2nd Life Guard Regiment (1)
  Life Guard Grenadier Battalion (1)
  Leib Grenadier Regiment (2)
2nd Brigade: Generalmajor Lagerbring
  Upland Infantry Regiment (2)
  Sondermanland Infantry Regiment (3)
  North Schonen Infantry Regiment (1)
  Pomeranian Foot Legion (72)

---

15   A further 120 detached.

Cavalry:
  Guard Dragoon Regiment (5)
  Pomeranian Horse Legion (1) (48)
  Kouteinikov #6 Cossack Regiment
Gotha Artillery Division: Edenhjelm (276)
  2—6-pdr Foot Batteries (6—6-pdrs and 1 how. ea.)
2nd Division: Generallieutenant Sandels
  (3rd, 4th and 6th Brigades—9,060)
3rd Brigade: Generalmajor Brandstroem
  West Gotha Infantry Regiment (2)
  Westmanland Infantry Regiment (2)
  Nerike Infantry Regiment (2)
4th Brigade: Generalmajor Reuterskjold
  Skaraborg Infantry Regiment (2)
  Elfsborg Infantry Regiment (2)
  Wermland Jäger Regiment (1)
6th Brigade: Generalmajor Boize
  Kronoborg Infantry Regiment (1)
  Calmar Infantry Regiment (1)
Cavalry Brigade: Generallieutenant Skjoldebrand
  (1,753 men)
  Guard Cuirassier Regiment (4)
  Schonen Hussar Regiment (6)
  Monter Hussar Regiment (5)
Artillery: Major Geist
  2—6-pdr Batteries (7 6-pdrs)
  1-6-pdr Horse Battery (6 6-pdrs) (79)
Reserve Artillery: Colonel Cardell (247)
  1 12-pdr Battery *Wendes* (8 guns)
  1 6-pdr Battery *Svea* (6 guns)
  1 Horse Battery *Wendes* (6 guns)
  Artillery Park
Attached:
  Rebrejev Don Cossack Regiment (362)
  British Rocket Battery (151)

POLISH RESERVE ARMY: GDK BENNIGSEN
Advanced Guard Division: Generallieutenant
Stroganov
Brigade: Generalmajor Glebow
  6th Jager Regiment (2) (1,724)
  41st Jager Regiment (2) (1,213)
  Horse Battery #10 (2 guns) (107)
  Light Battery #26 (12 guns) (189)
  Stander Sapper Company (108)
Brigade:
  1st Combined Hussar Regiment (5) (857)
  1st Combined Uhlan Regiment (5) (716)
  Platov #5 Don Cossack Regiment (535)
  Andreinov #3 Don Cossack Regiment (515)
  Vlassov #3 Don Cossack Regiment (400)
  4th Ural Cossack Regiment (241)
  2 Bashkir Regiments (681)
Brigade: Generalmajor Tenishev
  Simbirsk Foot Cossack Regiment (513)
  Pensa Foot Cossack Regiment (459)

Main Body: General of Infantry Docturov
12th Division: Generalmajor Chovansky
Brigade: Generalmajor Sanders
  Smolensk Infantry Regiment (2) (1,441)
  Narva Infantry Regiment (2) (1,483)
Brigade: Generalmajor Scheltuchin
  Alexopol Infantry Regiment (2) (1,438)
  New Ingremannland Infantry Regiment (2) (1,430)
Artillery:
  Position Battery #45 (12 guns) (263)
  Light Battery #1 (12 guns) (155)
26th Division: Generalmajor Paskievich
Brigade: Generalmajor Savonia
  Ladoga Infantry Regiment (2) (1,402)
  Poltava Infantry Regiment (2) (1,592)
Brigade: Colonel Schemtschuschnikoff
  Nivegorod Infantry Regiment (2) (1,512)
  Orel Infantry Regiment (2) (1,322)
Brigade:
  5th Jager Regiment (2) (1,506)
  42nd Jager Regiment (2) (1,261)
Artillery:
  Position Battery #26 (12 guns) (263)
  Light Battery #47 (161)
13th Division: Generalmajor Lindorfs
Brigade: Generalmajor Rossy
  Veliki-Loutzk Infantry Regiment (3) (2,204)
  Galitz Infantry Regiment (3) (1,013)
Brigade: Generalmajor Ivanov
  Saratov Infantry Regiment (3) (2,082)
  Pensa Infantry Regiment (2) (1,412)
Cavalry Division: Generallieutenant Tschaplitz
Brigade: Generalmajor Repninsky
  Combined Dragoon Regiment (5) (773)
  1st Converged Chasseurs à Cheval Regiment (4) (538)
  2nd Converged Chasseurs à Cheval Regiment (4)
  (625)
Brigade: Generalmajor Kreutz
  2nd Converged Uhlan Regiment (4) (567)
  Taganrog Uhlan Regiment (4) (646)
  Siberian Uhlan Regiment (2) (194)
  Jitomir Uhlan Regiment (2) (189)
Artillery:
  Horse Battery #2 (12 6-pdrs) (309)
Cavalry: Generalmajor Knorring (800)
  Tartar Uhlan Regiment (6)
  Radinov Don Cossack Regiment
  4th Poltava Foot Cossack Regiment
  14th Bashkir Regiment
Reserve Artillery: Colonel Kolotinsky
  Position Battery #22 (12 guns) (281)
  Light Battery #18 (12 guns) (167)
  Light Battery #48 (12 guns) (176)
  Light Battery #53 (12 guns) (180)
  Horse Battery #9 (12 guns) (292)
  Miner Company (1) (74)
  1st and 7th Pontooneer Companies (2)
Streifkorps Oberst Graf Mensdorf-Pouilly
  Erzherzog Ferdinand Hussar Regiment (2)

Hessen-Homburg Hussar Regiment (1)
Gorin #1 Don Cossack Regiment
Illowaiski #10 Don Cossack Regiment
Sreifkorps
3/Guard Jager Battalion
1/, 2/3rd Silesian Landwehr Cavalry Regiment
Rauch's Streifkorps (in Halle)
1/4th Silesian Landwehr Infantry Regiment
1/14th Silesian Landwehr Infantry Regiment
3/14th Silesian Landwehr Infantry Regiment
3/15th Silesian Landwehr Infantry Regiment
Reorganizing in Silesia
2/5th Silesian Landwehr Infantry Regiment
1/6th Silesian Landwehr Infantry Regiment
3/6th Silesian Landwehr Infantry Regiment
4/6th Silesian Landwehr Infantry Regiment

Sources: Fabry, *Étude sur les Operations de Maréchal Oudinot;* Zveguintov, *L' Armée Russe;* Austrian General Staff, *Befreiungskriege 1813;* von Quistorp, B., *Geschichte der Nord-Armee im Jahre 1813*

FRENCH OFFICER CASUALTIES

BATTLE OF LEIPZIG 16-19 OCTOBER 1813[16]

Imperial Guard
1st Division Old Guard: Général de division Friant
1st Chasseurs à Pied Regiment (0/2)
2nd Chasseurs à Pied Regiment (0/0)
1st Grenadier à Pied Regiment (0/5)
2nd Grenadier à Pied Regiment (0/2)
2nd Division Old Guard: Général de division Curial
Fusilier Chasseur Regiment (1/0)
Fusilier Grenadier Regiment (0/12)
Velites of Turin (0/5)
Velites of Florence (1/11)
Saxon Guard Regiment (0/0)
Polish Guard Battalion (0/0)
Westphalian Guard Grenadier Battalion (0/14)
I Corps Young Guard: Maréchal Oudinot
1st Division: Général de division Pacthod
1st Voltigeur Regiment (1/6)
2nd Voltigeur Regiment (0/8)
3rd Voltigeur Regiment (0/1)
6th Voltigeur Regiment (0/15)
7th Voltigeur Regiment (2/9)
11th Voltigeur Regiment (0/1)
3rd Division: Général de division Decouz

4th Voltigeur Regiment (1/3)
5th Voltigeur Regiment (0/13)
8th Voltigeur Regiment (1/10)
9th Voltigeur Regiment (0/3)
10th Voltigeur Regiment (1/6)
12th Voltigeur Regiment (0/1)
II Corps Young Guard: Maréchal Mortier
2nd Division: Général de division Barrois
1st Tirailleur Regiment (0/5)
2nd Tirailleur Regiment (0/6)
3rd Tirailleur Regiment (3/3)
6th Tirailleur Regiment (0/5)
7th Tirailleur Regiment (1/0)
4th Division: Général de division Roguet
Flanquer-Chasseur Regiment (0/7)
Flanquer-Grenadier Regiment (0/4)
4th Tirailleur Regiment (2/2)
5th Tirailleur Regiment (0/2)
8th Tirailleur Regiment (0/4)
9th Tirailleur Regiment (0/2)
10th Tirailleur Regiment (0/2)
Guard Cavalry Corps: Général de division Nansouty
1st Division: Général de division d'Ornano
Berg Lancer Regiment (5/12)
2eme Chevauléger-lancier (Dutch lancers) (1/3)
Empress Dragoon Regiment (Young Guard) (0/0)
2nd Division: Général de division Lefèbvre-Desnoëttes
1er Chevauléger-lancier (Polish Lancers) (0/0)
Chasseurs à Cheval de la Garde (Young Guard) (0/0)
Grenadiers à Cheval de la Garde (0/0)
3rd Division: Général de division Walther
1er Chevauléger-lancier Régiment de la Garde (Old Guard Polish lancers) (0/6)
4th Gardes d'Honneur Regiment (0/1)
Chasseurs à Cheval de la Garde (Old Guard) (1/6)
1st Gardes d'Honneur Regiment (0/1)
Empress Dragoon Regiment (Old Guard) (1/3)
2nd Gardes d'Honneur Regiment (0/1)
Grenadiers à Cheval de la Garde (Old Guard) (0/4)
3rd Gardes d'Honneur Regiment (0/4)
II Corps: Maréchal Victor
4th Division: Général de division Dubreton
24th Légère Regiment (5/17)
19th Line Regiment (5/24)
37th Line Regiment (3/36)
56th Line Regiment (7/17)
5th Division: Général de division Dufour
26th Légère Regiment (5/32)
93rd Line Regiment (7/16)
46th Line Regiment (0/7)
72nd Line Regiment (5/5)
6th Division: Général de division Vial
11th Légère Regiment (5/24)
2nd Line Regiment (2/13)
4th Line Regiment (7/23)
1/, 3/, 4/18th Line Regiment (0/18)

---

16   Figures are officers dead and officers wounded. In the absence of accurate figures, officer casualties give some idea of unit losses. Though very approximate, the numbers of total casualties can be estimated by assuming the ratio of officer casualties to enlisted casualties is 1:10.

III Corps: Général de division Souham
8th Division: Général de division Brayer
6th Provisional Légère Regiment (2/9)[17]
10th Provisional Légère Regiment (2/15)
14th Provisional Line Regiment (1/10)
19th Provisional Line Regiment (0/14)
21st Provisional Line Regiment (8/34)
24th Provisional Line Regiment (4/13)[18]
9th Division: Général de division Delmas
2nd Provisional Regiment (0/7)
29th Légère Regiment (1/12)[19]
1/, 2/, 3/136th Line Regiment (5/20)
1/, 2/, 3/138th Line Regiment (8/7)
1/, 2/, 3/145th Line Regiment (4/120)
11th Division: Général de division Ricard
3/, 4/9th Légère Regiment (0/7)
17th Provisional Regiment (5/12)
50th Line Regiment (0/14)
4/65th Line Regiment (4/6)
142nd Line Regiment (1/14)
144th Line Regiment (5/9)
23rd Light Cavalry Brigade Beurmann
10th Hussar Regiment (0/1)
Baden Dragoon Regiment (0/0)
IV Corps: Général de division Bertrand
12th Division: Général de division Morand
1/, 2/, 3/, 4/8th Légère Regiment (6/16)
1/, 2/, 3/, 4/13th Line Regiment (0/2)
1/, 2/, 4/23rd Line Regiment (0/10)
1/, 2/, 3/137th Line Regiment (0/10)
15th Division: Général de division Fontanelli
1st Italian Légère Regiment (0/0)
Milan Guard (0/3)
1st Italian Line Regiment (?)
4th Italian Line Regiment (?)
6th Italian Line Regiment (?)
7th Italian Line Regiment (?)
Mixed Division: Generalleutnant Franquemont
1st Württemberg Combined Line Battalion (?)
2nd Württemberg Combined Line Battalion (?)
3rd Württemberg Combined Line Battalion (?)
1st Württemberg Chevauleger Regiment *Prinz Adam (?)*
3rd Württemberg Chevauleger Regiment *Herzog Ludwig (?)*
Brigade: Général de brigade Wolff
Westphalian Chevauléger Regiment (0/6)
Hesse-Darmstadt Chevauléger Regiment (0/0)
V Corps: Général de division Lauriston
10th Division: Général de division Albert
4th Provisional Légère Regiment (2/12)
139th Line Regiment (2/28)

1/, 2/, 3/140th Line Regiment (4/14)
1/, 2/, 3/141st Line Regiment (5/22)
16th Division: Général de division Maison
1/, 2/, 3/152nd Line Regiment (0/15)
1/, 2/, 3/153rd Line Regiment (3/13)
1/, 2/, 3/154th Line Regiment (2/16)
17th Division: Général de division Rochambeau
1/, 2/, 3/135th Line Regiment (1/23)
1/, 2/, 3/150th Line Regiment (2/15)
1/, 2/, 3/155th Line Regiment (4/26)
6th Light Cavalry Brigade: GD Dermoncourt
2nd Chasseurs à Cheval Regiment (0/8)
3rd Chasseurs à Cheval Regiment (1/5)
6th Chasseurs à Cheval Regiment (2/1)
VI Corps: Maréchal Marmont
20th Division: Général de division Compans
3/, 4/32nd Légère Regiment (4/26)
1/, 2/, 3/, 4/, 5/1st Marine Infantry Regiment (11/39)
1/, 2/, 3/3rd Marine Regiment (10/34)
20th Provisional Regiment (4/30)
25th Provisional Regiment (4/9)
(includes losses of 2/86th Regiment assigned to XI Corps)
21st Division: Général de division Lagrange
1/, 2/, 3/, 4/37th Légère Regiment (3/24)
1/, 2/, 3/4th Marine Regiment (9/27)
1/Joseph Napoleon Regiment (0/6)
1/, 2/, 3/, 4/, 5/, 5/2nd Marine Regiment (11/51)
22nd Division: Général de division Friederichs
3/, 4/23rd Légère Regiment (3/7)
11th Provisional Regiment (2/17)
13th Provisional Regiment (10/19)
3/, 4/15th Line Regiment (1/11)
16th Provisional Regiment (4/9)
3/, 4/70th Line Regiment (1/15)
3/, 4/121st Line Regiment (7/14)
25th Light Cavalry Division: GB Normann
2nd Württemberg Chevauleger Regiment (?)
4th Württemberg Chevauleger Regiment (?)
5th Light Cavalry Division: Général de division Lorge
5th Chasseurs à Cheval Regiment
10th Chasseurs à Cheval Regiment
13th Chasseurs à Cheval Regiment
15th Chasseurs à Cheval Regiment
21st Chasseurs à Cheval Regiment
22nd Chasseurs à Cheval Regiment
VII Corps: Général de division Reynier
13th Division: Général de division Guilleminot
4/1st Légère Regiment (0/2)
2/, 6/18th Légère Regiment (0/6)
3/7th Line Regiment (0/0) (Not engaged)
156th Line Regiment (0/0) (Not engaged)
1/Illyrian Regiment (0/6) (Not engaged)
52nd Line Regiment (0/0) (Not engaged)
67th Line Regiment (0/0) (Not engaged)
101st Line Regiment (0/0) (Not engaged)

---

17 Includes casualties from 25th Légère in XI Corps/
18 Includes casualties from 103rd Line in Margaron's independent division.
19 Includes casualties from the battalion assigned to Lefol's Division.

32nd Division: Général de division Durutte
  35th Légère Regiment (1/2)
  131st Line Regiment (1/7)
  132nd Line Regiment (0/5)
  36th Légère Regiment (1/5)
  133rd Line Regiment (1/9)
  Würzburg Line Regiment (0/4)
24th Division: General von Zeschau
  Lecoq Light Battalion (0/1)
  Von Spiegel Grenadier Battalion (0/0)
  Von Steindal Infantry Regiment (0/2)
  Prinz Frederich Infantry Regiment (0/4)
  Von Rechten Infantry Regiment (0/1)
  Von Sahr Light Battalion (0/1)
  Von Anger Grenadier Battalion (0/0)
  Niesemeuschel Infantry Regiment (0/2)
  Saxon Jäger Company (?)
  Saxon Sapper Company (?)
26th Light Cavalry Brigade: von Lindenau
  Prinz Clement Uhlan Regiment (?)
  Saxon Hussar Regiment (?)
VIII Corps: Général de division Poniatowski
26th Division: Général de division Kamienecki
  Vistula Legion Regiment (1/16)
  1st Polish Line Regiment (0/10)
  16th Polish Line Regiment (0/17)
  8th Polish Line Regiment (0/15)
  15th Polish Line Regiment (0/13)
  12th Polish Line Regiment (0/14)
  14th Polish Line Regiment (0/15)
27th Light Cavalry Brigade: Général de brigade
Uminski
  14th Polish Cuirassier Regiment (0/8)
  Krakus Regiment (0/14)
XI Corps: Maréchal Macdonald
31th Division: Général de division Ledru
  11th Provisional Demi-brigade (0/7)
  13th Provisional Demi-brigade (6/17)
  1/, 2/8th Westphalian Line Regiment (0/7)
  4th Westphalian Light Battalion (0/4)
  Neapolitan Elite Regiment (0/8)
  1/, 2/4th Neapolitan Light Regiment (0/8)
35th Division: Général de division Gerard
  3/, 4/, 7/6th Line Regiment (1/22)
  1/, 2/, 3/, 4/112nd Line Regiment (2/23)
  3/, 4/2nd Italian Légère Regiment (0/5)
  1/, 2/, 3/, 4/5th Italian Line Regiment (0/4)
36th Division: Général de division Charpentier
  1/, 2/, 3/, 4/22nd Légère Regiment (1/22)
  4/, 6/10th Line Regiment (1/12)
  3/, 4/3rd Légère Regiment (2/13)
  3/, 4/, 7/14th Légère Regiment (7/28)
39th Division: Général de division Marchand
  1/, 2/1st Baden Line Regiment (0/0)
  1/, 2/3rd Baden Line Regiment (1/0)
  1/Hesse-Darmstadt Guard Fusilier Regiment (3/8)
  1/, 2/Hesse-Darmstadt Leibgarde Regiment (?)
  1/, 2/2nd Hesse-Darmstadt Infantry Regiment (1/1)

**28th Light Cavalry Brigade: Général de division
Montbrun**
  4th Italian Chasseurs à Cheval Regiment (?)
  Würzburg Chasseurs à Cheval Regiment (?)
  2nd Neapolitan Chasseurs à Cheval Regiment (0/4)
IX Corps: Maréchal Augereau
51st Division: Général de division ?
  32nd Provisional Demi-brigade (0/0)
  2/63rd Line Regiment (0/13)
  34th Provisional Demi-brigade (2/18)
  35th Provisional Demi-brigade (0/14)
52nd Division: Général de division Sémélé
  37th Provisional Demi-brigade (0/9)[20]
  2/39th Line Regiment (3/6)
  6/121st Line Regiment (0/0)
  (Losses listed in VI Corps)
  6/122nd Line Regiment (2/16)
  2/86th Line Regiment (0/0)[21]
Independent Divisions
Division: Général de division Lefol
  1st Erfurt Battalion (0/0)
  2nd Erfurt Battalion (0/0)
  2/54th Line Regiment (1/6)
  1 ½ Bataillon de Marche (0/10)[22]
Polish Division: Général de division Dombrowski
  2nd Polish Line Regiment (0/11)
  4th Polish Line Regiment (0/20)
  2nd Polish Uhlan Regiment (0/6)
  4th Polish Chasseurs à Cheval Regiment (0/7)
**Division Special "C": Général de division
Margaron**
  1/, 2/3rd Baden Line Regiment (0/0)
  1/36th Légère Regiment (listed in VII Corps)
  4/35th Légère Regiment (listed in VII Corps)
  2/96th Line Regiment (0/8)
  2/103rd Line Regiment (listed in 111 Corps)
  1/132nd Line Regiment (listed in III Corps)
I Cavalry Corps: GD Latour-Maubourg
**1st Light Cavalry Division: Général de division
Berkheim**
  16th Chasseurs à Cheval Regiment (4/7)
  1st Chevauléger-lancier Regiment (2/14)
  3rd Chevauléger-lancier Regiment (1/6)
  5th Chevauléger-lancier Regiment (0/3)
  8th Chevauléger-lancier Regiment (0/10)
2nd Light Cavalry Division: GD Corbineau
  6th Hussar Regiment (1/10)
  7th Hussar Regiment (0/6)
  8th Hussar Regiment (1/9)
**3rd Light Cavalry Division: Général de division
Chastel**

---

20 Casualties of the 17th and 29th Légère are listed
    in the III Corps.
21 Losses listed in VI Corps.
22 Casualties of the 29th Légère are listed in the III
    Corps.

8th Chasseurs à Cheval Regiment (0/1)
9th Chasseurs à Cheval Regiment (0/3)
1st Chasseurs à Cheval Regiment (0/5)
19th Chasseurs à Cheval Regiment (0/9)
25th Chasseurs à Cheval Regiment (3/4)

1st Cuirassier Division: Général de division Bordesoulle

2nd Cuirassier Regiment (2/6)
3rd Cuirassier Regiment (0/14)
6th Cuirassier Regiment (3/11)
9th Cuirassier Regiment (1/14)
11th Cuirassier Regiment (0/12)
12th Cuirassier Regiment (1/8)
Saxon Garde Cuirassier Regiment (1/5)
Saxon Zastrow Cuirassier Regiment (0/1)

3rd Cuirassier Division: Général de division Doumerc

4th Cuirassier Regiment (1/3)
7th Cuirassier Regiment (1/3)
14th Cuirassier Regiment (2/4)
Italian Napoleon Dragoon Regiment (3/9)
7th Dragoon Regiment (3/6)
23rd Dragoon Regiment (1/10)
28th Dragoon Regiment (0/6)
30th Dragoon Regiment (1/6)

II Cavalry Corps: Général de division Sébastiani
2nd Light Cavalry Division: GD Roussel d'Hurbal

2nd Chevauléger-lancier Regiment (0/2)
11th Chasseurs à Cheval Regiment (2/4)
12th Chasseurs à Cheval Regiment (1/6)
4th Chevauléger-lancier Regiment (1/3)
5th Hussar Regiment (1/4)
8th Hussar Regiment (0/3)

4th Light Cavalry Division: Général de division Exelmann

6th Chevauléger-lancier Regiment (0/12)
4th Chasseurs à Cheval Regiment (4/14)
7th Chasseurs à Cheval Regiment (5/10)
20th Chasseurs à Cheval Regiment (2/11)
23rd Chasseurs à Cheval Regiment (2/6)
24th Chasseurs à Cheval Regiment (0/10)
11th Hussar Regiment (1/8)

2nd Cuirassier Division: Général de division St-Germain

1st Carabinier Regiment (1/8)
2nd Carabinier Regiment (3/6)
1st Cuirassier Regiment (0/6)
5th Cuirassier Regiment (0/1)
8th Cuirassier Regiment (0/2)
10th Cuirassier Regiment (0/2)

III Cavalry Corps: Général de division Arrighi
5th Light Cavalry Division: Général de division Lorge

5th Chasseurs à Cheval Regiment (0/2)
10th Chasseurs à Cheval Regiment (0/3)
13th Chasseurs à Cheval Regiment (0/0)
15th Chasseurs à Cheval Regiment (0/2)
21st Chasseurs à Cheval Regiment (0/2)
22nd Chasseurs à Cheval Regiment (0/2)

6th Light Cavalry Division: Général de division Fournier

29th Chasseurs à Cheval Regiment (0/2)
31st Chasseurs à Cheval Regiment (0/4)
1st Hussar Regiment (1/1)
2nd Hussar Regiment (2/2)
4th Hussar Regiment (0/0)

4th Heavy Cavalry Division Général de division Defrance

12th Hussar Regiment (0/1)
4th Dragoon Regiment (1/1)
5th Dragoon Regiment (0/2)
14th Dragoon Regiment (0/0)
12th Dragoon Regiment (0/0)
24th Dragoon Regiment (0/0)
16th Dragoon Regiment (0/3)
17th Dragoon Regiment (1/0)
21st Dragoon Regiment (0/1)
26th Dragoon Regiment (0/1)
27th Dragoon Regiment (0/0)
13th Cuirassier Regiment (0/1)

IV Cavalry Corps: Général de division Sokolnicki
7th Light Cavalry Division:

1st Polish Chasseurs à Cheval Regiment (0/7)
3rd Polish Uhlan Regiment (0/6)

8th Light Cavalry Division: Général de division Sulkowski

6th Polish Uhlan Regiment (0/4)
8th Polish Uhlan Regiment (0/5)

V Cavalry Corps: Général de division Pajol
9th Light Cavalry Division: Général de division Subervie

3rd Hussar Regiment (1/4)
27th Chasseurs à Cheval Regiment (0/4)
14th Chasseurs à Cheval Regiment (2/2)
26th Chasseurs à Cheval Regiment (0/2)
13th Hussar Regiment (1/9)

5th Heavy Cavalry Division: Général de division l'Héritier

2nd Dragoon Regiment (3/8)
6th Dragoon Regiment (0/11)
11th Dragoon Regiment (0/2)
13th Dragoon Regiment (0/3)
15th Dragoon Regiment (1/11)

6th Heavy Cavalry Division: Général de division Milhaud

18th Dragoon Regiment (0/3)
19th Dragoon Regiment (0/2)
20th Dragoon Regiment (0/2)
22nd Dragoon Regiment (1/2)
25th Dragoon Regiment (1/3)

Von Quistorp, *Geschichte der Nord-Armee im Jahre 1813*

ALLIED CASUALTIES

ARMY OF BOHEMIA: GENERAL PRINZ SCHWARZENBERG
Losses unknown

ARMY OF SILESIA: GENERAL DER KAVALLERIE Blücher
1st Prussian Army Corps: GL von Yorck
Fus/1st East Prussian Infantry Regiment
  (0/1/1/9/0/2)[23]
Fus/2nd East Prussian Infantry Regiment
  (0/0/0/16/0/0)
Iagers, Leib Regiment (1/0/0/8/0/0)
Thüringer Battalion (0/0/1/6/0/0/)
11th Corps: Generalleutnant Osten-Sacken
10th Division: Generalmajor Lieven
Jaroslav Infantry Regiment (0/0)[24]
Crimea Infantry Regiment (192/0)
Bieloserk Infantry Regiment (2/0)
8th Jager Regiment (198/0)
39th Jager Regiment (302/0)
27th Division: Generalmajor Neverovski
Odessa Infantry Regiment (256/0)
Tarnopol Infantry Regiment (293/0)
Vilna Infantry Regiment (291/0)
Simbrisk Infantry Regiment (273/0)
49th Jager Regiment (189/0)
50th Jager Regiment (201/0)
16th Division: Generalmajor Repnin
Okhotski Infantry Regiment (94/0)
Kamchatka Infantry Regiment (256/0)
Corps Artillery:
Position Battery #10 (16/1)
Position Battery #13 (19/0)
Light Battery #24 (0/0)
Light Battery #35 (11/0)
Horse Battery #18 (6/22)
Corps Cavalry: Generallieutenant Vasil'chikov
Smolensk Dragoon Regiment (20/4)
Kourland Dragoon Regiment (2/3)
White Russia Hussar Regiment (21/93)
Akhtyrsk Hussar Regiment (49/105)
Mariupol Hussar Regiment (55/88)
Alexandria Hussar Regiment (65/97)
Cossacks: Generalmajor Karpov II
Karpov #2 Cossack Regiment (18/46)
Loukoffkin Cossack Regiment (16/110)
Kutainikov #4 Cossack Regiment (13/20)
Grekov Cossack Regiment (9/21)
Semencikov #4 Cossack Regiment (13/45)
Illowaiski #9 Cossack Regiment (12/28)
2nd Bashkir Regiment (0/7)

2nd Kalmuck Regiment (40/56)
Baron Bode Volunteer Regiment (1/8)
4th Ukrainian Cossack Regiment (10/11)
Army Corps: General of Infantry Count Langeron
Losses 18 October

	Officers	Men
Dead	27	545
Wounded	140	2,615
Missing	1	382

Losses 19 October

	Officers	Men
Dead	1	52
Wounded	25	391
Missing	0	125

ARMY OF THE NORTH: BERNADOTTE, CROWN PRINCE OF SWEDEN
3rd Prussian Army Corps: Generallieutenant Bülow
Staff   (1/0/0/1/0/0/0/0/0)[25]
3rd Brigade: Generalmajor Hesse-Homburg
2nd East Prussian Grenadier Bn
  (1/21/0/5/106/0/0/0)
1/3rd East Prussian Inf Regt (2/22/0/4/154/0/21/0)
2/3rd East Prussian Inf Regt 1/12/0/5/142/0/0/0)
Fus/3rd East Prussian Inf Regt (0/6/0/5/142/0/0/0/0)
1/4th Reserve Infantry Regt (0/6/0/4/113/0/0/0)
2/4th Reserve Infantry Regt (0/11/0/5/127/0/0/0)
3/4th Reserve Infantry Regt (1/0/00/213/0/0/0)
3rd East Prussian LW Regt (1/26/0/5/128/0/0/47/0)
5th Brigade: Oberstleutnant von Schoon
Pomeranian Grenadier Bn (1/14/0/2/243/0/0/0)
Iagers of above bn (0/12/0/2/16/0/0/0)
1/1st Pomeranian Inf Regt (1/2/0/1/62/0/0/0)
Iagers of above bn (0/0/0/0/5/0/0/0)
2/1st Pomeranian Inf Regt (2/5/0/1/94/0/0/7/0)
Fus/1st Pomeranian Inf Regt (3/20/0/2/178/0/0/8/0)
Iagers of above bn (0/11/0/2/22/0/0/10/0)
1/2nd Reserve Infantry Regt(0/6/0/2/97//0/0/0)
2/2nd Reserve Infantry Regt(1/3/0/0/106/0/0/0/0)
3/2nd Reserve Infantry Regt (1/13/0/2/121/0/0/0/0)
2nd Kurmark Landwehr Regt (0/0/0/2/13/0/0/0)
6th Brigade: Generalmajor Krafft
1/Colberg Infantry Regt   (0/5/0/2/41/0/0/0)
2/Colberg Infantry Regt   (0/1/0/1/10/0/0/0)
1/9th Reserve Infantry Regt (0/3/0/2/32/0/0/0)
3/1st Neumärk Landwehr Regt (0/0/0/0/5/0/0/0)
4/1st Neumärk Landwehr Regt (0/7/0/4/43/0/0/0)
Reserve Cavalry: Generalmajor Oppen
Königin Dragoon Regiment (0/0/3/0/0/0/0/0/1)
Brandenburg Dragoon Regiment (0/0/1/0/0/0/0/0/0)
2nd Kurmark LW Cavalry Regt (0/2/9/0/0/0/0/1/2)
4th Kurmark LW Cavalry Regt (0/1/11/0/3/1/0/1/3)

---

23   Losses are officers and men; dead, wounded, and missing.
24   Numbers are men and horses.
25   3rd Corps numbers are officers, men, horses; dead, wounded and missing.

2nd Pomeranian LW Cavalry (0/0/6/0/0/0/0/0/0)
1st Leib Hussar Regiment (0/1/4/1/6/1/0/0/0)
Artillery Reserve: Oberstleutnant Holtzendorf
12-pdr Foot Battery #4 (0/2/24/1/11/0/0/0/0)
12-pdr Foot Battery #5 (0/7/20/1/12/0/0/0/0)
6-pdr Foot Battery #5 (0/0/7/0/4/1/0/0/0)
6-pdr Foot Battery #10 (0/3/14/0/4/1/0/2/0)
6-pdr Foot Battery #16 (0/1/3/0/0/0/0/0/0)
Horse Battery #5 (0/0/15/1/6/6/0/0/0)
Horse Battery #6 (0/5/15/0/15/7/0/0/0)
6-pdr Horse Battery #11 (0/1/11/0/4/2/0/0/0)
Russian Troops:
Position Battery #7 and #21 (0/4/16/0/21/16/0/0/0)
Russian Corps: GL Baron Winzingerode
Losses on 18/19 October
Dead: 1 General, 2 Staff officers, 7 Sub officers, 163 men, 462 horses
Wounded: 4 Staff officers, 19 Sub officers, 244 men, 241 horses
Swedish Army: Field Marshal Stedingk
Losses 19 October

	Dead		Wounded	
	Officers	Men	Officers	Men
Staff	1	–	–	–
1st Division	–	21	3	70
2nd Division	2	21	1	55
Artillery	0	1	2	1

POLISH RESERVE ARMY: GDK BENNIGSEN

1 General, 6 staff officers, 63 officers, and 3,000 men killed, wounded, and missing.

Von Quistorp, *Geschichte der Nord-Armee im Jahre 1813*

PRUSSIAN 1ST CORPS REORGANIZED AFTER MÖCKERN 17 OCTOBER 1813

Commanding General: Generallieutenant von Yorck
Advanced Guard: Oberst von Katzeler
Infantry:
East Prussian Jägers (2 coys)
Landwehr Battalion, Major von Thiele
Landwehr Battalion, Major von Rekowsky
Landwehr Battalion, Major von Wedell
2/12th Reserve Infantry Regiment
1/Brandenburg Infantry Regiment
West Prussian Grenadier Battalion
Leib-Grenadier Battalion
Fus/West Prussian Infantry Regiment
Guard Jäger Battalion (1 coy)
6-pdr Foot Battery #12
Cavalry[26]
5th Silesian Landwehr Cavalry Regiment (4)

East Prussian National Cavalry Regiment (5)
Brandenburg Uhlan Regiment (4)
Brandenburg Hussar Regiment (3)
2nd Leib Hussar Regiment (2)
Horse Battery #2
Army Corps:
1st Division: Generalmajor von Hünerbein
1st Brigade: Oberst von Lothin
East Prussian Jäger Battalion (2) (230)
Silesian Grenadier Battalion (539)
1/4th Silesian Landwehr Regiment (545)
5th Silesian Landwehr Regiment (1 combined bn) (545)
13th Silesian Landwehr Regiment (1 combined bn) (516)
Combined Grenadier Battalion
1st East Prussian Grenadier Battalion (233)
West Prussian Grenadier Battalion (343)
Leib-Grenadier Battalion (492)
Leib Hussar Regiment (2) (385)
6-pdr Foot Battery #2 (8 guns) (114)
8th Brigade: Oberstleutnant von Gaza
Combined Battalion von Wiegand
Fus/1st East Prussian Infantry Regiment
1/12th Reserve Infantry Regiment[27]
14th Silesian Landwehr Regiment (1 combined Bn) (493)
1/, 2/Brandenburg Infantry Regiment (1 combined Bn) (810)
Battalion 2nd Converged Prussian Infantry Regiment
Brandenburg Hussar Regiment (4) (356)
6-pdr Foot Battery #15 (8 guns) (91)
2nd Division: Generalmajor von Horn
2nd Brigade: Generalmajor von Mecklenburg Strelitz
Combined Battalion von Rummel
Fus/1st East Prussian Infantry Regiment
Fus/2nd East Prussian Infantry Regiment
1/, 2/2nd East Prussian Infantry Regiment (664)
Fischer Bn/6th Silesian Landwehr Regiment (358)
1/, 2/1st East Prussian Infantry Regiment (828)
6-pdr Foot Battery #1 (8 guns) (110)
7th Brigade: Oberst von Weltzien
4/Guard Jäger Battalion (1 co) (108)
1/, 2/, Fus/Leib Infantry Regiment (1,494)
Thuringian Battalion (201)
15th Silesian Landwehr Regiment (1 combined bn) (770)
4th Silesian Landwehr Regiment (1 combined bn) (632)
3/, 4/3rd Silesian Landwehr Cavalry Regiment (94)
6-pdr Foot Battery #3 (8 guns) (128)
Cavalry Reserve: Oberst von Jürgass
Brigade: Oberst Graf Henckel von Donnersmark
Lithuanian Dragoon Regiment (5) (410)
West Prussian Dragoon Regiment (4) (269)

---

26 The Advanced Guard was broken out of the following forces, but is still included below.

27 Strength figures counted with rest of regts.

Brandenburg Uhlan Regiment (288)
East Prussian National Cavalry Regiment (373)
Landwehr Brigade: Major von Bieberstein
  5th Silesian Landwehr Cavalry Regiment (176)
  1st Neumärk Silesian Landwehr Cavalry Regiment (183)
  10th Silesian Landwehr Cavalry Regiment (194)
Artillery:
  Horse Battery #1 (8 guns) (111)
  Horse Battery #3 (8 guns) (119)
Reserve Artillery: Oberstleutnant von Schmidt
  12-pdr Foot Battery #1 (8 guns) (189)
  12-pdr Foot Battery #2 (8 guns) (189)
  6-pdr Foot Battery #12 (8 guns) (103)
  6-pdr Foot Battery #24 (8 guns) (117)
  3-pdr Foot Battery #1 (8 guns) (91)
  Horse Battery #3 (8 guns) (126)
  Horse Battery #12 (8 guns) (111)

Prussian General Staff, *Rectal des Plans des Combats et de Batailles livrées par l'Armée Prussienne Pendant les Campagnes des Années 1813, 14, et 15*

THE AUSTRO-BAVARIAN ARMY

AUSTRO-BAVARIAN ORDER OF BATTLE 15 OCTOBER 1813

Austrian 1st Corps: GdK von Frimont
Light Division: Feldmarschal-leutnant Graf Fresnel
1st Brigade: Generalmajor Graf Hardegg
  Szekler Grenz Regiment (2)
  Archduke Joseph Hussar Regiment (6)
2nd Brigade: Generalmajor von Volkmann
  Jäger Battalion #3
  Schwarzenberg Uhlan Regiment (6)
  6-pdr Cavalry Artillery Battery (6 6-pdrs)
Line Division: Generalmajor von Bach
Brigade: Generalmajor von Bach
  Archduke Rudolph Infantry Regiment (4)
  Jordis Infantry Regiment #59 (4)
  6-pdr Brigade Batteries (2) (8 6-pdrs ea.)
1st Reserve Division: FML von Trautenberg
1st Brigade: Generalmajor Graf Klenau
  Frisch Grenadier Battalions
  La Best Grenadier Battalions
  Berger Grenadier Battalions
  Putheany Grenadier Battalions
  6-pdr Brigade Battery (8 6-pdrs)
2nd Brigade: Generalmajor von Diemar
  Possmann Grenadier Battalion
  Kramer Grenadier Battalion
  Hromada Grenadier Battalion
  6-pdr Brigade Battery (8-3-pdrs)
Cavalry Reserve Division: FML von Splenyi
1st Brigade: Generalmajor Minutillo

Szekler Hussar Regiment (6)
Frimont Hussar Regiment (6) (en route)
2nd Brigade: Oberst von Flachenfeld
  Knesevich Dragoon Regiment (6)
  Liechtenstein Cuirassier Regiment (6)
  Cavalry Battery (6 6-pdrs)
Artillery: Generalmajor von Sertnik
  6-pdr Position Battery (6 6-pdrs)
  3 12-pdr Position Batteries (6 12-pdrs ea.)
Streifkorps Scheibler
  Szekler Hussar Regiment (2)
  2/Ansbach National-Feld-Bataillon
  6/7th Chevauléger Regiment
Extra Corps:
  Landwehr Staff Dragoons (2 sqns)
  Pioneer Company (1)
  Medical Companies (2)
  Det. Pontooneers
  Det. Pontoon Train

Bavarian 2nd Corps: GdKavallerie Graf Wrede
1st Infantry Division: Generalleutnant Graf Rechberg
1st Brigade: Generalmajor Prinz Karl of Bavaria
  1/, 2/1st Infantry Regiment
  1/3rd Infantry Regiment
  1/Oberdonait Kreis Regiment
  3rd Combined Jäger Battalion
2nd Brigade: Generalmajor von Maillot
  2/10th Infantry Regiment
  2/2nd Infantry Regiment
  2/Oberdonau Kreis Regiment
  1/Main Kreis Regiment
  2nd Converged Jäger Battalion
Artillery: Oberstleutnant Goschel
  Light Battery #4 (6 6-pdrs)
  6-pdr Foot Battery #5 (8 6-pdrs)
1st Light Cavalry Brigade: Generalmajor von Vieregg
  2/, 3/, 4/, 5/1st Chevauléger Regiment
  2/, 3/, 4/, 5/2nd Chevauléger Regiment
  1/, 2/, 3/, 5/7th Chevauléger Regiment
2nd Infantry Division: Generalleutnant Graf Beckers
1st Brigade: Generalmajor Graf Pappenheim
  1/, 2/4th Infantry Regiment
  Combined Salzach Kreis Battalion
  1/Regen Kreis Battalion
  4th Combined Jäger Battalion
2nd Brigade: Generalmajor Freiherr von Zoller
  1/, 2/6th Infantry Regiment
  2/Rezat Kreis Battalion
  1/Inn Kreis Battalion
  1st Jäger Battalion
Artillery: Major von Caspers
  Light Battery #2 (6-6prds)
  6-pdr Foot Battery #7 (8 6-pdrs)
2nd Light Cavalry Brigade: Generalmajor von Elbracht
  2/, 3/, 4/, 5/3rd Chevauléger Regiment
  2/, 3/, 4/, 5/6th Chevauléger Regiment

3rd Infantry Division: Generalmajor von Lamotte
1st Brigade: Generalmajor von dem Stockh
  1/, 2/11th Infantry Regiment
  1/7th Infantry Regiment
  1//Unterdonau Kreis Battalion
  1/Iller Kreis Battalion
2nd Brigade: Generalmajor Deroy
  1/8th Infantry Regiment
  1/9th Infantry Regiment
  1/5th Infantry Regiment
  1/Rezat Kreis Battalion
  2/Iller Kreis Battalion
  1/Isar Kreis Battalion
Artillery: Major Wagner
  Light Battery #3 (6-6prds)
  6-pdr Foot Battery #9 (8 6-pdrs)
3rd Light Cavalry Brigade: Oberst von Diez
  2/, 3/, 4/, 5/4th Chevauléger Regiment
  2/, 4/, 5/5th Chevauléger Regiment
Artillery Reserve: Oberstleutnant Maratini
  12-pdr Foot Battery #8 (6 12-pdrs)
  12-pdr Foot Battery #11 (6 12-pdrs)
  2 Foot Batteries (6 12-pdrs ea.)

Königlich Bayerische Kriegsarchiv, *Darstellungen aus der Bayerischen Kreigs-und Heeresgeschichte*; Frederich, R., *Geschichte des Herbstfeldzuges 1813*

BAVARIAN ARMY CORPS AT HANAU
29 OCTOBER 1813

COMMANDING OFFICER: GDK GRAF WREDE
Headquarters:
  Feldgendarmerie Squadron
  4/7th Chevauléger Regiment (Ordnance Squadron)
1st Cavalry Brigade: Generalmajor Freiherr von Vieregg
  2/, 3/, 4/, 5/1st Chevauleger Regiment (4)
  2/, 3/, 4/, 5/2nd Chevauleger Regiment (4)
  1/, 2/, 3/, 5/7th Chevauleger Regiment (4)
2nd Division: GL von Beckers von Westerstetten
1st Brigade: Generalmajor Graf Pappenheim
  1/, 2/4th Line Infantry Regiment
  5/, 6/4th Jäger Battalion
  Combined Salzach Kreis Battalion (part of 1st and 3rd Bns)
  Regen Kreis Battalion
2nd Brigade: Generalmajor Freiherr von Zoller
  1/, 2/6th Line Infantry Regiment
  1st Jäger Battalion
  1st Iller Kreis Battalion
  Combined (1st and 2nd) Rezat Kreis Battalion
2nd Cavalry Brigade: Generalmajor Elbracht
  2/, 4/, 5/3rd Chevauleger Regiment (3)
  2/, 3/, 4/, 5/6th Chevauleger Regiment (4)
2nd Artillery Commando: Major von Calpers
  7th 6-pdr Foot Battery
  2nd Wurst Battery (6-pdrs)

3rd Division: Generalleutnant von Freiherr von Lamotte
1st Brigade: Generalmajor Jason von der Stocky
  1/, 2/11th Line Infantry Regiment
  1/7th Line Infantry Regiment
  1st Iller Kreis Battalion (part of 1st and 3rd Battalions)
  1st Under-Donau Kreis Battalion (part of 1st **and** 2nd Bns)
2nd Brigade: Generalmajor von Deroy
  1/5th Line Infantry Regiment
  1/8th Line Infantry Regiment
  1/9th Line Infantry Regiment
  2nd Iller Kreis Battalion (part of 3rd and 4th Bns)
  1st Isar Kreis Battalion (part of 1st and 2nd Bns)
1st Cavalry Brigade: Oberst Diez
  2/, 4/, 5/4th Chevauléger Regiment (3)
  2/, 4/, 5/5th Chevauléger Regiment (3)
3rd Artillery Commando: Major Wagner
  9th 6-pdr Foot Battery
  1st Wurst Battery (6-pdrs)
Artillery Reserve: Hauptman Ulmer
  11th 12-pdr Foot Battery
  8th 12-pdr Foot Battery

Königlich Bayerische Kriegsarchiv, *Darstellungen aus der Bayerischen Kreigs- und Heeresgeschichte*, Munich, 1900-1914.

AUSTRIAN FORCES UNDER GdK FRIMONT
18 NOVEMBER 1813

Light Division: Feldmarschal-leutnant Graf Fresnet
1st Brigade: Generalmajor Graf Hardegg
  1st Szekler Grenz Regiment (2)
  Erzherzog Joseph Hussar Regiment (6)
2nd Brigade: Generalmajor Freiherr von Volkmann
  3rd Jäger Battalion
  Schwarzenberg Uhlan Regiment (6)
  Artillery Cavalry Battery (6 6-pdr guns)
Line Division: Generalmajor Freiherr von Bach
  Erzherzog Rudolph Infantry Regiment (4)
  Jordis Infantry Regiment (4)
Reserve Infantry Division: Feldmarschal-leutnant Freiherr von Trautenburg
1st Brigade: Generalmajor von Klenau
  Frisch Grenadier Battalion
  de Best Grenadier Battalion
  Berger Grenadier Battalion
  Putheany Grenadier Battalion
  6-pdr Brigade Battery (8 6-pdrs)
2nd Brigade: Generalmajor von Diemar
  Possmann Grenadier Battalion
  Kramer Grenadier Battalion
  Hromada Grenadier Battalion
  6-pdr Brigade Battery (8 6-pdrs)

Reserve Cavalry Division: Feldmarschal-leutnant von Splenyi
1st Brigade: Generalmajor Minutillo
  Szekler Hussar Regiment (6)
  Frimont Hussar Regiment (detached)
2nd Brigade: Oberst von Flachenfeld
  Knesevich Dragoon Regiment (6)
  Liechtenstein Cuirassier Regiment (4)
  Cavalry Battery (6 6-pdrs)
Artillery: Generalmajor von Swrtuik
  1 6-pdr Position Battery (6 6-pdrs)
  3 12-pdr Position Batteries (6 12-pdrs ea.)
Support Troops: Generalmajor von Geppert
  Pioneer Company
  Det. Pontooneers
  Pontoon Train (70 pontoons)
  Landwehr Staff Infantry Companies (2)
  Landwehr Staff Cavalry Squadrons (2)
  Landwehr Medical Companies (2)
Streifkorps: Oberst Scheibler
  Szekler Hussar Regiment (2 sqns)

Königlich Bayerische Kriegsarchiv, *Darstellungen aus der Bayerischen Kreigs- und Heeresgeschichte*, Munich, 1900-1914.

THE BATTLE OF SCHESTEDT 10 DECEMBER 1813

DANISH FORCES

General of Infantry Prince Frederick von Hesse

Advanced Guard: Général de brigade Lallemand
Light Brigade: Oberst von Waldeck
  2/Schleswig Jäger Corps
  1/, 2/Holstein Sharpshooter Corps
  1/3rd Jutland Infantry Regiment
  Louise Augusta Leibjäger Company
  6-pdr Foot Battery von Gerstenberg (8 guns)
  1/, 2/, 3/, 4/Holstein Heavy Cavalry Regiment
  1/, 2/17th Polish Lancer Regiment
Main Body: Prince Frederick von Hesse
1st Brigade: Generalmajor Graf Schulenburg
  1/, 4/Oldenburg Infantry Regiment
  2/Oldenburg Infantry Regiment (½ bn)
  Jäger Co. 3/Oldenburg Infantry Regiment
  1/Dronningen Infantry Regiment
  Jäger Co./Dronningen Infantry Regiment
  Altona Jäger-Grenadier Company
  3/, 4/Holstein Infantry Regiment
  Koye 6-pdr Foot Battery (8 guns)
  2/, 6/Jutland Hussar Regiment
  3-pdr Horse Battery von Gönner (8 guns)
2nd Brigade: Oberst von Abercron
  1/, 2/Fünen Infantry Regiment

1/Schleswig Infantry Regiment
2/, 3/, 4/Fünen Dragoon Regiment
6-pdr Foot Battery Früs (10 guns)
Rearguard:
Train: 500 Wagons
  2/Fünen Infantry Regiment
  2/Oldenburg Infantry Regiment (2 coys)
  1/Fünen Dragoon Regiment
  2/Schleswig Infantry Regiment[28]

Total—about 9,000 men

WALLMODEN'S CORPS

Division: Generalmajor Arentschildt
1st Brigade: Major von Natzmer
  1st Battalion Russo-German Legion (18/892)
  2nd Battalion Russo-German Legion (20/740)
  5th Battalion Russo-German Legion (20/814)
2nd Brigade
  6th Battalion Russo-German Legion (13/795)
  7th Battalion Russo-German Legion (19/624)
Division: Lyon
Line Brigade: Lt. Colonel Hackett
  Lauenberg Battalion (638)
  Langrehr Battalion (638)
  Bennigsen Battalion (638)
  Det/KGL Light (Holzermann) Brigade (150)
  Anhalt-Dessau Battalion (600)
  Hanoverian Jäger Detachment (40)
Division: Vegesack
Advanced Guard: Oberst Graf Osten-Sacken
  Mecklenburg Foot Jäger Battalion (375)
Cavalry:
  1st Hussar Regiment Russo-German Legion (17/470)
  Bremen-Verden Hussar Regiment (3 sqns) (300)
  Mecklenburg Mounted Jäger Regiment (3 sqns) (384)
Artillery:
  1st Horse Battery Russo-German Legion (6 guns)
  2nd Horse Battery Russo-German Legion (6 guns)
    Total 250 men
  Hanoverian Foot Battery (4 guns)
  KGL Horse Battery (1 section—2 guns)
    Total 160 men
Division: Generalmajor von Dörnberg
2nd Brigade: Oberstleutnant Wardenburg
  3rd Battalion Russo-German Legion
  4th Battalion Russo-German Legion
Hanoverian Light Brigade: Oberst Lieutenant Martin
  Lüneburg Battalion
  Bremen-Verden Battalion
  Combined Jäger Battalion
  Hanoverian Jägers (3 coys)

---

28 Detached to the rearguard from the main body after the battle started.

Russo-German Legion Jägers (1 co)
2nd Hussar Regiment Russo-German Legion
3rd Hussar Regiment King's German Legion
1st Horse Battery King's German Legion
2nd Horse Battery King's German Legion

Von Quistorp, B., *Geschichte der Nord-Armee im Jahre 1813*, Berlin, 1894.

ALLIED CASUALTIES

	Initial Strength		Killed and Wounded; Captured			Lost
	Off	Men	Off	Men	%	
Staff	?	0	0	1		
Arentschildt's Div. Staff	?	2	0	0		
RGL Brigade Staff		0	0	2		
1st Battalion RGL	18	892	2	55	8	7/0
2nd Battalion RGL	20	740	2	68	22	12
3rd Battalion RGL		3	93	27		
4th Battalion RGL		0	20	49		
5th Battalion RGL	20	814	0	15	229	30
6th Battalion RGL	13	795	2	75	44	15
7th Battalion RGL	19	624	0	47	48	15
Lauenberg Battalion		638	3	90	15	17
Langrehr Battalion		638	0	?	0	0
Dessau Battalion		600	0	?	100	17
Bennigsen Battalion		638	0	0	0	0
Bremen-Verden Bn			0	0	14	
Lüneburg Battalion			0	0	0	
Holtzermann's Det, KGL		150	1	?	6	5
Hanoverian Jägers		40	0	4	0	13
RGL Jägers	?		0	2	0	
Mecklenburg Fuss Jägers		375	3	14	?	4
1st RGL Hussar Regt	17	470	1	10	3	3
2nd RGL Hussar Regt			0	2	5	
3rd RG1 Hussar Regt			0	0	0	
Bremen Verden Hussar		300	0	0	3	
Mecklenburg Mtd Jägers		384	6	47	19	19
1st RGL Horse Battery			0	1	0	
2nd RGL Horse Battery			0	0	0	
	250					0
KGL Horse Battery			0	0	0	

Hanoverian Foot Battery			0	0	3	
	160					2
Total			25	543	598	

THE BESIEGED FORTRESSES

FRENCH GARRISON OF TORGAU 20 OCTOBER 1813

Staff (75/28)
Gendarmerie (1/28)
Artillery and Train (70/1,930)
4 Artillery Companies Det/Artisans
8 Pontooneer Companies
4 Train Companies
Engineering Troops (20/640)
1 Miner Company
2 Sapper Companies
Artisans (66)
2 Train Companies
2nd and 8th Marine Military Artisans (20/1,200)
1st Torgau Battalion (21/300)
1st, 2nd and 3rd Torgau Regiment (168/7,146)
Convalescents in Depots (60/1,000)
Polish Cossacks (4/100)
6th and 17th Military Equipage Battalions
  (20/1,240)
Hessians and Württembergers (36/1,800)

Augoyat, *Relation de la défense de Torgau par les troupes françaises en 1813*, Paris, 1840.

FRENCH FORCES IN DANZIG 29 NOVEMBER 1813

10th Corps: Général de division Count Rapp
Aides de camp: Chef d'escadron Turkheim,
  Capitaine Marnier
Chief of Staff: Général de brigade d'Hericourt
  General Staff: (25)
Gendarmerie: (0/8)
Imperial Guard: Chef d'escadron Martin-Laforest
  Mixed Guard Force (281)

7th Division: Général de division Grandjean (3,858)
1st Brigade: Général de division Bachelu
  1/, 2/13th Bavarian Line Regiment
  1/, 2/1st Westphalian Line Regiment
  1/, 2/, 3/10th Polish Line Regiment
2nd Brigade: Général de brigade Prince Radziwill
  1/, 2/, 3/5th Polish Line Regiment
  1/, 2/, 3/11th Polish Line Regiment

30th Division: Général de division Count Heudelet (3,556)
1st Brigade: Général de brigade Breissan
 1st Provisional Demi-Brigade
  4/2nd Légère Regiment
  4/4th Légère Regiment
  4/17th Légère Regiment
 6th Provisional Demi-Brigade
  4/16th Légère Regiment
  4/21st Légère Regiment
  4/23rd Légère Regiment
2nd Brigade: Général de brigade Husson
 7th Provisional Demi-Brigade
  4/8th Line Regiment
  4/14th Line Regiment
  4/94th Line Regiment
 8th Provisional Demi-Brigade
  4/24th Line Regiment
  4/45th Line Regiment
  4/59th Line Regiment
3rd Brigade: Général de brigade Gault
 9th Provisional Demi-Brigade
  4/54th Line Regiment
  4/88th Line Regiment
  4/95th Line Regiment
 17th Provisional Demi-Brigade
  6th Légère Regiment
  25th Légère Regiment
  39th Line Regiment

33rd Division: Lieutenant General Destres (1,594)
1st Brigade: Maréchal de camp Pepe
 1/, 2/5th Neapolitan Line Regiment
 1/, 2/6th Neapolitan Line Regiment
 1/, 2/7th Neapolitan Line Regiment

30th Division: Général de brigade Franceschi (1,341)
1st Brigade: Général de brigade Deviniers
 Provisional Regiment
  22nd Légère Regiment
  4/3rd Line Regiment
  4/29th Line Regiment
  4/105th Line Regiment
  4/113rd Line Regiment
 German Provisional Battalion
  Frankfurt Regiment
  4th Rhinbund (Saxon Ducal Houses) Regiment
  5th Rhinbund (Lippe and Anhalt) Regiment
  6th Rhinbund (Schwarzburg, Waldeck, Reuss) Regiment
 Depot 44th Line Regiment
 1/, 2/King of Rome Regiment
 French Commissariat Battalion

Cavalry Brigade: Général de brigade Cavaignac (1,078)
 1st Provisional Cavalry Regiment
  4/2nd Dragoon Regiment
  4/5th Dragoon Regiment
  4/12th Dragoon Regiment
  4/13th Dragoon Regiment
 2nd Provisional Cavalry Regiment
  4/14th Dragoon Regiment
  4/17th Dragoon Regiment
  4/19th Dragoon Regiment
  4/20th Dragoon Regiment
 3rd Provisional Cavalry Régiment de Marche
  3rd, 6th, 8th Cuirassier Regiments
  3rd, 7th, 11th, 19th, 23rd, 24th, 25th Chasseurs à Cheval Regiments
  7th, 8th Hussars, 28th Dragoons
  1/, 2/, 3/, 4/9th Polish Chevauléger-lancier Regiment

Artillery: Général de brigade Lepin (1,615)
 4/, 5/, 9/, 10/, 19/5th Foot Regiment
 7/, 12/, 17/, 22/7th Foot Regiment
 21/8th Foot Regiment
 6/, 18/9th Foot Regiment
 2/, 3/, 4/, 5/, 6/2nd Pontooneer Battalion
 6th Ouvrier Company
 3rd Armorer Company
 7th Principal Train Battalion
 11th Principal Train Battalion
 12th Principal Train Battalion
 1st (bis) Train Battalion
 9th (bis) Train Battalion
 11th (bis) Train Battalion
 2nd Bavarian Artillery Company
 5th Württemberg Artillery Company
 10th Saxon Artillery Company
 6th and 16th Polish Foot Artillery Companies
 1st Polish Horse Artillery Companies
 Regimental Artillery/29th Line and Regiments of 7th Division
 Powder Technicians

Engineers: Général de division Campredon (696)
 Engineering Staff
 2/1st Miner Battalion
 4/3rd Sapper Battalion
 Polish Sapper Battalion
 Spanish Pioneer Battalion

Marine: Contre-amiral Dumanoir (404)
 4th Équippage de Flotille
 17th Équippage de Flotille
 Danube Marine Artisan Battalion
 1st Escaut Marine Artisan Battalion
Customs: Directeur Bonneville (47)

d'Artois, *Relation de la Défense de Danzig en 1813 par le 10e corps de l'Armée Françaises, contre l'Armée combinée Russe et Prussienne.*

Notes

1 The Eye of the Hurricane September 1813

1 Clément, *Campagne de 1813*, p.405.
2 Bonaparte, *Correspondance de Napoléon*, #20497.
3 Bonaparte, *Correspondance de Napoléon*, #20512.
4 Clément, *Campagne de 1813*, p.407, & Bonaparte, *Correspondance de Napoléon*, #20510 & #20513.
5 Vassil'shikov commanded the 3rd Dragoon Division, 2nd Hussar Division and a force of 10 Cossack regiments.
6 Fabry, *Étude sur les Opérations 5 Septembre*, p.2.
7 Though not stated, this was probably a volley from the French light cavalry.
8 Fabry, *Étude sur les Opérations 5 Septembre*, p.3.
9 Fabry, *Étude sur les Opérations 5 Septembre*, p.4.
10 Fabry, *Étude sur les Opérations 5 Septembre*, p.5.
11 Clément, *Campagne de 1813*, p.413.
12 Kaisarov commanded a small force of three Cossack regiments.
13 Fabry, *Étude sur les Opérations 5 Septembre*, p.9.
14 Fabry, *Journal du Prince du Wurtemberg*, p.130.
15 Plotho was one of the early German authors to extensively write about this campaign. His four volume work on the 1813 campaign is an excellent source of details on the allied and, most particularly, the Prussian actions.
16 Plotho, *Krieg in Deutschland*, Vol II, pp.162-163.
17 Fabry, *Étude sur les Opérations 5 Septembre*, p.10.
18 Clément, *Campagne de 1813*, p.415.
19 St-Cyr, *Mémoires*, Vol II, p.141.
20 Clément, *Campagne de 1813*, p.418.
21 St-Cyr, *Mémoires*, Vol II, pp.142-143.
22 St-Cyr, *Mémoires*, Vol II, p.143.
23 St-Cyr, *Mémoires*, Vol II, p.146.
24 Clément, *Campagne de 1813*, p.419.
25 Fabry, *III et V Corps en 1813*, p.70.
26 This unit was also known as the Krakus Regiment. They were the Polish answer to Cossacks and served mostly in a reconnaissance role. Napoleon also once referred to them as "his pygmy cavalry" because of their small horses. Despite that joke, they were the terror of the Cossacks.
27 Poniatowski, *Correspondance*, Vol V, pp.402-405.
28 Clément, *Campagne de 1813*, p.422.
29 The Elbe, running north and south, provided an effective military barrier that, once crossed by the allies, would force him to abandon his Saxon and Bavarian allies. In addition, the cities along the Elbe were major industrial and commercial centers that supported Napoleon's war effort.
30 Clément, *Campagne de 1813*, p.424.
31 The 22nd Light Cavalry Brigade, assigned to the II Corps, was under Oberst von Hammerstein and consisted of the 1/1st and 2/2nd Westphalian Hussar Regiments. They were both defected on 18 September at Freiberg.
32 Fabry, *Étude sur les Operations 5 Septembre*, p.126.
33 Clément, *Campagne de 1813*, p.426.
34 Fabry, *Étude sur les Opérations 5 Septembre*, p.175.

35 Fabry, *Étude sur les Opérations 5 Septembre*, p.194.

36 Fabry, Fabry, *Étude sur les Opérations 5 Septembre*, p.195. There are contrary accounts of this battle and the work of some artists suggests that Blücher was taken prisoner during this engagement.

37 Fabry, *Étude sur les Operations 5 Septembre*, p.197.

38 Simon, *Kriegsereignisse Teplitz und Pirna*, p.83.

39 Fabry, *Étude sur les Opérations 5 Septembre*, p.212.

40 Fabry, *Étude sur les Opérations 5 Septembre*, p.213.

41 Fabry, *Étude sur les Opérations 5 Septembre*, p.214. & Thomas, *Régiment Rhénan*, p.70.

42 Simon, *Kriegsereignisse Teplitz und Pirna*, p.84.

43 Simon, *Kriegsereignisse Teplitz und Pirna*, p.85.

44 Fabry, *Étude sur les Operations 5 Septembre*, p.172.

45 The Army of the Reserve or Polish Reserve Army was a force of second line troops organized in Poland. It consisted of a large number of landwehr units, "combined" regiments (converged depot formations that were made into units usable in the field), and Russian militia units, with a small number of actual line formations.

46 Clément, *Campagne de 1813*, p.431.

47 Fabry, *Opérations 22 Septembre*, p.31.

48 Three squadrons each of the East Prussian National Cavalry Regiment, the Brandenburg Hussar Regiment, the Brandenburg Uhlans, and also two squadrons of Russian dragoons and some Cossacks.

49 Fabry, *Opérations 22 Septembre*, p.32.

50 Fabry, *Opérations 22 Septembre*, p.33.

51 The *geschwindschritt* was the attack pace or fastest marching pace used by the Prussians.

52 Fabry, *Opérations 22 Septembre*, p.34.

53 Fabry, *Opérations 22 Septembre*, p.35.

54 Bonaparte, *Correspondance de Napoléon*, #20626.

55 Clément, *Campagne de 1813*, p.434.

56 Clément, *Campagne de 1813*, p.436.

57 Clément, *Campagne de 1813*, p.438.

58 Czernichev had: Combined Hussar Regiment (3 sqns)(301), Isoum Hussar Regiment (3 sqns)(398), Finland Dragoons (2 sqns)(207), Sisoeff #3 Cossacks (335), Girov Cossack Regiment (298), Grekov #18 Cossack Regiment (334), Vlasov #3 Cossack Regiment (319),Valabin #2 Cossack Regiment (280), and half of a Russian horse battery with four 6-pdrs and two licornes served by about 100 men.

59 Czernicheff, *Königreich Westphalen*, p.105.

60 The garrison consisted of: Grenadiergarde Battalion (1,000), Chasseurgarde Battalion (840), Chasseur-Karabinier Battalion (160), Füsiliergarde Depot (160), Depot/2nd Line Regiment (150), Depot/5th Line Regiment (150), Cadre 2/7th Line Regiment (150), Depot/8th Line Regiment (150), Depots of 1st, 2nd, 3rd, and 4th Light Battalions (300), Garde du Korps (286), Depot/Chevauxlégergarde (140), Guard Hussar Regiment (450 including 300 mounted), Gendarmes (30), Guard 6-pdr Foot Battery (209), Artillery depots (24), Artisan Company (103). In addition, there were veteran and departmental companies, giving a total force of 3,060 infantry, 906 cavalry with 756 horses, and 34 guns.

61 Czernicheff, *Königreich Westphalen*, p.151.

62 Sporschil, *Die Grosse Chronik*, Vol I, p.732.

63 Czernicheff, *Königreich Westphalen*, pp.151-152.

64 Czernicheff, *Königreich Westphalen*, p.190.

65 Sporschil, *Die Grosse Chronik*, Vol I, p.733.

66 The Kassel garrison now consisted of 100 Chevaulégers, 250 Guard Hussars, 100 Chasseurgardes, 100 Chasseur-Karabiniers, 100 men of the 7th Infantry Regiment, Füsiliergarde (40 men), Depots of the 2nd, 5th, and 8th Infantry Regiments (120 men total), and 40 men from the depots of the light battalions. This was a total of 350 mounted cavalry, 500 infantry, and some artillerists and gendarmes.

67 Clément, *Campagne de 1813*, p.439.

68 Weil, *Campagne de 1813*, p.188.

69 Fabry, *Opérations 22 Septembre*, p.155.

70 Fabry, *Opérations 22 Septembre*, p.157.

71 Plotho, *Krieg in Deutschland*, Vol II, pp.233-234.

72   It is possible that this force was part of a provisional cavalry regiment, which could have contained some members of the 13th Cuirassier Regiment, but Fabry indicates that they were probably Guard Grenadiers à Cheval. If grenadiers, the losses are also exaggerated, for they lost only "4 officers and 50 men" in this engagement.

73   In this instance, *ordre serré* should be interpreted as meaning a closed formation in contrast to a loose or skirmish formation. This means that the Prussian cavalry rode with each man's boots touching the boots of the rider next to him.

74   Fabry, *Opérations 22 Septembre*, p.158.

75   Foucart, *Cavalerie Légère en 1813*, p.129.

76   Fabry, *Opérations 22 Septembre*, p.160.

77   Plotho, *Krieg in Deutschland*, Vol II, pp.233-234.

78   Foucart, *Cavalerie Légère en 1813*, p.130, & Martinien, *Tableaux Tués et Blessés*, p.24.

79   Poniatowski, *Correspondance*, Vol V, pp.436-437.

2 Operations on the Lower Elbe August–September 1813: The Battle of the Göhrde

1   Quistorp, *K.-Russisch-Deutsche Legion*, pp.56-57.

2   Bonaparte, *Correspondance de Napoléon*, #20357.

3   Clément, *Campagne de 1813*, p.440.

4   Quistorp, *K.-Russisch-Deutsche Legion*, p.60.

5   Clément, *Campagne de 1813*, p.441.

6   The Russo-German Legion was formed from German soldiers captured by the Russians from Napoleon's allies during the 1812 campaign.

7   The KGL was the King's German Legion formed from the remnants of the pre-1806 Hanoverian army. It fought extensively in Spain under Wellington. These units of the KGL, the 73rd Foot Regiment, and a rocket battery were the only British forces to participate in the 1813 campaign in Germany.

8   Quistorp, *K.-Russisch-Deutsche Legion*, p.62.

9   Quistorp, *K.-Russisch-Deutsche Legion*, pp.62-63.

10   Quistorp, *K.-Russisch-Deutsche Legion*, p.64.

11   A division of artillery consisted of two guns.

12   Quistorp, *K.-Russisch-Deutsche Legion*, p.65.

13   Quistorp, *K.-Russisch-Deutsche Legion*, pp.66-67.

14   Clément, *Campagne de 1813*, p.442.

15   The landsturm was a militia formation of a lower quality than the landwehr. The landsturm was not intended to take to the field, but was to garrison cities and other strong points, releasing regular forces from that duty, or act as guerrillas.

16   Clément, *Campagne de 1813*, p.444.

17   Bourgue, *3e Régiment d'Infanterie*, p.312.

18   Quistorp, *K.-Russisch-Deutsche Legion*, p.80.

19   Schussler, *Lützowischen Freikorps*, p.101.

20   Quistorp, *K.-Russisch-Deutsche Legion*, p.82.

21   Schussler, *Lützowischen Freikorps*, p.103.

22   Schussler, *Lützowischen Freikorps*, p.103.

23   Schwertfeger, *K.-Deutsche Legion*, Vol II, p.521.

24   Quistorp, *K.-Russisch-Deutsche Legion*, p.84.

25   Schussler, *Lützowischen Freikorps*, p.104.

26   Quistorp, *K.-Russisch-Deutsche Legion*, p.84.

27   Schwertfeger, *K.-Deutsche Legion*, Vol IL p.522.

28   Quistorp, *K.-Russisch-Deutsche Legion*, p.85.

29   Schwertfeger, *K.-Deutsche Legion*, Vol II, pp.522-3.

30   Quistorp, *K.-Russisch-Deutsche Legion*, p.86.

31   Quistorp, *K.-Russisch-Deutsche Legion*, p.87.

32   L.-G., *Aus Hannovers militarischer*, p.291.

33   Schwertfeger, *K.-Deutschen Legion*, Vol II, p.524.

34   Quistorp, *K.-Russisch-Deutsche Legion*, p.89.

35   Quistorp, *K.-Russisch-Deutsche Legion*, p.91.

36   Venzky, *Russisch-Deutsch Legion*, p.103.

37   Quistorp, *K.-Russisch-Deutsche Legion*, pp.94-95.

38   Quistorp, *K.-Russisch-Deutsche Legion*, p.96.

39   Quistorp, *K.-Russisch-Deutsche Legion*, p.99.

40   Quistorp, *K.-Russisch-Deutsche Legion*, p.101.

41   Quistorp, *K.-Russisch-Deutsche Legion*, p.102.

42   Licornes were a special Russian howitzer noted for its significantly longer barrel and greater accuracy than the howitzers used in the rest of Europe. There were 10-pdr and 20-pdr licornes. The smaller were assigned to the 6-pdr batteries and the heavier to the 12-pdr batteries.

43   Schussler, *Lützowischen Freikorps*, p.107 & L.-G., *Aus Hannovers militarischer*, pp.291-292 & Quistorp, *K.-Russisch-Deutsche Legion*, p.267.

44   Clément, *Campagne de 1813*, p.445.

3   The Allies Execute Their Plan to the North 1–15 October 1813: The Battle of Wartenburg

1   Clément, *Campagne de 1813*, p.451.

2   Mirus, *Das Treffen bei Wartenburg*, p.13.

3   Mirus, *Das Treffen bei Wartenburg*, p.40.

4   Mirus, *Das Treffen bei Wartenburg*, p.3.

5   Mirus, *Das Treffen bei Wartenburg*, p.41.

6   Mirus, *Das Treffen bei Wartenburg*, p.32.

7   Mirus, *Das Treffen bei Wartenburg*, p.44.

8   He was accompanied by the first platoon of 6-pdr Foot Battery #1 (four guns) under Lieutenant Baldauf. The remainder of the battery remained by Elster.

9   Mirus, *Das Treffen bei Wartenburg*, p.45.

10   Mirus, *Das Treffen bei Wartenburg*, p.46.

11   Mirus, *Das Treffen bei Wartenburg*, p.47.

12   Prussian General Staff, *Pläne der Schlachten and Treffen,* Vol II, p.60.

13   Mirus, *Das Treffen bei Wartenburg*, pp.48-49.

14   Mirus, *Das Treffen bei Wartenburg*, pp.49-50.

15   Mirus, *Das Treffen bei Wartenburg*, p.51.

16   Mirus, *Das Treffen bei Wartenburg*, p.53.

17   Mirus, *Das Treffen bei Wartenburg*, p.54.

18   Because of the high number of casualties in earlier engagements, the landwehr battalions of Knorr and Kotulinsky were combined into a single battalion.

19   Mirus, *Das Treffen bei Wartenburg*, p.55.

20   Rossler, *Tagebücher*, p.351.

21   Prussian General Staff, *Pläne der Schlachten and Treffen,* Vol II, p.60.

22   Mirus, *Das Treffen bei Wartenburg*, p.57.

23   Rossler, *Tagebücher*, p.353.

24   Prussian General Staff, *Pläne der Schlachten and Treffen,* Vol II, p.62.

25   Mirus, *Das Treffen bei Wartenburg*, p.58.

26   Mirus, *Das Treffen bei Wartenburg*, pp.60-61.

27   GD Beaumont commanded the corps cavalry that had been assigned to the XII Corps before the corps was disbanded. It contained the Westphalian Chevauléger-lanciers and Hessian Chevaulégers.

28   The number taken prisoner seems to vary widely, depending on the sources read, 200-500 being the range. On 15 August these two regiments had a total of 777 officers and men in seven squadrons, but by 15 October they could, between them, field only 221 officers and men in two squadrons. As the brigade did not engage in any significant combat before or after Wartenburg, the loss of 556 officers and men must be heavily attributed to this action, supporting the higher figure.

29   Minis, *Das Treffen bei Wartenburg*, pp.60-61 & Sporschil, *Die Grosse Chronik*, Vol I, p.701.

30   1st, 2nd, and 3rd Combined Battalions respectively.
31   Prussian General Staff, *Pläne der Schlachten and Treffen,* Vol II, p.63.
32   Rossler, *Tagebücher,* pp.355-6.
33   Prussian General Staff, *Pläne der Schlachten and Treffen,* Vol II, p.62. The corps of St.-Priest and Kapzevich were part of the Army of Silesia that Blücher did not engage in the battle.
34   Prussian General Staff, *Pläne der Schlachten and Treffen,* Vol II, p.61.
35   Mirus, *Das Treffen bei Wartenburg,* pp.82-85.
36   Clément, *Campagne de 1813,* p.454.
37   Clément, *Campagne de 1813,* p.459.
38   Clément, *Campagne de 1813,* p.460.
39   Clément, *Campagne de 1813,* p.462.
40   Clément, *Campagne de 1813,* p.467.
41   Clément, *Campagne de 1813,* p.472.
42   Napoleon's Correspondence, #20754.
43   Fabry, *III et V Corps,* p.80.
44   Fabry, *III et V Corps,* p.81.
45   Clément, *Campagne de 1813,* p.483.
46   Clément, *Campagne de 1813,* p.487.
47   Sporschil, *Die Grosse Chronik,* Vol I, p.650.
48   Sporschil, *Die Grosse Chronik,* Vol I, p.651.
49   Sporschil, *Die Grosse Chronik,* Vol I, p.652.
50   Sporschil, *Die Grosse Chronik,* Vol I, p.652.
51   Clément, *Campagne de 1813,* p.486.
52   K.u.K. Kriegsarchivs, *Befreiungskrieg,* Vol V, p.390.
53   Ordnance officer is the German term for an orderly or an aide-de-camp.
54   K.u.K. Kriegsarchiv, *Befreiungskrieg,* Vol V, p.391.
55   K.u.K. Kriegsarchiv, *Befreiungskrieg,* Vol V, p.392.
56   K.u.K. Kriegsarchiv, *Befreiungskrieg,* Vol V, p.393.
57   K.u.K. Kriegsarchiv, *Befreiungskrieg,* Vol V, p.394.
58   K.u.K. Kriegsarchiv, *Befreiungskrieg,* Vol V, p.395.

4 The Army of Bohemia in the South 1–15 October 1813: the Battle of Liebertwolkwitz

1   K.u.K. Kriegsarchiv, *Befreiungskrieg,* Vol V, p.139.
2   K.u.K. Kriegsarchiv, *Befreiungskrieg,* Vol V, p.140.
3   K.u.K. Kriegsarchiv, *Befreiungskrieg,* Vol V, p.141.
4   This Möckern is not the same Möckern where Eugène fought a battle in the spring of 1813.
5   K.u.K. Kriegsarchiv, *Befreiungskrieg,* Vol V, p.142.
6   Poniatowski, *Correspondance,* pp.446-447.
7   K.u.K. Kriegsarchiv, *Befreiungskrieg,* Vol V, p.143.
8   K.u.K. Kriegsarchiv, *Befreiungskrieg,* Vol V, p.144.
9   K.u.K. Kriegsarchiv, *Befreiungskrieg,* Vol V, p.145.
10   *Divisionsmasse* is a unique Austrian formation where two infantry companies broke themselves in half and formed the half-companies one behind the other, forming a dense column. Its use was principally as a defense against cavalry. It was, however, terribly vulnerable to artillery attack.
11   K.u.K. Kriegsarchiv, *Befreiungskrieg,* Vol V, p.146.
12   K.u.K. Kriegsarchiv, *Befreiungskrieg,* Vol V, p.147.
13   K.u.K. Kriegsarchiv, *Befreiungskrieg,* Vol V, p.148.
14   K.u.K. Kriegsarchiv, *Befreiungskrieg,* Vol V, p.149.
15   K.u.K. Kriegsarchiv, *Befreiungskrieg,* Vol V, p.181.
16   K.u.K. Kriegsarchiv, *Befreiungskrieg,* Vol V, p.182.
17   A "division" of infantry in this instance consists of two infantry companies, approximately 300 men if near full strength.

18   K.u.K. Kriegsarchiv, *Befreiungskrieg*, Vol V, p.183.

19   K.u.K. Kriegsarchiv, *Befreiungskrieg*, Vol V, p.184.

20   K.u.K. Kriegsarchiv, *Befreiungskrieg*, Vol V, p.185.

21   The IV Cavalry Corps consisted of the 7th and 8th Light Cavalry Divisions, which were formed entirely from Polish cavalry. The only non-Polish formations were the two horse batteries and train assigned to the 8th Light Cavalry Division.

22   K.u.K. Kriegsarchiv, *Befreiungskrieg*, Vol V, p.202.

23   Lefol's Division contained slightly over 2,000 men and was formed of the 1st and 2nd Erfurt Battalions, 2/54th Line Regiment, and a Bataillon de Marche formed from the 29th Légère, 25th, and 33rd Line Regiments.

24   K.u.K. Kriegsarchiv, *Befreiungskrieg*, Vol V, p.203.

25   K.u.K. Kriegsarchiv, *Befreiungskrieg*, Vol V, p.204.

26   K.u.K. Kriegsarchiv, *Befreiungskrieg*, Vol V, p.205.

27   K.u.K. Kriegsarchiv, *Befreiungskrieg*, Vol V, p.206.

28   K.u.K. Kriegsarchiv, *Befreiungskrieg*, Vol V, p.207.

29   K.u.K. Kriegsarchiv, *Befreiungskrieg*, Vol V, p.208.

30   K.u.K. Kriegsarchiv, *Befreiungskrieg*, Vol V, p.209.

31   K.u.K. Kriegsarchiv, *Befreiungskrieg*, Vol V, p.210.

32   Kandelsdorfer, *Feld-Jäger-Bataillons* No 7, p.84.

33   K.u.K. Kriegsarchiv, *Befreiungskrieg*, Vol V, p.212.

34   The Austrians consisted of two squadrons of the Hohenzollern Chevaulégers, one from the Klenau Chevaulégers, and one from the Kienmayer Hussars. The Prussians consisted of two squadrons each of the 2nd Silesian Hussars and the Silesian National Cavalry Regiment.

35   The 1st Jäger Battalion and the 1/Brod Grenz.

36   Three from the Levenehr Dragoons, four and a half from the Vincent Chevaulégers, and four from the Kaiser Chevaulégers.

37   K.u.K. Kriegsarchiv, *Befreiungskrieg*, Vol V, p.212.

38   Kandelsdorfer, *Feld-Jäger-Bataillons* No 7, p.85.

39   A "klumpen" was a quickly formed defensive formation designed to protect skirmishers from enemy cavalry. An officer or NCO would call his men to rally on him. They would place their backs against him and face outwards with their bayonets, forming a knot of men. It was absolutely immobile, but offered some credible defense against a surprise cavalry attack.

40   Kandelsdorfer, *Feld-Jäger-Bataillons* No 7., p.86.

41   K.u.K. Kriegsarchiv, *Befreiungskrieg*, Vol V, p.214.

42   K.u.K. Kriegsarchiv, *Befreiungskrieg*, Vol V, p.215.

43   During the battles around Wachau on the first day of the Battle of Leipzig, Napoleon came close to breaking the Austrian lines and forcing their withdrawal from the battlefield. Had he done so, he could have turned on and crushed the other allied armies that stood around Leipzig.

44   K.u.K. Kriegsarchiv, *Befreiungskrieg*, Vol V, p.396.

45   K.u.K. Kriegsarchiv, *Befreiungskrieg*, Vol V, pp.397-398.

46   von Seidel, *Affaire de Lindenau*, p.112.

47   von Seidel, *Affaire de Lindenau*, p.113.

48   von Seidel, *Affaire de Lindenau*, p.114.

49   Weil, *Campagne de 1813*, p.222. & Friederich, *Herbstfeldzuges*, Vol II, p.441.

50   Both the Neumärk Dragoons and the East Prussian Cuirassiers had four squadrons and a Jäger detachment. The Silesian Uhlans had only two squadrons, two squadrons apparently being detached. Their total force was about 1,000 men and eight cannon.

51   Weil, *Campagne de 1813*, p.223.

52   K.u.K. Kriegsarchiv, *Befreiungskrieg*, Vol V, p.376.

53   Weil, *Campagne de 1813*, p.223.

54   K.u.K. Kriegsarchiv, *Befreiungskrieg*, Vol V, p.377.

55   This is the same officer who precipitated the defection of the Prussian corps from the French army in 1812.

56   Weil, *Campagne de 1813*, p.223.

57 K.u.K. Kriegsarchiv, *Befreiungskrieg*, Vol V, p.378.

58 The 2nd Silesian Hussar Regiment and 2/, 3/Silesian Uhlan Regiment under the command of Major von Schmiedeberg.

59 K.u.K. Kriegsarchiv, *Befreiungskrieg*, Vol V, p.379.

60 Friederich, *Herbstfeldzuges*, Vol II, p.444.

61 Friederich, *Herbstfeldzuges*, Vol II, p.445.

62 K.u.K. Kriegsarchiv, *Befreiungskrieg*, Vol V, p.380.

63 Friederich, *Herbstfeldzuges*, Vol II, p.446.

64 Weil, *Campagne de 1813*, p.225. & K.u.K. Kriegsarchiv, *Befreiungskrieg*, Vol V, p.381.

65 K.u.K. Kriegsarchiv, *Befreiungskrieg*, Vol V, p.382.

66 K.u.K. Kriegsarchiv, *Befreiungskrieg*, Vol V, p.383.

67 Friederich, *Herbstfeldzuges*, Vol II, p.449.

68 K.u.K. Kriegsarchiv, *Befreiungskrieg*, Vol V, p.384.

69 Friederich, *Herbstfeldzuges*, Vol II, p.450.

70 Weil, *Campagne de 1813*, p.225.

71 K.u.K. Kriegsarchiv, *Befreiungskrieg*, Vol V, p.387.

72 This is an Austrian regiment, not one from the state of Württemberg. It was common practice in the Austrian army to name regiments after princes of the Holy Roman Empire, of which Württemberg was one.

73 K.u.K. Kriegsarchiv, *Befreiungskrieg*, Vol V, p.389.

74 Weil, *Campagne de 1813*, p.226.

5 The Battle to the South 16 October 1813

1 The allied figures presented are a compilation figures drawn from Quistorp and the Austrian Kriegsarchiv, which are on a regimental level. The French figures are drawn from-Quistorp and Rousset. There is considerable disparity in the various figures for the strengths of the armies present. A selection of those figures is:

		Total	Infantry	Cav.	Guns
Quistorp	Allies	193,920	154,185	39,735	778
	French	187,110	147,158	39,952	734
Sporschil	Allies	301,500			
	French	171,000			
Vaudoncourt	Allies	349,000			
	French	156,800			
Kausler	Allies	290,150			
	French	140,000			

2 The term "Armeeabteilung" is probably best translated as "Army Wing", though it can be interpreted to mean a "Corps". An "abteilung" is a division and, in the military sense, is normally interpreted as a "detachment" or, on occasions, as a "battalion". However, in this particular usage, where an "abteilung" contains "corps", "divisions", etc., the period term "wing" is the best interpretation.

3 Pelet, *Principales Opérations*, p.233.

4 K.u.K. Kriegsarchiv, *Befreiungskrieg*, Vol V, p.443.

5 Plotho, *Relation de la Bataille de Leipzig*, p.16.

6 Sporschil, *Die Grosse Chronik*, Vol I, p.774.

7 Barclay de Tolly was serving as a supernumerary officer and assigned to command this "wing" during the battle, but he did not have a regularly assigned command or position in the army's order of battle.

8 Sporschil, *Die Grosse Chronik*, Vol I, p.778.

9 This division consisted of the 8th, 16th, and Vistula Regiments.

10 Sporschil, *Die Grosse Chronik*, Vol I, p.771.

11 Pelet, *Principales Opérations*, p.231.

12 Pelet, *Principales Opérations*, p.232.

13 K.u.K. Kriegsarchiv, *Befreiungskrieg*, Vol V, p.444.

14 Plotho, Relation de la Bataille de Leipzig, p.17.

15 Sporschil, *Die Grosse Chronik*, Vol I, p.783.
16 K.u.K. Kriegsarchiv, *Befreiungskrieg*, Vol V, p.445.
17 K.u.K. Kriegsarchiv, *Befreiungskrieg*, Vol V, p.l44.
18 Sporschil, *Die Grosse Chronik*, Vol I, p.784.
19 This brigade contained the Krementsoug and Minsk Regiments.
20 Sporschil, *Die Grosse Chronik*, Vol I, p.785.
21 Sporschil, *Die Grosse Chronik*, Vol I, p.786.
22 Plotho, *Relation de la Bataille de Leipzig*, p.20.
23 K.u.K. Kriegsarchiv, *Befreiungskrieg*, Vol V, p.450.
24 Sporschil, *Die Grosse Chronik*, Vol I, p.787 & Plotho, *Relation de la Bataille de Leipzig*, p.21.
26 K.u.K. Kriegsarchiv, *Befreiungskrieg*, Vol V, p.449.
27 Plotho, *Relation de la Bataille de Leipzig*, p.22.
28 K.u.K. Kriegsarchiv, *Befreiungskrieg*, Vol V, p.449.
29 K.u.K. Kriegsarchiv, *Befreiungskrieg*, Vol V, p.450.
30 Pelet, *Principales Opérations*, p.239.
31 Sporschil, *Die Grosse Chronik*, Vol I, p.787.
32 Pelet, *Principales Opérations*, p.245.
33 K.u.K. Kriegsarchiv, *Befreiungskrieg*, Vol V, p.461.
34 K.u.K. Kriegsarchiv, *Befreiungskrieg*, Vol V, p.462.
35 Pelet, *Principales Opérations*, p.246.
36 Sporschil, *Die Grosse Chronik*, Vol I, p.788.
37 K.u.K. Kriegsarchiv, *Befreiungskrieg*, Vol V, p.464.
38 Sébastiani commanded the 2nd and 4th Light Cavalry Divisions and the 4th Heavy Cavalry Division.
39 "Windmühlenberg" is translated as "Windmill Heights", but research did not reveal if this is the name of a specific hill or a generic term used for any and every hill upon which a windmill sat.
40 K.u.K. Kriegsarchiv, *Befreiungskrieg*, Vol V, p.464.
41 Pelet, *Principales Opérations*, p.250.
42 In German "graben" means either ditch or canal. This is, therefore, the Pös ditch or canal. Unfortunately, it does not appear on any of the maps reviewed and its precise nature could not be determined. As it did not figure as a major obstacle it was probably little more than a drainage ditch.
43 This redoubt was, apparently, a work left over from either the Thirty Years War or the Great Northern War. It was not a new work and has no relationship with Bernadotte's Army of the North.
44 K.u.K. Kriegsarchiv, *Befreiungskrieg*, Vol V, p.465.
45 K.u.K. Kriegsarchiv, *Befreiungskrieg*, Vol V, p.466.
46 Plotho, *Relation de la Bataille de Leipzig*, pp.31-32.
47 K.u.K. Kriegsarchiv, *Befreiungskrieg*, Vol V, p.466.
48 K.u.K. Kriegsarchiv, *Befreiungskrieg*, Vol V, p.467.
49 K.u.K. *Kriegsarchiv, Befreiungskrieg*, Vol V, p.468.
50 The 2/2nd West Prussian Regiment and two battalions of the 9th Silesian Landwehr Regiment. The Silesians had been reorganized and the lst, 3rd, and 4th Battalions stood as a single converged battalion. The 2nd Battalion was still of sufficient strength to operate as a battalion.
51 K.u.K. Kriegsarchiv, *Befreiungskrieg*, Vol V, p.469.
52 Plotho, *Relation de la Bataille de Leipzig*, p.31.
53 These three battalions were the 2/2nd West Prussians and the two battalions of the 9th Silesian Landwehr Regiment under Major Troschke (combined lst, 3rd, and 4th Bns) and Captain Heugel (2nd Bn), who had replaced the badly wounded Major Below.
54 The attack pace or *skoryi szag* was 100 to 110 paces per minute and, in fact, slower than the French *pas de charge* which was 120 paces per minute.
55 Plotho, *Relation de la Bataille de Leipzig*, p.25.
56 Schvichov commanded the 1/2nd Silesian, 1/11th Reserve, and the 10th Silesian Landwehr Regiments.
57 K.u.K. Kriegsarchiv, *Befreiungskrieg*, Vol V, p.446.
38 K.u.K. Kriegsarchiv, *Befreiungskrieg*, Vol V, p.470.
59 Plotho, *Relation de la Bataille de Leipzig*, p.19.

60 Sporschil, *Die Grosse Chronik*, Vol I, p.796.

61 Sporschil, *Die Grosse Chronik*, Vol I, p.797 & Plotho, *Relation de la Bataille de Leipzig*, p.29.

62 K.u.K. Kriegsarchiv, *Befreiungskrieg*, Vol V, p.471.

63 K.u.K. Kriegsarchiv, *Befreiungskrieg*, Vol V, p.472.

64 Gudovich's Brigade consisted of the Military Order Cuirassier Regiment and the Little Russia Cuirassier Regiment.

65 Pelet, *Principales Opérations*, pp.252-253.

66 Plotho, *Relation de la Bataille de Leipzig*, p.26.

67 K.u.K. Kriegsarchiv, *Befreiungskrieg*, Vol V, p.474.

68 Each Austrian heavy cavalry regiment consisted of six squadrons. Squadrons were organized by pairs into "divisions". These divisions were named after various officer ranks, i.e. the Oberstendivision, Oberstleutnantsdivision, and Majorsdivision.

69 Sporschil, *Die Grosse Chronik*, Vol I, p.789.

70 Pelet, *Principales Opérations*, pp.252-253.

71 Martinien, *Tableaux*, pp.89-90.

72 K.u.K. Kriegsarchiv, *Befreiungskrieg*, Vol V, p.475.

73 Sporschil, *Die Grosse Chronik*, Vol I, p.790.

74 K.u.K. Kriegsarchiv, *Befreiungskrieg*, Vol V, p.476.

75 K.u.K. Kriegsarchiv, *Befreiungskrieg*, Vol V, p.477.

76 K.u.K. Kriegsarchiv, *Befreiungskrieg*, Vol V, p.477.

77 K.u.K. Kriegsarchiv, *Befreiungskrieg*, Vol V, p.478.

78 Pelet, *Principales Opérations*, p.254.

79 K.u.K. Kriegsarchiv, *Befreiungskrieg*, Vol V, p.479.

80 Pelet, *Principales Opérations*, p.251.

81 Sporschil, *Die Grosse Chronik*, Vol I, p.790.

82 Plotho, *Relation de la Bataille de Leipzig*, p.26.

83 K.u.K. Kriegsarchiv, *Befreiungskrieg*, Vol V, p.452.

84 K.u.K. Kriegsarchiv, *Befreiungskrieg*, Vol V, p.482.

85 Pelet, *Principales Opérations*, p.247.

86 Plotho, *Relation de la Bataille de Leipzig*, p.29.

87 K.u.K. Kriegsarchiv, *Befreiungskrieg*, Vol V, p.485.

88 This is probably Masson's battery. Masson had to retreat under fire and was unable to withdraw all of his battery in this attack due to dead horses and the impassible nature of the battlefield. He abandoned four guns and pushed them into a stream. Only two guns and three caissons were saved. Masson and most of his battery died, and the only survivors were an officer, a sergeant, and a few gunners.

89 Pelet, *Principales Opérations*, p.255.

90 K.u.K. Kriegsarchiv, *Befreiungskrieg*, Vol V, p.490.

91 K.u.K. Kriegsarchiv, *Befreiungskrieg*, Vol V, p.492.

92 K.u.K. Kriegsarchiv, *Befreiungskrieg*, Vol V, p.492.

93 Pelet, *Principales Opérations*, pp.259-260.

94 Fabry, *Opérations des III et V Corps*, p.83.

95 Fabry, *Opérations des III et V Corps*, pp.84-85.

96 Fabry, *Opérations des III et V Corps*, p.85.

97 Plotho, *Relation de la Bataille de Leipzig*, p.38.

98 Bistrom normally commanded the brigade containing the Ismailov Guard Infantry Regiment and Guard Jager Infantry Regiment, however, he now appears to be commanding the Guard Jagers, the Finland Guard Regiment, and the Pavlov Guard Grenadiers.

99 K.u.K. Kriegsarchiv, *Befreiungskrieg*, Vol V, p.493.

100 For details of Merveldt's capture see the next chapter.

101 K.u.K. Kriegsarchiv, *Befreiungskrieg*, Vol V, p.494.

102 Plotho, *Relation de la Bataille de Leipzig*, p.52.

103 Plotho, *Relation de la Bataille de Leipzig*, p.40.

104 Plotho, *Relation de la Bataille de Leipzig*, p.52.

6 The Battle to the West: Connewitz and Lindenau 16 October 1813

1   K.u.K. Kriegsarchiv, *Befreiungskrieg*, Vol V, p.453.

2   K.u.K. Kriegsarchiv, *Befreiungskrieg*, Vol V, p.454.

3   Plotho, *Relation de la Bataille de Leipzig*, p.23.

4   K.u.K. Kriegsarchiv, *Befreiungskrieg*, Vol V, p.455.

5   The term used in the original source was *Schloss* which can be translated as either a fortress, a palace, or a large country manor. As the specific meaning was not clear, the term *château* was used, as it has the same spectrum of meanings. In the case of Dölitz it was a substantial building with a large, two story gate house and an enclosed inner court. It had no developed military defenses, other than its inherently high, thick walls and numerous stone buildings.

6   It is probable, though not mentioned in the source document, that Peltzer was followed by a further force of greater strength.

7   Plotho, *Relation de la Bataille de Leipzig*, p.24.

8   K.u.K. Kriegsarchiv, *Befreiungskrieg*, Vol V, p.457.

9   K.u.K. Kriegsarchiv, *Befreiungskrieg*, Vol V, p.457.

10   K.u.K. Kriegsarchiv, *Befreiungskrieg*, Vol V, p.487.

11   K.u.K. Kriegsarchiv, *Befreiungskrieg*, Vol V, p.488.

12   This brigade contained Velites of Turin, Velites of Florence, 1/Saxon Guard Regiment, the Polish Guard Battalion, and the Westphalian Guard Fusilier Battalion.

13   Pelet, *Principales Opérations de la Campagne de 1813*, p.256.

14   K.u.K. Kriegsarchiv, *Befreiungskrieg*, Vol V, p.488.

15   Sporschil, *Die Grosse Chronik*, Vol I, p.802.

16   The *pas de course* was a dead run, though nominally established with a cadence of 250 paces per minute.

17   Zaremba, "Batalion polski Gwardii w 1813 r.", *Bron i Barwa*, p.6.

18   Pelet, *Principales Opérations de la Campagne de 1813*, p.256.

19   K.u.K. Kriegsarchiv, *Befreiungskrieg*, Vol V, p.487.

20   Plotho, *Relation de la Bataille de Leipzig*, p.32.

21   Sporschil, *Die Grosse Chronik*, Vol I, p.802.

22   K.u.K. Kriegsarchiv, *Befreiungskrieg*, Vol V, p.497.

23   K.u.K. Kriegsarchiv, *Befreiungskrieg*, Vol V, p.499.

24   K.u.K. Kriegsarchiv, *Befreiungskrieg*, Vol V, p.499.

25   K.u.K. Kriegsarchiv, *Befreiungskrieg*, Vol V, p.500.

26   Pelet, *Principales Opérations de la Campagne de 1813*, p.213.

27   Weigel's Brigade consisted of the Mariassy and I. Gyulai Infantry Regiments.

28   Von Seidel, *Affaire de Lindenau*, p.116.

29   The 2nd Column contained the 1/Warasdiner St-George Grenz and two battalions of the Fröhlich Infantry Regiment, and 11 Chevauléger squadrons. Two of the Chevauléger squadrons were detached as military police.

30   Liechtenstein's Division had a total of 2,657 men, including 1,857 cavalry. Two Jäger battalions were detached from his division to Hessen-Homburg's and Gyulai's Column. The 1/Broder Grenz, the Jäger Battalion #7, and some of the cavalry were detached to the third column.

31   Sporschil, *Die Grosse Chronik*, Vol I, p.806.

32   Czollich's Brigade contained three battalions of the Kottulinsky Regiment and two of the Kaiser Regiment.

33   Von Seidel, *Affaire de Lindenau*, p.117.

34   Pelet, *Principales Opérations de la Campagne de 1813*, 233.

35   K.u.K. Kriegsarchiv, *Befreiungskrieg*, Vol V, p.500.

36   Quinette commanded a brigade of Defrance's 4th Heavy Cavalry Division.

37   K.u.K. Kriegsarchiv, *Befreiungskrieg*, Vol V, p.502.

38   Von Seidel, *Affaire de Lindenau* , p.118.

39   K.u.K. Kriegsarchiv, *Befreiungskrieg*, Vol V, p.503.

40   K.u.K. Kriegsarchiv, *Befreiungskrieg*, Vol V, p.504.

41   The 8th Légère Regiment was assigned to Belair's Brigade, Morand's 12th Division.

42   Von Seidel, *Affaire de Lindenau*, p.119.

43   Plotho, *Relation de la Bataille de Leipzig*, p.33.
44   Pelet, *Principales Opérations de la Campagne de 1813*, p.235.
45   K.u.K. Kriegsarchiv, *Befreiungskrieg*, Vol V, p.506.
46   The divisionsmasse is a formation where an Austrian battalion breaks into three, two company divisions. These two company groups then break into four half-companies formed in a dense column one half-company wide and four deep. The outer three ranks then face outwards to defend against cavalry. In contrast, the klumpen (clump) is a quick square where the loose skirmishers rush together in a tight knot, all facing outwards. It is also to defend the infantry against cavalry attack.
47   Von Seidel, *Affaire de Lindenau*, p.119.
48   Sporschil, *Die Grosse Chronik*, Vol I, p.808.
49   K.u.K. Kriegsarchiv, Befreiungskrieg, Vol V, p.506.
50   Von Seidel, *Affaire de Lindenau*, p.120.
51   Plotho, *Relation de la Bataille de Leipzig*, p.35.
52   Von Seidel, *Affaire de Lindenau*, p.121.
53   Plotho, *Relation de la Bataille de Leipzig*, p.35 & von Seidel, *Affaire de Lindenau*, p.126.
54   Plotho, *Relation de la Bataille de Leipzig*, p.37.
55   Von Seidel, *Affaire de Lindenau*, p.126.

7 The Battle of Möckern 16 October 1813

1   K.u.K. Kriegsarchiv, *Befreiungskrieg*, Vol V, p.511.
2   K.u.K. Kriegsarchiv, *Befreiungskrieg*, Vol V, p.512.
3   K.u.K. Kriegsarchiv, *Befreiungskrieg*, Vol V, p.514.
4   K.u.K. Kriegsarchiv, *Befreiungskrieg*, Vol V, p.516.
5   K.u.K. Kriegsarchiv, *Befreiungskrieg*, Vol V, p.516.
6   K.u.K. Kriegsarchiv, *Befreiungskrieg*, Vol V, p.517.
7   Marmont, *Mémoires*, Vol V, p.283.
8   K.u.K. Kriegsarchiv, *Befreiungskrieg*, Vol V, p.518.
9   Plotho, *Relation de la Bataille de Leipzig*, p.41.
10   K.u.K. Kriegsarchiv, *Befreiungskrieg*, Vol V, p.519.
11   Plotho, *Relation de la Bataille de Leipzig*, pp.42-43.
12   K.u.K. Kriegsarchiv, *Befreiungskrieg*, Vol V, p.520.
13   K.u.K. Kriegsarchiv, *Befreiungskrieg*, Vol V, p.522.
14   K.u.K. Kriegsarchiv, *Befreiungskrieg*, Vol V, p.522.
15   K.u.K. Kriegsarchiv, *Befreiungskrieg*, Vol V, p.523.
16   K.u.K. Kriegsarchiv, *Befreiungskrieg*, Vol V, p.526.
17   These were the Tannenwald woods.
18   Plotho, *Relation de la Bataille de Leipzig*, p.45.
19   Marmont, *Mémoires*, Vol V, p.284 & Pelet, *Principales Opérations*, p.263.
20   Prussian General Staff, *Pläne der Schlachten und Treffen*, Vol II, p.82.
21   Prussian General Staff, *Pläne der Schlachten und Treffen*, Vol II, p.83.
22   A *point d'appui* is a strong point that provides support for a wing, i.e. a village, impenetrable woods, ridge line, etc.
23   K.u.K. Kriegsarchiv, *Befreiungskrieg*, Vol V, p.528.
24   K.u.K. Kriegsarchiv, *Befreiungskrieg*, Vol V, p.528.
25   Prussian General Staff, *Pläne der Schlachten und Treffen*, Vol II, p.83.
26   The Thuringian Battalion had, during the 1813 Spring campaign been formed as part of the French army, from troops from the Saxon Ducal Houses. However, its recruits were not well disposed towards serving with the French, and when caught on an isolated march, defected to the Prussian army.
27   Plotho, *Relation de la Bataille de Leipzig*, p.47.
28   K.u.K. Kriegsarchiv, *Befreiungskrieg*, Vol V, p.529.
29   K.u.K. Kriegsarchiv, *Befreiungskrieg*, Vol V, p.530.
30   Prussian General Staff, *Pläne der Schlachten und Treffen*, Vol II, p.84.

31   Prussian General Staff, *Pläne der Schlachten und Treffen*, Vol II, p.84.

32   *Vorhut* and *Nachhut* are best translated as "advanced guard" and "rearguard", but in this instance, the *Vorhut* is the advanced guard of the advanced guard, so the German term was left so as to minimize confusion.

33   K.u.K. Kriegsarchiv, *Befreiungskrieg*, Vol V, p.531.

34   This division had only six squadrons of light cavalry and five squadrons of dragoons, plus a half-horse battery.

35   This division was a division in name only. It had a strength of five squadrons of dragoons and one squadron from the 13th Cuirassier Regiment. In addition, it had a half-horse battery.

36   K.u.K. Kriegsarchiv, *Befreiungskrieg*, Vol V, p.532.

37   K.u.K. Kriegsarchiv, *Befreiungskrieg*, Vol V, p.526.

38   Prussian General Staff, *Pläne der Schlachten und Treffen*, Vol II, p.85.

39   Prussian General Staff, *Pläne der Schlachten und Treffen*, Vol II, p.86.

40   K.u.K. Kriegsarchiv, *Befreiungskrieg*, Vol V, p.533.

41   Marmont, *Mémoires*, Vol V, p.284 & Pelet, *Principales Opérations*, p.263.

42   Prussian General Staff, *Pläne der Schlachten und Treffen*, Vol II, p.88.

43   K.u.K. Kriegsarchiv, *Befreiungskrieg*, Vol V, p.534.

44   Plotho, *Relation de la Bataille de Leipzig*, p.48.

45   K.u.K. Kriegsarchiv, *Befreiungskrieg*, Vol V, p.353 & Plotho, *Relation de la Bataille de Leipzig*, p.49.

46   Marmont, *Mémoires*, Vol V, p.287.

47   K.u.K. Kriegsarchiv, *Befreiungskrieg*, Vol V, p.536.

48   These were probably the five squadrons of dragoons.

49   Prussian General Staff, *Pläne der Schlachten und Treffen*, Vol II, p.89.

50   Plotho, *Relation de la Bataille de Leipzig*, p.48.

51   The work *Pläne der Schlachten und Treffen* lists the New Russia Dragoon Regiment, but this is, in fact, either the Kargopol or Kinburn Dragoon Regiment. The New Russian Dragoons were serving in St.-Priest's Corps.

52   Prussian General Staff, *Pläne der Schlachten und Treffen*, Vol II, p.92.

53   Prussian General Staff, *Pläne der Schlachten und Treffen*, Vol II, p.93. This work indicates that it was the eagle of the 125th Line Regiment, but further research revealed that to be a typographical error and the actual eagle captured was that of the 145th.

54   Prussian General Staff, *Pläne der Schlachten und Treffen*, Vol II, p.94.

55   Marmont, *Mémoires*, Vol V, p.285.

56   K.u.K. Kriegsarchiv, *Befreiungskrieg*, Vol V, p.538.

57   Prussian General Staff, *Pläne der Schlachten und Treffen*, Vol II, p.90.

58   K.u.K. Kriegsarchiv, *Befreiungskrieg*, Vol V, p.539.

59   This maneuver is when platoons turn in inverted order to the right.

60   Prussian General Staff, *Pläne der Schlachten und Treffen*, Vol H, p.91.

61   This is the notorious "Guard Marine" Battalion whose eagle was captured. In fact, it was not an Imperial Guard unit, but a force of marine artillery converted into an infantry battalion, part of one of the 1st Marine Infantry Regiment, of Marmont's VI Corps.

62   Plotho, *Relation de la Bataille de Leipzig*, p.50.

63   Pelet, *Principales Opérations*, p.264.

64   K.u.K. Kriegsarchiv, *Befreiungskrieg*, Vol V, p.539.

65   K.u.K. Kriegsarchiv, *Befreiungskrieg*, Vol V, p.540.

66   Rossler, *Tagebücher*, p.361.

67   K.u.K. Kriegsarchiv, *Befreiungskrieg*, Vol V, p.541.

68   K.u.K. Kriegsarchiv, *Befreiungskrieg*, Vol V, p.542.

69   K.u.K. Kriegsarchiv, *Befreiungskrieg*, Vol V, p.542.

70   K.u.K. Kriegsarchiv, *Befreiungskrieg*, Vol V, p.543.

8 The Second Day of the Battle 17 October 1813

1   K.u.K. Kriegsarchiv, *Befreiungskrieg*, Vol V, p.544.

2   K.u.K. Kriegsarchiv, *Befreiungskrieg*, Vol V, p.545.

3 K.u.K. Kriegsarchiv, *Befreiungskrieg*, Vol V, p.546.
4 K.u.K. Kriegsarchiv, *Befreiungskrieg*, Vol V, p.547.
5 Plotho, *Relation de la Bataille de Leipzig*, p.54.
6 K.u.K. Kriegsarchiv, *Befreiungskrieg*, Vol V, p.547.
7 K.u.K. Kriegsarchiv, *Befreiungskrieg*, Vol V, p.548.
8 K.u.K. Kriegsarchiv, *Befreiungskrieg*, Vol V, p.549.
9 K.u.K. Kriegsarchiv, *Befreiungskrieg*, Vol V, p.550.
10 K.u.K. Kriegsarchiv, *Befreiungskrieg*, Vol V, p.550.
11 K.u.K. Kriegsarchiv, *Befreiungskrieg*, Vol V, p.552.
12 Plotho, *Relation de la Bataille de Leipzig*, p.55.
13 K.u.K. Kriegsarchiv, *Befreiungskrieg*, Vol V, pp.553-4.
14 K.u.K. Kriegsarchiv, *Befreiungskrieg*, Vol V, p.554.
15 K.u.K. Kriegsarchiv, *Befreiungskrieg*, Vol V, p.555.
16 Rossler, *Tagebücher*, p.361.
17 Von Quistorp, *Nord-Armee*, Vol II, p.223.
18 K.u.K. Kriegsarchiv, *Befreiungskrieg*, Vol V, p.556.
19 Tarotino was a battle fought shortly after the French occupation of Moscow in 1812, where the Russians surprised Murat and gave his army wing a serious thrashing.
20 Plotho, *Relation de la Bataille de Leipzig*, p.56.
21 K.u.K. Kriegsarchiv, *Befreiungskrieg*, Vol V, p.556.
22 K.u.K. Kriegsarchiv, *Befreiungskrieg*, Vol V, p.558.
23 K.u.K. Kriegsarchiv, *Befreiungskrieg*, Vol V, p.559.
24 K.u.K. Kriegsarchiv, *Befreiungskrieg*, Vol V, p.560.
25 A march of 42 kilometers (26.25 miles) in a single day by an Austrian column represents a massive effort by the Austrian army, which usually limited its marches to 15 or so miles per day. In contrast the French were known to march 50-60 or more miles on a single day and maintain rates of 30 miles per day for several days in a row.
26 K.u.K. Kriegsarchiv, *Befreiungskrieg*, Vol V, p.561.
27 K.u.K. Kriegsarchiv, *Befreiungskrieg*, Vol V, p.557.
28 Plotho, *Relation de la Bataille de Leipzig*, p.56.
29 Plotho, *Relation de la Bataille de Leipzig*, p.57.
30 Von Quistorp, *Nord-Armee*, Vol II, p.223.
31 Plotho, *Relation de la Bataille de Leipzig*, p.57.
32 K.u.K. Kriegsarchiv, *Befreiungskrieg*, Vol V, p.567.
33 Von Quistorp, *Nord-Armee*, Vol II, p.224.
34 Von Quistorp, *Nord-Armee*, Vol II, p.225.
35 K.u.K. Kriegsarchiv, *Befreiungskrieg*, Vol V, p.563.
36 K.u.K. Kriegsarchiv, *Befreiungskrieg*, Vol V, p.564.
37 K.u.K. Kriegsarchiv, *Befreiungskrieg*, Vol V, p.566.
38 K.u.K. Kriegsarchiv, *Befreiungskrieg*, Vol V, p.566.
39 K.u.K. Kriegsarchiv, *Befreiungskrieg*, Vol V, p.568.
40 K.u.K. Kriegsarchiv, *Befreiungskrieg*, Vol V, p.569.
41 K.u.K. Kriegsarchiv, *Befreiungskrieg*, Vol V, p.570.
42 K.u.K. Kriegsarchiv, *Befreiungskrieg*, Vol V, p.571.
43 K.u.K. Kriegsarchiv, *Befreiungskrieg*, Vol V, p.572.
44 K.u.K. Kriegsarchiv, *Befreiungskrieg*, Vol V, pp.573-4.
45 K.u.K. Kriegsarchiv, *Befreiungskrieg*, Vol V, p.575.
46 K.u.K. Kriegsarchiv, *Befreiungskrieg*, Vol V, pp.576-7.
47 K.u.K. Kriegsarchiv, *Befreiungskrieg*, Vol V, p.578.
48 Plotho, *Relation de la Bataille de Leipzig*, p.61.

9 The Battles to the South: the Third Day of Battle 18 October 1813

1   K.u.K. Kriegsarchiv, *Befreiungskrieg*, Vol V, p.587.
2   Plotho, *Relation de la Bataille de Leipzig*, p.62.
3   K.u.K. Kriegsarchiv, *Befreiungskrieg*, Vol V, p.588.
4   K.u.K. Kriegsarchiv, *Befreiungskrieg*, Vol V, p.589.
5   Plotho, *Relation de la Bataille de Leipzig*, p.63.
6   The actions of the columns of Bernadotte and Blücher are discussed in the next chapter.
7   Plotho, *Relation de la Bataille de Leipzig*, pp.64-65.
8   K.u.K. Kriegsarchiv, *Befreiungskrieg*, Vol V, p.596.
9   Pelet, *Principales Opérations*, p.290.
10   K.u.K. Kriegsarchiv, *Befreiungskrieg*, Vol V, p.597.
11   K.u.K. Kriegsarchiv, *Befreiungskrieg*, Vol V, p.599.
12   K.u.K. Kriegsarchiv, *Befreiungskrieg*, Vol V, p.600.
13   Plotho, *Relation de la Bataille de Leipzig*, p.68.
14   K.u.K. Kriegsarchiv, *Befreiungskrieg*, Vol V, p.601.
15   Pelet, *Principales Opérations*, p.293.
16   Then von Hessen-Homburg was replaced by General Colloredo.
17   K.u.K. Kriegsarchiv, *Befreiungskrieg*, Vol V, p.602.
18   K.u.K. Kriegsarchiv, *Befreiungskrieg*, Vol V, pp.603-4.
19   This hill received its name after the battle. *Monarchenhügel* means "monarch's hill" and commemorates their presence on this hill during the battle.
20   K.u.K. Kriegsarchiv, *Befreiungskrieg*, Vol V, pp.605-6.
21   The *geschwindschritt* means double quick pace.
22   Plotho, *Relation de la Bataille de Leipzig*, p.69.
23   Plotho, *Relation de la Bataille de Leipzig*, p.70.
24   K.u.K. Kriegsarchiv, *Befreiungskrieg*, Vol V, p.614.
25   K.u.K. Kriegsarchiv, *Befreiungskrieg*, Vol V, p.614.
26   Plotho, *Relation de la Bataille de Leipzig*, p.71.
27   Plotho, *Relation de la Bataille de Leipzig*, pp.71-72.
28   Though technically "regiments" these units seldom numbering more than a squadron apiece.
29   K.u.K. Kriegsarchiv, *Befreiungskrieg*, Vol V, pp.615-6.
30   K.u.K. Kriegsarchiv, *Befreiungskrieg*, Vol V, pp.590-1.
31   Plotho, *Relation de la Bataille de Leipzig*, p.74.
32   K.u.K. Kriegsarchiv, *Befreiungskrieg*, Vol V, p.591.
33   The identification of this formation is uncertain. It was probably Desfour's Brigade, which was assigned to Mayer's Division.
34   K.u.K. Kriegsarchiv, *Befreiungskrieg*, Vol V, pp.592-3.
35   In this instance, a division consists of two companies.
36   Plotho, *Relation de la Bataille de Leipzig*, p.75.
37   K.u.K. Kriegsarchiv, *Befreiungskrieg*, Vol V, p.594.
38   Von Barsewisch, *Grossherzoglich Badischen Leib-Grenadier-Regiments*, p.148.
39   K.u.K. Kriegsarchiv, *Befreiungskrieg*, Vol V, pp.595-6.
40   Plotho, *Relation de la Bataille de Leipzig*, p.77.
41   K.u.K. Kriegsarchiv, *Befreiungskrieg*, Vol V, pp.620-1.
42   Plotho, *Relation de la Bataille de Leipzig*, p.79.
43   K.u.K. Kriegsarchiv, *Befreiungskrieg*, Vol V, pp.617-8.
44   K.u.K. Kriegsarchiv, *Befreiungskrieg*, Vol V, pp.608-9.
45   Rossler, *Tagebücher*, p.361.
46   K.u.K. Kriegsarchiv, *Befreiungskrieg*, Vol V, pp.610-1.
47   K.u.K. Kriegsarchiv, *Befreiungskrieg*, Vol V, p.612.
48   Pelet, *Principales Opérations*, p.292.
49   Plotho, *Relation de la Bataille de Leipzig*, p.87.
50   Plotho, *Relation de la Bataille de Leipzig*, p.88.

10 The Battles to the North and West 18 October 1813

1   Plotho, *Relation de la Bataille de Leipzig*, p.80.
2   K.u.K. Kriegsarchiv, *Befreiungskrieg*, Vol V, p.618.
3   This was probably three normal Russian 12-pdr batteries. Each battery normally consisted of four 20-pdr licornes, four medium 12-pdr cannon, and four light 12-pdr cannon.
4   Plotho, *Relation de la Bataille de Leipzig*, p.81.
5   K.u.K. Kriegsarchiv, *Befreiungskrieg*, Vol V, p.620.
6   Von Quistorp, *Nord-Armee*, Vol II, p.230.
7   Guilleminot's 13th Division had been detached to join Bertrand.
8   Plotho, *Relation de la Bataille de Leipzig*, p.82.
9   Marmont, *Mémoires*, Vol V, p.292.
10   Marmont, *Mémoires*, Vol V, p.293.
11   Von Quistorp, *Nord-Armee*, Vol II, p.234.
12   Fabry, *Opérations des III et V Corps en 1813*, p.87.
13   Fabry, *Opérations des III et V Corps en* 1813, p.87.
14   K.u.K. Kriegsarchiv, *Befreiungskrieg*, Vol V, pp.621-2.
15   K.u.K. Kriegsarchiv, *Befreiungskrieg*, Vol V, p.623.
16   Von Quistorp, *Nord-Armee*, Vol II, p.237.
17   K.u.K. Kriegsarchiv, *Befreiungskrieg*, Vol V, pp.624-5.
18   Von Quistorp, *Nord-Armee*, Vol II, p.245.
19   K.u.K. Kriegsarchiv, *Befreiungskrieg*, Vol V, p.631.
20   Von Quistorp, *Nord-Armee*, Vol II, p.238.
21   Von Quistorp, *Nord-Armee*, Vol II, pp.245-246.
22   Bogue's Rocket Battery had been assigned to Wallmoden's Corps, but had been detached and sent south to join Bernadotte.
23   K.u.K. Kriegsarchiv, *Befreiungskrieg*, Vol V, p.627.
24   Von Quistorp, *Nord-Armee*, p.239.
25   K.u.K. Kriegsarchiv, *Befreiungskrieg*, Vol V, p.628.
26   The Saxon Hussar Regiment now had about 200 men.
27   Von Quistorp, *Nord-Armee*, Vol II, p.239.
28   When this unit defected, only two 6-pdr guns and two howitzers passed over to the allies.
29   K.u.K. Kriegsarchiv, *Befreiungskrieg*, Vol V, p.629.
30   Described as they were deployed, east to west.
31   Von Quistorp, *Nord-Armee*, Vol II, p.243.
32   Fabry, *Opérations des III et V Corps*, p.88.
33   Fabry, *Opérations des III et V Corps*, p.89.
34   Fabry, *Opérations des III et V Corps*, p.89.
35   Von Quistorp, *Nord-Armee*, Vol II, p.246.
36   Fabry, *Opérations des III et V Corps*, p.90.
37   Plotho, *Relation de la Bataille de Leipzig*, p.83.
38   Daugeranville's Brigade was from the 2nd Cuirassier Division, II Cavalry Corps, under Sébastiani.
39   Horse Batteries #5, #6, and #11: 24 guns; 6-pdr Foot Batteries #5, #10, and #16: 24 guns; 12-pdr Foot Batteries #4 and #5: 16 guns; Russian 12-pdr Position Battery #7: 12 guns
40

Rounds fired	Round shot	Shell	Canister
Horse Battery #5	126	36	–
Horse Battery #6	284	58	44
Horse Battery #11	197	58	76
6-pdr Foot Battery #5	361	100	154
6-pdr Foot Battery #10	149	35	52
6-pdr Foot Battery #16	280	28	–
12-pdr Foot Batteries #4	271	69	101
12-pdr Foot Batteries #5	191	47	6

41   K.u.K. Kriegsarchiv, *Befreiungskrieg*, Vol V, p.632.

42   Von Quistorp, *Nord-Armee*, Vol II, p.249.

43   Plotho, *Relation de la Bataille de Leipzig*, pp.83-84.

44   Von Quistorp, *Nord-Armee*, Vol II, p.249.

45   Von Quistorp, *Nord-Armee*, Vol II, p.251.

46   K.u.K. Kriegsarchiv, *Befreiungskrieg*, Vol V, p.635.

47   Von Quistorp, *Nord-Armee*, Vol II, p.257.

48   Plotho, *Relation de la Bataille de Leipzig*, p.85.

49   K.u.K. Kriegsarchiv, *Befreiungskrieg*, Vol V, p.626.

50   Fabry, *Opérations des III et V Corps*, p.87.

51   Von Quistorp, *Nord-Armee*, Vol II, p.258.

52   Von Quistorp, *Nord-Armee*, Vol II, p.259.

11 The French Retreat 19 October 1813

1   Plotho, *Relation de la Bataille de Leipzig*, p.89.

2   Marmont, *Mémoires*, Vol V, pp.297-298.

3   Plotho, *Relation de la Bataille de Leipzig*, p.90.

4   Plotho, *Relation de la Bataille de Leipzig*, p.91.

5   Von Barsewisch, *Grossherzoglich Badischen Leib-Grenadier-Regiments*, p.150.

6   Plotho, *Relation de la Bataille de Leipzig*, pp.94-95.

7   Plotho, *Relation de la Bataille de Leipzig*, p.96.

8   Marmont, *Mémoires*, Vol V, p.298.

9   Marmont, *Mémoires*, Vol V, p.299.

10   Plotho, *Relation de la Bataille de Leipzig*, p.97.

11   Marmont, *Mémoires*, Vol V, p.300.

12   Marmont, *Mémoires*, Vol V, p.302.

13   Martinien, *Tableau*, pp.14-15, 24-25.

14   Plotho, *Relation de la Bataille de Leipzig*, p.103.

12 The Fox and Hounds 20 October–29 October 1813

1   Dodge, *Napoleon*, Vol IV, p.273.

2   Bonaparte, *Correspondance*, #20817.

3   Sporschil, *Grosse Chronik*, Vol I, p.950.

4   Sporschil, *Grosse Chronik*, Vol I, p.951.

5   Sporschil, *Grosse Chronik*, Vol I, p.952.

6   Sporschil, *Grosse Chronik*, Vol I, p.955.

7   Sporschil, *Grosse Chronik*, Vol I, p.956.

8   Sporschil, *Grosse Chronik*, Vol I, p.953.

9   Dodge, *Napoleon*, Vol IV, p.274.

10   Sporschil, *Grosse Chronik*, Vol I, p.954.

11   Sporschil, *Grosse Chronik*, Vol I, p.957.

12   Sporschil, *Grosse Chronik*, Vol I, p.958.

13   Sporschil, *Grosse Chronik*, Vol I, p.959.

14   Sporschil, *Grosse Chronik*, Vol I, pp.960-961.

15   Sporschil, *Grosse Chronik*, Vol I, pp.962-963.

16   Sporschil, *Grosse Chronik*, Vol I, pp.964-965.

17   Sporschil, *Grosse Chronik*, Vol I, pp.966-967.

18   Sporschil, *Grosse Chronik*, Vol I, p.969.

19   Gilardone, *Bayerns Anteil am Herbstfeldzuge*, p.68.

20   Gilardone, *Bayerns Anteil am Herbstfeldzuge*, p.69.

21   The garrison of Würzburg consisted of:

1/, 2/113th Line Regiment—Italian
2/127th Line Regiment—French and Hanseatic
2/128th Line Regiment—French and Hanseatic
2 French artillery companies
70 Det 1/4th French Sapper Battalion
70 men from the 13th Hussar Regiment—Italians, 500 men from the Würzburg depot—mostly sick and invalided
100 Würzburg artillerists

22 Gilardone, *Bayerns Anteil am Herbstfeldzuge*, p.70.
23 Gilardone, *Bayerns Anteil am Herbstfeldzuge*, p.72.
24 Gilardone, *Bayerns Anteil am Herbstfeldzuge*, p.73.
25 A 12-pdr gun is a field gun and is quite incapable of any serious siege effort, if the fortress is at all maintained and consists of anything other than simple field earthworks. Napoleon found this to be so, when he attempted to take Smolensk in 1812 with nothing heavier than 12-pdr field guns.
26 Gilardone, *Bayerns Anteil am Herbstfeldzuge*, p.74.
27 Gilardone, *Bayerns Anteil am Herbstfeldzuge*, p.81.
28 Gilardone, *Bayerns Anteil am Herbstfeldzuge*, p.82.
29 Generals Grouvel and Guérin commanded the 56th Colonne de Marche and 55th Column de Marche respectively.
30 Gilardone, *Bayerns Anteil am Herbstfeldzuge*, p.83.
31 Sporschil, *Grosse Chronik*, Vol I, p.971.
32 Gilardone, *Bayerns Anteil am Herbstfeldzuge*, p.84.
33 Gilardone, *Bayerns Anteil am Herbstfeldzuge*, p.85.
31 Gilardone, *Bayerns Anteil am Herbstfeldzuge*, p.87.
35 Gilardone, *Bayerns Anteil am Herbstfeldzuge*, p.88.
36 These two regiments were part of Exelman's 4th Light Cavalry Division, Sébastiani's II Cavalry Corps.
37 Gilardone, *Bayerns Anteil am Herbstfeldzuge*, p.89.
38 Gilardone, *Bayerns Anteil am Herbstfeldzuge*, p.90.
39 Dodge, *Napoleon*, Vol IV, p.276.

13 The French Fall Back on the Rhine 28 October-31 December 1813: The Battle of Hanau

1   Gilardone, *Bayerns Anteil*, p.91.
2   Gilardone, *Bayerns Anteil*, p.92.
3   Von Guttenberg, *Bayerische Nationalgarde*, p.215.
4   Gilardone, *Bayerns Anteil*, p.93.
5   Gilardone, *Bayerns Anteil*, p.94.
6   Von Guttenberg, *Bayerische Nationalgarde*, p.216.
7   Gilardone, *Bayerns Anteil*, p.95.
8   Gilardone, *Bayerns Anteil*, p.96.
9   Gilardone, *Bayerns Anteil*, p.97.
10 Von Guttenberg, *Bayerische Nationalgarde*, p.217.
11 Gilardone, *Bayerns Anteil*, p.98.
12 Von Guttenberg, *Bayerische Nationalgarde*, p.218.
13 Plotho, *Combat de Hanau*, p.149.
14 Gilardone, *Bayerns Anteil*, p.99.
15 Gilardone, *Bayerns Anteil*, p.103.
16 Gilardone, *Bayerns Anteil*, p.104.
17 Sporschil, *Grosse Chronik*, Vol I, p.1012.
18 Plotho, Combat *de Hanau*, p.150.
19 Gilardone, *Bayerns Anteil*, p.105.
20 Gilardone, *Bayerns Anteil*, p.106.
21 Plotho, *Combat de Hanau*, p.151.

22 Gilardone, *Bayerns Anteil*, p.107.

23 Gilardone, *Bayerns Anteil*, p.108.

24 Gilardone, *Bayerns Anteil*, p.109.

25 Gilardone, *Bayerns Anteil*, p.110.

26 Gilardone, *Bayerns Anteil*, p.111.

27 Sporschil, *Grosse Chronik*, Vol I, p.1014.

28 In this action the 4th Bavarian Light Battalion lost 10 officers and 100 men dead and wounded out of a strength of 20 officers and 546 men present on 8 October.

29 Gilardone, *Bayerns Anteil*, p.112.

30 Von Guttenberg, *Bayerische Nationalgarde*, p.220.

31 Gilardone, *Bayerns Anteil*, p.113.

32 Plotho, *Combat de Hanau*, p.151.

33 Gilardone, *Bayerns Anteil*, p.115 and Sporschil, *Grosse Chronik*, Vol I, p.1016.

34 Gilardone, *Bayerns Anteil*, p.116

35 Gilardone, *Bayerns Anteil*, p.117

36 Gilardone, *Bayerns Anteil*, p.118

37 Sporschil, *Grosse Chronik*, Vol I, p.1016.

38 Plotho, *Combat de Hanau*, p.152.

39 Gilardone, *Bayerns Anteil*, p.119

40 Dodge, *Napoleon*, p.277.

41 Plotho, *Combat de Hanau*, p.152.

42 Gilardone, *Bayerns Anteil*, p.120.

43 Von Guttenberg, *Bayerische Nationalgarde*, p.223.

44 This is the same Cambronne, who at the Battle of Waterloo, reportedly responded to a British call to surrender with the "Mot de Cambronne" (Cambronne's word) or "Merde!"

45 Gilardone, *Bayerns Anteil*, p.122.

46 Marbot, *Mémoires de Baron de Marbot*, p.357.

47 Plotho, *Combat de Hanau*, p.153.

48 Gilardone, *Bayerns Anteil*, p.124.

49 Gilardone, *Bayerns Anteil*, p.123.

50 Gilardone, *Bayerns Anteil*, p.125.

51 Gilardone, *Bayerns Anteil*, p.126.

52 Gilardone, *Bayerns Anteil*, p.127.

53 Plotho, *Combat de Hanau*, p.153.

54 Gilardone, *Bayerns Anteil*, p.128.

55 Gilardone, *Bayerns Anteil*, p.130.

56 Plotho, *Combat de Hanau*, p.153.

57 Gilardone, *Bayerns Anteil*, p.132.

58 Gilardone, *Bayerns Anteil*, p.131.

59 Gilardone, *Bayerns Anteil*, p.133.

60 Von Guttenberg, *Bayerische Nationalgarde*, p.225.

61 Gilardone, *Bayerns Anteil*, p.134.

62 Gilardone, *Bayerns Anteil*, p.135.

63 Maciaga, *k.u.k. galizischen Infanterie-Regiments Feldmarschall Friedrich Josias Prinz zu Sachsen-Coburg-Saalfeld*, Nr. 57, p.375.

64 Plotho, *Combat de Hanau*, p.154.

65 Plotho, *Combat de Hanau*, p.155.

66 Gilardone, *Bayerns Anteil*, p.138.

67 Plotho, *Combat de Hanau*, p.156.

68 Gilardone, *Bayerns Anteil*, p.139.

69 Gilardone, *Bayerns Anteil*, p.140.

70 Gilardone, *Bayerns Anteil*, p.141.

71 Fabry, *Opérations des III et V Corps*, pp.103-4.

14 Operations on the Lower Elbe: Mecklenburg and Holstein October-December 1813

1 Quistorp, *Russisch-Deutsche Legion*, p.116.
2 Mazade, *Correspondance de Davout*, Vol IV, p.297.
3 Mazade, *Correspondance de Davout*, Vol IV, p.300.
4 According to Meddelser fra Krigsarkiverne, Vol 7, p.200, Wallmoden was threatened by Bernadotte in an effort to force Wallmoden to try breaking through the Ratzeburg position.
5 Quistorp, *Russisch-Deutsche Legion*, p.120.
6 Mazade, *Correspondance de Davout*, Vol IV, p.301.
7 Quistorp, *Russisch-Deutsche Legion*, p.121 and Meddelser fra Krigsarkiverne, Vol 7, pp.205.
8 Mazade, *Correspondance de Davout*, Vol IV, p.299.
9 Quistorp, *Russisch-Deutsche Legion*, p.120 and Meddelser fra Krigsarkiverne, Vol 7, pp.208-212.
10 Mazade, *Correspondance de Davout*, Vol IV, p.305.
11 Mazade, *Correspondance de Davout*, Vol IV, p.307.
12 Mazade, *Correspondance de Davout*, Vol IV, p.308.
13 Mazade, *Correspondance de Davout*, Vol IV, p.310.
14 In Danish Bornhöft is written "Bornhoved," but the German spelling has been used to facilitate reading by non-Danish speakers.
15 *Skarpskytterkorps* is translated as "sharpshooter corps." These men were apparently a specialized unit of marksmen.
16 Quistorp, *Nord-Armee*, Vol II, p.438-439.
17 The Danish accounts of this engagement are found in Meddelser fra Krigsarkiverne, Vol 7, pp.7-9.
18 Quistorp, *Russisch-Deutsche Legion*, p.167.
19 This force consisted of the 1/, 4/Oldenburg Regiment, the Jäger Company of the 3/Oldenburg Regiment, the Altona Jäger and Grenadier Companies, and half of the 2/Oldenburg Regiment.
20 The 1/Fünen and 1/Schleswig Infantry Regiments advanced, while the 2/Schleswig Regiment was detached to the rear.
21 Quistorp, *Russisch-Deutsche Legion*, p.169.
22 Quistorp, *Russisch-Deutsche Legion*, p.168.
23 Quistorp, *Russisch-Deutsche Legion*, p.169.
24 At this time 4/Oldenburg Regiment present consisted solely of two companies.
25 Quistorp, *Russisch-Deutsche Legion*, pp.173-174.
26 Quistorp, *Russisch-Deutsche Legion*, p.177.
27 This is probably a "hasty square" similar to the Austrian *klumpen* which was formed under these circumstances by the men crowding together and facing outwards. This type of anti-cavalry formation could not move or fire coordinated volleys.
28 Quistorp, *Russisch-Deutsche Legion*, p.179.
29 Quistorp, *Russisch-Deutsche Legion*, p.180.
30 Quistorp, *Russisch-Deutsche Legion*, pp.180-181.
31 Quistorp, *Russisch-Deutsche Legion*, p.182.
32 Quistorp, *Russisch-Deutsche Legion*, p.186.
33 Much of the Danish account of this battle comes from Meddelser fra Krigsarkiverne, Vol 7, pp.112-138.
34 Quistorp, *Russisch-Deutsche Legion*, p.188.
35 Quistorp, *Russisch-Deutsche Legion*, p.191.
36 In contrast, the Danes claim to have lost 66 dead, 326 wounded, 146 missing, and one howitzer left on the field. They claim to have killed 522 allies, taken 625 prisoners, and captured two guns.
37 von Quistorp, B.,Die Kaiserlich Russisch-Deutsche Legion, pg 213.

15 The Siege of Danzig 15 August-31 December 1813

1 De Vaudoncourt, *Prince Eugène Napoleon*, p.126.
2 Bonaparte, *Correspondance* #19697.
3 Tournes, *Campagne de Printemps*, pp.158-159.

4   D'Artois, *Défense de Danzig*, pp.204-205.

5   D'Artois, *Défense de Danzig*, pp.209-210.

6   M. de M*****, *Le Siège de Danzig*, pp.117-8.

7   This attack is indicated to have consisted of around 1,500 by M. de *****, *Le Siège de Danzig*, p.118.

8   Rapp, Memoirs, p.304.

9   D'Artois, *Défense de Danzig*, p.224 and M. de *****, *Le Siège de Danzig*, p.118.

10   Rapp, *Memoirs*, p.305.

11   Rapp, *Memoirs*, p.305.

12   D'Artois, *Défense de Danzig*, p.227.

13   D'Artois, *Défense de Danzig*, p.228.

14   Rapp, *Memoirs*, p.306.

15   This force of cavalry was a "regiment de marche" or an *ad hoc* formation organized for the purpose of transporting replacements to the front line. These units were very seldom employed in combat roles, because of their general lack of a full cadre of officers and NCOs.

16   D'Artois, *Défense de Danzig*, p.230.

17   General Rapp, in his memoirs, identifies this as a "battalion of the Vistula", but no portion of the Vistula Legion was present.

18   Rapp, *Memoirs*, p.308.

19   French Archives, Carton C2-708.

20   Rapp, *Memoirs*, p.309.

21   French Archives, Carton C2-708.

22   Apparently all three battalions were involved as Chefs de Bataillon Bellanger, Dupray, and Ellambert are indicated as being present by M. de M*****, *Le Siège de Danzig*, p.120.

23   M. de M*****, *Le Siège de Danzig*, p.119.

24   D'Artois, *Défense de Danzig*, p.234.

25   The extreme range of a field gun is about 2,000 meters, but this is reasonably within the effective range of siege guns.

26   D'Artois, *Défense de Danzig*, p.237.

27   D'Artois, *Défense de Danzig*, p.239.

28   Sporschil, *Grosse Chronik*, Vol I, p.1146 and M. de M*****, *Le Siège de Danzig*, p.121.

29   M. de M*****, *Le Siège de Danzig*, p.121.

30   This battery is identified as having two officers and 118 men on the 1 August 1813 (return found in the French Archives, Carton C2-708). It is probable that this was the combined remains of the old Polish 6th and 16th Foot Batteries, however the exact identity of the battery is unknown.

31   D'Artois, *Défense de Danzig*, p.242.

32   Sporschil, *Grosse Chronik*, Vol I, p.1146.

33   Rapp, *Memoirs*, p.314.

34   M. de M*****, *Le Siège de Danzig*, p.122.

35   Rapp, *Memoirs*, p.317.

36   Rapp, *Memoirs*, p.318.

37   *Möwenschanze* is translated as Seagull Field Work.

38   D'Artois, *Défense de Danzig*, p.257.

39   M. de M*****, *Le Siège de Danzig*, p.124.

40   D'Artois, *Défense de Danzig*, p.268.

41   D'Artois, *Défense de Danzig*, p.276.

42   D'Artois, *Défense de Danzig*, p.278.

43   D'Artois, *Défense de Danzig*, p.279.

44   D'Artois, *Défense de Danzig*, p.283.

45   D'Artois, *Défense de Danzig*, p.294.

46   Sporschil, *Grosse Chronik*, Vol I, p.1149.

47   M. de M*****, *Le Siège de Danzig*, p.128.

48   M. de M*****, *Le Siège de Danzig*, p.129.

49   D'Artois, *Défense de Danzig*, p.300.

50 The value of the mill was based on the necessity of processing unground grain held in Danzig's granaries. Without it the quality of the food rations would have been severely reduced and the ability of the garrison to continue diminished.

51 D'Artois, *Défense de Danzig*, p.314.

52 D'Artois, *Défense de Danzig*, p.331.

53 D'Artois, *Défense de Danzig*, p.335.

54 D'Artois, *Défense de Danzig*, p.339.

55 D'Artois, *Défense de Danzig*, p.359.

56 M. de M*****, *Le Siège de Danzig*, p.136.

57 M. de M*****, *Le Siège de Danzig*, pp.136-7.

58 D'Artois, *Défense de Danzig*, p.361.

59 24,299 metric hundred weights of grain, 108 of flour, 53 of rice, 228 of salt, and 404,880 biscuit rations were lost.

60 The French artillery in Bischofsberg consisted of 18 24-pdrs, 21 12-pdrs, 13 8-pdrs, 17 6-pdrs, one 4-pdr, seven 3-pdrs, four 6.4" howitzers, five 24-pdr howitzers, nine 10" mortars, and 13 6" mortars. This includes the artillery mounted on the lines of fortifications attached to Bischofsberg as well as the gate at Petershagen and Neugarten or Schidlitz.

61 D'Artois, *Défense de Danzig*, p.370.

62 D'Artois, *Défense de Danzig*, p.372.

63 D'Artois, *Défense de Danzig*, p.373.

64 D'Artois, *Défense de Danzig*, p.337.

65 D'Artois, *Défense de Danzig*, p.378.

66 D'Artois, *Défense de Danzig*, p.380 and Rapp, *Memoirs*, p.332.

67 D'Artois, *Défense de Danzig*, p.387.

68 D'Artois, *Défense de Danzig*, p.392.

69 D'Artois, *Défense de Danzig*, p.404.

70 Rapp, *Memoirs*, p.334.

71 D'Artois, *Défense de Danzig*, p.416.

72 M. de M*****, *Le Siège de Danzig*, pp.140-141.

73 The "honors of war" was a concept from the 18th century and earlier where a garrison under siege negotiated the surrender of the fortress, but the garrison marched off, free to rejoin its national army. They were allowed to take their personal arms and baggage with them, but not the masses of equipment generally found in a fortress. That was turned over to the victor of the siege.

74 D'Artois, *Défense de Danzig*, p.451.

75 Rapp, *Memoirs*, p.336.

76 D'Artois, *Défense de Danzig*, p.454.

16 The Other Sieges 15 August–31 December 1813

1 Bagés, *Siège de Glogau*, p.18.

2 Bagés, *Siège de Glogau*, pp.26-27.

3 Bagés, *Siège de Glogau*, pp.29-30.

4 Bagés, *Siège de Glogau*, p.31.

5 Bagés, *Siège de Glogau*, p.53.

6 St-Cyr, *Mémoires*, Vol II, p.196-197.

7 St-Cyr, *Mémoires*, Vol II, pp.200-201.

8 The Russian Reserve Army was also known as the Polish Reserve Army.

9 These three units were the Neuschelot Infantry Regiment, the 27th Jager Regiment, and the 43rd Jager Regiment.

10 Sporschil, *Grosse Chronik*, Vol I, p.1152.

11 St-Cyr, *Mémoires*, Vol II, p.213.

12 Sporschil, *Grosse Chronik*, Vol I, p.1153.

13 Chasteler, governor of Theresienstadt, brought with him the brigades of Generalmajors Krause and Dreschel,

which were formed from the landwehr and field battalions of the Kollowrath, Rainer, Argenteau, Erbach, Fröhlich, and Froon Infantry Regiments.

14 Sporschil, *Grosse Chronik*, Vol I, p.1154.
15 These sharpshooters were probably men drawn from the third rank of the line companies and not Jägers or grenzers.
16 Sporschil, *Grosse Chronik*, Vol I, p.1156.
17 Sporschil, *Grosse Chronik*, Vol I, p.1158.
18 O'Meara was an Irishman and former commander of the Irish Legion.
19 Sporschil, *Grosse Chronik*, Vol I, p.1160.
20 St-Cyr, *Mémoires*, Vol II, p.261.
21 Augoyat, *Défense de Torgau*, pp.3-5.
22 Augoyat, *Défense de Torgau*, p.10.
23 Augoyat, *Défense de Torgau*, p.13.
24 Augoyat, *Défense de Torgau*, p.15.
25 Augoyat, *Défense de Torgau*, p.19.
26 Augoyat, *Défense de Torgau*, pp.23-24.
27 Sporschil, *Grosse Chronik*, Vol I, p.1165.
28 Sporschil, *Grosse Chronik*, Vol I, p.1165.
29 The von Sahr and von Rechten Infantry Regiments had lost so many men that they were reduced to the strength of a single combined infantry battalion.
30 Sporschil, *Grosse Chronik*, Vol I, p.1166.
31 Augoyat, *Défense de Torgau*, p.37.
32 Augoyat, *Défense de Torgau*, p.38.
33 Augoyat, *Défense de Torgau*, p.47.
34 Sporschil, *Grosse Chronik*, Vol I, p.1168.
35 Augoyat, *Défense de Torgau*, p.50.
36 Augoyat, *Défense de Torgau*, p.52.
37 Augoyat, *Défense de Torgau*, p.55.
38 Sporschil, *Grosse Chronik*, Vol I, p.1172.
39 Sporschil, *Grosse Chronik*, Vol I, p.1172.
40 Augoyat, *Défense de Torgau*, p.58.
41 Augoyat, *Défense de Torgau*, p.61.
42 Augoyat, *Défense de Torgau*, p.64.
43 Augoyat, *Défense de Torgau*, p.56.
44 Augoyat, *Défense de Torgau*, p.63.
45 Augoyat, *Défense de Torgau*, p.65.
46 Sporschil, *Grosse Chronik*, Vol I, p.1182.
47 Sporschil, *Grosse Chronik*, Vol I, p.1183.
48 Sporschil, *Grosse Chronik*, Vol I, p.1184.
49 Sporschil, *Grosse Chronik*, Vol I, p.1185.
50 Grollman—1/4th Kurmark Landwehr Regiment
   Schwerin—3/4th Kurmark Landwehr Regiment
   Lavière—3/3rd Kurmark Landwehr Regiment
   Ozarowsky—2/7th Kurmark Landwehr Regiment
51 Sporschil, *Grosse Chronik*, Vol I, p.1188.
52 The system of measurements used in Germany at the beginning of the 18th century varied considerably, each state having its own system of measurements. A *centner* is a hundredweight, however the precise pound used in this hundredweight is uncertain.
53 Sporschil, *Grosse Chronik*, Vol I, p.1217.
54 Sporschil, *Grosse Chronik*, Vol I, p.1218.
55 Sporschil, *Grosse Chronik*, Vol I, p.1220.
56 Gilardone, *Bayerns Anteil*, p.75
57 Sporschil, *Grosse Chronik*, Vol I, pp.1120-1121.

58   Sporschil, *Grosse Chronik*, Vol I, p.1222.

59   Sporschil, *Grosse Chronik*, Vol I, p.1123.

60   The term "full military honors," as contrasted with "honors of war," means the surrendering force was "saluted" before it marched off to the prisoner of war camp. In contrast, "honors of war" means that the force surrendering the fortress has exchanged the fortress for its freedom and, unless the agreement is perfidiously broken as was done with Danzig and Dresden, the troops evacuating the fortress are entitled to march through the occupied territory until they are able to rejoin the rest of their army. Whether they were "paroled" or able to recommence operations at that point depends on what was negotiated.

61   Savary, *Défense de Hambourg*, p.31.

17 Italy and Spain, the Political Situation, and Retrospective September-December 1813

1   Fain, *Mil Huit Cent Treize*, p.352.

2   Sauzy, *Allemands Sous les Aigles Françaises*, Vol II, *Le Contingent Badois*, pp.90-96.

3   Sauzy, *Allemands Sous les Aigles Françaises*, Vol II, *Le Contingent Badois*, pp.96-97.

4   Sauzy, *Allemands Sous les Aigles Françaises*, Vol VI, *Les Soldats de Hesse et de Nassau*, pp.145-46.

Bibliography

d'Amonville, Cpt., *Les Cuirassiers du Roy, Le 8e Cuirassiers, Journal Historique du Régiment 1638-1892* (Paris: Lahure, 1892).

Anonymous, *Campagne de Prince Eugène en Italie pendant les années 1813 et 1814* (Paris: Plancher, 1817).

Anonymous, *Denkwürdigkeiten des Mecklenburg-Strelitzischen Husaren-Regiments in den jahren des Befreiungskampfes 1813 bis 1815* (Neubrandenburg: C. Brünslow, 1854).

Anonymous, *Geschichte des Magdeburgischen Husaren-Regiments Nr. 10* (Berlin: A. Duncker, 1863).

Anonymous, *Historique du 2ème Régiment d'Artillerie* (Grenoble: Librairie Dauphinoise, 1899).

Anonymous, *Historique du 3e Régiment de Cuirassiers, ci-devant du Commissaire Général 1645-1892* (Paris: Boussod, Valadon & Cie., 1893).

Anonymous, *Historique du 4e Régiment de Cuirassiers, 1643-1897* (Paris: Lahure, 1893).

Anonymous, *Historique du 127e Regiment d'Infanterie* (Valenciennes: P. & G. Girard, 1897).

von Ardenne, *Geschichte des Husaren-Regiments von Zieten (Brandenburgisches) Nr. 3* (Berlin: Mittler & Son, 1905).

Arthur, R., *A Legiao Portuguesa ao servico de Napoleo 1808-1813* (Lisbon: Livraria Ferin, 1901).

d'Artois, P.H., *Relation de la Défense de Danzig en 1813 par le 10e corps de l'Armée Française, contre l'Armée combinée Russe et Prussienne* (Paris: Ladrange, 1820).

Arvers, P., *Historique du 82e Régiment d'Infanterie de Ligne et du 7e Régiment d'Infanterie Légère, 1684-1876* (Paris: Typograhie Lahure, 1876).

Atteridge, A.H., *Joachim Murat* (New York: Brentano's, 1911).

Aubier, Lt., *Un Régiment de Cavalerie Légère de 1793 à 1815* (Paris: Berger-Levrault & Cie., 1888).

Augoyat, *Relation de la défense de Torgau par les troupes françaises en 1813* (Paris: Chez Leneveu, 1840).

Austro-Hungarian (K. u. K.) Kriegsarchiv, *Befreiungskrieg 1813 und 1814* (Vienna: Verlag von L.W. Seidel & Sohn, 1913).

Bagés, Cdt. G., *Le Siège de Glogau 1813-1814* (Paris: H. Charles-Lavauzelle, date unknown).

von Barsewisch, *Geschichte des Grossherzoglich Badischen Leib-Grenadier-Regiments (1803-1872)* (Karlsruhe: Chr. F. Muller, 1893).

de Behaine, Cdt L., *La Campagne de France, Napoléon et les Alliés sur le Rhin* (Paris: Perrin & Cie., 1913).

Beitzke, Dr. H., *Geschichte der Deutschen Freiheitskriege in den Jahren 1813 und 1814* (Berlin: Duncker & Humblot, 1864).

Belhomme, Lt. Col., *Histoire de l'Infanterie en France* (Paris: H. Charles-Lavauzelle, 1893-1902).

Bigge, W., *Geschichte des Infanterie-Régiments Kaiser Wilhelm (2. Grossherzoglich Hessisches) Nr. 116* (Berlin: Mittler & Son, 1893).

Bleibtreu, C., *Maschalle, Generale, Soldaten, Napoleons I* (Berlin: A. Schall, date unknown).

Bleibtreu, C., *Die Volkerschalcht bei Leipzig* (Leipzig: T. Thomas, 1907).

Blond, G., *La Grande Armée* (Paris: R. Laffont, 1979).

Bogdanovich, M.I., *Istoria Bojny 1813 Goda, Za Nezavisimost' Germanü po Dostobernym' Istochnikam' Sostabdena po Byso chayshchemy Pobeleniju* (St. Petersburg: 1863).

Bogdanovich, M.I., *Istorich Voin 1813 Goda Za Nezavicimost Germanü Po Dostovern'm' Istochnikam'* (St. Petersburg: 1963).

Bogdanovich, M.I., *Istorich Voin 1814 Goda Vo Frantsü i Nizlozhenich Napoleona I* (St. Petersburg: 1865).

Bonaparte, N., *Correspondance de Napoléon 1er* (Paris: H. Plon, 1868).

von Bonin, U., *Geschichte des Ingenieurkorps und der Pioniere in Preussen* (Wiesbaden: LTR Verlag, 1981).

Bonnières de Wierre, Cpt. A., *Historique du 3e Régiment de Dragons* (Nantes: Bourgeois, 1892).

Boppe, A., *Les Espagnols dans la Grande Armée; Le Division Romana (1808-1809); Le Régiment Joseph Napoléon (1809-1813)* (Paris: Berger-Levrault & Cie., 1899).

Boppe, A., *La Legion Portuguese (1808-1813)* (Paris: Berger-Levrault & Cie., 1897).

Bory, J.R., *Régiments Suisses au Service de France* (Freiburg: Collection "Le Shako", 1975).

Bouchard, S., *Historique du 28e Régiment de Dragons* (Paris: Berger-Levrault & Cie., 1893).

Boucquoy, E.L., *La cavalerie légère (les hussards, les chasseurs à cheval)* (Paris: J. Grancher, 1980).

Boucquoy, E.L., *Les Cuirassiers* (Paris: J. Grancher, 1978).

Boucquoy, E.L., *Dragons et Guides d'Etat-major* (Paris: J. Grancher, 1980).

Boucquoy, E.L., *Les Gardes d'honneur du Premier Empire* (Paris: A. Crepin-Leblond, 1908).

Boucquoy, E.L., *La Garde Impériale; Troupes à Pied* (Paris: J. Grancher, 1977).

Boucquoy, E.L., *La Garde Impériale; Troupes à Cheval* (Paris: J. Grancher, 1977).

Boucquoy, E.L., *L'infanterie* (Paris: J. Grancher, 1979).

Bourgue, Lt. M., *Historique du 3e Régiment d'Infanterie (ex-Piemont) 1569-1891* (Paris: Henri Charles-Lavauzelle, 1894).

von Boyen, Col., *Darstellung der Vorgang in der Schlacht von Dennewitz: Nach den Geschichten der betreffenden Regimenter Mit besonderer Berücksichtingung des Errinerungen des damaligen Generalstabschefs* (Berlin: Julius Sittenfeld, 1893).

Breton de la Martinière, M., *Campagnes de Buonaparte en 1812, 1813, et 1814 jusqu'à son Abdication* (Paris: J. Dentu, 1814).

Brett-James, A., *Europe Against Napoleon* (New York: McMillan, 1970).

Burghersh, Lord, *Memoir of the Operations of the Allied Operations under Prinz Schwarzenburg and Marschal Blücher During the Latter End of 1813 and the Year 1814* (London: J. Murray, 1922).

Burturlin, D., *Tableau de la Campagne d'Automne de 1813 en Allemagne, Depuis la Rupture de l'Armistice jusqu'au Passage du Rhin par l'Armée Française* (Paris: A. Bertrand & Magimel, Anselin & Pochard, 1817).

Calmon-Maison, J.J.R., *Le Général Maison et le 1er Corps de la Grande Armée; Campagne de Belgique (décembre 1813-avril 1814)* (Paris: 1870).

Camon, Col., *La guerre Napoléonienne, Les Batailles, Vol IV* (Paris: Librairie Militaire R. Chapelot, 1910).

du Casse, A., *Mémoires et Correspondance Politique et Militaire du Prince Eugène* (Paris: Michel Lévy Frères, 1859).

Cathcart, G., *Commentaries on the War in Russia and Germany in 1812 and 1813* (London: J. Murray, 1850).

Chandler, D., *The Campaigns of Napoleon* (New York: MacMillan, 1966).

Chandler, D., *Dictionary of the Napoleonic Wars* (New York: MacMillan, 1979).

Chandler, D., *Napoleon's Marshals* (New York: MacMillan, 1987).

Chapuis, Col., *Observation sur les Combats de Culm, des 29 et 30 Août 1813* (Paris: L. Martinet, 1853).

Charras, Lt. Col., *Histoire de la Guerre de 1813 en Allemagne* (Paris: 1870).

Chavane, J., *Histoire du 11e Cuirassiers* (Paris: C. Charavay, 1889).

Chuquet, A., *Inédits Napoléoniens* (Paris: Ancienne Librairie Fontemoing et Cie., 1914-1919).

Chuquet, A., *Ordres et Apostilles de Napoléon* (Paris: Librarie Ancienne Honoré Champion, 1912).

Clément, G., *Campagne de 1813* (Paris: H. Charles-Lavauzelle, date unknown).

Clerc, *Historique du 79e Régiment d'Infanterie* (Paris: Berger-Levrault & Cie., 1896).

von Conrady, C., *Geschichte des Königlich Preussischen Sechsten Infanterie-Regiments von seiner Stiftung im Jahr 1773 zu Ende des Jahres 1865* (Glogau: C. Flemming, 1857).

Corda, H., *Le Régiment de la Fère et le 1er Régiment d'Artillerie* (Paris: Berger-Levrault & Cie., 1906).

Cosse-Brissac, R., *Historique du 7e Régiment de Dragons 1673-1909* (Paris: Leroy, 1909).

Diamant-Berger, M., *Le 19e Régiment de Chasseurs à Cheval 1792-1826, 1872-1919* (Paris: Librairie Courtot, date unknown).

Dodge, T.A., *Napoleon* (Cambridge, MA: Houghton, Mifflin & Co., 1904).

Drexl, Dr F., *Die Befreiungskriege 1813-1815* (Regensberg: F. Habbel, 1913).

Dupré, Chef de Bataillon, *Les Fastes du 14e Régiment de Ligne* (Paris: Librairie Militaire d'Anselin, 1956).

Dupuy, Cmdt. R., *Historique du 12e Régiment de Chasseurs de 1788 à 1891* (Paris: E. Person, 1891).

Duroisel, Cpt. G., *Historique du 93 Régiment d'Infanterie Ancien Enghien et 18e Légère* (La Roche-sur-Yon: Ivonnet & Filles, 1893).

von Eck, *Geschichte des 2. Westfälischen Husaren-Régiments Nr. 11 und seiner Stammtruppen von 1807-1893* (Mainz: H. Kusittich, 1893).

d'Eckmuhl, *Le Maréchal Davout, Prince d'Eckmuhl, Correspondance inédite 1790-1815* (Paris: Perrin & Cie., 1887).

Esposito, Gen., *A Military History and Atlas of the Napoleonic Wars* (New York: AMS Press, 1978).

Fabry, G., *Étude sur les Opérations de l'Empereur 5 septembre au 21 septembre 1813* (Paris: Librairie Militaire, R. Chapelot & Cie., 1913).

Fabry, G., *Étude sur les Opérations de l'Empereur du 22 septembre au 3 octobre 1813* (Paris: Laval, Bameoud & Cie., 1913)

Fabry, G., *Étude sur les Opérations du Maréchal Macdonald du 22 août au 4 septembre 1813* (Paris: Librairie Militaire, R. Chapelot & Cie., 1910).

Fabry, G., *Étude sur les Opérations du Maréchal Oudinot du 15 août au 4 septembre 1813* (Paris: Librairie Militaire, R. Chapelot et Cie., 1910).

Fabry, G., *Journal des Campagnes du Prince du Wurtemberg* (Paris: Librairie Militaire R. Chapelot et Cie., 1907).

Fabry, G., *Journal des Opérations des III et V Corps en 1813* (Paris: Librairie Militaire R. Chapelot et Cie., 1902).

Fain, Baron, *Manuscrit de Mil Huit Cent Treize, Contenant le précis des Évenements de cette Année Pour Servir a l'Histoire de l'Empereur Napoléon* (Paris: Delaunay Librairie, 1824).

Fiffre, E., *Histoire des Troupes Étrangères au Service de France* (Paris: Librairie Militaire, 1854).

Foucart, Cmdt., *Une Division de Cavalerie Légère en 1813* (Paris: Librairie Militaire Berger-Levrault et Cie., 1891).

Freiherr von Holz, Col. G., *1813-1815 Osterreich in den Befreiungskriegen* (Vienna: A. Edlingers, 1912).

von Freytag-Loringhoven, *Kriegslehren nach Clausewitz aus den Feldzügen 1813 und 1814* (Berlin: E.S. Mittler & Sohn, 1908).

Friederich, E., *Die Befreiungskriege 1813-1815* (Berlin: E.S. Mittler & Sohn, 1913).

Friederich, R., *Die Schlacht an der Katzbachk* (Berlin: E.S. Mittler & Sohn, 1913).

von Fritz, K. & Ortenberg, G., *Hessisches Militar zur Zeit des Deutschen Bundes* (Beckum, Deutschen Gesellschaft für erreskunde e. V., 1984).

Galli, *L'Allemagne en 1813* (Paris: Gamier Frères, 1889).

Gasiorowski, M.W., *Mémoires militaires de Joseph Grabowski, Officier à l'état-major imperial de Napoléon 1er 1812-1813-1814* (Paris: Librairie Plon, 1907).

Giesse, K., *Kassel-Moskau-Kustrin 1812-1813* (Leipzig: Verlag der Dykschen Buchlandlung, 1912).

Gilardone, G., *Bayerns Anteil am Herbstfeldzuge 1813, Darstellungen aus der Bayerischen Kriegs-und Heeresgeschichte* (Munich: K. B. Kriegsarchive, 1913).

Gleich, *Die ersten 100 Jahren des Uhlanen-Regiments Ktinig Wilhelm (2 Württemberger) Nr. 20* (Stuttgart: Uhland'schen Buchdruckerei, GmbH, date unknown).

Grossen Generalstab Kreigsgeschichteliche Abteilung II Deutschland, *Pläne der Schlachten and Treffen welche von der preussischen Armee in den feldzügen der Jahre 1813,14, und 15 geliefertworden* (Berlin: G. Reimer, 1821).

Grossen Generalstab Kreigsgeschichteliche Abteilung II Deutschland, *Urkundlich Beiträge und Forschung zur Geschichte des Preussischen Herres: Die Gefechtsausbildung der Preussische Infanterie von 1806* (Wiesbaden: LTR-Verlag, 1982).

Grossen Generalstab Kreigsgeschichteliche Abteilung II Deutschland, *Urkundlich Beiträge und Forschung zur Geschichte des Preussischen Herres: Der Preussische Kavallerdienst von 1806* (Wiesbaden: LTR-Verlag, 1984).

Guillon, E., *Napoléon et la Suisse, 1803-1815* (Paris: Librairie Plon, 1910).

Gumtau, C.F, *Die Jäger und Schützen des Preussischen Heeres* (Berlin: E.S. Mittler, 1835).

von Guttenberg, E., "Die bayerische Nationalgarde II Classe in den Befreiungskriegen", *Darstellungen aus der Bayerischen Kriegs- und Heeresgeschichte* (Munich: 'Königlich Bayerische Kriegsarchiv, 1913).

Guye, A., *Le Bataillon de Neuchâtel, dit les Canaris au service de Napoléon* (Neuchâtel: À la Baconniere, 1964).

Henderson, E., *Blücher and the Uprising of Prussia against Napoleon 1806-1815* (New York: AIMS Press, 1978).

Henke, C., *Davout und die Festung Hamburg-Harburg 1813-14* (Berlin: E.S. Mittler & Sohn, 1911).

Heuman, Lt. Col., *Historique du 148e Régiment d'Infanterie* (Paris: H. Charles-Lavauzelle, date unknown).

von Holleben, Gen. Maj., *Geschichte des Frühjahrsfeldzuges 1813 und Vorgeschichte* (Berlin: E.S. Mittler & Sohn, 1904).

James, C., *An Universal Military Dictionary in English and French in which are explained the Terms of the Principal Sciences that are Necessary for the Information of an Officer* (London: T. Egerton, 1816).

Jerabek, R., *Die Kämpf in Südkärnten 1813* (Vienna: Heeresgeschichtliches Museum, 1986).

Jomini, Gen. Baron, *Histoire Critique et Militaire des Campagnes de la Revolution faisant suit au Traité des Grandes Opérations militaires* (Paris: Chez Magimel, Anselin & Pouchard, 1816).

Jomini, Gen. Baron, *Réplique du Colonel Jomini à Lord Londonderry (General Stuart) sur les évenements de la Campagne de Dresde en 1813* (publisher unknown, date unknown).

Jomini, Gen. Baron, *Traité des Grandes Opérations Militaires, Contenant l'Histoire Critique des Campagnes de Fréderic II, Comparés à celles de l'Empereur Napoléon* (Paris: Magimel, 1811).

de Juzancourt, G., *Historique du 7e Régiment de Cuirassiers (1659-1886)* (Paris: Berger-Levrault & Cie., 1887).

de Juzancourt, G., *Historique du 10e Régiment du Cuirassiers (1643-1891)* (Paris: Berger-Levrault & Cie., 1893).

K. und K. Kriegsarchivs, *Befreiungskrieg 1813 und 1814* (Vienna: Verlag von L.W. Seidel & Sohn, 1913).

Kandelsdorfer, K., *Geschichte des K. und K. Feld-Jäger-Bataillons No 7* (Vienna: Druck A.D. Mur, 1896).

Kircheisen, F., *Napoleon I und das Zeitalter der Befreiungskriege in Bildern* (Munich: G.Müller, 1914).

Klessman, E., *Die Befreiungskriege in Augenzeugenberichten* (Germany: Krag Rauch, 1967).

von Knobelsdorff-Brenkenhoff, B., *Briefe aus den Befreiungskriegen, Ein Beitrag zur Situation von Truppe und Heimat in den Jahren 1813/14* (Bonn: 1981).

Königlich Bayerischen Kriegsarchiv, *Darstellungen aus der Bayerischen Kriegs- und Heeresgeschichte* (Munich: Lindauersche, Buchhandlung, 1900-1914).

Kraft, *Die Württemberger in den Napoleonischen Kreigen* (Stuttgart: 1953).

von L.-G., B., *Aus Hannovers militärischer Vergangenheit* (Hannover: Buchdruckerei von Arnold Weichelt, 1880).

Lachouque, H., *The Anatomy of Glory* (Providence, RI: Brown University Press, 1962).

Léfèbvre de Behaine, *La Campagne de France, l'Invasion (décembre 1813–janvier 1814)* (Paris: Librairie Academique Perrin, 1934).

Leonard, K.C., *Geschichctliche Darstellung der Schlacht bei Hauau am 30. Oktober 1813* (Hanau: Fr.. König's Buchhandlung, 1913).

Lewinski & Brauchitsch, *Geschichte des Grenadier-Regiments König Wilhelm I (2. Westpreussischen) Nr. 7* (Glogau: C. Flemming, 1897).

zur Lippe-Weissenfeld, E. Graf, *Geschichte des koniglich Preussischen 6. Husaren-Regiments (ehedem 2. Schlesischen* (Berlin: Königlichen Geheimen Ober-Hofbuchdruckerei, 1860).

Louvat, Cpt., *Historique du 7ème Hussars* (Paris: Pairault & Cie., 1887).

Lumbroso, A., *Correspondance de Joachim Murat* (Turin: Roux Frassati et Cie., 1899).

Lunsman, F., *Die Armee des Königreichs Westfalen 1807-1813* (Berlin: C. Leddihn, 1935).

M. de M****, *Le siège de Dantzig en 1813* (Paris: 1814).

McQueen, J., *The Campaigns of 1812, 1813, and 1814* (Glasgow: E. Khull & Co., 1815).

Maag, Dr. A., *Geschichte der Schweizer Truppen in Franzosischen Dienst vom Ruckzug aus Russland bis zum zweiten Pariser Freiden* (Basel: E. Kuhn, 1894).

Mackensen, *Schwarz Husaren, Geschichte des 1. Leib-Husaren-Regiments Nr. 1 und des 2. Leib-Husaren-Regiments Kaiserin Nr. 2* (Berlin: E.S. Mittler & Sohn, 1892).

Madelin, L., *Histoire du Consulat et de l'Empire* (Paris: Librairie Hachette, 1950).

Marbot, Baron de, *Mémoires du Baron de Marbot* (Paris: Librairie Plon, 1892).

de Margon, Cmdt, *Historique du 8e Régiment de Chasseurs de 1788 à 1888* (Verdun: Benve-Lallemant, 1889).

de Marmont, A.F.L.V, *Mémoires du Maréchal Marmont, Duc de Raguse, de 1792 a 1841* (Paris: Perrotin, 1857).

de Martimprey, A., *Historique du 8e Régiment de Cuirassiers d'après les Archives du Corps, celles du Dépôt de Guerre, et autres Documents* (Paris: Berger-Levrault, 1888).

Martinet, M., *Historique du 9e Régiment de Dragons* (Paris: H.T. Hamel, 1883).

Martinien, A., *Tableaux par corps et par batailles des Officiers Tués et Blessés pendant les Guerres de l'Empire (1805-1815)* (Paris: Editions Militaires Européennes, 1984).

Mason, F., *Cavaliers de Napoléon* (Paris: Librairie Ollendorff, date unknown).

Maude, F.N., *1813: The Leipzig Campaign* (New York: MacMillan, 1908).

de Mazade, C., *Correspondance du Maréchal Davout, Prince d'Eckmühl 1801-1815* (Paris: Librairie Plon, 1885).

Meddelser fra Krigsarkiverne (Stockholm, various issues).

Mirus, R., *Das Treffen bei Wartenburg, am 3. Oktober 1813* (Berlin: E.S. Mittler & Sohn, 1863).

Mollard, J., *Historique du 63 Régiment d'Infanterie* (Paris: Berger-Levrault & Cie., 1887).

Müller-Leobnitz, A.D., *Die Schlacht an der Katzbach* (Liegnitz: Niederschlesische Tageszeitung, 1938).

Nafziger, G.F, *The Bavarian and Westphalian Armies, 1799-1815* (Cambridge, ON: RAFM, 1981, 1983).

Nafziger, G.F, *The Russian Army, 1800-1815* (Cambridge, ON: RAFM, 1983).

von Odeleben, O., *Napoleons Feldzug in Sachsen im Jahr 1813* (Meisenheim: Anton Hain K.G., 1970).

von der Oelsnitz, A.C., *Geschichte des Königlich Preussischen Ersten Infanterie-Regiments seit seiner Stiftung im Jahr 1619 bis zur Gegenwart* (Berlin: E.C. Mittler & Sohn, 1955).

Ore, C., *1er Régiment de Chasseurs 1651-1903* (Chateaudun: Laussedat, 1903).

Paret, P., *Yorck and the Era of Prussian Reform 1807-1815* (Princeton, NJ: Princton University Press, 1966).

Parquin, Cpt., *Souvenirs du Capitaine Parquin 1803-1814* (Paris: Boussod, Valadon, & Cie., 1892).

Paulig, F.R., *Geschichte der Befreiungskriege* (Frankfort: Frederich Paulig, 1891).

Pelet, Général, *Des Principales Opérations de la Campagne de 1813* (extracted from the Spectateur Militaire).

Petre, F.L., *Napoleon's Last Campaign in Germany: 1813* (New York: Hippocrene Books, 1974).

Pfister, A., *Aus dem Lager des Rheinsbundes 1812 und 1813* (Leipzig: Deutsche Verlags-Anstalt, 1897).

Pflug-Harttung, *1813-1815, Illustrierte Geschichte der Befreiungskriege* (Germany: Union Deutsche Verlagsgesellleschaft, 1913).

Phillippart, J., *Memoirs and Campaigns of Charles John, Prince Royal of Sweden* (London: C.J. Barrington, 1814).

Phillippart, J., *Napoleon's Campaign in Germany and France 1813-1814* (London: C.J. Barrington, 1814).

Pichard & Tuety, *Unpublished Correspondence of Napoleon I* (New York: Duffield & Co., 1913).

Pieron, Lt., *Histoire d'un Régiment, La 32me Demi-Brigade 1775-1890* (Paris: à le Vasseur et Cie., date unknown).

Pietsch, P. von, *Die Formations—und Uniformierungs Geschichte des Preussischen Heeres 1808-1914* (Hamburg: Verlag H. Gerhard Schulz, 1963).

Pitot, Lt., *Historique du 83e Rgiment d'Infanterie 1684-1891* (Toulouse: privately published, date unknown).

de Place, R., *Historique du 12e Cuirassiers (1668-1888)* (Paris: Lahure, 1889).

Plotho, C., *Combat de Hanau, livré le 30 octobre 1813.* (N.p., n.d.).

Plotho, C., *Der Krieg in Deutschland und Frankreich in den Jahren 1813 und 1814* (Berlin: Carl Friedrich, 1817).

Plotho, C., *Relation de la Bataille de Leipzig (16, 17, 18, & 19 octobre)* (Paris: J. Correard, 1840).

Poniatowski, J., *Correspondance du Prince Joseph Poniatowski avec la France* (Poznan: 1929).

Prussian General Staff, *Plan der Schlachten und Treffen Welche von der Preussischen Armee in den Feldzuge der Jahr 1813, 1814, und 1815* (Berlin: 1821).

von Quistorp, B., *Geschichte der Nord Armee im Jahre 1813* (Berlin: E.S. Mittler & Sohn, 1894).

von Quistorp, B., *Die Kaiserlich Russisch-Deutsche Legion Verlag* (Berlin: von Carl Heymann, 1860).

Rapp, Count, *Memoirs of General Count Rapp, First Aide-de-Camp to Napoleon* (London: Henry Colburn & Co., 1823).

Rehtwisch, T., *Grossgörschen 2 May 1813* (Leipzig: Turm Verlag, 1912).

Rossler, *Tagebücher aus den zehn Feldzügen der Württemberger ureter der Regierung Königs Friderich* (Ludwigsberg: Friedrich Nast, 1820).

Rothwiller, Baron, *Historique du Deuxième Régiment de Cuirassiers Ancien Royal de Cavalerie (1635-1876)* (Paris: Plon & Cie., 1877).

Roulin, Lt. Col., *125e Régiment d'Infanterie* (Orléans: George Jacob, 1890).

Rousset, C., *La Grande Armée de 1813* (Paris: Librairie Academique Didier, 1892).

Rousset, M.C., *Souvenirs du Maréchal Macdonald, Duc de Tarente* (Paris: Librairie Hachette & Cie., 1892).

Ruby, Col., & de Labeau, Cpt., *Historique du 2me Régiment de Cuirassiers (1668-1942)* (Marseille: Établissements Moullot Fils Aîné, 1944).

von Ruesch, von Lossow, von Gunther, & von l'Estocq, *Geschichte des königlichen Zweiten Ulanen-Regiments* (Potsdam: A. Stein, 1858).

St-Cyr, G., *Memoires du Maréchal Gouvion Saint-Cyr 1812-1813*, 1982, Paris, Remanences.

von St Rötha, *Die Königlich Preussische Reitende Artillerie von Jahre 1759 bis 1816*, 1981, Wiesbaden, LTR Verlag.

von Salisch, G., *Geschichte des Königlich Preussischen Siebenten Infanterie-Regiments von seiner Stiftung in Jahre 1797 bis zum lsten July 1854* (Glogau: C. Flemming, 1854).

Sauzey, Cpt., *Les Allemands sous les Aigles Françaises: Le Contingent Badois* (Paris: Librairie Militaire R. Chapelot et Cie., 1904).

Sauzey, Cpt., *Les Allemands sous les Aigles Françaises: Nos Allies les Bavarois* (Paris: Librairie Militaire R. Chapelot et Cie., 1910).

Sauzey, Cpt., *Les Allemands sous les Aigles Françaises: Le Regiment des Duches de Saxe* (Paris: Librairie Militaire R. Chapelot et Cie.,1908).

Sauzey, Cpt., *Les Allemands sous les Aigles Françaises: Les Saxons dans nos rangs* (Paris: Librairie Militaire R. Chapelot et Cie.,1907).

Sauzey, Cpt., *Les Allemands sous les Aigles Françaises: Les soldats de Hesse et Nassau* (Paris: Librairie Militaire R. Chapelot et Cie.,1912).

Savary, M., *Relation de la défense de Hambourg en 1813, et 1814, Extracted from the* Spectateur Militaire, *July 1846* (Paris: Bourgogne et Martinet, 1846).

Freiherr von Schauthroth, W.F., *Im Rheinbund-Regiment der Herzoglich Sachsischen Kontingente Koburg-Hildburghausen-Gotha-Weimar wahrend der Feldzüge in Tirol, Spainen und Russland, 1809-1813* (Berlin: E.S. Mittler & Sohn, 1905).

Schmidt, C., *Le Grand-Duché de Berg (1806-1813); Étude sur la Domination Française en Allemagne sous Napoléon 1er* (Paris: 1905).

Schmitt, Lt., *151e Régiment d'Infanterie* (Paris: 1901).

von Schöning, K.W., *Geschichte des Königlich Preussische Regiments Garde du Corps zu seinem hundertjährigen Jubelfest* (Berlin: 1840).

von Specht, F.A.K., *Das Königreich Westphalen und seine Armee im Jahr 1813, so wie die Auflösung desselben durch den kaiserlich russischen General Graf A. Czernicheff* (Kassel: 1848)Schussler, A., *Geschichte des Lazowischen Freikorps, Ein Beitrag zur Kriegsgeschichte der Jahre 1813 und 1814* (Berlin: E.S. Mittler, 1826).

Schuster, O. & Franke, F.A., *Geschichte der Sachsischen Armee von deren Errichtung bis auf die neuste Zeit* (Leipzig: 1855).

Schwertfeger, B., *Geschichte der Königlich Deutsch Legion 1803-1816* (Hannover: Hahn'sche Buchhandlung, 1907).

von Seidel, F., *Affair de Lindenau, Extracted from the Austrian Military Journal and translated by P. Himly* (Paris: J. Correard, 1840).

Shanahan, W.O., *Prussian Military Reforms 1786-1813* (New York: Columbia University Press, 1945).

von Sichart, A. und R., *Geschichte der Königlich-Hannoverschen Armee* (Hanover & Leipzig: Han'sche Buchhandlung, 1898).

Simon, G., *Die Kriegeserignisse zwischen Teplitz und Pirna im August and September des Jahres 1813. Die Schlacht bei Kuhn am 29. und 30. August 1813 und Das Gefechtbei Arbesau am 17. September 1813; Nach verläszlichen Quellen Bearbeitet* (Teplitz-Schonau: Emil Seewald, 1911).

Simond, E., *Le 28e de Ligne, Historique du Régiment* (Rouen: Megard & Cie., 1889).

Le Spectateur Militaire, "Premier Siege de Glogau, Mars 1813 a Juin 1813", Vol IX (Paris: H. Charles-Lavauzelle, 1905).

Sporschil, J., *Die Grosse Chronik, Geschichte des Krieges des Verbundeten Europas gegen Napoleon Bonaparte, in den Jähren 1813, 1814, und 1815* (Braunschweig: G. Westermann, 1841).

Stiegler, E., *Le Maréchal Oudinot Duc de Reggio* (Paris: Librairie Plon, 1894).

Suremain, *Mémoires du Lieutenant Général Suremain (1794-1815)* (Paris: Plon-Nourritt et Cie., 1902).

Suzanne, *Histoire de la Cavalerie Française* (Paris: C. Terana, 1984).

Temaux-Compans, M., *Le Général Compans (1769-1845)* (Paris: Librairie Plon, 1912).

Thomas, J., *Un régiment Rhénan sous Napoléon Premier* (Liège: H. Vaillant-Charmanne, 1928).

Tournes, R., *La Campagne de Printemps en 1813, Lützen* (Paris: Charles-Lavauzelle & Cie., 1931).

Vassal, Lt., *Historique du 11e Régiment d'Infanterie* (Montauban: Edouard Forestie, 1900).

de Vaudoncourt, Gen. G., *Histoire des Campagnes d'Italie en 1813 et 1814, avec un Atlas Militaire* (London: T. Egerton, 1817).

de Vaudoncourt, Gen. G., *Histoire Politique et Militaire du Prince Eugène Napoléon, Vice-roi d'Italie* (Paris: Librairie Universelle de P. Mongie, 1828).

Vaupell, O., *Den Danske Haers Historie til nutiden Og Den Norske Haers Historie indtil 1814* (Copenhagen: 1872).

Venzky, G., *Die Russisch-Deutsche Legion in den Jahren 1811-1815*, 1966, Wiesbaden, Otto Harrassowitz.

Viger, Count, *Davout, Maréchal d'Empire* (Paris: P. Ollendorff ed., Imprierie H. Bouilant, 1898).

Vitzthum von Eckstadt, *Die Hauptquartiere im Herbstfeldzuge 1813 auf dem Deutschen Kriegsschauplatze* (Berlin: E.S. Mittler & Sohn, 1910).

Vogel, F.L., *Theilnahme der König. Preuss. Artillerie an dem Kämpfe des Befreiungskriege* (Weisbaden: LTR Verlag, 1981).

Voigtlander, L., *Das Tagebuch des Johann Heinrich Lang aus Lübeck und die Feldzuge der Hanseaten in den Jähren 1813-1815* (Lübeck: Verlag Schmidt-Romhild, 1980).

Voisin, C., *Historique du 6e Hussards* (Libourne: G. Maleville, 1888).

Vollmer, U., *Die Bewaffnung der Armeendes Königsreichs Württemberg und des Grossherzogtums Baden* (Schwabisch Hall: Journal Verlag Schwend GmbH, 1981).

Wagner, A., *Recueil des Plans de Combat et de Batailles livrées par l'Armée Prussienne pendant les campagnes des Années 1813, 1814, et 1815 avec des éclaircissements Historiques* (Berlin: G. Reimer, 1821).

Weil, M.H, *Campagne de 1813, La Cavalerie des armées alliés* (Paris: Librairie Militaire de L. Baudoin, 1886).

Wilhelm, Duke of Brunswick, *Geschichte des Magdeburgischen Husaren-Regiments, Nr. 10* (Berlin: A. Duncker, 1863).

Wolf, A., *Historique du 10e Régiment de Chasseurs à Cheval depuis sa création jusqu'en 1890* (Paris: Librairie Militaire de L. Baudoin, 1890).

Wrangell, Baron G., *Mit Graf Pahlens Reiterei gegen Napoelon* (Berlin: E.S. Mittler & Sohn, 1910).

Zanoli, A., *Sulla Milizia Cisalpino-Italiana Cenni Storio-Statistici Dal 1796 al 1814* (Milan: Tipografi-Librairie Fonditori di Caratteri, 1845).

Zaremba, A., "Batalion polski Gwardü w 1813 r.", *Bron i Barwa*, London, 11 (1957).

Zweguintov, *L'Armée Russe* (Paris: privately published, 1969).

Index